Beyond Left & Right

Beyond Left & Right

Insurgency and the Establishment

David A. Horowitz

University of Illinois Press

Urbana and Chicago

Publication of this book was supported by a grant from the
Portland State University Foundation.

© 1997 by the Board of Trustees of the University of Illinois
Manufactured in the United States of America
1 2 3 4 5 C P 5 4 3 2 1

This book is printed on acid-free paper.
Library of Congress Cataloging-in-Publication Data
Horowitz, David A.
Beyond left and right : insurgency and the establishment / David
A. Horowitz.
       p.   cm.
Includes bibliographical references and index.
ISBN 0-252-02266-1 (cloth : acid-free paper). —
ISBN 0-252-06568-9 (pbk. : acid-free paper)
1. United States—Politics and government—20th century.
2. United States—Foreign relations—20th century. I. Title.
E743.H679   1997
306.2'0973—dc20   96-10032
CIP

To the memory of my mother and father,

Dorothy Levine Horowitz (1917–90)

and Nathan Horowitz (1908–94)

alright we are two nations.

John Dos Passos,
The Big Money, U.S.A.

Contents

Preface

"Two souls dwell in the bosom . . . of the American people," wrote the newspaper columnist Dorothy Thompson in 1938. One sought the abundant life of the corporate market. The other yearned for "former simplicities, for decentralization, for the interests of the 'little man.'" Attempts to reconcile order and liberty have long characterized the history of the United States. Twentieth-century Americans have dreamed of harmonizing the collective institutions of the political economy with traditional individualism and democracy. Accordingly, conflicts over concentrated power and centralized authority have played a pivotal role in national life. Yet scholars often approach American politics from a "left versus right" perspective that contrasts "liberal" or "progressive" campaigns for social justice and power sharing with "conservative" insistence on the status quo, order, elitism, and militarism.[1]

Historians have compounded these problems by showing little sensitivity to democratic and indigenous opponents of modern rationalism, urban liberalism, and cultural pluralism. The spread of European fascism and communism in the 1930s and 1940s convinced many intellectuals inside the United States of the dangers of grass-roots movements fueled by passion or ideology. Much of the work of the 1950s and 1960s portrayed critics of elite institutions and values as marginal agitators characterized by irrational anxieties, prejudices, ignorance, and bigotry. Richard Hofstadter, the nation's leading historian of the period, depicted the heirs of the populist and progressive legacies as alienated extremists infused with nativist "isolationism," narrow nationalism, and conspiratorial paranoia about the eastern intelligentsia. Intellectuals assumed, the historian Leo Ribuffo has noted, "that only vestigial 'backward-looking' groups rejected the dominant trends toward scientific rationalism, liberal reform, and reformed capitalism."[2]

Since the 1980s such scholars as Ribuffo, Alan Brinkley, Thomas Bender, David Thelen, Christopher Lasch, and Catherine McNicol Stock have called for a fusion of social and political history that embraces the lives of ordinary people and includes the independent producers of the "old" middle class. Nonelite conceptualizations of political and cultural development have prompted Thelen to speculate on "the power of tradition to inspire resistance." Meanwhile, Jackson Lears has asked scholars to consider the possibility that "the most profound radicalism is often the most profound conservatism." Perhaps the most significant example of revisionist thought has been Lasch's observation that "ideological distinctions between liberalism and conservatism" were "increasingly obscure" and no longer defined the lines of discourse.[3]

✦ ✦ ✦

Beyond Left and Right applies Lasch's insight to the study of American political culture in the twentieth century. The book combines the broadness of a general synthesis with the research details of a monograph. Rather than confine its scope to self-appointed leaders and ideologues, it concentrates on elected officeholders and the heads of popular social movements. The work supplements the public and private statements of these figures by sampling the contents of their constituent mail. Acknowledging the tension between belief and rhetoric, it proceeds on the premise that power and market needs coexist with ongoing ideological and cultural loyalties. By examining the experience of insurgent opponents of concentrated power in the established order, the study seeks to capture a lost history that simultaneously places politics, economic behavior, and foreign policy in a social and cultural framework.

The analysis focuses on "independent" competitors and citizens who eschewed formal political ideology for an indigenous populism that advanced traditional needs, interests, and values. Such affinities frequently included strong nationalist sentiments and cultural and ethnic identities. *Beyond Left and Right* describes people who reacted to innovations in corporate capitalism, the modern state, and consumer values by mounting assaults on centers of power in big business, organized labor, centralized government, and the professional elite.[4] Their mainstream challenge to an evolving establishment separates them from upper-class conservatives, fascist and racial theorists, intellectual libertarians, religious cultists, organized labor, socialist visionaries, New Deal reformers, civil rights advocates, New Left revolutionaries, radical feminists, and environmentalist lobbyists, none of whom is direct-ly addressed in this overview.

The main protagonists of *Beyond Left and Right* include William Jen-nings Bryan, Robert La Follette, William Borah, Hiram Johnson, George Norris, Burton Wheeler, Robert La Follette Jr., Gerald Nye, Wright Pat-man, Huey Long, Father Charles Coughlin, William Lemke, Charles Lindbergh, Robert Wood, John Flynn, Kenneth Wherry, Karl Mundt, Robert Taft, Douglas MacArthur, Joseph McCarthy, John Bricker, George Wallace, and Ronald Reagan. The book is not a collective biography, however; it is organized both chronologically and topically. The intro-ductory chapter sets the context for the study by surveying the liberal, republican, and producer values emerging from eighteenth- and nine-teenth-century America. It contrasts traditional precepts of individual freedom, self-reliance, and equality of opportunity with the rise of cor-porate capitalism, institutional complexity, and the modern state. The chapter concludes by showing how producer values and interests in-fluenced early twentieth-century populists and traditionally oriented pro-gressive reformers.

Chapter 2 describes the attempts of insurgent progressives and agrar-ian Democrats to oppose military and diplomatic interventionism be-tween 1914 and 1929. These critics of U.S. foreign policy feared the rise of military and governmental elites unresponsive to democratic control and suspected that war furthered the selfish goals of wealthy business interests. They tied these anxieties to continuing disquiet over Old World corruption and tyranny as well as nationalistic concerns for American independence. The chapter traces the efforts of congressional noninter-ventionists to halt military preparedness and keep the United States out of the Great War in Europe. It then turns to insurgent efforts to fight wartime conscription, censorship, and profiteering, as well as the excesses of the 1919 Red Scare. The chapter closes by outlining insurgent outrage against such international institutions as the League of Nations and the World Court and surveys the controversies over U.S. activities in Latin America in the 1920s.

Chapter 3 demonstrates the manner in which progressive insurgents in the Senate and elsewhere used continuing suspicions of concentrated power to support their allegations of collusion between government agen-cies and dominant corporate interests in the 1920s. Postwar attacks on economic and political privilege were fueled by a crisis in American ag-riculture, fears for the survival of small business, and continuing anxi-eties over survival of the producer ethic. Anticorporate progressives charged that Republican administrators showed favoritism to powerful railroads, Wall Street speculators, huge banking concerns, industrial giants, oil refiners, and influential monopolies. The political manifestation of these complaints emerged with the Progressive party of 1924. The chapter concludes by exploring the contradictions inherent in an insurgence that sought to combat the institutional clout of organized money without employing potentially oppressive forms of centralized political power.

Chapter 4 places the producer politics of 1920s insurgents within a traditionalist response to New Era consumerism and cosmopolitan social values. It explores rural mores, Prohibition, Protestant fundamentalism, nativism, immigration restriction, the Ku Klux Klan, anti-Hollywood activism, and the social conflicts associated with the presidential election of 1928. In doing so, it outlines the existence of a cultural insurgence that sought to reassert individual morality and community control over an increasingly secular and institutional society ruled by unaccountable elites.

Chapter 5 traces how some populist and progressive agitators responded to the Great Depression by advancing monetary and financial panaceas designed to rescue beleaguered independent farmers and small business proprietors. It describes William Lemke's farm mortgage relief proposals, anti–Wall Street fervor, the adversaries of chain banking, the advocates of inflation and public banking, and the money-based reforms Father Coughlin and Huey Long advanced. After emphasizing the way 1930s economic radicals addressed republican and middle-class hostility to "special interests," the chapter closes with an assessment of the Union party's role in the 1936 presidential campaign.

Chapter 6 focuses on the process by which small business interests turned to social movements and politics during the depression to combat economic concentration and threats to individual opportunity. It explores crusades against national chain stores and monopolies as well as efforts to oppose the National Recovery Administration for alleged favoritism to big business. Like the monetary and financial reformers, however, small business advocates often failed to distinguish between their own economic interests and the general welfare. By the end of the 1930s American society appeared to accept the loss of traditional economic individualism as a necessary price of market efficiency and future prosperity.

Just as the 1930s witnessed the eclipse of economic populism as a component of mainstream politics, so it experienced the final outburst of progressivism. Chapter 7 describes the process by which political insurgents began to break with the New Deal liberalism defined by a strong central government and alliance with organized labor. It follows traditional progressives' estrangement from Franklin Roosevelt by tracing

controversies over the Supreme Court, union sit-downs and labor legislation, government relief, federal taxes, deficit spending, and unaccountable executive power. It then describes the mix of nationalism, populism,
and producer values in Philip La Follette's National Progressives of
America. By 1940 most former progressives had shifted their focus from
big business to centralized government.

Chapter 8 once more shifts the scene to foreign policy, where insurgent concerns over concentrated power and regimentation played a substantial role in national debates over the prospective role of the United
States in the century's second European war. The chapter traces the insurgent contribution to controversies over World War I debts, the World
Court, and the Nye munitions hearings. It then describes congressional
consideration of neutrality legislation, the Ludlow amendment to require
referenda on any declaration of war, and conscription. The heart of this
chapter outlines the emergence of "democratic nationalism," the populist and noninterventionist ideology that substantially characterized the
approach of the America First Committee, the nation's leading antiwar
organization prior to Pearl Harbor.

Chapter 9 explains how the demands of World War II collective security and mobilization elicited an insurgent response that marshaled long-
standing precepts of nationalism, antistatism, and cultural populism. The
war led opponents of concentrated power to equate liberalism with military internationalism and to associate New Deal reform with elitism,
government centralization, and remote bureaucracy. This chapter addresses deep-seated congressional opposition to wartime executive agencies,
small business suspicion of federal bureaucracy, and hostility to evolving international institutions. It also outlines the origins of a deep-seated anticommunism among nationalists and middle-class populists representing the traditional producer economy.

Chapter 10 describes the emergence of a bipartisan coalition after
World War II that substituted nationalism for noninterventionism and free
enterprise for attacks on concentrated economic power. In conscious
opposition to organized labor and New Deal reform, middle-class insurgents of the late 1940s mounted an all-out attack on statism, cultural
elitism, and liberal internationalism. Their efforts helped define the prevailing anticommunism of cold war politics. This chapter ties the crusade against communism to populist concerns over remote bureaucracy,
internal security, the loyalty of elites, congressional prerogatives over
executive power, and the Truman administration's Europe-centered foreign policy. By 1949 the "loss" of China and widespread frustration over
the containment of communism tested the allegiance of Republican party nationalists to the cold war consensus.

Using the Korean War as context and White House protest mail as evidence, chapter 11 explores the nationalist agenda of the 1950s. After describing the end of foreign policy bipartisanship in 1950, it depicts Senator Joe McCarthy's exploitation of public frustration with the management of the cold war. The chapter then focuses on controversies over Secretary of State Dean Acheson and General Douglas MacArthur. After discussing Robert Taft's failure to obtain the Republican presidential nomination in 1952, it provides an account of nationalist critiques of the foreign policy of the Eisenhower administration. It concludes with a detailed view of the fight to pass the Bricker amendment, which restricted executive prerogative in foreign affairs.

Chapter 12 portrays Joe McCarthy's populist campaign to purge American life of diplomatic and intellectual elites not sufficiently committed to the moral crusade against communism. It explores popular aversion to the "new class" of "knowledge elites," whose professional expertise seemed to promote collectivism, social experiment, government bureaucracy, and liberal internationalism. The chapter then examines congressional inquiries into tax-exempt foundations and ties between corporate and academic power. It also describes ideological opposition to federal involvement in the civil rights struggle. It concludes with an analysis that places the John Birch Society on the margins of insurgence.

Chapter 13 begins with an account of the "social issues" raised by Barry Goldwater's 1964 race for the presidency. It then describes the response to Lyndon Johnson's sponsorship of civil rights reform. After analyzing the populist campaigns of George Wallace and the social and economic issues of the 1970s, the chapter explores antielitist aspects of the Christian Right and New Right, the Reagan-Bush administrations, and the centrist politics of the early 1990s. By the last decade of the twentieth century insurgents had completed the shift in their definition of "special interests" and the focus of their outrage. *Beyond Left and Right* closes with a conclusion that critically examines the insurgent legacy and reviews prospects for engaging in a political dialogue that goes beyond conventional political categories.

✦ ✦ ✦

The writings of LeRoy Ashby, Alan Brinkley, Stanley Coben, Wayne Cole, Justus D. Doenecke, Louis Filler, Eugene D. Genovese, Robert Griffith, Mona Harrington, Ellis W. Hawley, Richard Hofstadter, Don Kirschner, Christopher Lasch, Lawrence W. Levine, Leonard J. Moore, David W. Noble, Leo Ribuffo, Michael P. Rogin, David Thelen, William I. Thompson, William A. Williams, and Gene Wise are among the volumes of professional history that have played a central role in shaping the content, methodology, and spirit of this book. Influential analyses from outside the history discipline include works by Daniel Bell, Jeffrey Bell, E. J. Dionne Jr., Thomas B. Edsall, Jerome L. Himmelstein, Michael Novak, Kevin P. Phillips, and Edward A. Shils.

The author wishes to inform readers that all italics in quoted passages appear in the cited sources but minor spelling and punctuation errors have been corrected. References to "Mr." and "Mrs." in correspondence salutations have been omitted in chapter notes except when necessary to indicate gender identity. Full citations appear in the appropriate categories of the bibliography.

Brief passages in this volume have appeared in somewhat different form in the following journal articles: "The Perils of Western Farm Politics: Herbert Hoover, Gerald P. Nye, and Agricultural Reform, 1926–1932" (*North Dakota Quarterly* 53 [Fall 1985], 92–110); "White Southerners' Alienation and Civil Rights: The Response to Corporate Liberalism, 1956–1965" (*Journal of Southern History* 54 [May 1988], 173–200); "The Crusade against Chain Stores: Portland's Independent Merchants, 1928–1935" (*Oregon Historical Quarterly* 89 [Winter 1988], 341–68); and "Senator Borah's Crusade to Save Small Business from the New Deal" (*Historian* 55 [Summer 1993], 693–708).

✦ ✦ ✦

Institutional assistance proved invaluable in the completion of this project. Fellowships at Stanford University's Summer Faculty Renewal Program during August 1978 and July 1981 facilitated participation in Barton J. Bernstein's symposium entitled "Postwar America, 1945–1960." A summer stipend from the National Endowment of the Humanities permitted the author to attend Martin L. Fausold's seminar, "Reform and the 1920s," offered at the Herbert Hoover Presidential Library in 1979. A second summer award permitted inclusion in Robert A. Divine's "The Cold War: From Truman to Nixon," an NEH seminar given at the University of Texas at Austin in 1982. Further support came from a Hoover Scholar Research Grant from the Herbert Hoover Presidential Library Association in the spring of 1983 and a Summer Independent Research Grant from the Oregon Committee for the Humanities during the same year. Portland State University provided sabbatical leaves during 1982–83 and 1991–92 and a grant of paid released time during the fall of 1989. A subvention grant from the Portland State University Foundation facilitated publication of this book.

The author extends profound appreciation to the numerous librarians and archivists who went beyond the call of duty to assist in gathering materials for this study. He also wishes to thank Portland State's Diane

Gould, Lee Ellington, and Linda Schreiner-Mahoney for invaluable aid in manuscript preparation. Paul Copley, social studies chair at Sunset High School in Beaverton, Oregon, researched the materials surrounding the tax-exempt foundations. Michael G. Horowitz is to be acknowledged for helping with the title and the project's general orientation. Peter N. Carroll's reading of the manuscript generated wise and helpful advice and counsel. LeRoy Ashby and an anonymous reader, who meticulously reviewed the contents for University of Illinois Press, provided explicit and helpful recommendations for revision. Richard L. Wentworth, director of the press, deserves heartfelt commendation for both vision and persistence. Manuscript editor Jane Mohraz also proved to be an invaluable ally. Finally, Gloria E. Myers takes top billing as the writer's intellectual partner and confidante. As always, the author is responsible for all errors and matters of judgment.

1

Producer Values, Corporate Culture, and Progressive Politics

The task of progressive reform, Senator Robert M. La Follette proclaimed in 1916, was to combat "the encroachment of the powerful few upon the rights of the many."[1] La Follette's cry spoke to the sensibilities of a generation anxious about the hidden hands of privilege and the survival of individualism and democracy. Yet his denunciation of concentrated wealth and power mirrored central precepts of an American political legacy of some 150 years.

✦ ✦ ✦

Scholars have traced American antipathy to dependence and tyranny to two prominent ideologies associated with the American Revolution. The first embraced a "liberal" individualism that viewed government authority as a threat to freedom, autonomy, and justice. Borrowing notions from John Locke and Adam Smith, the liberal ethic equated personal liberty and happiness with natural rights to property and material pleasure. It pictured human labor and ingenuity as the source of wealth and viewed both governmental and market elites with suspicion. Eighteenth-century liberals believed that the economic autonomy of producers would promote the personal independence and freedom necessary for a just and stable society. Through the pursuit of self-interest, the public good would be served.[2]

A second ideological strand embraced the Atlantic tradition of republicanism or civic humanism, which some scholars have tied to classical antiquity and the Italian Renaissance. Adherents of republicanism asserted that material independence was the foundation of a virtuous citizenry. The people were the possessors of political sovereignty and the guarantors of social justice. Through their vigilance, republican governments could be protected against the aristocratic subversions of moral decadence, wealth, luxury, and corrupt power. Yet such states could survive only if they remained simple and austere, advanced equality of opportunity, and kept their constituents free from the tyrannies of bureaucracy and standing armies. Like economic liberalism, the republican ideal celebrated personal independence and liberation from the restraints of government and privilege. Northern and southern adherents of both philosophies joined the American Revolution because they equated British monarchy, aristocracy, and imperial authority with a corrupt assault on liberty.[3]

By the early nineteenth century the young nation adhered to a consensus republicanism that portrayed its government as simple, honest, and free from the influence of monarchy and European corruption. America's virtuous and independent citizens were said to live in conditions of general economic equality, broadly distributed authority, and localized control. Andrew Jackson and his Democratic followers played on this image by building a political movement advocating popular property rights, the sale of cheap government land, liberal incorporation laws, free trade, and opposition to centralized government. The main target of the Jacksonians turned out to be monopolistic and government-licensed corporations, though. By leading a successful campaign to terminate the charter of the Second Bank of the United States in 1832, President Jackson mobilized rampant suspicions about speculative finance. A movement to protect producers and combat concentrated economic power, Jacksonian democracy sought equality of opportunity by separating government from the marketplace.[4]

Denouncing slavery in the late 1850s, the Republican party of Abraham Lincoln incorporated the capitalist work ethic and ascetic values first advanced by Whig opponents of the Jackson presidency. But the new party also accepted the "libertarian republicanism" that Democrats had promoted since 1800. The synthesis created a northern middle-class ideology of producers that stressed hard work, thrift, business initiative, character, and sexual restraint. Grounded in local community and face-to-face relationships, American property holders of the mid-nineteenth century fashioned themselves the freest people in the world. Midwesterners of the period defined their region as the home of responsible, earnest, and industrious citizens free of obligatory ties to others. For many independent farmers, artisans, and small business competitors outside the South, commercial capitalism appeared to be a liberating way of life that offered equal liberty for all and special privileges or monopoly power to none.[5]

Just as the producer ethic appeared to triumph with the North's victory in the Civil War, the U.S. economy experienced an industrial and transportation revolution characterized by the growth of large private corporations. Managers of these new enterprises combined new productive technologies with expanded access to raw materials and control of distribution. Standardized business procedures and innovative administrative techniques facilitated organizational efficiency and the absorption of competitors. During the 1880s rapid expansion of the railroad, steel, and petroleum industries generated the fastest economic growth of any decade since the war. As net capital flow to the United States reached $1.5 billion between 1870 and 1895, a national market economy spread consumerism to all regions. By 1900 three hundred industrial trusts controlled two-fifths of the nation's manufacturing.[6]

"The system of corporate life is a new power for which our language contains no name," noted Charles Francis Adams Jr. in 1869. As the corporation became the "frontier of opportunity," a growth-oriented national market began to replace the nation's unconcentrated mercantile economy. Although corporate capitalism generated stable prices, employment, and investment opportunities for the new middle class, it created a bureaucratic order that established new hierarchies. By standardizing work procedures, the organizational revolution produced a white-collar culture of salaried professionals whose institutional loyalty was in marked contrast to the individualism of independent entrepreneurs. The railroads, the first prototype of business bureaucracy, dramatized these developments by paying employees for time instead of completed tasks. Requirements of interstate travel even led Congress to replace local clock settings with a national system of standardized time in 1883.[7]

As Steven L. Piott has suggested, the rise of business management helped engender the "corporate-dominated values and modes of modern, twentieth century America." Urban industrialism changed a predominantly rural and frontier nation into a metropolitan society. It created networks of secularized social relationships divorced from moral context and traditional roles and obligations. In particular, restraints on economic activity no longer prevailed. Americans found that membership in a specific profession or social class took precedence over ties to families, friends, and communities. Corporate culture helped loosen geographic boundaries, weaken the autonomy of traditional communities, and prepare people for custom-wrenching innovation and change.[8]

Late-nineteenth-century corporations sought to present themselves as the natural expression of self-reliance, independent initiative, and widespread opportunity. Even when firms absorbed competitors into "trusts" that dominated the industry, the judiciary tended to legitimize their operations. The Supreme Court's 1886 ruling in *Santa Clara County v. Southern Pacific Railroad* provided companies with the legal status of individuals under the Fifth and Fourteenth amendments. By classifying incorporated businesses as "natural" entities, the Court protected them against the state's arbitrarily depriving them of assets or earnings.[9]

Corporate interests played on public fears of government control to suggest that legal restrictions on enterprise would be "paternalistic" or "European." Nevertheless, Congress passed the Interstate Commerce Act of 1887, which prohibited discriminatory railroad pricing and established a federal regulatory commission to work with industry attorneys. Three years later the Sherman Antitrust Act outlawed restraints of trade against the public interest. Federal courts, however, continued to apply common-law distinctions between reasonable and unreasonable restraints of commerce and refused to rule that financial domination constituted a monopoly practice. In the *E. C. Knight Company* case of 1895 the Supreme Court held that the federal government had no antitrust jurisdiction over interstate manufacturing or processing. New Jersey soon legalized corporate holding companies, while Delaware and West Virginia allowed businesses to hold stock in other firms. Between 1898 and 1904 the U.S. economy experienced 236 industrial consolidations, involving $6 billion in capital.[10]

The Supreme Court finally resolved the trust issue in 1911. In a landmark decision the Court dissolved the Standard Oil and American Tobacco corporations but enunciated a "rule of reason" that distinguished between monopolies. Reverting to common-law antitrust interpretations, the tribunal established that restrictions on competition did not necessarily constitute illegal impediments to trade or attempts to monopolize. Restraint of trade, declared the Court, was confined to employing unfair methods designed to eliminate competitors and setting market prices and trade norms that violated public interest. Consequently, the Sherman Act applied only when violators sought to exclude or drive competitors from their right to compete. The Court concluded that any effort to guarantee free competition might infringe on liberty of contract and rights of property.[11]

✦ ✦ ✦

As corporate dominance increased after the Civil War, small producers worried about ruthless competitive practices, exploitive labor policies, questionable ethical standards, and excessive profit making. The heart of the issue concerned the fear that great corporations were stifling opportunity and enslaving individuals and communities to new forms of dependence. Beyond familiar controls, the huge concerns threatened what David Thelen has described as "remembered standards" of protective law and community sanction. Recurring late-nineteenth-century economic panics, such as the severe depression of 1893–97, threatened small enterprise and aggravated the problem. Once the ally of independent entrepreneurs, the Republican party became vulnerable to charges that it had extended "special privileges" to postwar industrialists and railroads. Public land grants, protective tariffs, and government corruption helped make "monopoly" the central issue of national politics.[12]

Anxious producers and small enterprisers associated monopoly with impersonal power, government favoritism, the primacy of wealth, and threats to economic independence and community autonomy. As the economic historian Stuart Bruchey has stated, antimonopoly became "a cry of protest on the part of individuals increasingly depersonalized and lost in corporate anonymity, of small towns increasingly invaded by the railroad, of small business and small farmers increasingly menaced by large-scale and distant competition." Jacksonians had opposed granting legal privileges to selected corporations as a violation of natural economic laws. Post–Civil War critics argued the free market had been perverted by special legislation that gave large enterprises "unjust advantages" and control over natural resources and public franchises. Antimonopolists further protested that corporate domination of transportation and banking robbed producers of the rewards of labor and threatened equality of opportunity.[13]

New York's Grover Cleveland, elected president in 1884 and 1892, captured the essence of antimonopoly sentiment when he remarked that "the communism of combined wealth and capital . . . insidiously undermines the justice and free integrity of free institutions." Notions of republican virtue and economic individualism permeated Henry George's *Progress and Poverty,* published in 1879. Fearing that collectivized wealth might divide the nation between a ruling elite and a permanent, degraded, landless proletariat, George proposed a single tax to preserve equality of opportunity. The scheme distinguished between productive and speculative income by limiting taxation to rent and "unearned increment" arising from land ownership. Its persistent popularity demonstrated widespread fear that privileged monopoly threatened the middle-class stake in competitive capitalism.[14]

Plains farmers in both the North and South ranked among the most bitter critics of corporate power. Such opposition surfaced even though many economic indicators actually favored agriculture. Prices for goods that farmers bought, for example, declined more than crop returns after 1869. Railroad rates also fell faster than farm product prices. The period witnessed easy credit, lower interest rates, and a moderate amount of agricultural debt in relation to equity. As farm gross product per worker rose in the late nineteenth century, growers escaped the systemic depressions that plagued the industrial economy. Nevertheless, independent farmers felt powerless before the impersonal forces of the national and global market. Rural producers worried about declines in commodity prices, complained of cheating and unfair pricing by warehouses and grain elevators, and resented the setting of erratic rates by monopolistic railroads. Nervous about rising debt, undercapitalized farmers feared a dependence on unpredictable markets and remote financial powers.[15]

Agrarian protest was rooted in the perception that monopolistic interests wielded illegitimate and unfair control over credit, transportation, distribution, and government policy. Farm agitation first surfaced in the 1870s when growers organized the Granger movement, a network of rural consumer cooperatives and mutual aid societies antagonistic to the railroads and middlemen. When falling crop prices and drought threatened the cooperative ideal in the next decade, small producers joined the Southern Alliance and the National Farmers' Alliance of the Northwest. Under the leadership of C. W. Macune, whose Texas organization swelled to a million members, the Southern Alliance attracted over four million followers by 1890. Viewing real wealth as the capacity to produce, southern agrarians sought to reconcile material self-interest with community welfare by defending worthy producers against unjust rule by financial and political elites.[16]

Both farmers' alliances functioned in a two-track capacity. First, organizers created a movement to serve isolated producers burdened by market dependence, confusion, and powerlessness. Their networks provided lectures, rallies, picnics, camp meetings, newspapers, and local purchasing and marketing cooperatives to free farmers from credit dependence and high production costs. Meanwhile, the movement followed a second track through national politics. Calling for a struggle of "the masses against the classes," Alliance leaders demanded federal regulation of a trust-directed "conspiracy against legitimate trade."[17]

Alliance political mobilization centered on the currency question. As the nation's population doubled between 1865 and 1895, its money supply actually diminished, leading to a tripling of the dollar's value. Critics targeted the "Crime of '73," a reference to Congress's demonetization of silver. By the 1880s inflationists, debtor interests, and agrarian agitators were demanding a bimetallic currency in which silver would be pegged at one-sixteenth the value of gold. Currency reformers believed that money should facilitate the exchange of wealth among producers and that its value should not arbitrarily be set by law. Monetarists consequently had no hesitancy in calling for increased quantities of circulated currency to stimulate economic activity and eliminate the power of elites to manipulate access to credit. William H. Harvey's *Coin's Financial School,* which argued these points, sold 300,000 copies within a year of its 1894 publication. The next year produced a similar discussion in Ignatius Donnelly's popular *American People's Money.*[18]

C. W. Macune's Southern Alliance incorporated monetary reform when it publicized a national agenda in 1889. The platform demanded the abolition of land monopoly and federal ownership of railroads and telephone and telegraph lines. It also replicated the Greenback Labor party's insistence that the government issue inflationary legal tender. Its most important plank, the subtreasury plan, addressed the idea of a circulating and flexible currency. This proposal called for growers to store nonperishable commodities in government warehouses and to receive 1 percent paper money loans for 80 percent of the value of those crops. By placing additional greenbacks in circulation, populists believed that money could keep pace with added population. They hoped that variations in commodity prices would be determined by the market's supply and demand instead of a contracting currency.[19]

Cooperation among Alliance officials, independent farmers, small-town merchants, and elements of organized labor led to the formation of the People's or Populist party in 1892. Focusing on land, transportation, and money, the party's Omaha convention anticipated important aspects of twentieth-century insurgence. It proposed that settlers be able to reclaim acreage formerly granted to the railroads. It also sought to outlaw foreigners' ownership of land and initiate government ownership of interstate transportation and communications. The Populists further demanded the creation of postal savings banks, a graduated federal income tax, an inflated national currency, and unlimited coinage of silver and gold at the 16-1 ratio. The convention recommended a one-term American presidency, the direct election of U.S. senators, and state adoption of the initiative and referendum. Finally, the People's party expressed sympathies for organized labor and a shorter working day.[20]

Populists sought a market society of producers sustained by government ownership of such distribution resources as the railroads and the money supply. Yet agrarian reformers seemed to embody a near-paralyzing ambiguity. On one hand, some Alliance activists hoped to use state power to curb monopoly and redistribute wealth across the social spectrum. On the other, deep-seated fears over the use of coercive government by wealthy plutocrats generated strong antistatist sentiments. Unable to resolve the dilemma, the People's party relied on the silver issue in 1892. The result produced a little more than a million votes (8.5 percent of the popular tally) for its presidential candidate, James B. Weaver. Meanwhile, the Populists elected ten congressional representatives, five U.S. senators, and three governors.[21]

✦ ✦ ✦

By the time the Democrats held their national convention in 1896, free silver partisans had taken control of the party machinery. A populist platform now condemned trusts, monopolies, and high protective tariffs and called for unlimited coinage of silver valued at a 16-1 ratio to gold. The currency debate reached a passionate climax when Nebraska's William Jennings Bryan electrified the Chicago assembly with a powerful denunciation of the gold standard. In a brilliant synthesis of republican moralism and agrarian radicalism, Bryan drew the classic distinction between "idle holders of capital" and "the struggling masses." "You shall not press down upon the brow of labor this crown of thorns," he thundered, "you shall not crucify mankind upon a cross of gold."[22]

Bryan perfectly embodied the Midwest's traditional producer values, fears of concentrated wealth and power, and commitment to majority rule and the rights of ordinary people. Born in 1860 in the prairie country of south-central Illinois, Bryan was reared in the culture of evangelical Baptism. His father was a politician and judge with strong republican sympathies. After studying law in Chicago, Bryan set up practice in Lincoln, Nebraska, in 1887. Turning to politics three years later, he rode a wave of agrarian protest to become only the second Democrat in the state's history to win a seat in Congress. Bryan never supported the public banking proposals of the Populists but strongly opposed the protective tariff and the gold standard. His first congressional speech used a metaphor of burglary to proclaim that the tariff showed government "favoritism" toward greedy manufacturers.[23]

By the time he began his second and last congressional term in 1893 Bryan had adopted the "eternal war" over the currency as his leading passion. He described the struggle for free silver as one fought for the common people in the interests of democracy and equality before the law. Arrayed against them were "the corporate interests of the nation, its moneyed institutions, its aggregations of wealth and capital, imperious, arrogant, compassionless." In the Jacksonian tradition, the Nebraska representative identified farmers as honest producers and bankers as parasitical speculators. "The poor man who takes property by force is called a thief," Bryan told the House, "but the creditor who can by legislation make a debtor pay a dollar twice as large as he borrowed is lauded as the friend of sound currency." Cotton and wheat farmers were expected to sell below their costs of production, he continued, so that the American gold supply could be replenished.[24]

Bryan lost a senatorial bid in 1894 but won national acclaim by traveling the lecture circuit in behalf of Democratic silver proponents. The "Cross of Gold" speech reiterated the argument that the issuance of currency was a government function, not a matter for private banks. Riding the crest of his reputation and convention oratory, the thirty-six-year-old Bryan replaced incumbent president Grover Cleveland by taking the nomination for the top slot on the ticket on the fifth ballot. He also won the endorsement of the Populists, although the splinter party named Georgia's Thomas E. Watson as its own vice presidential candidate.[25]

The "Boy Orator of the Platte" stumped the continent in a national campaign that approached the emotional intensity of an evangelical crusade. Bryan charged that the Republicans had collected an enormous campaign fund and that "money loaners," "corporate employers," and "trusts and syndicates" had resorted to threats and coercion to impose their party on the American people. In contrast, Republican candidate William McKinley ignored the ongoing economic depression and identified his campaign with progress and prosperity. By rejecting the pietism of the Bryan crusade, McKinley embraced a cultural pluralism that appealed to urban, ethnic, and working-class voters. On election day the Republicans triumphed with over 7.0 million votes (51.1 percent of the total) and an electoral college margin of 271 to 176. With nearly 6.5 million ballots, however, Bryan and the Democrats swept all of the South and most of the West, winning twenty-two states in all.[26]

Despite the setback, Bryan continued to represent populist suspicion of concentrated financial power. "There is no good monopoly in private hands," he told delegates to a Chicago conference on trusts in 1899. "Money is to be the servant of man, and I protest against all theories that enthrone money and debase mankind." Unlike humans, he insisted, soulless corporations were given perpetual life. Bryan also expressed republican animosity toward imperialist Britain and the European continent. Like Georgia's Tom Watson, who warned that overseas involvement served the "privileged classes," Bryan tied financial plutocracy to the European culture and pretensions of the eastern upper class. Some in the East, he complained, were "better acquainted with the beauties of the Alps than the grandeur of the Rockies, more accustomed to the sunny skies of Italy than the invigorating breezes of the Mississippi Valley."[27]

Bryan cleverly linked the monetary controversy to populist themes of American nationalism. He expressed fury at economic leaders who feared that abandonment of the gold standard would result in partial repudiation of the $4 billion in American securities held by British investors. Eastern financial elites, the Nebraskan told Congress in 1893, were not "willing to trust their fortunes and their destinies to American citizens."

"Shall we confess our inability to enact monetary laws?" an exasperated Bryan demanded of the House. "Are we an English colony or an independent people?" Writing in the *Arena* five years later, the populist warned that foreigners owned large amounts of stock in American railroads and other corporations and unduly influenced corporate policy and electoral politics. Adherence to the gold standard, he charged, was merely "an acknowledgment of subserviency to European dictation." Instead of a country, lamented Bryan, "we are but a province."[28]

Nationalist and republican sentiments penetrated the core of Bryan's opposition to overseas imperialism. Following the Spanish-American War of 1898, the former presidential candidate lobbied against the annexation of the Philippines. "Militarism is the very antithesis of Democracy," he preached. Bryan accepted a second Democratic nomination for what he intended to be a national referendum on formal empire in 1900. A self-governing republic "can have no subjects," he told the convention. "Every citizen is a sovereign but . . . no one cares to wear a crown." Believing that the United States should expand its influence through trade and the force of example, Bryan used the campaign to warn how standing armies threatened republican government. But despite brutal military suppression of an anticolonial insurrection in the Philippines, voters appeared to accept U.S. annexation as an accomplished fact. President McKinley and vice presidential candidate Theodore Roosevelt easily rode to a second Republican electoral triumph over the Great Commoner.[29]

When Bryan ran for the presidency a third time in 1908, he attempted to incorporate populist sentiments in a campaign focused on domestic issues. With "Shall the people rule?" as his slogan, the Democratic candidate embraced such familiar schemes as the direct primary, voter election of U.S. senators, the graduated income tax, and federal licensing for corporations. He also supported woman suffrage, campaign reform, and federal guarantees for bank deposits. Despite Bryan's call for improvement in the conditions of the "producing classes," Republican nominee William Howard Taft rolled to an easy 52-43 percent victory by promising to consolidate the reforms initiated by his predecessor, Theodore Roosevelt.[30]

Although the People's party never recovered from the fusion campaign of 1896, southern populists continued the struggle inside state Democratic movements. From the 1890s on, several southern states created railroad commissions, public utility agencies, and bank and insurance regulation. Others pursued antitrust policies, passed unfair business practice acts, and enacted safety and inspection laws for mines and factories. In North Carolina, Mississippi, Alabama, Georgia, and Arkansas reformers instituted the direct primary, initiative, referendum, recall, corrupt practices legislation, and antilobbying laws. Southern populists, such as Tom Watson, Mississippi's James Vardaman, and South Carolina's Ben ("Pitchfork") Tillman, combined demagogic white supremacy with adamant opposition to northern corporations and monopolies. Fusing anti-Catholicism and anti-Semitism with racism, Watson insisted on opposing the "privileged classes." Vardaman, in turn, described himself as a defender of the "great, silent, slow-thinking toiling multitude."[31]

✦ ✦ ✦

Southern populists believed that collusion between a corrupt white establishment and poor blacks served as a barrier to their success. Consequently, Watson, Vardaman, and Tillman pushed their states toward the enactment of racial ("Jim Crow") segregation laws and the disenfranchisement of black voters. In contrast farmers and small business interests in midwestern and western states focused on high railroad freight rates, exorbitant interest charges, and insufficient credit. Midwestern political ferment at the turn of the century resulted in the rise of a group of Republican insurgents whose roots lay in the devastating economic depression of the 1890s. Although most had rejected the People's party, these new leaders injected populist protest against concentrated power and remote government into Republican campaigns. Directly familiar with the threat of railroads, banks, middlemen, and industrialists to economic individualism, they crusaded with nineteenth-century fervor against corporate monopolies and trusts.[32]

Demands for economic opportunity and responsive government became a major theme of early progressive reform. South Dakotans elected Andrew E. Lee, a populist Republican, as governor in 1898. Seeking to make the political machinery more responsive to citizen needs and less amenable to special interests, Lee ushered in passage of the initiative and referendum. Nine years later the state legislature established a direct primary, strictly regulated lobbying, and outlawed corporate contributions to electoral campaigns. In Wisconsin Robert La Follette led University of Wisconsin reformers to purge state politics of corruption and capture the governor's seat in 1900. Seeking to tax the railroads, La Follette portrayed a struggle between "the people" who wanted justice and corporate interests seeking "special privilege." The legislature responded by creating state commissions regulating taxation, railroad rates, and civil service appointments. Wisconsin also passed a direct primary law, as did Oregon, Iowa, and Missouri.[33]

Missouri's Governor Joseph Folk turned to law as a device to restrain corporate power. Between 1905 and 1908 Folk packaged crusades against bribery, bossism, and selfish partisanship as the "Missouri Idea." His administration passed legislation for state regulation of lobbyists, rail-roads, and insurance companies and enabled municipalities to control utility costs. Meanwhile, Attorney General Herbert Hadley negotiated with insurance corporations for lower rates and greater competition. Hadley also sued International Harvester and the lumber interests for monopoly practices, prevented subsidiaries of Standard Oil from oper-ating in Missouri, and threatened to prosecute the railroads if they dis-obeyed new state rate laws.[34]

In the 1910s progressive insurgence took more militant forms in the Dakotas. South Dakota voters elected the well-driller Peter Norbeck to the governorship in 1916. A successful entrepreneur and one of the largest landholders in the state, Norbeck called for reformist programs that were "simply cooperative" instead of socialistic, "progressive, yet not radical." Rejecting state ownership, the South Dakotan nevertheless insisted that government should regulate monopolies producing unreasonable profits. Provided with a helpful "farmers legislature," the Norbeck regime en-acted a state rural credits program. The administration's second term brought the creation of a state cement plant and coal mine as well as government hail insurance and bonding programs.[35]

Neighboring North Dakota provided another example of how grass-roots populists were willing to use government to foster a competitive agrarian economy. By 1914, 89 percent of the state's population remained on farms or in small towns. Settled mainly by German and Scandinavian immigrants, North Dakota constituted the last agricultural frontier in the United States. Only when sufficient moisture produced high grain prices were farmers able to meet mortgage, interest, and survival demands. Initial settlement in the area had been underwritten by Minneapolis mill-ers and railroad promoters. These interests not only had furnished cap-ital for transportation and communications systems but also had laid out town sites, had advertised agricultural opportunities, and had become the region's political overlords. As a result, outside corporations came to own many of the state's banks, newspapers, and grain elevators. North Da-kotans, the regional historian Glenn H. Smith has concluded, perceived themselves to be "a colony of the milling and financial centers of the East."[36]

As a developing frontier whose raw materials and labor were exploited by distant interests, North Dakota was ripe for mobilizing "the people" against "the interests." Accordingly, wheat farmers organized a market-ing cooperative in 1907 that grew into the Equity Cooperative Exchange four years later. Equity hoped to eliminate the excessive profits of eleva-tor companies, grain exchanges, and futures speculators but found itself prevented from exerting trading rights on the Minneapolis Exchange.

Seeking to arrange the storage of sufficient wheat to create a market free from Minneapolis control, farmers used their numerical strength to rat- ify a 1914 amendment to the state constitution authorizing the construc- tion of a publicly owned terminal elevator. Nevertheless, the state legis- lature refused to authorize the building of the facility. One lawmaker purportedly told Equity members to leave the creation of statutes to leg- islators and "go home and slop the hogs."[37]

When national banks no longer lent on farm mortgages in the de- pressed North Dakota economy, independent wheat growers turned to politics in 1915 by organizing the Nonpartisan League (NPL), an insur- gent movement that attracted forty thousand members in a single year. The NPL emulated the farmers' alliances of the 1880s by creating its own cooperative newspapers, retail stores, and banks. It also used the direct primary to advance political candidates who supported government in- tervention to preserve a competitive economy. The NPL's platform of 1916 called for state-owned terminal elevators, flour mills, packing and cold storage plants, hail insurance, and rural credit banks. The league also insisted on reforming wheat grading practices and exempting farm improvements from taxation. Organizing farmers in a grass-roots cam- paign, the NPL used the Republican primary and the general election to sweep the one-time farmer and teacher Lynn Frazier into the governor- ship with a league-dominated legislature.[38]

The NPL's founder, Arthur C. Townley, a former Minnesota socialist, openly played on republican resentments in recruiting supporters. "If you put a lawyer, a banker, and an industrialist in a barrel and roll it down- hill," he told embittered farmers, "there'll always be a son-of-a-bitch on top." Like South Dakota's Norbeck, however, the NPL endorsed capi- talism and individual ownership. Townley, Frazier, and such league lead- ers as William Lemke and William Langer argued that state government could provide the independent economic force to offset the power of concentrated capital. The NPL promised to sustain free competition by establishing state control of money, banking, natural resources, and es- sential marketing facilities. Townley cleverly combined participatory democracy with individual economic self-interest. By 1918 the Nonpar- tisan League had spread to fourteen north-central and western mountain states and had attracted 220,000 followers.[39]

✦ ✦ ✦

Insurgent progressives, such as Robert La Follette, hoped to use nonpar- tisan commissions, civil service, and direct primaries to keep special in- terests out of politics. Yet these procedural reforms also won endorse- ment from urban professionals and middle-class activists seeking social stability and order in a tumultuous society. Accepting the modern corporation as the basis of an efficient and prosperous economy, modernizing reformers sought to apply rational planning, scientific expertise, efficiency, and professional administration to the management of early-twentieth-century government and society. Instead of prosecuting trusts, they wanted to regulate them in the public interest through nonpartisan government agencies. Meanwhile, a bipartisan coalition of "corporate" progressives hoped to use the initiative and the referendum to circumvent the power of political "bosses" and reinvigorate a responsible middle-class citizenry.[40]

The precepts of corporate progressivism were most explicitly outlined in Herbert Croly's influential *Promise of American Life* (1909). A California-born editor and intellectual, Croly sought to overcome widespread dissension over trusts. His plan embraced a "new nationalism," in which a "democratic elite" would administer an assertive federal welfare and regulatory bureaucracy. Croly argued that a strong central government could offset concentration in the market and protect the poor and working classes. Advocating the virtues of the corporate economy and social reform, he supported using academic and management experts in government service.[41]

On the state level Wisconsin led the way in implementing corporate progressivism. Under Governor Francis E. McGovern's administration between 1911 and 1915, the legislature approved constitutional provisions liberalizing the amendment procedure and authorizing the initiative, recall, and referendum. Lawmakers also enacted a state income tax, workers' compensation, regulation of working hours for women and children, a corrupt practices act, a state insurance system, and benefits to farmers. The most innovative policy of the McGovern administration involved its use of university scholars as drafters of legislation and as expert members of state nonpartisan commissions and regulatory agencies. The "Wisconsin Idea" represented the first successful combination of business and academic intelligence in the public interest. Accordingly, Governor McGovern created commissions to oversee industrial labor and education, railroads, tax collection, insurance, dairy farming, highway construction, forests, waterpower, and public administration.[42]

Corporate progressivism also permeated the politics of Theodore Roosevelt, a reformer who nevertheless insisted that large corporations were the inevitable consequences of modern industrialism. Although Roosevelt's presidency initiated over forty antitrust suits between 1901 and 1909, it preferred to use administrative agencies to negotiate "gentlemen's agreements" and accords with railroads and other enterprises. Out of office in 1911, Roosevelt dismissed those who had taken on "the impossible task of returning to the economic conditions that obtained sixty years ago." A disciple of Herbert Croly, he supported woman suffrage, social insurance, and a federal corporation commission in a 1912 run for the presidency on the Progressive party ticket. Woodrow Wilson, a Virginian who had served as president of Princeton University and governor of New Jersey, led the Democratic opposition by heralding a "new freedom" that would discipline inefficient and excessively large businesses.[43]

Once Wilson prevailed at the polls, he embraced the Croly and Roosevelt approach. Ratification of the Sixteenth Amendment enabled Congress to pass a graduated income tax to enhance federal revenues. Wilson signed the Federal Reserve Act, creating twelve regional depository banks, whose interest rates would be set by a Federal Reserve Board appointed by the president. To regularize market rules of competition, Congress created the five-member Federal Trade Commission (FTC). Besides winning the right to conduct investigations and require periodic corporation reports, the new agency was able to issue restraining orders to prevent "unfair methods of competition" and uphold antitrust laws. Congress also passed the Clayton Antitrust Act, which prohibited price discrimination and other practices discouraging competition. The Wilson administration subsequently created the nation's first farm loan program; approved federal regulation of working conditions for merchant seamen, railroad employees, and children; and authorized federal workers' compensation.[44]

✦ ✦ ✦

Woodrow Wilson's reforms would shape the nation's political economy for decades. Yet opponents of concentrated economic and political power continued to be nervous about coordination between a strong central government and big business. Led by Robert La Follette, insurgent progressives created the National Progressive Republican League in 1911. Designed to promote "popular government and progressive legislation," the league pushed for the direct election of U.S. senators, state procedural reforms, and a corrupt practices act. Passage of the Seventeenth Amendment two years later gave voters the right to elect senators and bolstered the insurgent cause. By 1917 such reformers as Iowa's Albert B. Cummins, Minnesota's Moses Clapp, North Dakota's Asle Gronna, Oregon's Harry Lane, and Washington's Miles Poindexter had made their way to the Senate.[45] Their presence was overshadowed by four giants of American insurgence, however: Nebraska's George W. Norris, California's Hiram W. Johnson, Idaho's William E. Borah, and Wisconsin's Robert La Follette.

George Norris was born in 1861 in Sandusky County, Ohio, attended college in Indiana, and began practicing law in Nebraska in the mid-1880s. Norris prospered in mortgage-loan dealings until the depression of the 1890s wrought havoc on Nebraska farmers and ranchers. After serving as a county prosecutor, the young attorney defeated a Populist by two votes to become a district judge. His court won a reputation for allowing local farmers to present evidence warranting postponement of mortgage foreclosures. Resisting the statewide Populist tide, Norris stuck with the Republicans and won election to Congress in 1902. He soon concerned himself with railroad rates, packing-house regulations, the sugar trust, and independent banking. After organizing a group of young Republican "insurgents" between 1908 and 1910, Norris succeeded in depriving House speaker Joe Cannon of unilateral power to make committee assignments. The highly publicized victory connected "insurgence" to open confrontation with established power and tied the Nebraskan's name to political independence.[46]

Sent to the Senate in 1912, Norris applied his progressive philosophy to the needs of wheat farmers by agitating for government-sponsored irrigation and electric power projects. He supported Wisconsin's Robert La Follette in the Republican presidential primaries in 1912 but switched his loyalty to the more viable Theodore Roosevelt candidacy. Norris criticized the Federal Reserve Board and the Federal Trade Commission bills for not sufficiently confronting concentrated financial power, but voted for them on the floor. After a conference committee eliminated criminal penalties for unfair trade violations from the Clayton antitrust bill, however, Norris opposed the measure in the Senate. A Republican independent who shied away from most alliances, the Nebraskan embodied the republican values of individualism, honest government, and nationalism.[47]

Hiram Johnson won election to the Senate in 1916. A civic-minded Republican, Johnson had opposed his own father by entering San Francisco reform politics in the 1890s. As public prosecutor for the city, he assisted in the conviction of Abraham Reuf, a Republican boss, for bribery in 1908. Two years later Johnson entered the California gubernatorial race. Touring the state in a red auto, he promised to combat the political influence of the Southern Pacific Railroad. As California's first progressive governor, Johnson pledged to fight "the interests" and provide political and economic opportunities for "the people." Between 1911 and 1917 he won enactment of the direct primary, referendum, recall, and ratification of the federal woman suffrage amendment. Johnson also signed bills authorizing workers' compensation, shorter laboring hours for women, regulation of public utilities and railroads, and civil service reform.[48]

The Johnson administration sought the use of scientific management in state affairs in an atmosphere devoid of partisan politics and class consciousness. Not surprisingly, the governor joined Theodore Roosevelt as the vice presidential candidate of the Progressive party in 1912. Johnson's cooperation with his idol, however, belied a strong yearning for nineteenth-century moral and economic traditions. Although state agencies worked to systematize public functions, the governor himself looked to the creation of a classless society sustained by such personal virtues as honesty, frugality, and moral character. Many of Johnson's constituents (60 percent in Los Angeles) were transplanted midwesterners. This helped provide the evangelical tone to his California crusades. Central to such traditional progressivism was the belief that the abolition of monopoly, corporate corruption, and economic privilege would bring prosperity to independent enterprisers in the manner Thomas Jefferson once promised.[49]

Like George Norris and Hiram Johnson, William Borah was a passionate admirer of Theodore Roosevelt. Unlike the others, however, Borah had supported the Bryan silver crusade of 1896. Born on a southern Illinois farm in 1865, he briefly attended college in Kansas before passing the bar in 1887. On his way to make his fortune in Seattle, Borah left the train at Boise for lack of funds. He settled in the Idaho capital and rose to leadership of the progressive wing of the state Republican party. Overlooked for selection to the Senate in 1903, Borah received the legislature's appointment three years later. He concentrated on domestic issues during his first two terms, leading the fight for constitutional amendments authorizing the income tax and direct election of senators. Borah also joined Norris and Johnson in opposing economic privilege. "Monopoly is at war with democratic institutions," he declared in 1913. Business and financial centralization, warned Borah, were "at variance with self-reliant, self-respecting, free, and independent citizenship."[50]

True to his republican and individualist roots, Borah opposed all concentrations of power, whether they rested in private monopoly or public bureaucracy. He objected to federal control of western waterpower and development, for example, and attacked the conservation programs of President Roosevelt's Forest Bureau. Borah also campaigned against creation of the Federal Reserve Board, charging that the agency delivered too much power to private bankers. Moreover, he voted against the FTC because it appeared to enable industrial monopolies to use government bureaucracy to evade antitrust laws. Such controversies combined with a rich voice and command of the language to make Borah one of the Senate's leading personalities and a mainstay of the anticorporate wing of the progressive movement.[51]

Wisconsin's Senator Robert La Follette, a short, stocky, square-jawed, and iron-willed dynamo, was the most recognized of the insurgent progressives. Born in a log cabin in 1855, La Follette graduated from the state university and went on to win a county district attorney election over the opposition of the local boss of his own Republican party. He continued to defy the party machine and served three congressional terms in the 1880s as an advocate of economy in government. After his third election as governor the Wisconsin legislature appointed La Follette to the Senate. He hoped to campaign for the presidency but faced disappointment when Theodore Roosevelt received the Progressive nomination in 1912. The rivalry with Roosevelt also reflected La Follette's preference for "corrupt practices" legislation instead of trust regulation by federal agencies. The differences between the two served as a microcosm of the ideological and political tensions between corporate and anticorporate progressivism.[52]

When Woodrow Wilson assumed the presidency in 1913, Robert La Follette was the nation's leading symbol of popular resistance to concentrated power. He opposed the Federal Reserve bill because it failed to attack the power of investment bankers. Joining many Democrats the next year, La Follette and independent Republicans defeated the Federal Reserve Board appointment of an International Harvester director under antitrust indictment. The Wisconsin progressive also objected to the FTC's loose definitions of unfair practices. Nevertheless, La Follette voted for the trade commission bill because it prohibited interlocking directorates. As he sought reelection to a third Senate term in 1916, La Follette confessed his belief that centers of financial power in New York controlled transportation, banking, industry, and commerce. America's greatest prosperity, he believed, had occurred in the nineteenth century, when the laws of supply, demand, and competition had enjoyed free rein.[53]

La Follette's republican views perfectly embodied an insurgent impulse framed by the depression of the 1890s and the moralistic response of populists and anticorporate progressives to economic and political privilege. Defending individual economic enterprise and political accountability against suspected concentrations of abusive power, dissident Republicans and Democratic allies nervously monitored the ever-widening agenda of the Wilson administration and its energetic president. Their confrontations with the former governor and university president would help create a legacy of insurgence in twentieth-century American political culture.

2

The Campaign against Internationalism, 1914–29

As war tensions mounted between the United States and Germany in March 1917, Senator George Norris ignored frantic pleas by advisers and rented the city auditorium in his hometown of Lincoln to address three thousand constituents. "I have come to Nebraska to tell you the truth," began Norris. Speaking without notes, the Republican insurgent lashed out at a Wall Street banking establishment that "sat behind mahogany desks" and calculated how the miseries of war "could be converted into gold for its filthy pockets." "You shall not coin into gold the life blood of our brothers," he cried. A week later the solon extended his tribute to William Jennings Bryan by telling the Senate that the nation was sinking into war "upon the command of gold." "I feel that we are about to put the dollar sign upon the American flag," protested Norris.[1]

✦ ✦ ✦

George Norris's outbursts reflected the discomfort of insurgent progressives and agrarian democrats with the use of force for overseas economic or political gain. Adherents of individual freedom, self-reliance, and equality of opportunity found it difficult to reconcile traditional republican values with foreign military adventurism and the corrupting centralization of government power. Populist agrarians particularly feared the rise of a military and professional elite unresponsive to democratic control. Nationalist fervor also figured in anxieties over diplomatic involvement in Europe. Geographically removed from European centers of controversy, many residents of the Midwest and the mountain states rejected the Old World and imperial Great Britain as festering centers of corruption and blood feuds.

Senator William Borah remembered British overtures to the Confederacy during the Civil War. Many western farm mortgagees also sustained memories of London's harsh nineteenth-century credit policies.[2]

Noninterventionist sentiments often were linked to agrarian discontent. Economic subservience of western farmers and ranchers to eastern banking and transportation interests helped engender severe distrust of national government and political leaders. Replicating their late-nineteenth-century experiences, agricultural producers usually defined their concerns as contrary to those of unseen economic elites in the East. Exploitation of labor and foreign imperialism appeared to serve the wealthy without providing anything for ordinary producers. Such thinking led the National Nonpartisan League to view the European war of 1914–18 primarily as a struggle between rival groups of monopolists seeking commercial supremacy. Even a far more moderate Idaho Grange leader complained to Senator Borah that American newspapers were controlled by big business and arms manufacturers wishing to force the United States into war.[3]

Although voting lines were not absolutely consistent, agrarian and western progressives tended to lead the opposition to Wilsonian foreign policy. Robert La Follette, George Norris, and Tom Watson bitterly opposed the occupation of Mexico's Vera Cruz in 1914. Borah, who supported the invasion, led the fight for Philippine independence and continued to denounce military intervention in Central America. "Our brutally taking possession of Nicaragua, actually carrying on war, killing hundreds of her people, taking possession of capital and forcing through a treaty greatly to our advantage," the Idaho senator complained to a constituent in 1916, "is one of the most shameless things in the history of our country." Between 1911 and 1917, one scholar has calculated, nine of the eleven least "imperial-minded" senators were progressives, while four out of the five "most progressive" were anti-imperialist.[4]

By 1917 a distinct anti-interventionist sentiment had emerged in Congress. Noninterventionists were opposed to committing U.S. armed forces to Europe and participating in overseas military alliances. Although some tied their foreign policy views to the pursuit of social or political reform at home, nationalism played a greater role in defining their perspective. "The national spirit seems to have given way very largely to the foreign or international spirit," lamented William Borah early in 1917. "I want to protect and advocate American rights," declared the senator, "if possible without war" and with "no alliances with foreign powers whatever." Reiterating a traditional republican belief, Borah insisted that the United States had no "more business with the entangling alliances of Europe and [its] dynastic and family quarrels . . . than we had a hundred years ago." "No more subtle, treacherous, unpatriotic scheme could be devised by which to betray the interests of the common people of this country," he concluded.[5]

The conflict over Wilsonian foreign policy first arose with the issue of military preparedness. Once Britain and France entered the war against Germany in 1914, the president supplemented his call for neutrality with requests for larger army forces, the creation of new reserves, and increases in naval battleship and cruiser strength. Democratic leaders supported Wilson's demands, but thirty members of the House, mostly midwestern and southern agrarians, joined William Jennings Bryan in denouncing the "same old gang" of "reactionaries and plutocrats" for stifling reform and profiting from military contracts. A House amendment to cut the number of new battleships from two to one failed by only fifteen votes early in 1915. Meanwhile, a coalition of thirty-seven rural Democrats and progressive Republicans sought to pass a Senate amendment to prohibit arms exports to European belligerents.[6]

Opposition to rearmament often coincided with traditional agrarian and republican fears of European corruption. Early in 1916 Democratic representative Isaac R. Sherman, a former Civil War general, a monetary inflationist, and the oldest member of the House, warned that militarism and imperialism were "a couplet of devious devils" that threatened orderly self-government. The call for U.S. intervention in Europe, asserted Mississippi's Senator James Vardaman, came from "all the militarist, the imperialistically inclined element, whose natural sympathies are with a strong centralized government as against democracy." Democratic Senate Foreign Relations Committee chair William J. Stone predicted that the European war would "be the worst thing that ever happened to this country" and that the nation would never again be the same.[7]

As the war deepened in Europe, William Jennings Bryan once again emerged as a key critic of U.S. foreign policy. Appointed President Wilson's secretary of state as a gesture to the agrarian wing of the Democratic party, Bryan sought to mediate U.S. maritime disputes with Germany. He also proposed a ban on all private loans to the European belligerents. Prospects for such policies deteriorated in May 1915, when a German submarine sank the British *Lusitania* and 1,198 passengers, 198 of them American, were lost. Resigning the next month, Bryan continued to assert that the erosion of U.S. neutrality rights and profits were secondary to the nation's self-interest in maintaining noninterventionism. As Wilson moved toward a preparedness program, the Nebraskan organized a summer tour of the Midwest, South, and Pacific Northwest to take his case to the nation.[8]

Bryan accused special interests of attempting to draw the United States into war. Among those who would profit from the conflict, he told audiences, were powerful bankers, armaments manufacturers, and the military interests. As he spoke before 100,000 people in San Francisco, the Great Commoner contrasted western "producers of wealth" with eastern financial and industrial interests. Emulating the rhetoric of the Populists and anticorporate progressives, he depicted the struggle as one of "the people vs. the special interests." The people "who do the dying should also do the deciding," cried Bryan. He then introduced audiences to the idea of a war referendum, a proposal calling for voters to approve congressional declarations of war unless the nation's borders were invaded.[9]

❖ ❖ ❖

By 1917 the Republican insurgents Robert La Follette and George Norris had replaced agrarian Democrats as the leading congressional critics of military intervention. La Follette had endorsed President Wilson's attempts to keep the United States out of the European war in 1914, but he became increasingly uneasy after Bryan's resignation. When Robert Lansing, the new secretary of state, authorized banks associated with J. P. Morgan to float the first war loans to Britain and France in August 1915, La Follette sharply denounced the maneuver. Such extension of credit, he admonished in *La Follette's Magazine,* was "underwriting the success of the cause of the Allies." During 1916 La Follette supported the House's McLemore Resolution, which requested the president to warn Americans not to travel on belligerent-owned ships moving through war zones. When Wilson denounced such efforts as a surrender of American rights and a challenge to presidential leadership, the House tabled the motion by a 276-142 margin.[10]

Like Bryan and other anti-imperialists, La Follette employed a literal definition of national defense. He contrasted limited coastal fortifications, artillery, and mobile forces to protect national boundaries with overseas armies rooted in the extension of economic privilege. Having based his political career on exposing ruthless self-interest in an unregulated market, the Wisconsin senator found it easy to see the dominant economic interests behind demands for military preparedness. He viewed the munitions trade as willing "to sacrifice human life for private gain" in the form of fat contracts, graft opportunities, and easy money. La Follette attributed militarism to European financial imperialism. He described a "scheme" by which dominant "financial interests" unlawfully wrung "surplus wealth" from the people and invested it in weaker nations. As a result, the Continent had become "a human slaughter pen," a land "cursed with a contagious and deadly plague" symbolized by the arming of twenty-one million men.[11]

Viewing war as "the most ghastly experience that can come to any country," La Follette warned that its consequences fell to ordinary people instead of "the handful of men in positions of power." Like Bryan, the Wisconsin senator embraced the idea of a war referendum. A bill he introduced in April 1916 would have required the Bureau of the Census to conduct an advisory referendum on war when the president severed diplomatic relations with a foreign power and 1 percent of the voters in twenty-five states signed petitions requesting the poll. La Follette also sought an embargo on all arms and ammunition bound for the European belligerents. Such views challenged presidential powers in international affairs. Wilson "assumes it to be the exclusive prerogative of the Executive to pursue any foreign policy" independent of congressional input, La Follette chided in 1916. Democratic control of such decisions, he warned, was essential to the establishment of world peace.[12]

Robert La Follette's battle with presidential foreign policy came to a head when Germany announced the resumption of unrestricted submarine warfare in January 1917. Interference with American shipping constituted a threat to international trade, which President Wilson viewed as a foundation of U.S. economic vitality and an essential national right. Wilson insisted that the nation's freedoms rested on expanding the base of economic prosperity through corporate growth, world trade, and the acceptance of democratic values. Yet the president's drift toward military involvement depressed La Follette, who viewed the war as a defeat for the world he sought to preserve. "One cannot shake off the feeling that an awful crisis is impending," he confided to his family as the Senate debated severing German diplomatic ties. When Wilson announced that the German ambassador had been handed his papers, La Follette reported that "all of the Progressive Republicans and Democrats were sick at heart," and he retreated to his office to be alone.[13]

William Jennings Bryan volunteered to speak at a mass antiwar rally in early February, but La Follette advised that he should quietly meet with Democrats while the senator talked with progressive Republicans. As Bryan quickly became discouraged with Congress, the Wisconsin insurgent realized that severing diplomatic ties was inevitable. Indeed, only two Republicans and two Democrats joined him in opposing the measure. Five days later La Follette introduced a resolution to prohibit the use of U.S. ports for the debarkation of armed merchant ships. Informing his family that he was "tired, depressed, and lonesome," La Follette wrote that he wished he could prove that the "jingo" newspapers had been "retained by the interests and are *now* being actually subsidized to force on the war." He then learned from a Hearst press editor that large steel and coffee interests supposedly were in Washington to urge the dissolution of the German sea embargo. "So we must have war to make business prosperous," La Follette wrote to his family with a sense of grim vindication.[14]

Pressure for military involvement escalated when the State Department released the "Zimmerman Note" on February 28. The document purported to involve Germany in a contingency alliance with Mexico that included plans for the reconquest of New Mexico, Arizona, and Texas. In response President Wilson asked Congress for authority to arm U.S. merchant ships. In the House Democratic loyalists easily defeated an amendment that sought to prohibit armed vessels from carrying munitions to belligerents. The president's bill then passed by a vote of 403 to 14. Hoping to prevent a Senate vote before the congressional recess, noninterventionists managed to postpone debate until two days before the end of the session. In the filibuster that followed, William Stone, chair of the Foreign Relations Committee, defied his own party by opposing the administration. Meanwhile La Follette learned that Democratic leaders planned to prevent him from speaking. After threatening that "someone would get hurt" if he was denied his Senate rights, La Follette stood in the center aisle and defied anyone to remove him.[15]

Although the Wisconsin insurgent never addressed the Senate on the bill, twelve Senate opponents of the armed ship bill managed to stop its passage before the Sixty-fourth Congress ended. Describing the proposal as "probably the most important measure that has come before the Senate in fifty years," La Follette called the victory "one of the greatest achievements of my public career." He insisted the Senate had postponed aggressive action that would have brought "the awful catastrophe" of war. President Wilson responded harshly. "A little group of willful men representing no opinion but their own," he announced, "have rendered the great Government of the United States helpless and contemptible." After the administration concluded that it already had the constitutional authority to place weapons on merchant ships traveling through war zones, the State Department issued such an order.[16]

When Wilson asked Congress for a declaration of war against Germany in early April, La Follette was the last opponent to speak in Senate debate. In a speech lasting nearly three hours in a hushed and tense chamber, the Wisconsin solon protested that Britain was equally guilty of neutrality violations, that war propaganda and loans to the Allies explained the nation's slide toward involvement, and that secret Allied treaties originally had precipitated the conflict. La Follette denied that national honor was at stake in either British or German provocations. In the final tally three Democrats, Harry Lane of Oregon, William Stone of Missouri, and James Vardaman of Mississippi, joined the Republicans Asle Gronna of North Dakota, George Norris, and La Follette on the minority side of an 82-6 vote. Later that night the House endorsed the measure by a vote of 373 to 50. As the Wisconsin insurgent left the Senate floor in silence, someone in the corridor handed him a rope.[17]

✦ ✦ ✦

La Follette never abandoned his conviction that the crusade "to make the world safe for democracy" was anything other than a triumph of Wall Street interests over the "instinct of the people." He noted in June 1917 that the president's supporters were beginning "to see a long and weary and very bloody road ahead of us now with the brunt of the fighting and financial burden almost sure to fall on us." A few progressive colleagues joined the Wisconsin insurgent in expressing skepticism over U.S. war aims. One day after voting to initiate hostilities, California's Senator Hiram Johnson confided that he was "depressed and disillusioned, so filled with disgust and pessimism" because of the rampant pretense and hypocrisy in the capital. "There is not a man in either branch of Congress who has the guts to express himself frankly and fearlessly," Johnson complained to a California reformer. Given such congressional submissiveness, the senator wondered how the president would ever be compelled to state the nation's war goals.[18]

Like La Follette, Johnson wondered if the country had any conception of the tremendous changes that would accompany war. "We never are going to be quite the same Nation again," the Californian warned in private letters to his family. "I doubt if the Republic as we have known it in the past . . . will ever return." Johnson worried about government coercion, the supremacy of bureaucratic expertise, and war-induced obsessions with efficiency. Noting the growth of administration review panels and industrial mobilization boards beyond congressional scrutiny, he questioned the expansion of executive power at the expense of legislative prerogative. Federal officials now used claims of national security to undercut the investigatory role of Congress, observed Johnson. Depressed and anxious about the erosion of a familiar world, the senator found his wartime nights plagued by insomnia.[19]

Johnson's discomfort increased with President Wilson's request for military conscription in June 1917. Both La Follette and Idaho's Borah voted against the draft as a violation of constitutional and republican principles. In contrast Johnson and George Norris grudgingly backed wartime conscription but complained about its consequences. Johnson described the draft as "miserable, rotten, horrible, engrafting upon a supposed democracy but a foul feudalism." "We are making the *world* safe for democracy with the enthusiasm of Peter of Serbia and the Mikado," he confessed to his son. The administration's request for wartime censorship also disturbed the insurgents. When Wilson asked Congress to permit the postmaster general to exclude objectionable materials from the mails under the proposed Espionage Act, Johnson and Norris led the unsuccessful effort to delete the controversial section. The Senate did vote 39 to 38 to support Johnson's motion to defeat the president's request to establish censorship of the press. "No free people should be subjected to undefined and indefensible laws," he told the Senate.[20]

Despite such rhetoric, Johnson eventually supported the amended Espionage Act. In contrast Norris and Borah continued to oppose the measure. Although Borah had voted for war, he assured constituents he was "not going to be swung off my feet by those who suppose that war in these modern times consists of gathering up a few hundred thousand men and putting them in uniform and getting a sufficient number of drums and flags and brass bands." Borah's skepticism of Wilson's crusade was reinforced by Edward C. Stokes, a New Jersey banker, former state governor, and frequent correspondent. The masses had not yet accepted the military conflict as "an American war," confided Stokes in July 1917. Ordinary people were mystified by its great expense and shared "a widespread feeling that this is a capitalistic war, brought on to protect loans abroad." Grass-roots opinion also blamed England for getting the United States into the conflict, reported Stokes. If a referendum were held, he speculated, a dazed and confused public would vote for peace.[21]

Borah's suspicions about U.S. policy carried over into the Espionage Act, "the spy bill" he dismissed as arbitrary, tyrannical, and unconstitutional. "While professing to be warring for democracy we have gone a long ways toward undermining our own democratic principles," the senator confided to an Idaho college professor. "It is [as] autocratic as anything in Prussia," he charged, and "would destroy free speech if enforced." Borah also feared that the espionage and conscription bills set dangerous precedents for excessive presidential power. "I do not want any man telling me that when I grant him dictatorial powers, that he will not abuse them," he wrote to a constituent. Ironically, the Idaho and California insurgents switched sides on the Sedition Act of 1918, which prohibited the use of profane, abusive, and scurrilous language about the government, the military, and the flag. While Borah defended the measure as a legal way of restraining irresponsible propagandists in wartime, Johnson opposed it as a suppression of legitimate dissent.[22]

La Follette, Borah, Norris, and Johnson also sought to frame war finance policy. As the Senate began consideration of a revenue bill in June 1917, insurgent progressives sought to tax war profits and wealth instead of authorizing the sale of government securities. "Every bond that is issued," La Follette told the Senate, "must some time be redeemed with interest out of the taxes that the people must pay." Releasing a 1913 government report that detailed annual earnings of over $3 million by twenty Americans, the Wisconsinite proposed to double the income tax. When the measure met a 58-21 defeat and another effort by Norris failed, La Follette sought a war-profits tax. Borah strongly supported this scheme, estimating that five months of hostilities had produced over $7 billion in war earnings. Johnson introduced a similar proposal. "Those who make swollen war profits out of this particular exigency," he declared, "are those who ought to pay for the cost of this war." The Senate, however, rejected La Follette's and Johnson's taxation schemes by better than 3-1 margins.[23]

Despite insurgent setbacks, the Revenue Act of 1917 embodied the principle that war costs generally should be borne by corporations and the affluent. The measure raised corporate and graduated income taxes and instituted an excess-profits levy on personal and corporate earnings. Government bonds ultimately accounted for a third of war spending and taxation the remainder. La Follette and the progressives sought to continue wartime tax schedules after the armistice, but only five Senate colleagues supported the Wisconsin senator's proposal to hold back a 25 percent cut in revenues and maintain what he called "the righteous taxation of the rich."[24]

✦ ✦ ✦

Robert La Follette and William Borah represented a producer culture that strongly disapproved of war profiteering. The 1.2 million member National Grange, for example, supported war-profits legislation. So did the Nonpartisan League (NPL). "Anti-profiteering is our big ace card out here," the Idaho NPL leader Ray McKaig informed Borah. In turn, the Idaho senator blamed the economic problems of farmers on profiteers, monopolists, and speculators. "Between those who want to murder us and those who want to rob us the honest American citizens are having a very serious experience in these days," he cracked. After Wisconsin's Society of Equity called for nationalization of distribution facilities and utilities, war profiteering became the major issue of the 1918 Republican primary for the state's second Senate seat. "The thieves and harpies that fatten off war must be scourged from the temples of government," declared James Thompson, the progressive candidate. Thompson lost the primary to Irving L. Lenroot by less than three thousand votes, but Wilson administration officials soon attacked the Republican victor as disloyal as well.[25]

Estimating that 70 percent of Wisconsin residents lacked sufficient loyalty, war promoters in the National Security League blamed the state's large German-American population. The chair of the Minneapolis Federal Reserve Bank held German farmers in North Dakota and Minnesota responsible for the region's indifference to "liberty loan" drives, although he admitted that the response of Scandinavians was no less "disappointing." He also noted that the "radical" agitation of North Dakota Nonpartisans provided "a formidable force" in discouraging bond sales. The state's NPL talked of financing the war by taxing the "swollen profits" of "food gamblers" and others who had benefited from it. "If we cannot pay the war debt as we go along," proclaimed NPL founder Arthur Townley, "then we will have to pay it when we get back." Failure to tax war profits, insisted Townley, would force Americans to "live for decades in the mire of national bondage" induced by debt. The NPL gathered its tax proposals in a 1918 pamphlet entitled *How to Finance the Great War.*[26]

The most famous attack on war finance came from the Minnesota Nonpartisan and former Republican House member Charles A. Lindbergh. The son of a prominent member of the Swedish Parliament, Lindbergh migrated to Minnesota as a child in 1860. After receiving a law degree from the University of Michigan, he was a small-town lawyer for twenty-three years. Elected to Congress in 1906, Lindbergh joined George Norris and other Republican insurgents in curtailing the powers of the autocratic House speaker Joe Cannon. He became the first representative to demand an investigation of the "money trust," which he considered the "father" of all monopoly. Known as the Pujo Committee, the House Banking and Currency panel conducted a sensational inquiry into the interlocking directorates of the Morgan and Rockefeller interests in 1912. Accordingly, it found a "great and rapidly growing concentration of control of money and credit."[27]

The Pujo inquiry helped ease passage of the Federal Reserve Act. Yet Lindbergh insisted that the new system of banking regulation served powerful financial interests. As a small-town lawyer experienced with commodity prices, mortgages, and land values, he viewed eastern investors as "speculative parasites" serving a "dollar plutocracy." Lindbergh believed that such interests had promoted the maritime controversies that led to war with Germany. After losing the 1916 Republican Senate primary, the Minnesotan waited until the United States entered the European conflict to release *Why Is Your Country at War and What Happens to You after the War and Related Subjects* (1917). A pocket book designed for wide distribution, the 220–page volume was a compilation of Lindbergh's congressional speeches and assorted writings. Focusing on such symbols of "special privilege" as Wall Street and the Federal Reserve, it held that world peace could be achieved only by nationalizing munitions, removing the profit from war, and separating commerce from speculative finance.[28]

Concerned about government repression, Lindbergh warned his daughter to "prepare to see me in prison and possibly shot." Indeed, the Bureau of Investigation conducted an inquiry into the disposition of the five thousand copies of *Why Is Your Country at War*. Locating a volume at a Socialist party bookstore in St. Paul, the Bureau of Investigation traced Lindbergh's connections to the Nonpartisan League. When government agents requested that he turn over all remaining copies to the Department of Justice for the duration of the war, the Minnesotan complied. Meanwhile, he won NPL endorsement for the 1918 Republican primary for governor. Local authorities, however, prevented his speaking in at least two locations. At a third, police arrested the candidate, released him, and drove him twenty miles out of town. Marginalized by law enforcement and political leaders, Lindbergh lost the primary. He mysteriously held Roman Catholics partially responsible.[29]

Robert La Follette also faced severe wartime recriminations. In September 1917 the Wisconsin senator addressed the last session of an NPL conclave in St. Paul. At the league's request, La Follette had substituted a speech on war-profits taxes for one on war aims. But when a heckler asked if the United States did not have grievances against Germany, La Follette responded that "the *comparatively* small privilege of the right of an American citizen to ride on a munition loaded ship flying a foreign flag is too small to involve this government in the loss of millions and millions of lives." He added that former Secretary of State Bryan had warned the president that the *Lusitania* had contained six million rounds of ammunition. La Follette then moved on to his familiar cry that war costs should be met by taxing surplus income and war profits. He concluded with the admonition that Americans had "the right to discuss freely . . . whether this war might not be terminated with honor."[30]

Troubles for La Follette mounted when the Associated Press quoted him as saying that the United States had "no grievances with Germany." The Minnesota Commission of Public Safety, a state body in charge of wartime loyalty and security, immediately petitioned the Senate to expel La Follette "as a teacher of disloyalty and sedition giving aid and comfort to our enemies." In Wisconsin both houses of the legislature passed loyalty resolutions sharply denouncing the senator by name. Demands for La Follette's expulsion surfaced at two meetings at the University of Wisconsin, where he subsequently was burned in effigy. When the university faculty met in January 1918 to endorse President Wilson's Fourteen Points, 399 instructors and professors signed a "round-robin" memorial that condemned the senator's failure to support the prosecution of the war. The reformist editor of the *Wisconsin State Journal* charged that La Follette was a "reactionary" unable to recognize that the military crusade had assumed "progressive lines" and was "spiritualizing our American sense of communism."[31]

La Follette did receive scattered support. The reformer Lincoln Steffens asked him to consider the nation's war mood as a sickness. North Dakota's Attorney General William Langer assured him that "no single man" in the nation had done more for the common people. Eugene V. Debs, head of the Socialist party, praised La Follette's "uncompromising courage" in facing down the "brutal prosecution" of "the plutocracy of Wall Street" and "their prostitute press." Moved by deference to war fervor, however, the Senate's Committee on Privileges and Elections began to organize a full inquiry in May 1918. Warren G. Harding, the Ohio Republican, may have captured the panel's mood when he noted that although the committee lacked sufficient evidence of disloyalty, La Follette's attitude had "made him a very dangerous public servant." Nevertheless, the November armistice brought a committee report that the speech in question did not justify any action and a 9-2 vote to dismiss the charges. In January 1919 the entire Senate sustained the finding by a vote of 50 to 21.[32]

✦ ✦ ✦

Like the depression of the 1890s, the bitter experience of World War I became part of an American insurgent legacy. Antiwar sentiment appeared strongest in the Midwest and the mountain states. As Christopher Gibbs has explained of Missouri, a "silent majority" of the region's citizens opposed involvement in the conflict and resisted bond drives, food pledge campaigns, and conscription. Long-standing traditions of localism, democracy, and suspicion of centralized power remained strong for many Americans. Midwesterners and others consequently found it easy to believe that special interests had drawn the country into war against majority will and were profiting while taxes and prices escalated at the expense of ordinary people. Insurgents, such as Hiram Johnson, George Norris, William Borah, and Robert La Follette, brought these issues to the national political stage. Sensitive to questions of power, they legitimized widespread concern over the consequences of internationalism, full-scale mobilization, and the dominance of the executive branch in a centralized state.[33]

As a progressive who opposed privileged concentrations of power, La Follette held Woodrow Wilson responsible for the "appalling destruction of everything democratic which had been gained in a twenty year struggle." On the eve of the armistice, the Wisconsin senator hoped to "get back to the normal" and discover "that the *great mass* of our people were not war mad." Yet as he observed the labor unrest that brought four million Americans out on strike in 1919, La Follette detected "a new era of savagery" that compelled "the rich" to shoot down workers protesting increased living costs. It was "hard to see much hope for the poor," he observed in April 1919. Convinced that wartime greed had brutalized the American ruling elite, the Wisconsin senator anticipated increased poverty, suffering, resentment, and open class warfare.[34]

Radicalized by wartime repression and frustrated by a climate of class tension and intolerance, La Follette toyed with the idea of peaceful revolution. He told his family in April 1919 that he had been invited to the home of the pacifist-socialist Scott Nearing to discuss constitutional and nonviolent means of revolutionary change. La Follette was fond of Nearing and urged his son Robert to read the radical's *Poverty and Riches* (1916). Yet the elder La Follette's democratic populism prevented him from embracing nonelectoral strategies. Reform by the ballot was slow and discouraging, he admitted. Yet if people did not have sufficient intelligence to change government by voting, he wondered, how would they ever conduct "a real democratic government after they had established it by force?" Although La Follette remained skeptical of a political system dominated by a "subservient" and "controlled" press, he saw no alternative to an electoral movement to bring "lasting reform." In May 1919 he declined an invitation to address Nearing's revolutionary socialists.[35]

As a passionate democrat, La Follette feared the "horrors" of "bloody revolution." He noted "a sort of frenzy among small groups of tense, passionate, and irresponsible types," whose activities elicited the repressive laws, state sedition statutes, and deportations associated with the postwar "Red Scare." Terrorists were the worst enemies of radical reform, he insisted. La Follette saw only "madness" in assassination attempts by American anarchists and other revolutionaries. He repeated such dire characterizations when the home of Attorney General A. Mitchell Palmer was bombed in June 1919.[36]

The prospect of European revolution produced a more complex response. As communist revolutions erupted in Russia and Germany between 1917 and 1918, La Follette blamed the violent upheavals on the strains of war. "These are the conditions that beget revolution," he wrote to his family. "I dread to see it and yet it may be necessary." Noting Secretary of the Treasury William McAdoo's Senate testimony that U.S. troops might have to remain in Europe if "anarchy" spread, La Follette anticipated the use of Allied forces to throttle democracy in the name of order. He warned that the Allies were threatening to starve Germany if it did not keep order by curbing socialism and bolshevism. "The plutocrats are wearing long faces these days," the veteran progressive noted with some humor. La Follette then belittled the administration's Russian food assistance program as a "shallow scheme" to fight communism without responding to underlying causes.[37]

While La Follette marveled at the manner in which wartime conscription had turned millions of Europeans and Americans against militarism, Hiram Johnson professed to be far more disturbed by the implications of bolshevist unrest. The materialist and social class dogmas of the Russian Revolution, declared Johnson, challenged both Christian conscience and political democracy. Yet Johnson joined La Follette in insisting that the

roots of revolution lay in the "neglected sore spots" of economic and social life. Bayonets, prisons, and arbitrary power were not answers to human aspirations for a better life, he lectured. As a consistent progressive,
Johnson portrayed the danger of "twin evils." On one side lay the "reactionary, panic-stricken profiteer"; on the other, "embittered, discouraged,
defeated revolutionaries who would wreck the gains of a thousand years
struggle upward for some ideal impossible of practical attainment."[38]

Johnson's distaste for European power politics and social upheaval
deepened when he learned in December 1918 of the presence of fourteen
thousand U.S. troops in northern Russia and Siberia. The California progressive Raymond Robins, a participant in the American Red Cross mission to the new Soviet Union, had supplied the senator with documents
purporting to connect the military occupation to Allied efforts to restore
the prerevolutionary order. Johnson adamantly opposed such involvement.
He told Robins that the deployment appeared to be part of a policy "of
subjugating or subduing nations or people who do not think as we do,"
an example of the permanent pattern of intervention brought by the war.
Portraying a "war against revolution in all countries, whether enemy or
ally," Johnson speculated that international bankers were behind the undeclared campaign against the Soviets. Privately, he spoke of "leaving
Europe to clean its own house and police its backyards."[39]

Seeking to call attention to U.S. involvement in northern Russia and
Siberia, Senator Johnson introduced a resolution in December 1918 that
asked for State Department clarification of the military deployment. A
subsequent proposal demanded outright withdrawal of the troops. "I am
opposed to American boys policing Europe and quelling riots in every new
nation's backyard," Johnson told his colleagues. He offered accounts of
U.S. soldiers advancing into the interior of Siberia, burning Russian towns,
and displacing local revolutionary councils. Intervention enabled the "gro-
tesque" Soviet government "to last far beyond its allotted time and to
exercise its despotic sway in the name of public safety," declared Johnson.
Assuring listeners that bolshevism never would find a foothold in the United
States, he nevertheless insisted that it was "impossible" to "shoot or hang
a state of mind." When the Senate deadlocked, Vice President Thomas R.
Marshall broke the tie with a negative vote. Johnson's proposal was ultimately defeated by five votes.[40]

As President Wilson and the Allies carried on peace talks at Versailles
between January and June 1919, Hiram Johnson, Robert La Follette, and
William Borah mocked the president's previous statements about open
diplomacy and self-determination. The senators insisted that World War
I had militarized American society and had involved the United States in
the imperial politics of Europe. They criticized Wilson for being account-

able only to himself and for carrying on personal diplomacy with the leaders of the imperial states that had precipitated the European holocaust. Noninterventionists viewed violent revolution and economic empire as dreaded consequences of the same problem. "I confess," Johnson confided to a California political associate, "I am unable to understand an American father or an American mother who would wish to enter into any arrangement with the bankrupt nations of the earth to maintain their tottering goals with American blood."[41]

La Follette's distaste for European imperialism underscored his skepticism over the peace process. Expressing his views in a series of letters to his family, the Wisconsinite portrayed a hypocritical Allied approach to Wilson's "peace without victory." The senator hoped that the settlement would compel Germany to abandon compulsory military training and adopt the war referendum. He reasoned that if Berlin insisted that all powers comply, the peace treaty would bring "the death knell of militarism and war." Yet La Follette feared that Germany would be reduced to a state of desperation that would make social revolution inevitable. The "scramble for spoils" through war reparations, he predicted, would sow all Europe with a hatred that would guarantee future autocracies and wars. The solon argued that England, France, and Italy demanded high indemnities because they feared the high taxation needed to pay for the war. The conditions imposed on Germany and "the barbaric measures resorted to in order to force acceptance," he protested, "will be our lasting shame."[42]

Much of La Follette's criticism rested on a midwestern aversion to British imperialism. England did not intend "to give up being the boss of the seas," he noted in a snide reference to Wilson's rhetoric concerning free navigation. La Follette foresaw British and U.S. cooperation in a "monster navy" that would protect investments and loans in "undeveloped" areas. Since small nations would be exploited and robbed, he predicted, the American people would have to be prepared for continual war. The senator sharply denounced Wilson's refusal to consult Congress while at Versailles. Having reduced the wartime Congress to "a mere automaton," charged La Follette, the chief executive now prepared to sacrifice his own Fourteen Points to placate the British. "And while Wilson is bowing and smiling and juggling with words," he complained, "England, France and Italy are settling all the terms." As the president and the Allies were about "to determine the fate of the world's future," declared La Follette, "we know *nothing about it*."[43]

Wisconsin's fiery senator admitted that he had "such a feeling of resentment against Wilson that it is not altogether easy to maintain a judicial tone when I write about him." He pictured the president as a shallow and amoral practitioner of modern public relations. "He is too much the phrase maker to have even passing convictions," lamented the veteran progressive. Comparing Wilson with "an intellectual crook," La Follette protested that the nation was "afloat in a sea of 'BUNK.'" He pleaded for Americans to see the president "slipping out of one thing after another which he has pledged over and over again—juggling with his fourteen points like a sleight-of-hand performer or a card sharp, groveling at the feet of the strong and bluffing the weak." La Follette pictured Wilson returning home "with a ship load of flim flam for suckers." Having undermined American democracy, bloated the national debt, and committed the nation to financing European bankruptcy, the president now sought to use "cheap pious cant" to impose "a spoils-grabbing compact of greed and hate."[44]

Seeking to create a stable global order in which disputes between nations might be resolved without violence, President Wilson had won the approval of Allied peace negotiators for a league of nations. Enforcement of world peace was to be maintained through a system of collective security. Article 10 of the League Covenant stipulated that member nations would be obligated to come to the military defense of victims of armed aggression. For Wilson the League of Nations provided the machinery for sustaining a rule of law among nations, an environment the president believed essential to the prevention of chaotic revolution and continuing war. In July 1919 he confidently submitted the League Covenant and the Versailles treaty for Senate approval. The resulting controversy marked one of the great foreign policy debates of American history.[45]

Although response to the League crossed party and ideological lines, western progressives played a major role in leading the opposition. Ten of the Senate's sixteen "irreconcilables" came from midwestern and mountain states that produced agricultural and mining commodities for the domestic market and had little interest in European affairs. The region's dominant republican ideology looked harshly on the military and financial imperialism associated with Europe. Open to suggestions that hidden financial interests had precipitated U.S. involvement in the war, western producers feared that international bankers and powerful interests might dominate the stable world system that Wilson sought. Such senators as Washington's Miles Poindexter and North Dakota's Asle Gronna joined better-known progressives in fretting about limitations on the nation's freedom of action. Others shared the region's suspicions over executive power and viewed the treaty process as a test of congressional participation in foreign policy.[46]

Although Hiram Johnson initially expressed interest in an international peace organization, William Borah convinced him that the League represented the triumph of British diplomacy. Indeed, Johnson's nationalism led him to complain that League proponents deemed it "a real offense to be an American" and "a sin" to be patriotic. The Californian focused on the mandatory collective security clause of Article 10, "to my mind the most vicious thing in the whole scheme." He argued that adherence to the provision would involve the United States in perpetual clashes with the forces of change and would require repeated intervention to suppress internal revolutions. Johnson portrayed the League as providing stability and legitimacy to an unjust peace settlement. "Shall American boys police the world?" he asked the Senate in a major address in June 1919. Johnson took the "old-fashioned gospel of straight Americanism" to New England, the Midwest, and the Pacific Coast in a summer and fall tour that attracted mass rallies and overflow crowds.[47]

Robert La Follette and George Norris joined Johnson in the League fight. William Borah provided the crusade's prestige and intellectual leadership. An expert in jurisprudence and a devout student of the Constitution, the Idaho senator had opposed talk of a proposed league three months before the United States entered the war. Borah objected to the scheme as a threat to the ideals of republican society. He insisted that efforts to guarantee the peace of the world would implicate the nation in a permanent alliance with European powers. The United States would become "a republic in arms," warned the senator, burdening Americans with taxation and distracting them from vital domestic questions. Borah predicted that the abandonment of George Washington's antipathy to European entanglements would bring about "the beginning of the end of the American Republic as we have known it."[48]

President Wilson paraded the internationalist cause in a triumphant national tour in September 1919 but then collapsed from nervous exhaustion and suffered a paralyzing stroke. Substantially incapacitated during the remainder of his term, Wilson failed to adjust to the newly elected Republican majority in the Senate. When the Foreign Relations Committee chair, Henry Cabot Lodge, introduced a treaty version that included reservations concerning American autonomy, the president ordered Democrats to reject the proposal. Nevertheless, the Senate adopted the Lodge reservations in March 1920, thereby eliminating Article 10 from the League Covenant. A combined vote of hard-line Wilsonians and irreconcilable League opponents then prevented the two-thirds majority necessary for ratification of the treaty.[49]

❖ ❖ ❖

Insurgent progressives and noninterventionists took pride in the fact that the United States never ratified the Treaty of Versailles or joined the League of Nations. Opposition by twenty-seven senators also may have weakened the Four-Power Treaty of 1922, which simply called for cooperation with the British, French, and Japanese in respecting mutual interests in the Pacific. More dramatic was the way in which Senate dissidents made payment of Allied war debts a central controversy of postwar U.S. foreign policy. Insurgents such as La Follette, Norris, Borah, and Johnson continued to believe that private banking loans had enabled France, Britain, and Italy to buy vast quantities of American munitions and supplies between 1914 and 1917. They argued that Allied inability to meet a $2 billion debt to the Morgan interests had precipitated involvement in the European conflict. La Follette further insisted that $10 billion of "liberty loans" had enabled the Allies to defeat Germany and maintain their ability to repay private loans owed to American bankers.[50]

Opponents of Wilsonian foreign policy contended that the Allies had created the League of Nations as a result of pressure from international financiers in the United States. La Follette and Borah reacted with fury when they learned that J. P. Morgan and his associates had received a copy of the Treaty of Versailles before U.S. senators had. La Follette believed that Wilson's link to the bankers had been established through Thomas Lamont, an affiliate of the House of Morgan who served as the president's financial adviser at Versailles. For the Wisconsin progressive the League of Nations represented a concord of interests "between the old imperialism of Great Britain and the new imperialism of our monopoly-controlled government." "Morgan and the group of Jew bankers," he confided in a 1919 tirade out of character with his customary ethnic tolerance, "expect to 'finance' the war settlements and rake down commissions."[51]

When the Warren Harding administration submitted bills to refund the $10 billion Allied war debt in 1921 and 1922, the noninterventionist bloc objected that deferral of interest payments might bring pressure for outright cancellation. Observing that "imperial finance is to my mind about as objectionable as militarism," William Borah dismissed the refunding effort as a device to permit European nations to repay their loans to private bankers. Congress compromised in 1922 by creating the World War Debt Funding Commission, with instructions to arrange European repayment of loans over twenty-five years at a minimum of 4.25 percent interest. All major European debtors negotiated agreements with the commission, but each accord had to be approved by Congress. According to a 1923 agreement the panel gave the British sixty-two years to pay off their obligation at 3.3 percent interest. Although the terms turned out to be the most stringent European debtors faced, nationalists still denounced the pact for tying the United States to Europe.[52]

Renegotiation of the war debts became an issue in the 1922 Senate elections when Henrik Shipstead, the Minnesota Farmer-Labor party candidate, demanded that the United States confine credit to nations willing to undertake wholesale disarmament. "If the governments want our money," declared the Minnesota dentist, "let them pay for it by guaranteeing world peace." Opponents maintained that debt refunding would enhance the credit of imperialistic European governments and permit them to secure fresh loans to sustain militarism. Such criticism resurfaced in 1926 after the House approved reduced Italian obligations and extended its loans at 2 percent interest over sixty-two years. Nebraska's Senator Norris objected that the federal government had borrowed funds from American citizens at 4.5 percent. In effect, the nation's taxpayers had been asked to underwrite the Italian loan, while Rome continued to pay 7 percent interest on a private loan extended by the Morgan bankers.[53]

Congressional approval of the Italian debt settlement elicited bitter condemnation by nationalist and progressive adversaries of U.S. globalism. The *Nation*'s William Hard, a self-proclaimed opponent of concentrated power, summed up such criticism in "Benito and I Save the St. Paul," a farcical commentary published in 1926. Hard portrayed Italy's Benito Mussolini as delighted to pay interest to leading private banks once Andrew Mellon had renegotiated the loans Washington extended. Parodying internationalist rhetoric, the author described "one" world beyond the "age of isolation." In a global market, mocked Hard, everyone had the "right to live off everybody else" since payment of debts reduced prosperity. Publication of the piece prompted Huey Long, chair of Louisiana's Public Service Commission, to request more of Hard's writings on the question.[54]

Opponents of imperial finance bitterly resisted U.S. participation in the World Court. The League had created the Permanent Court of International Justice in 1922 to resolve civil disputes between nations. A pet project of Elihu Root, the American jurist and former secretary of state, the tribunal received President Harding's strong endorsement. Once the administration attached a series of reservations ensuring U.S. sovereignty, it asked Congress to approve membership in 1923. *Collier's* magazine estimated that four-fifths of the nation supported U.S. participation. When the House backed the Court by a 303-28 margin in early 1925, the idea won overwhelming press endorsement and support from most of the large Protestant denominations, several Jewish organizations, the National Association of Manufacturers, the American Legion, and the American Federation of Labor. The Senate finally approved membership in 1926, but the American reservations were so extreme that other members of the Court objected and called for new negotiations.[55]

Before talks could proceed, however, seven Senate proponents of Court membership were defeated in the 1926 Republican primaries. Opposition to U.S. participation stemmed more from anxieties over internationalism than from concerns over actual membership. William Borah, who succeeded Henry Cabot Lodge as chair of the Senate Foreign Relations Committee in 1924, did not oppose the principle of international arbitration. Borah did, however, suspect that association with the World Court might involve the United States in the political considerations of the League of Nations. The Idaho senator insisted that American freedom of action could not be sustained if the tribunal was an adviser and attorney for the League and its protocols. America's "first and primary obligation," lectured Borah, was "to our own people." It was time for the United States to "experience a rebaptism of pride and vigilance and look after her own interests with decision and courage," he concluded.[56]

Populist discomfort with imperial finance underscored nationalist concerns over Court membership. The "real force" pushing U.S. participation, Borah explained, was the same influence and power that had been responsible for the League and "the imperialistic and unconscionable" war settlement. Nearly half the Republican opponents of the Court were western progressives or insurgents. Robert La Follette spoke for many when he charged that the tribunal was the product of a plan by international bankers to entangle the United States in European affairs. Financiers who knew no country "and serve only their own power and profit," insisted La Follette, sought to use American wealth and military prowess to safeguard the financial enterprises of the "tottering" nations of the Continent. With similar passion, Hiram Johnson derided the propaganda of "selfish interests" who sought "to make profit out of taking us into Europe," and he cited the *American Mercury*'s sardonic portrait of British influence in American country clubs and Ivy League colleges.[57]

The World Court controversy fit the political needs of western insurgents. Senator Henrik Shipstead consistently held that the tribunal's role was "to decide that loot acquired as a result of the last war has been legally acquired." Portraying the Court as providing legal machinery for the protection of foreign loans and investments, Shipstead insisted that anti-Christian ventures into imperial finance threatened the constitutional life of American democracy. Meanwhile, North Dakota's Gerald P. Nye, a former newspaper editor affiliated with the Nonpartisan League, won appointment to a vacant Senate position in 1926. When technical objections arose about Nye's seating, Borah and other allies used the nominee's hostility to the Court to elicit support. Nye's maiden speech depicted the tribunal as a "world-wide collection agency" for the same international bankers responsible for the credit problems of American farmers. Faced with a crucial loss of support after 1926, the White House abandoned the Court fight.[58]

✦   ✦   ✦

Although not all opponents of internationalism fell within the republican and populist legacy, its perspective frequently framed the terms of foreign policy debate in the 1920s. Hiram Johnson, for example, took particular pains to draw sharp distinctions between globalism and traditionally nationalist perspectives. Having used political bases in Sacramento and San Francisco to fight his way to the California governorship and the U.S. Senate, Johnson maintained strong ties to the cosmopolitan wing of the progressive movement. Consequently, even as the senator emerged as an "irreconcilable" opponent of the League, he maintained a rich political dialogue with Chester H. Rowell, a pro-League progressive. As the debate intensified, Rowell bombarded Johnson with sharply reasoned polemics in support of a "positive Americanism" that would reach beyond the United States. In an interrelated world in which isolation no longer proved viable, the League provided a "Constitution of the World," argued Rowell.[59]

Johnson responded to such assertions by insisting that conflicts in Russia, Poland, Italy, Yugoslavia, and East Asia did not concern the United States. He wondered why American nationalism received such negative treatment in the media. "There are certain individuals," the California progressive explained in a 1923 article written for the *New York Times Magazine*, "who hug to themselves the title 'intellectuals,' who contemptuously scorn all petty virtues, and who scoff at patriotism. In their superior wisdom, and their all embracing world desires, they forget their country and would even leave us naked and defenseless. These 'intellectuals' revel in the title of internationalists; and nationalism and patriotism are with them mere terms of reproach."[60]

In exploring the relationship between international banking and the foreign policy views of big-city newspapers, Johnson pressed his argument further. Despite $30 billion of debt and 250,000 graves, he charged in a 1925 weekly newsletter, the American people had no notion of the nation's overseas involvements. While international bankers consummated "master strokes of finance" and European loan settlements, ordinary citizens were "but fit to pay the price of war." Johnson asked why the metropolitan press consistently denounced critics of American globalism. "Is it because money must not be disturbed nor profits questioned?" he inquired. "If we could know what the House of Morgan has received for floating foreign loans," hinted Johnson, "perhaps we might find the answer."[61]

Noninterventionists portrayed imperialism, colonialism, militarism, and entangling alliances as interrelated phenomena that threatened the twin foundations of the American republic—democracy and nationalism. By the 1920s their strongest base of operations had shifted to the western plains states and the Republican party. Representatives of the northern hinterlands insisted that imperialism and war stemmed from the political influence of corporate finance and industry. Speaking for those who supplied raw materials, agricultural staples, and investment opportunities, western members of Congress viewed the regional economy in colonial terms. Senator Gerald Nye of North Dakota compared westerners with a colonial people who dedicated their labor and energy to the profits of others. Collusion between Wall Street and the State Department mirrored the ties between big money and government policies. Westerners often saw privileged interests dominating both agriculture and U.S. foreign affairs.[62]

Robert La Follette provided the most acerbic critiques of imperialism. La Follette carried on a substantial correspondence with a Yale professor of international law, Edwin Borchard, by no means an agrarian. Borchard insisted that modern economic prosperity stemmed from maintaining trade barriers, winning foreign markets, and ensuring access to raw materials. He argued that nations accomplished these tasks through colonies, protectorates, spheres of influence, or dominant roles as investors. Borchard described armaments as a means to protect a single nation's position in the struggle for prosperity and security. La Follette grafted such analysis onto his own midwestern moralism. In 1921 he responded to an administration request for new battleships by condemning "the determination of the industrial and financial masters of this country to put behind investments a guarantee of the Government of the United States." They hoped "to establish the precept that the flag follows the investor," charged La Follette, and to employ the navy "as an insurance collection agency for the investing classes."[63]

An exchange between William Borah and Will H. Hays, chair of the Motion Picture Producers and Distributors of America, clearly illustrated the depth of the noninterventionist critique of foreign policy. In an effort to improve the film industry's standing with Congress, Hays had written to Borah in 1926 to extol the motion picture's role in stimulating understanding among people of all backgrounds and nations. Wars came from those who did not comprehend each other's ideas, beliefs, and ambitions, he suggested. Borah responded that war was not the problem. Instead, he pointed to "the strong nations" that were "exploiting and literally robbing the weaker people of not only their wealth but their health and the modicum of liberty which they now have." Opposed to silent complicity in imperialism, Borah asked Hays to "turn your movies loose in behalf of the down-trodden."[64]

For progressive nationalists U.S. military intervention in Nicaragua turned out to be the most dramatic example of the imperialism they condemned. A small detachment of marines occupied Nicaragua between 1912 and 1925. Nebraska's George Norris ridiculed this deployment by charging that the United States had used force to impose a government on Nicaragua and then had won its agreement to continue the occupation. One year after the marines withdrew, they returned amid political violence to support the claims of a conservative ally to the Nicaraguan presidency. Western insurgents bitterly denounced the presence of troops, which lasted until 1933. The marines had returned to sustain a government that Americans originally had placed in power, charged Norris. "We are there without the consent of the people of Nicaragua," he declared in 1927, "without any right, moral or legal. We have, as a matter of fact, participated in a civil war in a foreign country by taking up one side of the controversy and lending moral and military assistance."[65]

Norris assumed the honorary presidency of the National Citizens' Committee on Relations with Latin America in 1927. Criticizing the State Department for secrecy and misleading propaganda, the group embraced a wide variety of reform leaders, including the journalist William Allen White, the educator John Dewey, Rabbi Stephen S. Wise, and Senator Gerald Nye. The United States had violated its own traditions by setting itself up "as a great Colossus on this hemisphere," declared Norris. He charged that Washington was "carrying on an unauthorized and indefensible war" against Nicaragua. William Borah noted that the Monroe Doctrine did not give the United States the right to interfere with the sovereignty of Latin American countries. Washington was smeared with selfishness and the most sordid brand of imperialism, charged Borah. By using military force only weeks after popular elections, he claimed, the United States had violated popular will. "We of all people in the world," he concluded, "ought not to undertake to impose upon the people of another nation a government which they do not want."[66]

President Adolpho Díaz had been placed in power, asserted Senator Burton K. Wheeler, a Montana Democrat, because he was "the most perfect instrument available to enable the New York bankers to have their will." This was the third time the dictator had been "warshipped" into office, he charged. The "rough-shod, antirepublican rule" of the State Department had robbed Nicaragua of its sovereignty. Minnesota's Senator Henrik Shipstead claimed that the 1926 coup followed the refusal of Nicaraguan officials to sell the national bank to a group of American investors led by a top officer of a Morgan affiliate. In 1928 Gerald Nye introduced a Senate resolution calling for a presidential declaration against the use of armed force to protect the foreign investments of U.S. citizens. Another proposal by Wisconsin's Senator John J. Blaine sought to exclude naval appropriations for maintaining the marines in Nicaragua. In a three-hour tirade Blaine demanded that U.S. investors comply with the laws of host nations and that no funds be used for intervention in friendly countries. Although anti-imperialist views did not dominate Congress, they contributed to the moderation of Latin America policy in an era when the banking community sought more stable relations in the hemisphere.[67]

Anti-imperialism shared its republican roots with nationalism and non-interventionism. "We should never forget," Nebraska's Norris reminded constituents, "that the right of revolution is, after all, a sacred right." North Dakota's Nye agreed with the father of a fallen marine who wrote that Nicaraguan rebels were defending the integrity of their nation in the tradition of Washington, Jefferson, and Lincoln. Similar themes pervaded the rhetoric of Senator John Blaine. The son of Norwegian and Scottish immigrants, the three-time governor of Wisconsin proclaimed to the chamber that the Declaration of Independence had been ravished by the diplomacy of the dollar.[68]

From 1914 through the 1920s a coalition of insurgent progressives and agrarian Democrats mounted an impassioned crusade against military and diplomatic internationalism. Connecting fears of Old World corruption and tyranny to nationalistic concerns for American independence, it cautioned against entry into the European war and opposed involvement in the League of Nations, the World Court, and Latin American imperialism. This mixture of progressives, nationalists, noninterventionists, and reformers would constitute an even more potent foreign policy force during the following decade of economic and international turmoil.

3

Anticorporate Progressives and the New Era, 1920–29

Exasperated by the continual disruptions of the Senate's Republican progressives in 1929, New Hampshire's venerable George H. Moses jauntily characterized his western colleagues as "sons of the wild jackass."[1] In a period in which New Era enthusiasts preached cooperation between corporate leaders and the federal government, the description was one that opponents of concentrated power could embrace with pride. Indeed, the selective prosperity of the 1920s provided the insurgents with unprecedented opportunities to tie deep-seated sectional and cultural animosities to an economic radicalism confronting privileged elites. Yet their individualist temperaments and reluctance to employ government coercion limited their impact on Jazz Age politics.

❖   ❖   ❖

During World War I the federal government's War Industries Board mobilized the economy by promoting industrial coordination and planning, scientific management, and enlightened labor relations. Many of these innovations were an extension of the organizational revolution already rationalizing responsibility and decision making in the marketplace. By the early 1920s New Era business journals were filled with talk of management ethics, corporate social responsibility, and enhanced public relations. Executives such as General Electric's Owen D. Young promised to end class conflict and improve living standards through mass production, technological innovation, and better marketing and distribution. Herbert C. Hoover, President Warren Harding's commerce secretary, embodied these aspirations with his attempt to create an "associative" economy, in which trade and professional associations worked with government agencies to promote efficient production, pricing, and competition.[2]

Robert La Follette was one of the first insurgents to acknowledge the human costs of the corporate revolution. "The individual is fast disappearing in the business world, and in his stead, is the corporation," noted La Follette in a draft of a 1917 speech. Predictably, the Wisconsin senator expressed his criticism through the lens of producer values and traditional individualism. He complained that corporate and monopolistic control of enterprise reduced people to "mere cogs in the wheels of a complicated mechanism" and replaced independent competitors who stamped their character on companies. As a result, individuality and business conscience "merged in the impersonal, intangible, corporate entity." La Follette described educated and able young people who found it difficult to rise above the first round of competition and were forced to remain in routine jobs without hope of advancement. Impersonal corporate hierarchy imposed a deadening influence on ambition and exerted a depressing effect on individual growth and development, he concluded.[3]

La Follette tied the impersonality of the corporation to the wartime rapacity of organized money. Corporate entities were the vehicles of "the most extensive swindling operation known in the history of finance," he charged. "The want of personal identity and the absence of moral responsibility" made the modern firm "a convenient cover" for "avaricious and unscrupulous conduct." For a traditional republican like La Follette, the organizational revolution merely disguised moral responsibility. The test of real prosperity continued to be success for the greatest numbers. "It is not the accumulation of wealth itself that need be feared," the senator reasoned, "but the wrongful use of this tremendous power in the hands of a few selfish men." La Follette wondered if Americans could salvage their democratic heritage, whether they would "become servants instead of masters of their boasted material progress and prosperity—victims of the colossal wealth this free land has fostered and protected."[4]

Discomfort with the corporate order overlapped the economic concerns of western enterprisers and farmers in need of capital. Angry about eastern concentrations of financial power, traditional producers were extremely sensitive to potential collusion between big banking interests and the federal government. After 1920 they increasingly turned their attention to the Federal Reserve Board. Since the system's inception in 1913, the powerful New York district bank had emerged as the guiding force of American finance. Because New York lenders controlled the flow of currency, critics charged that the Federal Reserve Board administered monetary policy in the interests of large capital. Local borrowers and enterprisers felt especially bitter about high discount or interest rates that the board passed on to smaller banks. Yet politicians could do little to influence fiscal policy once the Senate confirmed the president's nomination of the Federal Reserve Board's directors.[5]

Criticism of the banking panel escalated after World War I. Idaho's William Borah expressed a common view when he complained in 1920 that the system had failed to supply western capital needs at reasonable rates. Control over interest, asserted Borah, had given a few men the power to inflate or contract the currency and thereby regulate property values. Former New Jersey governor and banker Edward Stokes, a frequent Borah correspondent, described postwar loan rates as a "money crime" and "a conspiracy" against prosperity. "If you burn a man's house, you are punished," persisted Stokes, "but if you destroy the value of his property through control of the money market, you are regarded as a shrewd financier." Such conduct in high places helped foster the spirit of bolshevism, he contended. Noting the absence of any justification for a credit contraction, the former banker hypothesized that speculators sought to use high interest rates to force farmers and small investors to cover expensive loan payments by selling off stock and securities at bargain prices.[6]

Six months after Stokes's warning, the Federal Reserve Board initiated a period of monetary deflation by raising the discount rates it charged member banks. Higher interest rates discouraged borrowing by banks affiliated with the system and forced them to liquidate loans to individual customers. Pressed for working capital, local banks in rural areas found themselves unable to extend wartime loans. As Stokes had predicted, farm belt borrowers immediately sold off crops to realize quick returns and meet loan obligations. The forced sale of agricultural goods brought a dramatic drop in commodity prices. Wheat, which sold at over $2.50 a bushel in 1920, plummeted to $1.00 a bushel by the end of 1921. In South Dakota, where farmers owed over $300 million in debts to eastern note holders, land prices fell by a third to half their value. North Dakota livestock prices dropped by nearly half. Usher Burdick, a member of the Nonpartisan League, later recalled that the credit crunch dropped the value of his sheep from $8.00 a head to $0.50.[7]

Deflation, withdrawal of agricultural credit, and low commodity prices marked the rural economic depression that began in 1920. Five thousand independent banks failed in the first years of the decade. Between 1920 and 1929 the value of the nation's farm properties declined from $79 billion to $51 billion. Protests flooded the offices of western Federal Reserve banks and politicians. If farmers did not receive extended time to pay off their bank loans, a county agricultural agent warned Idaho's Senator Borah, many stood to lose their life earnings. "The simple fact," Nebraska's Governor Samuel A. McKelvie told the Federal Reserve, "is that the urgent demand for liquidation and the contraction of credit has imposed unusual and extraordinary hardships upon the farmers and the cattlemen." If Nebraska cattle raisers and feed growers did not receive reasonable credit at affordable rates, he predicted, their livelihood would be jeopardized. Without loans, added a prominent farm journal editor, growers would "drop out, drift to the cities, and swell the already overflowing ranks of unskilled labor."[8]

Western political leaders and their constituents suspected that the Federal Reserve sought to favor big business at the expense of rural producers. Nebraska's Senator George Norris privately fumed about the "wrongful manipulations" of the power vested in the banking board. Years later Wisconsin's Robert M. La Follette Jr. would describe the 1920s credit contraction as "one of the most colossal financial conspiracies of history." Such fears appeared to be validated when John Skelton Williams, President Wilson's comptroller of the currency and a former member of the Federal Reserve Board, asserted in 1921 that the previous administration believed farm commodity prices were too high and that board governors actually celebrated the decline of small banks. "Let 'em fail," one member supposedly had said of faltering rural lenders, "their condition is the result of their own misjudgment, and they can take the consequence of it." Williams charged that the Federal Reserve Board favored speculators over producers.[9]

Although farm and ranch operations often involved speculation in land and commodity values, western politicians maintained Jacksonian distinctions between honest production and manipulations of wealth. "I think it is an established principle adopted by economists and bankers," Minnesota's Henrik Shipstead told the Senate in 1927, "that credit should never be extended to speculation, that the legitimate extension of credit should . . . be for production and never for speculation or for luxury." Shipstead protested that the 1920 contraction required farmers to sell the "liberty bonds" many had purchased under wartime political pressure. Tax-exempt "liberty bonds" frequently found their way to institutional speculators since they drew a better return than farm loans. As South Dakota's Peter Norbeck pointed out, the federal government had urged wheat farmers to expand wartime production. Now the government's monetary policy penalized those who had borrowed money to invest in wartime land, machinery, and supplies.[10]

For such "moral agrarians" as George Norris, Peter Norbeck, and William Borah, the survival of republican and democratic values depended on prosperity for rural producers and independent enterprisers. Widespread farm bankruptcy, fretted Borah, would "reduce us to a level of the landlord and tenant system in this country and no more serious proposition than that could be stated." Such anxiety appeared justified when Congress passed the Esch-Cummins Transportation Act of 1920, legislation that threatened to raise agricultural shipping costs drastically. The omnibus bill facilitated the return of the nation's railroads to private hands after wartime management by the federal government. It also created a Railway Labor Board and expanded Interstate Commerce Commission (ICC) control over rates, corporate structure, profits, and financing. The law further empowered the ICC to permit consolidations and pooling arrangements among competitors and to create a revolving fund of excess profits to be reinvested in struggling lines.[11]

Treating the carriers as public utilities, the Transportation Act sought to build a more efficient national system and enhance investor stability by improving the financial condition of railroads whose equipment had deteriorated during the war. Accordingly, the law empowered the ICC to divide the nation into rate districts, where minimum instead of maximum charges would be set. For two years carriers were to be guaranteed an annual "fair return" equivalent to 6 percent of the value of their overall holdings. Western progressives protested that the arrangement appeared to extend unwarranted privileges to organized capital at the expense of competition and inexpensive freight rates. Robert La Follette, whose first Wisconsin political campaigns had targeted railroad exploitation, described the new rate increases as "by far the most gigantic in history." La Follette demanded restoration of rate-setting power by state commissions. Meanwhile, the American Farm Bureau Federation and grower cooperatives attributed the agricultural depression of the early 1920s to inflated transportation charges.[12]

Rural politicians argued that the Esch-Cummins Transportation Act permitted the railroads to base rate increases on assessments of corporate value inflated by Wall Street speculation. The "iniquitous terms" of the law, insisted La Follette, guaranteed the value of watered railroad securities owned by eastern bankers. Raising the specter of the "money power" once again, the Wisconsin senator won an easy reelection bid in 1922. The Transportation Act also served as the main target for Smith Wildman Brookhart's insurgent victory in the Iowa Republican Senate primary. In Montana Burton K. Wheeler ran a victorious campaign for the Senate with a pledge to work for the law's repeal. Wheeler, Brookhart, Lynn Frazier, and Edwin Ladd of North Dakota; Robert B. Howell and George Norris of Nebraska; and Magnus Johnson and Henrik Shipstead of Minnesota all punished Senate Interstate Commerce chair Albert Cummins by successfully opposing his reappointment. Yet critics were not strong enough to erase the legislation that seemed to symbolize the vulnerability of western producers.[13]

The political weakness of early 1920s agriculture inspired efforts to create a "farm bloc," whose goals frequently overlapped those of the western progressives and insurgent opponents of concentrated power. Agrarian interests had succeeded in establishing a federal farm loan program in 1916. Three years later rural members of Congress confronted President Wilson over his veto of a bill repealing daylight savings time. Wartime clocks had been set ahead to prolong evening daylight for urban "victory" gardeners and electric consumers. Farmers, however, habitually complained that the change of time forced them to perform morning chores in the dark and compelled them to hay and harvest before heavy dews dried. They suggested that city workers report to work an hour early to gain additional evening daylight for leisure activities. For farm leaders like John A. Simpson, president of the American Farmers' Union, the time issue amounted to another instance in which rural producers were asked to make greater sacrifices "than any other class." Other growers simply objected to the preference of "fad time" over "natural time."[14]

Congress authorized continuation of daylight savings time in the spring of 1919, but rural discontent and growing independence from Wilson soon produced a successful repeal bill. When the president vetoed the measure, citing convenience for industrial production, Congress promptly overrode him by substantial margins. Despite the minor victory, however, the first meeting of the congressional "farm bloc" did not take place until May 1921. Chaired by Iowa's Senator William S. Kenyon in the Washington offices of the American Farm Bureau Federation, the conclave attracted eleven other solons as well as advisers from the Farm Bureau and the Department of Agriculture. By the end of the year the group included nine senators and a hundred members of the House. Its new chair was Senator Arthur Capper, a Kansas Republican and Theodore Roosevelt progressive. Prior to his Senate election in 1918 Capper had fought railroad domination as a crusading publisher of an agricultural weekly and as the state's reform governor. The son of Quaker parents, he had opposed military preparedness but supported the war.[15]

The congressional farm bloc experienced another minor victory when President Harding signed a 1921 law extending federal loans to agricultural marketing associations. A more substantial triumph came in the meat-packing industry, where an oligarchy of five corporations allied with powerful banks to fix the prices stock raisers received. Because the huge processors also manipulated consumer prices, the farm bloc found the votes to pass the 1921 Packers and Stockyards Act. The law prohibited meat packers from monopolizing markets, controlling prices, or establishing territorial pools. A Grain Futures Act, passed in the same year, established similar controls over dealers in wheat and grain.[16]

✦ ✦ ✦

Independent farmers continued to hold their traditional adversaries in banking, transportation, and distribution responsible for the agricultural depression of the 1920s. Serious structural problems underlay the plight of New Era rural producers, though. More than forty million acres had been placed under cultivation during the emergency wartime mobilization. Meanwhile, tractor use increased from 85,000 in 1918 to 827,000 by 1929. As a result, farmers no longer needed twenty-four million acres to feed horses and mules. More important, mechanization and the increased acreage of the war years combined to produce an oversupply of commodities in a period in which a restored European agriculture and high tariffs reduced foreign demand. Farm earnings fell from 18.5 percent of the national income to 9.5 percent between 1919 and 1928. As agricultural land dropped in value, banks were compelled to call in promissory notes and foreclose on mortgages. Rural lenders who took possession of foreclosed land in a declining market found themselves on the brink of insolvency.[17]

Squeezed by rising costs and declining income, farm leaders looked to government legislation to solve their problems. Yet such a strategy required its promoters to overcome deep suspicions of federal power. South Dakota's Senator Peter Norbeck struggled with these issues in correspondence with Republican National Committee chair John T. Adams. Although Norbeck agreed that prices reflected supply and demand, he wondered how market laws could function when tariffs artificially subsidized manufacturers and the government guaranteed railroad profits. Farmers no longer accepted the notion that government could not bring relief from low farm prices, he protested in 1921. The Harding administration had "absolutely no comprehension of the economic problems of the northwest," the South Dakotan confided to a constituent. He warned a Republican colleague that the party could hold western farmers only with clean government and "progressive legislation." Norbeck concluded that the farmer needed to benefit from instead of becoming a "victim" of "artificial stimulants."[18]

Eastern political and economic interests were a favorite target of Norbeck's frustration. The South Dakota senator acknowledged the "education, culture, and wealth" of the Atlantic seaboard and commended the region's intelligent pursuit of its goals. Yet he professed rage at eastern ignorance of the economic problems of South Dakota and the northern plains. "The average Eastern Senator," wrote Norbeck to a South Dakota publisher, "is of the opinion that there is nothing the matter with the Northwest, except that we are less sensible and less thrifty than they are in the East." Hiram Johnson shared Norbeck's regional animosity. Johnson told the South Dakotan that "our distinguished New England brethren" disdained the politics of the western progressives because they believed that government served "its highest purposes when a few, already rich make more money out of it."[19]

Seeking a balanced approach to western agrarian politics, Norbeck criticized the Nonpartisan League and political radicals. "They have found it quite convenient," he wrote to an associate in 1923, "to limit themselves largely to an unfair discussion of economic issues to stir up the prejudices of the distressed farmers of the northwest rather than to find relief." Like Robert La Follette, the South Dakota senator dismissed radicals as people capable of obtaining power but not retaining it. Norbeck distinguished between dangerous radicalism and genuine protest against farm belt economic and political conditions. He acknowledged that Dakotans wanted a "new deal" but insisted that socialism would not bring the desired relief. "I am as progressive as anybody," declared Norbeck, "but I want to have my feet on the ground and stand only for the things that are sound and will work in practice." His three major concerns, he told a progressive activist in 1922, were lower freight rates, better farm marketing conditions, and more credit at lower interest rates.[20]

Although he admitted that half the "so-called 'Agricultural Bloc'" consisted of southern Democrats, Norbeck equated the congressional farm coalition with "western progressive sentiment." His correspondence in the early 1920s sought to clarify the nature of the insurgency in which he participated. Although he acknowledged that the United States was "probably the most conservative nation in the world," he depicted a recent trend "towards a certain radicalism." Nevertheless, Norbeck denied that American radicals veered "towards socialism." Instead, he equated 1920s insurgence with better distribution of wealth, individual rights, and personal opportunities. Once such terms were understood, he explained to a South Dakota banker in 1922, "the Progressive becomes a Radical." Such reasoning lay behind the alienation from eastern manufacturers and financiers that Norbeck shared with many western members of Congress. Predictably, he traced Democratic electoral victories in the East "to a protest against organized wealth, against tax evasion, against high car [transit] fares, and against white shirts generally."[21]

The McNary-Haugen bill of 1924 provided western farmers and politicians with the decade's most important test of concern for the independent producer. Like the free silver campaign in the 1890s, the measure answered a desperate call for full agricultural parity. It sought to create a government marketing cooperative to buy surplus commodities and sell them overseas at reduced rates. Government losses would be compensated through an "equalization fee" levied on each farmer's surplus. Proponents argued that crop prices would be sustained because the federal government could market unsold crops overseas. Plains "populist" and "mainstream" wheat growers saw the McNary-Haugen bill as a complement to the high tariffs that favored industrial interests. Yet Secretary of Commerce Hoover and President Calvin Coolidge opposed the measure on constitutional and economic grounds, and it failed to clear the House in 1924. Farm advocates responded bitterly. It did not satisfy growers, griped William Borah, "to say that a protective tariff is statesmanship and that the McNary-Haugen bill is cheap politics."[22]

✦ ✦ ✦

Congressional refusal to pass agricultural relief dramatized growing alienation between the hinterlands and eastern centers of capital and political power. Dissatisfaction throughout the country was alarming, Borah wrote to a Kansas City hardware supplier early in 1922. "I am not so sure," he speculated, that Americans were not "losing faith in their government. And you could not blame them." Failure to relieve the economic depression, explained the Idaho senator, was enough "to undermine anyone's faith." Peter Norbeck conveyed similar sentiments when he told a national Republican official that average voters saw the federal government as "inefficient, indifferent, and wasteful, if not largely corrupt." Even when cabinet members were not themselves "crooked," Norbeck assured a South Dakota banker, they "ran everything" for the benefit of big business. The Coolidge cabinet "would sell the oil fields, the forests, the coal mines, and even the ether in the air to big corporations—that is, to their own kind of people," he concluded in 1924.[23]

Animosity toward corporate domination of Washington came to a head over Secretary of the Treasury Andrew Mellon's attempt to stimulate investment by legislating tax relief for wealthy individuals and corporations. It was difficult to believe, Hiram Johnson wrote to Norbeck, "that the men with incomes of a half million or more are so concerned with my prosperity and yours that they want us to understand we can only retain it by permitting them to make more money." Johnson insisted that Mellon's proposals offered the supreme test of whether senators "stood for common humanity or for great fortunes." "The hearts of those who represented big business were set upon this plan," he explained. The measure consequently required "more courage . . . to stand up under the grueling drubbing for just common folks than in anything else which has been before the Congress in my time."[24]

Like Mellon's tax program, the Teapot Dome scandal suggested collusion between the federal government and powerful private interests. During 1921 the Harding administration had transferred government petroleum reserves at Wyoming's Teapot Dome and elsewhere from the navy to the Department of the Interior. Secretary of the Interior Albert B. Fall then leased the valuable lands to private oil operators. Disturbed that oil companies had been pressing for such privileges since 1913, Robert La Follette denounced the transfer as "absolutely detrimental to the public interest." The Wisconsin senator worked with the National Association of Independent Oil Producers, which worried that release of naval reserves would depress crude oil prices. Insisting there was "ample independent capital" to develop petroleum resources without granting rights to "monopolistic interests," the independents pushed La Follette into demanding a Senate inquiry into the relationship between the federal government and the large oil corporations.[25]

Under the leadership of Thomas J. Walsh, a Montana Democrat, the Senate Committee on Public Lands held open hearings in October 1923 that confirmed La Follette's suspicions. Evidence revealed that Secretary Fall had received over $400,000 in cash and bonds from oil corporations benefiting from government leases. Meanwhile, a Senate select committee, chaired by Smith Brookhart but energized by Burton Wheeler, exposed the corrupt activities and associations of Attorney General Harry M. Daugherty. For western progressives and critics of concentrated power, the Harding scandals suggested how corporate monopoly and greed corrupted government. The situation, noted William Borah, "has been so demoralizing that I hardly know how to express myself without appearing to be unreasonable." Beyond individual corruption, insisted Borah, lay a general condition of "waste, extravagance, and venality" that could not be overestimated. The United States had reached a point, the Idaho senator told a Connecticut judge, "where sordidness and corruption are equal to the condition which once tormented old Rome itself."[26]

Western progressives and insurgents generalized the lessons of Teapot Dome to conclude that powerful corporations dominated the presidency, judiciary, and federal bureaucracy. Independent Republicans such as George Norris contended that the Harding and Coolidge administrations had "packed and controlled" the regulatory agencies. Norris objected particularly to the big business slant of the Federal Trade Commission (FTC). Having supported the creation of the FTC in 1914, the Nebraskan recalled how the agency had exposed the "unholy methods" by which small competitors had been driven from business and the "unconscionable profit" extracted from consumers. Like Norris, Robert La Follette was an early FTC supporter who had fought against a proposed $100,000 cut in the agency's 1919 appropriations by suggesting that the bureau's "grilling" of the meat-packing monopoly had precipitated the attempt to cripple it.[27]

Both Norris and La Follette turned against the FTC when President Coolidge appointed William E. Humphrey, a stalwart Republican, corporate attorney, and lumber lobbyist, as the panel's fifth member in 1924. The appointment, charged Norris, changed the agency's majority from one that sided with the people to one that unthinkingly lined up with trusts, monopolies, and big business. Norris compared the panel's confidential deliberations to the secret treaties of wartime diplomacy. He also criticized the commission's dismissal of corporate infractions at the slightest promise of good behavior and condemned its refusal to impose penalties. Norris became particularly angered when the FTC abandoned a 1925 investigation of the electrical power industry that the Senate had requested at his initiative. The federal agency, he charged, had become "the refuge for monopoly, unfair competition, and unfair business methods." FTC investigators were "reactionary men" who used public taxes to approve the "devouring" of small producers by "criminals."[28]

La Follette joined Norris in denouncing the FTC. Citing the discontinuation of testimony from sworn hearings, the omission of verbatim records, and the exclusion of injured parties from proceedings, the Wisconsin senator declared that the commission was the last of the regulatory agencies "to be taken over by the forces it was intended to regulate." The panel's Republican majority, he protested, had "done vastly more to put honest business and the public at the mercy of profiteering and predatory wealth than was accomplished by Fall when he turned the naval reserves over to the oil monopoly." Once the FTC was "packed with its worst enemies," charged La Follette, independent regulation of corporate monopoly had become endangered.[29] For western progressives, Teapot Dome, the Mellon tax plan, and the "packing" of the FTC all suggested that Washington no longer addressed the needs of ordinary producers and enterprisers. Instead of serving as an ally of opponents of concentrated power, the federal government had become a dangerous antagonist.

❖ ❖ ❖

Disillusionment with Washington prompted western insurgents to improvise political strategy. In North Dakota and Minnesota farm, labor, and small business activists sought to build on the legacy of the Nonpartisan League (NPL). North Dakota Nonpartisans had captured the governorship and legislature in 1918 and created a state bank, a mill, and an elevator as well as an industrial commission, a workers' compensation bureau, and minimum wages and maximum hours for labor. NPL officials in Minnesota encouraged the creation of the Workingmen's Nonpartisan League as a vehicle for the common interests of producers in agriculture and labor. Both Minnesota leagues met in 1920 to appoint committees to draft a platform and nominate common candidates. Delegates agreed on Henrik Shipstead as their choice for governor.[30]

One of twelve children born to Norwegian homesteaders in central Minnesota, Shipstead practiced dentistry and in his spare time studied law. In 1916 he won election to the state legislature as a progressive Republican. When Shipstead failed to win his party's gubernatorial primary in 1920, both Minnesota leagues supported his candidacy on a separate Farmer-Labor ticket. Although he lost the election, both the new Farmer-Labor party and the NPL backed him two years later in a run for Frank B. Kellogg's Republican Senate seat. With help from Robert La Follette, who campaigned against Kellogg as the "steel trust senator," the Minnesota dentist swept to victory. Meanwhile, Magnus Johnson, the Farmer-Labor gubernatorial candidate, lost the 1922 election by only fifteen thousand votes. One year later the Swedish-born farmer and cooperative official astounded the nation by providing the Minnesota Farmer-Laborites with their second Senate seat in a special election to fill a vacancy.[31]

Despite the Minnesota victories, NPL leaders opposed the formation of a national Farmer-Labor ticket. Some worried that business and professional people might be frightened by the party name or that socialists might use it to build their own movement. Nonpartisans also feared that support for a third ticket could prove injurious in states where they successfully functioned within the two major parties. Nevertheless, the NPL continued to support the Farmer-Labor ticket in Minnesota and helped reiterate such old Populist demands as government control of an expanded currency and cooperative banks.[32]

The victories of Henrik Shipstead and Magnus Johnson expanded the influence of insurgent progressives. Johnson's election, proclaimed William Borah, "was a distressed voice telling the American people of the tragedy that is being enacted on the farmer." If foreign markets were not open to their products, he warned, "Minnesota will prove to be little more than the first rumbling of a political revolution." Riding the tide of agrarian discontent, Robert La Follette swept all but one Wisconsin county in 1922 to return to the Senate with the most overwhelming electoral victory in the state's history. Other successful Senate candidates included Republicans Robert Howell, a Nebraska progressive and former schoolteacher; Lynn Frazier, a Nonpartisan from North Dakota; and Smith Brookhart, an independent supporter of agrarian interests from Iowa. Democrats Clarence C. Dill, a Washington progressive with Farmer-Labor support, and Burton Wheeler, a Montana attorney with strong antimonopoly leanings, joined the other Senate insurgents.[33]

Despite the progressive orientation of Democrats Dill and Wheeler, most western insurgents were Republicans. Yet party loyalty proved difficult to sustain as three successive New Era administrations aligned themselves with big business. No one tried harder to bridge the gap between progressive faith and party discipline than Hiram Johnson, Theodore Roosevelt's vice presidential partner in the Progressive crusade of 1912. Sensing that Americans rejected splinter political movements, Johnson consistently sought to "progressivize" Republicans. He speculated privately in 1917 that party leaders probably would resist change and retain their power. Yet Johnson detected "the fallow soil of progressivism" in the rank and file. Estimating his chances at one in a million in 1919, the senator encouraged reorganization of the remnants of the California Progressive party into a small presidential campaign committee.[34]

Opening his 1920 Republican presidential campaign in Brooklyn, New York, Johnson criticized the League of Nations, the Allied intervention in the Soviet Union, and the Red Scare raids. Midwestern and western support followed. In North Dakota the Nonpartisan League endorsed the candidate. Meanwhile, Johnson finished a strong third in the South Dakota primary, running only 680 votes behind frontrunner Governor Frank Lowden of Illinois. In Michigan, where William Borah came to assist him, the California insurgent won a stunning primary upset. He followed this triumph with April victories in Nebraska and Montana. In New Jersey the candidate's first foray in the East, Johnson barely lost to General Leonard Wood. With George Norris supporting him in Indiana, the Californian came within 6,000 votes of Wood. Finally, Johnson overcame poor organization and labor and civic support for the League of Nations to carry his home state by 160,000 votes.[35]

Hiram Johnson came within 344 votes of the presidential nomination at the 1920 Republican convention but peaked on the third ballot when party regulars swung behind Ohio's Senator Warren Harding. Offered unanimous backing for the vice presidency, the California insurgent declined. He also rejected a postelection role in the inner circles of the Harding administration, confiding to his sons that "I just have to go my own way." When he was invited to a White House dinner in December 1922, Johnson noted with bitterness that those with whom he sat governed "the richest and most powerful nation on earth." None of them, he concluded, embodied "vision nor statesmanship."[36]

By late 1923 Johnson once again became convinced that the Republican party would remain permanently "reactionary" or be revitalized by a rank-and-file progressivism. Launching a second presidential campaign midway between "static reaction" and "destructive radicalism," the California politician directed a populist attack on Andrew Mellon's 20 percent tax reduction on incomes over $300,000. Johnson also demanded an adjusted veterans' bonus, lower railroad freight rates, and passage of the

McNary-Haugen bill. In foreign affairs he renewed the call for nonpartic-
ipation in the League of Nations and the World Court. The senator won
the support of his colleague Peter Norbeck, who defied the Republican
organization by proselytizing for the candidate in a 2,500-mile auto tour
of South Dakota. With Norbeck's help and the backing of NPL leaders in
North Dakota, Johnson won primaries in both states.[37]

Despite such triumphs, the Californian's campaign suffered from meager funding, poor organization, and little press support. Demoralized,
Johnson all but withdrew from the contest in April 1924. "The Republican party is dominated by the unholy alliance between crooked big business and crooked politics," he proclaimed in a written statement. "This
alliance must be smashed and the party revitalized and regenerated. The
nation must be purged of those in power who divide their allegiance with
special or corrupt interests." In private Johnson despaired. "Big business
is in the saddle as it hasn't been before during my life," he wrote to his
son. With "a venal press" and cleverly managed propaganda at its disposal,
organized money had learned "to disseminate propaganda cunningly and
scientifically." Coolidge would simply buy the election, confided Johnson.
Publicly, the disappointed candidate issued a press release reiterating the
faith that progressivism was "still cherished by the great inarticulate mass,
is yet enshrined in the hearts of millions."[38]

✦ ✦ ✦

Like Hiram Johnson, Robert La Follette held presidential aspirations while
viewing himself as a loner. In 1919 La Follette dismissed Senate insurgents
as "soft-shell progressives" who sought committee chairs instead of organizing for control of legislative policy. The Wisconsin insurgent confided
to his son that he expected to be "the one radical of the Senate in the future as in the past." Nevertheless, La Follette began efforts to build a progressive movement inside and outside Congress. In 1920 he cooperated
with sixteen railroad brotherhoods to create the Bureau of Research and
Publicity, a lobby designed to repeal the Esch-Cummins Transportation Act
and support independent congressional candidates. Evolving into the People's Legislative Service, the group responded to La Follette's urging by
holding two Conferences for Progressive Political Action (CPPA) in 1922.
The meetings attracted all the new Senate progressives and received William Jennings Bryan's endorsement as a tool against Wall Street influence
in politics.[39]

Despite his disappointment with third-party politics in 1912, La Follette believed there was "enough general disgust with both of the old organizations" that a new party might represent "the millions who want real
democracy." As he groomed himself for a potential presidential bid, ur-

ban progressives formed the Committee of 48 in 1919 that called for government ownership of railroads and natural resources. When socialists and labor groups dominated a subsequent convention, however, the NPL wing of the movement deserted the cause, and La Follette denounced efforts to create a farmer-labor party based on socialist principles. Opting to run as a Republican, the Wisconsin senator swept his state in the party's 1920 presidential primary. With support from labor reformers and Nonpartisans, he finished strongly among urban wage earners, middle-class liberals, and rural Scandinavians. La Follette's successful 1922 Senate campaign expanded this base to German-American socialists and farmers.[40]

As the 1924 election approached, the Committee of 48 sought to negotiate a third-party candidacy by William Borah but failed. In late 1923 the People's Progressive Party Convention in Detroit tried to draft the industrialist Henry Ford on a "Save America First" program, with similar results. The following June the farmer-labor movement convened a national convention in St. Paul, but La Follette lashed out at the involvement of communists as "absolutely repugnant to democratic ideals and to all American aspirations." Insisting that he would pursue a presidential bid only as an independent, the Wisconsin insurgent finally agreed to run as a Progressive when the CPPA reconvened in Cleveland the following month.[41]

The Progressive convention included Republican insurgents, western agrarians, old populists, urban liberals and socialists, women peace activists, and railroad and trade union leaders. Its platform called for public waterpower, cheap electricity, conservation of natural resources, and eventual government ownership of rail lines. The Progressives also embraced familiar La Follette tax reform measures, federal aid to farmers, popular election of federal judges, a constitutional amendment to permit Congress to override Supreme Court decisions, and the abolition of antilabor injunctions. The platform further proposed the adoption of an anti-imperial foreign policy and legislation to outlaw war and conscription. The heart of the document, however, was its suggestion that "the great issue before the American today is control of government and industry by private monopoly." Monopoly, it asserted, "crushed competition, stifled private initiative and independent enterprise, and . . . now extracts extortionate profits upon every necessity of life consumed by the public."[42]

La Follette and the CPPA executive committee chose forty-two year-old Burton Wheeler as vice presidential candidate. The tenth child of a Quaker father and a Methodist purity crusader, Wheeler was born in Massachusetts in 1882. He worked his way through the University of Michigan law school and settled in Butte in 1905, when he missed a train while engaged in a losing poker game. There he practiced law in the shadow of the giant Anaconda mining company. Wheeler went to the state legislature in 1911 and became a federal district attorney two years later. The prosecutor's distaste for pursuing wartime dissenters led to his resignation in 1918. Two years later both the Nonpartisan League and the Montana Labor League endorsed Wheeler for governor in a Democratic primary that pitted him against Anaconda. Wheeler lost the election but Farmer-Labor party support helped send him to the Senate in 1922. Concerned with the exploitation of natural resources and corporate monopoly, the Montana Democrat chaired the corruption investigations of the Department of Justice.[43]

Wheeler believed that Thomas Jefferson, Abraham Lincoln, and Robert La Follette were the three greatest Americans of all time. His political philosophy embraced a worldwide class struggle epitomized by the conflict between the East and West in the United States. Like La Follette, the Montana Democrat portrayed corporate power and international bankers as the cause of the nation's domestic problems and its overseas imperialism. Wheeler supported government ownership of railroads and waterpower because private enterprise and government regulation appeared ineffective. He endorsed government aid to labor and farmers because big business already received such benefits. But the senator also saw big government as a dreaded form of concentrated power. In the opening speech of the campaign Wheeler told a Boston Commons audience that Americans were "living under the dictatorship of a small class that controls the financial resources of the country." As long as political parties were dominated by economic interests, he warned, the nation must expect corruption in government.[44]

La Follette and Wheeler viewed the 1924 election as an opportunity for the nation's producers to participate in the first referendum on the corporate manner of doing business. For years the Wisconsin senator had portrayed an "invisible government," a financial oligarchy that dominated small business, government, both parties, the legislative process, and the courts. Now La Follette and Wheeler rallied audiences against the concentration of economic wealth and the abuse of power. The Wisconsinite insisted that the campaign sought "to restore government to the people," but he faced overwhelming obstacles. Almost seventy years old and outspent nearly twentyfold by the Republicans, La Follette lacked the energy and organization to mount a credible run. He also faced withdrawal of aid from the American Federation of Labor, which had supported an independent candidacy but refused to back a third party.[45]

Recurring disunity among Senate progressives and insurgents proved extremely harmful to Progressive prospects. Although Henrik Shipstead and Hiram Johnson endorsed the ticket, only Smith Brookhart and North

Dakota's Edwin Ladd and Lynn Frazier provided active support. Meanwhile, Robert Howell refused to bolt the Republican party, George Norris remained neutral, William Borah gave lukewarm support to Coolidge, and Peter Norbeck openly sided with the president. On election day La Follette and Wheeler received 4.8 million votes, or 16.6 percent of the popular tally. Although the Progressives carried only Wisconsin, they amassed 49 percent of ballots cast in thirteen midwestern and western agricultural states. The ticket came in second in California, Idaho, Iowa, Minnesota, Montana, Nevada, Washington, Wyoming, and the Dakotas. It also finished behind the winner in sixty-seven industrial counties in the Northeast and Midwest.[46]

❖ ❖ ❖

Despite its limitations, the Progressive campaign pointed to widespread dissatisfaction with conventional politics. William Borah noted that "almost one-fifth of all who cast a ballot . . . registered their convictions that neither of the old parties were longer fit to administer the affairs of government." Burton Wheeler went further, arguing that the Progressive vote demonstrated that prewar "radicalism" still survived. La Follette supporters were not the "Wall Street progressives" who had voted for Theodore Roosevelt in 1912, advised Wheeler. Instead, their insurgence involved "a class struggle" against "vested interests." Postwar progressives, he told a reform symposium in 1926, would continue "to check the growing arrogance of the executive department and restore government to the people."[47]

President Coolidge's nomination of Charles B. Warren for attorney general provided the perfect test of Wheeler's prognosis. The controversy provided insurgents with a unity that the Progressive party had failed to achieve. Indeed, Hiram Johnson wrote Peter Norbeck that approval of the Mellon tax plan and the Warren vote were the era's two greatest tests of Senate integrity. Reformers first mistrusted the nominee because he had been chief solicitor for the Republican presidential campaign of 1920. Organizing the largest collection of campaign funds in history, Warren had sent a circular letter to powerful business leaders asking them to "determine promptly what the value of Republican success means to you and your corporate interests."[48]

Insurgents were further outraged by Warren's ties to the sugar trust. The prospective attorney general had represented the American Sugar Refining Company while it sought to consolidate control over manufacturing, sales, and distribution. Warren's activities as president of its Michigan sugar beet subsidiary had resulted in federal charges of unlawful combination. When the nomination came before the Senate, the antitrust case was still before the FTC. Nebraska's George Norris, a longtime foe of the sugar interests, expressed the heart of the insurgent view of corporate privilege in an impassioned letter to a constituent. The sugar monopoly, exclaimed Norris, was "one of the most wicked trusts in existence, because it dealt in a necessity of life. It levied its unholy tribute upon every table in every humble home in the land. It took from the poor of the country by pennies, enough to make fortunes for those who sit around mahogany tables and do nothing but profit by the toil and sweat of others."[49]

Responding to criticism by some Nebraska Republicans, Norris insisted that the party rank and file did not "favor putting into office those who organize trusts and thus increase the burdens of our people." The nomination of a trust organizer to prosecute monopolies, he complained in the *Nation,* amounted to "nullification" of the antitrust laws. "Mr. Warren is not in reality a lawyer," charged Hiram Johnson, but "a negotiator, connubiator, manipulator, fixer, promoter." "The record," he asserted, "established that his whole career has been devoted to making the necessaries of life a little dearer for the common people in order that a few very rich may be a little richer. . . . he believes that government is for a favored class and that it is perfectly legitimate . . . to crowd others out of business, stifle competition, increase the cost of a necessary of life, and make those who have little and who are least able to pay, pay the price of increased fortunes for those who already have much."[50]

As western insurgents prepared to combat the Warren nomination in 1925, they confronted the anger of the Republican hierarchy. Party leaders already had excluded La Follette and Progressive defectors from Senate caucuses. The chamber soon voted 65 to 11 to strip third-party supporters of their committee seniority. On the same day, insurgents joined with Democrats to block a session on the Warren nomination by a single vote. When the Senate finally addressed the issue, William Borah led the opposition and prevailed on Peter Norbeck to side with the dissidents. In turn, Norbeck convinced his fellow South Dakotan, William H. McMaster, to join the cause. When the first roll call brought a 41-39 defeat for the administration, President Coolidge threatened to make a recess appointment. Both Borah and La Follette responded that the ultimatum violated constitutional separation of powers and pitted democracy against dictatorship. When a second roll call brought a 46-39 rejection of the nomination, the administration backed down. This was the first congressional veto of a cabinet appointment since 1868.[51]

Three months after the dramatic victory Robert La Follette died. Although his race for the presidency had divided western insurgents, La Follette remained the nation's leading symbol of an anticorporate politics that united small farmers, laborers, and the old middle class. As William Borah told the Senate in tribute, the creed of the Wisconsin reformer stemmed from a populist "faith in the average common sense of the masses." "There were no silk hats and broad cloth suits" among the mourners, noted George Norris. Burton Wheeler promised that La Follette's death would inspire the Senate to prepare "for the irrepressible conflict before us."[52]

Robert M. La Follette Jr. succeeded his namesake. The younger La Follette had served as his father's political aide and been vice-chair of the Progressive campaign of 1924. Easily winning a special election at the age of thirty, he became the youngest member of the Senate since Henry Clay. Early in 1926 La Follette was joined by thirty-three-year-old Gerald Nye of North Dakota. A country newspaper editor aligned with the Nonpartisan League, Nye had lost a 1924 run for Congress as a progressive Republican. The following year the governor appointed him to fill the Senate seat of the late Edwin Ladd. Since North Dakota had updated its laws to require the direct elections of senators, stalwart Senate Republicans succeeded in raising legal questions about seating the unknown Nonpartisan. A concerted effort by William Borah and other progressives managed to obtain a 41-39 vote to certify Nye's appointment. Emulating Robert La Follette Jr., the North Dakotan attacked the World Court in his first Senate address.[53]

✦ ✦ ✦

Rooted in a republican political culture that distrusted complicity between high finance and centralized government, western insurgents continued to challenge ties between Wall Street and Washington. Accordingly, 1920s anticorporate progressives joined the operators of independent lending institutions in opposing federal legislation to legalize branch banking. When the Wilson administration had proposed such a measure in 1918, small lenders reminded William Borah of his consistent denunciation of industrial and banking concentration. Branch banking was "entirely foreign to the traditions and spirit of this country," the president of a Spokane, Washington, depository pleaded. Independent bankers argued that centrally managed institutions could not be responsive to local conditions and needs. Such objections intensified when Pennsylvania's Representative Louis McFadden introduced legislation in 1922 to permit national banks to obtain up to twelve branches with approval from the affiliated lenders.[54]

McFadden limited his bill's coverage to the twenty-two states that already permitted state bank branches. Nevertheless, opponents contended that branch banking would drive independent lenders out of business and produce monopolistic control of credit. They insisted that independent banking prevented centralization of financial power in the same way that democracy worked against consolidated political power. Employing a moral yardstick for banking success, branch detractors asserted that lending institutions should attract business by the quality of their service instead of the circumstances of their location. "It is the difference between cordial, man-to-man service," declared a pamphlet of an independent Missouri bank association, "and the indirect, we'll see-what-the-head office-says mode of branch banking contact." Independent lenders portrayed their locally owned institutions as fostering business initiative in communities their officers knew intimately.[55]

Senator Arthur Capper from Kansas led the opposition to the McFadden bill with a proposal to prevent the establishment of national bank branches in states that did not expressly permit them. The measure also enabled states to repeal authorizations for branch banking. When Congress still had not passed legislation by 1924, the American Bankers Association (ABA) voted on a compromise to confine branch banking to states where it already was legal. Yet both sides retreated to their original positions at the 1926 ABA convention. Never had Senator Thomas Walsh, an opponent of branch banking, seen association officers "so determined to 'put over a proposition' regardless of the desire of the delegates as on this occasion." McFadden supporters, asserted Walsh, sought to give the nation's industrial centers financial power over agricultural regions. "The policy of those in control of national affairs since the World War," charged the Montana Democrat, had been "to centralize the functions of both government and business," contrary to American tradition.[56]

The House passed the ABA banking compromise in 1926, only to reverse itself 228 to 166 the following January. By then Senate opposition to the McFadden bill had hardened. Burton Wheeler, for example, not only objected to the measure's provisions for branch banking but also opposed its grant of additional investment powers to national and Federal Reserve banks. Henrik Shipstead joined Wheeler by noting that more than 3,500 banks had closed their doors between 1920 and 1925, 95 percent in agricultural communities. Branch banking, warned Shipstead, raised the question of whether independent bankers would survive or be entirely eliminated. Congress compromised on the issue by legislating the McFadden-Pepper Act of 1927. The new law enabled national banks to make long-term loans on real estate and engage in investment banking. It also allowed national banks to operate branch offices in cities where state bankers had similar privileges. The bill further stipulated that no state bank belonging to the Federal Reserve could establish out-of-town branches.[57]

Insurgent suspicions of high finance generated pointed criticism of Andrew Mellon's policies at the Treasury Department. Minnesota's Shipstead, one of Wall Street's harshest critics, warned in 1924 that Mellon had issued $21.5 billion of government securities at interest rates higher than private banks offered. As a result, large lenders were investing their funds in tax-exempt and high-interest government bonds. Washington had paid out $1 billion in public debt interest in fiscal 1923, the former dentist told the Senate. He argued that high returns on government securities led to increases in the discount rate that the Federal Reserve charged to member banks. Local institutions were consequently forced to raise loan rates to farmers and merchants. In contrast, Shipstead charged, the Federal Reserve had lowered "call loan" rates to banks investing in the stock market. The resulting "orgy of stock sales" had produced an average 25 percent "price inflation" among leading securities, another boon to speculators at the expense of small enterprisers.[58]

The conflict between local producers and concentrated capital found expression in the protests of Iowa's Smith Brookhart. Born in a Missouri log cabin to German-Swiss parents, Brookhart entered an Iowa law practice in the 1890s that often pitted him against railroad and corporate interests. An admirer of Theodore Roosevelt, he lost the Republican Senate primary to the incumbent, Albert Cummins, in 1920. Two years later Brookhart won a special election to fill Iowa's vacant second seat. He barely defeated several competitors for the full term in 1924, but an alliance of Democrats and stalwart Republicans successfully contested the election. Undaunted, the plodding Iowan defeated Cummins in the 1926 primary and returned to the Senate. A proud midwesterner who wore blue denim overalls and a straw hat at home, Brookhart lashed out at local banks that refused to lend funds to Iowans while the cities enjoyed prosperity. Farm loans once considered the safest in the world, he complained, now took second priority to speculation in the New York money market, where he estimated 74 percent of Iowa's money was invested.[59]

Seeking to compel the return of capital to local communities, Brookhart proposed that the Federal Reserve be forced to deposit all its funds with regional units instead of 25 percent. He also sought to prohibit member banks from making loans for stock and bond speculation. As such investment reached $4 billion in 1928, Wisconsin's Robert La Follette Jr. joined Brookhart in calling for restrictive legislation. In hearings before a Senate banking and currency subcommittee, however, the Harvard economist W. M. Sprague testified that local banks were making Wall Street investments because they could not negotiate a sufficient number of loans in their own regions. The economic distress of the Midwest, charged the professor, stemmed from an overabundance of small banks. Shaky lending institutions had invested too heavily in community enterprises and now were attempting to diversify their risks free from local conditions and prejudices. Rural land speculation, concluded the expert witness, lay at the heart of the region's economic dislocation.[60]

Despite Sprague's warnings, La Follette's resolution won crucial support from Brookhart, North Dakota's Lynn Frazier, and Banking and Currency Committee chair Peter Norbeck. Clearing the committee by a scant 7-5 vote, however, the measure was never considered by the Senate. Meanwhile, South Dakota's William McMaster, a Republican small-town banker himself, worked with Norbeck to introduce a proposal to require a 50 percent tax on call loans. McMaster denounced the "wild orgy of speculation" that limited profits to the rich, yet he mustered only eighteen supporters on a roll-call vote, twelve of them western progressives. The best that insurgents could manage was participation in Senate approval of a 1929 resolution by J. Thomas Heflin, an Alabama Democrat, compelling the Federal Reserve Board to provide information on "illegitimate and harmful speculation" for legislative purposes.[61]

Although insurgent ranks of the late 1920s were strengthened by the addition of Robert La Follette Jr., Gerald Nye, and Wisconsin's John Blaine, western progressives found it difficult to unify on a common political strategy and program. Early in 1927 La Follette confided that he hoped to take advantage of the Republicans' tenuous 49-47 Senate majority to advance progressive principles. Stung by President Coolidge's first veto of the McNary-Haugen bill, North Dakota's Nye soon followed by publicly calling for the formation of a "militant" Senate bloc of progressives. His platform sought to combine agricultural relief with federal flood control, public power, inland waterway improvement, abolition of branch banking, restrictions on the Federal Reserve, equitable freight rates, and reduction of government debt. Nye warned the Chamber of Commerce that sectional prejudice would produce a new party alignment if the East continued to ignore western needs.[62]

The fall of 1927 brought efforts by William Borah, Smith Brookhart, George Norris, Lynn Frazier, and Gerald Nye to fashion a common agenda for western progressives. The movement climaxed in December when Brookhart, Frazier, and Nye joined Robert La Follette Jr. and John Blaine in drafting a public letter to the Republican party that demanded endorsement of the McNary-Haugen bill. Shortly thereafter Nebraska's Robert Howell and Minnesota's Henrik Shipstead posed with the seven western progressives for a collective photograph designed to advertise the heightened political influence of the West. The test of such strength came with the contest for the Republican presidential nomination in 1928. Nye led the opposition to former Illinois governor Frank C. Lowden, a keen supporter of the McNary-Haugen legislation but no progressive. Insurgents preferred George Norris, a reformer whose concern for western interests went beyond farm relief, although he shared Brookhart's criticism of the McNary-Haugen bill's equalization tax as an unconstitutional deprivation of property rights.[63]

As the 1928 Republican convention approached, splits over presidential preferences and farm relief played havoc with the progressive bloc. Shortly after President Coolidge's second veto of the McNary-Haugen bill, twenty-eight midwestern farm organizations coalesced to form the Corn Belt Committee, which criticized administration agricultural policy. Calling for 100,000 producers to march on the convention to protest the veto, the committee warned that Republicans must nominate a candidate sympathetic to agriculture or lose the Midwest. Mainstream Republicans dismissed the rebels as fanatics and noisy "hangovers" from the Populist and Nonpartisan movements. Indeed, when the anticipated demonstration fizzled and William Borah denounced the McNary-Haugen legislation as unconstitutional, delegates rejected endorsement of the farm bill by a substantial margin of 806 to 278. Taking the defeat as a sign of his political weakness, Frank Lowden facilitated the nomination of Commerce Secretary Herbert Hoover.[64]

Senate progressives responded differently to the Republican party. Robert La Follette Jr., who heard catcalls when he introduced a Wisconsin minority report on taxation, remained neutral in the fall campaign, as did Henrik Shipstead. Peter Norbeck stayed in the Republican camp but refused to endorse Hoover. George Norris, who had won the Nebraska presidential primary without campaigning, rejected vice presidential overtures and eventually joined Wisconsin's John Blaine in supporting the Democrats. Only Smith Brookhart, Lynn Frazier, Robert Howell, Hiram Johnson, Gerald Nye, and William Borah backed Hoover. Borah played a major role in convention affairs and met with the nominee almost daily. The Idaho senator served on the resolutions committee and wrote the Republican planks on prohibition, campaign funds, and the outlawry of war. He also composed sections of the farm and labor platforms. As a gesture to agriculture, Borah pressed the party to extend the vice presidential nomination to Senator Charles Curtis from Kansas.[65]

As Congress moved toward higher industrial tariffs by the end of the decade, western progressives sought to provide equal protection for small farmers. Nine insurgents met in September 1929 to press for lower duties on manufactured goods and higher levies on agricultural commodities. Their actions inspired George Moses's outburst about their being "sons of the wild jackass." Moses was not alone in mocking Senate insurgents. Except for George Norris and Thomas Walsh, wrote the *American Mercury*'s H. L. Mencken, the progressives were "a sorry bunch of weaklings and time-servers," a "small, forlorn, and measly gang of false leaders." Detecting "little intellectual or moral fibre in any of them," Mencken ridiculed the reformers as men who "pother, trim, and hedge." "They sit back," he complained, "wail a bit, shake their heads, demand investigations, introduce endless . . . and inane resolutions, and then take it out by 'voting right.'" Mencken dismissed the insurgents as hypocrites limited to "face-saving devices."[66]

Western progressives were aware of such criticism. As early as 1926 George Norris had acknowledged that his colleagues had "been run over, rolled over, tumbled over, defeated, abused, maligned, and misrepresented." Yet Norris pleaded with a constituent to "realize that we have accomplished some good . . . in favor of the great suffering public." For years the Nebraskan had focused attention on public power. In 1921 he successfully used his clout as chair of the Senate Agriculture and Forestry Committee to defeat Henry Ford's plan to purchase a string of government nitrate plants and lease the Muscle Shoals Dam on the Tennessee River. Norris insisted that cheap government electric power should someday serve farmers and consumers and permit small producers to compete with corporate giants. Unwilling to enrich private concerns "at the expense of the taxpayers," he won congressional approval for government development of the Tennessee River valley in 1928 and 1929, although two Republican presidents vetoed the bill without an override.[67]

Norris's commitment to democratic goals typified insurgent ideology. As Robert La Follette Jr. explained to a radio audience in 1928, progressives sought to restore the representative government of Jefferson and Lincoln. Their movement, insisted William Borah, rested on "militant liberalism, not radicalism," and was designed to provide "clean and economic government . . . in the interests of the whole people." Although South Dakota's Peter Norbeck depicted progressive Republicans as the "Radical group" on the tariff, he joined Borah in rejecting "radicalism." Indeed, postwar insurgents shared a general suspicion of state control. "Liberty is what we are for. That's why we're progressive," the reform ally William Hard noted in the *Nation* in 1924. "Because we're progressive, and because we're for liberty, we're against governmentalization," he declared. Two years later Hard lamented that federal regulatory agencies once energized by "radicals" had fallen into the hands of "reactionaries."[68]

Progressive insurgents suffered from an inability to apply the individualist values of producer republicanism to the needs of a corporate and urbanized society. Such contradictions were compounded by the failure to distinguish between the economic needs of western agriculture and the requirements of a broader public interest. Farmer-labor disunity further reduced prospects for success. "The farmers and the laborers ought to be together . . . they are fighting the same battle," George Norris told the managing editor of *Labor* magazine in 1929. Norris quickly admitted, however, that both groups looked at politics from a selfish viewpoint focused on temporary gain.[69]

Western agricultural interests dominated the 1920s progressive agenda, while organized labor, urban reformers, and middle-class professionals appeared to be outside the fold. By 1929 insurgent progressives still disagreed on how to combat the institutional clout of organized money without employing oppressive forms of political power. What were the means of implementing the republican traditions of equal rights for all and special privileges to none in modern society? Could private investment be monitored and regulated in a market originally defined by economic liberty? How could the public good be addressed in an economy energized by individual and corporate self-interest? Were suspicions of high finance and institutional power mere hangovers from an agrarian past? Paralyzed by the implications of their political philosophy and values, Senate progressives found it difficult to maintain intellectual legitimacy. When Smith Brookhart warned a Senate subcommittee in 1928 that Wall Street speculation would push the country toward "the greatest panic in the history of the world," Joseph Stagg Lawrence, an expert witness from Princeton University, dismissed the outburst as the "curious emissions of a provincial mind."[70]

4

Two Nations: The Cultural Contradictions of the Jazz Age

During 1924 an Atlanta editor called on the citizens of the United States to assimilate "into a solidified American electorate expressing the will of the American people." Citing the need for better law enforcement, improved public schooling, and clean politics, the writer held out the vision of a "nonpartisan crusade" to ensure "purification of political action."[1] The *Imperial Night-Hawk,* the national organ of the Ku Klux Klan, constituted one of many voices that continued to honor producer values and republican morality in the 1920s. While New Era consumerism generated cosmopolitan social values and integrated ethnic groups into the national identity, it induced a confrontation between modern and traditional affinities that helped shape the postwar battle between insurgents and the established order.

❖ ❖ ❖

Corporate capitalists of the 1920s used the expertise of the professional middle class to refine the continental market and consumer culture created after the Civil War. Stimulated by the automobile, radio, electrical appliances, motion pictures, packaged foods, synthetic fibers, installment buying, nationwide advertising, and chain stores, New Era Americans learned how to transfer psychological energies from work to leisure. As an emerging recreational culture reinforced hedonistic pursuits of self-liberation and self-fulfillment, college youth, women, and ethnic minorities were among those who found role models in movie stars, musicians, dancers, and popular writers. Corporate advertisers, as Warren Susman has observed, encouraged people to mold themselves into a "performing self" infused with "personality." Between 1909 and 1929 household spending tripled, with amusements, clothing, furniture, and automobiles experiencing the greatest increases. Outlays for cosmetics, beauty aids, and home decoration multiplied eight times between 1914 and 1924.[2]

As the consumer economy spread from metropolitan centers, many Americans perceived a frightening collapse of traditions and institutions. "Acids of modernity," wrote the commentator Walter Lippmann, were eating away at customary definitions of status, obligation, and identity. Rejecting the moral relativism and pursuit of pleasure associated with popular culture, traditionalists talked of such virtues as duty, self-discipline, sacrifice, family obligation, and community cohesion. When mass communications and transportation replaced the practices and mores of insulated communities with the standardized patterns of urban culture, local institutions appeared to be endangered. Critics complained that the family had been weakened and that the cherished home had become nothing more than a service station for self-indulgent members. Millions of Americans responded to the exciting innovations of the New Era and Jazz Age with a heightened sense of loss, frustration, and antipathy.[3]

The critique of consumer culture often found expression in rural America, where independent producers struggled to survive a corporatized economy and severe postwar agricultural depression. As ruralites linked their harsh economic plight to the dominance of urban values and practices, bitter legislative confrontations emerged in such states as Iowa and Illinois. Midwestern farmers fought for farm-to-market roads, while urbanites pressed for intercity highways. While urban renters and salaried voters battled to maintain taxes on rural land and tangible assets, agricultural interests called for progressive levies on the income and liquid holdings of city dwellers. Fearing their revenues supported government programs that benefited urban centers or interfered with local trades, farming interests frequently opposed escalating salaries and expenses for state education and regulatory bureaucracies.[4]

While large cities and towns often prevailed in tax and highway matters, rural districts predominated on such cultural matters as liquor law enforcement, Sunday sports bans, and strict regulation of gambling. Ruralites equated urban spectator sports, such as boxing and horse racing, with cheap commercialism, unearned income, and ethnic gambling and crime. As farming and small-town populations declined in the 1920s, provincial opinion leaders sharply criticized the spread of urban consumer values. Traditionalists perpetuated a republican legacy that viewed cities as homes of the decadent rich and the corrupt working class. Rural midwestern newspapers pictured such places as Chicago and New York as oppressively congested and artificial towns dominated by immigrant crime, political machines, radical labor unions, salacious entertainment, and snide cosmopolitanism. Many Americans, the historian Richard Hofstadter explained, looked upon the postwar city as "the home of liquor and bootleggers, jazz and Sunday golf, wild parties and divorce."[5]

Western insurgents also feared urban "death chambers of civilization." As early as 1913 George Norris dismissed cities as places "where poverty prevails, where crime spreads, where misery lives, where disease is located, where anarchy is born." He might be "something of an old fogey," mused Norris years later, but the deterioration of urban morals appeared to be part of the decline of civilization plaguing society since the end of World War I. The elder Robert La Follette shared such views. Writing to his family after the close of hostilities, La Follette worried about veterans "flocking in great droves to the cities and white lights." Pointing to "the surfeit of sensationalism" that had "been doped out" during the war, the progressive hoped that the public was ready "for something besides 'Follies' and 'Jazz bands.'" La Follette wondered if newspapers, magazines, and billboards created a "repeated impression upon the mind . . . in overcoming and subduing all resistance even against one's positive knowledge and settled convictions."[6]

Notions of urban cultural decadence frequently appeared in the private musings of the insurgents. Writing to his sons in 1921, Hiram Johnson remarked on the desertion of the capital for a New Jersey boxing match. In this fight between "brutes," observed Johnson, the combatants would earn what "a lifetime of earnest, active, and honest endeavor" ordinarily would bring. Noting that five thousand women would attend the event, the California senator wondered "whether there was a reversion of the race." No lady would have patronized a fight in the days of his youth, he reminisced. Though he might be an "old fogey," admitted Johnson, he much preferred "the womanhood of old to the non-childbearing, smoking, drinking, and neurotic creature" who characterized the new era. "Since the war," he observed in a subsequent letter, "the American people have been gradually disintegrating into a moronic race. They have lost the capacity to reason."[7]

Jazz Age cultural confrontations did not always fall into simple urban-rural configurations. The immense struggle over national Prohibition, which took effect early in 1920, graphically illustrated this point. Except for Hiram Johnson and Robert La Follette, western progressives embraced the Eighteenth Amendment because they viewed liquor and the saloon as the primary symbols of cultural decadence and political corruption. Iowa's Senator Smith Brookhart denounced the evils of drink with the same fervor with which he condemned monopolistic trusts and banks. Idaho's William Borah, a passionate constitutionalist and protector of independent business, never departed from his profound commitment to Prohibition. In North Dakota, a dry state since its admission to the Union in 1889, leaders of the populist Nonpartisan League ranked among the foremost opponents of liquor.[8]

Prohibition crusaders portrayed the saloon as a product of greed, market competition, and corruption. Believing that industrial society had eroded traditional morality and family solidarity, reformers saw drinking as a symbol of the disorder inherent to modern secular life. Once the Eighteenth Amendment took effect, lax enforcement showed that popular will could easily be thwarted. Such themes found perfect expression in William Jennings Bryan. Convinced that abstinence from liquor elevated and liberated the individual, Bryan envisioned Prohibition as a form of Christian rebirth. As a follower of the social gospel, the Great Commoner also insisted that the "noble experiment" worked to safeguard the democratic fabric and cement the social order. Bryan pictured the liquor lobby as a nefarious example of a selfish interest that placed private profit above human welfare and thrived on the helplessness of the common people. The enactment of antiliquor laws thus represented the triumph of the democratic majority over corrupt defenders of the status quo.[9]

Prohibitionists joined moral-purity crusaders in seeking to regulate new urban amusements. North Dakota, for example, forbade the sale of cigarettes between 1895 and 1925. Voters upheld a nine-year ban on Sunday movies in 1920 while deciding to limit Sunday baseball to afternoons. Three years later a bill outlawed sabbath dancing, and a 1925 measure prohibited dancing in dark quarters or places "detrimental to public morals." North Dakota purity reform gathered its strength from the state's strict Norwegian Lutherans, but moral crusades encompassed the entire nation in the 1920s. The Methodist Central Sabbath Crusade Committee, for example, lobbied William Borah and others for a national Sunday observance bill. This proposal sought to prohibit the publication and circulation of Sunday newspapers, the operation of Sunday trains and all interstate traffic, and the use of all labor and amusements conducted for profit on the Christian sabbath. Bryan and the Methodists supported another bill to ban the interstate transmission of gambling information.[10]

Traditionalists found the automobile particularly troubling. Car advertisements promised to bring the family together with weekend outings and shared recreation, but moral authorities expressed concern over the activities of unchaperoned youth on secluded country roads. A modernist pastor in a large southwestern city insisted that new moral dangers crept into American life when married couples began the custom of exchanging partners in seating arrangements while out for evening motor rides. The mobility provided by the auto also threatened to disrupt the harmonies of community life. Critics worried about the loss of family and social cohesion that resulted from holidays and leisure time spent far from home. Religious officials wondered about the effect of Sunday outings on church attendance. More ominously, Nashville's Salvation Army reported that a majority of the women in its home for unwed mothers were victims of "the predatory drivers of automobiles."[11] In 1921 an Atlanta grand jury investigated the link between cars and moral degeneration.

Like the prohibitionists, religious fundamentalists derived support from urban and rural bastions ranging from Los Angeles to the Midwest to the South. Opposed to the "modernist" influence in Protestant denominations, fundamentalists insisted on a literal reading of the Book of Genesis. They argued that denial of human beings' divine origin and the Bible's teachings encouraged a slide to atheism, gross immorality, and a harsh, naturalistic world ruled by force instead of love. The Christian evangelist Gerald B. Winrod insisted that such "animalism" already pervaded New Era popular culture. Successful in shaping traditionalist theology among Baptists, Presbyterians, and others, fundamentalists vowed to purge modernism from the public schools by eliminating the teaching of Darwinian theories of human evolution.[12]

Once antievolutionists made substantial strides in Oklahoma, Florida, and North Carolina, the Tennessee legislature prohibited the teaching of evolution in public schools in 1925. Although supporters had passed an essentially symbolic gesture, the American Civil Liberties Union (ACLU) sought to overturn the statute's constitutionality by setting up a test case. As a result, authorities in Dayton, Tennessee, arrested John Scopes, a local high school teacher, for a classroom reading of a recent biology textbook that included evolution. When the ACLU retained the labor attorney Clarence Darrow to defend Scopes, the World Christian Fundamentals Association asked William Jennings Bryan to assist in the prosecution. Dayton now became the site for the decade's most dramatic confrontation between theological traditionalism and modernism.[13]

A veteran of the silver campaigns of the 1890s and crusades against imperialism and war in 1899 and 1917, Bryan had been converted to prohibitionism in 1910. The Great Commoner saw no contradiction between religion and reform politics and hoped to combine the two in an "applied Christianity." He insisted that Prohibition and fundamentalism were the two great moral issues of the 1920s. Bryan objected to Darwinism because he believed that it replaced love with the survival of the strongest. Evolution put people on a brute basis, he contended. Once humans abandoned their absolute faith in God, reasoned the Nebraska reformer, all morality and virtue were in jeopardy. Observing Jazz Age America, Bryan saw materialism, hedonism, and selfishness replacing God, church, and conscience. If students learned that people evolved from beasts, that there was no divine plan for the universe, and that morality was simply artificially made, faith would be destroyed. Teaching the brain, concluded Bryan, was not as important as educating the soul.[14]

The evolution controversy also spoke to populist distrust of expert educators responsible for the socialization of children. If public schools provided the bridge between the family and society, control over textbooks remained one way for parents to assert influence over their offspring. Bryan was particularly sensitive to these issues. He worried that consumer values threatened the work ethic and "the moral base of American life." Blaming social and economic elites for cultural corruption, Bryan objected to the role of experts in determining matters of faith and values. Arrogant intellectuals, he protested, endangered the nation's basic beliefs by supporting the predominance of an "oligarchy" of scientists in matters of common wisdom.[15]

Bryan saw antievolution laws as a matter of majority rule. He argued that free speech protections did not apply when parents and taxpayers refused to pay instructors to teach doctrines they found undesirable. "The *right* of the *People* speaking through the legislature, to control the schools which they *create* and *support*," explained Bryan in a personal letter in 1925, "is the real issue as I see it." The Great Commoner spoke of a "democracy of the heart" and interpreted the electoral mandate of the people as the voice of God. Indeed, his last appearance at a Democratic National Convention in 1924 had contained a plea for delegates "to stand together to fight the battles of religion in this land." Bryan's defense of fundamentalism reflected a conviction that government should be run by average citizens and should mirror their values. "I have had only the plain people to back me, and the rich interests have always been against me," he once reflected.[16]

The Scopes trial ended with a jury conviction and a $100 fine, which a higher court later remitted on a technicality. Portrayed by the urban press as a pathetic embodiment of narrow-minded bigotry and ignorance, Bryan died a few days later. John Scopes went on to a career as a professional geologist.[17] Although the event resolved nothing, the confrontation over Darwinism graphically illustrated the conflicting calls of modernism and tradition. While corporate and educational professionals gravitated to secular notions of science and pluralism, religious populists like William Jennings Bryan upheld the democratic wisdom of rooted communities. Not all traditionalists or insurgents embraced fundamentalist precepts. Yet the division between local communities and national elites continued to provide a significant backdrop for American political and cultural conflict.

✦ ✦ ✦

One of the Jazz Age's most divisive controversies involved the crusade that purity reformers and independent theater owners mounted against Hollywood's motion picture industry. American movies traced their origins to turn-of-the-century penny arcades and nickelodeons catering to non-English-speaking immigrants. Moving into the production of full-length features, the industry's Jewish entrepreneurs found financing from the Bank of Italy and New York's Kuhn and Loeb. The burgeoning studios moved to Los Angeles during the 1910s. By 1920 such silent screen stars as Charles Chaplin, Lillian Gish, Douglas Fairbanks, and Mary Pickford had brought respectability to an entertainment once based in working-class vice districts. As Americans began to attend movies more frequently than church, postwar screenplays mirrored consumer fascination with personal fulfillment, leisure, and romantic sexuality. Produced for mass appeal, Hollywood's "emotion pictures," such as *Forbidden Fruit* (1921) or *The House of Youth* (1924), often sought to entice viewers with sexually provocative features.[18]

The issue of movie content drew the attention of postwar social workers, ministers, educators, and women's organizations. Intent on imposing urban social discipline and order on working-class immigrants and rural newcomers, purity crusaders of the Progressive Era had sought state regulation of the sale of liquor, prostitution, sexual hygiene, and "modern" amusements. Following the formation of the National Board of Censorship, an advisory panel to set moral standards for the movies, one hundred cities and eight states enacted forms of film censorship between 1910 and 1930. Motion picture reformers claimed to be disturbed by the covert nature of film communication. Unlike books or plays, contended one critic, movies created "a mental atmosphere which is absorbed by the viewer without conscious mental effort. It requires neither literacy nor interpreter to understand it." William Sheafe Chase, an Episcopal canon, maintained that motion pictures appealed "to the baser passions and obsessions of the lower human nature" and were the nation's worst form of commercialized vice.[19]

Congressional action to reform the movie industry began when the House Education Committee held hearings on a proposal to establish a federal motion picture commission in 1916. Describing film as an article of interstate commerce, the committee favorably reported the bill to the full House. The measure never came to a vote, however. Four years later another offering sought to prohibit the interstate transportation of movies depicting crime, violence, and lawlessness, but it died in committee. Still another bill, offered by Representative Joseph Walsh of New Bedford, Massachusetts, proposed to outlaw the interstate distribution of indecent, lascivious, or lewd films. Walsh hoped to expand existing bans on "obscene" printed and graphic material to include motion pictures. Despite passage by both houses on two occasions in 1920, President Wilson refused to sign a censorship measure. The following year Indiana's Oscar E. Bland sought to regulate interstate shipment of immoral movies, but the House Judiciary Committee buried the proposal.[20]

By 1922 the movie industry faced censorship bills in thirty-two states. When a series of sensational Hollywood drug and sex scandals compounded the threat, the major studios quickly established the Motion Pictures Producers and Distributors Association (MPPDA) and appointed Will Harrison Hays, the former chair of the Republican party and Warren Harding's postmaster general, as president. The MPPDA sought to arbitrate internal industry disputes through film boards of trade. Its most important work, however, came in external publicity campaigns to restore the industry's reputation and combat government regulation and censorship. Advised by the public relations innovator Ivy Lee, Hays set out to acclimate the studios to reform concerns. An Indiana prohibitionist and Presbyterian elder, he appealed to the organized women's purity movement to make Hollywood more responsive to public needs.[21]

The Hays Office initiated its reform program by instituting moral background checks on performers and advising producers of their employment suitability. In 1925 Hays created the Studio Relations Department to preview films for morally offensive material. Two years later the studios accepted the bureau's "Don'ts and Be Carefuls" as the industry standard for eliminating "vulgarity and suggestiveness" in movies and for emphasizing "good taste." Still not satisfied, Hays asked Daniel A. Lord, a Jesuit priest and college teacher, to draft a more stringent set of standards. The resulting production code, approved by the MPPDA board in 1930, provided a uniform set of review and enforcement standards. The code prohibited nudity, regulated set locations and film titles, and demanded respect for marriage, home, religion, and law. It also introduced the doctrine of "compensating moral value," a yardstick by which "good" and "evil" never were to be confused in movie scripts.[22]

Midway between license and state control, the Production Code of 1930 reflected Hays's desire to involve women's organizations, civic groups, and educational leaders in a consensual program of voluntary regulation. Such purity groups as the Boy Scouts, the Daughters of the American Revolution, and the YMCA cooperated with the Hays Office and joined many social workers in rejecting government censorship. Other movie reformers, however, distrusted Hollywood voluntarism and persistently sought to mount external controls. As early as 1922 Henry L. Myers, a Montana Democrat, had ridiculed the prospect of studio self-regulation by noting that Hollywood prosperity thrived off "the sensual, the sordid, the prurient, the phases of fast life, the ways of extravagance, the risque." Between 1924 and 1925 the National Congress of Parents and Teachers (PTA) and the General Federation of Women's Clubs (GFWC) stopped cooperating with the Hays Office. Delegates to a Presbyterian conference on film then formed the Federal Motion Picture Council in America (FMPC).[23]

The FMPC found effective leaders in Canon Chase and the Minneapolis social worker Catheryne Cooke Gilman. Convinced that the powerful motion picture industry reflected the frightening amorality of American corporate life, Gilman pleaded that home influence no longer could survive the onslaught of "commercialized recreational profiteers." Purity crusaders like Chase and Gilman sought federal legislation to regulate movie content. They feared that emotionally expressive film characters embodied the lack of self-control associated with immigrants and children, two groups they sought to protect from Hollywood's influence. Youth workers and other professionals were particularly concerned that impressionable youngsters might equate licentious and irresponsible on-screen behavior with the normal practices of adulthood. "This is an age," a Methodist pastor and movie reformer warned the Maryland women's federation, "of fearlessness, of questioning, of shattered customs, smashed traditions, and good-by conventions."[24]

Reformers insisted that children who regularly attended movies developed less respect for authority, were sexually precocious, and disregarded the virtues of home life. As early as 1920 the child psychologist L. A. Averill had condemned films for depicting marital fickleness, "false and unhappy notions of life," and a "hazy, uncertain glamor." William Marston Seabury, a former industry counsel, expressed similar concerns in *The Public and the Motion Picture Industry* (1926). Two years later the Reverend William H. Short received a Payne Foundation grant to study the effects of movies on youth. Short's Motion Picture Research Council (MPRC) authorized twelve social science inquiries between 1929 and 1933, and tentative conclusions suggested that young moviegoers were selfish, materialistic, and exhibited a "gang spirit or mob mind." The Payne scholars condemned Hollywood for providing adolescents with emotional fantasy without the perspective to evaluate it. Meanwhile, Fred Eastman of the *Christian Century* charged that the "social sewage" of movies menaced American youth.[25]

✤   ✤   ✤

Independent theater owners joined purity crusaders in attacking the dominance of the major film studios. Capitalized at over $1 billion by 1920 and up to $2 billion by 1931, eight industry giants accounted for 90 percent of the eight hundred motion pictures produced each year in the United States. Centralized booking, national advertising, and systemwide accounting provided enormous financial advantages to the Hollywood studios. Paramount, alone, held over a thousand movie theaters by 1930. Warner Bros., RKO, the Fox syndicate, and Loew's-MGM followed by adopting chain-store methods of retailing. By the 1930s the five "majors" accounted for three-quarters of nationwide film revenue.[26]

Studio domination of distribution threatened independent exhibitors. Only Hollywood-affiliated theaters or large chains normally accessed profitable first-run films. Contracts compelled independents to accept "blind selling," a practice by which exhibitors were forced to run films of unknown content. "Block booking" arrangements obliged theater owners to purchase entire lines of movies instead of selected features. The studios also insisted that exhibitors commit themselves in advance to particular "play dates." These practices prompted independent theater owners to plead their case as local entrepreneurs victimized by Hollywood monopolists. Cleverly linking their plight to film audiences, they maintained that studios imposed immoral products on exhibitors and moviegoers alike. Industry interests constituted "the most corrupt trusts ever known," an independent operator complained to Montana's Senator Thomas Walsh in 1929. This "gigantic octopus," he pleaded, "ruthlessly" defeated the best intentions of theater owners.[27]

The Hays Office hoped to minimize trade controversies by controlling such exhibitor organizations as the Motion Picture Theater Owners of America (MPTOA), but Sidney S. Cohen, a New York exhibitor who served as the MPTOA's founding president between 1920 and 1925, frequently locked horns with the Hollywood establishment. As early as 1921 Cohen scored film producers for misreading public taste and demand with "exaggerated sex appeal." He asserted that much of movie content amounted to "a sin against the common decency of the American people." A 1925 MPTOA press release declared that patrons "should be supplied only with clean and wholesome pictures" appropriate to "a community institution." The theater owners lambasted "sinister control" by studios that sought "to terrorize and coerce" independent exhibitors. Condemning a "manufacturer's monopoly" over retail distribution, the MPTOA promised to "safeguard the people against the trustification of our Industry." Weeks later Cohen left to become chair of New York's Theater Owners Chamber of Commerce.[28]

Sidney Cohen's departure led to charges that the MPTOA functioned as a front for the Hollywood studios. In response, the trade activist Abraham F. Myers formed the Allied States Association of Motion Picture Exhibitors (ASAMPE) in 1929, an organization that quickly embraced six thousand independent exhibitor groups and soon represented nonaffiliated theater operators in contract negotiations with the MPPDA. Offering to protect communities from Hollywood "filth" and "indecency," the new trade group sought to eliminate compulsory block booking and blind selling. ASAMPE condemned "the forced showing" of "poor quality pictures" it described as "unfit for exhibit to the public, particularly in the neighborhood and small town theaters which comprise a large part of the seating capacity of the country."[29]

ASAMPE's rhetoric succeeded in winning the support of those women's clubs and censorship groups that sought federal regulation of motion picture content. In turn, moral crusaders used evidence of Hollywood coercion in the distribution system to validate a portrait of the studios as greedy and insensitive to the public welfare. "The character of the film is so dependent upon the trade practices," Catheryne Gilman wrote to a colleague in 1927, "that it is necessary for us to consider them." The following year Gilman told the Reverend Short that she would rather regulate movie trade practices and production standards than use censorship power to remove films once they were advertised. "With an open market restored to America," exulted the MPRC, "the local exhibitor will have no excuse for exploiting motion pictures in defiance of the wishes of his community and of his patrons." This kind of reasoning led such purity reformers as Canon Chase to demand federal regulation of a corrupt and oligarchic "Movie Trust," whose "moral poison" appeared dangerous to the nation's children.[30]

Small business and elite reform interests joined forces by supporting the creation of a government motion picture agency to oversee trade practices and the licensing of interstate film distribution. The proposed commission also was to frame moral standards governing movie production. Congress first considered such a proposal when New Jersey's T. Frank Appleby introduced a House bill in 1922 to create a new division of film regulation in the Bureau of Education. Between 1924 and 1926 Representative William D. Upshaw, a devout Baptist and vice president of the Georgia Anti-Saloon League, proposed several measures empowering the education bureau to license, censor, and supervise film production and distribution. For the first time in ten years the House Education Committee held hearings on movie reform in 1926. Meanwhile, William I. Swoope, a former Pennsylvania deputy attorney general, submitted his own bill for a federal motion picture commission. By 1927 the Hays Office counted 103 movie censorship bills in twenty-nine states.[31]

As purity activists like Catheryne Gilman continued to insist on the moral parameters of trade practice reform, the Federal Trade Commission (FTC) published the results of a six-year study in 1927. Detecting a conspiracy to monopolize the motion picture industry, the agency called for the separation of production, distribution, and exhibition. It also charged Paramount with coercive theater acquisitions and exclusionary distribution policies. As a result, the FTC issued a "cease and desist" order against the studio and condemned its block-booking system. A 1927 trade practice conference resulted in industrywide agreement on fifteen distribution practices. When the majors refused to accept an order against block booking, however, the Department of Justice mounted a suit against the standard uniform contract and film boards of trade. The agency also pressed antitrust suits against Warner Bros. and the Fox interests. Responding to these pressures, the Hays Office made arbitration voluntary instead of compulsory in 1930.[32]

With less emphasis on government prosecution of the studios in the late 1920s, antimonopoly reformers stepped up the campaign against Hollywood. In 1928 Montana's Thomas Walsh, a Democrat, demanded a Senate investigation of FTC and Department of Justice dealings with the movie industry. Three years later another Democrat, Clarence Dill from Washington, proposed that a select committee look into the operations of the Hays Office. Meanwhile, the Republican insurgent Smith Brookhart sought to outlaw blind selling and block booking and to place settlement of trade disputes in a federal regulatory commission. Republican Grant M. Hudson of Michigan, a lay Baptist leader and former Anti-Saloon League official, introduced a companion measure in the House. In 1930 Hudson embraced the idea of a presidentially appointed independent motion picture commission, four of whose nine members would be women. The proposed bureau was to license films according to Hays Office standards, compel the divestiture of studio-owned theaters, prohibit exclusive movie leases, and supervise all trade disagreements.[33]

Movie reformers gained an important ally in 1929 when the Hearst newspaper chain came out for a federal board of film censors. The *Churchman,* the national weekly of the Episcopal church, soon attacked Will Hays as a "window dresser" who shielded millionaire "panderers" selling "vice, crime, and sexual suggestion." The censorship issue split the reform movement, though. Catheryne Gilman resigned as chair of the National Council of Women's Motion Picture Committee in 1927 because she believed that the organization worked too closely with the Hays Office. The Federation of Women's Clubs opposed censorship, a position dramatized by the hiring of Alice Ames Winter, one of its former presidents, as MPPDA director of public relations in 1929. In such a climate even Gilman confessed that introducing such legislation as the Hudson bill was "almost political suicide." Indeed, New York's Representative Loring M. Black Jr. denounced movie reform measures as "medieval atrocities" seeking to make a "religion" of Americanism and establish "a pulpit parliament."[34]

Movie reform brought together a strained alliance. On one side were upper-class purity crusaders and professionals whose progressive emphasis on uplift brought demands for government regulation of social morality. On the other were independent theater owners who turned to the state to enact market constraints against economic adversaries. Ironically, both groups saw themselves as insurgents battling dangerous concentrations of power. By attacking the motion picture industry on both moral and economic grounds, reformers implicitly acknowledged the connection between nineteenth-century producer values and the competitive market. The movie reform movement questioned the hedonistic consumerism of the silver screen. It also romanticized independent entrepreneurs as servants of local communities and advocates of an antimonopoly populism. Like Jazz Age prohibitionists, fundamentalists, and cultural traditionalists, anti-Hollywood partisans acted as defenders of the people's virtue against the selfish forces of secular modernism and corporate rationality.

✦ ✦ ✦

Hollywood critics like Canon Chase targeted "the Jewish money czars of moviedom" for using motion pictures to subvert Christian family morality. In an era of rampant anxieties over conspiracies against republican precepts, anti-Semitism often framed the response to an industry in which Jews owned and managed the eight leading competitors. Fears that Jews covertly sought to create their own superstate permeated many areas of American life. Milo Reno of the Iowa Farmers Union repeatedly blamed the Midwest's agrarian difficulties on international Jewish bankers. Rural newspapers in the region often pictured Jews as dishonest, greedy, cruel, and gluttonous middlemen who exploited virtuous producers. Jews also were castigated as radical proponents of social change. Such themes found classic expression in Henry Ford's *International Jew,* a four-volume tract taken from a series of articles that appeared in the automaker's *Dearborn Independent* between 1920 and 1922.[35]

A progressive and populist, the Michigan entrepreneur sought to prove that a conspiracy of Jewish financial interests had sworn to control the world. Ford based his work on *The Protocols of the Elders of Zion,* a series of fabrications produced at the beginning of the century by a secret police agent for the czar of Russia. Jews were "the conscious enemies" of Anglo-Saxon civilization, wrote the automaker. Ford charged that Jewish financial interests used the liquor trade and immoral women to weaken the physique of gentiles and stimulate a postwar relaxation of morals. Jewish clothing concerns, he argued, created the decadent flapper skirt, while other Jews promoted gambling, played "skunk cabbage" jazz, wrote salacious prose, performed in cabarets, and produced cheap Hollywood movies. *The International Jew* sold half a million copies.[36]

Anti-Semitism also found expression in such western progressives as Hiram Johnson. When the California senator traveled on vacation to New Jersey's Atlantic City, he marveled that rich, assertive, and self-sufficient Jews stayed at the best hotels. They included, he wrote to his sons, "short, swarthy men, . . . squatly, dumpy women, and the innumerable daughters . . . bursting into overblown maturity." Confiding that he felt like "a stranger almost in a strange land," Johnson wondered if he were not witnessing "the conquest of this country by God's chosen people." In time, he concluded, the Jews would "make this country theirs."[37]

While republican anxieties over modernism sometimes resulted in anti-Semitic diatribes, they also spilled over into nativist assaults on Roman Catholics and other working-class immigrants. As Don Kirschner has suggested, cultural critics placed less emphasis on immoral behavior than on the kind of people who acted improperly. Traditionalists often portrayed Americans as white, Protestant farmers and middle-class residents of towns and tended to view city dwellers, industrial workers, ethnics, and racial minorities as outsiders who shared nothing with "original stock" citizens. Stereotypes described "new" immigrants from southern, eastern, and central Europe as dirty, radical, and vice-prone opponents of "the American way." Rural newspapers insisted that the newcomers would have to be "Americanized" to standards of honesty and compassion. The United States was "too good to become the resting place for gangmen and racketeers from Sicily," protested one Iowa editor.[38]

Nationalists like Hiram Johnson worried about the high proportion of non-Protestants and non-English-speakers who arrived in the United States at a rate of one million a year between 1900 and 1915. Concern over ethnic loyalty reached fever pitch during World War I and the "Red Scare" that followed it. Following a dramatic resumption of European immigration after the war, Congress passed an emergency restriction measure in 1921. In the Senate Johnson joined the western progressives William Borah, Arthur Capper, Robert La Follette, Peter Norbeck, and George Norris in the overwhelming 78-1 vote. Three years later Congress considered a bill to create a permanent restriction system based on national quotas.[39]

The 1924 immigration debate raised profound questions about national and cultural identity. Idaho's Borah, who favored "a drastic law" aimed at the "uneducated hordes of any foreign government," insisted that a nation had the right to determine who might come to its borders and become citizens. South Dakota's Peter Norbeck privately noted that "the purity of the race" necessitated that the United States unilaterally determine its immigration policy. Similar considerations marked Senator Capper's observation that a third of the nation's whites was of foreign birth or parentage. With ten million immigrants in the past two decades, he mused, the capacity of the melting pot had been "sadly overtaxed." Capper repeated the nativist suspicion that the new immigrants lacked interest in the duties of U.S. citizenship. Newcomers seemed to be setting up barriers against Americanization by encouraging and perpetuating foreign customs and alien prejudices, he told the Senate.[40]

Like his progressive colleagues, Nebraska's George Norris reiterated the distinction between the "old" immigration from northern and western Europe and the more recent arrivals from the southern and eastern sectors of the continent. Hiram Johnson was more concerned with the Japanese influx in California. Seeking to use federal law to discourage the immigration of those he believed to be unassimilable, Johnson supported a clause in the 1924 bill that barred all arrivals from China and Japan. Since naturalization laws already disqualified Asians from U.S. citizenship, the former California governor viewed the new provision as consistent with the nation's right to protect itself.[41]

The national origins bill passed the Senate by a one-sided margin of 62 to 6. Insurgent supporters included William Borah, Arthur Capper, Hiram Johnson, George Norris, Smith Brookhart, Thomas Walsh, Henrik Shipstead, and Magnus Johnson. Robert La Follette, Peter Norbeck, Robert Howell, Burton Wheeler, Lynn Frazier, and Edwin Ladd deferred to ethnic constituencies by declining to vote. Setting a national immigration agenda that lasted for forty years, the law eventually limited annual admissions from outside the Western Hemisphere to 150,000. It also imposed yearly quotas based on the number of each nation's immigrants already living in the United States. As a result, federal policy encouraged migrants from northwestern Europe and limited arrivals from predominantly Catholic and Jewish regions. The National Origins Act of 1924 institutionalized the fear of a foreign peasantry and proletariat shared by nativists and republicans alike.[42]

✢   ✢   ✢

The most important nativist influence of the 1920s was the Ku Klux Klan. The KKK's popularity, however, represented a curious mixture of ethnocentrism and insurgence. Reborn in Atlanta in 1915, the second Klan attracted between two and six million members during the postwar decade, half of them from cities with at least fifty thousand inhabitants. The secret movement began as a fraternal society with a sentimental reverence for the southern Klan of the 1860s. Like its predecessor, it required confidential loyalty oaths, staged rituals with white robes and hoods, and confined membership to white, native-born Protestant men. The order prohibited allegiance to any entity other than the U.S. government and itself. It professed dedication to pure womanhood, white supremacy, the Constitution, uncorrupted religion, freedom of speech, the common people, and public education. Klaverns employed economic boycotts, social ostracism, and political pressures to build a network of support for "one hundred percent Americanism" and "traditional values."[43]

A series of newspaper exposés and congressional hearings helped publicize the Klan in 1921. The following year Hiram Wesley Evans assumed national leadership. An Alabama-born graduate of Vanderbilt University, a thirty-two-degree Mason, and a member of the Disciples of Christ, the Dallas dentist transformed the Invisible Empire from a confederation of local vigilantes into a centralized and powerful political movement. With 200,000 members in Texas, the South and Southwest accounted for 41 percent of the Klan's numerical strength. Yet by 1924 Indiana, Illinois, and Ohio had contributed another 40 percent of the order's following. Other Klan strongholds included New York, Pennsylvania, Kansas, Oklahoma, Colorado, California, and Oregon. Seeking patronage favors and an agenda of Prohibition enforcement, immigration restriction, and support for public schools, the Klan helped elect seven governors and three U.S. senators. In Indiana Klansmen provided key support to more than half the members of the 1924 state legislature.[44]

The 1920s Klan took the American flag, the Constitution, and the Bible as the keystones of its principles. Official KKK publications fused racial and religious doctrine into a mystical nationalistic code that portrayed American cultural ideals as unique contributions to world progress. Americanism embraced principles of democracy, fair play, impartial justice, equal opportunity, individual responsibility, enlightened conscience, and loyalty to family, nation, race, and God. Klan ideology held that the nation's culture embodied a distinct racial and religious legacy that could be retained only by the descendants of its Anglo-Protestant pioneers. Leaders of the Invisible Empire equated Anglo-Saxon civilization with popular liberty and free institutions. Resistant to tyranny, Anglo-Saxons had perfected American democracy, religious freedom, and free and universal education.[45]

Imperial Wizard Hiram Wesley Evans linked patriotism and racial pride to the "spiritual independence" of Protestant Christianity. "It is the expression in religion of the same spirit of independence, self-reliance, and freedom which are the highest achievement of the Nordic race," Evans told readers of the *North American Review*. Protestantism, he declared, uniquely permitted unhampered individual development and conscience. Its spirit formed the basis of "our national soul." The Klan saw itself as a force of unity among Protestant denominations. Individual klaverns donated funds to Protestant institutions and congregations and participated as units in special church services. "The Old Rugged Cross" was the near-official hymn of the order. As the editor of the *Imperial Night-Hawk* proclaimed in 1924, the Klan had devoted itself to the "national redemption" of the United States.[46]

Leaders of the Invisible Empire described their movement as a crusade to restore individual, community, and national vitality. Klaverns administered fraternal oaths that required members to honor secrecy, loyalty, obedience, and solidarity with other Klansmen. The Klan's program of moral revitalization sought to perpetuate the internalized attributes of self-control and discipline associated with traditional producerism. It also attempted to create a social identity through language and symbolism. The order's rituals described inductees as "aliens," who experienced rites of passage similar to those of overseas immigrants. Officials explained that the lodge's white robes suggested the sanctity of saints and the equality of all members. Masks were to ensure dedication to the secret order and anonymity to protect them from their adversaries. Even controversial cross burnings were defended as signs of sacrifice, service, and Christian purity. With the aid of women's auxiliaries, klaverns also provided members with a variety of music, picnics, fireworks, camp-outs, sporting events, and rallies.[47]

Despite the assertive features of the Klan's subculture, the secret order expressed a sense of powerlessness when it viewed the nation's immigrants. Klan leaders insisted that recent migrants had divided allegiances and resisted assimilation to the American way of life. Dismissing Catholic and Jewish Europeans as "the tenement herd," Imperial Wizard Evans charged that new immigrants lacked the individual consciousness to be "genuine Americans." Klan literature depicted the Jews as unscrupulous middlemen and profiteers who lacked public spirit. Historically divorced from the land, the Jewish people lived for the moment and centered their existence on material success. Furthermore, Jewish exclusiveness threatened the cohesion of American culture. Klan hostility to Catholicism centered on the spiritual autocracy and institutional power of the Catholic church. KKK leaders painted an image of an Old World priesthood enslaving the minds of the young in parochial schools and cementing allegiance to a foreign religious oligarchy through urban political machines.[48]

Klan officials insisted that ethnic voters held the balance of power in national elections and forced their demands on corrupt politicians. Amid "a conglomerate mass of aliens," proclaimed Colorado's grand dragon, Anglo-Protestants were "now outlaws in the land of their forefathers." This theme reverberated consistently in postwar Klan rhetoric. "*As a people and a nation we are face to face with dissolution,*" the second KKK founder, William Joseph Simmons, anguished in a 1924 treatise. "*We are perishing as a people and the land of our fathers shall presently know us no more.*" An Ohio organizer proclaimed that the Klan wanted the nation "ruled by the sort of people who originally settled it; this is *our* country and we alone are responsible for its future." "You own this country," Imperial Wizard Evans told his grand dragons in 1923. "If you propose

to allow anyone to take it away from you, it can mean nothing to you."
Three years later the Klan's leading officer publicly complained that the
Nordic-American felt like "a stranger in large parts of the land his fathers
gave him."[49]

Evans asserted that a nation of diverse racial and ethnic groups could
never achieve the unity necessary for progress. He insisted that aliens be
taught fundamental American principles before admitting "further masses of ignorant, superstitious, religious devotees." The Klan placed its substantial political clout behind the immigration restriction movement.
Meanwhile, state and local units encouraged the membership to back "100
percent Americans" in business and at the polls. Klan leaders also contem-
plated prohibiting foreign-language newspapers and magazines and toyed
with the idea of requiring aliens to speak the national language in a specific
period of time. A KKK constitutional expert advised the organization to
maintain support for the electoral college to maintain a balance of power
against the "foreign-made section of the country" in the East. Colorado's
grand dragon even suggested that immigrants should live in the country
twenty-one years before voting, as native-born Americans did.[50]

Klansmen undoubtedly embraced and articulated the racial and ethnic
prejudices of postwar America. Yet, as Eckard V. Toy Jr. has suggested,
followers of the Invisible Empire "were not always against individual
aliens, Roman Catholics, Jews, or Negroes, but feared the abstract, almost
incomprehensible, symbol of stereotypes." Toy's analysis helps explain
decreasing KKK vigilantism in the 1920s. Although Klan whippings, brand-
ings, tarrings, and other assaults occurred in Texas, Oklahoma, Alabama,
Louisiana, Illinois, and Oregon, Hiram Evans claimed to nearly end such
practices after 1922. "The Klan will not engage in mobs or lynchings,"
the *Imperial Night-Hawk* instructed in 1924, "nor will they permit others to do so if they can prevent it." Indeed, Evans credited the Klan for
halving southern lynchings during his first year of office between 1922 and
1923. Illegal hangings of black men in the South dropped from seventy-
six in 1919 to twenty-nine in 1923 and seven in 1929.[51]

✦ ✦ ✦

Although race and ethnicity framed the Klan's perspective, the movement
manifested itself through a purity crusade against the social and cultural
consequences of New Era consumerism. Hiram Evans viewed American
society through the lens of a jeremiad. A 1924 pamphlet denounced postwar society as a wilderness of "stealth" and "vindictiveness" and condemned "*lawlessness, disrupting strife and controversy, propaganda instead of truth, and the economic inequities that increasingly threaten the
very stability of society.*" Truth had "*become a vagrant,*" declared Evans,

"ragged, distorted, and discredited by selfishness as never before in human history." Two years later the imperial wizard used the pages of the *North American Review* to point to "moral breakdown" across the nation. "One by one all our traditional moral standards went by the boards," he observed. The Klan's leader complained of ridicule faced by those who sought to defend the sacredness of the sabbath, chastity, and the right to teach children "fundamental facts and truths" in the public schools.[52]

Evans pictured an urban marketplace "taken over by strangers, who stacked the cards of success and prosperity" against Nordic-Americans. He also pointed to the "alien ideas" of the intelligentsia and professional classes. The imperial wizard contrasted the emotional and instinctive qualities of the Nordic to "the fine-haired reasoning of the denatured intellectuals." Klansmen, he proclaimed in a 1924 interview, were "wholeheartedly Christian, implacably opposed to atheistic intellectualism, and to all the amatory and erotic tendencies of modern degeneracy." Evans denounced liberals for fostering a groundless logic that led to "Communistic universalism" and a deterioration of willpower. He contended that their rejection of common sense and instincts had led to an abandonment of conscience, standards, and convictions. Such amorality, insisted the imperial wizard, corrupted the morals of the young, perverted education, and destroyed religion.[53]

As self-professed protectors of public propriety, Klan leaders vowed to restore traditional social morality. Stanley Coben has described the Invisible Empire as "the most visible and powerful guardian" of Victorian morals and cultural values in postwar America. Hooded followers of both sexes sought to uphold such domestic virtues as premarital chastity, marital fidelity, and family unity. In Indiana Klan women preached temperance and sought to regulate dance halls. Pennsylvania members of the secret order forced loafing husbands or deserters to support their families. In Oregon the KKK's grand dragon called for prosecution of "the careless father and gadabout mother." Meanwhile, klavern officials in the state's eastern railroad hub referred complaints of child neglect to the county health nurse and encouraged followers to be deputized for police sweeps of "intemperate activity." Klansmen in southern Oregon went so far as to abduct and threaten the life of a piano merchant known for consorting with young women. In Alabama the Klan patrolled country roads for parked couples.[54]

Maintenance of middle-class producer values set the Klan against potential disrupters of the community. An anonymous Idaho KKK broadside demanded the expulsion of "drunkards, bootleggers, whoremongers, adulterers, thieves, liars, murderers, haters of God, haters of Christ, haters of American ideals, obscene persons, willfully ignorant or illiterate persons," and other suspect people. In Dallas County, Texas, where the sheriff, chief of police, and district attorney were Klansmen, the secret order issued a proclamation that targeted "the gambler, the trickster, the moral degenerate, and the man who lives by his wits and is without visible means of support." The state's Klan leader listed bootleggers, thieves, robbers, rapists, wife-beaters, vagabonds, and adulterers as the order's chief enemies. The Klan in the region's booming oil towns demanded that police enforce laws against prostitutes, pimps, gamblers, and saloon-keepers. In Oregon the Klan ran a Christmas message in a coastal newspaper warning that "crooked" citizens would not escape its wrath.[55]

Klansmen frequently associated vice, crime, and immoral behavior with urban newcomers, such as ethnics and blacks. In the industrial area surrounding Youngstown, Ohio, the Invisible Empire confronted southern and eastern Europeans over Prohibition and related morals codes. Denver's secret order mushroomed to seventeen thousand by promising to end bootlegging, prostitution, and the sale of drugs in the city's Italian and Jewish underworld. In Pueblo, Colorado, the Klan vowed to expel foreign-born lawbreakers, bootleggers, and roadhouses. Oregon's Portland and Astoria klaverns attributed Prohibition violations and other vice offenses to Catholics and Finns, respectively. In Sacramento a Klan Methodist minister insisted that "nearly all the bawdy houses, bootleg joints, and other dives are owned or controlled by Romanists." In similar fashion the El Paso klavern in Texas mobilized Anglo-Protestants by addressing concerns over Prohibition violations by the Mexican-Americans of the border city.[56]

Despite such instances of ethnic conflict, maintenance of traditional values and law enforcement may have played a more central role in the secret order's affairs. The Invisible Empire sought power by promising to place purity crusaders in control of government, police, and schools. Such activities often precipitated greater confrontations with political and economic elites than with urban immigrants and allowed the Klan to function as a "populist" interest group for average white Protestants. Reacting to New Era economic and cultural consolidation and the local elites who profited from the consumer market, Klan members sought to revitalize social and civic unity through grass-roots purity reform. The Klan, the social historian Leonard J. Moore has suggested, often provided "the most organized means for resisting the social and economic forces" altering community life, undermining traditional values, and isolating and disempowering citizens who deemed themselves defenseless.[57]

Hiram Evans portrayed the fears of many Klansmen to readers of the *North American Review.* The Invisible Empire, he declared, spoke for "the plain people" of "pioneer stock" and a "progressive conservatism." Many Klan members were "hicks," "rubes," and "drivers of second hand Fords," acknowledged Evans, "very weak in the matter of culture, intellectual support, and trained leadership." Yet the imperial wizard insisted that the Invisible Empire would ensure "a return of power into the hands of the everyday, not highly cultured, not overly intellectualized, but entirely unspoiled and not de-Americanized average citizen." The Klan, promised Evans, had the power "to lead the common people of America."[58]

KKK crusades in Youngstown, Salt Lake City, California's Anaheim, and cities across Indiana, Texas, and Colorado targeted business and political elites who stood in the way of government and purity reform. In the secret order's home city of Atlanta a Klansman triumphed in the 1922 mayoralty run-off by defeating a three-time incumbent the respectable Civic Forum had endorsed. The next year a Klan candidate for mayor asked blacks and poor whites in Memphis to end the control of city politics by aristocrats and newly affluent elites. In statewide contests the support of the Invisible Empire helped send the Georgia populist Tom Watson to the Senate when the candidate denounced the American Legion as upper class. In Oregon the honorary Klansman and agrarian reformer Walter M. Pierce won the governorship with KKK backing in 1922 and then approved tax reform and an alien land law. Pierce also joined the Klan in endorsing a state initiative to compel children to attend public schools. Abolition of private and religious academies, he promised, would end "snobbery and bigotry."[59]

KKK insurgents sometimes supported labor and progressive movements. In La Grande, Oregon, where 37 percent of identifiable Klan members worked for the Union Pacific, the klavern supported the 1922 walkout of railroad shopcraft workers and appointed a committee to investigate Klan strikebreaking. Two years later the Progressive Robert La Follette won substantial support from western farmer-labor activists who were members of the Invisible Empire. Although Imperial Wizard Evans had referred to La Follette as an "arch enemy" for criticizing the secret order, Progressive party officials later acknowledged that economic issues drew some Klan members to their cause. In a parallel case a Minnesota Farmer-Labor candidate found himself accused of wrecking his party in 1926 after urging it to denounce the Klan. Henrik Shipstead and Gerald Nye won covert assurances of KKK support for their attacks on the World Court during the same election campaign.[60]

By the late 1920s revelations of Klan-related graft in Indiana and KKK violence in Alabama seriously narrowed the movement's influence and following. Nonetheless, the Invisible Empire left a major mark on the postwar era. Although prominent citizens sometimes joined the secret order, most analyses point to a predominance of low-level white-collar and skilled working-class members. They often saw themselves as "outsiders" seeking to reassert community control over social conduct in a world in which the rules seemed to be rapidly changing. Sharing some of the producer and republican values of political progressives, Klan activists confronted a society in which individual morality appeared to be replaced by institutional and secular power. Accordingly, leaders like Hiram Evans targeted the professional and intellectual elites in education and media who seemed to be setting the new social standards. As cultural insurgents, the hooded figures of the Ku Klux Klan sought to force accountability on national and community leaders and to reassert a traditional coherence in American life.[61]

✦   ✦   ✦

Jazz Age contradictions between cosmopolitanism and traditionalism surfaced in politics when New York's Governor Alfred E. Smith ran for the Democratic presidential nomination in 1924. An Irish-Catholic born in a tenement on New York City's Lower East Side, Smith quit school at the age of fifteen to work at the Fulton Fish Market. Soon he joined the Tammany Hall Democratic machine and advanced to the state legislature. In 1918 the plucky New Yorker won election to the governorship, where he earned a reputation as a skillful administrator and social welfare reformer. Smith's presidential political fortunes, however, floundered on bitter cultural splits among the Democrats. Seeking to keep the party unified and contain "religious or racial dissensions," William Jennings Bryan urged the defeat of a convention resolution singling out the Ku Klux Klan for bigotry. Once the measure lost by 1 vote out of 1,083 cast, the party's southern and western wing refused to support Smith. Hopelessly split, delegates agreed on a weak third nominee on the 103d ballot.[62]

Four years later the Democrats rallied behind Al Smith's presidential bid. The electorate, however, maintained misgivings over an ethnic Catholic identified so directly with urban popular culture. Smith viewed Prohibition as an attack on the customs and practices of non-Protestant immigrants, and the New Yorker's outspoken mockery of the Eighteenth Amendment tied him to an interconnected set of symbols that included liquor, political corruption, crime, immigration, and Roman Catholicism. The Kansas newspaper editor William Allen White observed that Smith hailed from a city "maggot-eaten with saloons." The nominee's salty speech, brown derby, and cigar only added to the threatening image. *Christian Century* described him as "a representative of an alien culture." Smith's opponents, noted Walter Lippmann, were "inspired by the feeling that the clamorous life of the city should not be acknowledged as the American ideal." The candidate's world, quipped H. L. Mencken, began at Coney Island and ended at Buffalo.[63]

Al Smith sought to broaden his political appeal by reasserting states' rights and promising to curb the expansion of federal taxes, legislation, and regulatory commissions. Despite the mobilization of Catholics and a 67.5 percent turnout of eligible voters, Smith received only fifteen million votes to Herbert Hoover's twenty-one million. As the Republican candidate split the once-solid Democratic South, he swept to an easy 444-87 victory in the electoral college. Reared outside small towns in Iowa and Oregon, Hoover seemed to embody rural Protestant and producer virtues. Yet he also represented the corporate ethic of New Era capitalism and the consumer-oriented market. Since cultural and political conflicts appeared to have prevented the emergence of effective progressive coalitions by the end of the decade, Republican insurgents and their allies hoped that the new president would act to restore agricultural prosperity and address the interests and social concerns of independent competitors.[64]

Indeed, many of the period's cultural controversies appeared to be waning as the 1920s closed. Fundamentalism no longer received national attention in the years after the Scopes trial. Immigration restriction took the edge off nativist anxieties and contributed to the reduced influence of the Ku Klux Klan. Two months in office, President Hoover appointed a national commission to recommend policies for defusing the explosive Prohibition issue. Gradually, Americans seemed to be accepting automobiles, telephones, radios, electric appliances, movies, and other fruits of New Era consumerism. While provincial newspapers continued to scapegoat urbanites and ethnics, their editorials curiously ignored examples of rural drinking, gambling, sexual misconduct, and violence. Advertisements in the rural press appeared to demonstrate the possibility that readers were more attracted than repelled by urban culture and the new consumer life.[65]

Much of the cultural conflict of the 1920s originated in the confrontation between modern consumerism and the traditions associated with the producer economy and social order. Acceptance of the corporate market often threatened cherished notions of simple living, self-reliance, community solidarity, and loyalty to organized religion. New Era critics worried that the hedonistic energies unleashed by consumerism and popular culture could destroy the discipline required for work and moral activism. They fretted that the shift from character and work to personality and lifestyle undermined the foundations of middle-class respectability, civility, and social progress.[66] Yet such preoccupations rested on the assumption that relative prosperity would continue to offer Americans elements of choice in cultural matters. As the decade ended, however, insurgents found new audiences for the populist economic anxieties once primarily directed at rural constituencies.

5

Farmers, the Money Power, and Depression Radicals, 1929–36

Confiding to the philanthropist Cornelius Vanderbilt Jr. in 1934 the diffi-culties of gaining mortgage bankruptcy relief for plains farmers, North Dakota's William Lemke lashed out at "idiotic class division" and the "stupidity" of the rich. Representative Lemke shared the fundamental populist faith that money was "a yardstick with which we measure the energy of our people."[1] His beliefs had been confirmed by the stock mar-ket crash of 1929 and the ensuing depression. Deflation, unemployment, and sinking demand led to breadlines, soup kitchens, and evictions in the cities. In the countryside rotting surplus and foreclosed farms provided further proof of the catastrophe. The collapse of investment, which wiped out thousands of banks and billions in savings, vindicated the views of monetary reformers like Lemke, who represented independent producers. As an obsession with wealth and money power continued to grip the na-tion, a new third party sought to combine economic radicalism and tradi-tional values.

✦ ✦ ✦

Depression conditions took on frightening implications in 1932 when the Farmers Holiday Association began to barricade Iowa highways to stop underpriced milk from getting to market. The action quickly spread across the Midwest. As farmers faced a winter of desperation, they reacted with violence. In Wisconsin, Iowa, Minnesota, Nebraska, and South Dakota, growers formed vigilante gangs to break up foreclosure proceedings. Gov-ernors in North Dakota, Iowa, and Minnesota issued proclamations in early 1933 that placed moratoriums on further forced sales. Drought, dust storms, and grasshopper plagues aggravated the disaster on the northern plains. Between 1929 and 1933 annual farm receipts in the United States dropped from $11.3 billion to $4.8 billion.[2]

Horrified at the economic disaster and worried about their political survival, leaders from agricultural regions used the depression to dramatize long-held views. "I think it is the most dangerous situation that has ever obtained at any one time in the history of this country," the monetary reformer William Borah wrote to an Idaho farm organizer. North Dakota's Gerald Nye accused the bankers of "squeezing the original capital" out of agriculture. Warning the Senate in 1932 of the need for "drastic action" to restore commodity prices, Nye insisted that delay would require more extreme solutions. A country banker from Colorado told Nebraska's Senator George Norris that unless the incoming administration relieved the farm crisis, there would be "without doubt, revolution."[3]

South Dakota's Peter Norbeck, no revolutionary, responded to depression conditions by reminding a banker from his home state that national prosperity depended on equalizing the purchasing power of farmers and industry. This view was reflected in the platform of the National Farmers Union, which demanded that the federal government act to guarantee cost-of-production prices for growers. It also coincided with the long-standing agenda of Oregon's Senator Charles McNary, chair of the Senate Agriculture Committee and cosponsor of key farm aid legislation in the 1920s. Farm prices, declared McNary in 1932, were dependent on the level of industrial production and urban purchasing power. The combination of sinking commodity prices and a worldwide collapse of credit, he warned, had produced the most serious crisis in agricultural history.[4]

At President Hoover's request, Congress had passed the Agricultural Marketing Act of 1929. The law authorized a federal board to loan $500 million to farm marketing associations and cooperatives. It also empowered the panel to create commodity stabilization corporations to regulate crop prices. The program ran into trouble when competing distributors, grain elevator operators, and cooperatives resisted a large Minnesota cooperative's domination of the grain stabilization program. Unable to convince wheat growers to reduce acreage, the agency ended its grain purchase program in 1931. By the next year the Federal Farm Board had lost $500 million.[5]

Charles McNary responded to the failure of the farm program by resurrecting the cost-of-production solution. In 1932 the Oregon senator introduced three amendments to the marketing act. He proposed to levy an equalization fee on exported surplus when farmers were unable to sell their crops at cost. In turn, commodity exporters would receive debentures from the Treasury Department to be used in buying imported goods. Under a domestic allotment plan first proposed by the National Farmers Union, the Federal Farm Board would set prices for agricultural commodities sold in the domestic market.[6]

North Dakota's Nye viewed the McNary amendments as the "turning point in the legislative battle for the American farmer." For once western progressives agreed. The McNary amendments won support from Senators Smith Brookhart of Iowa, Arthur Capper of Kansas, Lynn Frazier of North Dakota, Robert La Follette Jr. of Wisconsin, Henrik Shipstead of Minnesota, and Thomas Walsh and Burton Wheeler of Montana, as well as Norbeck and Norris. None of these proponents of the competitive economy favored price-fixing. But as Nye reasoned, the agricultural emergency forced the federal government to guarantee farmers the cost of production. Brookhart explained his departure from free-market economics by noting that Congress already had involved the government in private business with creation of the Reconstruction Finance Corporation in 1932, a government agency authorized to loan $1.5 billion to banks, insurance companies, and railroads. Despite such arguments, however, a 38-28 vote on the Senate floor sent all three proposals to committee.[7]

Failing to receive congressional aid in bolstering agricultural prices, the Farmers Holiday Association scheduled a national strike for June 1933. One day before the union proposed halting the distribution of farm commodities, Congress passed the most comprehensive agricultural reform package in U.S. history. The Agricultural Adjustment Act was the keystone of the farm policy Franklin D. Roosevelt's New Deal administration adopted. Based on the premise that overproduction and surplus were the primary obstacles to farm survival, the legislation offered government subsidies to those who agreed to restrict cultivated acreage. The new Agricultural Adjustment Administration (AAA) financed the program by levying a processing tax on marketed crops. The program sought to guarantee the same relative purchasing power or parity that farm income commanded between 1909 and 1914.[8]

The AAA met farmer demands by restricting supply and ensuring a system of government benefit payments. Reaction among western progressives varied. Gerald Nye, Lynn Frazier, and William Borah actually voted against the legislation. On the day the Senate Agriculture Committee sent the bill to the floor, former committee chairman Charles McNary laconically noted that the proposal "may do a lot toward restoring normal conditions and it may not." Peter Norbeck agreed that AAA embodied elements of his domestic allotment plan, but he wanted the government to purchase surplus agricultural land and take it out of production. Montana's Burton Wheeler objected to the unprecedented power that a passive Congress had given to an executive agency. "The Department of Agriculture and a few professors up there who sit around the office and never saw a bushel of wheat in their lives," complained Wheeler, "ask that we shall give the Secretary of Agriculture the greatest amount of power that has ever been granted in any bill in the history of the United States."[9]

Beneath the rhetoric of the western dissenters lay the insistence that overproduction was not the major cause of the agricultural crisis or the depression. Even the cautious constitutionalist William Borah revealed his commitment to a producer economy by picturing the restoration of mass purchasing power and a more equitable distribution of wealth as the most reliable roads to recovery. "What we have overproduction of," agreed Farmers Union president John A. Simpson, "is empty stomachs and bare backs." Angered by the Roosevelt administration's success in eliminating a cost-of-production rider from the AAA bill, Simpson attacked White House power brokers. "The best your 'Brain Trust' could produce," taunted the former Oklahoma farmer and country banker, was "summed up in three words: drink, borrow, and destroy." Instead of more loans, he complained, farmers needed monetary reform and cost-of-production guarantees to enable them to pay off what they already had borrowed.[10]

✦ ✦ ✦

Perhaps it was no accident that North Dakota, the militant Nonpartisan League's strongest base, inaugurated the most sweeping calls for agrarian reform in the 1930s. Foreclosures would wipe out a third of the state's farmers between 1930 and 1944. North Dakota's William Lemke, a first-year House Republican, brought national attention to the mortgage crisis when he sponsored a series of radical banking bills in 1934. No charismatic leader, Lemke was a short, chunky, freckled, and nearly bald man with a glass left eye and a right one that focused with difficulty. He spoke in flat and monotonous tones heavily marked by a German accent and appeared to fit the caricature of a "hick." Reared in the populist culture of the 1890s, Lemke worked his way through the University of North Dakota and graduated from Yale law school. After suffering serious losses in a series of Mexican land deals, he began to consider the populist monetary theories of W. H. (Coin) Harvey and Charles A. Lindbergh.[11]

Lemke began his political career in the World War I era as attorney for a farm cooperative, whose bankruptcy led to creation of the Nonpartisan League (NPL). He authored the program that swept the NPL candidate Lynn Frazier into the governor's chair in 1916. Four years later Lemke used the NPL's endorsement to become the state's attorney general and targeted the railroads and public utilities for law suits. Recalled with Frazier and a third NPL official in a bitter election in 1921, he rewrote a state grain-grading law that had been declared unconstitutional. Lemke also helped elect Frazier to the U.S. Senate. Nevertheless, NPL foes and mainstream Republicans frustrated his ambitions for public office until a league sweep sent him to Congress in 1932.[12]

Having campaigned for the Democrat Roosevelt, Lemke expressed disappointment with New Deal agricultural policy. Although he supported AAA as "a toe-hold and a beginning," the North Dakotan denounced it as an illegitimate stopgap "drawn by professors." Early in 1934 he told the House that farmers "do not believe that anyone reared and trained in the shadow of the temples of the money changers . . . can serve the best interests of agriculture." Lemke's impatience with the New Deal reflected growing distrust between metropolis and hinterland. He attacked Department of Agriculture attorneys who seemed more interested in social reform than in raising farm prices. When he learned that some Department of Agriculture officials had organized a Communist cell, he began a life-long habit of associating bureaucrats with communism. "These New York professors do not understand the agricultural problem of the nation," Lemke complained to constituents. Meanwhile, his letters home linked the Roosevelt "brains trust" to Wall Street finance.[13]

Lemke hoped to convince Congress that the Constitution granted the federal government control of monetary and banking affairs. Arguing that the agrarian crisis stemmed from underconsumption, not overproduction, he insisted that debtors needed to be protected from creditors anxious to capitalize on the economic contraction. Like the western progressives, Lemke held that small producers needed government aid if the competitive economy was to survive. He supported the Farmers Holiday Association's cost-of-production amendment to fix commodity prices. Lemke's real passion was mortgage refinance, though. He proposed that farmers whose debts exceeded the current value of their property be allowed to pay off their mortgages at 1 percent interest. Foreclosures then would be postponed for five years if debtors continued to make fair and reasonable payments. Lemke explained to the monetarist "Coin" Harvey that the proposal was "simply an emergency measure to keep the farmers on the farms" until the government assumed control over money and credit.[14]

Lynn Frazier had begun to introduce the mortgage refinance idea to the Senate in 1931, although his attempt to amend the AAA bill resulted in a 44-25 defeat two years later. Nevertheless, Lemke managed to win endorsements from Charles McNary, Gerald Nye, and North Dakota's Representative James H. Sinclair. After a nationwide tour sponsored by the National Farmers Union, twenty-one state legislatures called for passage of the bill. By 1934, when Lemke mobilized to push his legislation through Congress, the Roosevelt administration prepared to defeat it as a $14 billion threat to the nation's credit structure. To circumvent the unsympathetic House Rules Committee, Lemke and supporters collected 145 signatures (a third of the House) on a discharge petition to dislodge the measure from committee.[15]

As organizers neared their goal, Speaker of the House Henry T. Rainey warned that the Frazier-Lemke bill was "a direct plunge into communism" and appealed for administration pressure on petitioners to withdraw their endorsements. In response, Roosevelt cabinet officials and administration leaders contacted petition signers. "If this type of wild legislation passes," Roosevelt publicly warned in April 1934, "the responsibility for wrecking recovery will be squarely on the Congress." Unflappable, Lemke arranged a network radio broadcast through the National Farmers Union. Members of the House would face a severe reaction from their constituents, predicted the North Dakotan, if they failed to sign and stick by the discharge petition. The confrontation with Roosevelt worked, and Lemke succeeded in supervising passage of the bill in both houses. Fearing political reaction, the president ignored advice from financiers and signed the bill. Significantly, telegrams to the White House overwhelmingly supported Roosevelt's action.[16]

The Frazier-Lemke legislation faced further difficulties when the insurance industry tested its constitutionality in the federal courts. Lemke cooperated with government attorneys defending the measure and took part in opposing John W. Davis, the Democrats' 1924 presidential contender, in proceedings before the Supreme Court in 1935. But the Court ruled the Frazier-Lemke legislation unconstitutional because it deprived creditors of property without due process. Lemke then set out to redraft the legislation to meet legal objections. The Frazier-Lemke bill of 1935 placed a three-year moratorium on foreclosures instead of five and framed itself as an emergency measure. It also placed farm property more fully within the discretion of the courts.[17]

Despite these concessions and a favorable 18-5 vote in the House Agriculture Committee, the Rules Committee continued to deny a hearing for the second version of the bill. Lemke once again resorted to a discharge petition, but new rules now required 218 signatures (half the House). Noting that twenty-two states had now passed resolutions in favor of the measure, Representative Charles G. Binderup from Nebraska likened the North Dakotan's stand against House leaders to former campaigns by George Norris and William Jennings Bryan. When the administration proved helpless to stop the groundswell, President Roosevelt quietly signed the bill after it passed in 1935. The legislation again faced constitutional challenges, and Lemke soon responded to twenty federal law suits. These efforts were finally vindicated when the Supreme Court unanimously upheld the constitutionality of the Frazier-Lemke legislation in 1937.[18]

❖ ❖ ❖

William Lemke had prevailed against powerful adversaries and overwhelming odds. But the mortgage bankruptcy act constituted only the first step in the North Dakotan's struggle to radicalize the relationship between the individual producer and the nation's financial apparatus. Going beyond short-term mortgage relief, Lemke hoped to legislate long-term and fundamental agricultural debt refinancing. First introduced early in 1934, the Frazier-Lemke farm refinance bill proposed permitting the Farm Credit Administration to supply cash for farmers to pay off mortgages or buy back recently foreclosed properties. The new mortgages would be amortized over forty-seven years and used as security for low-interest federal bonds that would be issued to finance them. If no purchasers were found for the bonds, the Federal Reserve would be ordered to take them and issue up to $3 billion in currency, with the bonds as backing.[19]

Lemke believed that issuance of Federal Reserve notes would provide capital for farm refinance and increase the price of agricultural commodities, but he denied that the plan was inflationary. Inflation was an illusion, he explained to a constituent early in 1935, because bank or credit money was imaginary and not "real." The North Dakotan insisted that the refinance bill would put sufficient money into circulation to do the nation's business. The measure's purpose was to loosen up the frozen assets of the insurance companies and end the depression's "strike" of investment capital. Lemke painted his panacea as an attempt to mobilize the credit resources of the federal government to aid farm victims of deflation instead of private bankers.[20]

The Frazier-Lemke farm refinance bill had the support of the National Farmers Union, local farm bureaus, the Grange, and Father Charles E. Coughlin's National Union for Social Justice. But Lemke once again faced strong administration pressure and succeeded in collecting only 212 of the necessary 218 signatures for a House discharge petition in 1935. When the North Dakotan defied the Roosevelt leadership to gather 218 names the following year, he revised the bill to meet some objections. The opposition was adamant, however. The bankruptcy act was "bad enough," one Cincinnati insurance agent wrote to the White House, "but this one is simply impossible and the last straw." The Farm Credit Administration sent a memorandum to every representative noting that 1.5 percent bonds could not be sold to the investing public and that the refinance bill would apply to only 15 percent of the nation's farmers.[21]

The night before the fateful vote, Lemke went on radio to deliver an impassioned address. This time, however, he was not able to erase a lingering suspicion that his bill would undermine or destroy the U.S. economy. American Federation of Labor president William Green added to these doubts in a letter informing every House member of organized labor's objections to the inflationary features of the proposal. After a rare debate on the floor, the Frazier-Lemke refinance bill suffered a 235-142 defeat when fifty-eight of those signing the discharge petition switched sides. Lemke was devastated, but the desertion of organized labor particularly upset him. "I too was sorry that union labor was lined up with the coupon clippers," he admitted to a sympathetic constituent late in 1936.[22]

✦   ✦   ✦

Lemke's crusades for agricultural producers combined the rational needs of an economic interest group with a deep-seated distrust of financial elites. Although not all western progressives supported the details of the North Dakotan's panaceas, depression conditions sharpened their critiques of entrenched privilege. Six Senate insurgents opposed the 1930 reappointment of the corporate attorney Charles Evans Hughes to the Supreme Court. Two years later Hiram Johnson presided over a Senate inquiry into international bankers' flotation of foreign bonds and securities. Johnson's probe revealed that graft, fraud, and unethical practices had resulted in the loss of hundreds of millions of dollars in depreciated and defaulted securities. The controversy in turn motivated President Hoover to ask the Senate Banking and Currency Committee to investigate the New York Stock Exchange.[23]

As panel chair Peter Norbeck blamed the market for the "general sharpening of the depression and, perhaps for precipitating it," Ferdinand Pecora, the committee's chief counsel, grilled exchange officers and exposed insider trading, "pegged" stock prices, and improper merchandising of questionable stocks. When Norbeck took to national radio, Republicans heard a member of their own party describe Wall Street as "the worst crap game in the country." The investigation continued in 1933 after the Democrats assumed control of the Senate. Pecora now subpoenaed the investment tycoon J. P. Morgan, whose banking competitors supported Roosevelt. Upholding views long held by his father, Robert La Follette Jr. noted that the inquiry demonstrated "the despotic hold" that Morgan and New York City "interests" had on the economy. Nebraska's George Norris posited similar conclusions when he confronted the Senate with "the Spider Web of Wall Street," an eight-foot chart depicting control of 120 major corporations by interlocking directorates traced to eight New York banks.[24]

Suspicion of the investment community also surfaced when President Roosevelt asked Congress to pass the Emergency Banking Act of 1933. Faced with a panic, Roosevelt closed the nation's banks his first week in office. Days later he requested the power to halt monetary transactions, license institutions under a system of government scrutiny, and invest Treasury funds in private lenders. Despite unanimous approval for the bill in the House, Senator La Follette complained that the administration had failed to grasp the opportunity to nationalize the banks and end the financial dictatorship of New York investors. Viewing the vote over the banking proposal as the most important since the declaration of World War I, La Follette joined William Borah, Gerald Nye, and Henrik Shipstead in opposition, and Lynn Frazier and Peter Norbeck registered their disapproval by abstaining. Once the measure passed the Senate, William Lemke observed that Roosevelt had driven the international bankers "out of the temples by giving them . . . four billion dollars of Uncle Sam's good money."[25]

Similar concerns over financial centralization contributed to the debate over the Glass-Steagall banking bill of May 1933. This proposal sought to separate commercial and investment banking and establish a federal deposit insurance system, but it also included a branch banking clause for national lenders that angered defenders of independent business. Chain banking had been a central issue in Philip F. La Follette's successful drive for the Wisconsin governorship. La Follette, the son of Robert M. La Follette, told his state legislature in 1931 that the controversy involved a choice between "democratic or autocratic control of our credit system." In the Senate Louisiana's Huey Long took up the crusade against chain banking when he introduced an amendment to prohibit banks from establishing branches outside their home cities. Long then initiated a three-week filibuster to delay the bill. Once a new session began under New Deal leadership, however, the full banking measure won unanimous approval by senators anxious to reform the financial system and protect small depositors.[26]

Angered by the findings of the Pecora investigation, insurgents like the La Follettes endorsed the administration's Securities Act of 1933. This law regulated the issuance of new stock and required statements of relevant financial information. The following year Congress created the Securities and Exchange Commission and placed stock-trading practices and registration under stringent federal regulation. Progressives and monetary inflationists also agreed to Roosevelt's Banking Act of 1935, which gave the Federal Reserve Board direct control of open market operations and extended federal deposit insurance to some state banks. Such insurgents as Robert La Follette Jr. and Peter Norbeck objected to the seating of private bankers on the Board of Governors and opposed the underwriting of stock market securities by reserve banks. Despite continued calls for nationalized banking, monetary critics supported the legislation because it provided a start to publicly controlled finance.[27]

✦ ✦ ✦

Anger toward the financial community stemmed from the hurtful effect of deflation and constricted credit on rural debtors and entrepreneurs dependent on outside capital. No one better understood this than Robert E. Wood, the dynamic president of the Sears, Roebuck retail and mail-order empire. A quartermaster during World War I, Wood started his career with Montgomery Ward, the nation's pioneer mail-order merchandiser. When the company failed to respond to its competitor's development of retail outlets, Wood joined the more innovative Sears. By 1933 he had helped build a successful chain of Sears department stores. Meanwhile, Wood supported the New Deal in hopes that it would put the unemployed to work, distribute purchasing power, and counter deflation.[28]

As a retailer who served the consumer needs of the rural population, Wood concurred with radical critiques of the monied powers. "I think the monetary unit is the very root of our trouble," he wrote to Robert La Follette Jr. in 1933. Wood pressed for a silver-based currency and spending programs to generate inflation and higher prices. Predicting the onslaught of wholesale bankruptcies and receiverships, he warned Franklin Roosevelt early in 1933 that bankers and conservatives did not realize the consequences of deflation. One month after Roosevelt assumed office, Wood complained to Secretary of the Treasury William H. Woodin that farmers lacked the cash to buy goods. Sears mail-order receipts were running 50 percent below par, he reported. Portraying the Roosevelt administration's recovery efforts as inadequate, the merchandising executive accused New Dealers of trying "to make omelets without breaking any eggs."[29]

Robert Wood's hopes focused on a reinvigorated monetary system, with a revaluated dollar and a rise in farm commodity prices. Wood told La Follette that he hoped the next governor of the Federal Reserve Board would not be a New Yorker "bound by tradition in his views" on monetary questions and inflation. The Sears executive endorsed many New Deal reforms as necessary social measures, but the only two he held responsible for economic recovery were the 1933 abandonment of the gold standard and the consequent devaluation of the dollar. "I believe that the price of gold and our monetary policy have a more profound effect on the welfare of the masses," wrote Wood to the president in 1934, "than any other single measure that has been introduced."[30]

By supporting inflation, Wood mirrored the views of depression monetarists who contended that the free issuance, wide distribution, and rapid circulation of money would restore prosperity and security. California's Dr. Francis E. Townsend spoke for this impulse when he devised the "Old

Age Revolving Pension Plan" late in 1933. Townsend proposed supplying $200 monthly stipends to Americans over fifty-nine if the recipients spent the entire sum each month. The program was to be financed by a 2 percent tax on all business transactions. Townsend claimed that the addition of $20 billion of annual purchasing power would offset the initial cost, but economists countered that the plan would devour nearly half of national income and raise retail prices by 75 percent. The financial burden also would fall on already distressed young jobholders. Nevertheless, thousands of Townsend clubs sprang up across the nation, and organizers claimed support from twenty-five million petitioners. An evangelical crusade of sorts, the Townsend movement sought to cleanse the United States of bankers and "brain trust professors."[31]

Inflation served the needs of rural producers, who pleaded with the Roosevelt administration to restore price levels and general purchasing power through a circulation of more money and credit. A key element of these proposals was remonetization of silver. Populist leaders had argued since the 1890s that the free coinage of silver would put more dollars in circulation, provide debt relief, and discourage financial concentration by powerful banks. By the early 1930s Montana's Burton Wheeler had joined Nevada's Key Pittman in Senate leadership of the free silver campaign. Montana produced 16 percent of the nation's silver, much of it mined by small entrepreneurs. But Wheeler promised that a silver-based currency would benefit everyone by devaluing the dollar, thereby quadrupling the purchasing power of foreign consumers of U.S. exports. When Wheeler introduced a bimetallist amendment to a 1933 banking bill, the Senate found itself voting on a silver proposal for the first time since the 1890s.[32]

Three months after Wheeler's amendment was tabled, he introduced a silver rider to the AAA bill. The Montana progressive promised that silver remonetization would deprive dishonest bankers of control of the gold-based currency and simultaneously increase commodity prices to ensure the cost of production in agriculture. Despite enormous pressure from the administration, Wheeler and the silver forces came within ten votes (43 to 33) of victory. Meanwhile, nearly half the House signed a petition calling for the printing of paper money. These grass-roots pressures led President Roosevelt to agree to a compromise version of an inflationary proposal forwarded by Senator Elmer Thomas, a Democrat from Oklahoma. Introduced in April 1933 as an amendment to the AAA package, Thomsas's legislation authorized the president to induce inflation by remonetizing silver, printing paper money, or altering the gold content of the dollar. When the amendment passed the Senate by a 64-21 margin, Roosevelt quickly announced that the United States had abandoned the gold standard.[33]

Although the Thomas amendment provided a victory for producers attracted to inflationary solutions to the depression, western insurgents condemned the compromise by which the president received discretionary powers over the currency. In allowing the chief executive to fix the gold content of the dollar, Burton Wheeler warned the Senate, Congress had "come mighty close to setting up a dictatorship in the White House." During the fall of 1933 President Roosevelt experimented with government gold purchases designed to devalue the dollar and issued an executive order requiring government acquisition of domestic silver above the market price. Bimetallists like William Borah were not satisfied, though. Congress should have issued legal tender notes instead of delegating the power to the president, confided Borah to his Idaho constituents early in 1934. The country needed remonetization, he explained, but "the powers which are opposed to putting a larger volume of money into circulation are tremendous."[34]

William Borah expressed western producers' conviction that reduced output amounted to treason. Responding to an infuriated Illinois agricultural processor, the Idahoan attributed sinking crop prices, unstable consumer costs, credit scarcity, and small business stagnation to the administration's refusal to address the "money question." Such pressures led the Senate in early 1934 to come within two votes of adopting a Wheeler proposal to require government purchase of another billion ounces of silver to be used as the basis for additional paper money. Pressed by a coalition of interests, President Roosevelt signed another bill, the Silver Purchase Act. Supported by all western progressives, the law authorized the Treasury Department to buy silver until it constituted one-fourth of the national monetary reserve or until the world price escalated. In 1935 the administration raised the price of silver to eighty-one cents an ounce. In doing so, Roosevelt succeeded in separating mining interests from monetary reformers and helped dilute the call for a populist restructuring of the nation's currency.[35]

❖ ❖ ❖

No one carried the banner of monetary reform with more skill and self-conviction than Representative Wright Patman from Texas. A descendant of seventeenth-century English immigrants, Patman was raised by East Texas tenant farmers in 1890s poverty. Working as a janitor at the high school he attended, he prepared for law school with a two-year correspondence course. After receiving his degree in 1916 from Cumberland University in Tennessee, Patman returned to East Texas to practice law and become a founder of the local Boy Scouts. Elected to a brief stint in the state legislature, he was appointed Texarkana district attorney in 1924.

Patman promptly took on the city's gambling, prostitution, and bootleg-ging syndicates. Four years later he successfully ran for Congress by cam-paigning in a Model A Ford. The candidate promised to serve small farm-ers, independent business interests, and veterans by checking Wall Street, big corporations, and docile government agencies.[36]

A life-long Democrat, Wright Patman inherited a populist worldview defined by the struggle for equal opportunity and by hostility to special in-terests. During the Hoover presidency the Texas representative focused on antitrust agitation and elimination of loopholes from the tax code. In 1932 Patman single-handedly compelled the House Judiciary Committee to con-sider the impeachment of Secretary of the Treasury Andrew Mellon for conflict of interest involving favors for a petroleum conglomerate. When President Hoover appointed Mellon ambassador to Great Britain, Patman claimed victory. The East Texas firebrand supported the institutional reforms of the New Deal but tried to push the Roosevelt administration into more open conflict with concentrated capital. Taking on a perennial adversary of the struggling cotton farmers in his district, Patman denounced government complicity in the cottonseed trust. His agitation helped bring about a Fed-eral Trade Commission investigation of alleged pricing collusion.[37]

Appointed to a special House committee investigating monetary affairs in 1933, Patman campaigned for complete government ownership of the Federal Reserve banks through a scheme in which the Treasury Depart-ment would purchase necessary stock from member banks. The Texan also pushed a veterans' bonus bill, first introduced in 1929. The bonus plan called for immediately cashing $2 billion in life insurance compensation that Congress had granted World War I service members in the early 1920s. Although payment was scheduled for 1945, Patman demanded a program of "reflation" by which the federal government would issue new currency to pay the bonus at once. Under President Roosevelt, the House passed the bonus bill three times before the Senate finally approved it in 1935. After the chief executive twice vetoed the bill as inflationary, populist pres-sure for purchasing power led to an override by both houses in 1936.[38]

Wright Patman's obsession with the bonus reflected a profound com-mitment to currency and banking reform. The East Texan catalogued these sentiments in a small 1934 volume entitled *Banketeering, Bonuseering, Melloneering.* "Who shall control the issue and circulation of money is the greatest question before the people today," he began. Patman's call to ac-tion depicted a populist nightmare of "powerful monopolies and gigantic corporations" running the nation's finances, managing its industries, and dictating government policy. "This unbridled capitalistic combination," he warned, "must be brought under the direction and control of our Gov-ernment if FREE America is to survive."[39]

Banketeering repeated the populist protest that power over the coinage and regulation of money belonged to Congress, not private bankers. The volume of money controlled the exchange of goods and services, reasoned Patman. Yet its flow depended on the extension of credit by corporate lenders "subsidized" by the federal government. Patman contended that the current system allowed the private banks of the Federal Reserve to release government-printed notes. These were redeemable through a credit that permitted banks to buy interest-bearing government bonds. Upon presenting the bonds for redemption to the Treasury Department, corporate lenders collected tax-free interest in the form of freshly printed government money. Patman asserted that private banks held $12 billion in government bonds and received $400 million in annual interest from them by 1934. Nearly half the federal debt was owed to banks. Subsidized through government interest, lenders no longer sought to invest in trade and production.[40]

Patman's pet project became the creation of a national bank that could issue government money to enhance credit, curtail speculation, stimulate production, and inflate prices. In 1935 he attempted to win support for the idea by chairing a national monetary conference. Patman received encouragement from Robert E. Hemphill, a former member of the Federal Reserve Board, who asserted that Americans had "to borrow from the banks the entire circulation of the country." Robert L. Owen, a former senator from Oklahoma and the coauthor of the Federal Reserve Act, phrased the question that concerned Patman. "*Who shall control our money and credit,*" he asked, "*the private banks or the people?*" Representative Usher Burdick of North Dakota also attended the conference. A progressive Republican who liked to describe interest as "the cancer that has eaten up our economic structure," Burdick looked back to Abraham Lincoln's policy of paying Union army soldiers with $300 million worth of Treasury bills.[41]

Opponents of the financial establishment used the nation's large private bankers as symbols of concentrated economic power and privilege. In the words of a North Dakota county judge advising William Lemke, "the money question" remained "the keystone that holds intact the arch of special privilege, greed, injustice, militarism, and all the kindred deformities . . . [of] civilization." Like Patman, Lemke looked to the creation of a national bank as the solution to the depression credit crunch. Weeks after arriving in the House, the North Dakotan introduced a proposal to create a national bank and replace the Federal Reserve Board. Loans for the new bank would be secured by government bonds, their interest not to exceed 1 percent. Lemke claimed that federal monetary direction would ensure a sound and elastic national currency, an "honest dollar" that would not burden debtors with increased values. Nevertheless, he objected to using the term "nationalization," preferring to argue that his bank embodied public, not state, ownership.[42]

Lemke's proposal never made it out of committee. Secretary of the Treasury Woodin advised the chair of the Senate Banking and Currency Committee that it would be impossible to retire debt and obtain long-term credit at 1 percent interest. Despite such hostility, Patman sent all members of the House a plea for a nationalized monetary system as they prepared to debate President Roosevelt's banking bill of 1935. Meanwhile, allies of Father Charles Coughlin, the parish priest from Royal Oak, Michigan, whose sociopolitical commentary drew enormous radio audiences, introduced legislation to restructure the Federal Reserve and give the government direct control over banking. Senate progressives, such as Lynn Frazier, Robert La Follette Jr., Gerald Nye, Henrik Shipstead, Burton Wheeler, and New Mexico's Bronson M. Cutting, rallied to the cause. In July 1935 Nye introduced an amendment incorporating Coughlin's call for a national bank that would be the depository of all investment funds, the sole fiscal agent of the federal government, and the exclusive source of currency through issuance of its own notes.[43]

Despite Coughlin's highly publicized efforts, the Nye-Sweeney bill suffered an overwhelming 59-10 defeat in the Senate and became the last national banking alternative the body ever considered. During 1937 and 1938 Patman introduced bills for government ownership of Federal Reserve banks and claimed to have the support of 160 Democrats, all the progressives, and many Republicans. The fiery East Texan asserted that twenty-four large banks owned nearly 31 percent of the resources held by the nation's lending institutions. He argued that such concentration required that the open-market committee of the proposed public bank be composed solely of government officials. Patman hoped that amendments to his bill would give the Federal Reserve the power to adjust the purchasing power of the dollar to 1926 levels. But Roosevelt's banking reforms and the administration's turn toward inflationary deficit spending removed the urgency from monetary schemes, and Patman's proposal died in committee.[44]

✤ ✤ ✤

The depression's most powerful expression of antibanking sentiment came in Father Coughlin's weekly radio commentaries. Coughlin began broadcasting Sunday sermons in 1926, and within four years the CBS network had syndicated his social and political talks on eighteen stations. By 1932 Coughlin had organized his own network of thirty outlets, serving ten million people in the East and Midwest. With ten thousand letters a day pouring into his headquarters, Coughlin received more mail than anyone else in the United States. The Michigan priest achieved such fame by tying international bankers to the problems of the depression. American democracy had become "a plutocracy," he preached, in which "the power of wealth dominates." The root of the economic collapse, raged Coughlin, lay with the greedy bankers and financiers who subverted the economy by monopolizing control over money. The solution was to remove the system from the hands of the plutocrats by pumping more and cheaper currency into the economy.[45]

Insisting that money and banking were the key issues in American politics, Coughlin provided an urban and ethnic counterpart to agrarian populists and western progressives. Like the rural insurgents, he focused on currency revaluation and helped lead crusades for remonetization of silver and a national bank. Coughlin's version of the federal lending institution featured an elected board of directors to represent each state. This "financial democracy" would replace the Federal Reserve Board and would be authorized to issue currency and retire all outstanding paper money issued by other institutions. Coughlin agreed with agrarian inflationists who sought to raise prices to maintain the livelihood of producers and allow them to liquidate debt. He hoped to accomplish this by recalling nonproductive government bonds and paying them off with federal notes. Bankers and investors presumably would invest federal notes in industry or productive securities instead of debt bonds.[46]

Father Coughlin's appeal surpassed the economic message of an inflationist. In a charming and persuasive voice, the radio priest targeted elites whose arrogance and power seemed responsible for stifling individuality and opportunity in modern society. He denounced "banksters" and other masters of financial intrigue, Ivy League attorneys who served Wall Street, and remote government bureaucrats. "It is the Morgans, Mellons, Baruchs, Achesons, Douglasses, and Wallaces," he told radio listeners, "who want unsound money, and by wanting it, also want your farm, your business, your job, your cheap wheat, and your high debts."[47]

Charles Coughlin's following proved strongest among working-class and middle-class Catholics of German, Irish, and Italian background in the predominantly urban East and Midwest. Embracing second-generation Americans as "the people," he offered "outsiders" an opportunity to participate in populist politics. Coughlin brilliantly reversed nativist attacks on "disloyal" immigrants by focusing on the establishment itself. The real aliens, he implied, were the cunning Anglo-Protestants who had sacrificed the country to greed and such "communist" social evils as divorce, birth control, and free love. The radio priest persistently contrasted haughty and manipulative elites with virtuous farmers, independent business people, manual laborers, and white-collar employees. Coughlin offered not simple economic and political justice but revenge.[48]

The Michigan cleric initially portrayed himself as a "Christian radical" seeking to inject social justice into an oppressive market. If property holders failed to meet their social responsibility, he reasoned, the state should intervene to enforce a program of Christian socialism. A bitter anticommunist, Coughlin nevertheless espoused public ownership of those things "too important to be entrusted in private hands." This endorsement of state capitalism permitted him initially to support Franklin Roosevelt and the New Deal. By 1934, however, Coughlin had turned against his former ally, accusing the Treasury Department of playing into the hands of the international bankers. "Our Government still upholds one of the worst evils of decadent capitalism," he exclaimed, "namely, that production must be only at a profit for the owners, for the capitalist, and not for the laborer." By 1935 Coughlin was telling radio audiences that compromise and "marked cards" characterized the first two years of the New Deal. Roosevelt had failed to drive the money changers from the temple.[49]

Father Coughlin's answer to New Deal failures and his own inability to influence the president was the National Union for Social Justice (NUSJ). Founded in November 1934, the new movement dedicated itself to a fair and equitable distribution of wealth and profits and to the right to life, liberty, and happiness. The NUSJ spoke of breaking down the concentration of wealth, eliminating abuses identified with capitalism, and working for "social justice" legislation to preserve individual opportunity. Coughlin pictured his organization as a unified lobby of the people designed to bring pressure on Washington. Using the first sermon of the fall broadcasting season, which fell on Armistice Day, he pleaded with listeners to employ "the medium of the radio" to pass their wishes on to Congress. The radio, he later instructed, provided "a newer concept of democracy whereby you need not be satisfied with the mere casting of a vote."[50]

The National Union for Social Justice combined Father Coughlin's Christian socialism with elements of insurgent radicalism. Its pamphlets described "an absolute break-down of the old economic system" in which abuses dominated capitalism. The American Bourbons of banking and industry simply wished to patch up a dying system, proclaimed the NUSJ. The organization contrasted its own position with that of the Communists, whom it accused of desiring the abolition of private property and the nationalization of commerce under a government oligarchy of powerful commissars. Coughlin insisted that the nation could be rebuilt on "age old principles of positive morality" and that the "regimented poverty of communism and the created poverty of capitalism" were both unnecessary. His solution was a sixteen-point agenda, which skillfully synthesized the populist, progressive, agrarian, and insurgent political creeds that had defined hostility to corporate American for half a century.[51]

✦ ✦ ✦

Coughlin's program called for abolition of the Federal Reserve System and the creation of a government-owned central bank. It anticipated the restoration of congressional control over coinage and the regulation of money. The NUSJ promised to maintain stable cost-of-living levels and consistent dollar-exchange values by nationalizing banking, credit, and currency operations. Coughlin also proposed to abolish tax-exempt bonds and recall all nonproductive securities, such as war bonds. Meanwhile, the government would assert ownership of all public utilities and natural resources, shift tax burdens to the rich, and conscript wealth in time of war. The radio priest promised that his program would elevate human rights over property rights, ensure just wages, and demonstrate concern for the poor.[52]

"Sixteen Principles of Social Justice" marked a transition from reforms that sought to alter the composition of the currency to proposals that would change control of the money supply. Coughlin also became involved in presidential politics. Claiming an organizational membership of 8.5 million by 1935, the radio priest spoke of enrolling ten million new voters before the next year's election. A dramatic tour propelled the Michigan priest toward his goal. In New York City's Madison Square Garden an overflow crowd of thirty thousand showed up to hear him denounce President Roosevelt and the financiers J. P. Morgan, Bernard Baruch, and James Warburg as "enemies" of the people. If relief work brought recipients only $15 or even $50 a month, thundered Coughlin, "then this plutocratic system must be constitutionally voted out of existence."[53]

Charles Coughlin's support of three congressional reform measures brought him into alliance with some of the leading progressives and insurgents of the 1930s. Coughlin backed the Patman bonus plan, named the Nye-Sweeney banking and monetary control bill in 1935, and endorsed the Frazier-Lemke mortgage refinance scheme as "the last hope for financial reform under the New Deal." His congressional supporters included Republican senator Nye of North Dakota, Democratic senator Elmer Thomas of Oklahoma, Democratic representative Martin Sweeney of Ohio, and Republican representative Louis McFadden of Pennsylvania. He also won acclaim from Nebraska's George Norris, Idaho's William Borah, and Montana's Burton Wheeler. Huey Long and nine other senators petitioned President Roosevelt to appoint Coughlin as adviser to the U.S. delegation to the London Economic Conference in 1933.[54]

Membership in the NUSJ meant little more than being part of Father Coughlin's radio audience and mailing list. Nevertheless, followers expressed an intense loyalty to the Michigan priest. The Roosevelt administration reported that the Royal Oak post office cashed 16,558 money orders worth $54,616 in one month during 1935. When a Philadelphia radio station asked listeners to choose between carrying Coughlin or the New York Philharmonic on Sunday afternoons, telephone callers favored the controversial commentator by a margin of 187,000 to 12,000. Coughlin's supporters tended to express alienation from American society, the New Deal, and established institutions, including the Catholic church itself. Neither "liberal" nor "conservative," these frustrated Americans saw Father Coughlin as the nation's only spokesman of justice and economic reform.[55]

Before 1935 White House mail suggested that many Coughlin followers viewed the controversial cleric and President Roosevelt as a team. "I deeply admire the man in Detroit," one self-announced Baptist informed Roosevelt right after his inauguration, because he had "the courage to tell the people of the United States about the true condition of the financial structure." A woman from Cleveland warned the president that "average folks are sick and tired of the way things have been handled." Instead of catering to the wealthy, she advised, the "fearless priest" told people "the truth and not 'bunk.'"[56]

Many of the priest's supporters, however, came to share William Lemke's fear that New Deal liberals were in league with organized money. A Coughlin follower informed Roosevelt in 1935 that the New Deal had "deceived the working men of the United States and favored big business and huge corporations," catering "to the men who have concentrated the wealth of the nation in the hands of the few." Many identified with the underdog and believed that ordinary people, particularly the young, had been betrayed by Roosevelt policies.[57]

❖ ❖ ❖

While Father Coughlin proposed to restructure banking, Louisiana's Huey Pierce Long preached to depression-weary Americans about a plan to redistribute wealth. After traversing the South and Midwest for four years as a traveling cottonseed-oil salesman, Long passed the Louisiana bar and opened a private law practice in 1915. Attracted to politics, he toured the state and won election to the Railroad Commission three years later. Long used the position to attack railroads, telephone and telegraph companies, and pipeline and other utilities. Meanwhile, he managed to reduce rates and improve services. The young commissioner attempted to exploit populist appeals to win the governorship in 1924 but gained less than a third of the Democratic primary vote. Four years later he forged a successful constituency by focusing on economic divisions between rich and poor. His campaign slogan, "Every Man a King, But No One Wears a Crown," borrowed a memorable phrase from William Jennings Bryan.[58]

As governor, Huey Long spent millions on highways and hospitals, provided free textbooks for schools, and created night classes for poor whites and blacks. To finance the program, he revised the levy on extracted natural resources. When Long proposed a license tax on every barrel of Louisiana-refined petroleum in 1929, he faced impeachment proceedings that Standard Oil and other regional energy corporations had initiated. Once chances for conviction languished in the state senate, the "Kingfish" tightened personal control over patronage, the police and militia, the courts, the tax board, the public service commission, and election agencies. By the early 1930s critics charged that Louisiana's corrupt and authoritarian government resembled a fascist dictatorship.[59]

Huey Long ran successfully for the U.S. Senate in 1930 but declined to take his seat for sixteen months, preferring to help a handpicked successor win election back home. Once a senator, Long focused on the populist themes that endeared him to the Cajun, redneck, and hillbilly farmers and villagers of Louisiana. "Unless we provide for the redistribution of wealth in this country," he announced in one of his first floor speeches, "the country is doomed." The nation must either limit large fortunes and guarantee a decent life for citizens, warned Long, or wait for the otherwise inevitable revolution. The "blind financial powers," he told constituents in one form letter, "would let the country and all its people go slap damn to hell . . . before they would surrender their mastery of money control. . . ." Our "sole hope of salvation," declared Long, is "to cut these big fortunes down to reasonable size and spread the money and wealth among the people generally." In the spring of 1933 the irrepressible Louisianan introduced a Senate resolution to confiscate incomes over $1 million and inheritances over $5 million.[60]

To disseminate his views on redistributed wealth and create the framework for a national constituency, Long began to publish a weekly and then monthly newspaper called *American Progress*. Distributed free to 300,000 mail recipients from 1935 on, the journal dramatized populist economics with moralistic imagery and ordinary language. "To have allowed people to starve in the land of plenty," proclaimed the editors, was "a crime of a greed that must be held within limits to save our civilization." Meanwhile, Long distributed eighty thousand free copies of his gold-covered and folksy autobiography, *Every Man a King*, first issued in 1933.[61]

The culmination of Huey Long's Senate career came with the formation of the Share Our Wealth Plan in 1934 and the creation of a national organization to popularize its eight-point program. Share Our Wealth (SOW) depended on a capital levy that would tax away wealth on a sliding scale until it reduced fortunes to less than $4 million. Meanwhile, the government would confiscate all yearly income and inheritances over $1 million. Long's program endorsed government public works and purchase of agricultural surplus, Wright Patman's veterans' bonus, and the Townsend pension plan. It also promised every family a $5,000 annual income, a home, an automobile, a radio, and a free college education for all qualified students.[62]

Long took the Share Our Wealth crusade to the radio in 1935. The former Roosevelt supporter now denounced the New Deal for ignoring hunger, suffering, and unemployment and for allowing Wall Street to continue to define government policy. "Maybe you see a little change in the man waiting on the tables," proclaimed Long, "but back in the kitchen the same set of cooks are fixing up the victuals for us that cooked up the mess under Hoover." He cited 1930 Federal Trade Commission statistics to demonstrate that three-quarters of the nation's people lacked the resources to pay their debts. Called "the best radio speaker" in the United States by one opponent, Long received sixty thousand letters a week from listeners.[63]

As the historian Alan Brinkley has pointed out, Share Our Wealth contained fatal economic flaws. It included no plan to convert resources, mines, highways, schools, and transportation systems into wealth that could be redistributed to the needy. It ignored the fact that most of the rich's holdings were in capital investments that could not readily be assessed and liquidated. Without proposing a way to alter the corporate structure that provided wealth for the affluent, Long had no means to attack the concentrated power he detested. Redistribution of wealth required far more drastic solutions because there was not sufficient surplus to divide among the poor. One study suggested that if all wealth over $1 million were redistributed among those worth less than $5,000, recipients would have received only $400 each.[64]

Yet Huey Long was no socialist. His goal was to attack monopoly control and greed without destroying individual initiative and the freedom of entrepreneurs. Acting within nineteenth-century populist traditions, the Kingfish sought to gain acknowledgment that concentration of wealth was a fundamental defect of the U.S. economy. He assailed bankers and wealthy tycoons like the Rockefellers with vivid personal abuse, describing them as bloated plutocrats and "pigs swilling in the trough of luxury." By 1935 Long headquarters claimed over twenty-seven thousand SOW clubs and millions of nationwide followers, although support centered in the South, West, and Midwest (particularly Louisiana, California, and Minnesota). Although movement officials often came from the leadership ranks of local civic, veterans, and religious organizations, Long enthusiasts perceived themselves to be ordinary Americans opposed to special privilege and monopoly. "He had more friends among the common people than any man who has lived in this country in the last half century," Representative Usher Burdick observed of his ally in 1936.[65]

The Kingfish frightened eastern progressives and intellectuals associated with the League for Independent Political Action, an alliance of democratic socialists organized in 1929. Led by the philosopher John Dewey and the urban critic Lewis Mumford, the league sought to establish working alliances with activists in the Midwest. After organizing the Farmer-Labor Political Federation in Chicago in 1935, however, Dewey and the reformers learned that rank-and-file populists leaned toward Father Coughlin and Huey Long. Farmer-Laborites also began to flood the *Progressive* with letters praising the two men. In 1935 the La Follette family journal reversed its assessment by stating hearty agreement with the priest's and the senator's desire to redistribute the country's wealth. Meanwhile, the Farmer-Labor Political Federation found itself repeatedly confronted with rank-and-file demands that Long and Coughlin be included in its plans.[66]

Long established fruitful alliances with western progressives and agrarian reformers. In 1935 Milo Reno invited the senator to address over ten thousand people at the Farmers Holiday Association convention in Des Moines. An overwhelming majority quickly voted to endorse the idea of a third party for the next year's presidential election. Long proclaimed that the Republican William Borah was his first choice for president and that he could support the insurgent Republicans George Norris, Gerald Nye, and Lynn Frazier. He also spoke favorably of Elmer Thomas and Burton Wheeler, both Democrats. As Brinkley has shown, Long's 1934–35 roll-call votes corresponded to those of progressive senators in dramatic fashion: Borah, 74 percent; Nye, 80 percent; Frazier, 77 percent; Norris, 62 percent; Thomas, 63 percent; and Wheeler, 74 percent. Even Hiram Johnson, who admitted that "Long was not my sort," acknowledged that the Louisianan's wealth scheme sought to help the unprivileged and poor. His theory "sounds a little foolish on the face of it," admitted North Dakota's Usher Burdick in 1935, but Burdick relished Huey Long's attacks on wealth and "special privileges."[67]

❖   ❖   ❖

If the two major parties failed to provide a true choice, Long announced in August 1935, he might choose to run his own presidential campaign. Indeed, a secret poll by the nervous Democratic National Committee revealed that an independent Long candidacy could capture nearly 11 percent of the popular vote and conceivably control the electoral balance of power. In September 1935, however, an enraged relative of a Louisiana adversary shot the Kingfish to death in the halls of the capitol in Baton Rouge. Although not personal friends, Long and Coughlin had been moving toward cooperation. The cleric had endorsed redistribution of wealth as an important part of his program and *American Progress* sold well at Coughlin appearances. In June 1936 the Michigan priest proclaimed creation of a "united front" of followers of the NUSJ, the Townsend pension plan, Share Our Wealth, and the "farm bloc." Three days later William Lemke announced that he would run for president as candidate of the newly formed Union party.[68]

The Union party platform borrowed substantially from the NUSJ program and the groups to which Coughlin referred. As the social historian David Bennett has suggested, it incorporated "a potpourri of the monetary panaceas of the time." Lemke sought to use the campaign to popularize his mortgage refinance plan. He also hoped to transcend the limitations of past agrarian movements by finding common cause with Coughlin's predominantly urban, Catholic, and working-class constituency. Coalition politics proved very difficult, though. Once Farmers Holiday Association leader Milo Reno died in 1935, Lemke lost influence in the organization and efforts to endorse him led to bitter leadership splits. Similar divisions plagued the National Farmers Union, the Minnesota Farmer-Labor party, and the Wisconsin Farmer-Labor Progressive Federation. Such progressive leaders as Robert La Follette Jr. and Philip La Follette stuck with President Roosevelt in 1936. Among congressional progressives, only Usher Burdick and Lynn Frazier, Lemke's fellow North Dakotans, rallied to the Union party cause.[69]

Father Coughlin preached that Wall Street and the international bankers had taken control of both major parties, and he argued that only the Union party could keep the country from communist collectivism. Rejecting the consensus mode of liberal politics, the radio priest attempted to cultivate a raw populist nerve among those alienated from the American power structure. When he addressed a national conference of Townsend supporters in July 1936, Coughlin ripped off his coat and clerical collar and shouted that the NUSJ would not endorse any candidate who supported "the great betrayer and liar, Franklin D. Roosevelt. . . . I mean Franklin Double-Crossing Roosevelt." Two months later Coughlin told a Union party rally in Cincinnati that Roosevelt was "anti-God," a "scab president." The radio priest talked of using bullets when an "upstart dictator . . . succeeds in making a one-party government and when the ballot is useless." By 1936 Coughlin and Gerald L. K. Smith, a former Long aide, had begun to lace their rhetoric with the violent posturing and scapegoating found in the authoritarian fascist movements of Europe.[70]

While plodding and lifeless, William Lemke's speeches embraced their own stamp of exaggeration and hyperbole. With poor organization and little financing, the Union party floundered. Despite the attempt to build a "consensus of despair" among a diverse constituency of urban Catholics, agrarian radicals, poor southern whites, and the elderly, Lemke collected less than 900,000 votes (2 percent of the total tally). The Union party did best in heavily Irish-Catholic and German-Catholic cities, such as Cincinnati, St. Paul, and Boston, but averaged only about 10 percent in those strongholds. In the end Franklin Roosevelt's political skill and the substantive reforms of the New Deal eroded third-party appeals. When it came to a national election, many Union sympathizers were not willing to choose Father Coughlin over President Roosevelt.[71]

Like agrarian radicals, monetarists, and western progressives, Union party leaders tied economic radicalism to attacks on such elite institutions as Wall Street and the Ivy League. Grass-roots dissidents of the 1930s built skillfully on republican and populist hostility to "special interests" and the remoteness and inaccessibility of hidden institutions. But unlike the urban liberals of the New Deal, radical insurgents translated their identification with the common people into anger toward government bureaucrats as well as financial despots. Recoiling from communism and statism, they offered cooperative solutions to the depression, not collectivist blueprints. In an insurgency reminiscent of the Populist crusades of the 1890s, dissidents sought to overcome powerlessness by affirming traditional individual and social ideals.[72]

6

"Natural Man vs. Corporate Man": Battling for Small Business in the 1930s

On Armistice Day 1930 a platoon of armed and steel-helmeted World War I veterans marched on the local A&P chain store in St. Clairsville, Ohio, and sent customers fleeing with tear gas. The veterans were protesting the market's failure to close for the holiday as a mayoral proclamation requested. Their action captured common frustration over chain stores' lack of community spirit. By the Great Depression the spread of chain merchandising had sparked a national debate that touched on the fundamentals of the economic system and its values. As Leo Ribuffo has suggested, the traumas of the 1930s produced a test of American faith and morals that made it "a cultural as well as an economic crisis."[1]

❖ ❖ ❖

Chains were normally defined as four or more retail stores of the same type under central ownership. By 1931 they accounted for 18 percent of national retail sales and 45 percent of retail grocery receipts. A&P, the Great Atlantic and Pacific Company, annually sold over $1 billion of groceries through fifteen thousand outlets. Variety, drug, tobacco, clothing, and department store syndicates also captured significant portions of the nation's retail trade. The chain system fed on growing consumer mobility and the uniformity of national taste brought about by advertising, magazines, and movies. By eliminating the "middleman," introducing economies of scale, and terminating credit and delivery services, chains sought to reduce distribution costs and consumer prices.[2]

Chain store defenders boasted that they had applied the "rational" and "scientific" procedures of mass production to distribution. They pointed to standardized equipment, ample stocks of merchandise, professionalized business procedures, and well-conceived management routines. Their stores also featured systematized employee training, strategic location and selling methods, and effective advertising. "Our people know that the production and distribution of goods on a large scale is not wrong," Secretary of Commerce Herbert Hoover declared in 1928. "Many of the most important comforts of our people are only possible by mass production and distribution."[3]

Independent merchants were not comforted by such assurances. Many saw Wall Street behind the wave of chain mergers and expansion in the late 1920s. Critics argued that absentee corporations took money out of local communities and threatened individual proprietors. Some asserted that chains paid low wages, that they did not assume a fair share of local taxes, and that "loss leaders" falsely attracted customers in search of discount prices. Independent retailers also maintained that chains used their size to compel price concessions from manufacturers and that monopoly practices ultimately would lead to higher prices for consumers. Other critics questioned the effects of depersonalized chain management and standardized products on the spiritual life of towns and communities.[4]

Since distribution appeared to be the last preserve of the local independent, the battle over chain stores took on dramatic proportions. As early as 1922 the National Association of Retail Grocers introduced the idea of special license taxes on chain stores to limit their number. Missouri considered the first chain tax in 1923. Meanwhile, retailers formed independent merchant associations, established their own newspapers and radio stations, and lobbied politicians. By the beginning of 1931 ten states had enacted tax laws that calculated assessments according to the number of stores that chains maintained within their boundaries. Legislatures considered another 175 antichain tax bills that year.[5]

The economic depression intensified antichain sentiment by increasing the number of subsistence businesses competing for shrinking demand. "Those who would be independent," wrote the historian Walter Prescott Webb, "have been driven to the highways to set up hamburger stands, tourist camps, novelty shops, whiskey dispensaries, and roadhouses." Retail sales fell by nearly half between 1929 and 1933. In the year following October 1929 four hundred trade-at-home campaigns blossomed across the hinterland. The *New Republic* journalist John T. Flynn noted a virulence among independent business interests that had not been expressed since the 1890s. By 1931 he counted 291 national antichain organizations and 24 antichain newspapers. "A new battle of evolution is raging in the South," a Louisville department store manager told the *Nation,* "between the smaller retailer, taking the fundamentalist position, against the chain store, the exponent of modernism in distribution."[6]

Like beleaguered farmers, independent merchants sought to universalize their plight by appealing to the core values of the American republican tradition. "This country has grown and prospered by the middle class," the leader of a California retailer's association declared in a trade journal, "and when we take from our boys the ambition to . . . own their own business, we are undermining the very structure that has made this nation the greatest on the face of the earth." A New Jersey correspondent sent the following verse to President Franklin Roosevelt in 1933:

The chain stores all have come to town,
It seems they have control,
And it seems as if a man
Doesn't own his body or his soul.

Oh yes, their stores are pretty,
And their windows have a flash,
But they never know a person,
If they haven't got the cash.

For their bosses live on Wall Street,
And we're a bunch of fools,
If we think these fellows give a damn,
About our church and schools.

Now listen folks,
can we afford to sacrifice our rights?
Shall we neglect our townmen
to feed these parasites?[7]

❖   ❖   ❖

Many independent retailers protested that chain stores threatened to mechanize American business. "The greater portion of their thinking is done for 'em at the head office," a Minnesota merchant complained of chain store managers in 1929, "—all they need is a soldier of obedience and routine will do the rest." "An 'efficient' chain *can't* have a heart," he concluded. Montaville Flowers, a West Coast antichain radio evangelist, portrayed the "chain system" as "a duplication of the machine." "It is a parasite," declared Flowers. "Its god is money, its process is annihilation, its purpose to master the world."[8]

Small business crusaders frequently employed biological metaphors of parasitism to express the fear of economic extinction. Speaking on KWKH, a clear-channel, antichain radio station in Shreveport, Louisiana, that broadcast across the South and Midwest, Alabama's attorney general described "foreign" Wall Street chain stores sucking the life blood out of home-owned businesses. A Texas antichain association portrayed the "heroic struggle to free rugged individualism . . . from the fetters of foreign chain store monopoly" and to "battle this monster that is sucking the blood of independent business." "If you draw the blood from the veins of a human body," a Minnesota retail group warned, "that body will die."[9]

"Fightin' Bob" Duncan, the self-proclaimed "Oregon Wild Cat" and "chain store Nemesis," ranked among the most colorful of the depression's small business activists. Duncan had run in the 1922 Democratic congressional primary as a populist seeking to restore government to the people and "check monopolistic rapacity." Eight years later he filed for the same seat in the Republican primary. By 1930 the Portland businessman had turned his monthly *Duncan's Trade Register* into a vehicle for "giving chainstores hell." "This is a business revolution," he declared. "And it will not down until the business of this great nation is safely in the hands of the people." Duncan called for local boycotts against food distributors he accused of complicity in the Wall Street chain system.[10]

In 1930 Duncan took to the radio to describe merchants who cooperated with the chains as "skunks," "scabs," and "traitors" and vowed, "I'm going to shoot the next crook that comes into my office to bully me." Such language raised the ire of the Better Business Bureau and the Republican *Oregon Voter,* which denounced him as "an irresponsible nuisance" who used terroristic and racketeering methods to extort financial support. These controversies led to a conviction on federal charges of broadcast profanity in October 1930 and a six-month sentence in the county jail.[11]

Beneath Robert Duncan's excesses lay a reaction to the routinization of retail trade. "Why do we not standardize the human race," asked the *Trade Register,* and "eliminate all this cost of patterns and colors and styles?" Duncan decried a system in which Americans had their "bread baked by a Wall Street monopoly, out of monopoly flour, by a bunch of scab bakers . . . and distributed through Pay'n'Takit junk goods." He drew distinctions between the individual merchant, or "natural man," and the "corporate chain store man," whom he described as "an unnatural monster created . . . to accumulate filthy lucre." "Corporations project themselves through several generations," declared Duncan. A soulless "dragon devouring the people," they defied competition or outside control. It was time, concluded the *Trade Register,* "to restrict our monstrous corporations and restrain their rapacity before they master their creators." If these "man-made organizations" could not be contained, warned Duncan, they should be "exterminated."[12]

A combination of popular entertainment and the nightly antichain diatribes of William K. Henderson, the owner of KWKH, made it the most popular radio outlet in the South in 1930. "I'll whip hell out of them if you will support me," Henderson assured listeners as he accused chains of systematic short weighting, short changing, and other illegal practices to offset price cuts. The radio evangelist also outlined the chain system in larger terms, depicting its goal as "suppression of competition by unified management." Henderson pleaded that antitrust laws be directed against an "orgy of consolidations and trusts" conceived in Wall Street. Their purpose was "to crucify liberty-loving American citizens upon a cross builded by heartless and greedy rich." Such rhetoric appealed to depression-weary Americans in the nation's heartland. By the end of 1930 Henderson had raised over $373,000 from 35,000 contributors to his Merchants' Minute Men.[13]

Such populists as Louisiana's Huey Long and Wisconsin's Philip La Follette incorporated antichain rhetoric into their gubernatorial regimes in the early 1930s. The crusade against chain stores reached a turning point when the Supreme Court ruled in 1931 that states could tax chains and independents differently. During the next six years twenty-six states enacted graduated taxes on chain store outlets. By 1939 seventeen cities (sixteen in the South) had passed municipal levies.[14]

Congressional antichain action began when Representative Melville Clyde Kelly from Pennsylvania introduced a bill to regulate resale prices in 1925. Kelly hoped to prevent chains from exacting preferential prices from suppliers and underselling independent retailers. A House subcommittee reported the bill favorably in 1928. A week later the Senate consented to Iowa Republican Smith Brookhart's call for the Federal Trade Commission (FTC) to investigate chain stores. Originated at the behest of the National Association of Retail Grocers, the Brookhart resolution asked the FTC to determine if chains violated antitrust laws and how they might be regulated by Congress and federal agencies. Kelly reintroduced the price-fixing bill in 1929. "If present conditions continue," warned the Pennsylvania Republican, "we must accept the transformation of our land of opportunity into a land of hired men, with workers known as numbers, not as individuals."[15]

Meanwhile, Arthur Capper, a Kansas Republican and farm journal editor, brought a companion measure to the Senate. Capper's bill died in committee, but the House passed an amended version of Kelly's offering in 1931. Capper then resubmitted a "fair trade" bill to the Senate the next year. This proposal sought to eliminate chain price-cutting by permitting owners of trade-mark brands to stipulate that their products could not be used as retail loss leaders.[16]

Bemoaning the extinction of the middle class, Capper asserted that "predatory competition" had destroyed 400,000 merchants since 1925.

The Kansas Republican predicted that the farmer might be "turned into a peasant, the mechanic into a proletarian, and the merchant into a clerk!" Current law, he charged, had "elevated and sanctified property ownership so as to allow it privileges by which it is devouring us." Capper promised that his bill would "restore the equality of opportunity for the smaller business man in his competition with the big corporation." Although Senate debate produced no action, support for the Capper-Kelly measures transcended ideological lines. In the House Brooklyn's Emanuel Celler, a "liberal" Democrat, backed the Republican measure and introduced his own proposal for a graduated tax on chain stores in Washington, D.C. Royal S. Copeland, New York's "conservative" Democratic senator, endorsed the effort in the Senate. "I pray that I shall never see the day," declared Copeland, "when great corporate middlemen shall have displaced the individual merchant."[17]

The antichain crusade also won support from the North Dakota progressive Gerald Nye. The "independent force which has made our country great is being crushed," Nye told the Senate in 1931. A "juggernaut of greed" dictated that "no man may live who chooses to remain independent, for opportunity is gone. There is nothing left except to travel a blind alley in the status of an employee." Monopoly was a "pestilence," exclaimed Nye, "a cancer, spreading and devouring as it goes, the whole tissue of the nation's economic body." The North Dakotan sought a remedy for independent business in stricter antitrust enforcement by the FTC. During 1931 and 1932 he submitted bills to allow the agency to give legal standing to the "fair trade" provisions of industry conferences on competitive practices. Nye also called for FTC power to prosecute violations of trade rules as restraints of trade. He further argued that specially created trade courts could act to eliminate price discrimination, below-cost selling, and "unfair methods of competition."[18]

Between 1932 and 1935 the FTC released thirty-three reports and concluded its extended chain store investigation. The commission acknowledged that chains were increasing in size, that higher profit rates accompanied this trend, and that chains maintained an advantage over independents by averaging profits over a wide territory. Yet the agency confirmed that people shopped at chain outlets for lower prices. Pointing out that expanding chains acquired other chain units, not independent businesses, the FTC recommended against punitive taxation. "To tax out of existence the advantage of chain stores over competitors," it concluded, was to eliminate "the advantages which the consuming public have found in patronizing them."[19]

Although the FTC absolved chains of monopoly or antitrust violations under current law, it offered conclusions about controversial chain trade

practices. Acknowledging complaints about misbranded goods and misleading advertising, the commission noted the use of "specials" or "loss
leaders" to provide the appearance of reduced prices. Accordingly, its report recommended that Congress empower the FTC to prosecute unfair
or deceptive practices. The agency also dealt with allegations that chains
received special purchasing discounts and allowances from manufacturers. Concluding that such practices "may lessen competition and tend to
the creation of monopoly," the FTC asked Congress to amend the Clayton Antitrust Act to prohibit unfair price discrimination.[20]

✦ ✦ ✦

As California became the first of twenty-eight states to prohibit below-cost
sales in 1935, Congress entertained several federal proposals against price
discrimination. Meanwhile, Representative Wright Patman from Texas
organized a special investigation of the chain store lobby. Patman cleverly
exploited documents that federal officials had seized from the Washington office of the American Retail Federation. The evidence showed that
investment bankers routinely sat on the boards of retail chains, that chain
groceries used price-conscious women's organizations to oppose state taxation, and that chain officials sought to trade local newspaper advertising
for favorable coverage and editorials. Testimony also indicated that A&P
had received over $8 million in advertising allowances, rebates, and bro-
kerage allowances in the previous year. Depicting the chain adversary as
a "Goliath" sapping the civic life of local communities, Patman proclaimed
a "battle of the century."[21]

In June 1935 Representative Patman and Senator Joseph T. Robinson
introduced legislation drafted by the U.S. Wholesale Grocers Association.
The Robinson-Patman bill enabled the FTC to prosecute chains for using
their size to win discounts and other pricing allowances from suppliers.
Robinson announced that the measure sought "to prevent monopoly" and
protect the public against "oppressive practices." Yet once the Senate Judiciary Committee reported it favorably in February 1936, opposition
escalated. Chain representatives maintained that the Robinson-Patman
measure would amount to "a subsidy for the benefit of a relatively small
group of wasteful and extravagant distributors." Sears, Roebuck's Robert Wood told the White House that the proposal set "the economic clock
backward" by discouraging cost-saving efficiency in mass distribution. "It
is directly against what you are working for," the department store innovator Edward A. Filene wrote to President Roosevelt, "—a better distribution of wealth for the masses."[22]

Patman responded sharply to industry criticism. Early in 1936 the Texan
joined the Montana Democrat Burton Wheeler in appealing for support

from thousands of delegates attending several grocery conferences in Chicago. Two months later Patman rallied with Senators Robinson, William
Borah, and Millard F. Tydings at a Washington gathering of fifteen hundred independent retailers. "This bill has the opposition of all cheaters,
bribe-takers, bribe-givers, and the greedy," a Patman press release declared.
After the fiery populist took the crusade to save small retailers to a national
radio audience in April, Congress passed the Robinson-Patman bill. Yet it
also tacked on an amendment by Borah and Representative Frederick Van
Nuys from Indiana that imposed criminal penalties for violations but narrowed their application to explicit practices threatening competition. In
the end a stymied Congress left enforcement of the contradictory legislation to the FTC.[23]

"Fair trade" soon provided politicians with another chance to endorse
small business. Backed by the National Association of Retail Druggists,
forty-two states passed laws by 1937 that required retailers to uphold resale prices set by manufacturers. The legislation specifically aimed to avoid
loss leaders and other price-cutting measures by cut-rate retailers and department stores. Once the Senate supported Millard Tydings's bill to protect such laws from antitrust action, John E. Miller, an Arkansas Democrat, successfully introduced a companion measure in the House. "New
forces, strange forces, forces alien to the true American way of doing
things," warned Miller, "have long been at work chiseling away the foundation upon which the country rests." Pointing to centralized wealth,
monopoly, and absentee ownership, he pleaded that the "special privilege"
and "despotic powers" of retail monopoly challenged "all the finer things
America was meant to be." The nation, concluded Miller, was in danger
"of a new feudal system," with a small minority in complete control.[24]

Wright Patman sought to marshal sympathy for small business to enact a national chain store tax. Introduced with seventy-five cosponsors in
February 1938, the Patman bill won the enthusiastic backing of the National Association of Retail Grocers. The proposal placed a sharply graduated tax on nationwide chains of ten or more outlets. Tax amounts also
were to reflect the number of states in which chains operated. In endorsing the measure at their national convention, the independent grocers decried "regimentation" of the nation's wealth through monopoly-controlled
corporations. Patman pursued similar populist themes when he spoke on
the issue of "absentee ownership" at the independent druggists' convention, an address broadcast over two national radio networks and reprinted in *Vital Speeches of the Day*.[25]

When the House failed to act on the Patman tax bill, the Texan reintroduced it in 1939 but added a two-year grace period in which chains
could dispose of outlets. He also exempted individually owned coopera-

tives from its provisions. Continuing his assault, the Texarkana populist charged that profits from the dismissal of thousands of traveling salesmen went "to a few Wall Street bankers and New York and to a few charming ladies who go overseas and marry some count." Patman argued that the Robinson-Patman Act did not prevent chains from using earnings from one town to squeeze out independent merchants in another. He also quoted Franklin Roosevelt's warning that "there are values in local independence and responsibility which are being sacrificed to balance-sheet values." When inaction by the House Ways and Means Committee forced Patman to introduce the bill again in 1940, he quoted Roosevelt's admonition that a democracy could not tolerate "unfair competition against the little man."[26]

Despite Patman's efforts, the chain store tax never made it out of committee and died as a national issue after 1940. Lack of flexibility and diversity contributed to a decline in chain store sales in many states after 1935. This might have influenced a 1939 poll by *Fortune* that found over 47 percent of respondents preferred to leave the chains alone while only 43 percent sought to further tax them. The crusade against the chains also conflicted with the consumerist approach of the Roosevelt administration and retail innovators. "Opposition to chain stores is based largely on an emotional and sentimental appeal," a midwestern miller observed to Senator George Norris. A variety store official agreed, boasting to William Borah that "the most fundamental element" in chain store success was "the high average level" of store management. Writing in the *Journal of Marketing* in 1939, a distribution expert denied that the antichain crusade marked "a progressive policy." Rather, he insisted, it reflected an "increasing desire to protect existing institutions and the old ways of doing things . . . against the disturbing effects of change."[27]

Small business activists never were able to overcome the fact that chain stores tended to sell goods at lower prices than independents did. Studies showed that price remained the most important concern of chain consumers, followed by the conveniences of self-service and accessibility. "The success of the modern chain store," attorneys for Safeway argued in an Oregon court case in 1934, was largely due to its role as a "poor man's store," where frugal citizens could buy the necessities of life. When Emanuel Celler engaged Wright Patman in House debate in 1939, the Brooklyn representative defended chains as a benefit to consumers threatened by "special interests . . . unable to fend for themselves."[28]

Organized labor took a similar approach. "Throughout the depression the chain store has been a friend of the poor man," explained *Labor World,* "because the cost of living has been kept within reason." The 1938 convention of the American Federation of Labor cited consumer savings as the main reason for its opposition to the Patman bill, even though it had condemned chains the previous year for driving down manufacturers' prices. The Roosevelt administration also acknowledged chain store efficiency in distributing food when war in Europe threatened economic instability. Chains cooperated with the Department of Agriculture's food stamp program to supply surplus commodities to the nation's poor.[29]

Both sides agreed that chain stores were efficient and economical, but antichain activists insisted that moral and social issues took precedence over market performance. The question of saving a few cents, argued a writer for the *Progressive Grocer,* "fades into insignificance when compared with the economic disadvantages of unemployment, monopoly, concentration of money and credit, and the destruction of local communities." Despite such assertions, chain store opponents were no more able to universalize their particular economic interests than were independent farmers. Their crusade to preserve individual proprietorship and traditional economic values reached its limits when it collided with New Deal commitment to urban consumers and market recovery. Not surprisingly, all four Democrats on the House Ways and Means Committee helped provide the final burial of Wright Patman's chain outlet tax in 1940.[30]

✦ ✦ ✦

When the 1930s historian Walter Prescott Webb described the dominance of chain stores in his home city of Austin, Texas, he used Paramount's string of motion picture theaters as a prime example. The depression accentuated long-standing tensions between the studios and independent exhibitors, and the impact of sound technology intensified the efforts of Hollywood's purity critics. Between 1930 and 1934 leaders of the Methodists, Presbyterians, and Federal Council of Churches all stepped up attacks on the moral content of movies, but their efforts were eclipsed by the Roman Catholic church's Legion of Decency. Stung by increasing sexual frankness, explicit dialogue, and sensational themes in Hollywood films, the church hierarchy asked followers to boycott all motion pictures except those that did not offend "decency" and Christian morality. Between late 1933 and the spring of 1934 Catholic bishops claimed to have gathered eleven million pledges of allegiance.[31]

Protestant reformers, such as the social worker Catheryne Cooke Gilman, enthusiastically embraced the Legion of Decency's campaign. "It is a spectacular move and will make an impression on the thoughtless which some of us do not influence so easily," wrote Gilman to a Canadian associate. In 1934 the Presbyterian general assembly joined the fray by demanding a censorship board to prevent the exhibition of films that portrayed vice as the normal condition of life. Will Hays, the Presbyterian elder who headed the Motion Pictures Producers and Distributors of America (MP-PDA), responded to the combined assault of Catholics and Protestants by organizing the Production Code Administration (PCA). Distribution of Hollywood films now depended on mandatory certificates of approval from the new bureau. PCA head Joseph I. Breen, a Catholic and former trade journalist, pledged to enforce the moral strictures of the Hays Code of 1930, which set industry standards. Tightening previous policy, Hays ordered that appeals be handed by the MPPDA's board of directors instead of producer juries.[32]

Although Hollywood appeared to respond to moral criticism in the mid-1930s, independent exhibitors continued to protest the dominance of the major studios and resulting trade practices. Purity reformers such as Catheryne Gilman and William Sheafe Chase, moreover, remained skeptical of industry intentions. Gilman lectured PTA and civic groups in twenty-two eastern and southern cities at mid-decade. Her focal point was the need for a federal regulatory commission to advise film producers, thereby avoiding censorship once movies were in circulation. Gilman and Chase supported a 1934 bill by Wright Patman to prohibit block booking and require federal regulators to issue film plot summaries to exhibitors. The social worker acknowledged, however, that the Roosevelt administration would not antagonize its recovery program supporters in the motion picture industry, and Patman soon lost interest in the project.[33]

Representative Francis D. Culkin from Upstate New York resumed Patman's efforts. A Republican, former district attorney, county judge, and antimonopoly activist, Culkin embraced the reform notion of a federal commission to regulate cinema as a public utility. The New York politician liked to describe the "Movie Trust" as the fourth largest industry in the nation, "the most powerful instrument for the communication of thought that mankind has devised." Warning that motion pictures threatened "uplifting ideals of the home, school, and pulpit," he introduced legislation between 1934 and 1939 that combined prohibitions of block booking and blind selling with government distribution of film plot summaries to exhibitors. Despite endorsement from Gilman and Chase, the Culkin measures languished. Meanwhile, the movie crusader William Short sought a compromise that would remove the federal government from the supervision of motion pictures. Short found his answer in a 1936 House bill introduced by Samuel B. Pettengill, an Indiana Democrat. The Pettengill measure proposed to outlaw block booking and blind selling and allow the studios to provide written synopses to theater owners without government involvement.[34]

As supporters praised the Pettengill scheme's reliance on grass-roots judgment, however, Matthew M. Neely, a West Virginia Democrat and religious prohibitionist, introduced a Senate counterpart that focused exclusively on outlawing offensive trade practices. Neely's approach won key backing from exhibitor groups without losing the endorsement of most purity reformers. At hearings in 1939, testimony from twenty-nine civic and educational organizations reestablished the link between monopoly and indecent motion pictures. "We believe it is a basic right of the American community," proclaimed one movie reform leader, "to determine the kind of entertainment that is going to be shown by its neighborhood theaters."[35]

Overcoming industry opposition and organized labor's concerns that the motion picture work force might be reduced, the Senate passed the Neely bill. As the Justice Department prepared antitrust charges against the five major studios in 1940, however, Will Hays convinced Neely that punitive legislation no longer was necessary. Accordingly, the senator withdrew his bill just before a scheduled House vote. Despite the apparent setback, a 1940 consent decree between the federal government and Hollywood's five largest studios helped precipitate the changes reformers sought. The decree strictly limited block booking and blind selling and temporarily ended expansion by the Big Five. Significantly, the Justice Department asked for outright separation of film industry production and distribution in 1944. Five years later the *Paramount* decision ended studio ownership of theaters and permanently outlawed the trade practices formerly denounced by exhibitors and purity activists.[36]

✦ ✦ ✦

Far from taking a populist position, patronizing movie reformers such as Catheryne Gilman sought government protection for "weak and inarticulate communities" besieged by the moral contamination of consumerism. "I have no more confidence in the exhibitors as a group than I have in the producers," confided Gilman in 1934.[37] Yet even the most elitist purity activists were willing to strike an alliance with independent theater groups fighting concentrated economic power. Accordingly, the struggle against Hollywood decadence and financial hegemony offered an instructive example of the intersection of producer moral virtues and small business interests. Despite its contradictions, the movement provided a curious variant of the insurgent spirit that left a lasting impact on motion picture content and finance.

Like the movie studio controversy, Franklin Roosevelt's National Recovery Administration (NRA) generated continued protest over the survival of traditional morality and economic individualism. Established in 1933 as the administration's first industrial rehabilitation agency, the NRA sought to promote trade self-regulation and union collective bargaining under federal supervision. Although the program initially won support from independent merchants, organized labor, and planning activists, it faced censure from those who objected to delegating congressional power to an executive bureau. Harsher condemnation came from critics opposed to provisions that permitted trade associations to create industry code authorities exempt from antitrust restrictions on price-fixing and other practices.[38]

Western progressives such as Idaho's William Borah played a major role in confronting the NRA. A veteran of the antitrust wars of the 1910s and 1920s, Borah insisted that freedom for independent business provided the key to democracy. He offered a classic explanation of this view in a 1934 letter to a Colorado merchant association. "I look upon the fight for the preservation of the 'little man,' for the small, independent producer and manufacturer," wrote Borah, "as a fight for a sound, wholesome, economic national life." "When you have destroyed small business," he continued, "you have destroyed our towns and our country life, and you have guaranteed and made permanent the concentration of economic power. . . . The concentration of wealth always leads . . . to the concentration of political power. Monopoly and bureaucracy are twin whelps from the same kennel."[39]

Borah insisted that he did not fight corporations in principle but merely condemned such monopoly practices as price-fixing. "I am opposed to giving industrialists power to fix their own regulations as to fair competition," he wrote to an Idaho journalist, "because it means the destruction of every 'independent' who does not see fit to come in . . . it is a gigantic scheme to give unlimited power to monopoly." The Idaho senator never accepted administration claims that the NRA would stabilize prices, raise consumer purchasing power, and enable small businesses to survive larger competition by practicing efficiency and coordination. Instead, a long-held fear of collusion between powerful governmental and corporate institutions prompted Borah to see the NRA as a tool of elite economic interests, "a very advanced step toward the ultimate concentration of wealth."[40]

The Idaho solon assumed leadership of the NRA opposition as the Senate debated its formation in June 1933. Sharply attacking the proposed suspension of antitrust laws, Borah observed that "we are to have trusts and combines and monopolies but we are not to call them such." Unless the millennium arrived, he noted with sarcasm, powerful firms in each industry would dominate the creation of trade codes. "You will have vast combines and monopolies controlled by political machinery," warned Borah. "You not only propose to let big business organize into trusts and combines," he shouted, "but you propose to let them invoke the law, make criminals out of and send to jail those who do not conform to their codes!" Once Senate Democrats consented to a Borah amendment prohibiting "combinations in restraint of trade, price-fixing, or other monopolistic practices," the bill passed. The Idahoan refused to vote for it, though. When a conference panel struck out the explicit prohibition on price-fixing, seven progressives also joined the minority opposition.[41]

Pressed by Borah and North Dakota's Gerald Nye, the Roosevelt administration created a government oversight board to safeguard small business interests under the NRA. The panel began hearings on industry pricing in January 1934. Large retailers, farm organizations, and consumer groups testified that trade codes had resulted in uniform bidding and unjustified price increases. Responding to complaints about antitrust violations, the president quickly issued an executive order that permitted small businesses to appeal the decisions of federal administrators to the FTC or to request aid from the Justice Department. In February the Senate accepted a Borah motion to require the trade commission to investigate price-fixing under the steel code and price hikes under the petroleum agreement. The Idaho crusader soon took to network radio to gather support for an amendment to restore antitrust provisions to the NRA charter. Domination by trusts and monopolies, he declared, was a "travesty upon justice" whether one called it "rugged individualism" or "planned industrialism."[42]

Sensitive to free enterprise issues, President Roosevelt created the National Recovery Review Board in March 1934. Chaired by the labor attorney Clarence Darrow, the commission sought to discover whether NRA codes promoted monopoly or discriminated against small businesses. Meanwhile, the FTC's report on steel price-fixing depicted "control by the larger producing interests." Borah now referred to NRA monopolies as "economic feudalism" and pictured their practices as "almost a complete scheme for elimination of small business . . . under color of law." When the review board published its conclusions in May, it found that giant corporations dominated eight code authorities and that the NRA encouraged monopoly in six of the industries it reviewed. The panel recommended the elimination of most price and production provisions and called for major changes among code authorities. In response, the NRA affirmed its commitment to competitive ideals, mandated safeguards against price-fixing, and created the Industrial Appeals Board to handle small business complaints.[43]

Although the Roosevelt administration appeared willing to address substantive complaints Borah and others advanced, the Idaho senator never abandoned his basic criticism. "I have about come to the conclusion that small business cannot be protected under the NRA as it is now organized," he explained to a New Haven retailer in April 1934. Borah summarized his views to Representative Allen T. Treadway from Massachusetts by noting that "prices are fixed on the basis of large overcapitalization and heavy overhead charges and the small business man is not permitted to take advantage of his small capitalization and his lighter overhead." To dramatize his fury at government bureaucracy in August 1934, Borah promised to provide free legal counsel to an Idaho baker who refused to follow NRA orders to raise the price of white bread by one cent.[44]

New Dealers pictured Borah's opposition to the NRA as the work of a reactionary unable to come to terms with the modern state. Yet his defense of small producers and retailers helped make the Idaho senator a near-legend among struggling entrepreneurs who believed themselves threatened by big business. "According to what I have read and heard over the radio," a small-town Oregon grocer wrote in 1934, "you are the only man that we have down at Washington that is really trying to do something for the little fellow." "You are the most level headed, conscientious advocate of the people of the United States," proclaimed another small business admirer. A radio service and sales operator promised "that the small business man here in California is with you 100–percent in your fight." "Your public utterances in defense of the small business men have been so clear and to the point," exulted the officer of a Michigan independent refiners' association, "that we have come to look upon you as the ablest, and perhaps the only, champion of our cause."[45]

Between October 1933 and March 1934 Borah's office reported receiving some fourteen thousand small business complaints about the NRA, sometimes three hundred a day. His description of the agency's impact on independent business, a small sawmill operator suggested, was "but to state the case mildly." A lumber operator from Arkansas complained that the unjust timber codes seemed to have been "hatched in the middle of Russia." In New York a manufacturer claimed that administrators of the shoe agreement came out of the industry trade association and permitted the larger interests to continue discount orders and below-cost selling. Similarly, a Utah hat producer charged that New York millinery producers dominated his code authority and priced western consumers out of the market.[46]

Replete with charges of racketeering and bureaucratic imperialism, Borah's mail appeared to contradict administration optimism about the NRA. In April 1934 the manager of a Cincinnati engineering firm wrote to protest that executives of big corporations used code powers for fixing prices, restraining production, shutting out new competitors, and merging more businesses into fewer hands. The NRA gave them "judicial, executive, and taxing powers," he objected. Two months later a Maryland oil distributor reported that he had been taken into court for violations of the petroleum code. "While the rights of . . . individual operators were threatened," he charged, large companies had been granted "a monopoly which I consider almost imperialistic." In February 1935 a Massachusetts lumber dealer claimed to be paying $2–$5 in fees to code authorities for every $1,000 worth of sales. Small lumber operators resented such "tribute," he declared, and wanted to be left alone.[47]

Although subsequent research has suggested that the NRA Petroleum Code Authority frequently worked against the interests of the major companies, Borah received many letters from disgruntled independent producers and retailers. Allocation of production, complained one Arkansas oil refiner, placed independents at the mercy of major petroleum interests with huge cash surpluses and extensive facilities. This refiner noted that code provisions required small operators to reduce output, thereby forcing them to raise prices to meet expenses. A similar complaint came from an Indiana service station operator, who objected that the petroleum code permitted large oil corporations to discount prices for most commercial customers while prohibiting independent retailers from doing likewise. The *New York Times* reported in February 1935 that Borah received a telegram from the Retail Petroleum Dealers Association asserting that twenty-eight hundred independent service stations in southern California demanded an investigation of "oil industry price-fixing."[48]

Price-fixing remained the most common complaint of Senator Borah's small business correspondents. In May 1934 a hardware retailer from Worcester, Massachusetts, protested that code agreements favored the chain stores by classifying them as jobbers, thereby allowing them to qualify for lucrative discounts. But small businesses also objected when codes prevented them from setting prices below those of larger competitors. A neighborhood dry-cleaning shop in Meridian, Mississippi, complained that NRA minimum prices made it impossible to undersell competitors at the more convenient downtown locations. As a result, the operators claimed to have lost nearly 65 percent of their business. The beleaguered dry cleaner asserted that three similar establishments in town already had gone out of business.[49]

Borah remained an important conduit for independent enterprisers who felt victimized by the "twin whelps" of monopoly and bureaucracy. Rather than limit his appraisals to the health of the independent business community, however, the Idaho insurgent was careful to emphasize that ordinary people suffered when "monopoly" benefited from political favoritism. In a November 1933 speech Borah cited price-fixing by "combines and monopolies" as the reason for a 63 to 120 percent increase in the cost of consumer essentials. As long as industrialists had the power "to sit about a table and fix prices," he asserted early in 1934, they would "continue to raise their prices in order to keep a little ahead of the rise in the prices of commodities." In a February radio speech that seemed to ridicule New Deal concern for consumers, the Idaho senator bemoaned price increases in working-class commodities, such as cotton towels, men's overalls, and children's hose.[50]

Senator Borah's views resonated in a depression culture in which many believed that special privilege, not economic efficiency, ensured corporate size and success. Vocal Senate opponents of the NRA included not only North Dakota's Nye but also Louisiana's Huey Long, Minnesota's Henrik Shipstead, Wisconsin's Robert La Follette Jr., South Dakota's Peter Norbeck, and even the Roosevelt enthusiast George Norris of Nebraska. Outside Congress, Father Charles Coughlin taunted President Roosevelt by claiming that the "vast majority" of his nearly 200,000 correspondents had little faith in the NRA. Popular journalists, such as John Flynn and Mark Sullivan, concurred. "The little business man is the true 'rugged individualist,'" declared Sullivan in a piece reprinted in the *Congressional Digest* early in 1935, "and the tendency to exterminate him by Government policies seems to me tragic."[51]

Suspicion over federal bureaucracy and sentiment favoring small business contributed to the resignation of NRA administrator Hugh Johnson in September 1934. The following January Borah renewed efforts to win congressional approval for a bill eliminating price-fixing. Accordingly, the Senate Judiciary Committee held closed hearings on the NRA's impact on small business. Battle lines were drawn. Donald R. Richberg, a New Deal economic adviser, warned the public to distinguish between "good" and "bad" monopolies. Meanwhile, Johnson publicly proclaimed that President Roosevelt had "saved more little men under NRA than Senators Borah and Nye ever preached about."[52]

Responding to the onslaught from New Deal partisans, the Idaho senator took to the floor in March 1935 to summarize the case against the NRA and to restate a progressive faith in individual business initiative. "It is not alone a question of how many have been driven out of business," he argued, "but whether small business enterprises have been compelled to live on the ragged edge of bankruptcy while the larger enterprises are enjoying vast profits." He was "not opposed to big business as such," reiterated the Idahoan, but only to "those practices which none but the highwayman can justify." Borah restated his request that "small business be permitted to exist under just and equal laws." If independent enterprise was "making its last struggle," he proclaimed, "it should be permitted to do so under fair laws." "You must permit a fair distribution to all according to his effort," the senator lectured. "If you do not," he concluded, "you do not have a republic."[53]

The Senate voted 43 to 33 to defeat Borah's amendment to strip NRA of antitrust exemptions. In May, however, Bennett Champ Clark, a Missouri Democrat, won approval of a resolution that limited the agency's tenure to ten months and stripped it of intrastate and most price-fixing powers. The Supreme Court then invalidated the entire National Industrial Recovery Act, declaring in the *Schechter* case that the code-making authority constituted an unconstitutional delegation of legislative power. When the House soon renewed the charter of the weakened NRA, the Senate acceded but added the Borah antitrust proviso. In June 1935 President Roosevelt asked congressional leaders to accept the amendment to save the overall package. After a fifteen-hour filibuster by Senator Long, both chambers agreed to limit the extension of the NRA to April 1936. Congress also refused to provide the agency with code-making or enforcement powers. Meanwhile, the Borah amendment permitted the president to approve only those voluntary agreements that did not violate antitrust laws.[54]

✦ ✦ ✦

Seeking to explain antimonopoly partisans' success in destroying the recovery agency, Rexford Tugwell, a former Roosevelt adviser, once observed that NRA collectivism "met head-on the tight-fisted orthodoxy of Presbyterian corner grocers." Yet more was at stake. William Borah, Gerald Nye, Huey Long, and other progressives graphically expressed their generation's profound distrust of an impersonal corporate economy and a remote government bureaucracy. Many independent producers and retailers shared the belief that only conspiratorial forces prevented individual success in a free market. They tended to view chain stores and banks, Hollywood studios, Wall Street finance, and powerful government bureaucracies as precisely the sort of institutions that were destroying American traditions of economic opportunity and fair play. Faced with the decimation of their communities, progressive leaders and other insurgents staked their political careers on invoking the specter of monopoly and saving small business.[55]

Certainly no revolutionary, Senator Borah played the monopoly theme with great skill in the anti-NRA campaign. In a series of radio broadcasts during the summer and fall of 1934, the Idahoan echoed old Bob La Follette in proclaiming that monopoly was the most critical problem facing the country. Recovery from the depression, he asserted on the Fourth of July, had been retarded by the "arbitrary treatment of men who made this country." Three weeks later the senator told celebrants of Idaho's Mormon Pioneer Day that monopolies were "economic Hitlers." Once the NRA was gone, Borah continued to invoke the trust issue, declaring it to be the central issue of the 1936 presidential election. Speaking in Peoria, Illinois, the Idaho Republican attacked the du Ponts and Standard Oil. "You'll likely hear that I am a radical," he declared. "That is because I say the greatest question before us is how to save the independent small businessman, and the only way to do it is to destroy monopoly."[56]

Borah also proved influential in shaping the denunciation of monopoly in the 1936 Republican platform. The senator previously had proposed that the party call for legislation to prevent monopolistic corporations from engaging in interstate commerce. But because he believed that compromise would be "pure political cowardice," he refused to participate in the actual drafting of the document. The result was a weaker platform that denounced monopolies as "indefensible and intolerable" and called for "vigorous enforcement of the criminal laws" against them. Meanwhile, Republican presidential candidate Alfred M. Landon demanded an end to the "tyranny of economic dictatorship" as well as the "bondage of bureaucracy."[57]

In the Senate Borah fought the antimonopoly battle by introducing a national corporate licensing bill in 1935. Under its provisions the FTC would license all interstate corporations except unlawful trusts, combinations, and monopolies. Applicants were to prove that they did not engage in monopoly practices or restraints of trade. It was "monopolistic control" of the economy that bred discontent and lawlessness, insisted Borah. Meanwhile, Wyoming's Senator Joseph C. O'Mahoney proposed a national corporation registry. Taking to network radio in August 1935, O'Mahoney described the U.S. economic system as feudal rather than democratic and complained that Americans confused corporate prerogatives with individual rights. The western Democrat warned that checks and balances had never been placed on the governance of corporations. As a result, he charged, "a few ambitious and irresponsible men in positions of corporate authority have the power to destroy the security of our entire industrial and commercial structure."[58]

As the economy slid into the "Roosevelt recession" in late 1937 and early 1938, Senators O'Mahoney and Borah produced a joint proposal that required corporate licensees to observe antitrust laws and stop deceptive practices. The bill permitted the FTC to withdraw permits if it found violations of fair labor and trade procedures. Just as the Senate Judiciary Committee prepared to conduct legislative hearings, Assistant Attorney General Robert H. Jackson delivered a blistering December 1937 radio address in which he held "monopolistic prices" accountable for the recent economic downturn. When Roosevelt invited Borah to a White House luncheon the next month and hinted at antitrust law revision, speculation held that a recession-wary White House might sponsor a corporate licensing bill. The president's April 1938 message to Congress furthered such conjecture. "Private enterprise in the United States is ceasing to be free enterprise," exclaimed Roosevelt, "and is becoming a cluster of private collectivisms . . . a concealed cartel after the European manner."[59]

Instead of embracing corporate licensing, however, the president announced the creation of the Temporary National Economic Committee (TNEC) to study monopoly. Roosevelt appointed Joseph O'Mahoney as chair, William Borah as the only Republican, four other members of Congress, and six administration officials. As he inaugurated the first monetary investigation since the Pujo inquiry of 1912, the chief executive described "a concentration of private power without equal in history." The TNEC never lived up to expectations, though. Preliminary testimony by Willard L. Thorp, chief economist for Dun and Bradstreet and senior researcher for the Commerce Department, dramatically compromised the antitrust position by demonstrating that the mere size of a corporation did not imply monopoly, an actual "rarity" in American business. Price competition, cautioned Thorp, was merely one means by which companies competed. In a mature economy there was "actually no manner in which you can measure the extent of unlawful agreements and combinations," he warned.[60]

Split between various schools of economic thought, the TNEC produced a final report that confined itself to technical changes in antitrust and patent procedures. Borah and Mahoney introduced another corporate licensing bill in 1939, but the measure never survived committee. By January 1940 "the Great Opposer" from Idaho was dead, and a new decade had emerged in which antimonopoly rhetoric would be considered mere bombast.[61]

❖ ❖ ❖

President Roosevelt's flirtation with antitrust demonstrated the political complexities of the issue in a corporate society whose core traditions embraced freedom of enterprise. New Deal administrators repeatedly found themselves compelled to balance the diverse needs of consumers, large corporations, and independent competitors. The difficulties of doing so could be challenging. In 1934 chain store executives protested to the White House about a documentary film that used a picture of the president to link the fight against the depression to agitation for a tax on chains. Written and produced by Frank R. Wilson, a former government publicist and NRA official, and distributed through local retail organizations, the five-reel *Forward America* was dedicated to the American housewife. Wilson's polemic depicted chain magnates as "hogs" and "traitors" and asked audiences to support the New Deal to "drive out the chain store crooks." Following the uproar, the FTC filed a complaint against the producer for unfair competition.[62]

The White House heard from small business operators. Some, like the successful New England stationery manufacturer Henry S. Dennison, simply reiterated the need for competition on equal terms without price discrimination. Others sharply attacked the New Deal. "Your talk about helping the small business man," a California wholesaler wrote to the president in 1936, "has proven itself to be a joke." A Georgia clothing retailer who described himself as "a poor dumb hardworking small town merchant" asked how he could compete with a chain store that worked its help over seventy hours a week. From East Chicago, Indiana, a dairy wholesaler pleaded for restriction of chain store loss leaders. "Whatever help has come for general business," he observed, "has apparently gone to the big capitalists and industrialists."[63]

Although Roosevelt made ritualistic overtures to small business in political campaigns and press conferences, passage of the 1936 Robinson-Patman Act seemed to provide the political moment of awakening for the independent business community. By 1938 small business interests had begun to move beyond narrowly defined trade associations to create more ambitious political lobbies. When the Department of Commerce issued a thousand invitations to a conference on small business that year, rebellious delegates formed their own council and sharply criticized their New Deal hosts. Among their demands were a government agency to issue small business loans, enactment of fair trade laws, antitrust enforcement, and regulation of chain store competition.[64]

Within a year of the Washington meeting, fifty small business organizations sprang into existence, five competing for national leadership. By 1942 two groups had emerged as key lobbies: the National Federation of Independent Business and the Conference of American Small Business Organizations. Under the leadership of C. Wilson Harder, a former motor company owner, the National Federation of Independent Business became a lobby for antitrust enforcement and regulation of large corporations. The Conference of American Small Business Organizations, chaired by the Chicago publisher Frederick A. Virkus, established itself as a consortium of small business associations.[65] Interest groups now pictured independent enterprise as a unique institution with its own political agenda and worldview. Perceiving the New Deal as too friendly to labor and large corporations, small business groups joined critics of the federal bureaucracy while simultaneously lamenting government failure to address their needs.

Independent enterprisers embodied other contradictions as well. Turning to politics to protect competition and individual opportunity, retailers and others often failed to distinguish between strengthening competition and protecting their own market position. Restrictions on brokerage payments and advertising allowances, for example, damaged food dealers more frequently than corporate chains. Moreover, protective laws like Robinson-Patman and Miller-Tydings tended to hamper production and hold up prices. Aware of such paradoxes, New Deal officials and economists tended to dismiss small business as a risky and unwise investment, particularly in the overbuilt and excessively competitive service and distribution fields. They also realized that Americans often followed the dollar when confronted with the choice between small enterprise and cost efficiency.[66]

Yet the story of small business insurgence went beyond the use of politics to protect specific economic interests. Like other depression-era Americans, independent competitors were overwhelmed by a mystifying economic catastrophe that heightened fears of powerlessness, dependence, and rule by impersonal institutions. Traumatized, they strove to defend the market freedoms of a traditional way of life. Their values taught that liberty lay in the chance to place creative energies in a self-owned enterprise reflecting the personality of the owner. Old-fashioned entrepreneurs saw concrete, localized, and personalized businesses as empowering institutions that stimulated character as well as community cohesion. Adherents of the republican tradition and democratic ideology, they believed that equality of opportunity, individual improvement, and social mobility were the keys to America's material richness and spiritual health.

Two communications to President Roosevelt illustrated such views in 1936. First, an anti–chain store pamphlet by the rural Missouri publisher William Hirth paid romantic homage to "the vanishing traveling salesman" or "drummer." Hirth recalled how the objects of his nostalgia contributed to economic well-being by moving the products of wholesale houses, factories, and mills. But he also remembered how sellers "scattered good cheer and good fellowship" throughout the hotels and railroads they patronized. A second letter came from someone in Chattanooga. "What has become of the old country blacksmith who could do anything from fix a plow or wagon to make a fiddle?" the correspondent asked the president. "We need more small industries scattered nearer to their market. We need them in our communities. They were our American backbone."[67]

The 1930s depression heightened long-standing cultural anxieties over concentrated power and wealth. As many Americans perceived chain stores, monopolies, and government bureaucracies as threats to traditional market liberties, a series of economic crusades intersected the decade's political life. Independent merchants and other individual competitors played major roles in such efforts. These middle-class insurgents struggled to realize the good life of accessible commodities while upholding the values of a rooted social order. The contradictions of such dualism were difficult to sustain, though. Despite the continuing hold the free enterprise idea had on the national psyche and persistent economic concentration among leading corporations, concerns for material security hereafter relegated economic populism to a distinctly minor role in American life and politics.[68]

7

The Last Progressives: Breaking with New Deal Liberalism, 1936–40

"To this day," proclaimed the economics consultant Willis James Ballinger in 1941, "the most ardent advocates of unlimited bigness are found among high finance men and Communists." Ballinger had served as a regional organizer for Robert La Follette's 1924 presidential campaign and as an adviser to the Federal Trade Commission in the late 1930s. The economist now pictured supposed ideological opposites as united in the belief that centralized planning and operation were "necessary for efficiency."[1] Such antistatism epitomized the views of old progressives who equated economic individualism with democracy. By the eve of World War II anti-institutional sentiments of this kind made it difficult for these former Roosevelt allies to remain within the bounds of New Deal liberalism and the president's political coalition.

✦   ✦   ✦

Progressive cooperation with Franklin Roosevelt had long crossed party lines. As early as 1931 Senators George Norris, Robert La Follette Jr., and Bronson Cutting, all Republicans, sponsored the Progressive Conference on the Depression, which called for unemployment relief and public works under the Hoover presidency. "Never before in history has monopoly and organized wealth so completely controlled our governmental affairs as at the present time," declared Norris. California's Senator Hiram Johnson joined the three reformers in endorsing Roosevelt's candidacy the following year, as did Senators Lynn Frazier and Henrik Shipstead. The National Progressive Republican League rallied progressives and independents to the Roosevelt cause. The Democratic front-runner even expropriated

Johnson's invocation of "the forgotten man." Celebrating Roosevelt's victory, the Californian remarked that the president-elect brought "renewed optimism and hope" to a "dispirited and despairing people."[2]

Hiram Johnson was among four Senate Republican progressives the new administration approached with cabinet positions. Each refused, but Roosevelt consulted several western insurgents on political and patronage issues and provided Democratic support in 1934 for the reelection of Robert La Follette Jr. and Hiram Johnson. While La Follette played an instrumental role in championing New Deal public works, Nebraska's Norris worked with the administration to create the Tennessee Valley Authority, a multipurpose public power project near Muscle Shoals. The progressive bloc, including the Republicans William Borah, Arthur Capper, Peter Norbeck, and Michigan's James Couzens, supported such Roosevelt reforms as the Social Security Act, the Banking Act, the creation of the Works Progress Administration (WPA), and the National Labor Relations (Wagner) Act. Progressives also helped Roosevelt pass the Public Utility Holding Act of 1935, a measure containing a "death sentence" provision for monopoly power syndicates. Insurgents further aided passage of new excess profit taxes.[3]

William Borah attempted to parlay insurgency into a progressive alternative to the New Deal by making a run for the Republican presidential nomination in 1936. Borah consistently had demanded that his own party purge itself of "reactionary leaders" and restore "liberal principles." During the summer of 1935 his supporters castigated both parties for surrendering to the "forces of massed capital." The progressive Kansas newspaper editor William Allen White heralded the Idaho politician as "the only Republican who could at this minute beat Roosevelt." Borah won endorsements from the western progressives Gerald Nye, Lynn Frazier, Peter Norbeck, and Henrik Shipstead and scored well in primaries in Pennsylvania, Wisconsin, Illinois, Oregon, and Idaho. Yet the poorly funded candidate was no match for a Republican Old Guard furious at his denunciations of corporate privilege and monopoly, and his quest for the nomination ended by convention time.[4]

Unable to influence the Republican nomination process, Borah, Hiram Johnson, and Gerald Nye remained neutral in the 1936 presidential race. Five Republican insurgents—James Couzens, Peter Norbeck, Henrik Shipstead, Robert La Follette Jr., and George Norris—supported the Democratic ticket. Two—La Follette and Norris—agreed to lead the Progressive National Committee, a revival of the National Progressive League of 1932. Norris told a 1936 conference of progressives that Roosevelt represented "the common man" and the fight against "human greed, selfish interests, and . . . heartless monopoly." La Follette, once rumored to have been

Roosevelt's vice presidential choice, used a radio broadcast on the eve of the election to rally listeners to help the Democratic candidate defeat the "desperate, organized drive of blind reactionaries for power." Burton Wheeler, the progressive Democrat from Montana, also continued to be a strong Roosevelt supporter.[5]

✦ ✦ ✦

As Democrats increased their hold to a 334-89 majority in the House and a 75-17 majority in the Senate, Franklin Roosevelt won the 1936 election with 60.4 percent of the popular vote and an overwhelming 523-8 vote in the electoral college (all but Maine and Vermont). The importance of city voters and corporate support in the landslide appeared to free Roosevelt from dependence on mainly nonurban congressional progressives. As opponents of concentrated economic and political power began to worry about the president's accountability, Roosevelt proposed reorganizing the federal judiciary in February 1937. In the previous twenty months the Supreme Court had struck down laws establishing the National Recovery Administration, the Agricultural Adjustment Administration, and state minimum wage standards. Fearing the invalidation of other New Deal legislation, the president sought the right to name additional federal judges for every unretired justice over seventy years of age. The proposal would have immediately given him the right to name forty-four judges to the federal bench and to expand the size of the Supreme Court by six.[6]

Among progressives, Robert La Follette Jr. and George Norris welcomed judicial reform as an attempt to serve New Deal ends. Most Senate progressives reacted with fury, however. Within days an open letter to Congress by the long-time reformer Amos Pinchot accused the president of attempting to "control the political and economic life of the country." Senator Borah soon joined the fray. Four days before the Roosevelt announcement the Idahoan had gone on network radio to ask for Supreme Court reform through constitutional amendment. The Court provided for a government of law, not men, he declared, a place where the humblest citizen might seek justice free from the influence of dictatorial power. The fiery solon soon confided to Idaho political associates that he had "never felt more deeply about any subject, unless it was the League." If the Supreme Court could "be made a tool to change the Constitution without the consent of the people," he wrote to a constituent, "then the people have lost control of their government."[7]

Three days after President Roosevelt's speech Borah consulted with Hiram Johnson and conferred with mainstream Republicans. The Idaho politician saw no contradiction in cooperating with Old Guard elements of his own party. "To talk about conservatism and liberalism is to make use of mere worn-out shibboleths," he explained. Preservation of the judicial system, predicted Borah, "would wipe out all lines of cleavage between liberals and conservatives." Indeed, a broad Senate coalition of conservative and moderate Democrats and conservative and progressive Republicans quickly emerged to oppose the "court packing" bill. Western progressives and insurgents, such as Borah, Hiram Johnson, Arthur Capper, Lynn Frazier, and Gerald Nye, helped mount an alliance strategy and set the emotional tone of the campaign's rhetoric.[8]

Once Republican Senate leaders realized that hostility to the Court plan spanned ideological and party barriers, they deferred to such Democrats as Burton Wheeler. After lining up Senators Nye and Frazier, Wheeler forged an alliance with Frank E. Gannett, a Borah financial supporter and newspaper publisher, whose National Committee to Uphold Constitutional Government distributed ten million mailings in six months. An early Roosevelt supporter, Wheeler hoped to amend the Constitution to permit Congress to override Supreme Court decisions by two-thirds majorities. As an opponent of concentrated power, however, Wheeler shared insurgent suspicions about executive prerogative. He reminded a national radio audience in February 1937 that labor and farm activists had turned to the Court for free speech protections during World War I. "Make the Court subservient to one man or make it subservient to mob rule," warned Wheeler, "and you destroy the liberties of the minorities of this country." The Court debate, he insisted, was "the most important public constitutional question raised since the Civil War."[9]

As the Senate Judiciary Committee prepared for the March 1937 hearings, a poll of nearly 300,000 newspaper readers in 203 cities found respondents opposed to the Court plan by nearly two to one. By April Hiram Johnson claimed to have received 75,000 petition signatures protesting the measure. Gallup polls revealed 53 percent opposed it, with even larger margins of hostility in such farm states as North Dakota, Kansas, Idaho, and Oregon. Rural criticism coincided with condemnation by the National Grange and lack of unified support for judicial reform in the American Farm Bureau and the National Farmers Union. Gallup surveys showed that among Roosevelt supporters the greatest opposition came from average and above-average income groups in farm and small-town regions.[10]

Franklin Roosevelt's attempt to reorganize the judiciary tapped deep-seated feelings in the national psyche. Many Americans looked to the Supreme Court as a symbol of security and stability. It was "one solid thing to hold to in a world of unrest," a California shopkeeper told the president. Describing himself as "a bitter democrat and a rank conservative," the correspondent pictured the federal government as efficient as a nation-wide chain store but too large to serve human needs. Those fearing abuse by consolidated economic and political power believed that the checks and balances of an independent judiciary served as protection in a dangerous time. "I cannot conceive how any one man, progressively inclined," a protester wrote to Senator La Follette, "can find any argument for the deliberate changing of the Supreme Court to a political body." "At a time when dictatorships are running rife in Europe," a concerned woman informed Gerald Nye, "we rightly shudder at the prospect of any change in our government which tends to place more power in the hands of one man."[11]

Public mail on the Court plan revealed that many Americans questioned President Roosevelt's motivation. "I have heard nothing but emergencies for the last four years," a Beloit attorney complained to La Follette. A farm wife explained to Senator Nye that her family was "seething with indignation, raging against our helplessness." Roosevelt had broken his mandate to preserve democracy and had substituted his own judgment for the people's will, she concluded. An anonymous office worker pleaded for the president to admit that his supporters did not believe the Court plan was right. Roosevelt's record was "so grand," the writer explained, that such a statement "would forever silence" those who claimed he planned a "dictatorship." The real "reactionaries," a Grange leader from Washington lectured Wisconsin's Governor Philip La Follette, were not Senators Johnson, Borah, and Wheeler but those who would destroy the independence of the judiciary.[12]

Many protests also revealed the social anxieties of the old middle class. If the Supreme Court were subordinated to Congress and the president, warned a Minneapolis glue manufacturer, large industrial groups would gain greater control over small business. The powerful did not require the Constitution or Supreme Court, explained a Pennsylvanian to Senator Nye; only the poor and weak needed the Court to prevent their oppression by the strong. The actuary of a small life insurance company tied hostility toward the Roosevelt proposal to fears that an unrestricted New Deal would pander to the working class. Denying that his annual income of $7,800 made him an economic royalist, he reiterated the importance of such producer values as thrift and self-denial. "Is this doctrine of class hatred to go on," an Idaho probate judge asked Senator Borah, "until the great middle class, which really constitutes the backbone of the country, is to be submerged, and labor and the have-nots are the only ones to receive consideration at the hands of the government?"[13]

As sit-down strikes by the Congress of Industrial Organizations (CIO) dominated headlines in March and April 1937, a distinct antilabor message crept into protests against the Court bill. Opponents described worker occupation of factory property as unpunished violations of law and connected such laxity to presidential influence on the judicial process. "The breakdown of respect for law and order and property rights is very, very serious," an opponent of the Court plan explained to President Roosevelt. A self-described Republican progressive wrote to tell Senator Norris that industrial strife, disrespect for law, and politicalization of the Supreme Court were all connected. What was at stake, a New York woman lectured the president, was a system in which impartial juries decided cases on evidence only. Other writers contended White House commitment to legislation on wages and hours was connected to a desire to circumvent the judiciary and pass the "court packing" bill.[14]

Hearings on judicial reform climaxed when Burton Wheeler read a letter from Chief Justice Charles Evans Hughes denying that the Court was overworked. Soon after, the high tribunal validated a state minimum wage law and the Wagner Act. In May 1937 the Senate Judiciary Committee defeated the Court proposal by a 10-8 vote, and Justice Willis Van Devanter, an opponent of the New Deal, announced his retirement. Six days later the Court upheld the Social Security Act. White House fortunes deteriorated when Joseph T. Robinson, the Senate majority leader, died of a heart attack in July. The administration then pressed for a compromise to limit presidential appointment powers to two justices, but Wheeler was adamant about demonstrating Senate anger over lost power and prestige. "We must teach that man in the White House a lesson," he declared. "We must show him that the United States Senate has to be consulted and is going to have something to say about how this government is run." After consultations between Wheeler and Roosevelt officials in July, the Senate recommitted the Court bill to committee by a 70-20 vote.[15]

✦ ✦ ✦

The Court defeat had a profound effect on many of Franklin Roosevelt's progressive allies. "It is the first time that he has misjudged public sentiment," observed Robert Wood, the president of Sears, Roebuck. Insurgents such as Hiram Johnson, Gerald Nye, and William Borah rarely again supported New Deal initiatives. Burton Wheeler may have experienced the most dramatic break with Roosevelt. Wheeler's greatest fear was once bigness in industry and business. After 1937, however, the progressive Democrat saw little difference between an unregulated corporation and the regimentation fostered by an executive not accountable to the people.[16]

Wheeler's opposition to judicial reform brought him into disagreement with Montana labor groups for the first time in his career. Roosevelt loyalists played up the conflict, warning local unions of "decoy liberals" aligned with "economic royalists." Most Republican insurgents had voted for the Wagner Act and generally sided with labor struggles against monopolistic corporations. Yet progressives like Wheeler increasingly criticized unions in the late 1930s as being part of a web of powerful institutions that threatened the old middle class. They complained that New Deal labor reform appeared to assist city-based unions at the expense of rural producers and small business operators. Representatives of agricultural constituencies, such as Gerald Nye, objected to extending government "favoritism" and "special privileges" to both corporate and union interests. It was hard to achieve harmony among agriculture, labor, and industry, explained South Dakota's Peter Norbeck, when each clamored for the same federal dollar.[17]

Many western progressives had been disillusioned by organized labor's failure to support agrarian monetary and marketing reforms. The union movement, moreover, had remained cool to monopoly complaints against chain stores, banks, and other corporations. Representatives of independent farmers and traditional enterprisers therefore had ample reason to suspect that labor's immediate needs had prompted it to desert democratic values and act against the interests of the struggling middle class. Ruralites also resented the unionization of farm cooperatives. The problem for liberals in Minnesota, a Democratic state judge confessed to Senator Wheeler in 1940, was "ill feeling created by the coercive methods" of local dairy unions. The judge supported New Deal domestic programs but noted that farmers in the Old Northwest were "just about convinced . . . that organized labor is a racket." Why should labor union leaders "be telling you boys what to do," a Minnesotan asked Henrik Shipstead.[18]

Such sentiments explain widespread discomfort with CIO sit-down strikes in mass-production industries in 1937. Among western progressives, only Robert La Follette Jr., whose Senate Civil Liberties Committee investigated corporate violations of the Wagner Act, defended the tactics of the strikers. Hiram Johnson lashed out at the administration's refusal to preserve the rule of law. Johnson charged that President Roosevelt was unwilling to antagonize CIO financial supporters and that the same ties explained the attempt to stack the Supreme Court. Warning that "dictatorship lurks down the road," he called the sit-downs "the most ominous thing in our national life today." Although Johnson and Charles McNary were the only western progressives to back the failed Senate attempt to denounce the strikes, insurgents such as Burton Wheeler and William Borah opposed the sit-downs as wrong in principle. While refusing to single out labor "and leave capital free to pursue its illegal methods," Borah predicted that public opinion would turn against union actions that were contrary to law.[19]

Introduction of the 1937 bill on fair labor standards dramatized the disparities between New Deal liberalism and progressive insurgency. Robert La Follette Jr., George Norris, and Henrik Shipstead unequivocally supported the effort to create federal wage and hours regulations and outlaw most child labor, but other Senate progressives balked. Rural politicians feared that increased wages penalized farmers by raising the price of manufactured goods while making agricultural labor prohibitively expensive. William Borah led a group of rural senators in exempting farm labor from the wage and hours bill. Insurgents such as Borah received the same sort of small employer complaints that had marked the campaign against the NRA. "If you are for the small fellow and against the 'big interests,'" a Massachusetts manufacturer of machine knives wrote to Borah, "you'll oppose the Wages and Hours bill." Because small plants could not arrange forty-hour weeks throughout the year, protested the writer, they would be forced to pay overtime. Other correspondents complained that national standards could not take into account "peculiar conditions."[20]

For progressives the most controversial part of the legislation involved creation of a Fair Labor Standards Board to set regional labor requirements. Borah condemned the bureau as "a little NRA" and recoiled from granting authority to an executive commission. Burton Wheeler, Arthur Capper, and Gerald Nye agreed that government agencies should not assume arbitrary control over employment conditions. Hiram Johnson perhaps best expressed such suspicions when he explained in August 1937 that he "never again would give unlimited powers to an undisclosed board." To leave wage and hour measures to a Washington bureau, he asserted, "would be one more way of turning over the economic life of the country to the President for him to exercise at his own sweet will." Despite opposition by six Republican progressives, the measure carried the Senate in 1937 and passed the House in an amended version the next year.[21]

✦ ✦ ✦

Progressive suspicions of executive power combined with western economic interests to stir bitter controversy over the Reciprocal Trade Agreements Act. First enacted as "an emergency program" in 1934, the trade law gave the president the power to conduct tariff negotiations and reduce duties without Senate approval. It specifically allowed him to halve tariffs when trading partners reduced import taxes on U.S. products. Shippers, exporters, bankers, auto manufacturers, cotton producers, and the national Chamber of Commerce enthusiastically supported this boon to international trade. Agricultural, lumber, and mining interests west of the Mississippi, however, feared an onslaught of foreign imports into their domestic markets. They saw reciprocal trade as a device to encourage the export of eastern industrial products in exchange for a flood of farm and mineral imports to the West. Small manufacturers in the East also sought to maintain protective tariffs against foreign competition.[22]

Hoping to open up overseas markets to ease the depression at home,

six Senate progressives (Arthur Capper, Robert La Follette Jr., Peter Norbeck, George Norris, Henrik Shipstead, and Burton Wheeler) endorsed the
reciprocal trade bill of 1934. Nevertheless, Hiram Johnson won support
from several insurgents with an amendment excluding agricultural products from the bill's provisions. Picturing New Deal administrators as "internationalists" and irresponsible "freetraders," Johnson joined William
Borah and Gerald Nye in condemning the delegation of congressional
authority to the executive branch. "An emergency adds nothing to and
takes nothing from the Constitution," admonished Borah. The Idahoan
complained that the trade bill stripped Congress of its taxing power and
empowered administration "theorists" to destroy regional industries they
deemed inefficient. Despite these attempts, Johnson's amendment failed,
and the opposition of six progressives (Bronson Cutting, Lynn Frazier,
Huey Long, Johnson, Nye, and Borah) was not sufficient to defeat the bill.[23]

When reciprocity came up for renewal in 1937, Arthur Capper and
Joseph O'Mahoney, an antimonopolist from Wyoming, joined the opposition. By now the Court fight had increased progressive sensitivity to presidential power and given substance to William Borah's fears about delegating congressional authority. All insurgents except Robert La Follette Jr.
and George Norris supported a Republican amendment to require a two-
thirds vote of the Senate to ratify trade treaties. When the proviso failed,
the bill passed by a wider margin than in 1934. Progressives found themselves caught between loyalty to local producers and concern about urban
consumers. Wisconsin's La Follette supported reciprocal trade. Yet all seven
of the state's House Progressives opposed the measure in order to protect
local dairy farmers and penalize eastern industrialists. Montana's Burton
Wheeler voted for reciprocity in both 1934 and 1937 because he hoped
to lower the price of manufactured goods for western consumers, but the
senator also sought higher duties on raw materials to bolster the purchasing power of western miners.[24]

When the trade bill came up for still another extension in 1940, progressives joined other Roosevelt critics in attacking the president's executive power and growing internationalism. As opponents linked the economist interests of small producers to constitutional criticism of presidential
treaty making, they moved toward outright nationalism. Representative
Allen Treadway, the ranking Republican member of the House Ways and
Means Committee, called for an amendment to guarantee that home producers had the same opportunities that foreign competitors had. Millard
D. Brown, president of Continental Mills, accused the administration of
reducing U.S. living standards to the levels of Italy, Japan, "or other so-
called favored nations." "Is it any wonder," persisted Brown, "that the once
conservative Democratic party has fallen into the hands of men who are

purposely sabotaging our American system?" Robert La Follette Jr., Henrik Shipstead, and Burton Wheeler joined Senate opposition to the 1940 tariff bill, but the administration prevailed in a tight 42-37 vote.[25]

Franklin Roosevelt's executive reorganization plan triggered similar fears of presidential dictatorship. Ignored by Congress during the Court controversy of 1937, the reorganization bill came before the Senate early the next year. It sought to expand the White House staff, strengthen the management agencies of the federal government, and authorize the president to create new cabinet departments with independent agencies under their supervision. Its most controversial provision, however, required a two-thirds vote by Congress to reject future presidential reorganization proposals. William Borah and Burton Wheeler once again rallied Senate opponents. "The problem which confronts us," the Idahoan proclaimed, "is the restraining and controlling of the remarkable bureaucratic growth in this country." Borah attacked bureaucracy as a taxpayer burden destructive of democratic government. Concurring, Wheeler predicted to the *New York Times* that "some professor from Dartmouth, or Yale, or Harvard, or Columbia" would direct the White House program.[26]

New Dealers dismissed reorganization opponents as enemies of liberalism. The president himself privately described Senator Wheeler as a "New England conservative, the same as Calvin Coolidge." For similar reasons a North Dakota Democrat painted Gerald Nye as "a candidate of the reactionaries." Yet progressives consistently tied their resistance to government centralization and executive power to their belief in democratic values. Harry Sauthoff, a Progressive from Wisconsin, attacked reorganization for granting "one man the power, not only to reorganize 130 different agencies, but to completely abolish any or all of them without any veto power in the legislative branch." Sauthoff summarized the sentiments of Wisconsin's four other House Progressives when he declared the measure "too strong for me to swallow." Sentiment across the nation split over the issue, with 17 percent of a national sample backing more power for the president, 42 percent favoring less, and 41 percent wanting no change.[27]

Senate western dissidents such as Arthur Capper, Hiram Johnson, and Henrik Shipstead shared the obsession with executive bureaucracy and joined all the other insurgents except Robert La Follette Jr. and George Norris in voting to recommit the reorganization scheme to committee. When the motion failed by a 48-43 vote, administration leaders pushed through approval of the bill by a vote of 49 to 42. The measure faced stiff opposition by anti-Roosevelt forces in the House, however. Under fire from demonstrations and telegram campaigns organized by the National Committee to Uphold Constitutional Government and Father Coughlin, the president compromised by reducing the proposed congressional veto from two-thirds to a bare majority. Nevertheless, opponents succeeded in returning the measure to committee in a close 204-196 vote. It was not until 1939 that a diluted version of the executive reorganization bill finally passed House scrutiny.[28]

Concerns over arbitrary power, executive prerogative, taxation, and spending all jelled in the specter of the federal bureaucracy. "The New Deal administration is on the wrong track," Senator Capper from Kansas declared on the radio in 1938: "It is attempting to attain worthwhile objectives by . . . regimentation of the individual, concentration of all powers of the federal government in the hands of the executive, and substitution of a central government at Washington for state and local government." Insurgents joined conservatives in complaining that regulatory commissions often carried out instructions from the executive branch instead of fulfilling their obligation to implement congressional will. A 1940 staff memo from the office of Robert A. Taft, the Republican senator from Ohio, questioned the delegation of legislative power to administrative agencies, the exercise of judicial power by politically appointed administrators, and the issuance of regulations without statutory or judicial standing in law.[29]

New Deal critics tied accusations of bloated bureaucracy to complaints about excessive taxation of ordinary producers. A 1938 study by the Republican National Committee asserted that taxes diverted 23 percent of national income and that levies on consumption particularly hurt low-income groups. Such evidence suggested an emerging concert of interest between the besieged middle class and the more affluent. The new alliance surfaced in 1938 when Congress refused an administration request to raise personal income taxes and remove tax exemptions on federal securities. Although Senators Borah, La Follette Jr., and Norris managed to win approval for a flat 18 percent levy on corporate income, Congress erased the undistributed profits tax, lowered capital gains rates, and insisted on special tax exemptions for small business. Enraged, Roosevelt let the measure become law without a signature.[30]

✦ ✦ ✦

By the late 1930s rising public expenditures had become a central focus of a coalition of insurgent progressives and antigovernment forces in both parties. Sixty-one percent of a 1939 national sample thought federal spending was too high. Many members of Congress had supported New Deal legislation as emergency measures, not permanent programs. Government spending, Henrik Shipstead told the Senate, was "merely a temporary palliative to give us a breathing spell," not a solution to the problems of purchasing power and prosperity. Noting that relief had been designed as a temporary response to joblessness and hunger, Hiram Johnson warned that "the thing that most perils our form of government has been the yielding of the power of Congress under the stress of emergency."[31]

Progressives shared New Deal critics' contention that heavy relief allotments benefited urban and working-class areas at the expense of agricultural and middle-class sectors of the economy. Once they believed that the worst of the depression had abated in their own constituencies, many members of Congress resisted federal relief. Gerald Nye recalled that by 1937 he sensed that the New Deal's temporary emergency measures had become permanent, costly, and burdensome. From the perspective of progressive insurgents, New Deal liberalism appeared to spawn interest group conflict and class warfare at the expense of the independent middle class. Henrik Shipstead expressed this view when he observed that administration methods were "brewed in the cauldron of economic ignorance and class hatreds." "Prejudices generated by the New Deal," complained Shipstead, "leave our people more divided than at any time throughout our whole history."[32]

Many Americans responded to the threat of government spending, bureaucracy, and taxation by reasserting traditional producer values. North Dakota's William Lemke noted with impatience that the New Deal's $54 billion budget had "done nothing towards making men and women self-supporting." Constituent mail resonated with similar themes. The loudest Roosevelt supporters in town, two Wisconsinites told Senator La Follette, were not fit to influence anyone imbued with honesty, ambition, and courage. With the president's "soft palaver and great promises," they complained, he had "gained the confidence of all the riff-raff, nit-wits, have-nots, dumb-bells, and so, and got their votes, and then has the crust to always be talking about a mandate from the people." Letters poured into Henrik Shipstead's office on the topic of relief. "The regimentation on the part of our government has destroyed confidence, paralyzed business, and trespassed upon our individual liberty," complained a St. Paul writer. "So many people have become content to be dependent on the government that the morale of the people has been lowered."[33]

Such evocations of the producer ethic frequently came from those who identified themselves as ordinary Americans. "If the president could get his ear close enough to the ground to hear the ever-growing rumble against all this relief from all we common 'in between people,'" a Minnesota farm couple wrote to Senator Shipstead, "he would not ask for more money to be passed out to the class of people who are on relief." The correspondents asked that welfare be confined to necessary food instead of cash that allowed recipients to run cars, buy gas, go to dances, and consume beer. In a similar fashion, the struggling wife of a St. Paul restaurant owner vented her frustrations:

It is so depressing when we have to work so many hours as poor small business people—no union regulates hours for us—nor helps us get a wage minimum—no government cares where we drum up the business to pay compensation and taxes. I have no fit dress to attend church. My children wear old patched underwear that was cast off by relief clients who got new things from the government agencies. The dolesters' children can throw fresh tomatoes at 8¢ a piece around in the alleys while our children must economize on milk. The criminal waste makes any sensible honest person weep.[34]

Insurgent discomfort with relief aggravated the growing rift with the White House. When Roosevelt asked for more than $3 billion for work relief in the recession year of 1938, both Arthur Capper and the New Deal loyalist George Norris questioned the wisdom of the request. Only when the Appropriations Committee added some $300 million in farm parity payments did the Senate approve the measure. Hiram Johnson was one of eight senators to oppose the bill. Bitterly against any extension of government power, the Californian listed "horrid implications" to spending, such as totalitarianism, inflation, and repudiation of national debts. The following year insurgents split over the administration's unsuccessful attempt to restore $150 million to the WPA budget. Ultimately, only Robert La Follette Jr., George Norris, and Burton Wheeler sided with Roosevelt. Meanwhile, progressives unanimously supported the Hatch Act of 1939, which struck out at the administration by, among other things, outlawing the use of relief funds for electoral purposes.[35]

The deepening alienation between insurgents and President Roosevelt spilled over into agricultural issues. Western progressives of the 1930s straddled a curious contradiction. They hoped to limit government assistance to temporary economic emergencies and not engender a federal bureaucracy they deeply distrusted, yet rural members of Congress maintained government aid to small farmers was shamefully inadequate. In 1938 all the western progressives except Robert La Follette Jr. and George Norris voted to limit application of the administration's farm bill to two years. Although the legislation set up a new AAA that limited crop acreage in exchange for commodity loans and parity payments, insurgents and other rural congressional leaders insisted that cost-of-production guarantees should replace marketing quotas. They also attacked the second AAA as a nonemergency program drafted by bureaucrats who compromised farmers' independence.[36]

Fears of centralized power and suspicion of White House motives led to insurgent denunciations of Franklin Roosevelt in the 1938 congressional elections. The chief executive's call for voters to choose "liberals" and reject anti–New Dealers in the Democratic primaries led to charges that he was emulating Joseph Stalin's dictatorial "purge" of the Soviet Communist party. The "ruthlessness of the president," protested Hiram Johnson, "seems to me compelling proof that he has reached such a despotic and unreasonable state of mind that he will tolerate no man who disagrees with him." With 61 percent of a national sample critical of Roosevelt's actions, the primary strategy failed in most cases. In the general election Republicans gained six seats in the Senate and eighty-one in the House. Most Republican advances came in the Midwest and West, where the recession eroded confidence in the administration's ability to restore prosperity. Among the new Republican members of Congress were Senator Robert Taft of Ohio and Representative Karl E. Mundt of South Dakota.[37]

✦ ✦ ✦

Not all western insurgents sought political alternatives to urban liberalism and the New Deal by embracing outright conservatism. In Minnesota the thirty-nine-year-old sensation Floyd B. Olson won the 1930 governor's race on the Farmer-Labor ticket. An attorney who had worked as a manual laborer in shipyards, railroads, and mines, Olson advocated agricultural cost of production, state ownership of utilities, exemption of low-income families from property taxes, and a government-owned central bank. In 1932 the governor declared a moratorium on mortgage sales until the legislature acted. When opponents tried to defeat a relief bill, he threatened martial law. "I am a radical," explained Olson. Nevertheless, the three-term governor cut spending to its lowest point since 1921 and followed a reformist program of establishing business cooperatives, increasing public regulation of utilities, and initiating environmental legislation.[38]

North Dakota's William ("Wild Bill") Langer provided another midwestern mixture of agrarian radicalism and traditional values. Running for governor in 1932 as a Republican endorsed by the Nonpartisan League, Langer confronted a state economy racked by a three-year drought, $25 million in unpaid taxes, and a third to half of its people on relief. The candidate denounced eastern chain banks and promised to make tax and budget cuts, restore farm prices, and create jobs. Once in office, he acted to salvage state credit by transferring gasoline tax receipts to a bond retirement fund. Meanwhile, Langer approved a 52 percent cut in state property levies and agreed to a sales tax (subsequently rescinded by voters). The governor also declared a state bank holiday and a moratorium on all debts and mortgage foreclosures. Under the leadership of Langer and the populist Usher Burdick, a Farm Holiday convention instructed producers to establish county councils of defense against court takeovers. The governor completed his program by issuing embargoes on the sale of wheat and livestock, although a federal court later invalidated the order.[39]

Beset by the midwestern farm crisis, Langer, Olson, and the governors of South Dakota and Iowa met in Des Moines in October 1933 to map joint agricultural policies. When President Roosevelt rejected their plan for price-fixing, the North Dakotan exploded: "We just voted one son-of-a-bitch out of office and can do it again." Such outbursts reflected the distrust many of the region's farmers felt toward New Deal Washington. Roosevelt Democrats returned the hostility. As Langer carried on a primary fight for reelection in 1934, a federal court convicted him of illegally soliciting campaign contributions from state employees who handled federal relief funds. Two days after his primary victory, Langer faced an eighteen-month prison sentence. The state supreme court subsequently ruled him disqualified for office.[40]

The Langer case demonstrated how regional leaders could exploit grassroots anger toward Washington. After a reversal by a federal appeals panel, a hung jury in a second trial, and an acquittal in a third, the North Dakota politician returned to the governorship in a successful independent candidacy in 1936. He soon extended the sales tax, set up state unemployment insurance, expanded relief programs, and established soil conservation districts. Yet questionable bond transactions and a purge of faculty at the state agricultural college renewed charges that Langer was building a corrupt political machine. These controversies plagued the North Dakotan when he declared his candidacy for the Senate in 1940.[41]

The clearest embodiment of 1930s progressive insurgence came in the Wisconsin governorships of Philip F. La Follette, son of the state's late and celebrated progressive senator. At thirty-one, the intense and enthusiastic La Follette became the youngest governor in Wisconsin history in 1930. His inaugural address noted the dislocating effects of "new forms of credit control, new forms of power development and distribution, and new forms of corporate organization." La Follette signed a steeply graduated income tax, dropped a state tax on farm income, approved state unemployment compensation, expanded relief and public works, and created plans for public power and tighter regulation of utilities. In 1932, however, Republican regulars charged that Wisconsin government was inundated by communists, and they defeated the incumbent in the party primary. Democrats followed national trends by sweeping to power.[42]

Seeking to explore a realignment of national politics in 1933, Philip La Follette hosted a Chicago conference of some twenty-five progressive leaders, including his brother, Senator Robert La Follette Jr., and the insurgent solons Bronson Cutting, Lynn Frazier, Hiram Johnson, George Norris, Gerald Nye, and Henrik Shipstead. On the ninth anniversary of their father's death the following year, the La Follettes announced the formation of the Wisconsin Progressive party. Senator La Follette told the group's opening conference that the nation needed a third party free from control of organized wealth. But his brother set the tone for the movement when he noted that "the great bulk of our people are not farmers first or laborers first—we must appeal to them as Americans, and not to them on the basis of their occupations. . . . I think it is a fatal error, an irretrievable blunder, to launch this as a class party."[43]

The Progressive party's fourteen-point declaration called for publicly owned utilities and banks, debt moratorium laws, full employment, nationwide unemployment insurance and social security, protection for collective bargaining, and taxes on corporate dividends and inheritances. As Senator La Follette accepted the Progressive designation for his reelection race, Philip announced his intention to seek the governorship on the party ticket. Insurgent senators flocked to Wisconsin to support the La Follette team. "People are realizing," the North Dakotan Lynn Frazier told crowds, "that the working people, farmers, and small business men have been discriminated against and that there must be a general readjustment before we can get back to normal times." The La Follette organization pioneered the use of mass mailings geared to recipients' particular interests. Voters responded to its message by electing both brothers, sending seven Progressives to the House of Representatives, and providing the party with a plurality in the Wisconsin lower house.[44]

Philip La Follette's second governorship advanced unemployment insurance, mortgage relief, public works, the graduated income tax, property tax relief, and banking reform. The governor sought to use the profit motive to make business regulate itself. Wisconsin workers' compensation and unemployment programs, for example, raised premiums on factories with high accident and turnover rates and rewarded employers with better records. La Follette easily won reelection in 1936 with a record tally. Meanwhile, the Farmer-Labor party of neighboring Minnesota sent Elmer A. Benson to the state house. These triumphs led the progressive *Madison Capital Times* to anticipate "a new political realignment in the nation which will defeat the reactionary forces."[45]

✦ ✦ ✦

A combination of tactical and ideological considerations had long prevented Governor La Follette from identifying with such third-party movements as the Farmer-Labor Progressive Federation. Formed in 1933 by radical intellectuals seeking humane alternatives to capitalism, the federation helped create Wisconsin's Progressive party in 1934. La Follette never joined because he worried that such slogans as "production for use" symbolized socialism and big government to ruralites and old-time progressives who sought to preserve traditional values. The governor also remained loyal to President Roosevelt's New Deal. As recession returned to the economy in the summer of 1937, however, the Wisconsinite became convinced that White House policies had destroyed the president's prestige. In July Roosevelt told La Follette that he opposed more work relief programs because the depression was over. The governor began to question such administration policies as deficit spending, the restriction of agricultural production, and unproductive welfare payments.[46]

The basic difference between the New Deal and midwestern progressivism, Philip La Follette noted in his memoirs, was progressives' determination to use the nation's productive power to overcome economic stagnation. By 1938 the Wisconsin leader hoped to move government to "stimulate individual initiative through collective action." He told the *Nation*'s Max Lerner that he had never been more than a New Deal "fellow traveler." President Roosevelt's response to the depression, observed La Follette, was merely "a cross between socialism, technocracy, and what used to be called . . . 'the new capitalism.'" The governor criticized state collectivism and rejected the language of class conflict. "The way out is not by division of our wealth," he told the Economic Club of New York in February 1938, "but by multiplying it." Calling for a new realignment that fused the individualism of Republicans with the common action of Democrats, La Follette sought to broaden the Progressive movement's electoral base of farmers, workers, and small business people.[47]

After meetings with Wisconsin Progressive party leaders in March 1938, Governor La Follette consulted with labor, farm, student, publishing, and business groups as well as midwestern progressives. Ensuing correspondence confirmed the leader's suspicions about independent producers' grievances. One writer pointed out that tax-exempt bonds had produced $37 billion in federal obligations and had contributed to a national debt of more than $90 million a day. A Farmer-Labor congressional representative from Minnesota concurred with La Follette's criticism of President Roosevelt's spending and borrowing policies. Others pleaded the case for small banks and businesses against financial consolidations and monopolies and pointed to insufficient credit extended by chain lenders. Farmers protested high interest rates, excessive relief expenditures, and "artificially created scarcity." A Milwaukee attorney called for a new party to place the needs of producers and consumers before the profit of owners.[48]

Sentiment for a national progressive party, built "from the bottom up," appeared to support Philip La Follette's aspirations. In April 1938 he took a major step toward this goal by delivering four network radio addresses. The Wisconsin governor called for reorganization of the national economy so that unemployed Americans might support themselves and contribute to the country's wealth. "Are we going to get down to business and really master our difficulties," he asked, "or are we going to go on tinkering and patching?" La Follette accused both Herbert Hoover and Franklin Roosevelt of using deficit spending and public works "to mark time until prosperity returned." He insisted that economic well-being resulted from the unrestricted industrial and agricultural production of "real wealth."[49]

La Follette soon announced the convening of an April 28 meeting to discuss the future of progressivism. As four to five thousand people gathered for the evening event at the University of Wisconsin's livestock pavilion, the National Guard stood by, a color guard and drum and bugle corps circled the arena, and a band played patriotic songs. University athletes in red and white letter-sweaters served as ushers. Philip La Follette ascended the banner-draped stage amid flags, cheers, and spotlights to deliver an emotional hundred-minute speech. The governor blamed the rise of global military dictatorships on the widespread failure to produce enough real wealth to support secure living standards. La Follette rejected the autocratic dictatorships of communism and fascism and criticized socialism for rewarding individual needs instead of individual contributions. Old-fashioned capitalism had failed, he warned, but socialists were unable to understand that human nature had not changed.[50]

Rejecting old models, La Follette promised a "new frontier" at home, "a new economic order" in which the nation could use sound investment and economic reform to create increased demand for its products. The real difference among Americans, he asserted, was one between producers or earners of wealth and those who collected it. The governor argued that abundance must be created by useful work, not by curbing production or going into debt. He attacked New Deal "coddling or spoon feeding" and insisted that government could take collective action for "orderly progress" without destroying individual initiative.[51]

La Follette's answer to the challenge of the Great Depression and modern alienation was the National Progressives of America (NPA), a new political party whose insignia would be a blue X set in a white background and surrounded by a red circle. The governor explained how the cross symbolized the ballot, equality, and the multiplication of wealth while the circle represented unity. The NPA's organizing principles included government-controlled banks and monetary policy to stimulate investment, safeguards against the executive branch's arbitrary use of power, a guaranteed annual income, and nonintervention in European affairs. "Whatever it may cost, so help us God," he cried, "we shall use the power of the United States to restore to every American the opportunity to help himself." "In the best sense," concluded La Follette, "this new crusade is a religious cause."[52]

✦ ✦ ✦

Within a month the charismatic governor had received twenty-five thousand letters of support. During the summer and fall of 1938 organizing tours carried the dynamic speaker across the Northeast and Midwest. Brother Robert endorsed the effort by proclaiming that Progressives sought a functional "middle way." Nevertheless, the NPA faced serious difficulties. As an action-oriented pragmatist, La Follette had openly expressed impatience with bickering liberals and intellectuals, whom he expected would resent any challenge to their leadership. Perhaps this explained why New York City mayor Fiorello La Guardia was the only progressive of national standing that La Follette had consulted. Union leaders immediately perceived that the governor had failed to follow his father's 1924 strategy of winning third-party endorsements from the railroad brotherhoods and national labor organizations. The *Nation*'s Max Lerner warned that CIO leaders would remember that "a party that starts out to keep clear of the labor stigma may end by fighting labor."[53]

Liberal journals such as the *Nation* criticized the middle-class base of the NPA and noted the absence of support from such groups as the Farmer-Labor Progressive Federation. "Of course, we can both understand," an NPA supporter and New York municipal judge wrote to La Follette, "how progressive labor leaders who have gained so much through the Roosevelt administration hate to consider anything . . . that might jeopardize their present gains." New Deal loyalists, such as Senator Norris and the Wisconsin newspaper editor William T. Evjue, also feared disruption of the progressive alliance with liberals. A third party was premature, editorialized *Common Sense*, the voice of the democratic left, in reference to the conviction among labor and liberal intellectuals that any new political alignment must coalesce around the New Deal. "Roosevelt has got your and my cause further ahead in half a decade than we together and alone could have done in two decades," an Illinois legislator and Democratic reformer lectured La Follette.[54]

Urban progressives and liberals also objected to Philip La Follette's broad attacks on relief, monetary policy, and internationalism. Writing to University of Chicago president Robert M. Hutchins, a retired businessman suggested that the governor's "hoary and meaningless" monetarism could only be compatible "with a totalitarian regime." Others, such as the sympathetic William Benton, called for La Follette to abandon "opportunism" and focus on specifics. A friend at the *New York Times* privately noted that the governor was "talking a language that at the moment is strange to most people." No one was clear "where he was going or how he proposed to get there," concluded the *Nation*'s Max

Lerner. The editor of the liberal *New Republic* actually sent La Follette a questionnaire eliciting his views on relief, social security, crop restrictions, farm parity prices, and labor issues. What positive measures besides nationalized banks, he asked, did the governor favor that were not already included in Roosevelt's programs?[55]

Philip La Follette believed that only liberal intellectuals cared about specific programs and that ordinary people sought qualities of leadership rather than blueprints. He told Max Lerner that a broad-based movement could not afford to offend potential supporters with premature details. But urban progressives and liberals mistrusted La Follette's invocations of "rugged individualism." They also recoiled at the frank use of mystical nationalism, which the governor described as "a deep and slumbering force . . . with enormous power for evoking middle-class and mass support." In a period in which many sensed the danger of Germany's National Socialists, talk of a single, united political party stirred serious misgivings.[56]

Aware of the powerful effects of pageantry and symbolism in Europe's dictatorships of the 1930s, La Follette understood that people sought meaning and a sense of belonging in political movements. The *New York Herald Tribune* columnist Dorothy Thompson brilliantly captured this aspect of the NPA's strategy. "How refreshing it is to hear a speech from the non-Marxist left," exulted Thompson, "cut itself loose from the social work, settlement house, and benevolent feudal landlord mentality that has dominated the New Deal." Thompson noted that La Follette had learned the psychological appeal of fascism, which made demands on its followers instead of offering benefits. The leader of the NPA embodied the technique of modern politics, she observed, by appealing to the vast unorganized masses as individuals.[57]

Philip La Follette consciously devised the NPA insignia to embody an imagery appropriate to mass democracy. Yet critics from *Time* and *Life* to *Common Sense* mocked the emblem as a "circumscribed swastika" reminiscent of Nazi Germany or as a religiously exclusive Christian cross. "Some feel that it's . . . taking a page from the fascist book," a La Follette loyalist reported, "some think it's frankly absurd. Others . . . that it's out of place in American politics." President Roosevelt privately wondered whether the United States would soon see a movement with some "new form of arm salute." Thompson also expressed serious reservations. "The banners, the crusade, the exaggerated emotional appeal, and the exaggerated nationalism are all somewhat disturbing," she wrote. Mixing economics and mysticism, warned Thompson, could ignite an intolerance resulting in fanatical totalitarianism.[58]

As the 1938 elections neared, the NPA seemed to divide the progressive movement. National polls suggested that the party could take no more than 7 percent of the vote in a presidential election. In Iowa Farmer-Laborites split on whether to endorse La Follette's party. Minnesota's Farmer-Labor governor Benson refused it any assistance. In California the NPA supported its own candidate against a Democrat backed by organized labor and urban liberals. At home in Wisconsin La Follette had to best a Farmer-Labor candidate for the gubernatorial nomination of his own party. Once he won the primary, he faced a fusion candidate backed by both Democrats and Republicans. On election day, Julius P. Heil, a stalwart Republican, defeated the head of the NPA ticket by 183,000 votes. The Progressive delegation lost five of its seven House seats in Washington and twenty-four of a combined sixty-seven in the state legislature.[59]

Within weeks the NPA was dead, and Philip La Follette was gone from electoral politics. When the Minnesota Farmer-Labor party invited him to address its 1940 convention, a state industrial union official protested that the former governor was "a crackpot." La Follette delivered his normal recipe of NPA principles, but he also told the delegates that their activities were "worth more to the rank and file of Minnesota and America than all the high-falutin' dissertations of languid liberals and rocking-chair radicals combined." La Follette had tried to unite New Deal supporters and opponents, urbanites and ruralites, the working and middle class. But the charismatic leader's refusal to communicate in customary definitions of liberalism and conservatism appeared to confuse potential allies. His fusion of producer values and mystical nationalism also contravened loyalties to consumerism and the welfare state shared by urban intellectuals, labor leaders, corporate officials, and New Deal administrators. By 1940 Philip La Follette was a leader without a movement, a populist without a party.[60]

✦ ✦ ✦

The political scientist David Green has suggested that Franklin Roosevelt set the terms of 1930s political discourse by equating conservatism with limited government for the few and liberalism with generous welfare for the multitude. Yet as the president sought to sustain the alliance between loyal Democrats and progressives, his efforts became increasingly problematic. New Dealers never sufficiently understood the social historian Catherine McNicol Stock's insight that the depression and 1930s political reform empowered a "new" middle class. Farm mechanization, class polarization, the growth of professions, and creeping bureaucracy had been shaping the nation's hinterland since the 1880s. The county agricultural agents, relief officials, social workers, academic experts, attorneys, advertisers, and chain store managers of the depression decade supplied explicit examples of the erosion of community control that had been occurring for half a century.[61]

As Alan Brinkley has argued, the Great Depression forced Americans to acknowledge the transition of economic power from small, local interests to private and public bureaucracies of national scope. As modernism took its toll, individual communities struggled to retain control of their destinies. The loss of autonomy particularly threatened small-town bankers, merchants, manufacturers, and others in the "old" middle class. For these citizens and others, an intrusive federal government symbolized the daily threat to individual and traditional values. The twin evils of New Deal collectivism and egalitarianism also were tied to White House intellectuals and planners whose interests lay with urban ethnic minorities, organized labor, and northern blacks. Outside the privileged sectors of the metropolitan market and national power structure, the insurgent constituency found its economic interests, political concerns, and social prestige in jeopardy.[62]

By the late 1930s old progressives thought New Deal reform was defined by urban liberals looking to a consumer democracy of abundance instead of a republic of citizen producers. In an era increasingly molded by the corporate culture of private and public organizations, recalcitrant elements struck out at the emerging network of impersonal institutions and relationships. Ideologically opposed to concentrations of economic and political power, insurgents portrayed New Deal intervention as illegitimate "statism" harmful to American character and democracy and the interests of their constituents. As they expressed the complaints of the middle-class producers and businesspeople who continued to dominate their home bases, insurgents turned their ire on centralized government and bureaucracy.[63]

The estrangement between the Roosevelt administration and old progressives certainly was gradual. Although the president sometimes grumbled that progressive senators were unreliable individualists, in the end they supported the New Deal in more than a third of key roll-call votes. In contrast, less than a fifth of the votes of the ten most conservative Democratic senators backed Roosevelt on the same issues. The entire Republican delegation cast less than 4 percent of comparable votes for the administration. Nevertheless, by 1938 William Borah, Arthur Capper, Lynn Frazier, Hiram Johnson, Gerald Nye, and Henrik Shipstead all supported mainstream Republicans in their home states. In North Dakota Nye attacked government spending and presidential power in a successful reelection bid that depended on contributions from stalwart Republicans.[64]

More dramatic evidence of insurgent turnabouts came in Montana, where Burton Wheeler, long a Roosevelt ally, charged in 1938 that Representative Jerry J. O'Connell, a Democrat who supported the president's Court plan, had become the administration's exclusive recipient of local patronage. When O'Connell worked with organized labor to undermine the senator's power base, Wheeler helped a conservative Republican defeat him in a stunning November upset. Minnesota's Henrik Shipstead appeared to follow a similar path when he left the Farmer-Labor party in 1940 to run for reelection as a Republican, although he insisted he would campaign on "progressive principles." Meanwhile, the White House predicted that Senator La Follette would face defeat in 1940 if Wisconsin Progressives failed to cooperate with the Democrats, and Roosevelt speculated about finding a candidate to defeat Hiram Johnson.[65]

By 1938, one scholar has concluded, the views of progressive Republicans were "indistinguishable from those of conservatives of both parties." Yet such judgments use Franklin Roosevelt's definitions of political discourse as their basis. Burton Wheeler addressed this issue in his autobiography when he insisted on equating "liberalism" with resistance to concentrated political and economic power and the guarantee of equal opportunity. Although associated with "liberal" and "progressive" politics, recalled the senator, he consistently thought of himself as a "conservative" defender of the American heritage. Wheeler denied that he ever made the "classic swing from left to right." Instead, he argued that "while the times, the issues, and the leaders have changed, my basic outlook has remained the same. I don't know if there is a label for this philosophy; I never felt one was necessary. . . . I agree with the 'liberals' when they are on the side of justice for the individual and against the concentration of economic power and I agree with the 'conservatives' in their opposition to the buildup of centralized power in the federal government."[66]

Wheeler's views on liberalism found resonance in the political ideas of Karl Mundt, the Republican from South Dakota. A high school and college speech teacher, Mundt fashioned a successful 1938 campaign for the House on opposition to New Deal principles. In one of his first speeches as a senator, the South Dakotan defined liberalism as a philosophy of self-government that protected the common people from monopoly. New Dealers masqueraded as "liberals," "progressives," or "moderns," argued Mundt, but they really were "tories" opposed to self-rule. Like Wheeler and the western insurgents, Mundt saw no difference between the abuses of economic monopolists and those of political overlords. One of the first to describe government centralization as "statist," he accused the Roosevelt administration of importing "Old World economic ideals and political policies." The New Deal, contended Mundt, provided bureaucrats with management rights belonging to producers and average citizens.[67]

Mundt's politics expressed a profound midwestern suspicion of concentrated power. As early as 1935 regional Republicans had convened a conference of "grass-rooters" to seek constructive alternatives to the New Deal.

Attacking "unsound, un-American, and unconstitutional" policies implemented by "demagogic methods and academic theorists," the participants had demanded recovery along "sane, sound, and American lines." By 1939 anti-Washington sentiment had become a central tenet of national politics. A Gallup poll of that year reported that 52 percent of Americans saw themselves as conservative and 46 percent as liberal. Meanwhile, another survey found that 88 percent of respondents viewed themselves as middle class.[68] As the depression decade closed, politicians representing traditional producers and enterprisers adopted an increasingly critical approach to centralized political power. Equally fundamental schisms were emerging over foreign policy. Their lasting impact would complete the rupture between New Deal liberalism and insurgent progressivism.

8

The Noninterventionist Insurgency, 1935–41

"We cannot and we must not ask American boys to die upon the bloody battlefields of Europe and Asia," Montana's Burton K. Wheeler warned the Senate in the summer of 1941, "in order to establish liberty denied to the people of the United States."[1] Wheeler's plea encapsuled fears that a war against foreign dictatorships might accelerate the trend to totalitarianism in the United States. Beleaguered by economic depression and repelled by European posturing and instability, many Americans preferred an "isolationist" approach to international diplomacy in the 1930s. Noninterventionists hoped to substitute unilateral conduct of foreign policy for overseas alliances and military commitments. As a substantial antiwar movement crested before Pearl Harbor, activists recycled many of the domestic concerns of New Deal critics. Anxieties over concentrated power and regimentation contributed significantly to the "great debate" over war and peace. For both internationalists and noninterventionists the stakes appeared enormous.

❖ ❖ ❖

Herbert Hoover and Franklin Roosevelt had both been compelled to deal with the continuing unpopularity of American commitments to Europe. Although Allied war debts had been converted to long-term, low-interest notes in the 1920s, European governments were unable to repay them in a depressed market. Hoover attempted to alleviate the problem by agreeing to a one-year debt moratorium in 1931. But such insurgent progressives as Hiram Johnson feared that this action would lead to outright cancellation. Johnson chaired a Senate inquiry into the investment community in 1931 and 1932. He charged that the State Department had helped arrange questionable loans to Latin American governments without alerting small banks that purchased the notes from New York lenders. Johnson's investigation also disclosed that J. P. Morgan and other investors wanted to cancel government loans to Europe so that private obligations could be repaid. An outspoken critic of government and corporate cooperation in the 1920s, the California senator concluded that the State Department continued to serve the interests of international bankers.[2]

Johnson responded to the abuses uncovered by his inquiry by introducing the debt default bill in 1932. The measure prohibited private loans or bond sales to foreign governments in default of obligations to the United States. Although the proposal initially targeted Latin American governments, Johnson shifted focus when he began to fear that Roosevelt might move to cancel the European debt. Denouncing investment bankers, the internationalist press, and cosmopolitan intellectuals, the California insurgent charged that removal of the obligations would compel American taxpayers to foot the bill that Europeans were unwilling to pay. As a proud nationalist, Johnson reminded listeners that only Congress could settle the debt question.[3]

Once President Roosevelt took office in 1933, Congress postponed action on a newly drafted version of Johnson's bill. The following year the senator accepted a proviso that limited the measure's applicability to governments that had defaulted on Treasury obligations. Johnson also agreed that the law would not apply to nations that previously had ceased debt payments. When both houses easily passed the Johnson bill, the president reluctantly signed it. The Californian believed that despite its compromises the act succeeded in undermining the nefarious connections between international finance and war. Like William Borah and Henrik Shipstead, he argued that loans enabled the governments of Europe to militarize and conduct senseless wars. Johnson also reasoned that the United States would have no grounds for armed intervention if financial investments were not at stake. The first sampling of American public opinion on the issue in 1938 revealed divided sentiment, with 47 percent supporting full collection of obligations, 42 percent favoring reduction, and 11 percent desiring cancellation.[4]

Rampant suspicions of elite intrigue underlay the war debts controversy. Western progressives such as Hiram Johnson touched a sensitive chord when they associated international finance with the manipulation of wealth instead of its production. A similar mix of populist economics and culture defined continuing opposition to U.S. membership in the World Court. President Calvin Coolidge had abandoned the campaign for a U.S. seat on the tribunal in 1926, but four years later Herbert Hoover submitted a reworked version of Court protocols. The Senate Foreign Relations Committee waited until 1932 to approve the proposal by a bare 11-9 majority. After three more years of delay the panel reported the bill to the floor, with reservations on the Court's ability to issue advisory opinions affecting the United States.[5]

Many of the nation's leading corporate executives, law professors, educators, and social workers supported U.S. membership on the Court as a step toward international peace and stability, but western insurgents continued their bitter denunciation of the tribunal throughout the Roosevelt administration. As in the 1920s, Republican progressives William Borah, Lynn Frazier, Hiram Johnson, Gerald Nye, Robert La Follette Jr., Peter Norbeck, George Norris, and Henrik Shipstead opposed Court membership. Democrats Huey Long and Burton Wheeler joined the opponents in 1935. Wheeler went on national radio to share his concern over unsettled conditions in Europe and the Court's connection to the League of Nations. The tribunal's decisions, "with their sanctions of force," he warned, "will be virtually breeding war." The Montana senator also noted that the European powers were hostile to reservations protecting U.S. autonomy.[6]

As the insurgents Hiram Johnson and William Borah led the anti-Court campaign on the Senate floor in 1935, William Randolph Hearst joined the fray with generous doses of nationalist sentiment in his nationwide chain of daily newspapers. But it was the compelling rhetoric of the radio priest Charles Coughlin that mobilized tens of thousands of telegrams imploring senators to defeat the protocols. Coughlin consistently equated internationalism with both communism and the global banking community. Two days before the final vote he initiated his first confrontation with the Roosevelt administration by delivering a broadcast sermon entitled "The Menace of the World Court." The Michigan cleric repeated charges that involvement with international bankers and European affairs would sacrifice U.S. sovereignty. Unwilling to risk political capital on the fight, President Roosevelt stood by as the Senate came seven votes shy of the two-thirds required for ratification. Twenty Democrats joined Court opponents in defeating the president's request for membership.[7]

✦   ✦   ✦

While the Senate resisted membership in the World Court, it moved to examine controversial ties between foreign policy and corporate interests. By 1934 a broad coalition of reformers had joined the call to eliminate profit making from war and prevent munitions dealers and financiers from encouraging its outbreak. The alliance not only embraced pacifists, church groups, and such liberal organs as the *Nation* and *New Republic* but also included the conservative American Legion and Henry Luce, publisher of *Fortune*. In March 1934 the American Legion and the Women's International League for Peace and Freedom backed a Senate resolution jointly sponsored by Gerald Nye and Michigan's Arthur H. Vandenberg Jr. The proposal called for legislation to decommercialize war and an investigation to determine if existing laws adequately controlled arms traffic. Nye's maneuvers resulted in the creation of a special Senate committee to carry out the inquiry. Once the Democratic leadership named its members, the panel chose Republican Nye as chair.[8]

A western progressive critical of high finance and the international trade in munitions, Gerald Nye used national radio to portray war profits as a challenge to global peace. In September 1934 he described the wartime gains of military contractors as "ungodly." The following month Nye dismissed munitions dealers as "nothing more than international racketeers bent upon gaining profit through a game of arming the world to fight itself." Doing away with financial incentives, he reasoned, "would materially remove the danger of more war." Nye subsequently told a radio audience that World War I had cost the nation an inflationary $33 billion, two-thirds of which the government borrowed.[9]

Between September 1934 and February 1936 the Nye Munitions Committee conducted some twenty-six weeks of public hearings. Its witness list included such arms producers as the Du Pont corporation, shipbuilders, aircraft manufacturers, industrial suppliers, and the investment banker J. P. Morgan. After issuing a preliminary bulletin in April 1935, the panel produced seven final reports in the next fourteen months. It concluded that bribery of government officials and collusive contract bidding had contributed to exorbitant profiteering in shipbuilding and other defense industries. The committee described an "alliance of the military with powerful economic groups to secure appropriations . . . for a constantly increasing military and naval establishment." It contended that the use of armed force served the economic interests of industrialists who supplied global arsenals. World peace, warned the panel, could not be achieved when munitions interests were "left free to goad and frighten nations into military activity."[10]

J. P. Morgan's testimony took the inquiry into the causes of U.S. involvement in World War I. The Nye committee concluded that private credits to the British and French gave "the great commercial and financial interests" a "vested interest in allied success." "Loans to belligerents militate against neutrality," observed the panel. Nye revealed his own reading of events by commenting that "bankers were in the heart and center of a system that made our going to war inevitable." The panel, however, assigned major responsibility to the executive branch of government. First, it noted that Washington had encouraged private arms sales to foreign governments and had provided technical assistance to military contractors. Second, the committee concluded that President Woodrow Wilson had consciously acted to protect U.S. economic interests in Europe. Despite the president's sincere devotion to peace and democracy, it declared, the situation created by munitions interests and bankers led him "to follow the course from which he dared not deviate."[11]

Nye's committee experiences led him to surmise that the executive branch played a central role in decisions of war and peace. Although the senator raised a furor when he referred to documents on record that indicated that President Wilson had "falsified" prior knowledge of Allied secret understandings, the controversy barely figured in the panel's final recommendations. The committee summary called for greater congressional power to tax war profits and eliminate tax exemptions for government bonds. It proposed (by a 4-3 vote) government ownership of munitions companies during peace. It also recommended the extension of existing neutrality protections, which included embargoes on the sale of arms to belligerents, prohibitions against loans and exports to warring nations, and bans against travel by U.S. citizens on belligerent ships. The lessons of the past seemed to indicate that armed conflict might be avoided by curtailing commerce with those at war.[12]

✦ ✦ ✦

As Gerald Nye described "giant fortunes carved by men and corporations out of war while millions died," the munitions inquiry gave unprecedented exposure to the noninterventionist position and helped make the Senate a major arena for national dialogue over foreign policy. Events in Europe also contributed to a sense of urgency. In 1935 Germany's Adolf Hitler repudiated the Treaty of Versailles and initiated rearmament under the direction of the National Socialists. An Italian invasion of Ethiopia also appeared likely. By the spring of 1935 the Nye hearings had yet to go beyond study of the munitions trade and profiteering by military contractors. Nevertheless, Nye and Bennett Champ Clark, a Democratic committee member from Missouri, moved toward a broader agenda by presenting the Senate with a set of proposals designed to keep the United States out of war.[13]

The Nye-Clark resolutions sought to cut off military equipment, loans, and American travel to warring nations. Although the Foreign Relations Committee struck out the proviso on loans, noninterventionists joined bill sponsors in filibustering until the Senate approved the measure before adjournment. Despite misgivings, Hiram Johnson supported the resolution as a statement of American intention "to keep out of European controversies, European wars, and European difficulties." Gerald Nye had reservations as well but called the package the most important piece of legislation of the current Congress. In August 1935 the legislation passed both houses without debate and received President Roosevelt's signature. It established a mandatory embargo on arms to nations at war, organized the licensing of military suppliers, and restricted travel on the ships of belligerents. Compromises limited the law to six months and gave the president discretion in determining the timing of its provisions.[14]

Gerald Nye and the noninterventionists resumed the campaign for strict neutrality just as J. P. Morgan testified before the munitions inquiry in January 1936. "It is utterly impossible for us to enjoy the profits from other people's wars," declared Nye, "and maintain a resolve to stay out of that war; impossible to be economically in a war while politically out of it." Nye and Champ Clark now proposed to extend the arms embargo against belligerents to a ban on loans and credits. Once again a compromise was reached when President Roosevelt signed the bill in February. The Neutrality Act of 1936 incorporated the loan prohibition and strengthened the arms embargo provisions, but it also gave the president discretion in determining when a state of war existed and limited the law's application to fourteen months.[15]

With backing from Nye, Arthur Vandenberg, and the Washington Democrat Homer T. Bone, Champ Clark introduced an amendment to the neutrality statute in February 1937. A former national commander of the American Legion, the Missouri Democrat sought a permanent law discouraging U.S. participation in foreign wars. With the outbreak of the Spanish civil war and increasing Japanese presence in China, noninterventionist opinion split on the details of the proposal. As a result, the Senate Foreign Relations Committee hammered out another compromise, which Congress passed and Roosevelt signed. While maintaining features of previous neutrality legislation, the 1937 law prohibited the arming of merchant ships involved in trade with belligerents. It also outlawed the use of U.S. vessels for transporting arms to warring nations. A two-year provision gave the president discretionary power to place the sale of nonmilitary goods to belligerents on a "cash-and-carry" basis.[16]

As world tensions escalated in 1937, Congress overrode the objections of such western noninterventionists as Arthur Capper, Lynn Frazier, Robert La Follette Jr., and Gerald Nye to approve an administration naval appropriation of more than $1 billion. When undeclared war broke out between China and Japan, Roosevelt critics called for invocation of the Neutrality Act. The president responded by forbidding government ships to transport arms to the belligerents. In October his "quarantine address" proposed international efforts to restrain lawlessness by aggressor nations.

Two months later the Japanese attacked an American gunboat escorting Standard Oil tankers on the Yangtze River.[17]

Threats of global war mobilized noninterventionist leaders. William Borah, who strenuously defended neutral rights of trade, nevertheless cautioned that democracies had no business "running around over the world trying to placate every situation and adjust every controversy." We must not be "missionaries with bayonets," warned Minnesota's Henrik Shipstead. Such concerns led to the recycling of the progressive concept of the war referendum early in 1938. Introduced as an amendment to the Constitution by Representative Louis Ludlow, a Democrat from Indiana, the proposal sought to ensure that congressional declarations of war would be subject to ratification by a majority of the electorate. The procedure was not to apply in cases of imminent or actual attack. A pet scheme of William Jennings Bryan, Charles Lindbergh Sr., and Robert La Follette, the war referendum had first been considered in 1917 and appeared as a plank in the Progressive party platform of 1924. Ludlow pictured his amendment as an attempt "to democratize the war power" among those who bore the "burdens and costs" of military conflict.[18]

Having seen his proposal die twice in committee since 1935, the Indiana representative sought and obtained the 218 House signatures necessary for discharge. As the date of congressional consideration approached, Ludlow organized a broad coalition of religious leaders, editors, educators, and retired military officers into the National Committee for the War Referendum. Although the Methodist and former rural journalist cleverly expropriated New Deal democratic rhetoric, a presidential message to the House rejected the amendment as "impracticable in its application and incompatible with our representative form of government." The Ludlow amendment "would cripple any president in his conduct of our foreign relations," warned Roosevelt, and make war more likely by encouraging others to "violate American rights with impunity." Despite strong support from the Great Plains and upper Mississippi valley, the House voted 209 to 188 to return the amendment to committee. An attempt by Robert La Follette Jr. and Gerald Nye to check "unlimited executive power" with a Senate version also failed.[19]

In October 1938, 68 percent of a national sample continued to support the Ludlow amendment, but deteriorating conditions in Europe complicated the noninterventionist argument. In the spring of 1938 Nazi Germany absorbed the nation of Austria. When the Germans threatened Czechoslovakia six months later, the British and French agreed to permit Berlin to annex the Sudetenland. A Gallup poll found that 59 percent of American respondents supported the Munich accords as a step toward peace. When the Nazis invaded the rest of Czechoslovakia in March 1939, Gallup found only 17 percent of its sample willing to send the U.S. military to help Britain and France if hostilities erupted. Convinced that threats of war required strict U.S. impartiality, Gerald Nye led efforts to retain the arms embargo and cash-and-carry. As the Senate Foreign Relations Committee held hearings on neutrality, however, an opinion survey found 57 percent supported legislation permitting the sale of military goods to Britain and France in the event of war. In May 1939 the Roosevelt administration called for repeal of the Neutrality Act.[20]

The House responded positively to Roosevelt's request but retained the arms embargo. In July Gerald Nye, Champ Clark, Robert La Follette Jr., and Hiram Johnson organized opposition to repeal in the Senate. The single purpose of the neutrality law, explained Nye to the journalist Walter Lippmann, was "to help keep us out of other people's wars." La Follette concurred, telling a national radio audience that selling military equipment to one side would be "the first fatal step that will lead to our being drawn into war." Drawing on hostility to presidential power in the domestic arena, the Senate Foreign Relations Committee voted 12 to 11 to postpone consideration of repeal, with the progressives William Borah, Arthur Capper, Henrik Shipstead, Johnson, and La Follette siding with the majority. Yet the noninterventionist triumph appeared fragile when the Soviet Union and Nazi Germany signed a nonaggression pact in August 1939 and the Germans invaded Poland the following month. The violation of the Polish border brought prompt declarations of war by Britain and France.[21]

President Roosevelt responded to the outbreak of hostilities by requesting a special session of Congress to reconsider repeal of the neutrality laws. By October 1939, 62 percent of sampled opinion approved of legislation to enable the British and French to buy American war supplies. The president, however, confronted noninterventionists, who insisted that Congress had to act to prevent him from dragging the nation into European squabbles. "The real nub of the neutrality controversy," declared Gerald Nye, was "presidential power, presidential discretion, presidential chance to commit the country in a way that makes staying out of war exceedingly difficult." Hiram Johnson used nationalist terms to describe the arms embargo as "a people's law . . . an American law enacted by Americans for the protection of America and Americans." For William Borah, who reported receiving two thousand letters a day on the issue, neutrality meant commitment to the nation's freedom of action.[22]

Senate debate on repeal involved the most dramatic foreign policy confrontation since the struggle over the League of Nations. Western progressives played an instrumental role in generating noninterventionist strategy and rhetoric. William Borah attacked the "war hounds of Europe" and "power politics." Robert La Follette Jr. recalled his father's resistance to war in 1917. Gerald Nye painted the conflict as a struggle for empire in Europe and profit at home. Hiram Johnson saw the nation "walking down the bloody path of war." Fearing any indirect aid to European dictators, George Norris became the only western progressive to endorse repeal. The final vote revoked the arms embargo by a 55-24 margin (243 to 172 in the House) and authorized cash-and-carry. The next day the Senate approved the Neutrality Act of 1939 by 63 to 30 (243 to 181 in the House).[23]

✤ ✤ ✤

By December 1939, 47 percent of a national poll thought the country's most important problem was keeping out of war. The next year brought a shift in attitudes, though. In April 1940 Nazi armies occupied Denmark and Norway. The following month the Germans stormed into Luxembourg, Belgium, and Holland. In June Paris fell to the Third Reich. By August and September the German air force was attacking British population centers in preparation for a possible invasion. President Roosevelt had long considered western Europe to be America's first line of defense. He responded to the defeat of France by appointing the Republican Henry L. Stimson as secretary of war and the Republican Frank Knox as secretary of the navy and instructed them to begin military preparedness. In September the president issued an executive order that authorized the exchange of fifty American destroyers for access to British bases in the Western Hemisphere. He also endorsed legislation to create the nation's first peacetime military selective service system.[24]

Both White House supporters and critics were aware of public opinion changes. The fall of France had increased support for military conscription from half to nearly two-thirds in national samples. In September 1940 President Roosevelt reviewed confidential polls revealing that majorities now believed it more important to help Britain than to avoid armed conflict. Yet more than 90 percent of all Americans opposed a declaration of war and overseas deployment. Many, moreover, viewed a peacetime draft as a European form of oppression incompatible with individualistic democracy. As the Socialist Norman Thomas told the president, the selective service bill embodied "a revolutionary change in the American way of life." The draft, protested one White House letter writer, was the work of "the same gang of pseudo-Americans and internationalists that caused the murder of thousands of young fellows in the 'war to end wars.'" Other opponents criticized "Soviet inspired law" or "fascist-nazi policy" that would create "a goose-stepping beehive" of "robots."[25]

Senate noninterventionists fought the draft with a fury reminiscent of the 1917 struggle. Gerald Nye, the most active opponent, maintained the proposal was the result of hysteria and propaganda advanced by indus-

trialists and military contractors. A modern army needed quality techni-
cians, not mass numbers, he argued. Burton Wheeler addressed antidraft
rallies and radio audiences with the cry that conscription was the "greatest step toward regimentation and militarism ever taken by Congress."
Wheeler insisted that the draft violated constitutional freedoms and threatened the American economic and social system. "If you pass this bill," he
warned a radio audience, "you slit the throat of the last democracy still
living." For the first time in years George Norris joined all the western
progressives except Charles McNary in opposing the Roosevelt administration. Yet the conference report passed the Senate 47 to 25 and the House
233 to 124. The bill's final version provided that men between the ages of
twenty-one and thirty-six register for a lottery. A maximum of 900,000
would draw one year's service in the Western Hemisphere.[26]

President Roosevelt publicly backed conscription in the same speech in
which he accepted the Democratic nomination for a third term. Nineteen
months earlier only 30 percent of a national sample had approved severing the two-term precedent. When the president simultaneously endorsed
the peacetime draft and abandoned the two-term tradition, he left himself open to predictable criticism. Most western insurgents already claimed
that the New Deal abused executive power. Possibilities of a third term
encouraged such noninterventionists as Burton Wheeler to picture
Roosevelt as a greater threat to American democracy than Hitler or Benito Mussolini was. Wheeler had assured friends in late 1939 that the president would not seek reelection because of the aversion of rural and other
Americans to a third term. As late as April 1940 the Montana senator
reported Roosevelt's agreement that "it was a mistake to run."[27]

Assuming that Franklin Roosevelt would retire, Wheeler permitted the
formation of a presidential campaign committee in his name. Supporters
included Democratic senators Edwin C. Johnson, Elmer Thomas, and D.
Worth Clark, CIO leader John L. Lewis, and Father Coughlin. During the
spring of 1940 Wheeler raised his political profile through a series of nationwide addresses. In Chapel Hill, North Carolina, he paraphrased Britain's Lord Acton to complain that political and economic power "begets
power." As Nazi forces marched on Paris in early June, a Wheeler radio
talk condemned the fabrication of "mad hysteria" in New York and Washington. Another speech described Henry Stimson and Frank Knox as "high-
class, conservative, reactionary Republicans" whom President Roosevelt
had incorporated into a "War Cabinet." In a late-June radio address entitled "Keep Out of War," Wheeler bemoaned the capture of the Republican convention by international bankers and warmongers and suggested
that a third party might be needed to address antiwar issues.[28]

Burton Wheeler received predictable support from Philip La Follette, who offered to take to the radio to deliver "a genuine American appeal" for the candidate. Yet Wheeler acknowledged that many "liberals" remained loyal to Roosevelt. "It amuses me," he wrote to a Kentucky newspaper publisher early in 1940, "when I find some of these ultra-New Dealers calling me a conservative, and the president a great liberal." North Dakota's Governor John Moses confided that although Wheeler had the friendship "of a large, liberal progressive element" and some conservatives in the state, most Democrats awaited Roosevelt's instructions. By the summer of 1940 the noninterventionist Make Europe Pay War Debts Committee supported Wheeler's nomination for president but warned against a futile third-party attempt, stressing the importance of his reelection to the Senate. Once Franklin Roosevelt's renomination seemed clear, Wheeler withdrew his name from contention and indicated unwillingness to accept a vice presidential slot.[29]

Issues of war and peace also split the Republican party. The noninterventionists William Borah, Arthur Capper, and Gerald Nye first turned to Arthur Vandenberg, a member of the Munitions Committee, to oppose President Roosevelt. Nye took to the campaign trail in the spring of 1940 to remind farmers in the Great Plains that Vandenberg had led the fight against reciprocal trade. Other noninterventionists favored Ohio's Senator Robert Taft. By convention time in June, however, Wendell Willkie, an interventionist, emerged as the Republican favorite. A former Indiana Democrat and public utilities attorney, Willkie mounted a well-financed and well-organized nomination campaign climaxed by a sixth ballot victory. Insurgents such as Henrik Shipstead fumed that a Wall Street holding company lawyer and conscription supporter had taken over the party. Representative Usher Burdick from North Dakota tied the nomination to such international financiers as Ogden Reid and Thomas Lamont, whom he accused of warmongering to protect European investments.[30]

To offset Wendell Willkie's internationalism, the Republicans chose Oregon's Senator Charles McNary for vice president. Building on a reputation for progressive politics and agrarian values, McNary hoped to attract the vote normally won by western insurgents. The Republican platform scored the nation's preparations for territorial protection as inadequate and promised that aid to the Allies would conform to international law and U.S. defense requirements. In contrast to the Republicans, the Democrats chose an internationalist, Secretary of Agriculture Henry A. Wallace, for the second slot. Yet the Democratic platform opposed intervention in the war, and President Roosevelt concluded the election campaign by promising that American soldiers would not "be sent into any foreign war."[31]

Wendell Willkie and Charles McNary won the support of all of President Roosevelt's former insurgent allies except George Norris and Robert

La Follette Jr. A last-minute radio appeal by Gerald Nye insisted that the real emergency was the domestic economic crisis resulting from participation in World War I. The North Dakotan accused the Roosevelt administration of leading the nation to world conquest with a far-flung empire that would cost billions to maintain against the resentments of an angry world. Nye, Arthur Capper, and Henrik Shipstead all campaigned for Willkie. Meanwhile, Hiram Johnson won renomination to the Senate on California's Republican, Democratic, and Progressive tickets and denounced a third-term presidency as more dangerous than war. Cut off from White House support, Johnson offered a lukewarm endorsement of the Republican presidential nominee while cooperating with Nye to provide strong backing to Shipstead's reelection as a Republican instead of a Farmer-Laborite.[32]

Burton Wheeler also sought Senate reelection without President Roosevelt's help. The fiery Montanan had a strong base among the state's railroad brotherhoods, farmers, and miners. Yet much of organized labor resented his escalating disputes with the White House and New Deal policymakers. Wheeler had promised to campaign for the president when the Democrats incorporated elements of his foreign policy positions into the platform. In the end, however, the senator stayed out of the presidential race and quietly voted for the Socialist Norman Thomas. Meanwhile, he carried Montana with 73 percent of the vote and tripled Roosevelt's vote. In the nationwide contest the president took all but ten states and nearly 55 percent of the popular vote. "This probably may be the last ceremony of the inauguration of a president that we'll ever have," a glum Hiram Johnson noted weeks later.[33]

✦ ✦ ✦

By 1941 the Roosevelt administration was convinced of the seriousness of the Nazi threat. The president told the governing board of the Pan-American Union in May that the German economic challenge would force competition with slave labor, fixed farm prices, and prohibitive tariffs. Hitler threatened the system of open trade upon which American political and economic stability depended. As Mark L. Chadwin has observed, international business leaders were particularly concerned about access to markets and raw materials in the British Commonwealth, the Continent, and Europe's colonies. Both the administration and the corporate community feared that Latin America might fall to German economic expansion and Nazi-inspired political revolutions. As a result, the flow of materials to the United States could easily be terminated. Both groups saw similar consequences if Germany used the navy of a defeated Britain to take control of the Atlantic seaways.[34]

Concerns for long-range economic stability prompted leading members of the corporate community to support government internationalism. During the summer and fall of 1940 a group of influential figures in business, banking, law, publishing, and journalism constituted itself as the Century Group and held weekly New York gatherings to press the United States to intervene. Many cooperated with the newly formed Committee to Defend America by Aiding the Allies. Others were among the 170 distinguished names supporting an open letter to Congress that condemned "indifference and apathy toward what is happening in the world." Published in major newspapers in January 1941 as a telegram to the president, the protest focused on "the irreconcilable nature of the forces" involved in the world war. It warned that conflict "threatens to wipe out the salt of Christian civilization in which men may be free from the restraints of intolerance, from the fear of injustice, and from the menace of arbitrary power."[35]

As the rhetoric of the open letter suggested, internationalists mixed a concern for national interest with a commitment to the democratic and humane values associated with Western civilization. The newspaper columnist Dorothy Thompson tapped this blend when she begged Senator Borah to support neutrality revision in 1939. "What is at stake," urged Thompson, "is world sovereignty and world revolution." She charged that the Germans were about "to let loose the most awful carnage that the world has ever seen . . . total, terrific, absolutely unlimited war against the West with every instrument of horror and destruction." Donald Richberg, a New Dealer, set the same tone in a letter to Robert La Follette Jr. Asserting that "the security of our lives and the perpetuity of our institutions" were menaced by the alliance between totalitarian Germany and the Soviet Union, Richberg pleaded for help in stopping Germany's "armed march" across Europe.[36]

German invasion of the Low Countries in May 1940 led the financier Thomas Lamont and others to form the Committee to Defend America by Aiding the Allies. Lamont confided to President Roosevelt that the aggression provided "the final conclusive proof that civilization as free nations know it has entered a struggle for life or death." With the Kansas editor William Allen White as chair, the committee enrolled hundreds of thousands in a grass-roots effort to support the administration's foreign policy. Its mix of strategic interest and democratic fervor complemented the president's approach. As early as October 1939 Roosevelt had lectured Norman Thomas on "our obligations to a civilization to which we owe so much and of which we are an integral part." Two months later the president told White that he feared an Axis victory would threaten both world trade and Western civilization. In July 1940 Roosevelt warned Thomas that dictatorships would segregate the United States until it was vulnerable to final attack.[37]

Noninterventionists replied strongly to such charges. The signers of the open telegram, one antiwar activist complained, were not *"leaders"* but "special *pleaders"* who were "egging us on to war." The American people were "lethargic toward defense," she asserted, because they were reluctant "to wage an offensive war in behalf of the British Empire." In response to interventionist pressures on President Roosevelt and Congress in late 1940, the Iowa newspaper editor Verne Marshall used his own funds to organize the No Foreign War Committee (NFWC). Marshall saw the new lobby as a response of the "common people" to the "raucous shouting" of White's Committee to Defend America and other internationalist efforts. Describing supporters as "just every-day, red-blooded, patriotic Americans" who put the United States first, Marshall quickly collected nearly twelve thousand signatures on telegrams that asked the president to keep the nation out of the European war. Such Senate noninterventionists as Gerald Nye, Arthur Vandenberg, and Burton Wheeler also backed the NFWC.[38]

Marshall's rank-and-file lobby failed to generate the necessary finances to remain a factor in antiwar politics. The leading noninterventionist force in American life was the America First Committee (AFC), formed in September 1940. A Minnesota loyalty organization had used a similar name during World War I. The new group grew out of a Yale University student association started by R. Douglas Stuart Jr., the son of a Quaker Oats executive. Stuart prevailed on General Robert Wood of Sears, Roebuck to serve as national chair of the Chicago-based committee. A supporter of New Deal inflationary programs designed to bolster purchasing power, Wood turned against the Roosevelt administration during the judicial reorganization controversy. He opposed the third-term presidency as a dangerous concentration of executive power and feared that U.S. intervention in the war would bring the destruction of worldwide capitalism.[39]

America First drew two-thirds of its 800,000 members from within three hundred miles of Chicago. Most of its officers and major financial contributors were prominent midwestern business and law figures, often associated with manufacturing and processing for a domestic market. The AFC's national committee listed the regional bankers J. Sanford Otis and Hanford MacNider; the manufacturers William H. Regnery, J. C. Hormel, and Sterling Morton; the agricultural leaders Ray McKaig, Frank O. Lowden, and George N. Peek; and such progressive veterans as John Flynn, Amos Pinchot, the novelist Kathleen Norris, and Mrs. Burton Wheeler. Major advisers included Philip La Follette; Samuel Pettengill, a former House member; William Benton, vice president of the University of Chicago; and Chester Bowles, an advertising executive. Additional funds came from Herbert Hoover, Henry Ford, and the publishers Robert R. McCormick of the *Chicago Tribune* and J. M. Patterson of the *New York News*. Philip La Follette and Senators Burton Wheeler and Gerald Nye frequently addressed AFC rallies.[40]

Advertising itself as a nonpartisan organization of patriotic citizens, America First advocated a strong national defense as its first priority. It insisted that military aid to the Allies weakened the United States and that American liberties could best be preserved by keeping out of European and Asian wars. Denying that Britain was fighting to preserve democracy, it urged a negotiated peace in western Europe. The AFC called for a foreign policy that did not impair the U.S. form of government or its standard of living. In this spirit, the organization opposed conscription and supported a national advisory referendum before war could be declared.[41]

❖   ❖   ❖

As Wayne Cole has indicated, liberals and conservatives took both sides in the foreign policy debates of 1940–41. Interventionists included New Deal reformers and intellectuals, tradition-minded southerners, and banking and corporate leaders. Noninterventionists rallied midwestern business interests and other New Deal foes but found support among socialists, intellectuals, progressives, and former insurgents. Meanwhile, such Wall Street figures as the investment consultant William J. Baxter joined the movement against intervention. Such contradictions were compounded by the fact that few agreed on terms for defining the international debate. The antiwar activist Philip La Follette, for example, attacked the use of such labels as "isolationists" and "interventionists" as misleading epithets. Others, such as Gerald Nye, depicted noninterventionists as progressives on the international front and wore the "isolationist" label proudly."[42]

Noninterventionists liked to believe they represented the "rank and file" of the American people. On a western auto trip in the summer of 1940, a Chicago railroad executive reported that one-fifth of the working people and four-fifths of the small-town middle class with whom he talked held anti-Roosevelt views. The antiwar movement contained a diversity of backgrounds and political viewpoints. Yet certain patterns of support emerged by 1941. Such groups as America First did well outside the South among small farmers, light manufacturers, independent retailers, and basic service providers. Strong in rural and small-town environments, they also attracted Americans of Irish, German, Italian, and Scandinavian ethnicity. Noninterventionist views were disproportionately popular among women and people with limited formal education.[43]

The movement against military involvement in Europe espoused an ideology of democratic nationalism, particularly in its largest power bases in the economically and socially marginal Midwest and Great Plains. Even in good times, the region's family-financed manufacturers, agricultural processors, and service providers remained outside eastern banking ties and targeted mainly hemispheric markets. Infused with distrust of Europe and Washington, midwestern business leaders cared little about British, French, or Chinese independence. Nor did they benefit from reciprocal trade links to a global economy. Instead, regional producers and allies resisted outside financial control and sought protection from the advantages that unstable currencies and low wages afforded foreign competition. Domestic economic interests were threatened by the prospect of war-induced inflation, national debt, conscription, taxation, labor monopoly, and state controls.[44]

Economic concerns helped to distance such groups as the National Association of Manufacturers and the Chicago Association of Commerce from interventionist policies. Progressives such as Usher Burdick, Robert La Follette Jr., Gerald Nye, and Burton Wheeler had argued that eastern bankers and munitions makers were partially responsible for U.S. involvement in World War I. By 1941 many midwestern business leaders had come to see the earlier war as a disaster brought on by selfish interests at home and abroad. Noninterventionists now asserted that the dislocations of the unnecessary global conflict had contributed to the agricultural depression of the 1920s, the economic collapse of the 1930s, and the chaotic slide toward a second world war. Business attacks on militarism led Robert Wood to taunt the White House that its "pink friends" had incorrectly "preached that every war is brought on by the capitalists and their desire for profit."[45]

Such arguments helped emphasize the importance of defending the Western Hemisphere instead of Europe as the source of American strength, a view that reinforced existing suspicions of the cosmopolitan, internationalized world of high finance and diplomacy. William Borah had once predicted that an alliance with London would involve the United States "with every controversy which may arise anywhere." Aversion to overseas entanglements also tapped traditional American fears of "Old World" power politics, blood feuds, and imperialism. There was "not much choice," a New Yorker from Queens explained to Gerald Nye, "between Nazism, Fascism, and Communism."[46]

Denunciations of European ideology and plutocracy frequently concentrated on British colonialism and aristocracy. The war was a power play over empire, not a moral or ideological struggle between democracy and autocracy, insisted Hiram Johnson. Antiwar activists often expanded on Irish and German rage at the British Empire. "When did England or France ever care about the United States?" a constituent asked William Borah late in 1939. A St. Paul supporter of Father Coughlin instructed Henrik Shipstead to tell "the big mouths in Washington" to "quit worrying about poor, old chiseling England." "Americanism and British Traditions," a North Dakota judge warned Usher Burdick, "do not mix any better than Whiskey and Gasoline."[47]

Democratic nationalism embodied strong pressures for the United States to isolate itself from European militarism and diplomacy. "I will never give my vote to sending American boys to fight and die on the foreign battle fields of the Old World," Robert La Follette Jr. proclaimed in a 1940 form letter. When an Oregon constituent asked Charles McNary to "help us to keep *America's hands clean*," the senator sent back a form reply that pledged to keep the country out of war and "entangling alliances." Antiwar senators, such as Gerald Nye and Henrik Shipstead, assured nervous correspondents of their belief that democracy could not be upheld through armed force. Nye publicly argued that the United States lacked the physical strength to make itself the guardian of international virtue. As Philip La Follette noted, the foreign policy debate centered on whether democracy could best be defended by fighting overseas dictators or by protecting it with all necessary means at home and in the Western Hemisphere.[48]

Noninterventionists believed that militarism stemmed from political and economic causes within society. In turn, they insisted that war could destroy democracy by legitimizing regimentation and dictatorship. The call for U.S. intervention, proclaimed an Idaho pamphleteer, amounted to "a plea that in order to save democracy in the world, we must destroy it at home." Robert McCormick's *Chicago Daily Tribune* used similar reasoning to predict that involvement in the war would produce "bankruptcy and a centralized, despotic government different in no essential detail from Hitler's despotism." Not surprisingly, insurgents who had led the opposition to New Deal centralism played a major role in these denunciations. Henrik Shipstead warned that war would destroy democracy and constitutional government. Burton Wheeler often used the same themes. "The issue is the preservation of our way of life here in America," Wheeler told a national radio audience in August 1940.[49]

Political arguments for democratic nationalism emphasized the dangers of the World War I precedent. In November 1939, 68 percent of a Gallup poll expressed the opinion that American involvement in the earlier conflict had been a mistake. Noninterventionists never tired of reminding Americans of Woodrow Wilson's desire to "make the world safe for democracy." Such rhetoric, Robert La Follette Jr. declared in 1941, was "merely the cloak behind which the eternal European struggle for power was concealed." The propaganda of the last war read "like ghoulish humor,"

Hiram Johnson informed the Senate. To dramatize his conviction that the United States was preparing to repeat the errors of 1917, Johnson quoted the following passage from the writer John T. Flynn: "We have been told we are in an emergency. Then the president starts a spy scare and hunt. Then he announces that submarines are prowling off our coasts. Then he invokes the old Espionage Act. People are asked to adjourn politics. The result is they adjourn almost everything."[50]

Noninterventionists mobilized ordinary citizens to defeat the powerful propaganda of the administration and eastern internationalists. "The plain people of America," declared Philip La Follette at a Wisconsin America First meeting, were "determined to stay out of war." This theme resonated through antiwar pronouncements. During 1939 Charles McNary mailed out constituent form letters that assured readers that overwhelming majorities of Congress and the American people opposed military conflict and declarations of war. Noninterventionists continued to cite polls estimating that 80 percent or more of the population rejected direct U.S. involvement in the conflict. Never abandoning the democratic war-making proposals of the Ludlow amendment, critics of Roosevelt foreign policy looked upon militarism as a tool of elite interests. Only "the common people" could save the United States from the propaganda of "warmongers and interventionists."[51]

❖ ❖ ❖

Lend-lease aid to Britain presented America First with its paramount challenge. In response to London's plea that it no longer could afford to meet the cash-and-carry provisions of the Neutrality Act, President Roosevelt delivered a "fireside chat" at the end of 1940. Declaring that the British were fighting for American security, the chief executive announced his intention to make the United States "the great arsenal of democracy." A week later Roosevelt's annual message to Congress asked for authority to turn military supplies over to nations at war with aggressors. The president envisioned "a world founded upon four essential human freedoms"— freedom of speech and religion and freedom from want and fear. Introduced in January 1941, the lend-lease bill permitted the chief executive to sell, transfer, exchange, lend, or lease food and war supplies to any nation whose protection he considered vital to the defense of the United States.[52]

Robert Wood initiated America First's attack on lend-lease. The legislation was so broad, declared Wood, that it gave the president unilateral control over U.S. laws and liberties. In the Senate Burton Wheeler led the assault with customary gusto. Lend-lease promised totalitarian dictatorship and war to please economic and foreign royalists, fumed Wheeler before a national radio audience. The New Deal's "triple-A foreign policy" would "plow under every fourth American boy." Noninterventionist colleagues joined Wheeler in appealing for mass support over the radio and on the Senate floor. Henrik Shipstead described the bill as "a blank check upon the entire resources of our country." Robert La Follette Jr. charged that its "sweeping" powers created a "rubber stamp Congress" that might permit the president "to get us into war by the back door." Gerald Nye proclaimed that the unprecedented legislation encroached on constitutional prerogatives and subverted government process.[53]

Midwestern and western noninterventionists focused on fears that military mobilization would bring increased statism at home. These concerns became clear when Colonel Charles A. Lindbergh testified before the foreign relations committees of both houses of Congress. An aviation expert and former consultant to the Air Corps, Lindbergh minimized the threat of a German air attack on the United States. The colonel insisted that aid to Britain would weaken American defenses and move the nation "a step away from the system of government in which most of us in this country believe." "I do not believe that the danger to America lies in an invasion abroad," he concluded. "I believe it lies here at home in our own midst."[54]

The House Foreign Affairs Committee's minority report noted that lend-lease was "the most important and far-reaching bill this house has ever considered," a proposal involving "a complete change in the way of life of our republic." Nevertheless, the legislation easily passed the House by 260 to 165. Hiram Johnson organized the noninterventionist side in the Senate. After three weeks of debate, including a twelve-hour address by Gerald Nye, senators voted 60 to 31 in favor of the bill. In March 1941 Congress appropriated $7 billion of lend-lease to Great Britain.[55]

One month after the passage of lend-lease, Charles Lindbergh joined the national committee of America First. The son of the Minnesota Nonpartisan Leaguer Charles A. Lindbergh Sr., the outspoken colonel won national acclaim in 1927 with the first solo air flight across the Atlantic. Extensive tours of European aviation facilities in the late 1930s gave Lindbergh credibility on matters of air power. As war broke out in 1939, all three networks carried his first American radio address, a plea that "the destiny of this country does not call for involvement in European wars." Lindbergh never departed from this initial message. In a "Letter to Americans," which Collier's published in March 1941, he asked readers to help maintain national independence from foreign interests. Interventionists sought to "beguile" Americans into supporting steps that would lead to war without offering a feasible plan for victory, charged Lindbergh.[56]

As Lindbergh began to address huge America First rallies, the Roosevelt administration accused him of appeasement. He responded by resigning his commission in the Army Air Corps Reserve. When Germany invaded its former ally, the Soviet Union, in June 1941, America First ridiculed the idea of going to the aid of Joseph Stalin's dictatorship. In San Francisco Lindbergh told an overflow audience of twelve thousand that "I would a hundred times rather see my country ally herself with England, or even with Germany with all her faults, than with the cruelty, the Godlessness, and the barbarism that exist in the Soviet Union." He insisted that an alliance with Moscow "should be opposed by every American, every Christian, and by every humanitarian in this country." Nothing ever changed Lindbergh's earlier view that the fratricidal conflict was "simply one more of those age old quarrels within our family of nations."[57]

Between April and December 1941 Charles Lindbergh's cross-country appearances made him America First's prime attraction. As the homespun orator himself later suggested, he did not advance his father's agrarian radicalism by attacking "special interests" associated with financial despotism. Nevertheless, Lindbergh's democratic nationalism echoed many of the political and cultural attitudes associated with anti-New Deal and midwestern insurgence. "We must face the fact," he told a gathering at Fort Wayne, Indiana, "that you and I and our generation have lost our American heritage." Lindbergh clung to such producer values as abstinence, frugality, fortitude, and discipline. "We Americans are a primitive people," he complained in an August 1941 article in *Life* magazine: "We do not have discipline. Our moral standards are low. It shows up in the private lives of people . . . , their drinking and behavior with women. It shows in the newspapers, the morbid curiosity over crimes and murder trials."[58]

Although Lindbergh was not an agrarian populist, he seemed to embody his father's distaste for urban culture as a center of decadent wealth and artificial intellect. In a piece in *Reader's Digest* in 1939, the controversial aviator warned of the "spiritual decline" that accompanied "the mineral-like quality" of industrial life. His crusade against military intervention embraced an attempt to recover such lost virtues as self-reliance, independent control of individual personality, and "national destiny." In Minneapolis Lindbergh addressed a May 1941 gathering that included two hundred editors of regional country newspapers. He used the opportunity to remind listeners of his father's belief "that the future of American lay more in the farms of the Mississippi Valley than on the battlefields across the sea." Appropriately, the meeting's solicitation for America First accompanied the singing of "Jingle Bells" and other traditional favorites.[59]

When Charles Lindbergh met President Roosevelt in 1939, he confessed that it was difficult to talk to a person who wore a mask. This impression seemed to work its way into later charges that the chief executive promised peace but led the nation to war. Lindbergh accused the Roosevelt administration of "government by subterfuge." "As a nation," he charged

in Fort Wayne, "we have been led along like children, with sugared promises and candied pills." Lindbergh complained that the 1940 presidential
election had denied voters the chance to vote on matters of war and peace.
He questioned whether Roosevelt would use the threat of war to justify
restriction of congressional power and "assumption of dictatorial procedures." Democratic prosperity was far more essential, proclaimed the
aviator, than foreign crusades "for freedoms that are tottering in our own
country." The place to save democracy, he concluded, was "right here in
America."[60]

✦   ✦   ✦

Insisting that Western civilization depended on united racial strength
against "Asiatic hordes" and other inferiors, Lindbergh pictured the European war as a "white man's quarrel" that represented "racial suicide by
internal conflict." Critics saw similar ethnic stereotyping in Lindbergh's
attacks on "war agitators." In a major America First speech in Des Moines,
Iowa, in September 1941 the controversial aviator declared that "the three
most important groups who have been pressing this country toward war
are the British, the Jewish, and the Roosevelt administration." Lindbergh's
remarks extended to "a number of capitalists, Anglophiles, and intellectuals" who identified with British interests. Although he empathized with
Jewish desires to overthrow the Nazis and condemned Berlin's persecution
of European Jews, he appeared to echo Hitler's propaganda by charging
that the Jews' "greatest danger to this country" came in "their large ownership and influence in our motion pictures, our press, our radio, and our
government."[61]

Charles Lindbergh's questioning of Jewish influence coincided with a
Senate investigation of interventionist propaganda in the motion picture
industry. Western insurgents, such as Gerald Nye, had long been critical
of Hollywood's monopolistic practices and cultural influences, but the
controversy took a political turn when Burton Wheeler complained that
filmed news documentaries were not covering both sides of the lend-lease
debate. Wheeler threatened government regulation if the industry did not
abandon its "violent propaganda campaign" to incite the nation to war.
In August 1941 Champ Clark and Nye used a resolution drafted by John
Flynn, a former munitions inquiry staffer, to call for a Senate investigation. On the same day, Nye delivered a St. Louis speech that blasted movies as "the most gigantic engines of propaganda in existence to rouse the
war fever in America." The senator then read out a list of predominantly
Jewish studio heads.[62]

Senate Commerce Committee chair Burton Wheeler appointed D. Worth
Clark, a noninterventionist Democrat from Idaho, to lead the inquiry, and

hearings began in September. A grant from America First allowed John Flynn to organize the investigation. Most of the fireworks, however, came from the testimony of Champ Clark and Gerald Nye. Clark emphasized the influence of mass communications on public debate. Seventeen thousand movie theaters nationwide, he charged, had been turned over to "daily and nightly mass meetings for war." Freedom of discussion had been "seized and monopolized by a few men." Nye denied charges of anti-Semitism but argued that foreign-born Jews had colored entertainment with their "inborn hatreds" and "vengeful spirits." Such movies as *Convoy, Flight Command,* and *Escape,* he argued, sought to break down American determination to stay out of the war by inducing hatred. War movies, testified Nye, constituted "the most vicious propaganda that has ever been unloosed upon a civilized people."[63]

The North Dakota senator also attacked such documentary features as the weekly *March of Time.* Pointing to the manipulation of newsreel images, verbal narratives, and titles, Nye argued that movies could "be perverted into instruments of propaganda with ease." He asserted that the Roosevelt administration encouraged the politicalization of entertainment and pointed to European dictatorships' "complete dominance and control" of radio and film. Nye claimed, moreover, that Hollywood molded movies to suit the British market, which provided the industry's margin of profit. Wendell Willkie, the industry's counsel, acknowledged that the movie colony opposed Nazism and voluntarily cooperated with government defense efforts, but he insisted that features simply reflected prevailing tastes. Noninterventionists dismissed the former presidential candidate as a proponent of war and a recently appointed director of Lehman Brothers, a Jewish-owned international investment firm.[64]

Antiwar activists adamantly denied the Lindbergh speech or the Hollywood inquiry had anti-Semitic motives. Like the aviator himself, America First professed to understand Jewish desires to defeat the Nazis. Yet Gerald Nye spoke for many when he charged that Jews and other interventionists were trying to destroy the movement by smearing it as anti-Semitic. In turn, Jewish leaders, administration supporters, and some noninterventionists questioned the premises of such arguments and insisted that Jews were as divided about the war as other Americans. The columnist Dorothy Thompson pointed out that the movie industry was owned by the nation's largest and non-Jewish banks. Only one of America's eleven most influential interventionist newspapers, noted Thompson, was Jewish-owned. Among the twenty-six directors of the radio networks, she observed, only two were Jews. Only two of the nation's thirty leading interventionists were Jewish. Moreover, internationalists were as likely as their ideological opposites to portray Jewish Americans in negative stereotypes.[65]

America First leaders openly courted Jewish support and disassociated the organization from anti-Semitic contributors, publications, and speakers. Nevertheless, headquarters could not always control life at the chapter level. In eastern cities followers of Father Coughlin's anti-Semitic Christian Front played such a significant role that the New York chapter head, John Flynn, feared America First might be taken over by fascists. In Portland, Oregon, Richard Neuberger, a Jewish journalist and noninterventionist, reported that the chapter chair had publicly uttered crude anti-Semitic slurs.[66]

Noninterventionist leaders such as John Flynn acknowledged that anti-Semitism had penetrated the antiwar movement. "It is not to be denied," Flynn warned Robert Wood in June 1941, "that there is a powerful anti-semitic under-current moving around the country." National polls sustained this view. In 1938, 31 percent of a sample saw Jews as less patriotic than other citizens, and 41 percent believed they had "too much power." Two years later 17 percent of Gallup respondents named Jews as a "menace to America." Since the Populist movement of the 1890s, anti-Semitism had thrived in antielitist movements as well as privileged circles. Some Americans believed that the transnational composition of the Jewish people and their strong cultural traditions mitigated against nationalistic loyalties. In a private aside, California's Hiram Johnson castigated Jews who wanted to risk American lives to protect European brethren "who neither live here, nor have anything in common with our country." Both noninterventionists and internationalists hoped to protect the United States from communism and Nazi espionage by limiting the immigration of German-Jewish refugees.[67]

Twentieth-century anti-Semitism embodied republican suspicions of commercialism and competitive values. Viewed as "overbearing," "materialist," and a "corrupt race," Jews were accused of "trying to run everything and everybody." "What is to become of Christian America," a Long Island woman asked William Borah, "if any more of this obnoxious, aggressive, exploiting race of vultures are admitted to this country?" Leo Ribuffo has discussed the modern perception that Jews avoided physical labor, manipulated money without engaging in production, valued profit more than life, and destroyed ethical standards in the professions. Senator William Langer of North Dakota captured these sentiments when in 1941 he noted in a secret manuscript that Jews were persecuted because they arrogantly assumed positions as "wealth absorbers" while relegating Gentiles to "common" labor.[68]

Anti-Semitic animosities found expression in the image of the international banker, a phrase used by Hitler to describe interlocking Jewish finance. Few antiwar officeholders were as explicit as Mississippi's Representative John Rankin in linking Wall Street interventionism to "a little group of our international Jewish brethren." Only such isolated politicians as Oregon's Representative Rufus C. Holman were willing to praise Hitler for breaking the hold of international bankers over Germany's common people. Yet such mainstream noninterventionists as Usher Burdick, Burton Wheeler, and Gerald Nye often held New York and London banking interests responsible for scarce currency and the push to war. In a rhetorical burst cited in a 1941 FBI report, Wheeler specifically listed "the Rothschilds and the Warburgs of Europe" as major culprits. Although noninterventionist leaders were not pro-Nazi or anti-Semites, their rhetoric occasionally played into the hands of extremists and helped marginalize the antiwar message.[69]

Charles Lindbergh's Des Moines speech compounded these problems. When two members of the governing board of the New York chapter of America First immediately resigned, John Flynn, the chair, sent Lindbergh an urgent message. Although he had engineered the investigation of movie propaganda, Flynn had been concerned with Hollywood's abuse of power, not its allegiance to Jewish interests. Anyone who denounced "the Jews" as war-makers, he now cautioned the controversial aviator, incurred the guilt of intolerance and placed the movement on the defensive. In the weeks following the Des Moines speech and the Hollywood investigation, America First faced crippling internal division and an increasingly hostile press. The Roosevelt administration already charged that Hitler's deadliest weapon was anti-Semitism. From the fall of 1941 America First found it impossible to overcome accusations that it echoed Berlin's propaganda and thereby served as an agent of Nazi subversion.[70]

❖ ❖ ❖

Since the summer of 1940 President Roosevelt had portrayed noninterventionists as "appeaser fifth columnists." Once Charles Lindbergh represented America First, the chief executive publicly attacked the aviator as a disloyal "copperhead." Meanwhile, Secretary of the Interior Harold Ickes denounced Lindbergh as a Nazi "fellow traveler." As the administration extended aid to Britain in 1941, it increasingly portrayed domestic critics as parties to a foreign, totalitarian conspiracy. In April noninterventionists were unable to stop Roosevelt from ordering U.S. warships to trail German submarines in all waters. After the president extended the patrols, the United States took over Iceland's defense and convoyed British ships. Powerless to reverse the escalation, Burton Wheeler sent out a million postcards urging recipients to oppose U.S. entry into the war. When two hundred soldiers received the franked cards, however, Secretary of War Henry Stimson charged that Wheeler had come close "to the line of subversive activities . . . if not treason."[71]

In August 1941 President Roosevelt and Winston Churchill subscribed to the Atlantic Charter, an agreement to press for postwar global freedoms. Days later the House passed an eighteen-month extension of the draft by a single vote (203 to 202). The following month the president issued "shoot-on-sight" orders regarding Axis ships. In November the White House requested repeal of the Neutrality Act to arm merchant vessels carrying lend-lease supplies. Despite vociferous noninterventionist dissent, the administration prevailed by margins of 50 to 37 in the Senate and 212 to 94 in the House. "The whole vote," Burton Wheeler wrote to John Flynn, "was a defeat for the people and a victory for administration power, patronage, and pap." By the fall of 1941 the noninterventionist movement found itself helpless to halt the concentration of executive power it associated with war. America First, declared its vice-chair, Hanford MacNider, had "come to the end of the road."[72]

Although Charles Lindbergh feared that President Roosevelt might postpone or cancel the 1942 congressional elections, America First began to prepare by calling a November 1941 meeting of chapter heads. Philip La Follette, the keynote speaker, declared that the only two planks of the noninterventionist cause were the Declaration of Independence and the Constitution. "Our motto," thundered La Follette, was "I am an American." The following month Lindbergh made one of his most comprehensive denunciations: "If we do not know what our government is doing or what it intends to do; if we have no right to vote upon the issue of foreign war; if our news is to be censored and mixed with propaganda, as in the totalitarian states; if our citizens are to be drafted, and our national economy upset, by a president who ran for his first term on promises of economy, and for his third term on promises of peace, then ours is no longer a free and democratic nation." "The battle cry of freedom is being used to regiment our people," declared the aviator.[73]

Lindbergh intended to call for a new political movement based on integrity and American traditions, but Japan attacked Pearl Harbor the day after he drafted his speech. On December 8 Congress declared war on Japan, with Republican House member Jeanette Rankin casting the only negative vote. A former Nonpartisan Leaguer, Rankin had voted against entry into World War I and returned to the House in 1940 when Burton Wheeler supported her race against the Montana New Dealer Jerry O'Connell. On December 11 Italy and Germany declared war on the United States, and Congress unanimously reciprocated. The national committee of America First immediately voted to dissolve so that it could support the military effort and avoid a takeover by extremists.[74]

"I am sure we were right and I am sure that history will prove we were right," Robert Wood wrote to Charles Lindbergh the next day.[75] Bitter in defeat, noninterventionists failed to appreciate the idealistic component to the internationalist cause. Such neglect opened antiwar campaigns to charges of callousness. In the end the American people sided with Franklin Roosevelt's use of force as a response to overseas totalitarianism. For the democratic nationalists of the noninterventionist camp, however, war meant fulfillment of their worst nightmares. Sensing the end of an era in U.S. history, many expected that Roosevelt would irreversibly doom the nation to international militarism, collective regimentation, and moral decay.

9

Democratic Nationalism and the Assault on Collectivism, 1941–46

Viewing World War II from the perspective of hindsight, Charles Lindbergh observed that the conflict marked "the beginning of our western civilization's breakdown." Lindbergh captured noninterventionists' pessimism about the global military crusade. War opponents particularly feared the domestic consequences of the conflict. Burton Wheeler liked to quote from William E. Barrett's stark pamphlet *War, America.* While the nation would love war "as men love whiskey," Barrett had predicted, its bleak realities would include fatherless children, illegitimate offspring, and a chilling moral bankruptcy.[1] Wartime response to the demands of collective security reinforced narrow partisan interests, but it also tapped the mix of traditional, populist, antistatist, and noninterventionist sentiments that defined democratic nationalism. By 1946 a coalition of bipartisan insurgents prepared to engage in full-scale confrontation with the remnants of elite New Dealism and liberal internationalism.

❖ ❖ ❖

"This war does not belong to a little clique," the North Dakotan William Lemke lectured the House in 1943. "It belongs to all of us. It is not a social event for the international 400. It is a war in which our sons are dying. . . ." Despite assurances of unity following Pearl Harbor, nationalists and former war opponents continued to advance their own conception of the conflict without appearing to endorse Axis propaganda. "While everyone wants to contribute to the winning of the war," Gerald Nye wrote to America First founder R. Douglas Stuart Jr., "it doesn't necessarily follow that everyone is willing to see our country sold out while engaged in winning the war." For Nye and other critics of New Deal internationalism this meant an insistence that American war aims not extend beyond the Western Hemisphere.[2]

The demand for a nationalist foreign policy won endorsement from a broad spectrum of political leaders. The group included such mainstream Republicans as Herbert Hoover and Senator Robert Taft but extended to such old progressives and early New Deal supporters as Gerald Nye, Henrik Shipstead, Burton Wheeler, and George Peek. All backed Taft's admonition that the United States should not pursue "a crusade" to impose the four freedoms throughout the world. Indeed, Peek accused Franklin Roosevelt of emulating Adolf Hitler and the Japanese by using the war to "impose his views upon other nations." Administration policy, in the words of Representative Hamilton Fish, a noninterventionist Republican from Upstate New York, amounted to "a glorified world-wide WPA" draining essential national resources. The danger with Washington's broad war aims, argued the Republican economist and strategist Lawrence Dennis, was that a struggle for "permanent world peace" could become "a permanent American war."[3]

Opponents of Roosevelt internationalism questioned military and diplomatic strategy by subjecting the nation's allies to harsh criticism. Nearly four-fifths of a 1942 public opinion sample affirmed that the United States needed the help of allies to win the war. The same survey found that 77 percent anticipated postwar cooperation with Britain. Yet Americans continued to distrust the Allies. A 1942 Gallup poll showed half the sample skeptical of Britain's motives and a majority believing that London could have prevented the war. One-quarter of respondents held British propaganda responsible for U.S. entry. Nearly one-third of those questioned in another survey thought that Britain would try to get the United States to do most of the fighting. A 1942 poll by the Office of Facts and Figures found 48 percent of respondents in the rural Midwest and 40 percent in five large American cities had major grievances against the British.[4]

Attitudes toward the Soviet Union were mixed. A majority favored aid to Moscow, and 88 percent believed that the Soviets were doing all they could to win the war. Yet only 45 percent expected Soviet-American postwar cooperation. Indeed, a 1942 Gallup poll found two-thirds of the sample wanted Washington to do everything possible to keep the Soviets from spreading communism once European hostilities ended. One-third of the respondents thought that Moscow would try to impose communism on the United States through secret agents. The Office of Facts and Figures found that 34 percent of rural midwesterners and 30 percent of urbanites expressed anti-Soviet sentiment. Meanwhile, opinion samples showed that 83 percent of respondents expected postwar cooperation with China and that Americans ranked the Chinese second among the Allies in terms of wartime effort and leadership caliber.[5]

Foreign policy nationalists were suspicious of both the Soviet Union and Great Britain. Minnesota's Henrik Shipstead, for example, pictured the United States as the "Company" that paid the bills for "Britain-Russia & Co., Ltd." Was it the goal of the New Deal, asked Shipstead, "to Anglicize the Declaration of Independence and Sovietize the Constitution of the United States?" Representative Overton Brooks, a Louisiana Democrat, violated party discipline in 1944 by complaining that "the American people did not send their sons abroad to fight and die for the safety of Great Britain or . . . for the triumph and extension of Russian influence." The United States was caught between "John Bull and the Russian Bear," protested the Washington columnist John O'Donnell.[6]

Criticism of Britain concentrated on London's imperial aspirations. As early as February 1942 the White House feared that Wisconsin's Senator Robert La Follette Jr. intended to call for the suspension of lend-lease to Britain until India won its independence. When President Roosevelt privately assured La Follette that Indian nationhood would be negotiated after the war and pleaded for wartime cooperation, the senator backed off. That summer Prime Minister Winston Churchill proclaimed he did not intend to "preside at the liquidation of the British Empire." Churchill's outburst prompted strong pleas for Indian independence from such nationalists as Robert R. Reynolds, chair of the Senate Military Affairs Committee. Five members of the committee charged in 1943 that Britain was using lend-lease to pursue colonial policies in the Middle East and East Asia. When Congress renewed the lend-lease program the next year, Roosevelt foreign policy opponents insisted on an understanding that funds be limited to wartime military necessities.[7]

Relations with the Soviets came under greater fire from pre–Pearl Harbor noninterventionists. When Hitler invaded Russia in June 1941, Secretary of the Interior Harold Ickes acknowledged that public sentiment was "terribly confused." Ickes feared that an alliance with the Communist power would provoke domestic attacks on international commitments and endanger the struggle against fascism. Demands for Allied unity minimized anti-Soviet criticism, yet, as the *Chicago Tribune* noted, the Soviet Union was also an agent of a subversive and violent state collectivism. "We all thrill at Russian success" against the Nazis, observed the *Tribune* in June 1942. Nevertheless, the newspaper pointed to the "specter of revolutionary communism" hanging over Europe. The alliance with Moscow strained President Roosevelt's wartime consensus by suggesting, as Robert Wood had predicted, that the military conflict would result in the exchange of "a Nazi-dominated Europe for a Communist Europe" and continentwide impoverishment.[8]

Discomfort with the Soviet Union escalated with the Moscow Conference of Foreign Ministers in 1943, in which the United States and Britain joined the Soviets in laying the groundwork for European postwar planning. Republican foreign policy critics noted that the accord failed to set the western boundaries of the Soviet Union or to recognize the Polish government in exile. Senator Arthur Vandenberg from Michigan led his party in accusing the administration of secretly handing over central and eastern Europe to Moscow to satisfy Roosevelt's own dreams of world order. The Republican Nationalist Revival Committee, organized in Chicago in 1943 to combat the Wendell Willkie's internationalist influence on the party, condemned the Moscow Declaration as the "unconditional surrender of the United States to Europe."[9]

The response to the Moscow Declaration revealed the continuity between pre–Pearl Harbor noninterventionism, nationalism, and anticommunism. Significantly, William Langer, the Nonpartisan Leaguer from North Dakota, placed the *Chicago American*'s defining editorial on the matter in the *Congressional Record*. Entitled "Sacrifices to Communism," the piece charged that the accord "doomed the peoples of eastern Europe to Communist slavery when they have been 'liberated' from Nazi thralldom." The pact nullified the Atlantic Charter, asserted the *American,* and "fertilized the seeds of World War No. 3" by allowing the Soviet Union to determine the territorial future of Poland, Finland, and the Baltic states. Postwar interim governments would be administered by whichever army occupied them, declared the editorial. It charged American leaders with agreeing to postpone application of self-determination until the Allies had set national boundaries for eastern Europe. Quoting the American Roman Catholic archbishops, the newspaper pictured the Moscow agreement as the result of "tragic compromises and a fateful repudiation of sound principles."[10]

Nationalist hostility toward the Soviet Union was tied to the perception that Japan constituted the foremost and nearest enemy and that Asia, not Europe, provided the most important arena of U.S. interests. Pacific-minded noninterventionists distrusted Winston Churchill's potential influence and celebrated General Douglas MacArthur's Philippine exploits instead. Accusing a "wolf pack of communistic smearers and radical New Deal and fellow traveler stooges" with attacking the nation's "greatest fighting general," such foreign policy critics as Hamilton Fish successfully sought MacArthur's appointment as commander in chief of Allied forces in East Asia. The Japan-first strategy, supported by the former progressives

Burton Wheeler and Henrik Shipstead, prompted Senator Albert B. Chandler, a Democrat from Kentucky, to speculate that Tokyo could be quickly defeated if Stalin allowed the United States to use Siberian air bases.[11]

❖   ❖   ❖

Soviet pressure for a European second front contributed to suspicion of Communist activities in the United States. Pennsylvania's Representative Charles I. Faddis, a Democrat, noted that the Soviets already had exploited Nazi aggression to take over Finland, the Baltics, and part of Poland. The timing of the second front, Faddis told the House, would depend on military strategy, not the political "yammering" of Communist "parasites" at home. Anticommunist newspapers, such as the Catholic *Tablet* of New York and the *Washington Daily News,* ran unfavorable accounts of speeches by American Communist party leaders who suggested that wartime cooperation with the Soviets was a "turning point in world history." Such reports validated a view of communism as subversive of nationalist goals. Elmer Davis, director of the Office of War Information (OWI), liked to say that communists were those in favor of collective security before August 1939, opposed during the Russo-German pact, and in favor again after the Nazis attacked the Soviet Union.[12]

Martin Dies, chair of the Special House Committee on Un-American Activities, alerted President Roosevelt in the fall of 1941 that Joseph Stalin and the American Communist party were "conducting one of the most insidious propaganda campaigns ever turned loose upon the American people." Dies suggested that the party hoped "to convert the anti-Nazi feelings of the American people into pro-Soviet sentiments." In response to a press conference reference by the president to a "freedom of religion" clause in the Soviet Constitution, the Texas Democrat asked Roosevelt to make it clear that the Stalinist regime was "utterably repugnant to the American people" and only made a "cruel pretense to freedom of religion worship." The similarities between Stalin and Hitler were "far more striking than any of their differences," he asserted. Several months later Dies repeated Winston Churchill's characterization of communism as "absolute rule of a self-chosen priesthood according to the dogmas it has learned by rote."[13]

Expanding on Dies's warnings, such Republican nationalists as Hamilton Fish complained that Communists were spreading un-American propaganda through "Trojan-horse methods and organizations." Fish claimed that the "insidious use of false fronts, deception, and camouflage . . . beguiles and fools loyal Americans." To support his point, the New Yorker provided a newspaper clipping of the Young Communist League's change of name to American Youth for Democracy. The *Tablet* story reported that the new group's founders called for postwar universal military training to build "a people's army" to drive out American "fascists and anti-communists." The ex-radical Max Eastman used the pages of *Reader's Digest* to attack communist propaganda in *Mission to Moscow,* a Hollywood version of former ambassador Joseph E. Davies's early campaign for a Soviet alliance. Eastman accused the film of ignoring the judicial murders, mass deportations, and state-planned famines that had solidified Soviet totalitarianism. The movie was merely "a compendium of what the Soviet government wants the American people to believe," he charged.[14]

Concern over communist propaganda surfaced with the controversy over the 1942 foreign agent registration bill. The measure compelled foreign intelligence services to register with the Department of Justice and account for their American operations. Convinced that the Communists had mounted a "foreign conspiracy masked as a political party," Dies managed to win House passage for an amendment requiring registration of Communist party officers and members. The proviso never survived the legislative process, but the agent registration bill overcame White House objections and passed both houses early in 1942. Portraying the measure as "a hang-over of isolationism" that prevented intelligence officials from protecting foreign information sources and cooperating with British, Chinese, and Soviet services, administration aides convinced President Roosevelt to veto the proposal. Both houses soon approved a successor that allowed the president to exempt operatives of nations he deemed essential to the national defense.[15]

Anticommunists, such as Representative Fred E. Busbey from Illinois, claimed that many of their colleagues had silenced themselves because they feared undermining the war effort or being smeared as pro-Nazi. Pre–Pearl Harbor noninterventionists from Lawrence Dennis to Burton Wheeler warned that New Dealers would use the pretext of war to marginalize opponents of internationalism. Concerns for patriotic unity prompted the militantly nationalist *Chicago Tribune* to disassociate itself from anticommunists who adhered to bigotry and fascist tenets. Nevertheless, both Roosevelt officials and the Communist party portrayed such Republican newspapers as the *Tribune,* the *New York Journal-American,* and the *New York Daily News* as "defeatists" and unwitting Axis collaborators. As Leo Ribuffo has suggested, the administration reacted to anxiety about "fifth column" subversion by mounting a wartime "brown scare." Government officials depicted nationalists and former antiwar activists as "divisionists" who served Nazi desires to reduce U.S. military effectiveness. Such charges linked criticism of the Allies, the Jews, and New Deal social philosophy to Axis treason and totalitarianism.[16]

From May 1940 President Roosevelt directed the FBI to monitor telegrams critical of defense policies, authorized the attorney general to use listening devices on those suspected of subversive activities or espionage, and persistently badgered the Justice Department to convene a grand jury to probe the source of America First's funding. An FBI inquiry found no foreign donations to AFC and only occasional crossover between its members and those of pro-Nazi groups. Yet the administration continued to hound such "fringe" leaders as Father Charles Coughlin, William Pelley, Gerald L. K. Smith, and Gerald Winrod, whom it accused of being conscious agents of the "conspiracy against our way of life."[17]

Father Coughlin had turned to anti-Semitism in late 1938 when his radio broadcasts began to describe nazism as a defense against a communist threat created by Jewish radicals and international bankers. Meanwhile, Coughlin augmented a forty-station radio network of thirteen million listeners by organizing the Christian Front. The Christian Front attracted working-class youth in heavily Catholic cities in the Northeast and specifically targeted Jews for sporadic vandalism and street violence. By 1940 Coughlin was praising Hitler for imposing a new moral purity, reforming Germany's financial system, and purging communists and subversives. When the Justice Department moved to ban the *Social Justice* newspaper from the mails in the spring of 1942, the periodical had an estimated 200,000 circulation. Under pressure from President Roosevelt, the Catholic church ordered the radical priest to cease all political publishing and broadcasting.[18]

Once the government had silenced Father Coughlin, it convened a Washington grand jury that indicted William Pelley, Gerald Winrod, Lawrence Dennis, Elizabeth Dilling, George Sylvester Viereck, and others for conspiring with the Third Reich to impair the loyalty, morale, and discipline of the armed forces. Two subsequent indictments expanded the list to thirty defendants. The sedition trial targeted Nazi agents, members of the German-American Bund, such fascist theorists as Dennis and Dilling, and such leaders of extremist and anti-Semitic organizations as Pelley and Winrod. Pelley's Silver Shirts castigated Jews as symbols of urban liberalism, collectivism, and internationalism. Winrod's Defenders of the Christian Faith combined evangelical fundamentalism, anti-Semitism, and small business populism. Dennis ignored the Jewish issue and called for a benevolent fascism that would nationalize banks and monopolies, subsidize small enterprises and farms, use progressive taxation to redistribute wealth and income, and establish one-party rule.[19]

Because the defendants had expressed explicit hostility to the New Deal and Roosevelt internationalism, critics accused the administration of conducting a political trial. The government's priority, explained Lawrence Dennis to former American First chair Robert Wood, was to link "anti-

Semitism and isolationism" with nazism. Gerald Nye told the Senate that most of the defendants were "no more guilty of conspiracy than I am," no more punishable "than millions of other Americans who gave voice to antiwar feelings before Pearl Harbor." William Langer, his North Dakotan colleague, concurred by noting that the alleged conspirators had "no more influence than a rooster." The case was "a legal farce," concluded Langer, "a perversion of justice."[20]

Noninterventionists such as Gerald Nye, Robert Taft, Burton Wheeler, and William Langer pictured the sedition trial as a predictable example of the repression that accompanied expanding government power in wartime. Although Justice Department attorneys privately acknowledged the legal weaknesses of the case, they stressed that it *must be won at all costs.* Undoubtedly, the administration hoped to use the prosecution to help legitimize a consensus on an international order based on human rights and collective security. Yet the trial was marred by inadequate evidence and the prosecution's violation of civil liberties. After extensive delays and chaotic courtroom testimony, the case ended in a mistrial in November 1944 when the presiding judge died.[21]

✦ ✦ ✦

Concerned with morale and unity in a war directed against an ideological foe, such government leaders as Vice President Henry Wallace painted the conflict as a "fight to the death between the free world and the slave world." Roosevelt established the Office of War Information to coordinate propaganda in 1942. The OWI's radio messages, leaflets, booklets, films, and magazines were designed to celebrate the American way of life and extol the liberal sentiments of the "four freedoms" and the Atlantic Charter. By sustaining morale, the information agency sought to minimize the social disorder noninterventionists saw as the inevitable result of war.[22] Yet the OWI symbolized the fusion of government propaganda, alien philosophy, and oppressive bureaucracy that fueled the wartime anti-Roosevelt coalition.

Congressional opposition to a government propaganda agency was not long in coming. Joe Starnes, an Alabama Democrat, protested in 1943 that taxpayers who had spent $300 billion on the military crusade did not need to be reminded "why we are fighting in this war." Domestic propaganda, proclaimed Starnes, was "a stench to the nostrils of a democratic people." The nation "needs no [Joseph] Goebbels sitting in Washington to tell the American press what to publish," he insisted. Senator Styles Bridges, a Republican from New Hampshire, stressed the same theme. The administration had created "the first United States Government propaganda bureau of a kind used in the dictator countries," cautioned Bridges. With its "growing collection of misfits, political hirelings, and radical journalists," he suggested, the OWI was like "the cuttlefish which drowns itself in its own ink."[23]

Accusations of politicalization inundated the OWI. Objecting to the implications of racial equality that characterized agency publications, some southern Democrats detected a "distinct socialistic tinge" to the agency. Hamilton Fish pointed out that even some elements of organized labor had complained that communists and "fellow-travelers" in the overseas branch were broadcasting Soviet propaganda to the people of occupied Europe. Republicans tied these allegations to a portrait of the OWI as a propaganda tool of the Democrats. The first demand of a collectivist state, Fred Bradley, a Michigan Republican, reminded the House, was suppression of free speech and control of communications. When the agency's overseas magazine described President Roosevelt as a benevolent opponent of "toryism" at home, Republicans screamed that the OWI was campaigning for New Deal platforms and a presidential fourth term.[24]

Congressional funding hearings produced major problems for the OWI in 1943 when the House approved Joe Starnes's motion to abolish the domestic branch. After Elmer Davis, the agency's director, threatened to resign, the House and President Roosevelt agreed on a compromise that permitted restoring the unit as an office to coordinate between other bureaus and the communications industry. Meanwhile, no OWI funds would be spent on printed literature or motion pictures in the United States. Despite repeated congressional threats to liquidate the OWI or investigate its usefulness, the beleaguered agency survived until August 1945, when it was abolished by executive order.[25]

The Office of Civilian Defense (OCD), organized in 1942 to prepare Americans for enemy attack and to bolster civilian morale, came under similar fire. Republican and other New Deal adversaries protested that the OCD's programs disguised a "collectivist" agenda. Critics objected to volunteer coordinator Eleanor Roosevelt's hiring "leftists" and using a modern dancer to teach physical fitness. The House soon voted to abolish the OCD as a separate agency and place it in the War Department. Although the House ultimately rescinded the move, it insisted on prohibiting agency funding for "aesthetic diversions," such as "fan dancing" or "street shows," and the first lady resigned her post. House investigators also compelled OCD administrators to concentrate on citizen defense and abandon morale building. Not satisfied, Michigan's Fred Bradley compared the agency's block-by-block discussion groups the following year to Communist cells and complained about academic lecturers who advocated "the surrender of American independence" to "some super world state" in training sessions for organizers.[26]

✦ ✦ ✦

The controversy over government responsibility for civilian morale demonstrated the fear that wartime Washington was intruding on the once-private area of personal values and social relations. Nationalists, populists, former noninterventionists, and other anti–New Dealers also objected to control by burgeoning government bureaucracies. The Executive Reorganization Act of 1939 had created the Office of Emergency Management, which organized such wartime agencies as the Office of Price Administration (OPA) and the War Production Board (WPB) through executive orders. Draft boards, civil defense groups, and rationing agencies led to a tripling of federal civilian employment between 1939 and mid-1943. By 1945 there were nearly four million such workers. Federal budget expenses leaped from less than $9 billion in 1939 to over $95 billion in 1945. Meanwhile, the federal debt climbed from less than $58 billion in 1941 to more than $260 billion by the end of the war.[27]

Some objection to Washington's power appeared trivial. In Ohio the Republican governor, John W. Bricker, received floods of mail from constituents who opposed a 1942 federal law that sought to conserve evening daylight and energy by requiring that all clocks be set forward an hour (the measure supplemented summer daylight savings time). As in World War I, the dispute pit the "fast" time of the cities against the "slow" time of the countryside. "No human being can change time," protested one traditionalist to the Ohio legislature. But there were practical implications to the controversy as well. "Cows eat, drink and rest and produce milk by God's time," a Grange official explained to Bricker. When the legislature heard repeated complaints that predawn darkness brought hardships to schoolchildren, factory workers, and agricultural laborers, it voted overwhelmingly to return to prewar time in 1943. Nevertheless, such Ohio cities as Akron and Cincinnati stayed on war time. The fiasco demonstrated the difficulties of adjusting to Washington's demands amid total military mobilization.[28]

Anxieties over federal power focused on efforts to prevent wartime inflation through price regulation. Congress passed the Emergency Price Control Act in January 1942. Using polls indicating public support, the OPA soon ordered a retail price freeze on nonfarm goods. By the end of the year the agency had enacted ten major rationing programs and printed coupon books for such commodities as gasoline, coffee, canned foods, and shoes. In October Congress passed the Emergency Anti-Inflation Act, giving the president the authority to stabilize wages, prices, and salaries affecting the cost of living. Compromising with the farm bloc, the Senate allowed the OPA to impose limits on agricultural prices within 90 percent of parity. When President Roosevelt quickly issued an executive order that froze most farm commodity prices, rural producers and their congressional allies protested that he had exceeded his powers, and the Senate voted 78 to 2 to rescind the order. Only when the chief executive agreed to forbid further wage and salary increases did the Senate retreat.[29]

Roosevelt issued the anticipated wage and salary order in April 1943, but he sought to hold down the cost of living and preserve labor peace by initiating a consumer subsidy program that allowed the federal government to buy agricultural commodities at market prices and sell them to distributors below cost. Critics of the executive branch protested that Congress never authorized the program. Farm groups complained that it raised the federal debt and pandered to urban and labor interests. Predictably, both chambers voted in June to prohibit the program. After Roosevelt vetoed the legislation, however, the House fell eighty votes short of an override. Committed to farm price supports, Congress had to accept continuation of the consumer subsidies.[30]

The Emergency Anti-Inflation Act of 1942 also authorized the president to correct inequities in wages and salaries. Roosevelt soon issued an executive order that set a $25,000 after-tax ($67,000 gross) limit on salaries. Although the largely symbolic action affected few Americans, public opinion supported the action by a 2-1 margin. Nevertheless, Republican members of Congress attacked policymaking by executive order. Arguing that the cap destroyed incentive, established precedent for a socialized economy, and violated congressional intent, the House Ways and Means Committee revoked the proviso in March 1943. The full chamber then voted to support the committee, with nearly all Republicans siding with the majority. In the Senate such former progressives as Gerald Nye opposed the "dictatorial executive order," as did Robert La Follette Jr., Hiram Johnson, Joseph O'Mahoney, and Henrik Shipstead. One month after the Senate reversed Roosevelt's action by an overwhelming 74-3 vote, the president caved in and abandoned his scheme.[31]

Congressional suspicion of the OPA led to the creation of the House Select Committee to Investigate Acts of Executive Agencies beyond the Scope of Their Authority. The inquiry stemmed from a proposal advanced in February 1943 by Representative Howard W. Smith, a Virginia Democrat. Republicans hoped an investigation would show how federal bureaucracy imperiled constitutional government, free enterprise, and the American way of life. But even such Roosevelt Democrats as California's Jerry Voorhis supported the review as a way of ensuring the implementation of congressional will. The Smith resolution passed the House by a resounding 294-50 vote. As the committee turned to the OPA, the Virginia representative warned that New Dealers were trying to force changes in American business practices.[32]

OPA's anti-inflation program addressed the needs of consumers, not producers. Predictably, small business competitors often objected. Traveling salespeople in the East, for example, protested that gas rationing permitted them to cover only a third of their normal mileage. In Minnesota fish suppliers argued against restrictions on motor boat fuel. Until the Petroleum Administration for War allowed them to apply for exemptions, independent truckers objected to the cancellation of credit cards for gas purchases. An order limiting meat slaughters to 70 percent of 1941 output prompted small wholesalers and processors to charge that large packinghouses no longer sold to them. Dairy producers, millers, bakers, and canners complained that increased labor and supply costs made it impossible to honor commodity price ceilings.[33]

Wary members of Congress tied such inequities to centralized government control and executive threats to congressional power. Representative Everett M. Dirksen, a Republican from Illinois, noted, for example, that federal courts did not have jurisdiction over OPA appeals because Congress had created emergency panels to review the agency's decisions. In a similar fashion, Representative John Jennings, Jr., a Tennessee Republican, complained that OPA officials ran "kangaroo courts" to perpetuate their "outrages." Rules, regulations, price ceilings, sanctions, and penalties, protested Jennings, "have harassed and tormented our people." William Lemke, a Nonpartisan Leaguer from North Dakota, described the OPA "as an un-American illegitimate child put over by an official clique in Washington that think more of foreign institutions than our own." The House Committee on Un-American Activities even suggested that some OPA officials were Communists.[34]

The Smith committee exploited these sentiments by focusing on the alleged arrogance of unqualified bureaucrats. "Congress is trying to rid the government of a lot of power-drunk theorists," declared Florida's Representative Robert L. F. Sikes. Their "far-fetched rulings," charged Sikes, were "the despair of businessmen, . . . an American gestapo, waiting to crack down upon the unwary." Minnesota's Walter Judd touched a similar theme when he told constituents that the country was mounting a "rebellion" against arbitrary rulings by theorists who lacked firsthand business experience. Charles W. Vursell, a House Republican from Illinois, reiterated the point by noting that the Smith committee had exposed OPA official J. Kenneth Galbraith as a professional economist with no business experience. The controversy led William Langer to claim that the OPA had 2,700 lawyers in the field. When the government insisted there were only 1,700, Langer pointed to the agency's "wasteful squandering of funds" and stated that whatever the number, there were "several thousand too many."[35]

As the Smith committee proceeded to compel OPA officials to testify in

June 1943, the House passed three amendments introduced by Everett Dirksen. The first sought to ensure "business-like operations" through a 20 percent ($35 million) cut in OPA funding. The second erased salaries for agency officials who awarded subsidy payments. The third required price policy administrators to have five continuous years of business experience in the field they regulated.[36]

❖ ❖ ❖

Congressional disciplining of the OPA reflected widespread discomfort with the intrusions of wartime bureaucracy. Total war required "rationing of nearly everything and regimentation of nearly everyone," charged the Republican dissident Lawrence Dennis. The complaint appeared to be widespread. "I feel that you people in Washington have a very poor understanding of the average American," a Californian wrote to the White House in 1942. The protester contended that most people attributed unnecessary gas and rubber rationing to the whims of "some 'damn fool' in Washington." He asked the federal government to explain the persistence of rubber shortages when auto and tire producers had converted to synthetic substitutes. Most citizens believed that the war could be won without sacrificing standards of living. "Washington's indirect and deceitful way of dealing with the American people," declared the correspondent, was destroying public confidence in government.[37]

As rationing and price controls took effect, dissatisfaction with the government grew. In mid-1942 more than a fourth of a sample of rural midwesterners held the administration responsible for problems with the war effort (30 percent held business management accountable). That September 19 percent of a national poll asserted Washington had too much control over the nation's way of doing business. Three months later the figure jumped to 27 percent. By January 1943, 41 percent of Americans surveyed believed that government should have less control over everyday commerce. George B. Schwabe, an Oklahoma Republican, felt moved to exclaim that the nation was suffering from "bureauitis."[38]

Such Republicans as Kentucky's Representative John M. Robsion bemoaned the waste involved in the "useless" regimentation of the federal bureaucracy. Robsion also criticized the fact that 300,000 single men and childless husbands remained as civilian employees of the government during wartime. Other members of Congress, such as Senator Millard F. Tydings, a Maryland Democrat, castigated the nearly three thousand Washington publicists whose "drivel" addressed nonessential needs. Yet opponents of bureaucracy went beyond issues of efficiency to picture systemic flaws in the U.S. form of government. In most cases they blamed the problem on New Deal agencies that had "sprung up like mushrooms." The nation, asserted Roy O. Woodruff, a Michigan Republican, was "paying deeply for the past follies of foolish politicians, selfish bureaucrats, and irresponsible, ill-advised theorists as well as would-be autocrats." Woodruff reasoned that the hardships of the home front had their sources in New Deal "political experimentation" and the policies of a "clique" exploiting world affairs for its own political purposes.[39]

Congress insisted that the expansion of executive prerogative lay at the root of the nation's problems. Representative Robert F. Jones, an Ohio Republican, defined the enemy as the "invisible government of planners outside of the control of Congress." For the former dentist Henrik Shipstead, the danger lay in the fact that "long-haired men and short-haired women," the self-styled "brainy people," had taken over government and presumed to do the thinking for the American people. Representative Walter Judd, a Minnesota physician, followed a similar line. By assuming that "everybody but themselves is a crook," the newly elected Judd wrote to a constituent, New Dealers had made "millions of Americans so angry that they are coming to regard Washington as more of an enemy than Hitler and Japan." Expanding on a popular Republican theme, Senate party leader Kenneth S. Wherry declared in 1945 that only Congress stood between the nation "and a form of bureaucratic, dictated, coupon-rationed life which would combine the worst features of all known social systems."[40]

Former populists and progressives shared the hostility to bureaucracy that permeated Congress. Louis Ludlow, an Indiana Democrat, twice introduced House resolutions to investigate the matter. William Lemke, a fellow noninterventionist, remained one of the House's staunchest critics of government agencies. In a 1943 floor speech Lemke painted the administration as "top heavy with book-educated specialists from Harvard, Cornell, and Columbia . . . woefully lacking in experience and common horse sense." Bureaucracy produced mainly "bluff, bluster, blunder, and deception," he charged. Substituting "their own egotistical ignorance for law," government officials had used "red tape" to "hamper, harass, and hamstring" the nation's working people. Congress now sensed that the bureaucratic system was vaguely "un-American," declared Lemke.[41]

Robert La Follette Jr. provided a broader analysis of the problem. Although La Follette believed that "dollar-a-year monopolists" were responsible for the worst abuses of the wartime agencies, he acknowledged that bureaucracy itself was placing representative government "on trial for its life." Writing in the *Atlantic Monthly* in July 1943, the senator warned that a "multitude of agencies" was "reaching into the homes and lives of each and every citizen, affecting what he shall eat, what he shall wear, how warm or cold his home shall be, where he shall work, how he shall do business, what prices he shall charge . . . what he shall raise and what he will get to do with it." La Follette argued that the technical nature of problems required a growing body of administrative law drafted and implemented by the executive branch. Accordingly, it was difficult to check how agencies spent appropriations. The legislature was obliged, he concluded, to limit "the excesses of a relatively irresponsible bureaucracy operating under vast designated powers."[42]

Congress confronted the issue of executive rule in 1940 when it passed the Walter-Logan bill. Proposed by Senator M. M. Logan from Kentucky and Representative Francis Walter from Pennsylvania, both Democrats, the legislation sought to permit unconditional judicial review of most federal agencies' orders. Walter insisted that the measure was designed to stop "administration bureaucracies" from exercising "autocratic powers" and controlling the legislative and judicial branches of government. Other supporters argued that the bill would rejuvenate congressional authority, safeguard a government of laws, and control "administrative absolutism." Although the House failed to override President Roosevelt's year-end veto, the Walter-Logan episode revealed how hostility toward New Deal regulatory policy divided both Democrats and Congress.[43]

Accusations of communism in the federal agencies contributed sharply to antigovernment sentiment. Martin Dies's House Committee on Un-American Activities (HUAC) saw its mission as purging the executive departments of a "united front of radicals and crackpots." Such panel supporters as Eugene Cox, a Democrat from Georgia, portrayed the subversive "enemy within our own borders" as harshly as he did foreign foes. After Dies warned in February 1943 that forty-three employees of the federal government had Communist affiliations, the House voted to renew HUAC for two years. Meanwhile, a special House appropriations panel investigated Dies's charges and recommended the dismissal of three government officials known as left-wing professors. The House then voted overwhelmingly to fire the three until the president sought Senate approval for reappointment. Despite objections, both Roosevelt and the Senate signed onto the House action. In July 1943 the Senate toyed with the idea of requiring war agency officials making an annual salary of at least $4,500 to come before it for confirmation.[44]

Wartime demands for efficiency led the Senate to chose Missouri's Harry S. Truman in 1941 to lead the Special Committee Investigating the National Defense Program. Antibureaucracy feeling also spilled over into campaigns against perceived New Deal threats to private enterprise and economic opportunity. During 1942 and 1943 Congress eliminated the Civilian Conservation Corps, the Works Progress Administration, and the National Youth Administration and drastically reduced funding for the Farm Security Administration. The House also abolished the National

Resources Planning Board (NRPB), an executive agency whose postwar blueprint called for deficit financing of expanded medical care, education, housing, social insurance, and public works. The Joint Committee on Reduction of Nonessential Federal Expenditures, chaired by Senator Harry F. Byrd, a Virginia Democrat, played a major role in the assault on the NRPB. When Congress created a joint panel on postwar economic policy in 1943, it called for the removal of wartime controls and enactment of such investment incentives as tax reduction.[45]

✦ ✦ ✦

Much of the conflict over government regulation revolved around the welfare of small or independent enterprise. Like many others, Wright Patman, a Texas Democrat, equated small business with reliance on the initiative and resourcefulness of individual proprietors. Wartime economic concentration and government defense policy exacerbated their concerns about the survival of small firms. Under the direction of "dollar-a-year" executives on leave from private corporations, the War Production Board centralized economic mobilization and conversion to military production. Defense priorities for rapid production ensured cost-plus contracts, enabling corporate after-tax earnings to leap from $6.4 billion in 1940 to $10.8 billion four years later. Wartime tax codes allowed industrialists to amortize expansion costs over five years. Moreover, widespread antitrust immunity encouraged big war contractors to use pools and cooperative arrangements for efficiency.[46]

Since large corporations had the plants, technology, and managerial expertise for wartime production, they received most government defense contracts. In the eighteen months after May 1940 the nation's one hundred largest companies won over three-fourths of the primary war supply contracts. More than half the $175 billion in prime awards between 1940 and 1944 went to the top thirty-three corporations. Most subcontracts were given to other large companies or to smaller outfits bound to terms set by the giants. The result of these trends was dramatic. Firms with less than a hundred workers saw their portion of total manufacturing employment slip from 26 percent to 19 percent between 1939 and 1944. By the end of 1943 small manufacturers were merging or selling their factories at more than twice the rate of 1939. Altogether, over 324,000 business firms folded between 1940 and 1945, more than 10 percent of the total existing before the war.[47]

As the nation's industrial machinery geared up for military production in the summer of 1940, Senator James E. Murray, a Montana Democrat, called for the creation of a Senate small business committee. Murray rejected the idea of "an inquisitorial investigation or witch hunt" against the chains and big business. Instead, he promised to explore how small business could be aided by providing risk capital and loans and simplifying reports to the government. A Roosevelt loyalist, Murray warned the president that Republicans had "set the small businessmen of the country against you." Although the White House asked him to postpone the resolution until completion of the Temporary National Economic Committee (TNEC) report on independent enterprise, the Montanan pushed ahead. In October 1940 the Senate established its Special Committee to Study the Problems of American Small Business and named Murray as chair. Three days before Pearl Harbor, the House agreed to set up its own small business panel, with Wright Patman, the Texas populist, as presiding officer.[48]

Truman committee hearings in 1941 had revealed that government defense agencies had largely failed to steer military contracts to smaller firms. Senator Murray enlisted the aid of Robert Taft and Arthur Capper, both advocates for independent businesses, to focus the attention of the Small Business Committee on equitable access to military contracts and raw materials. Unless Washington offered relief, suggested a panel report, big business would dominate postwar industry. Such an outcome would create the conditions for a "totalitarian system" of government collectivism. Murray also reported that wartime banks and lending institutions were not extending loans to small entrepreneurs. If administrative agencies did not have adequate representation of independent business, he argued, they would not understand that "the future of free enterprise" depended on "the maintenance of small business."[49]

Both James Murray and Wright Patman put the weight of their committees behind legislation to force the War Production Board to mobilize the capacity of small operators. The Murray-Patman bill, which passed both houses unanimously in May 1942, also provided the Smaller War Plants Corporation with $150 million to loan to independent manufacturers. By November 1943 the agency claimed to have granted nearly $1.5 billion in contracts and $40 million in financial assistance. Yet a provision of the Murray-Patman Act permitted violations of antitrust laws when the WPB certified that contracts were necessary to the war effort and the public interest.[50]

As military procurement reached a plateau in 1944, the Senate small business panel focused on the inability of independent manufacturers to gain access to materials for peacetime reconversion. Frustration exploded in a dramatic confrontation between Kenneth Wherry, a Nebraskan Republican on the committee, and a WPB official. Wherry had defeated George Norris in a three-way race in 1942 by depicting big government and bureaucracy as hostile concentrations of remote power. Appointed to the Small Business Committee, the new senator accompanied a North

Carolina furniture manufacturer to WPB headquarters to complain about inadequate fiberboard allocations. As Wherry identified himself to a paper-shuffling official, the bureaucrat announced that he was studying a set of outhouse blueprints and was tired of senators asking for favors. According to his own account, the Nebraskan seized the man by the throat and flung him into his chair. Later that day Wherry subpoenaed the official and the WPB's vice-chair. The agency apologized and resolved its problems with the manufacturer.[51]

In 1944 the Senate easily approved a Murray and Wherry proposal to meet reconversion needs by increasing the capital stock of the Smaller War Plants Corporation to $350 million. A report by the Small Business Committee had suggested that large producers received special government funding for conversion to wartime production. The bill now sought to stimulate public and private loans to independent business and facilitate small competitors' access to government resources, patents, and surplus war property sales. After hearing the noninterventionist Hamilton Fish assert that a million small businesses with four or less employees had gone bankrupt in the past two years, the House approved the measure, and the president signed it at the end of the year. The Smaller War Plants Corporation eventually won the status of an independent agency and lasted until the end of 1946. Meanwhile, the Smaller War Plants Division of the WPB attempted to aid small businesses by allowing them to reconvert to civilian production ahead of the large military contractors.[52]

Despite gains, the small business coalition was split by partisan and ideological differences as the military conflict came to an end. The 1941 TNEC report had attempted to chart a consensus on economic opportunity for individual competitors. Unlike communism or fascism, concluded the TNEC, democracy afforded the masses the hope of using their own property to maintain their economic existence. Yet Americans found it difficult to adjust the plight of the individual to organized economy. Since the 1890s, the report read, the nation had "failed to protect individual rights against the growing power of groups." Collective agencies had produced centralized business, labor, agriculture, and government, forcing small business to deal with bureaucracy and monopoly. Framed by Democratic chair Joseph O'Mahoney, the TNEC report called for national standards for corporate competition and financing.[53]

Both the TNEC and the congressional small business panels supported the Roosevelt administration's insistence that government activism could aid independent enterprise. A loyal Democrat, House committee chair Wright Patman was one of the few small business advocates to support the OPA's extension in 1945. Patman also pointed out that twelve years of Republican rule had produced 50 percent more business failures than eleven years of the New Deal had. The Texan continued to win the support of retail trade associations for aggressive attacks on large distributors. After a Small Business Committee inquiry in 1943, Patman introduced legislation to ensure that small distributors had access to war surpluses. The effort to achieve reconversion equity won the panel editorial acclaim as "an effective court of appeal for the little fellow."[54]

Despite strong allies, the Patman committee almost had its funding eliminated in 1945. The panel's failure to focus on the threat of government competition, cooperatives, and labor unions angered such groups as the National Small Business Men's Association (NSBMA) and the Conference of American Small Business Organizations (CASBO). These lobbies shared Robert Taft's fear that big business units could easily be taken over by a socialist-leaning government. Frederick Virkus, leader of the CASBO, complained that large interests used the planned economy to postpone small producers' reconversion. Moreover, Patman's suspicion of eastern banks, investment houses, and large corporations produced an independence that alienated administration officials. Despite a temporary funding cutoff, however, the House small business panel prevailed when such retail trade associations as the National Association of Retail Druggists (NARD) came to its rescue and Congress responded.[55]

✦ ✦ ✦

As World War II drew to a close, conflicts between nationalist and internationalist commitments resurfaced as a defining wedge in American politics. In July 1944 President Roosevelt invited the representatives of forty-four nations to a monetary and financial conference at Bretton Woods, New Hampshire. The meeting laid the groundwork for establishing the International Monetary Fund (IMF), the International Bank for Reconstruction and Development (World Bank), and the General Agreement on Tariffs and Trade (GATT). Capitalized at $8.8 billion, the IMF created a central pool of currencies and gold from which member nations could borrow to settle international trade balances. The World Bank used a $9.1 billion fund to make and guarantee long-term international investments for productive purposes. GATT created the structure for negotiating multinational tariff concessions.[56]

Secretary of the Treasury Henry Morgenthau Jr., the conference president, announced that these actions were designed to eradicate the evils of competitive currency devaluation and destructive trade barriers. The world's people "must be enabled to produce and to sell if they are to be able to purchase and consume," argued Morgenthau. The war had taught leaders, he insisted in the radio broadcast that concluded the meeting, that national interests were best protected through international cooperation.

Proclaiming the end of an era of "extreme nationalism," Morgenthau pictured the people of the earth as "inseparably linked to one another by a deep, underlying community of purpose."[57]

Robert Wagner, a New York Democrat, introduced legislation to support the IMF in February 1945. The proposal won endorsement from the Business and Industry Committee for Bretton Woods, an association of over a hundred leading business and banking executives. Yet traditional noninterventionists continued to question the purpose of global monetary reform. Their concerns were perhaps best captured by the constituent who warned Minnesota's Henrik Shipstead that the agreement would result in "enslavement of the world to the international banking gang." A "financial regimentation" that forced other nations to take out loans and repay them in dollars, agreed Shipstead, would compel an American police force to counter global resentment. North Dakota's William Langer argued that the United States should not join the IMF until it agreed to prohibit loans for military purposes. A bipartisan coalition of senators from western mining areas denounced the fund's unwillingness to expand the money supply by remonetizing silver.[58]

Republican critics of Bretton Woods built on a wartime legacy of economic nationalism that pictured international trade agreements as threats to living standards in the United States. Lawrence Dennis, a party strategist, embodied these sentiments most clearly in a secret position paper in 1942. Attempts to "save, run, and uplift the world, to enforce peace, plenty, and security for everybody, everywhere," complained Dennis, would come about only "by leveling down" the quality of American life. Reimposing the gold standard on the world, he warned, would only restore the international finance capitalism that died in 1929. Dennis dismissed Republican internationalism as the product of Wall Street, the Bank of England, the major foundations, and U.S. universities, "all propaganda agencies for the British internationalist idea in finance and trade." Republicans would have to choose, he insisted, between the economic nationalism that made their party and the economic internationalism that defined Franklin Roosevelt's New Deal.[59]

The journalist John Flynn, a veteran antimonopolist and noninterventionist, built on the nationalist critique to mount a detailed attack on the IMF. In a 1945 pamphlet entitled *You Better Know about Bretton Woods,* Flynn argued that the United States would contribute 77 percent of the fund's lendable assets because all U.S. investment would be in gold and dollars. Borrowers would control 75 percent of the board of governors, he advised. Furthermore, currency scarcities could compel the United States to pour more dollars into the fund and trade only with nations that had been rationed dollars. Flynn also reminded Americans that four-fifths of their $3 billion World Bank contribution would make up losses on guaranteed private loans.[60]

Senator Robert Taft proved to be the leading adversary of the Bretton Woods plan. Taft argued that a vast exchange fund could not stabilize international trade and that the United States should not support faltering currencies before recipients returned to civilian existence. He insisted that Washington first reach agreement with Britain on the relative value of the pound and then provide temporary credits to individual nations. Taft emphasized that the United States "should involve itself in no long-range program." Citing the opposition of the American Bankers Association and domestic business interests, the Ohioan pictured the IMF as part of a New Deal program to create new methods of deficit spending. He questioned exclusive presidential control of foreign exchange transactions and the gold value of the dollar. In June 1945, however, the Bretton Woods proposal passed the House 345 to 18. The next month it won Senate approval, with William Langer, Arthur Capper, Burton Wheeler, Kenneth Wherry, and Taft among the minority.[61]

Most members of Congress supported international trade agreements because they believed it important to demonstrate Allied wartime unity. Nevertheless, such Republican nationalists as Representative Raymond E. Willis from Indiana continued to complain about the Roosevelt administration's attempts "to indoctrinate" the nation with propaganda legitimizing the international economy. "We are being told . . . that we must cease to be nationalists," protested Kenneth Wherry, a defender of Nebraska livestock and sugar beet producers hurt by tariff reductions. In a similar fashion, George Peek, a farm machinery entrepreneur, warned that global trade concessions would lead to the abandonment of wage and price levels in the United States and the loss of the nation's independence of political action. Peek joined Wherry in mocking American Communist party leader Earl Browder's prophecy of a postwar "new world order" of free trade. Such a future, warned the former New Dealer, would benefit international bankers while destroying the nation.[62]

Congressional concern for agricultural producers and administration reliance on "executive agreements" surfaced repeatedly during the debates over renewal of reciprocal trade in 1943 and 1945. White House assumption of congressional prerogative, charged Senator Alexander Wiley, a Wisconsin Republican, provided an example of "collectivism on the march." A tirade by North Dakota's William Langer summarized the frustration of nationalist critics. "The academic bureaucrats who label themselves as experts," declared Langer, had "wormed their way into high places of non-elective government" and usurped the power of Congress. These "sixth columnist internationalists" sought to rule "by directive, decrees, regulations, and dictatorial practices." Unschooled in manual labor, "young callow college graduate fledglings" had implemented trade policies that resulted in foreigners' replacing American vegetable growers.[63]

Concern for independent producers in industry and agriculture led nine Republicans on the House Ways and Means Committee to file a minority report when the panel called for bipartisan endorsement of the trade bill in 1943. Yet only sixty-five representatives opposed the legislation on the final vote. After amendments shortened the renewal period from three to two years, Republicans voted 18 to 15 to support the bill in the Senate. Two years later a measure permitting presidential discretion in halving tariffs passed the Senate Finance Committee by a single vote before it was approved by the entire body. Dissenters on this round included Arthur Capper, William Langer, Joseph O'Mahoney, Henrik Shipstead, Robert Taft, and Kenneth Wherry.[64]

❖ ❖ ❖

Although the allure of international cooperation enabled the White House to persevere on the Bretton Woods proposals and reciprocal trade, the issue of executive power continued to complicate wartime policymaking. Early in 1943 Senator Arthur Vandenberg from Michigan renewed the call for the president's "strict accountability" to Congress. As Republican members of Congress placed lend-lease and other administrative programs under close scrutiny, Vandenberg charged that the administration planned to implement postwar international agreements by simple congressional majorities instead of the two-thirds vote needed for Senate ratification of treaties. John Flynn pleaded with the senator to lead Congress in "implacable" resistance to the president's "invasions." Roosevelt critics in the press, such as John O'Donnell of the *Washington Times-Herald,* complained that Americans knew less about White House war and peace aims than did the people of Great Britain.[65]

Congressional and nationalist will faced a severe test in March 1943, when four bipartisan sponsors introduced a House resolution calling on the United States to take the lead in forming a permanent international organization with military policing power. OWI studies showed that popular opinion overwhelmingly favored the creation of a postwar global association. A Gallup survey of 1942 found 59 percent of the sample supported a new league of nations (73 percent of all with an opinion). Aware of the negative political consequences of their rejection of U.S. membership in the League of Nations in the 1920s, Republican leaders moved cautiously toward bipartisan endorsement of a postwar peacekeeping unit. Yet suspicion of Allied war aims and anxieties over administration political goals helped kill the league proposal in committee.[66]

In June 1943 J. William Fulbright, an Arkansas Democrat, submitted a new House resolution that called for "appropriate international machinery," with adequate power to maintain a "just and lasting" postwar peace. When an amendment guaranteed that U.S. participation would be predicated on "constitutional processes," the measure won the support of such noninterventionists as Hamilton Fish. The September vote produced an overwhelming 360-29 endorsement. Tom Connally, a Texas Democrat, immediately introduced a Senate resolution proposing the establishment of a general international organization for maintaining "peace and security." Connally's final offering contained three significant qualifications: there would be no world police force, the "sovereignty" of member states would be preserved, and U.S. membership would depend on the two-thirds Senate vote needed to ratify treaties. The measure passed with only five dissenting votes in November.[67]

Despite such consensus, the prospect of U.S. membership in an international organization disturbed many noninterventionists and nationalists. Representative Usher Burdick from North Dakota, a Republican veteran of the Nonpartisan League wars, had insisted as early as 1941 that "One Worlders in the United Nations" would destroy the sovereignty of the only democracy on earth. Five weeks after Pearl Harbor Representative Clare Hoffman, a Michigan Republican, warned of the danger of "surrendering our independence" and "submerging our nationality" to become part "of a new supergovernment, a United States of the World." Burton Wheeler, a Democrat, suggested in 1943 that Europe needed less nationalism and the United States "more Americanism." The nation was not "isolationist," Wheeler assured Robert Wood the following April; it was simply opposed to a world police force or "supergovernment."[68]

John Flynn's writings provided a clear example of the application of democratic nationalism to foreign policy. A staff member and adviser to the Pecora and Nye investigations of the 1930s as well as a former America First official, Flynn published *As We Go Marching* in 1944. The book argued that New Deal planners had created an "autarchical corporative state" to alleviate unemployment through deficit spending. This expanding bureaucracy soon turned to militarism and imperialism to solve internal contradictions. Flynn saw the United Nations as "an international security program" run by "the huge military establishments of a few imperialist nations." Sharing these views, North Dakota's Gerald Nye criticized the Connally resolution because he feared a repeat of the Versailles treaty's attempt to freeze peace accords by force. When the Soviets, British, and Americans met at Dumbarton Oaks in 1944, the former Nonpartisan Leaguer denounced the gathering as "a military alliance between the great powers to rule the world by means of regional understandings."[69]

Like John Flynn, Gerald Nye predicted that the United States would soon have a standing army, huge debt, and a militarized educational system. Nye also warned that the balance-of-power system would pressure Americans to intervene in another European war to keep the Soviet Union from expanding. Concern over Soviet hegemony in eastern Europe had prompted North Carolina's Robert Reynolds to submit an unsuccessful amendment to the Connally resolution that called for recognizing the postwar independence of subjugated nations. When President Roosevelt returned from the three-power meeting in Yalta in February 1945, congressional representatives from Polish-American districts led other nationalists in questioning the failure to address Soviet wartime gains. By tolerating the "unilateral dismemberment" of Poland, declared Thad F. Wasielewski, a Democrat from Milwaukee, Yalta violated the stated war aim of achieving peace based on national self-determination. "Why must we yield with silence to the demands of our allies again and again and again?" asked Wasielewski.[70]

Following Franklin Roosevelt's death in April 1945, President Harry Truman moved the nation toward a key role in the creation of the United Nations. Careful to appoint congressional delegates from both parties to the San Francisco organizing conference, Truman asked the Senate to ratify the UN treaty in July. Few spoke against the proposal. Burton Wheeler noted that the UN Charter failed to include "one single clear specific provision for the protection of the individual human personality." Wheeler compared the charter and the UN treaty with the Fourteen Points and the Versailles accord. Henrik Shipstead, another traditional noninterventionist, argued that the concentrated military, political, and economic power of a superstate would crush the American middle class and impose world market requirements on the nation's economy. In the end Shipstead and William Langer were the only two senators to vote against the UN treaty. Langer later claimed that seven senators privately confided that he had voted correctly.[71]

✦ ✦ ✦

Wartime electoral politics helped replace veteran congressional noninterventionists with a new breed of younger nationalists lacking New Deal ties. Resentment of the OPA, freezes on farm prices, and the continuing war contributed to a twenty-two million drop in voter turnout in 1942. Republicans benefited from the "anti-Washington wave" by gaining forty-four seats in the House and nine in the Senate. Among the casualties was George Norris, the Nebraska progressive and World War I opponent who at the age of eighty-one reversed his decision to retire and ran as an independent. Kenneth Wherry, the Republican who won Norris's Senate seat, was a former auto dealer, attorney, and funeral director who had once worked for the man he defeated. A "maverick" who denounced Wall Street's manipulation of agricultural credit, Wherry turned the populist rage of the Great Plains against the unpopular rulers of a distant central government.[72]

Weeks after the 1942 election Lawrence Dennis drafted a Republican position paper. "The two great American issues of the twentieth century have been internationalism versus isolation and individualism versus collectivism," declared Dennis. Condemning the Republican party's abandonment of economic nationalism and isolation, he belittled bipartisan attempts to reconstruct the world through American credit. Dennis insisted that both Franklin Roosevelt and Wendell Willkie sought to commit the nation to an internationalism that would destroy the two-party system and require totalitarian controls. Only if the war ended before 1944, he predicted, could Republicans regain the presidency "on a wave of reaction" against "ration cards and radio propaganda."[73]

Robert Wood and other Republican nationalists embraced the Dennis memo. Yet as the party prepared for the 1944 presidential election, Wendell Willkie demanded that Republicans repudiate the party's noninterventionist wing. For such nationalists as Wood and John Flynn, Willkie was "a fifth columnist" who represented New York's international bankers. Accordingly, a group including Wood, Arthur Vandenberg, the publishers Frank Gannett and Roy Howard, the former America First official Lansing Hoyt, and *Progressive* editor Isabel B. La Follette sought to undercut Willkie by promoting the presidential candidacy of General Douglas MacArthur. After taking 74 percent of the Illinois Republican primary, however, MacArthur's strength tapered off, and the general withdrew. The Republican convention chose Thomas E. Dewey, the internationalist governor of New York, to contest President Roosevelt's quest for a fourth term. Although Ohio's Governor John W. Bricker won the vice presidential nomination, midwestern nationalists found themselves on the fringes of the Republican machinery once again.[74]

The Democrats swept to victory in 1944 with over 53 percent of the popular vote. Simultaneously, the ranks of former noninterventionists shrank with the defeats of Representative Hamilton Fish and Senators Bennett Champ Clark and Gerald Nye. Two years later Robert La Follette Jr. lost a tight Wisconsin Republican primary, Burton Wheeler failed to win the Democratic contest in Montana, and Minnesota's Henrik Shipstead lost in the general election. For opponents of New Deal internationalism and statism, the world had turned upside down. The editorialist Paul Jones, a Roosevelt critic, wondered how the "orthodox total liberal" could maintain "a superstitious belief in the healing virtue of centralized authority."

Wheeler noted the irony of treating corporate supporters of global interventionism as "liberals" while "lifelong progressives" were denounced as "reactionary" for opposing it. The source of "special privilege," insisted Philip La Follette, had shifted to "phony liberals" and "sap-headed internationalists."[75]

With the death of Hiram Johnson in 1946, William Langer and Arthur Capper remained the only Senate survivors of prewar progressivism and noninterventionism. Nevertheless, a bipartisan coalition of insurgent heirs came to dominate Congress in succeeding years. Substituting nationalism for noninterventionism and free enterprise for attacks on concentrated economic power, the new congressional majority mounted an assault on government power, liberal internationalism, and cultural cosmopolitanism that would define the domestic politics of the cold war.

10

Crisis of the Old Order: The Revolt against Liberal Elites, 1945–50

A 1945 report by the House Military Affairs Committee tersely observed that "Communist interests have coincided with the country's interests while the United States was at war with Germany."[1] The contradictions of the World War II alliance with the Soviet Union cast an immense shadow over postwar American politics and foreign policy. As war turned to cold peace, populist, nationalist, and democratic politicians continued to express frustration over New Deal collectivism, bureaucracy, and financial internationalism. But as the nation mobilized for a confrontation with global communism, they increasingly questioned the loyalty and moral discipline of the nation's intelligentsia and governing elites. By 1949 cold war reversals so infuriated Truman administration opponents that they prepared to disrupt a temporary foreign policy consensus and expose the perceived treachery of the established order.

✦ ✦ ✦

The close of World War II brought increased attacks on the Office of Price Administration (OPA) by longstanding critics of government bureaucracy. House Republicans, such as Nebraska's A. L. Miller and Ohio's Thomas A. Jenkins, insisted that OPA bureaucrats sought to "blueprint and regiment the citizen" through permanent price control. In the Senate W. Lee O'Daniel, a Texas Democrat, demanded the agency's "unconditional surrender" so that "free enterprise" might be restored to a peacetime economy. By the winter of 1946 the OPA had ended all rationing programs except sugar. Although polls indicated that nearly three-fourths of Americans supported the maintenance of price ceilings, legislation to extend the agency's life confronted crippling amendments, particularly from midwestern members of Congress.[2]

The OPA controversy prompted such politicians as Nebraska's Kenneth Wherry to complain that Washington paid more attention to the interests of urban workers and consumers than to the concerns of rural producers. Wherry fought to gain cost-of-production protection for livestock and other farm products and then sought to exempt agricultural commodities from price ceilings altogether. The senator also sought to compel the OPA to include distributor acquisition costs and prewar profit margins in retail pricing calculations. In November 1945 the Senate Small Business Committee reported that while individual proprietors feared inflation, they protested the lack of "elbow room" generated by price and trade restrictions. Inflexible price controls usually favored large buyers over small operators. When John Bricker, an Ohio senatorial candidate, surveyed small business constituents in mid-1946, respondents complained that price ceilings did not allow them sufficient profit to survive. Bricker accused the OPA of surrounding itself with "a small gestapo bent on persecuting the little merchant."[3]

Balancing business interests and the desire to control inflation, the Senate passed a restricted OPA renewal bill in June 1946. The measure included amendments originating with Robert Taft, Kenneth Wherry, and Michigan's Representative Fred L. Crawford that allowed manufacturers, distributors, and some retailers to adjust prices to wages and other costs. In protest, Chester Bowles, the director of the Economic Stabilization Board, resigned, and President Truman vetoed the bill as inflationary. A House-Senate conference then fashioned a compromise that exempted tobacco, petroleum products, and many agricultural commodities from price ceilings and allowed most producers to work costs into their prices. Anxious to preserve at least a skeletal OPA, Truman signed the legislation. Partisan pressures, small business lobbying, and ideological objections to government activism had succeeded in vitiating the last symbol of wartime controls.[4]

Despite the victory over the OPA, advocates for independent enterprisers insisted that vestiges of the war economy remained. Small manufacturers in the rubber industry objected to continuing government purchase and storage of raw materials. Arguing that taxpayers absorbed $250,000 a month in warehouse charges to ensure supplies and price stability for huge companies, Senator Bricker and Representative Crawford succeeded in ending the purchase program for natural rubber in 1947. The following year the two fashioned a compromise by which Washington would maintain control of synthetic rubber until 1950. Meanwhile, Kenneth Wherry led the Senate Small Business Committee in hearings in 1947 that exposed how the federal government permitted major oil refiners to deny supplies to independent processors. Wherry subsequently denounced the "government-controlled cartel allocation of raw materials and markets."[5]

The postwar attack on New Deal bureaucracy found its most eloquent champion in John Bricker, a small-town Republican lawyer and business leader who had served as Ohio's public utility commissioner, attorney general, and governor. Bricker skillfully parlayed wartime resentment of bureaucracy and controls into a 1946 run for the Senate. "They have assumed to tell us where we will work, what we will be paid, the clothing we shall wear, the food we shall eat," the 1944 vice presidential candidate told campaign audiences. Bricker insisted taxation (30 percent of postwar annual income) was a greater threat than military invasion and held it responsible for high interest rates, inflation, and public debt. Speaking to the interests of a beleaguered middle class, he accused "power-seeking, office-grabbing bureaucratic experimenters" of trying to turn back the liberation of the market by making government once again "the master of men."[6]

Bricker charged that alien and subversive philosophies had infiltrated labor and government and had reverted to "old world jargon" by references to a political "right" and "left." He rejected these categories by equating liberalism with human rights, middle-class opportunity, and less government power. Bricker described the New Deal as the "most reactionary force in history." Republicans pledged themselves, he declared, to self-government and a system of law that recognized the individual soul and conscience. Unlike the interwar insurgents whose coalitions frequently embraced labor, the Ohio crusader appealed to the New Deal's "forgotten" clerks, bookkeepers, schoolteachers, stenographers, pensioners, and other fixed-income people victimized by inflation and taxation. These middle-class Americans were the individuals who furnished the nation's civic leadership, he maintained. Unorganized, they found themselves the "chief victims" of state planning.[7]

Postwar opponents of the New Deal from both parties positioned themselves as insurgent foes of a decadent bureaucracy. Their politics attested to the strength of nineteenth-century notions of self-help and free enterprise. Such middle-class traditionalists as Henrik Shipstead, a Minnesota dentist nurtured in the farmer-labor activism of the 1920s, maintained an intense suspicion of "the impersonal, collective wisdom of public authority." The state had become "the center of economic policy," complained Shipstead in 1946, "as both lawgiver and baton-wielder, anesthetist, surgeon, and psychiatrist all in one." Representative Walter Judd, a mainstream Republican from Minnesota, held the same views, instructing constituents that both centralized business and government destroyed individual responsibility, self-reliance, independence of spirit, and the incentive to experiment. Similar fear of the power of "the modern state and super-state" characterized the speeches of Pat McCarran, a Democratic senator from Nevada.[8]

❖   ❖   ❖

The passionate antistatism of postwar critics coincided with an enhanced anticommunism, some of it fed by embittered pre–Pearl Harbor noninterventionists. Such former war opponents as Burton Wheeler used Soviet occupation of Eastern Europe to justify their original positions. Reminding colleagues and constituents that he had predicted that the military conflict would only make the world "safe for communism," Wheeler proclaimed in 1945 that "what we went to war to prevent Germany and Japan from achieving, we are now permitting to become a Russian triumph." "It is a tragic irony of history," added Henrik Shipstead the next year, "that Russia, who started this war by helping Hitler, ended up as our ally with all the loot of the Axis empires in her possession." Philip La Follette, former Progressive governor of Wisconsin and an early supporter of America First, noted in a 1946 radio speech that the Soviet Union was the world's last great dictatorship.[9]

Noninterventionists also resented the way communists and other internationalists had smeared American war opponents after June 1941. Burton Wheeler predicted to the journalist John Flynn that such behavior would "react against them when this war is over." Robert La Follette Jr. clearly embodied the anger over wartime propaganda. After leading the Wisconsin Progressive party to a nationalist foreign policy platform in 1944, La Follette lashed out at the Soviet Union and its domestic allies. In a bitter Senate speech in May 1945 he accused Moscow of violating the Yalta accords, destroying self-determination in Eastern Europe, and threatening a permanent peace with imperialist ambitions. Warning against appeasement, La Follette denounced a small minority of Americans for using Hitler-like tactics to discredit criticism of the Soviet Union. Their methods, he insisted, included "the big lie, the big smear, and the wholesale impugning of motives and character."[10]

For such progressives as Senators La Follette and Wheeler, the agents of world communism had replaced financial capitalists as the alien threats to a democratic heritage. Many anticommunists portrayed their foes as elite and privileged subverters of popular will and virtue. Communism denied that people had "a spiritual side," complained George A. Dondero, a Republican from Michigan. Its totalitarian concept, he charged, sought "to keep the common man common." This populist theme surfaced in the commonly expressed warning that communism threatened the basic economic freedoms of American capitalism, "the great revolutionary force of modern times." "Communism would be the great leveller," observed Usher Burdick, a Republican from North Dakota, years after the war. In terms reminiscent of Abraham Lincoln, Burdick warned that only capitalism permitted individuals the fruits of their labor. Emphasizing the coercive elements of a command economy, Ohio's John Bricker declared that the welfare state led to the police state.[11]

❖ ❖ ❖

Republicans played on popular animosity to government bureaucracy and communism in a concerted effort to retrieve control of Congress for the first time since 1930. Building on an agenda fashioned during the war, their candidates attacked unlimited government, executive dominance over Congress, and New Deal departures from political and constitutional tradition. "Stick to your high principles," a hopeful John Flynn advised Robert Taft; the country was "sick and tired of cheap politics and cheap politicians." For his part, Taft denounced excessive government spending and bureaucratic threats to personal liberty. A Democratic victory, warned Republican House minority leader Joseph W. Martin, would ensure "the same crushing bureaucracy, arrogance, and waste; the same deceit and trick phrases, the same distortion and weird construction of law; the same kind of secret government at home and secret diplomacy abroad."[12]

Anxious to exploit popular impatience with government regulations and bureaucracy, Republican candidates used the 1946 congressional elections to draw links between alleged betrayals of American principles at home and overseas. By election time Republican strategists had exploded the communist issue into a major threat. Democratic domestic policies, asserted B. Carroll Reece, chair of the Republican National Committee, bore "a definite made-in Moscow label. That is why . . . the choice that confronts Americans this year is between communism and republicanism." Minority leader Martin vowed that Congress would "ferret out all those who sought to destroy the American way of life." Robert Taft accused the Democrats of "appeasing the Russians abroad and of fostering Communism at home." Representative Charles Vursell, a Republican from Illinois, complained that the New Deal stood for "confusion, control, corruption, and communism."[13]

With Nebraska's Senator Kenneth Wherry heralding the 1946 election as a "crusade," party leaders marketed such slogans as "Had Enough? Vote Republican." Postwar inflation, strikes by 4.6 million American workers, delayed military demobilization, and tensions with the Soviets contributed to the Republicans' capturing a 245-188 majority in the House and a 51-45 plurality in the Senate. The new group included Ohio's John Bricker, Utah's Arthur Watkins, Indiana's William E. Jenner, California's William F. Knowland, Missouri's James Kem, Nevada's George W. Malone, and Wisconsin's Joseph R. McCarthy. McCarthy had defeated Robert La Follette Jr. in the Republican primary when organized labor refused to follow the senator's switch from the Progressive party. In the general election the former marine won by less than six thousand votes when he attacked New Deal bureaucracy and garnered financial support from American Action, a group of Chicago nationalists led by Robert Wood.[14]

Disturbed at Communist influence in the CIO unions, the defeated La Follette warned readers of *Collier's* magazine that party machinations and "fellow-traveler" activity were "a serious menace to our democracy." As the Soviet Union tightened its grip on Eastern Europe in the postwar years, fears of Moscow-inspired subversion gained legitimacy. Anticommunists easily exploited concerns that the Roosevelt and Truman administrations had failed to check the wartime activities of domestic Communist allies. Critics pointed to the 1945 discovery of more than a thousand classified government documents at the offices of *Amerasia*, a Washington bimonthly sympathetic to the cause of Chinese Communists. Although charges of espionage failed to stick, the case pointed to a link between State Department officials and Communist propaganda. The following year fourteen Canadian public officials and leaders were convicted of passing samples of enriched uranium and data about radar to Soviet agents.[15]

Gallup polls of 1946 revealed that 36 percent of the sample believed that Communists should be killed or imprisoned, 16 percent wished to render them inactive, and 7 percent wanted to watch them carefully. In another survey 48 percent thought that Communist party members had greater loyalty to the Soviet Union than to the United States. Another study showed 78 percent of respondents believing that Russian spies operated within U.S. borders. Only 17 percent of an August 1946 sample thought that Communists should be permitted to hold civil service jobs (69 percent disagreed). Certainly President Truman could not have been surprised when Pennsylvania's Governor George H. Earle reminded him of the "intense dislike and fear of communism by a vast majority of the American people."[16]

Although Communist employment in the federal government never surpassed seventy-five out of a work force of half a million, administration critics dramatized the *Amerasia* and Canadian cases to warn of subversive dangers to internal security. In October 1946 Representative J. Parnell Thomas, a Republican from New Jersey, urged federal prosecutors to "immediately crack down on the Moscow-directed fifth column operating in the United States." "Only the batblind can fail to be aware of the Communist invasion of our country," Francis J. Spellman, New York's Roman Catholic cardinal, declared the next month. Meanwhile, FBI director J. Edgar Hoover charged that 100,000 Communists already had infiltrated the nation's institutions.[17]

President Truman responded to the domestic subversion controversy in November 1946 by creating a Temporary Commission on Employee Loyalty. The following March the president established a permanent federal program. Under its terms, regional branches of federal agencies and departments used FBI files to conduct loyalty investigations of government employees. Membership in any one of an attorney general's list of subversive organizations could be grounds for further inquiry. Dismissals were to be issued when investigators found "reasonable grounds" for suspicion of loyalty, subject to approval by a central review board. In effect, the wartime domestic "fascist menace" had been replaced with a Communist threat of internal subversion.[18]

❖ ❖ ❖

Just as the temporary loyalty commission was setting a permanent program in place in the winter of 1947, the Senate started confirmation hearings for David E. Lilienthal's nomination as the first chair of the new Atomic Energy Commission (AEC). The tumultuous debates surrounding the appointment showed how anticommunism frequently buttressed an antielitist attack on government bureaucracy and managerial expertise. The former head of the Tennessee Valley Authority (TVA), Lilienthal won the support of the secretary of war, Under Secretary of State Dean Acheson, the industrialist Owen D. Young, the financier Bernard Baruch, several university presidents, and Philip La Follette. Yet the nominee confronted profound congressional anxiety over civilian control of nuclear facilities and potential threats to atomic secrecy. These concerns combined with Lilienthal's ties to New Deal planning to produce a stormy nomination process.[19]

The debate began when Senate members of the Joint Congressional Committee on Atomic Energy permitted Kenneth McKellar, a Tennessee Democrat, to participate in confirmation hearings. McKellar, who was a TVA opponent and Lilienthal's longtime adversary on patronage matters, grilled the nominee on past political affiliations, Communist activity in the TVA, attitudes toward the internationalization of atomic energy, public power philosophy, and even his Jewish ancestry. The senator implored the committee to deny the nomination if even one member of the panel became concerned about Lilienthal's Americanism or character. To bolster his case that the nominee did not understand that democracy meant "government by the people," McKellar prevailed on the committee to subpoena Arthur E. Morgan, Lilienthal's predecessor at the TVA.[20]

As Thomas K. McCraw has shown, the two TVA directors had feuded bitterly. While Morgan sought to reconcile private and public utilities in power-pooling negotiations, Lilienthal, who was a board member at that time, joined the progressives George Norris and Robert La Follette Jr. in opposing the scheme. When the Roosevelt administration backed the public power faction, the president fired Morgan in 1938 and replaced him with Lilienthal. Testifying nine years later, the ousted agency head insisted that Roosevelt had taken the action to cover up Morgan's charges of collusion, mismanagement, and conspiracy against Lilienthal and his allies. His rival customarily had resorted to intrigue, politics, and misrepresentation, Morgan told the committee. He asserted that Lilienthal had faked electric power reports, altered official agency minutes, colluded with the aluminum monopoly, and surreptitiously undermined his authority. Morgan's central criticism, however, rested on Lilienthal's character.[21]

The ousted TVA head viewed his former rival as a man "without ethical principle," an "actor" who could "almost instantly play any part to perfection." Morgan scored Lilienthal's covert methods because he believed that secrecy easily became "the shelter of self-interest." The nominee was not a liberal by conviction, Morgan told his hometown newspaper, Ohio's *Yellow Springs News,* but merely one who used liberalism to further his own ambitions. "He constantly preaches local autonomy," the former engineer explained to Robert Taft, "yet absolutely dictates the terms under which municipalities sell TVA current." Morgan concluded that Lilienthal could not be trusted to head the AEC.[22]

Senate members of the Atomic Energy Committee voted 8 to 1 to recommend the Lilienthal appointment, with only John Bricker dissenting. Yet Arthur Morgan's accusations of intellectual dishonesty hurt the nomination. When Republican leaders Kenneth Wherry and Robert Taft proclaimed opposition to the appointment in February 1947, the *New York Times* reported the possibility of "all-out partisan warfare between the majority and minority parties in Congress." Taft issued a statement that called the nominee "too soft" on issues connected with communism and the Soviet Union. Using a theme increasingly effective among Republican critics of the New Deal, the Ohio senator criticized Lilienthal for failing to exclude Communist employees from TVA's nuclear installations and other facilities. He also described the former bureau head as "temperamentally unfitted to head any important executive agency in a democratic government." "He is a man," advised Taft, "who does not care what means he uses to reach the end which he thinks happens to be desirable."[23]

Raising what he called "an issue of governmental philosophy," the Ohioan described David Lilienthal as a "power-hungry bureaucrat," capable of defying Congress and stretching executive power beyond the parameters of the statutes. Taft insisted that the Atomic Energy Act was so broad that its administrators had to be people who would not press their powers "to the very limit." Lilienthal, he observed, was part of "a small group of men who largely dominated the so-called New Deal." Opposed by a majority of the current Congress, these bureaucrats sought to defeat private enterprise through constant expansion of federal power. To prove his point, Taft quoted Lilienthal's definition of "modern management" as a process that gave administrators "wide freedom for judgment" in defining goals, assessing tasks, and determining operational methods.[24]

By portraying the nominee as a coarse instrumentalist who used elitist techniques to advance both the government's and his own power, Taft reiterated a theme that antistatists had been advancing since World War II. But by tying David Lilienthal's preference of ends over means to charges that he failed to respond adequately to the presence of Communists in his agency, the Republican leader subtly suggested a compatibility between manipulative New Deal administrators and ruthless totalitarians. Senator McKellar made the connection explicit in a brief comment on the floor. Professing that Lilienthal's "every real inclination" was "communistic," the crusty Tennessee Democrat drew a picture of a bureaucrat "so slick, so double-dealing, so double-appearing, ever trying to agree with the opinions of anyone whom he wants to curry favor with, he might well be a member of that party."[25]

Lilienthal also came under fire from Homer Ferguson, a Republican reform judge from Detroit elected to the Senate in 1942. An early foe of government bureaucracy, Ferguson proclaimed that those who pushed for federal planning, ownership, controls, and paternalism were "traveling the road to totalitarianism." The senator addressed the Lilienthal nomination by targeting agency managers who were "not scrupulous about the tactics they use . . . and follow the dangerous doctrine that the end justifies the means." The nominee was a "social aristocrat," asserted the senator—"socialistic" because of his belief in government ownership and control, "aristocratic" because he thought that experts should be the new governing class. Although Ferguson acknowledged that Lilienthal was well-intentioned and no Communist, he insisted that New Deal approaches to government would result in "benevolent despotism" and eventual tyranny.[26]

The AEC appointee provided the perfect foil for Republicans and others who presented themselves as insurgent opponents of government privilege. Such men as Lilienthal, asserted Ferguson, "believe that this is the day of the experts of special managerial class to whom the people must grant broad powers. They imply . . . that they know best what is good for the people, and that the people are to do what they are told to do." Seeking more and more power, experts would build an "authoritarian state" by constructing government agencies with limitless authority. "It progresses step by step," warned Ferguson, "to the point where the people are progressively the wards of the managers." Development of the atom bomb, concluded the former judge, should not be in the hands of those of the "authoritarian frame of mind."[27]

By linking Lilienthal to the New Deal and threats of communism and totalitarianism, Republicans managed to reopen a confirmation process that had once appeared resolved. By the time Senator Bricker moved to recommit the nomination to committee in early April, the Lilienthal appointment had become what the *New York Times* described as "one of the bitterest issues in recent United States history." Bricker's resolution lost by a relatively close 52-38 margin. Six days later the nomination carried by a 50-31 vote, with twenty-six Republicans and five Democrats in opposition. The Truman administration's victory, however, had taken its toll.[28]

✦ ✦ ✦

The Lilienthal confirmation battle helped inspire the Republican Congress to propose thirty-five investigations of administration agencies. State Department loyalty files and officials received attention from both a House appropriations subcommittee and the Committee on Expenditures in the Executive Departments. The House Committee on Education and Labor conducted hearings to expose Communist infiltration of trade unions. The Senate Committee on Expenditures in the Executive Departments questioned the loyalty of officials in the Department of Commerce. Yet none of these inquiries reached the explosive proportions of the highly publicized investigations the House Committee on Un-American Activities (HUAC) conducted.[29]

As far back as 1930 the New York Republican Hamilton Fish had chaired a congressional investigation of the activities of the American Communist party. Four years later Democrats pushed the House to create the Special Committee on Un-American Activities. The new panel continued to expose Communists but also focused on the German-American Bund and William Pelley's Silver Shirts. In 1938 the House reconstituted the committee as a temporary investigating unit and named Martin Dies, a Texas Democrat, as chair. Dies directed most of the panel's attention to the alleged role of Communists in the CIO, federal work programs, public colleges, the farmer-labor movement, and the American Civil Liberties Union. In 1945 Mississippi's John Rankin led a coalition of southern Democrats and northern Republicans in a 207-186 vote to make HUAC a standing committee of the House. Over the next two years John Wood, a Georgia Democrat who chaired the committee, conducted hearings designed to expose the use of subversive propaganda in OPA radio broadcasts and questioned present and former Communist party officials about their ties to foreign agents.[30]

When the Eightieth Congress convened in 1947, it named J. Parnell Thomas as HUAC's chair. Thomas hoped to discredit New Deal philosophy and supporters by demonstrating communist influence on both. The committee opened proceedings with a vain attempt to question a German immigrant, whom it cited as the chief American representative of the Communist International. It then explored whether his refugee brother had benefited from Immigration Bureau favoritism. HUAC also conducted hearings on Communist party involvement in the CIO. Its greatest interest, however, lay in the danger of communist subversion of American values. Since the committee pictured communism as a system that destroyed free thought and required people to take "orders from the government without question," it viewed propaganda as threatening as actual violence. The obsession with ideas explained former *Daily Worker* editor Louis F. Budenz's 1946 testimony that intellectual liberals were "the first line of defense" for the Communists.[31]

Focused on ideology, HUAC investigators turned to the motion picture industry in 1947. Suspicion of the giant Hollywood studios dated back to the antimonopoly and purity crusades of the interwar period. Burton Wheeler and Gerald Nye had used highly publicized Senate hearings in 1941 to attack the industry's alleged internationalist bias. Four years later John Rankin condemned the movies as the nation's "greatest hotbed of subversive activities" and called for exposing those who used "un-American" propaganda to "poison the minds" of children. As the hearings began, Thomas announced that committee inquiries already revealed that Communist screenwriters and directors had infiltrated the motion picture community and that the Roosevelt administration had pressured wartime Hollywood to produce pro-Soviet films, such as *Mission to Moscow* (1943). Thomas charged that Communist influence continued to result in subversive propaganda in films.[32]

To bolster its assertions, HUAC elicited testimony from several "friendly" allies in the film community. When this proved inconclusive, it issued subpoenas to eleven of seventeen "unfriendly" witnesses. After one left the country, the remaining ten appeared before the panel, invoked First Amendment rights, and refused to answer if they had ever been members of the Communist party. Committee investigators placed registration cards and other evidence of Communist activity into the record. They also produced a confessional article by the screenwriter Albert Maltz that shamelessly recanted his own previous attempt to rescue literary criticism from Marxist ideology. In November 1947 HUAC voted to cite the Hollywood Ten for contempt of Congress. When a meeting of industry executives quickly acted to ban the ten and all other "communists and subversives" from the movies, few dared to defend individuals perceived as arrogant parrots of the party line. Public opinion polls backed punishment of the Hollywood figures by margins of 47 percent to 39 percent.[33]

Anticommunism addressed a complex of fears associated with power-lessness. As Michael P. Rogin has suggested, it tied the cosmopolitan influence of intellectuals to centralized New Deal bureaucracy and internal subversion by the totalitarian left. The Department of State served as a perfect target for such anxieties. As early as 1946 Representative Edward Cox of Georgia had complained of "too many undesirable people holding important places" in the department. The same year Senators Pat McCarran, Kenneth Wherry, and Kenneth McKellar called for a State Department purge. HUAC backed into the area of internal security when it heard testimony in 1948 from Elizabeth Bentley and Whittaker Chambers, two self-confessed former Communist agents. Bentley described two major wartime espionage rings in the OPA and other government agencies. She also accused William Remington, an Ivy League graduate in the wartime Department of Commerce, of passing secrets to her for Soviet use.[34]

Whittaker Chambers's testimony proved more spectacular. Chambers described himself as a former writer for Communist publications who left the party around 1938. In apocalyptic terms, he proclaimed communism a form of totalitarianism, whose triumph meant slavery and "spiritual night to the human mind and soul." Chambers outlined the growth of Communist affinity groups in federal agencies during the 1930s and seconded Bentley's account of wartime espionage. Like Bentley, he charged that Harry Dexter White, a Harvard economist who served as the executive director of the International Monetary Fund, had passed secret information to a wartime Communist spy ring. Days later Chambers implicated Alger Hiss, the president of the Carnegie Endowment for International Peace and the secretary-general of the 1945 United Nations Conference at San Francisco, as a Communist associate during the 1930s.[35]

A Harvard law school graduate who had clerked with Justice Oliver Wendell Holmes Jr., Alger Hiss began a brilliant New Deal career in the Agricultural Adjustment Administration. Moving on to serve as a State Department assistant for East Asia affairs, he became President Roosevelt's translator at the symbolically important Yalta Conference. Categorically denying Chambers's charges, the former diplomat immediately appeared before HUAC as a voluntary witness. Days later he met his accuser in a private session and challenged him to repeat the allegations in public. When Chambers complied, Hiss filed a defamation suit. In pretrial examination by the plaintiff's attorneys, Chambers produced copies of State Department documents that Hiss allegedly had transmitted to him in the 1930s. Subpoenaed for further evidence of espionage in December 1948, Chambers took investigators to a hollow pumpkin on his Maryland farm in which he had hidden five microfilmed rolls of papers, most from Hiss's State Department office.[36]

The celebrated "pumpkin papers" led to the convening of a grand jury and Hiss's indictment on two counts of perjury. In the highly publicized trial, two Supreme Court justices submitted character references for the defense. Nevertheless, prosecutors managed to prove that many of the Chambers documents had been typed on a machine that Hiss once had owned. In May 1949 the jury deadlocked in an 8-4 vote. A second trial, however, resulted in a guilty verdict, and in January 1950 Hiss was sentenced to five years in prison.[37]

Seventeen years out of the White House, New Deal opponents eagerly seized on the symbolism of the Alger Hiss conviction. Karl Mundt, a Republican from South Dakota and the former chair of the HUAC subcommittee that had investigated the "pumpkin papers," rose to deliver a lengthy Senate diatribe on "what the Hiss trial actually means." While helping to set U.S. policy in China and Eastern Europe, declared Mundt, the discredited diplomat had placed a foreign creed above his duties to the nation. There were still people in the country, he marveled, who believed "it inconceivable that a man who looks so smooth and so intelligent and speaks such an effective Harvard accent" could be guilty of such charges. Noting how Hiss had contemptuously corrected the pronunciation and grammar of prosecutors, the *Detroit Free Press* joined Mundt in mocking the defendant's supporters. Despite the condescension of the "intelligentsia" and "parlor pinks" of Greenwich Village and Park Avenue, rejoiced the newspaper, a "battered old typewriter" with "no Groton-Harvard accent" had proven Hiss's guilt.[38]

✦   ✦   ✦

As Victor S. Navasky has observed, the Hiss proceeding placed the New Deal on trial. It "established the fundamental cold war assumption that to be a Communist was to be an agent of a foreign power." The conviction validated the anticommunist suspicion that Soviet conspiracies threatened to subvert the U.S. government and internal security. The case also bolstered the impression that New Deal bureaucracy had provided a haven for elitist enemies of the American way of life. These perceptions legitimized HUAC's role as monitor of a supposedly lax executive branch. They further countered cries by some administration leaders and liberals that the committee merely embodied the narrowest forms of provincial bigotry and anti-intellectualism.[39]

Karl Mundt's summation of the Hiss case included a sharp attack on President Truman for creating "more sizable obstacles than ever before confronted a congressional committee." The dispute with the president originated in March 1948, when HUAC targeted Edward U. Condon, director of the National Bureau of Standards, as "one of the weakest links in our atomic security." A supporter of civilian control of nuclear energy and an advocate of cooperation with the Soviet Union, Condon had participated in the American-Soviet Science Society and had made social contacts with members of Communist Poland's embassy. After learning of the nuclear physicist's clearance by a Commerce Department loyalty board, HUAC requested the files. When the department refused, Truman issued an executive order banning congressional access to classified material without presidential approval. Undaunted, the House passed a resolution offered by Clare Hoffman demanding that the executive branch yield whatever information Congress needed to perform its duties.[40]

The Senate never acted on Hoffman's motion. Nevertheless, HUAC's anticommunism resonated deeply among segments of the nation. In March 1947 Secretary of Labor Louis B. Schwellenback proposed making the Communist party illegal. Although the White House received protests from big city labor groups and others, it also heard from a variety of Americans who supported the scheme. Take the Communists "off the air, movies, and unions," wrote a man from Williamsport, Pennsylvania. "We did not fight for freedom to have another ism come along." A Michigan auto worker promised to donate $218.96 of back pay to help President Truman combat the "menace of enemies and undermining influences such as communism." Early in 1948 a Truman Democrat with an Irish-American name warned that "if you and the rest of your bunch don't quit pampering those Red rats and clean 'em out of our government, there's going to be some changes made!" Why, the correspondent asked, did the president allow Communists to "insult our country, spy on us, and trample on the world just as they damned well please?"[41]

Fears of Soviet subversion multiplied in February 1948, when Communist domination of key trade unions and government ministries resulted in a pro-Moscow coup in Czechoslovakia. Soon after, Communist-inspired strikes paralyzed France and Italy, only to be followed by the Soviet blockade of Berlin. "Cold fear is gripping people hereabouts," wrote an observer of the United States. In 1947, 55 percent of a national sample had expressed the belief that Russia sought to dominate the world. In the winter of 1948, 54 percent feared that Washington would find itself at war with Moscow within ten years. By summer 69 percent described U.S. policy toward the Soviets as "too soft." In the heightened tension of the period, White House disputes with HUAC appeared suspect, particularly when the president referred to the Hiss inquiry as a "red herring" designed to distract attention from the congressional agenda. Truman's "*faux pas,*" exulted HUAC's Karl Mundt to John Flynn, "was one his worst in a long series of bad blunders."[42]

Karl Mundt's characterization was echoed in White House mail. "The people feel that there must be something more than politics back of all this," observed one woman. "Can't you at least express publicly that you are shocked to learn that disloyal men have held high positions in your government?" asked another. "When people are aroused as they are about communism," warned a Florida congressional candidate, "apologies and talk of Red Herrings" surely would defeat the president's chance for re-election. Among "common, every-day folks" sharing a "grave concern" over communist dangers, explained another correspondent, "anything that indicates a withholding of information of any kind" aroused suspicion. "You will certainly agree," advised one protester, "that the public has the right to protect itself against irresponsible officials and those who do not always consider their country first." A federal attorney in Brooklyn, New York, reported young Catholic men in the taverns and soda shops believed that Washington was "infested with commies" and that Truman was "trying to cover them up."[43]

Communist party membership peaked at 75,000 during World War II and was less than half that by 1950. Nevertheless, a combination of partisan maneuvering and the desire to assuage public anxiety prompted congressional Republicans to lead the effort to legislate control of the communist "menace." The Taft-Hartley Act of 1947, for example, included a provision requiring union officers to sign oaths denying party membership. Pushing further, Karl Mundt introduced a measure calling for "Communist political organizations" to register the names of their officers and members with the attorney general. Mundt's proposal also sought to outlaw participation in any act, movement, or conspiracy directed toward the establishment of a foreign-controlled dictatorship in the United States. Representative Richard M. Nixon from California, who signed on as a cosponsor in 1948, chaired the HUAC subcommittee that held hearings on the bill.[44]

Mundt insisted that communism was not a legitimate political movement but an international conspiracy, "the left flank" of the drive toward "a tyrannical fascist state." Instead of outlawing the Communist party, as 69 percent of a national sample advocated in 1947, the South Dakotan hoped to drive Moscow functionaries above ground. By August 1948 the Mundt-Nixon proposal had earned a 63 percent approval rating in national polls. Despite objections to its vague definition of communist activity, the measure passed the House by an overwhelming vote of 319 to 58. In the Senate, however, it encountered an ambivalent response from Republican leader Robert Taft. Taft worried that some of the bill's provisions might prohibit free expression. But since he believed that it would be difficult to prove that the legislation's target organizations were actually conspiring to overthrow the government, he preferred to register all groups "tinged with a communist connection." Without the powerful Ohio senator's support, the Mundt-Nixon bill stalled in committee.[45]

✦ ✦ ✦

Although economic populism no longer played the central role it had in the 1930s, postwar leaders and politicians were compelled to acknowledge the problems of small producers and enterprisers. The Federal Trade Commission warned in 1946 that the "concentration of economic power" constituted the "greatest domestic challenge to the American theory of competitive enterprise" and "way of life." Studies showed that 2,450 formerly independent manufacturing and mining companies had disappeared as a result of mergers and acquisitions between 1940 and 1947. Eight large banking houses dominated and controlled two-thirds of the combined assets of the country's 250 largest nonfinancial corporations. Warning that a "free economy in the American tradition" could not be "regimented by either private or public power," the Joint Economic Committee of Congress condemned "monopolistic restrictions and the concentration of unbridled economic power in private hands." Modern monopolies, it concluded, were setting the organizing pattern for "a collectivist state."[46]

Such groups as the National Federation of Independent Business (NFIB) pleaded with Congress to save free enterprise "from the growing domination of monopoly business, big, monopolistic labor, and big, bureaucratic government." Both houses unanimously approved a 1947 resolution calling for equal representation of small competitors on government commissions and agencies. Yet the independent business lobby was sharply divided over Kenneth Wherry's attempt to gain legislative authority for his Senate Small Business Committee. Undaunted by the opposition of two of the NFIB's rivals, the Wherry panel issued a scathing report on endangered free enterprise in 1949. The "persistent march of monopoly finance and corporation merger," it declared, confronted Americans "with a far graver and vastly more complex concentration of financial and economic power than ever before in history." Independent competitors, the panel concluded, were threatened "by the exploitive abuses of concentrated economic power in the hands of 'big finance' and 'big business' and by new developments of economic power in 'big labor' and 'big government.'"[47]

Although the Wherry committee's charter expired in 1949, the Senate restored it the next year. One of the Nebraskan's closest small business allies turned out to be Robert Taft. A consistent opponent of reciprocal trade, Taft fused cold war nationalism with ongoing support of free enterprise for domestic producers. As a potential presidential candidate, the Senate leader also endorsed such reforms as hospital construction, state grants for health programs, federal aid to state education, and a national housing proposal. Yet Taft's self-defined "liberalism" placed freedom over coercion. Outlining his "political credo" in 1948, the Ohio Republican focused on individual liberty, equal justice under the law, equality of opportunity, and maintenance of decent living standards. Because true liberals believed in freedom, he declared, they rejected state action as the answer to all problems.[48]

Having lost the two previous presidential nominations to the internationalist and corporate wing of the party, Republican nationalists sought to make Robert Taft their candidate in 1948. Citing the Ohioan's stands on reduced government costs and taxes, regulation of labor unions, and a nationalistic foreign policy, Sterling Morton, a Chicago industrialist and former America First leader, labeled Taft "the best qualified man available for the presidency." Robert R. McCormick, publisher of the *Chicago Tribune*, agreed, pleading for Republicans to abandon the "eastern internationalists" and bankers who backed a bipartisan foreign policy. Even former Democratic senator Burton Wheeler endorsed Taft. "While he is hailed as an ultra reactionary," wrote Wheeler to Robert Wood, Taft was "an honest conservative who would not be pushed around by Wall Street or by the unintelligent reactionaries."[49]

Attempting to position himself as an enlightened nationalist and reformer, Taft sought to take the Republican presidential nomination away from Thomas Dewey and Harold E. Stassen, both internationalists. Taft Republicans derided the free trade doctrines of the party's eastern wing and portrayed Dewey's and Stassen's globalism as dangerous to the nation's producers. They reminded primary voters how the nationalist branch of the party had led the fight against New Deal "communism, controls, corruption, and confusion." Americans had elected a Republican Congress in 1946, John Bricker told the party convention, because they wanted "less bureaucracy and more of individual liberty." The nation "demanded that we stop building up power in Washington, keep it closer home, curb unbridled bureaucracy and the overweening love of power characterized by the New Deal." Taft was "a stalwart leader," proclaimed Bricker, who would reject "any foreign philosophy of government" and not compromise on the principle that freedom was universal.[50]

Like Philip La Follette, Robert Taft faced difficulties in defining himself. In a 1948 public opinion poll 40 percent labeled the senator a "conservative," but another 51 percent had no opinion about his ideology. Although Taft won his own Ohio primary, he placed a poor third in Nebraska when he expressed coolness toward farm supports. Weak in the

Northeast and West and unable to unite the anti-Dewey forces, the senator withdrew from the race before the third convention ballot. He nevertheless joined the campaign against the Democrats. In "The Case against President Truman," published in the *Saturday Evening Post,* the Ohio crusader attacked the White House's "wide latitude of discretion" in foreign policy and characterized executive regulatory bureaucracies and high taxes as oppressive to Congress, small business operators, and the American people. When Truman prevailed in the contest and the Democrats regained control of Congress, Republican nationalists and anti–New Dealers believed they had suffered a devastating blow.[51]

✦ ✦ ✦

While anti-Washington activists sought to combat the dangers of collectivism at home, they anguished over the proper responses to external challenges and threats. Hostile to New Deal globalism, persistent ties to European finance, and escalating federal expenditures, Republican nationalists and their allies remained highly skeptical of President Truman's efforts to define an assertive foreign policy. Lacking the export commodities of the South, Northeast, and West, farmers, processors, and manufacturers in the Midwest continued to serve mainly domestic customers. Accordingly, heartland business leaders opposed government spending and taxation, distrusted high finance, and sought regional trade protections from the global market. Such concerns also played into historic suspicions of European military entanglements and reluctance to commit U.S. resources to unreliable allies.[52]

The first postwar challenge to nationalism occurred in December 1945, when the United States and Great Britain signed an agreement extending $3.75 billion in low-interest loans to London. Although the pact sought to end British exchange restrictions and Commonwealth barriers to trade, an estimated 70 percent of Americans opposed it. In Congress a bipartisan coalition quickly attacked the loan on two grounds. Some representatives—such as Marion T. Bennett, a Republican from Missouri; Gerald W. Landis, a Republican from Indiana; Leon H. Gavin, a Republican from Pennsylvania; Karl Mundt, a Republican from South Dakota; and Emanuel Celler, a Democrat from New York—complained about burdening the debt-ridden economy with risky foreign obligations. Others—such as Representative Overton Brooks, a Louisiana Democrat; Representative Harold Knutson, a Minnesota Republican; and Senator Homer E. Capehart, an Indiana Republican—objected to subsidizing the British Labour party's program to nationalize banks, railroads, and mines. These critics of socialism found it hard to believe Truman administration assurances that a solvent Britain would help the West contain Soviet communism.[53]

Senator William Langer offered the most passionate denunciation of the British loan. A self-styled "isolationist" Republican, Langer believed in "enforced exclusion" from international councils of power. Speaking for the needs of rural North Dakotans, the independent solon had denounced sending the Soviet Union farm machinery in 1944. The following year he sought to ban lend-lease export of all agricultural equipment. Langer argued that American producers did not need overseas customers when they had an ample market at home. But he most strenuously objected to the loan because it supposedly permitted Britain to preserve "the outmoded antiquated machinery of imperialism." Langer insisted that U.S. funds would enable the British to buy weaponry to preserve control over colonies. London's enhanced financial clout would keep the empire dependent, stagnate the world economy, and endanger peace.[54]

As North Dakota historians have suggested, residents of the Midwest tended to identify with colonial subjects, whose labor and resources were exploited. Since postwar Britain appeared to combine imperialism and aristocracy with a socialist government, the region was deeply antipathetic to London. "Tell them go paddle their own canoe and borrow money from their own colonies," an indignant constituent advised Langer. When Winston Churchill delivered his "Iron Curtain" speech in Missouri in March 1946, Gallup polls indicated 57 percent supported the British loan. Nevertheless, midwestern Anglophobia and postwar fiscal concerns continued to play a major role in the debate over congressional approval. When the Truman administration sought to cut off Senate discussion after a month of acrimonious exchanges, closure never even approached the necessary two-thirds majority. Only after a Langer filibuster in the Senate and eleven attempts to defeat the measure in the House did Congress finally approve the credits, with close votes in both chambers.[55]

President Truman's $400 million of military and economic aid for Greece and Turkey gained far easier congressional endorsement in March 1947. Designed to halt the spread of Soviet communism in the Mediterranean, the request accompanied the Truman Doctrine, which pledged "to support free peoples" resisting subjugation by outside forces. By depicting the struggle in anticommunist terms, the president won the support of two-thirds of the World War II noninterventionists remaining in the Senate and more than half of those still in the House. Yet Senate Republicans such as Kenneth Wherry, George Malone, William Langer, and John Bricker refused to sign on. Langer accused the administration of exaggerating the Soviet threat, ignoring Germany, and abetting European militarism with U.S. funds needed at home. Bricker warned that the United States could best fight communism by preserving the strength of its domestic economy and driving subversives from government.[56]

Truman Doctrine appropriations won substantial victories of 67 to 23 in the Senate and 287 to 107 in the House. Nationalists, former noninterventionists, and militant anticommunists had misgivings about the administration's response to the perceived Soviet threat, however. In a 1946 speech at Kenyon College Robert Taft had derided the idea that the world was "to be ruled by the power and policy of the great nations" instead of international law. Although Taft reluctantly supported aid to Greece and Turkey, he joined other critics in questioning the militarization of U.S. foreign policy. Phrasing his opposition in antistatist terms, the Ohio senator questioned administration requests for conscription and universal military training. Congress extended the draft for one-year terms in 1946 and 1947, but it refused to endorse Truman's call for compulsory military instruction, which Taft described as a "totalitarian measure" placing young men "under the absolute control of the federal government" in their formative years.[57]

Robert Taft's insistence that universal training provided "the key" to the nation's militarization won him support from veteran antiwar activists, such as Oswald Garrison Villard, John Flynn, and the Socialist Norman Thomas. Yet to combat the Soviet threat, the president called a joint session of Congress in March 1948, at which he requested over $3 billion for universal military training and a renewed draft. Between 1947 and 1948 about three-fourths of national polling samples indicated support for civilian training. Nevertheless, Taft took the lead in campaigning against that segment of Truman's request. American freedom and the maintenance of peace, not provocative stands on global controversies, argued the senator in a major Nebraska address, were the main purposes of foreign policy. A huge military, he warned, would destroy the "free life" and well-being of the nation's people and produce "the very regimentation we are trying to avoid." Distrustful of Washington's New Deal heirs, Taft later predicted that "a militarized nation" would bring "a police state."[58]

Although Congress never considered universal military training, it debated the Truman draft request in June 1948. In the Senate William Langer, a longtime draft foe, denounced conscription as an instrument of autocracy and sought to embarrass draft advocates by introducing amendments to desegregate the army and force racial integration at all training facilities. After defeating at least five hostile amendments, the upper house easily passed a two-year draft bill, with John Bricker, Kenneth Wherry, and William Langer among the ten dissenting. Meanwhile, the House overcame the opposition of seventy-seven midwesterners to approve its own twenty-one-month measure. As Congress sought to reconcile the two bills, Langer joined a filibuster begun by the cold war critic and small business advocate Glen H. Taylor, an Idaho Democrat. The turbulent session finally climaxed when both houses agreed to a twenty-one-month draft of men between nineteen and twenty-five and the administration pledged to postpone inductions until 1949.[59]

✦   ✦   ✦

Small business interests, manufacturers for a domestic market, and ideological nationalists ardently opposed internationalist programs. By 1948 military spending and foreign aid accounted for more than three-fourths the annual federal budget and 92 percent of the increase in appropriations since 1941. Senate critics pointed to the inflationary impact of these programs and criticized them for increasing debt and depleting the nation's resources. William Langer spoke for many nationalists when he asked why the State Department was subsidizing foreign competitors who undermined living standards in the United States. Criticism of reciprocal trade took similar lines of argument. George Malone sent a special message to the Senate in 1949 arguing that tariffs served as a "floor under the American wage-living standard." The Nevadan told Langer that "Economic One Worlders" wanted to flood the United States with the overseas products of cheap labor.[60]

Despite such sentiments, President Truman used a special address to Congress in late 1947 to request a $17 billion European aid package. First outlined at Harvard University's commencement by Secretary of State George C. Marshall, the massive recovery program sought to keep Europe from economic collapse, bolster its resistance to communism, and cultivate a market for U.S. exports. A November 1947 Gallup poll found 61 percent of the sample familiar with the Marshall Plan and 47 percent of those favorable. Big business, farm, and labor groups saw the program as a stimulant to foreign trade and domestic prosperity. Yet the proposal generated opposition from nationalists, small producer interests, and anticollectivists fixated on the internal communist threat. Robert Taft originally reserved judgment, noting to a corporate food processor that he had "never run into a subject where there is such a wide difference of opinion." But Taft soon concluded that dollars could not fight communism and that overseas spending threatened inflation and regimentation at home.[61]

Many nationalists viewed the people of Europe as socialists and imperialists undeserving of U.S. aid. "How can anyone believe that this government should pay billions of dollars for the purpose of supporting socialistic governments in Europe and helping England to re-establish her vast empire is beyond my comprehension," a South Bend attorney complained to Senator Homer Capehart. The Indiana senator told his constituents that Europeans needed to fight communism by applying American principles of free enterprise, not state socialism. William Langer thundered at "international 'bank nights' and give-away contests, 'Queen for a day' contests in which we give to everyone but ourselves." Langer opposed the Marshall Plan, he explained to constituents, because Americans needed their own economic development and because foreign aid never served the poor who deserved it.[62]

Nationalist and antisocialist opposition to the Marshall Plan appeared strongest among small business interests, for whom European prosperity seemed irrelevant. Such groups as the Conference of American Small Business Organizations, the National Federation of Independent Business, the National Small Business Men's Association, the Illinois Manufacturers Association, and the National Association of Retail Grocers saw the scheme as a harbinger of greater taxation and bureaucratic interference with the free market. Independent business operators viewed themselves as threatened by international bankers and financiers, giant oil corporations, government agencies, and organized labor, all of whom they pictured as beneficiaries of foreign aid and the global market. When the anti–New Deal *Chicago Tribune* admonished that the Marshall Plan was a "venture into international pocket picking" that would ensure "bureaucratic tyranny" at home, the warning made sense to these groups.[63]

Although large agricultural groups, such as the Grange and the American Farm Bureau Federation, supported the Marshall Plan, family operators in the National Farmers Union remained critical of the program. Small farmers objected to the prospect of shipping agricultural implements to Europe while supplies dwindled in the United States. William Langer repeatedly complained that foreign programs denied tractors, combines, and trucks to western food growers. Essential raw materials, finished goods, and machinery, added Langer, would soon be diverted to Europe. Robert Taft joined the critics with a press release detailing the manner in which foreign aid reduced domestic supplies of fertilizer and agricultural machinery. Export programs had raised the price of grain so high, asserted Taft, that ranchers found it impossible to feed livestock and provide an adequate supply of meat.[64]

Small producer concerns led Homer Capehart to propose an alternative to the Marshall Plan. Before coming to the Senate in 1945, Capehart had sold farm implements, run an advertising agency, and owned companies that manufactured popcorn vending machines, jukeboxes, radio-phonographs, and wartime machine parts. These entrepreneurial experiences left the Indianan hostile to both New Deal regulation and Wall Street finance. Although Capehart supported the United Nations and the Truman Doctrine, he opposed foreign aid as a violation of the free market. The senator intended to avoid the Marshall Plan's reliance on government by creating an international division of the Reconstruction Finance Corporation (RFC). Once the United States and participating nations contributed matching funds, European manufacturers could directly buy materials and tools from suppliers with RFC letters of credit. The program would be supplemented by an outright relief grant of $2 billion. Capehart insisted that his proposal gave recipient governments a financial interest in the plan, that elimination of government purchases would cut costs, and that American taxpayers might earn interest on repaid loans.[65]

Seeking to distinguish between government relief and market-induced recovery, the Indiana senator presented his amendment as "the common horse sense of an American individual." With support from small business nationalists, such as John Bricker, William Langer, Kenneth Wherry, and William C. Revercomb, a West Virginia Republican, the Capehart proviso won twenty-two votes in the Senate. Nonetheless, the upper house approved the Marshall Plan by a substantial 69-17 margin, with two-thirds of the World War II noninterventionists in agreement. In the House the Truman proposal won an overwhelming 329-74 endorsement, with half the surviving noninterventionists supporting it.[66]

C. Wilson Harder, a small business leader, dissented from this consensus by warning that Washington bureaucrats were siphoning off domestic supplies to create an emergency that would justify restoring price controls and other regulations. George J. Burger, director of the National Federation of Small Business, agreed, speculating that "foreign relief" internationalists had "made up their minds" to eradicate U.S. surpluses. Enactment of the aid plan validated such anxieties. Aluminum users argued that when the Economic Cooperation Administration (ECA) subsidized low-cost shipments to Europe, it reduced supplies in the United States and increased prices. The ECA ignored small business in setting export strategies, charged Senator William Jenner from Indiana. To prove his point, Jenner produced an agency memo detailing price discussions among leading corporate exporters. "Listen, small businessmen of America," taunted the Indianan, the "list of conferees looks like a Who's Who of big business."[67]

Independent producers complained bitterly about the Marshall Plan. Small manufacturers of tractors and agricultural implements, for example, protested that European officials ignored ECA guidelines and granted import licenses only to the large American suppliers. Machinery suppliers asserted that the Europeans were illegally transferring sales contracts from firms inside the United States to companies on the Continent. Producers of lumber and sawmill goods told Homer Capehart that Greece was using over $500,000 of ECA funding to buy from their competitors in Communist Yugoslavia. Such policies led Robert Taft to declare that the Marshall Plan used public funds to assist European firms that competed with American companies. Disappointed that the recovery program was not aiding independent manufacturers and suppliers in the United States, J. Harry McGregor, a House Republican, asked Wright Patman, the chair of the Small Business Committee, to investigate why congressional intent had not been honored.[68]

✦ ✦ ✦

Controversy over the North Atlantic Treaty Organization (NATO) surpassed that of the Marshall Plan. A mutual defense pact signed in April 1949 by the United States, Canada, and ten Western European nations, NATO was the first peacetime military alliance in U.S. history. It signaled the Truman administration's transition from economic to armed containment of the Soviet Union. Disturbed by the previous year's Czechoslovakian coup and the Berlin blockade, 76 percent of Gallup poll samples indicated support for U.S. participation.[69]

NATO separated internationalist Republicans who saw the Soviets as a European security threat from those who viewed communism as a moral danger. The latter argued that the home front provided the proper arena for the battle against communism. Desiring to cut government spending and limit presidential power, such critics as Representative Lawrence H. Smith, a Republican from Wisconsin, mocked the utility of defense treaties and antiquated armies. Predictably, William Langer attacked NATO as a costly product of secret diplomacy. The United States would be plunged into European affairs, complained Langer, without any control over the billions of dollars it would squander. This "barren military alliance," he protested, violated the UN Charter and would do nothing to stop Soviet penetration of the political structures of Western Europe.[70]

The Senate Foreign Relations Committee already had anticipated criticism by amending the NATO treaty to include language guaranteeing the use of "constitutional processes" in ratifying and enforcing the agreement. Nevertheless, Robert Taft reasserted his role as the Truman administration's leading foreign policy opponent. Emphasizing that the conflict with the Soviet Union was more ideological than military, Taft accused the United States of "a tendency to interfere in the affairs of other nations, to assume we are a kind of demigod and Santa Claus to solve the problems of the world." The Ohioan warned that U.S. bellicosity threatened to involve the nation in disputes where its "liberty is not in fact concerned." The administration, he warned, had made war "an instrument of public policy rather than its last resort."[71]

Depicting NATO as a "prior undertaking by the most powerful nation in the world to arm half the world against the other," the Ohio senator joined with Kenneth Wherry and Arthur Watkins, a Utah Republican, to

cosponsor an important treaty reservation. This proviso sought to separate the mutual defense pact from the transfer of arms to Europe by denying that the United States had a moral or legal commitment to arm the
Continent. Once the reservation received only twenty-one votes, however, it became clear that the treaty would easily pass in the Senate. In July
1949 the upper house approved the NATO defense pact in a 82-13 vote,
with Robert Taft, William Langer, Kenneth Wherry, George Malone, and
Edwin Johnson, a Colorado Democrat, among the dissenters. The overwhelming defeat revealed how President Truman could use anticommunist sentiment to co-opt insurgent criticism of the administration's foreign
policy.[72]

Following the ratification of NATO, the cold war appeared to unravel
beyond the control of the Truman administration. In August 1949 Secretary of State Dean G. Acheson issued a white paper on China's civil war.
Although the United States had supported the Nationalist government of
Chiang Kai-shek with $2 billion in aid since 1946, the Chinese Commu-
nists were about to take over the country. Internal forces beyond U.S. control, stated Acheson, had made it impossible to stop a Communist victory
over a repressive regime. The State Department now announced its refusal to sanction intervention in behalf of a government that had "lost the
confidence of its own troops and its own people." One month after the
white paper was issued, President Truman gravely announced that the
Soviet Union had exploded an atomic bomb. In December the Chinese
Nationalists fled to the island of Formosa, and Communist revolutionaries ruled the largest nation on earth.[73]

Opponents of New Deal statism and internationalism had been questioning Washington's oppressive taxation, centralized rule, and interference
with the free market for the past ten years. They could now argue that the
administration's expensive foreign aid and military programs had failed
to accomplish their purpose of stopping the Communist tide.[74] The government's cold war reversals enabled critics to insist that it had failed to
summon the will to combat communism at home and abroad. For nationalists and anticollectivists, the trouble could lie only with leaders who were
not yet convinced of the dangers of the international peril. After the "loss"
of China and the explosion of a Soviet atomic bomb, American politics
once again would experience a populist insurgence directed at elites who
appeared as morally unreliable as the nation's European allies.

11

The Nationalist Critique of Bipartisan Foreign Policy, 1949–55

Speaking at Marquette University on the day after the Maoists took control of China, Joseph McCarthy, the Republican senator from Wisconsin, warned the students of his alma mater that the "Christian nations" were losing the "war" with "the Communist and atheistic world."[1] The "fall" of China appeared to signal that Washington had failed to contain the Communist threat in Asia, an area that such nationalists as Robert Taft, Karl Mundt, and Kenneth Wherry believed to be more important to future peace than Europe was. The success of the Chinese Revolution reawakened frustrations over the delayed opening of the Asian front in World War II and confirmed suspicions that only the Soviet Union had benefited from the global conflict. After 1949 Republican nationalists managed to distance their party from the bipartisan consensus on containment. Their continuing critiques of internationalist foreign policy would leave lasting marks on American society and mark a high point of insurgent influence.

✦ ✦ ✦

By the end of 1949 public alarm had risen sharply over the perceived threats of communism, the Soviet Union, and nuclear war. Following the October conspiracy convictions of eleven top American Communist party leaders, Judith Coplon, an aide in the Justice Department, went to trial in January on charges of spying for the Soviets. A Gallup poll soon revealed that 70 percent of the sample believed Moscow was building itself up to be the ruling power of the world. On January 21 Alger Hiss was convicted of perjury and sentenced to federal prison. Not long after, the physicist Klaus Fuchs was arrested in England for atomic espionage connected with his earlier work at Los Alamos.[2]

Republican nationalists held the Democratic State Department responsible for America's perceived decline abroad and vulnerability at home. Many traced the loss of China to the secret terms of the Yalta pact, a symbol of New Deal deceit and duplicity. "FDR sold Chiang Kai-shek down the river to get Joe Stalin into the Jap war," confided Arthur Vandenberg to his wife after reading the white paper on China. Truman critics, such as Minnesota's Representative Walter Judd, a former medical missionary to China, fumed that the administration had used collective security against communism in Europe but retreated behind appeasement in Asia. A frustrated Kenneth Wherry denounced the president's "determination to go forward with blundering policies that please the communists." Others saw the victory of the Chinese Maoists as a conscious and deliberate result of administration policy.[3]

Militant Senate nationalists, such as George Malone and William Langer, never had subscribed to the qualified consensus that defined postwar U.S. foreign policy. "I find myself," revealed Malone in a 1948 press release, "in complete disagreement with the temporizing tactics of those speaking for either or both parties who cloak their shilly shally position under the label of bipartisanship." "Our whole American foreign policy is crumbling around our heads," Langer warned the Senate early the next year; "our most vital interests are being forsaken, our prestige is being irreparably threatened, and our principles have been trampled under foot." "There isn't any bipartisan foreign policy," declared Robert Taft in a January 1950 radio speech, "and there hasn't been for the past year."[4]

Nationalist politicians sought a "Fortress America" to protect the nation from European entanglements and strengthen its unilateral response to the Communist threat. Many joined former president Herbert Hoover in calling for the withdrawal of military and economic resources from Europe. Accepting the necessity of huge military budgets, they nevertheless placed priorities on air and sea power instead of ground troops. By doing away with landed armies, conscription, and military alliances, advised the House Republican Lawrence Smith, air power transcended "the sordid hates, . . . prejudices, and intrigues of the Old World." Republican critics of the Truman administration also sought to maintain congressional prerogatives in the creation of international policy.[5]

The conflict between the White House and Congress came to a head in December 1950, when President Truman announced his intention to send troops to participate in NATO's West European defense command. This precipitated the "Great Debate" of 1951, another chapter in the half-century discourse over executive power in foreign policy. Robert Taft struck the first blow in the Senate. Condemning the appeasement of the Soviets in the 1930s and 1940s through executive secret policies, Taft claimed that a bipartisan consensus prevented criticism of international strategy. The Ohioan called for the United States to lead "the battle to prevent the spread of communism" and to defend liberty against the totalitarian Soviet Union, but he pictured the cold war as an ideological struggle that could not be won on "vast land areas." If the United States militarized containment in Europe and sought to reform the world, he warned, Americans would be overwhelmed by dictatorship, inflation, and domestic turmoil.[6]

Three days after Taft's speech Senator Wherry introduced a resolution calling for congressional approval of any troop movements to Europe. The Nebraskan repeated the nationalist dictum that air and sea power provided more security than land armies. Insisting that national defense embraced all aspects of American life, Wherry emphasized the constitutional responsibility of the legislature to shape the nature of foreign economic and military aid. "We cannot just fold our hands and salve our conscience," he pleaded, "with the thought that the military experts will take care of these matters." In the end the Senate compromised by passing two nonbinding resolutions. One approved the dispatch of four military divisions to Europe if the president issued semiannual reports on the implementation of the NATO treaty. The second called for congressional approval of any policy requiring the assignment of U.S. troops to NATO duty. Fifty-eight percent of a Gallup sample endorsed the right of Congress to limit the number of troops sent abroad.[7]

❖ ❖ ❖

Six days after the February 1950 arrest of Klaus Fuchs, Senator McCarthy began a political tour of the American heartland by appearing before the Women's Republican Club in Wheeling, West Virginia. When McCarthy told his Wheeling audience that he possessed a list of current State Department Communists, he immediately began to receive headline attention from a nation beset by cold war doubt and anxiety. Summoning the basic attack of the anticommunist crusade, the senator described "a war between two diametrically opposed ideologies, . . . a final, all-out battle." The United States could have been "a beacon in the desert of destruction," charged McCarthy, "a shining living proof that civilization was not yet ready to destroy itself." But Americans found themselves "in a position of impotency" because the State Department was filled with dupes and traitors who supported the enemy.[8]

Joe McCarthy questioned the loyalty of such State Department professionals as John Stewart Service and Gustavo Duran, but his greatest venom was reserved for Alger Hiss and Secretary of State Dean Acheson. Hiss had "sold out the Christian world to the atheistic world." Acheson, his patron, was a "pompous diplomat in striped pants with a phony British accent." Expressing the hostility to the eastern upper class that would mark his leadership of the anticommunist crusade, the Wisconsin solon warned against the "traitorous actions of those who have been treated so well by this nation . . . those who have had all the benefits that the wealthiest nation on earth has had to offer—the finest homes, the finest college education, and the finest jobs in government we can give. . . . The bright young men who are born with silver spoons in their mouths are the ones who have been worst."[9]

Two weeks after speaking in Wheeling, McCarthy took to the Senate floor with what he claimed to be a list of eighty-one State Department officials guilty of treason or espionage. The senator's accusations catapulted him to national attention and a revered place in the Republican party. "We haven't had such a fighter since Old Bob La Follette," exulted a Wisconsin party leader. In contrast President Truman used a March 1950 press conference to charge that McCarthy was "the best asset the Kremlin has." The following month the chief executive held the senator responsible for the "sabotage" of U.S. foreign policy.[10]

In response to the sensational charges from the Wisconsin Republican, the Senate Foreign Relations Committee asked Millard F. Tydings, a Maryland Democrat, to chair a special subcommittee to review the evidence. When the Tydings panel held tumultuous hearings in March 1950, McCarthy questioned the background of John Stewart Service and Philip C. Jessup, high State Department officials, and raised allegations about seven others. Once these charges fizzled, the Wisconsin senator attempted to reestablish credibility by focusing on the alleged Communist ties of Owen Lattimore, a State Department consultant and Asia scholar.[11]

The director of the Walter Hines Pages School of International Relations at Johns Hopkins University, Lattimore had had a distinguished career as a friendly adviser to China's Chiang Kai-shek, as head of Pacific Relations for the Office of War Information, and as conductor of top government seminars on Asia policy. By the mid-1940s he began to caution that the Chinese Nationalists could not prevail over the Communists and called for flexibility in Washington's Asia policy. Lattimore also proposed U.S. withdrawal from South Korea in 1949. These controversial recommendations led such anticommunists as the former Marxist Louis Budenz, the Asia-firster Alfred Kohlberg, and Senator William Knowland to focus on Lattimore's past ties to the Institute of Pacific Relations and the editorial board of *Amerasia*. Prompted by such information, McCarthy announced that he would use the Tydings committee hearings to name the "top Russian espionage agent" in the United States. After testifying in private session, the senator told reporters that he would "stand or fall on this one."[12]

McCarthy failed to produce any information that tied Lattimore to Communist activities. Yet he managed to sustain interest in the case by asserting that the scholar was "the principal architect of our far-eastern policy" and a contributor to the subversion of American and Chinese interests. To buttress his point, McCarthy read from a letter of "pro-Communist inclinations" that Lattimore had written in 1943. Meanwhile, William Knowland delivered a major Senate speech that attacked the academic's publications for adhering to the Communist party "line." Following Lattimore's public testimony, McCarthy subpoenaed Louis Budenz. The former editor of the *Daily Worker* testified that the Johns Hopkins scholar had been a member of a Communist cell at the Institute of Pacific Relations, that he had been told "to consider" Lattimore a Communist, and that he had been informed that the professor had been "of service" to the party in the *Amerasia* case.[13]

Although Budenz and McCarthy failed to substantiate their assertions, the Tydings hearings deepened the chasm between anticommunist activists and the Truman administration. Nationalist critics insisted that the Maryland Democrat sought to destroy McCarthy at the behest of the White House and the State Department. "It's the best job of smearing," wrote the columnist John O'Donnell, "since the days of World War I, when the Senate and, to their shame, members of the Washington press ganged up on the late Wisconsin senator Robert M. La Follette." O'Donnell reiterated the common Republican complaint that Tydings was the son-in-law of Joseph Davies, a former ambassador to the Soviet Union and the author of the infamous *Mission to Moscow.* McCarthy thrived off the confrontation with "dilettante diplomats" who "whined" and "whimpered" and "cringed" before communism, and he vowed to expose all the "egg-sucking phony liberals" whose "pitiful squealing . . . would hold sacrosanct those Communists and queers" who had sold China into "atheistic slavery."[14]

Distrust of the executive agencies and promise of political advantage prompted Joe McCarthy and other Republicans to insist that President Truman reverse himself by opening State Department loyalty files to the Tydings committee. This demand touched a nerve among those Americans who believed that the Democrats had appeased Communists at home and abroad. "How can the public be sure that Mr. Acheson is not covering up some more traitors of the Alger Hiss breed?" one correspondent demanded of Truman. "Give the people the facts," demanded another, "or you are in for plenty of trouble. They are tired of being fooled." White House critics succeeded in turning the controversy into one involving the right of the people to learn the facts about potentially disloyal federal employees. Under political pressure Truman compromised and allowed the Tydings committee members to inspect the files at the White House without taking notes.[15]

Although McCarthy could make few claims to accuracy, he succeeded in mobilizing massive mistrust of executive bureaucracy in an era of increasing danger in global affairs. By May 1950 George Gallup reported that 39 percent of Americans believed the senator's charges to be good for the country (29 percent disagreed). A constituent of Senator James P. Kem, a Missouri Republican, asked him to "please take a moment to pat Senator Joe McCarthy on the back for me and tell him that the plain people of America are grateful to him. We fully understand the obstacles placed in his path, but we are concerned with his motives more than with his methods, and we think he has performed and is performing a great service." In July 1950, when the Tydings committee issued its final report, Gallup noted that 31 percent of a national sample believed McCarthy's assertions about Communists in government to be literally true.[16]

The Tydings Report portrayed McCarthy's accusations as "a fraud and a hoax, . . . perhaps the most nefarious campaign of half-truths and untruths in the history of this republic." Yet only panel Democrats signed the document, and the Senate Foreign Relations Committee transmitted it to the floor without comment. The ensuing debate divided the Senate on partisan lines. "How can we get the Reds out of Korea if we can't get them out of Washington?" Indiana's William Jenner heckled the Democrats. His fellow Republican Kenneth Wherry called committee counsel Edward Morgan a "son of a bitch" and swung at him at the rear of the Senate floor. In turn, Tydings delivered an emotional tirade that described McCarthy as a charlatan whose reckless assertions exploited his office. The real traitors, he charged, were nationalists such as Jenner, who encouraged Soviet aggression by opposing the Marshall Plan and NATO. The following day Jenner countered by linking Tydings to "a select inner circle of a new political aristocracy" and foreign policy elite.[17]

✦ ✦ ✦

By the time the Tydings committee delivered its report, the United States was involved in the Korean War. The conflict began in June 1950, when the troops of Soviet-sponsored North Korea sought to reunify the peninsula by crossing the 38th parallel to invade South Korea. With the Soviets absent from the United Nations Security Council, the UN declared a "breach of peace." Since President Truman believed that the Communists had moved from subversion to territorial aggression, he unilaterally ordered the use of military force to protect the South Korean allies of the United States and avoid the appearance of appeasement. Under the leadership of General Douglas MacArthur and backed by Security Council endorsement, UN troops mounted a successful ground offensive that reversed North Korean occupation of much of South Korea. Ignoring the protests of neighboring China, however, Truman ordered Allied troops to move deep into North Korea. The Chinese responded in October 1950 by committing large numbers of soldiers to the conflict and turning the war into a bloody stalemate.[18]

The Korean "police action" required the kind of domestic restrictions many small business and nationalist critics opposed. In July 1950 Congress gave the president discretionary ability to combat wartime inflation by imposing price, wage, and rent controls. Truman implemented these powers when he declared a state of national emergency at the end of the year. Some administration adversaries, such as Representative Usher Burdick from North Dakota and Senator Homer Capehart from Indiana, complained about foreign spending and "governmental red tape and regulations" but reluctantly supported price controls to contain inflation. Others, such as Senator George Malone from Nevada, saw the Korean emergency as a pretext for instituting a managed economy and the goals of "socialistic plotters against things American." In a similar fashion, Senator James Kem expressed the fear that Truman's domestic and foreign policies would cement his place in history "as the president who presided at the final liquidation of the American way of life."[19]

While the Korean conflict brought controversial restrictions in the domestic economy, wartime animosity toward communism helped validate the long-standing demand for internal security legislation. Following the announcement of the Soviet explosion of an atomic bomb in December 1949, the Gallup poll found that 77 percent of a national sample favored registration of the American Communist party. Five months later FBI director J. Edgar Hoover publicly sanctioned the idea by announcing that tolerance for "tyranny" was "absurd." In July 1950 the FBI arrested two party members, Julius and Ethel Rosenberg, for conspiracy to pass atomic secrets to the Soviets. Meanwhile, President Truman gave the FBI authority over national security measures. A few days later a Justice Department press release asked the public to work with the FBI to stop Communists from using peace and civil rights groups "to achieve their sinister purposes." The following month Nevada's Pat McCarran, a Democrat, asked for Senate support of an omnibus internal security bill.[20]

As chair of Judiciary's Subcommittee on Immigration and Naturalization, McCarran already had introduced legislation to exclude and deport "subversive" aliens he considered the mainstay of the American Communist movement. He now combined his own measure with a new version of the Mundt-Nixon bill of 1948. Since the Senate's failure to act on his pet proposal, North Dakota's Karl Mundt had campaigned strenuously for a bill to require registration of Communist party functionaries and the labeling of Communist propaganda. Viewing communism as a dictatorial "way of life" supporting worldwide control by the Soviet Union, Mundt proclaimed it was time to quit "coddling" subversives at home while U.S. troops were dying in Korea. McCarran's package went beyond Mundt's proposals by requiring the delineation of "Communist-action" and "Communist-front" groups by the new Subversive Activities Control Board and their registration with the attorney general. Communists were to be denied passports and government and defense jobs and were to be subject to tighter espionage and sabotage laws.[21]

The McCarran bill won strong support among those who saw communism as an alien philosophy furthered by corrupt and privileged elites. A Nebraska woman spoke for many when she protested to the president that it was "impossible for us to allow communism here, and the same time send our boys to fight and *die* on foreign soil in an armed conflict against it." A Boston engineer concurred: "This is a two front war. In Korea and at home." Noting that her son-in-law was in Korea, a West Virginia woman asked Truman to run the Communists out of the country or put them in jail. A couple from Daytona Beach, Florida, also worked the populist theme by chastising the president for permitting Communists to "get by with murder practically by *paying* their way out of investigations or having good connections and going scot free on some *puny* loophole!" The men who made and enforced laws were "physical, mental, and moral cowards" for allowing Communist infiltration, a woman from Louisville wrote the White House. Such sentiments led a Texas housewife to propose a mass protest demanding that the president develop a program to deal with the Communist menace.[22]

Anticommunists such as Minnesota's Walter Judd denied that the McCarran bill punished people for their beliefs. Instead, they focused on the measure's registration requirements as a means for exposing those who sought to deny others their freedom and rights. Anxious to appear vigilant during wartime, the House voted 354 to 20 to approve the legislation. In the Senate liberals pressed for a substitute version authorizing the attorney general to intern sabotage and espionage risks during a national emergency, but the chamber merely incorporated the competing proposals in one package and passed it by a 70-7 margin. When Truman vetoed the McCarran bill on constitutional grounds, the House overrode the president by a vote of 248 to 48. Following William Langer's five-hour filibuster, the Senate concurred in a 57-10 vote.[23]

President Truman claimed that White House mail sustained his rejection of the McCarran bill by a 20-1 margin. Many Americans disputed these figures, however. "You are all either a bunch of fools or absolutely dishonest," a Montana department store owner wrote the president. "It's time some of you in the White House found out what the rank and file American is thinking about and quit listening to the pinks in the State Department." An Indiana welfare official argued that most White House correspondence emanated from administration supporters and "the Communist tribe who are organized for letter writing and all propaganda."[24]

Fortified by public concern over the communist issue, HUAC subpoenaed 110 Hollywood witnesses in 1951, 58 of whom admitted party involvement. Meanwhile, Pat McCarran, chair of the Senate Judiciary Committee, worked with the nationalists Homer Ferguson and William Jenner to organize the Internal Security Subcommittee. Insisting that the best educated and most brilliant people lent themselves to communist methods and thinking, McCarran sought to explain the "loss" of China by exposing ties between the State Department and the Institute of Pacific Relations. Following hearings, the Nevada senator announced that Owen Lattimore was "a conscious and articulate instrument of the Soviet conspiracy." President Truman responded to these pressures by issuing a 1951 executive order broadening federal loyalty board standards for dismissing government employees. Within months John Stewart Service, a McCarthy target, was declared a security risk and fired from the State Department. John Carter Vincent, another object of nationalist ire, was classified a loyalty risk in the same year.[25]

✦ ✦ ✦

Despite President Truman's attempts to assuage anxieties over internal security, the Korean War intensified mistrust of the administration. "Highly placed Red counselors in the State Department," proclaimed Senator McCarthy, "are far more deadly than Red machine gunners." McCarthy insisted that "Communists within our borders" played a larger role in the party's overseas successes than even the Soviet Union did. During the 1950 congressional campaign, the Wisconsinite carried his assault on Truman policy to fifteen states and pledged to drive from government "the Communists dupes, and fellow-travelers" who "plotted the Communist victory in Asia." Using the rhetoric of Ed Nellor, the creator of the Wheeling speech, McCarthy lambasted the "Commiecrats" who were "prisoners of a bureaucratic Communistic Frankenstein" as well as the "parlor pinks and parlor punks" who "still danced to the Moscow tune." In Maryland a successful McCarthy fund-raising effort and a distortion-filled brochure helped send Millard Tydings to shocking defeat.[26]

As the introduction of Chinese troops brought a bloody stalemate in Korea, public opinion turned against U.S. involvement. In December 1950 more than half a Gallup sample of Americans expressed the opinion that the United States had allowed itself to become involved in another world war. The following month nearly two-thirds called for immediate U.S. withdrawal. In February 1951, 30 percent asserted that the Soviets were winning the cold war. The next month half of Gallup respondents viewed involvement in the Korean hostilities as a mistake. By November 56 percent agreed that the conflict was a "useless war."[27]

Extension of conscription authorization and the lowering of the draft age contributed to the unpopularity of the Korean involvement. Compulsory military service particularly disturbed farm families in the north central states, a labor-scarce region to which immigrants had fled from European conscription and taxation. Many rural midwesterners shared the suspicion that State Department ineptitude had committed U.S. soldiers to an Asian land war in which the United States did not belong and could not win. "Russia must smile when she sees how we are falling into her trap of self-destruction," wrote a North Dakota woman to Senator Milton Young. The constituent mail of the state's congressional delegation turned against the war in December 1950, just as Young endorsed immediate withdrawal. By January 1951 an overwhelming majority of letters sought to "bring our boys home from Korea and mind our own business." That same month the North Dakota legislature sent Congress a resolution urging total military withdrawal.[28]

Other Americans were puzzled by the political nature of a limited and undeclared war conducted as a UN "police action." A California journalist reported to the White House that many people refused to believe the United States could be fighting communism while sitting with the Soviets in the United Nations. "They can't understand our breaking bread with Russia in the parlor while Russia is very obviously screwing us in the kitchen," he noted. A California woman asked President Truman if the nation was at war, with whom it was fighting, if communism was really a threat to national security, and if the administration was preserving American sovereignty or world government. The president's secretary responded, "This may not be war in the legal sense, but the struggle is just as real."[29]

Despite administration assurances, White House mail revealed the depth of frustration over the lack of success in a war that appeared to have no tangible goal. "Why don't you stop talking out of both corners of your mouth simultaneously?" inquired a Dallas woman, who saw the president as "a Caspar Milquetoast" unwilling to use nuclear weapons in "the greatest emergency in our national history." "Why don't you quit playing politics?" asked an Ohio woman disturbed at President Truman's alleged protection of "left-wingers in high government positions" and tolerance for allies like the British who conducted trade with Communist China. A former American Legion commander from Denver mocked White House insistence that the nation was not at war with Beijing by calling for troop withdrawal from Korea, where soldiers had "succumbed to the bullets of presumably friendly Chinese." Both the legionnaire and a retired Oklahoma schoolteacher accused Truman of submitting young Americans to "the butchery of Korea" in a halfhearted effort without purpose.[30]

Nationalist displeasure with the Korean War came to a head with President Truman's firing of General MacArthur. A near-legend for his World War II exploits as commander of U.S. forces in the Pacific, MacArthur had accepted the Japanese surrender and had won acclaim for administering a democratic and free-market occupation of Japan. "I have enormous admiration for him," proclaimed the progressive Philip La Follette, "and look upon him as the greatest living American." La Follette, a former MacArthur aide, insisted that the general embodied the leadership qualities that had characterized La Follette's father, whom MacArthur referred to as an old friend. The former Wisconsin governor told Republican colleagues in 1948 that the general had demonstrated how to stop Soviet penetration without hysteria or war, by encouraging Japanese cooperatives, smashing monopolies, legitimizing labor unions, launching land reform, safeguarding civil and religious liberties, and helping place a flat prohibition of war and militarism in Japan's constitution.[31]

With La Follette's guidance, Robert Wood and a group of midwestern business leaders attempted to organize a second MacArthur presidential bid in 1948. When the general refused to meet with party officials and only permitted his name to be entered in the Wisconsin primary, however, the candidacy failed to materialize. Two years later the Korean command once again placed MacArthur at the center of national attention. Yet the general's nationalist orientation collided with the Europe-centered globalism of the Truman administration. The president saw the Korean conflict as a symbolic anticommunist rallying point for the "free world." He hoped to show that territorial aggression would not be tolerated, that the United States honored its commitments, that collective security worked, that the political and military prestige of Communist powers was illusory, and that a Western arms buildup was essential. Truman's most important concerns were the protection of the security and interests of Japan and Western Europe and the avoidance of nuclear war.[32]

In contrast General MacArthur saw Europe as part of a dying system and believed that Asia would determine the world's future. Capitulation in the East, he warned the Joint Chiefs of Staff in December 1950, "could not fail to insure later defeat in Europe itself." Faced with a retreat below the 38th parallel spurred by the introduction of 200,000 Chinese troops, MacArthur sought to expand the Korean War by blockading China's coast and bombarding strategic sites, using Formosan soldiers in combat, and permitting diversionary actions and a possible counter-invasion of the Chinese mainland by Nationalist China. Once UN forces fought back to the 38th parallel in early 1951, however, the Truman administration rejected the general's requests and prepared to enter into truce talks. Determined to scuttle the negotiations, MacArthur sent a letter to House Republican leader Joseph Martin rejecting compromise. "Communist conspirators have elected to make their play for global conquest" in Asia, he asserted. Under such circumstances, "there is no substitute for victory."[33]

Citing the need for civilian control over the military, President Truman relieved Douglas MacArthur of his command in April 1951. The chief executive announced that the general had committed insubordination by publicly disagreeing with Korean War strategy and failing to clear policy statements. But MacArthur and his supporters saw a philosophical, not a tactical, basis to the controversy. "Strange voices are heard across the land," the general later would reflect in his memoirs. MacArthur could not abide by new notions that decried proven concepts of patriotism and suggested a higher destiny of internationalism. Americans now were called on to sacrifice their sons and daughters in a "halfhearted and indecisive war" disguised by "some more euphemistic and gentler name," he would write, until "we, the strongest military nation in the world, have suddenly become dependent upon others for our security and even our welfare."[34]

✦ ✦ ✦

As Gallup polls revealed that nearly two-thirds of respondents opposed President Truman's dismissal of MacArthur, the general returned home to spectacular and adoring crowds. Of the 10,000 constituent letters on the subject sent to Ohio's Senator John Bricker, three-quarters called for the impeachment of Truman, Dean Acheson, or Secretary of Defense George Marshall. Ohio's Robert Taft reported that 99 percent of the 3,500 telegrams and 12,000 letters sent to his office supported the general. By the end of the first week of May 1951 the White House had received 46,389 pro-MacArthur telegrams and 37,708 in favor of the president.[35]

Protests over the MacArthur firing often expressed bitter frustration over limited war and strategic foreign policy. "Bring our sons home from that game of tag or see-saw going on in Korea. Our sons' lives are being sacrificed for nothing," a Queens, New York, woman informed the president. Many correspondents accepted the logic that carrying the battle to the enemy would minimize the loss of American lives. "We do resent having our sons placed in an untenable strategic position," explained one letter writer, "to serve an unsuccessful diplomatic policy. . . . One can neither be a little bit pregnant nor involved a little bit in battle."[36]

"Thank God General MacArthur came back and has given us a rally-ing point," exclaimed a Pennsylvania veteran in a letter to Senator Ken-neth Wherry. Another protester told President Truman that he had "dis-charged the only MAN in this country who really had the interest of the COMMON PEOPLE at heart." "Where Mac walks, there goes America," a New Yorker wrote to his congressional representative, "and we have no man outside Mac who is pleading for this country." MacArthur's firing proved Joe McCarthy's assertions about Communist influence in the State Department, a St. Louis critic complained to Truman. The White House also received a clipping from the *Cleveland American* entitled "Football rules a la Truman." "No effort shall be made to win the game," it read, "the object is to show other possible opponents how good the home team is so that they won't want to risk a match at any time in the future."[37]

Congressional anticommunists used the MacArthur controversy as fresh ammunition for harsh attacks on the administration's national and inter-nal security record. Referring to the president, Joe McCarthy declared, "The son of a bitch should be impeached." McCarthy told reporters that Dean Acheson and "the old Hiss crowd" influenced President Truman at late-night sessions by plying him with bourbon and benedictine. "Some-one should hang for high treason for the needless loss of life in this war—where our only object is killing more of them than they do of us," the sen-ator proclaimed to a Wisconsin rally honoring a fallen soldier. Tying frustration with the war to his own charges of lax internal security, Mc-Carthy described "a leadership which whines, whimpers, cringes in fear, and urges that we dare not win a war which it started" because it shrank from nuclear retaliation made possible by "secrets stolen from us by spies which, according to the president, never existed."[38]

Joe McCarthy's cries mirrored the nationalist critique. Indiana's William Jenner pleaded with the Senate to "cut this whole cancerous conspiracy" by unseating the president and uncovering "the secret invisible government which has so clearly led our country down the road to destruction." Karl Mundt denounced "the Truman-Acheson cabal" and concluded that the chief executive lacked "the good judgment and the stability so needed to cope with the problems of his position." After attacking the United Nations for "indecision, incompetence, and culpability," North Dakota's William Langer prepared constituents for a presidential impeachment. The Asia-first activ-ist Walter Judd called MacArthur's removal "the Kremlin's greatest victory since Yalta." The general was "a giant whom the pygmies cannot tolerate because he has been so consistently right about Asia and they so consistent-ly wrong," charged Judd. Fear of appeasement in Asia and the loss of U.S. influence beyond the Pacific, explained Robert Taft, had "aroused Mac-Arthur and the country."[39]

Nationalists who saw the cold war policy as weak and vacillating viewed Secretary of State Dean Acheson as the major culprit. Born into a family with a social register background, Acheson graduated from Groton, Yale, and Harvard law school before becoming a senior partner in a prestigious Washington firm involved in international finance law. After serving as a top State Department official between 1941 and 1947, Acheson received Truman's nomination to head the department in January 1949. With public opinion nervous about the Communist menace, the Foreign Relations Committee invited the entire Senate to participate in the first public confirmation hearing ever held for the office. Testimony from former State Department colleagues suggested that Acheson had opposed hard-line confrontations with the Soviet Union. Kenneth Wherry, who had cast the lone vote against the diplomat's 1945 appointment as under secretary of state, told the Senate that Acheson should be defeated for his internationalist record and for the appeasement of Communists in Asia.[40]

Nationalists like Wherry saw Dean Acheson as a symbol of weak inaction, part of a cabal of elite policymakers who retreated into diplomatic double-talk. Homer Capehart pleaded with the Senate in 1949 to follow the American people and expel "this Wall Streeter who is a partner to loans to Communist-dominated countries, to Arabian oil interests, and to other international money-making enterprises." "All of us so-called 'little people' are very uneasy about the Communist menace here," agreed an Ohio housewife who wrote to President Truman. "Dean Acheson is too closely associated with pro-Russian thinking to be secretary of state." In a speech he never delivered, William Langer accused the nominee of holding an "alien internationalist philosophy" that could "destroy our form of government and our way of life." Langer voted with fellow Republicans Homer Capehart, Kenneth Wherry, William Jenner, William Knowland, and New Hampshire's Styles Bridges to deny the nomination, but the final result was a one-sided 83 to 6 for confirmation.[41]

Nationalist criticism of Acheson escalated following the Chinese Revolution. The State Department's white paper, charged the Michigan Republican Clare Hoffman, raised questions about whether the secretary was "a friend of the Communists, seeks to placate them, or is just dumb." Representative Walter Judd, who claimed to be the first in public life to call for Acheson's resignation, wrote constituents that it "irks me beyond words" to have witnessed "a war lost by supposed diplomats so soon after it has been won with such sacrifice by the fighting men." Senator Hugh Butler from Nebraska summarized the fury of the Republican attack on Acheson. "I look at that fellow," declared Butler, "I watch his smart-aleck manner and his British clothes and that New Dealism, everlasting New Dealism in everything he says and does, and I want to shout, Get out, Get out, you stand for everything that has been wrong with the United States."[42]

Acheson's long-standing association with Alger Hiss further infuriated critics. Soon after Hiss's perjury conviction, Acheson told reporters that he would not "turn my back" on the career diplomat. Minnesota's Walter Judd decried the secretary's statement as a betrayal of trust and an example of "personal government." White House protest letters suggested that Acheson had placed friendship above loyalty to country. "It is a terrific strain on the patriotism of the man in the street to hear such dissertations," wrote an Upstate New Yorker to President Truman. "Now that he has turned over China to the Reds and has shown his colors by standing by a Communist and convicted traitor," urged another, "kick him out of your cabinet in a good old-fashioned American way."[43]

✦   ✦   ✦

As the frustrations of the Korean War demonstrated the difficulties of sustaining the global crusade against communism, Acheson became the object of ridicule for Americans who still clung to republican and populist sensibilities. "The plain fact is—we don't trust him," a Long Island woman informed the president in July 1950. "When men are giving their lives as a result of the flagrant blunders of someone—don't you think it's time to try to rectify partially such blunders?" a Dallas protester asked the White House. "He speaks out for America but he talks another language to the Communists," admonished an Ohio woman. By the end of 1950, as the war was going badly in Korea, only 20 percent of a Gallup poll gave Acheson a favorable rating (31 percent were unfavorable, and 34 percent were unfamiliar with his name). "You have succumbed to the blandishments of the wax moustache, the perfumed handkerchief, and the British accent in the person of Acheson," a traveling salesman from New York's Flushing complained to the White House. Other letters pictured the secretary as a "mealy mouthed" intellectual and appeaser.[44]

When the war in Korea deteriorated into a stalemate in the spring of 1951, mail to the White House continued to portray Acheson as an elite Anglophile who lacked the moral courage to act decisively. "If Mr. Acheson can't evolve a positive comprehensive policy for Asia," a New Yorker admonished the president, "fire the pussy footer." A Chicago insurance company executive was more explicit. "You thought you were going to shove Acheson down the throats of the American people," he exclaimed, "but now you are going to find the American people are going to shove him down your throat—striped pants, frock tailed coat, bow tie, and boutonniere. Even though he may be pretty smooth and slippery he's going to be pretty hard for you to swallow." Get rid of Acheson, an Ohio letter writer warned the president, "and his whole troupe of 'pink-lotus-eaters.' . . . Harry, the universal judgments of the American people are never wrong."[45]

Nationalists and anticommunists alternated between demanding the use of atomic weapons in Korea and urging total withdrawal. A membership poll of the nominally conservative Committee for Constitutional Government found that a bare majority (419-408) opposed military withdrawal. Representative Judd privately summarized the issue's complexity when he noted that Acheson had written off the defense of Asia and then insisted "we walk into the trap" by sending U.S. troops back to Korea. Nationalists like Homer Capehart asserted that the United Nations limited the Korean police action. "President Truman has either forfeited American sovereignty, or he is forfeiting American lives by his own incompetence or negligence," exclaimed Capehart in 1950. "Under our present policy," complained Usher Burdick, "our boys cannot go in and fight for victory. We can't win and don't want to lose, so we are in an impossible situation." Karl Mundt declared the conflict "the bloodiest undeclared war" in U.S. history.[46]

Republican nationalists saw General MacArthur's triumphant return to the United States as a pretext for a congressional review of U.S. foreign policy. Senate minority leader Kenneth Wherry used the occasion to denounce the "holding action" in Korea and won quick support for a resolution requesting the general's appearance before a joint session of Congress. In an eloquent April 1951 address witnessed by sixty million television viewers, the former commander warned against administration defeatism and bid an emotional farewell. Wherry and Republican leaders seized the moment and convinced the Senate to establish a special panel to hold hearings on the MacArthur dismissal and overall East Asia policy. The Nebraska senator also hoped to broaden the proceedings to include evaluation of the executive's role in making foreign policy. Nevertheless, the Truman administration managed to contain the inquiry and used military testimony to assert that MacArthur's strategy would produce full-scale war with China and split the Allies. When it disbanded in August 1951, the special panel voted 20 to 3 against issuing a final report.[47]

Korean peace negotiations began in July 1951 but faltered when President Truman opposed forced repatriation of Communist prisoners of war. Seeking a psychological victory to compensate for the military stalemate, the White House hoped to show that Communist leaders could not depend on the loyalty of their troops. Nationalists continued to pound the administration by insisting that State Department appeasement had led to the North Korean invasion. To compound matters, they charged, Truman had failed to consult Congress when committing troops, "a complete usurpation" of presidential military authority, commented Robert Taft. Denouncing Democratic appeasement of "countries that have laughed and mocked us for decades," William Langer asked if any senator had been "consulted about having a war in Korea." "It is plain the American people have had enough," proclaimed Kenneth Wherry in July 1951, "enough of the Hisses and Achesons in the State Department; enough of international power politics and secret alliances."[48]

Frustrated by the futility of checking the executive power of the Democratic administration, nationalist Republicans once again hoped to advance Robert Taft as the party's 1952 presidential nominee. As David Green has suggested, the Ohio senator appeared to be a McCarthy at home and a MacArthur abroad. Taft repeated his 1948 pledge to pursue "liberty" instead of "socialism" in domestic affairs. But the eastern wing of the Republican party, as Justus Doenecke has noted, saw the Ohioan's foreign policy as too risky in Asia and too cautious in Europe. Seeking a balanced international strategy and the popularity of a winner, party leaders turned to Dwight David Eisenhower, supreme commander of the Allies in Europe. In 1951, 43 percent of Democratic voters had picked Eisenhower as the first choice for their party's presidential nomination. By February 1952 Republican voters were evenly split between Taft and the affable general.[49]

Nationalists such as Robert Wood and the *Chicago Tribune*'s Robert McCormick joined such Republican senators as William Jenner, Everett Dirksen, and John Bricker in seeking to reverse the internationalist tide that had dominated the party's three previous national conventions. Critics fiercely attacked General Eisenhower's association with the domestic and foreign policies of Truman Democrats. "If Eisenhower is nominated," Wood warned Douglas MacArthur in July 1952, "he will be in the control of the same crowd of men who are the backers of the New Deal." Yet even a keynote address by MacArthur failed to keep the convention from nominating the European commander on the first ballot. At first Robert Taft charged that Eisenhower had been installed by "the power of the New York financial interests" and fourth-fifths of the nation's leading newspapers. But after a congenial meeting at which the nominee promised lower government spending, the Ohioan agreed to support the Republican ticket.[50]

Nationalist and anticommunist sentiment played a major role in the 1952 campaign. Joseph McCarthy delivered a major convention address, campaigned with General Eisenhower in Wisconsin, and took to television to tie Adlai Stevenson, the Democratic candidate, to Alger Hiss and denounce Truman's "deliberate planned retreat from victory." Eisenhower and Richard Nixon, his vice presidential nominee, pledged to houseclean the State Department, repudiate Yalta, counter secrecy in presidential foreign policy and internal security, support the liberation of Eastern Europe, and "unleash" Chiang Kai-shek. After targeting communism, government corruption, and the Korean stalemate, the popular Eisenhower swept to victory. Republicans also regained control of Congress by slight majorities in both houses. "Forces of good and evil are massed and armed and opposed as rarely before in history," the new president remarked as he took office. The war against communism, asserted freshly appointed Secretary of State John Foster Dulles, involved "an irreconcilable conflict."[51]

Despite Dulles's rhetoric, most Republican nationalists remained skeptical of the new administration's intentions. Constituting more than half their party's strength in the new Congress, nationalists sensed that President Eisenhower shared the basic precepts of the Truman White House. Like his Democratic predecessors, the new chief executive endorsed the notion that the federal government could promote growth in the corporate economy and thereby minimize social conflict. Positioning himself as a proponent of "dynamic conservatism" and "progressive moderation," Eisenhower pursued a robust internationalism to protect U.S. global interests and contain communism. The president shared the assumption of Truman officials that U.S. security rested on a stable and friendly Europe. Rather than portray the cold war as a crusade against evil, Eisenhower preferred to treat it as a problem to be managed with calm leadership. The Korean armistice and Joseph Stalin's death in 1953 both contributed to reduced U.S.-Soviet tensions.[52]

✦ ✦ ✦

Traditional noninterventionists had always suspected commitments to what Charles Lindbergh called "the equality of internationalism." Many, including Lindbergh, Robert Wood of Sears, Roebuck, the journalist John Flynn, and Alfred Kohlberg, continued to denounce British influence on U.S. foreign policy in the 1950s. Flynn professed amazement at the extent to which President Eisenhower's inaugural address identified with "One-Worlders." For critics like the retired brigadier general who wrote to Senator John Bricker in 1953, eastern internationalists were more dangerous than the Kremlin because they were the "Hand Maidens of Communism." Kohlberg, an exporter and Asia-firster, expressed similar sentiments in a personal letter to the directors of American Telephone and Telegraph after their photograph was featured in a two-page advertisement in the May 1954 *Saturday Evening Post*. In the face of frightening ideological and military dangers in the world, chastised Kohlberg, the nation's corporate elite had "failed" the country by withdrawing "into an ivory tower of business, philanthropy, and finance" and refusing to assume leadership.[53]

Portrayed as an agent of global government, Secretary of State Dulles became a lightning rod for nationalist discontent. Senator William Jenner ignored Republican discipline to condemn Dulles publicly for ties to Wall

Street, contempt for Chiang Kai-shek, pro-NATO sentiments, and a Hiss-tainted trusteeship with the Carnegie Endowment. Arthur H. Dean, Eisenhower's special ambassador to Korea, received similar treatment from Senator Herman Welker of Idaho. Elected in 1950, Welker had a reputation for confronting Communists, New Dealers, and "One-Worlders." Dean had raised the possibility that Chinese Maoists were more interested in economic development than in international communism. Nationalists perceived strategic analysis of this kind as an example of the moral and spiritual vacuousness associated with Truman's foreign policy. Accordingly, Welker dramatically criticized Dean's comments by pointing to the diplomat's ties to the ill-fated Institute of Pacific Relations. The outburst reflected nationalist impatience with such Democratic legacies as Korea, the United Nations, and European foreign aid.[54]

Eisenhower internationalism also embraced hotly debated economic policies. Besides support of the World Bank and the International Monetary Fund, the administration sought the continuation of Truman reciprocal trade agreements. After Congress granted a succession of temporary extensions, it finally approved a four-year program in 1958. The compromise bill required a two-thirds vote of both houses to override presidential rejections of Tariff Commission recommendations. Foreign aid proved to be an even more contentious issue. Pushed by Republican critics of Truman policy, the Eisenhower administration backed reduced overseas assistance while proposing mutual security bills for Europe and Asia. The president hoped to reorient the security programs to economic aid in order to strengthen endangered allies against the Communist threat. Nationalist strains in the Republican party and growing hostility to foreign aid among southern Democrats, however, made it very difficult for the chief executive to sell his plan to Congress.[55]

William Langer of North Dakota remained one of the staunchest Senate critics of internationalism. Although like-minded colleagues often sided with him, the colorful Langer had no equal in drawing out the populist connotations in the nationalist perspective. In 1944 the North Dakotan had cast the only negative vote against the confirmation of Secretary of State Edward Stettinius because of the nominee's ties to the House of Morgan. Not long after, he charged that the State Department was dominated by "a clique of appeasement-minded cookie pushers." During Senate Foreign Relations Committee hearings on mutual security in 1954, Langer continued to ridicule the department for its remoteness from the American people. He dismissed it as "a refuge for career people of the social register" who were corrupted by "Europeanism" and "shop-worn social theories." Because they were "cosmopolites and less American than international," charged the senator, diplomats only saw the interests of their European friends.[56]

Langer's greatest criticism involved foreign aid for Britain and Western Europe. When Winston Churchill planned a 1952 visit to seek a loan, the North Dakotan sent a telegram to Boston's Old Church imploring that two lanterns be hung in the belfry to warn that the British were returning. The senator never dropped the nationalist contention that postwar Europe represented aristocracy and socialism at home and war and imperialism abroad. "Somehow we will have to get these people off our necks and their hands out of our pockets," he told the Foreign Relations Committee in 1954. Seeing no difference between Democratic and Republican "one worldism," Langer mocked the notion "that our security can be increased directly in proportion to the amount of money we spend abroad." Overseas assistance, he insisted, was not "a universal substitute for sound diplomacy and realistic thinking," particularly when it bankrupted the nation and diverted funds from such worthy programs as farm aid.[57]

Nationalists urgently opposed President Eisenhower's mutual security programs. The fund for Asian economic development, charged William Jenner in 1955, reflected the myth that "American spending in poor areas of the world will prevent Communists from getting in." Others contended that mutual security aid produced permanent dependency among developing nations. Congress granted the president only half of a proposed $200 million Asian development fund in 1955. The following year it eliminated the Asian program, slashed $1 billion from the mutual security package, and stipulated that 80 percent of development assistance be in the form of loans instead of grants. When committees in both houses conducted hearings on foreign aid and harshly criticized mutual security in 1957, legislators cut overseas assistance by another $1 billion. It was 1960 before administration lobbying produced a substantial $3.78 billion appropriation for foreign aid.[58]

As early as 1954 Gallup polls suggested that 61 percent of Americans identified themselves as "internationalists." By that same year, Gary Reichard has estimated, some 75 percent of the Republican members of Congress staked out similar positions on mutual security appropriations and tariff flexibility. The Eisenhower administration sought to cement the emerging consensus by combining talk of "trade and aid." Yet Republican internationalists persistently confronted resistance among large sections of the party's rank and file. One manifestation of this discontent was the formation in 1954 of Colonel Robert McCormick's For America, an anti-interventionist lobby pledged to an "enlightened nationalism."[59] Far more substantial was grass-roots enthusiasm and congressional support for Senator John Bricker's attempts to amend the Constitution's provisions for treaty making.

First proposed in 1951, the Bricker amendment sought to ensure that international treaties reflect fundamental precepts of American legality. It also required federal legislation to give overseas accords the status of international law. The amendment further mandated congressional approval of executive agreements with international agencies and other nations. Senator Bricker believed that Democratic presidents had conducted diplomatic and military policy without congressional sanction. He also feared that protocols introduced by "Godless and socialistic members" of the United Nations might threaten American domestic law and traditional rights. Citing such agreements as the UN Covenant on Human Rights and the Genocide Convention, Frank E. Holman, the former president of the American Bar Association, already had declared that treaty law had "become omnipotent, a kind of 'Frankenstein' instrumentality." Bricker explained that the "crux of the problem" lay in "the novel theory" that government guarantees of political and economic rights should be replaced by the direct application of international law to individuals.[60]

Fearing that UN treaties might require compulsory national health insurance and federal programs to end racial segregation, small business and southern industrial interests actively supported the Bricker amendment. When the American Bar Association endorsed the proposal in 1952, Bricker found fifty-eight Senate cosponsors. The next year the solon defied the Eisenhower administration by attracting sixty-three cosponsors and eliciting two months of legislative hearings. Bricker claimed that 400,000 Americans had signed petitions endorsing his measure. A Gallup poll of October 1953, however, found that only 19 percent of the sample even knew about the proposal. The Senate defeated the scheme by a 50-44 vote in February 1954. But when Walter George, a Georgia Democrat who was the ranking member of the Senate Foreign Relations Committee, introduced a reworked version, the measure received sixty of the sixty-one votes required for a two-thirds majority. A bipartisan coalition of southerners and midwesterners and every Republican nationalist supported the Bricker amendment.[61]

✦ ✦ ✦

Drawing on a populist nationalism that associated Europe with imperialism, tyranny, privilege, and ideological rigidity, critics of postwar internationalism sought to disrupt a carefully constructed foreign policy consensus. Some dissidents contended that professional diplomats represented the financial interests of Wall Street and powerful corporations whose business crossed national boundaries. The most important theme of bipartisan criticism, however, centered on the conviction that expert practitioners of modern diplomacy separated strategic matters from moral issues and thereby betrayed the true concerns of the American people. These anxieties were supplemented by questions concerning the federal government's commitment to the anticommunist crusade, its dedication to the free market of small competitors, and its ability to restrain itself from interfering in the personal lives of its citizens. Such themes would dominate much of the political controversy of the remaining years of the 1950s.

12

On the Edge: Confronting Communist Conspiracy, Corporate Consolidation, and Civil Rights, 1953–63

Addressing the bland consensus of the 1950s, one outsider complained that the nation's leaders were composed of "the soft-spoken and the soft-brained, the well-mannered and the lukewarm, the genteel and half-educated asses." In a world in which traditional verities were treated as "figments of a superstitious imagination," he charged, American political leaders placed "the genteel rules of a vulgar game above life itself." William S. Schlamm's diatribe in the conservative *National Review* expressed the growing alienation of nationalists, free-market advocates, anticollectivists, and opponents of government coercion. By the early 1960s, however, the waning of the domestic anticommunist crusade, the isolation of small business, and the growing popularity of civil rights reform placed such dissidents in a marginal position within the American political spectrum.[1]

❖ ❖ ❖

Energized by the anticommunist fervor of Republican nationalists, the Eisenhower administration had sought to strengthen internal security. Under an April 1953 executive order, government security risks could be discharged for reasons other than actual disloyalty, and hearing and review procedures were abolished. A second mandate permitted dismissal of witnesses using the Fifth Amendment. As Secretary of State John Foster Dulles stepped up the purge, John Carter Vincent, declared a loyalty risk in 1951, resigned. Meanwhile, increased security concerns resulted in denying security clearance to the Atomic Energy Commission consultant J. Robert Oppenheimer. A freethinking Berkeley professor who had Communist family and social ties dating back to the 1930s, Oppenheimer had headed the Los Alamos atomic laboratory. When he opposed strategic air and hydrogen bomb programs after World War II, the physicist fell under suspicion. Accusations by Oppenheimer critics prompted Eisenhower to initiate an inquiry. In June 1954 a majority of the Atomic Energy Commission cited the scientist for "fundamental defects of character and imprudent dangerous associations."[2]

The new administration also stirred the anticommunist pot when Attorney General Herbert Brownell Jr. announced that FBI records showed President Truman had known about Harry Dexter White's "spying activities for the Soviet government" before promoting him to executive director of the International Monetary Fund in 1946. Meanwhile, the Republican-led House Committee on Un-American Activities questioned over 650 witnesses in unions, churches, and the entertainment industry between 1953 and 1954. President Eisenhower signed the Communist Control Act in 1954, which explicitly outlawed the party as an "agency of a hostile foreign power" not entitled to the "rights, privileges, and immunities" of U.S. law. The chief executive also refused to grant clemency to Julius and Ethel Rosenberg, who were executed for conspiracy to commit atomic espionage in June 1953.[3]

Although outpolled in Wisconsin by Dwight Eisenhower, Joe McCarthy returned to a Republican-run Senate in 1953. Assigned chairmanship of the Committee on Government Operations, McCarthy named himself head of the panel's Permanent Subcommittee on Investigations. He soon joined the Republican nationalists Styles Bridges, Everett Dirksen, William Jenner, and Herman Welker in opposing the Eisenhower administration's nomination of Charles E. Bohlen as ambassador to the Soviet Union. A private school and Harvard graduate, Bohlen had served in the Moscow embassy in the 1930s and had participated in the major diplomatic conferences of World War II. To the dismay of critics, he defended Yalta and Truman administration policies in testimony before the Foreign Relations Committee. "We will never keep in power men who played an important role in selling out the people of Europe and Asia to the Soviet dictatorship," McCarthy warned the Senate. The Wisconsin solon demanded that Secretary of State Dulles testify about whether he had overruled department security staffers to provide Bohlen's clearance.[4]

The Bohlen nomination provided the first indication of the split between Joe McCarthy and Eisenhower Republicans. Militant nationalists feared that the new administration shared its predecessor's assumptions about the Soviets and was not sufficiently vigilant about potential disloyalty or lax security. In contrast the White House insisted that the Bohlen controversy had elicited an irresponsible assault on professional diplomacy. When McCarthy prepared to call the State Department's security chief before his committee, Eisenhower officials quickly squelched the effort. Meanwhile, the president gave Robert Taft access to Bohlen's loyalty files, and the Ohio senator assured colleagues of the nominee's trustworthiness. Only twelve other senators joined McCarthy in opposing the appointment on the roll-call vote. Temporarily eclipsed, the Wisconsinite responded by announcing two days later that he had personally arranged a secret pact with Greek ship owners to halt trade with Communist China and North Korea.[5]

McCarthy first directed his subcommittee to hearings on State Department publicity and propaganda agencies. He began by investigating alleged Communist infiltration of key departments in the Voice of America. The senator then subpoenaed former Communists and fellow travelers whose books appeared in the overseas libraries of the U.S. Information Agency (USIA). Although both inquiries fizzled, McCarthy delighted in exposing the past political ties of beleaguered bureaucrats and writers. Tapping additional targets in July 1953, he sought to subpoena William P. Bundy, a top official at the Central Intelligence Agency. A graduate of Groton and Harvard, Bundy was a corporate attorney who happened to be the son-in-law of Dean Acheson. McCarthy threatened a full-scale exposé of the CIA if he could not question Bundy on a $400 contribution to the Hiss Defense Fund. The senator backed off, however, when Vice President Nixon indicated that the White House would not permit the agency to submit to public investigations.[6]

Turning his attention to the army and the Defense Department, McCarthy investigated clearance procedures for civilian employees. He next asserted that an army intelligence study of Soviet Siberia contained Communist propaganda. To buttress his point, the senator elicited testimony from Louis Budenz, the former editor of the *Daily Worker,* which suggested that several writers listed in the study's bibliography were Communists. Cross-examining the army's chief intelligence officer, McCarthy declared that the major general was "completely incompetent." In October 1953 the Wisconsinite announced that his committee would show that a spy ring was operating among civilian scientists at the Army Signal Corps Engineering Labs at Fort Monmouth, New Jersey, the installation where Julius Rosenberg had worked during World War II. All that McCarthy uncovered, however, were the political ties, beliefs, and histories of former employees. Undaunted, the senator demanded the names of members of the loyalty board "who cleared men with clear-cut Communist connections."[7]

When former president Truman accused the Eisenhower administration of embracing McCarthyism in November 1953, it was the Wisconsin solon who responded. At first the senator warned that Eisenhower's team had failed to reverse the "whining, whimpering appeasement" of Democratic predecessors. The next month he took a more conciliatory tone by asking Americans respectfully to communicate their displeasure over European trade with Communist China (the White House received fifty thousand telegrams and letters). By the end of 1953, 50 percent of a Gallup sample had favorable views of McCarthy, while 29 percent did not and 21 percent had no opinion. Polls showed insufficient militance in expelling Communist officeholders to be the most common criticism of the Eisenhower administration.[8]

✦ ✦ ✦

Never one to practice caution, Senator McCarthy courted political danger by taking on the army and the popular President Eisenhower. The confrontation stemmed from the case of Irving Peress, a New York dentist with Communist affiliations. As he pursued the matter of army security clearances, McCarthy learned that Peress had been promoted to the rank of major and then had received an honorable discharge despite compromising security information in his personnel file. To demonstrate the army's lack of clear security policies and the bureaucratic confusion involved in implementing them, the Wisconsin senator compelled the closed-door testimony of General Ralph Zwicker, Peress's last commanding officer. When Zwicker hedged in responding to a question, the chair reminded the general that he was "an employee of the people." Not satisfied with a subsequent answer, McCarthy exploded that Zwicker "should be removed from any command" and that he was "not fit to wear that uniform."[9]

After General Zwicker's testimony Secretary of the Army Robert T. Stevens telephoned McCarthy to say that military officers would not be granted permission to appear before the senator's committee if they were going to be abused. Unperturbed, McCarthy answered, "I am going to kick the brains out of anyone who protects Communists. . . . I am all through with this covering up of Communists." The two had lunch together, but Stevens failed to obtain any concessions from the chair. After a mild rebuke from President Eisenhower in March 1954, McCarthy held a press conference to state that if "a stupid, arrogant, or witless man in a position of power appears before our committee and is found aiding the Communist party he will be exposed." He also announced that "the president and I *now* agree on the necessity of getting rid of Communists." When Vice President Nixon went on television to criticize reckless attempts to expose subversives, McCarthy responded, "I don't intend to treat traitors like gentlemen."[10]

McCarthy's conflict with the military was exacerbated by charges that the senator's office had sought special treatment for David Shine, the committee assistant who had been inducted into the army in November 1953. In turn, the Wisconsinite asserted that military brass had used Shine as a "hostage" to discourage further inquiries into army security practices. Once the White House released the army's accusations against McCarthy in March 1954, the Permanent Subcommittee on Investigations organized a public inquiry. Although McCarthy stepped down as chair, he retained the right of cross-examination. Beginning in April, the televised Army-McCarthy hearings presented a graphic illustration of the stark differences between the anticommunist insurgence and the Eisenhower commonwealth. John Adams, the army counsel, admitted that high-level White House meetings had been held to coordinate strategy on McCarthy. When the president cited the separation of powers in a public statement, however, executive branch officials were prohibited from testifying about such talks.[11]

Exploiting the executive wing's hostility, McCarthy dramatically positioned himself as a crusader against amoral, unaccountable, and secret government bureaucrats. As the hearings began, he objected to a brief filed by the "Department of the Army." It was only the work of a "few Pentagon politicians attempting to disrupt our investigation," protested McCarthy. "I maintain it is a disgrace . . . to let a few civilians who are trying . . . to hold up an investigation of Communists label themselves as the Department of the Army." More fireworks erupted in May when the army counsel asked the senator to reveal the source of a purported J. Edgar Hoover warning of lax security at Fort Monmouth. "There is no way on earth," answered McCarthy, "that any committee, any force, can get me to violate the confidence of the people who give me information from within the government."[12]

Once Attorney General Brownell refused to release Justice Department documents, the Wisconsin solon openly encouraged government employees to break federal law and usurp the authority of their superiors. "I will continue to receive information," declared McCarthy. "There's no power on earth can change that. Again, I want to compliment individuals [who] give me information even though some little bureaucrat has stamped it 'secret' to defend himself. . . . I would like to notify two million federal employees that it is their duty to give us the information they have about graft, corruption, Communists, and treason, and that there is no loyalty to a superior officer that can tower above their loyalty to their country. . . . I just will not abide by any secrecy directive of anyone."[13]

After privately noting that the statement amounted to "wholesale subversion of the public service," President Eisenhower publicly warned against those who set themselves "above the laws of the land." Although the Army-McCarthy hearings damaged both sides, television seemed to underscore the Wisconsin solon's outbursts, crude attacks, and distortions. By June 1954 Joe McCarthy's favorable ratings had slipped from 50 percent to 34 percent. Significantly, 59 percent of professional and business respondents and 62 percent of the college-educated sample registered negative opinions. Among the most intense McCarthy opponents was a group of corporate and political leaders in the Committee for Economic Development (CED). Formed in 1942 by Vermont's Ralph Flanders and a group of Republican internationalists who accepted the New Deal, the organization had strong ties to the Eisenhower White House.[14]

President Eisenhower long had objected to McCarthy's methods. As early as June 1950 the general had used his position as head of Columbia University to declare that Americans should not be suckered into calling anyone a communist "who may be just a little brighter than ourselves." Eisenhower also had expressed private outrage at McCarthy's June 1951 Senate denunciation of General George Marshall. In a sixty-thousand-word diatribe questioning the defense secretary's loyalty to the nation, the Wisconsin senator had traced Washington's cold war difficulties to "a conspiracy so immense and an infamy so black as to dwarf any previous such venture in the history of man." Opposed to the distractions and chaos of populist politics, Eisenhower worked closely with the CED to counteract the influence of Wisconsin's junior senator.[15]

Senator Flanders formally asked colleagues to censure McCarthy in July 1954. The Flanders resolution cited the Wisconsinite for conduct unbecoming a senator, behavior violating Senate traditions, and actions that tended to bring the body into disrepute. The response was predictably mixed. "We cannot condemn the one man who the American people think is trying to do something about Communism," pleaded Indiana's Homer Capehart. In contrast, John McClellan, an Arkansas Democrat, confided that "I'm fond of Joe McCarthy, but he's getting out of hand, and we have to do something to control him." In a compromise the Senate voted to create a bipartisan fact-finding panel appointed by the vice president. Following the November elections the Watkins select committee recommended censure for McCarthy's abuse of General Zwicker and his contempt of the Senate panel that had sought to examine his activities during the 1950 elections. McCarthy had failed to respect "the dignity, honor, authority, and powers of the Senate," concluded the committee, thereby inducing a loss of faith in "persons of high places" and "our form of government."[16]

Joe McCarthy responded by referring to himself as "the symbol of resistance to Communist subversion." Claiming that the Communist party had achieved a major victory, McCarthy explained that a powerful and ruthless "anti-anti-Communism" extended to the "greater part of opinion-molding machinery" in the nation. The real strength of the Communist party, he contended, was its "ability to influence the American mind" and persuade people that government should let up on efforts to clean out subversives. McCarthy concluded that the party had "now extended its tentacles" to the U.S. Senate, where the Watkins committee imitated its methods and had become "its unwitting handmaiden." Refusing to compromise or apologize, McCarthy was unable to prevent action on censure in December 1954. Two counts cited the solon for failing to cooperate with a Senate committee and for denouncing the Watkins panel. Five days after the 67-22 vote, McCarthy publicly apologized for the "unintentional deception" of endorsing General Eisenhower for president as a vigorous foe of communism.[17]

✦ ✦ ✦

Joe McCarthy cast opponents as advocates of European security at the expense of American strength. Predictably, Republican nationalists figured prominently in the senator's defense. Supporters included John Bricker and Homer Capehart as well as Styles Bridges, Everett Dirksen, William Jenner, William Langer, Karl Mundt, William Knowland, Herman Welker, and George Malone. Although Bricker sometimes distanced himself from McCarthy's methods, he joined the debate by charging that the solon's critics could not tolerate attacks on communism because their vision was "strikingly similar to socialism and other collectivisms." The Ohioan's constituents tended to agree, seeing the anticommunist's censure, in one woman's words, as a "diabolic attempt to silence the one man who has the courage to try to save us in spite of ourselves." The anti–New Deal activist John Flynn, who joined Robert Wood in donating money to McCarthy, placed the blame on President Eisenhower, whom he derided as "a collectivist" without "an intelligent idea in his head" about communism and socialism.[18]

McCarthy's antagonism toward the eastern elite won him the support of the former progressive Burton Wheeler, who compared the senator's exposés with his own experiences with Teapot Dome. "When you are dealing with crooks and spies," explained Wheeler, "you have to be tough." The Wisconsin senator's appeal extended to a wide array of western entrepreneurs and oil interests, small business and farm enterprisers, midwestern noninterventionists, blue-collar and white ethnic workers, evangelical Protestants, remnants of the eastern aristocracy, and anticommunist intellectuals and activists. As David Oshinsky has suggested, McCarthy united diverse Americans who shared an animosity to remote centers of power in Moscow, Washington, and New York. This "coalition of the aggrieved," as Richard Rovere described it, could not forgive New Deal liberals for permitting Communist infiltration of government and the perpetuation of a British-oriented internationalism. In McCarthy's hands foreign policy became a matter of patriotism versus cosmopolitan treason.[19]

Joe McCarthy succeeded in dramatizing the need to tighten up the federal government's loyalty-security standards and compelled Americans to see communism as a political-military conspiracy instead of a legitimate movement for change. Beyond his explanation of the nation's perceived decline, however, the senator had no significant ideology, program, or personal ambition and had little impact on electoral politics. As the political analyst Peter Viereck observed during the debate over censure, McCarthy's anticommunism was not as central to his mission as his "radical anticonservatism" regarding the nation's cultural elite. Viereck noted a supporter's prediction that the solon would "be redeemed" when the people retrieved their government from "the criminal alliance of Communists, Socialists, new Dealers, and the Eisenhower-Dewey Republicans." "His targets were not really Communists," David Oshinsky has concluded, "they were the well-dressed, well-educated managers of modern society."[20]

By focusing on such mainstream institutions as the army, the civil service, the diplomatic corps, and the Ivy League universities, the McCarthy crusade intuitively blended modes of populist insurgency with the sentiments of Republican nationalism. As the sociologist Talcott Parsons suggested, support for the movement by powerful interests did not erase the fact that McCarthyism embodied "a popular revolt against the upper classes." Beneath the senator's antics lay the classic populist demand that the will of the people impose justice and morality on powerful institutions and protected individuals. A militant anticommunist, McCarthy promised to rescue Americans from secret conspiracies emanating from privileged corners of the cultural landscape. As one student of the movement noted, the irreverent solon "turned Progressive ideology inside out." Ignoring the standard economic targets of the 1930s, McCarthy focused on an elitist cabal of old-stock Americans in the heart of the nation's political and cultural life.[21]

The Wisconsin senator took particular delight in contrasting his crudely masculine persona and tough-minded "horse sense" with an allegedly effete, weak, and effeminate intelligentsia. McCarthyites often portrayed professional, technical, and academic elites as unfit to lead a free society because they supposedly had flirted with Marxism and relativist moral codes during the economic crisis of the 1930s. When the intellectual classes mocked such traditional virtues as patriotism, individualism, and adherence to custom, McCarthy supporters detected a hidden agenda of globalism, collectivism, rational secularism, and unregulated social change. Followers of the Wisconsin senator were not surprised, therefore, when overeducated "egg-heads" and social snobs rejected the common sense of the American people and proceeded to "sell out" the country to the Communists. Images of elite betrayal and treason provided populist-oriented nationalists and dissidents a chance to strike at the very groups they had distrusted since the Great Depression.[22]

As one scholar of McCarthyism has suggested, "the image of the enemy was *not* the Russian spy, but . . . the American intellectual with an Ivy League accent." Edward Shils, a pluralist social scientist, explored this issue with clarity. Hostility to secrecy in Washington, argued Shils, stemmed from popular distrust of aristocrats, whose snobbery, aloofness, and self-restraint appeared to be replicated in government scientists, intellectuals, and professionals. Shils portrayed ordinary Americans' animosity toward "the more sophisticated person who . . . stands apart and does not share what is on his mind . . . , who thinks he is better than they are, and secretly might be thinking of subverting them." In a nation in which loyalty involved a conscious affirmation of ideals, the remoteness of thoughts, moral sentiments, and allegiances could be interpreted in a conspiratorial framework. This may explain why McCarthy and his supporters placed more emphasis on attitudes and associations than on overt actions.[23]

The anticommunist crusade also responded to social strains in postwar America. As Jerome Himmelstein has noted, the McCarthy movement maintained ties to conservative intellectuals, elements of the business community, and established political channels. Yet its attacks on the amorality of the "eastern liberal establishment" expressed a profound antielitist "rebelliousness." Despite the crusade's diverse sources of support, McCarthy followers seemed to share a resentment of professionals and managers who manipulated symbols and harnessed their intellect to institutional power. Members of Congress especially distrusted officials of the executive branch who appeared to seek management roles free from the populist influence of politicians. "Congress must realize," a frustrated correspondent advised Senator Bricker in 1952, "that this atheistic communism is not a working class movement . . . and never has been. It is a movement of frustrated intellectuals who are out to seize power."[24]

Although Michael Rogin has shown that the McCarthy movement did not embrace the class demands and statist solutions of earlier forms of agrarian agitation, it did mount a radical critique of the American establishment. The Wisconsin senator succeeded in drawing insidious connections between the postwar U.S. power structure and the Communists. McCarthy and the nationalists accomplished this by portraying social engineering, rational management, and expert rule as elite devices of both liberal and Marxist operatives. Anticommunists positioned themselves as populist insurgents who confronted the privileges of faceless bureaucracy by insisting on direct communication, individual responsibility, and the moral consequence of choices.[25]

Sentiments of this kind surfaced when supporters mourned McCarthy's early death in 1957. Representative Wint Smith from Kansas contrasted the cantankerous solon with "a world which has lost its understanding of the concepts of right and wrong, truth and error, good and evil, and seeks only to adjust itself to what is expedient." The *National Review*'s William Schlamm castigated the intelligentsia for minimizing the urgency of the war against communism. Modern society's loss of values, concluded Schlamm, was driven by the delusion that "man is intellectually an eternal child and morally a vegetable."[26]

✦ ✦ ✦

The labor historian Steve Fraser has observed that U.S. anticommunism was a "profoundly anticapitalist" movement that "rebelled against the corporate, bureaucratic, centralizing, and statist tendencies of the modern industrial order." Joe McCarthy's supporters illustrated such qualities by lashing out at the "knowledge elites" who had come to define public policy since the New Deal. Tied to centralized rule, collectivist ideas, and cosmopolitan social values, members of the "new class" attracted a populist ire formerly confined to business and banking targets. As diverse "out" groups faced the erosion of their own interests and morality in the years after World War II, academic intellectuals, professionals, planning activists, and government officials faced an indigenous uprising closely tied to the anticommunist crusade. The antielitist and antirationalist tone of such dissidence separated it from a bipartisan political establishment primarily concerned with stability and the orderly conciliation of differences.[27]

Anxiety over the influence of centralized finance remained one of the most persistent themes of American political culture. When congressional inquiries into communism produced a growing interest in tax-exempt foundations in the 1950s, however, concerns about corporate power merged with fears about collectivism and the reliability of academic elites. Spurred by Alger Hiss's former service as president of the Carnegie Endowment for International Peace, Pat McCarran's Senate Subcommittee on Internal Security conducted hearings in 1951 and 1952 that exposed the endowment's support for Owen Lattimore, the State Department consultant who had been accused of Communist inclinations. The investigation also revealed that the Rockefeller Foundation had subsidized the suspect Institute of Pacific Relations (IPR) for twenty-five years. In 1952 the House chose Judge Eugene E. Cox, a Georgia Democrat, as chair of the newly created Select Committee to Investigate Tax-Exempt Foundations. After brief hearings, the panel's report concluded that some Communists and sympathizers had obtained influential positions in the foundations, while such "subversive" individuals and groups as the IPR had benefited from foundation funding.[28]

Because the Cox investigation had failed to establish that foundations systematically followed the "Communist line," such militant nationalists as the New York exporter and Asia-firster Alfred Kohlberg insisted that the inquiry had "proven a dud." The veteran investigator John Flynn, who admitted that corporate foundations were "an old preoccupation of mine," was more optimistic, however. Flynn acknowledged that "the socialist revolution now under way . . . has been financed almost entirely by American big business," but he warned that the public was reluctant to believe that such "eminent" monied interests as the Rockefellers, Carnegies, and Fords "were actually supporting Red propaganda." Flynn argued that it was essential to understand that Communists did not use foundation money to advance specific declarations. Their program, he indicated to Brazilla Carroll Reece, the Tennessee Republican who was on the Cox panel, limited itself to general goals, such as discrediting capitalism and promoting planned economies.[29]

A former economics professor, member of Roosevelt's Temporary National Economic Committee, and southern campaign manager for Robert Taft, Reece took the House floor in April 1953 to criticize the Cox inquiry and call for a new select panel. Three months later he outlined "a diabolical conspiracy" to use the largest fortunes of U.S. capitalism to finance communism and socialism. The Republican House agreed to back the investigation in a close 209-162 vote that blurred party lines (sixty-nine Democrats in favor, forty-nine Republicans opposed). Brief hearings took place between May and July 1954, followed by a staff report by Norman Dodd, the panel's director of research. Foundations, education, and the government formed "a triangle of influences," asserted Dodd, and were responsible for an "evolving collectivism." The committee soon responded to Democratic complaints of bias by abandoning oral testimony. Nevertheless, a year-end final report insisted that elite foundations and academic agents threatened traditional American values and practices.[30]

Dodd's summary noted that seven thousand tax-exempt organizations accounted for $7.5 billion in assets but that a mere handful controlled a third of that amount. The report focused on "The Interlock," an "intellectual cartel" of major foundations and intermediary research organizations held together by intertwining directorates and joint projects. Reece panel investigators outlined a concert of interests among professors, politicians, and lawyers by describing the manner in which foundation-supported agencies helped select the federal government's academic consultants. The report noted that Washington invested an annual $150 million to $250 million in social scientists, making the government their leading employer. The heart of Dodd's document, however, lay in the contention that foundations were socializing the American people into a collectivist way of life.[31]

The Reece committee argued that foundation revenues once used for charity now were employed to influence or change American political thought and values. The result, it insisted, was corporate financing of socialism and social revolution, practices and ideas pictured as "incompatible with fundamental concepts in the Constitution." Foundation critics charged that grant money seldom went to studies critical of socialism. Instead, as the committee counsel René Wormser asserted, funding validated the efforts of those "fog-bound intellectuals" who embraced collectivist "fashions of thought." The panel's final report accused the granting agencies of supporting only those studies that endorsed the erosion of economic individualism and repudiated laissez-faire government. Too many stipends went to those promoting planning, control, and social engineering, it protested.[32]

By portraying foundation scholarship as conducive to the ideological needs of the nation's elite institutions, the Reece inquiry made a radical charge. One staff report cited a Carnegie-funded assessment of social studies that celebrated "a notable waning of the once widespread popular faith in economic individualism" and indicated that leaders and the public demanded "ever wider measures of planning and control" in "a new age of collectivism." An "age of transition" would lead to a "consciously integrated society" in which individual economic actions and property rights would be "altered and abridged." To prepare for the "new social order," the Carnegie study recommended that such academic disciplines as history and sociology be consolidated into social studies. The Reece staff also cited an educational report calling for teachers to impart respect for the social engineering needed "to solve the problems of human relations" and to secure acceptance of the internationalist concept of "one world" as part of "a new way of thinking."[33]

The "moral relativism" of foundation programs provided another lucrative target for the Reece inquiry, which accused social scientists of unsettling traditional social values and public rituals. Reece personally singled out the Ford Foundation's $15 million Fund for the Republic for sponsoring studies of censorship and blacklisting as well as workshops on racial tolerance. The panel also questioned foundation preference for empirical research over more "qualitative" theoretical experiments. Empiricism, testified the sociologist Albert H. Hobbs, ignored "moral precepts, principles, and established or accepted norms of behavior" and sought to base conclusions solely on sensory data. Hobbs pointed to Alfred C. Kinsey's 1948 and 1953 reports on human sexuality, initially supported by Rockefeller grants. Kinsey treated sexual norms as "rationalizations," he observed, while portraying "deviant" sexuality as "normal." The result was "a persistent questioning" of traditional codes and laws relating to sexual behavior, including homosexuality.[34]

Penn State's Hobbs and other social science critics contended that the foundations supported research sanctioning collectivism at the expense of moral notions of free will and self-autonomy. Analyzing Stuart Chase's *Proper Study of Mankind* (1948), written with Carnegie financial support, Hobbs objected to the implication "that man is essentially a puppet of the culture" and not responsible for his or her actions. Wormser, the committee's counsel, complained that impractical and idealistic intellectuals were remote from economic realities. But he also scored the granting institutions for supporting change for its own sake, referring to "a pathological" rejection of the judgment of the great majority of Americans. Wormser charged that the foundations and social scientists were "subversive" and "un-American" because they sought to destroy the nation's institutions and way of life before its people had agreed on a substitute.[35]

The Reece report declared that Americans should be "made aware of the impact of foundation influence on our accepted way of life." It also asserted that the Internal Revenue Service lacked the ability to oversee tax-exempt agencies engaging in "political" activity. The committee's solution was legislation that denied tax exemption to any charity holding more than 5 to 10 percent of its capital in the securities of a single enterprise and that required government representatives on foundation boards. Amid charges that the investigation of tax-exempt organizations had sought to impose thought control, however, the Reece proposals died in committee.[36]

✤ ✤ ✤

Attempts by independent competitors to check large corporations and banks did not prove any more successful than the effort to rein in the tax-exempt foundations had. By 1960 only 16 percent of the U.S. labor force was self-employed, while 38 percent worked for companies with at least five hundred employees. Congress created a Small Business Administration (SBA) to replace the Reconstruction Finance Corporation in 1953, but the new agency functioned with a strictly regulated and reduced loan program for independent enterprisers. In its first three years of existence, the SBA managed to process barely more than a thousand loans from 300,000 applications. Congress sought to remedy the logjam by converting the agency into a permanent agency with a $250 million revolving loan fund in 1958.[37]

Independent retailers' concerns over competition induced the House Small Business Committee to issue a 1952 report on price-cutting. In the *Schwegmann* decision of the previous year, the Supreme Court had ruled that antitrust provisions prevented states from using the Miller-Tydings Act to require interstate mail-order houses to abide by "fair trade" price agreements they had not signed. John A. McGuire, a Connecticut Democrat, now proposed federal legislation to strengthen the hands of the forty-five states with "fair trade" requirements. A coalition of farm, labor, consumer, and corporate interests opposed the elimination of retail price competition and demanded "free trade" instead of "price-fixing." In response, such independent business and retail lobbyists as Ed Wimmer, vice president of the National Federation of Independent Business, insisted on the need to relate prices to "competitive value." Wimmer sought to fight "gangsterism in the market place" and protect retailers from "predatory competition" by demanding the elimination of loss leaders.[38]

Independents argued that retail price protection was no different from federal rate control of transportation or labor. Although he did "not believe in government control of business," one merchant explained to North Dakota's Usher Burdick in 1953, rules were essential to "give everyone a fair chance in the game." A food distributor pleaded with Burdick to ensure the Jacksonian ideal of "EQUALITY TO ALL AND PRIVILEGES TO NONE." Small business advocates, such as Burdick, Senator Estes Kefauver from Tennessee, and Wright Patman from Texas, often invoked such populist expressions as the "equality of opportunity to compete" to defend trade policy. "Either the dry rot of monopoly will set in," Patman warned a 1954 food brokers convention, "or there will be a divided nation of big and monopolistically-inclined business on one side opposed by small independent business on the other." Sensitivity to free enterprise and respect for the clout of retail trade groups contributed to the overwhelming passage of the 1952 Fair Trade Act by margins of 196 to 10 in the House and 64 to 16 in the Senate.[39]

Despite such success, Wright Patman and his allies had far more difficulty strengthening the Robinson-Patman Act's strictures against price discrimination. The Supreme Court had ruled in *Standard Oil v. FTC* (1951) that quantity purchasers could mount a "good faith" defense of special price arrangements with manufacturers. First filed in 1955, Patman's bill sought to make the "good faith" defense inapplicable if price discrimination lessened competition or tended to monopoly. While his proposal languished in committee, the East Texan mounted a successful campaign in 1956 to gather the necessary 218 signatures for a discharge petition. At the same time, the Judiciary Committee reported out a similar measure, which the House passed 394 to 3. When Estes Kefauver brought a comparable offering to the Senate floor, however, the proposal became entangled with a bill on corporate mergers and died with adjournment. Two years later a more modest attempt to curb price discrimination in food, drugs, and cosmetics failed to elicit a vote in either house.[40]

Antimonopoly activists faced an uphill struggle in an Eisenhower administration friendly to corporate allies. Antitrusters had gained a victory when, in the *Paramount* decision of 1949, federal courts ended ownership of motion picture theaters by the five largest studios and outlawed industrywide block booking, blind selling, and discriminatory pricing. Nevertheless, a monopoly subcommittee of the Senate Small Business Committee felt compelled to hold full hearings on the continuing problems of independent exhibitors during 1953 and 1956. The Eisenhower team backed away from antitrust enforcement, preferring to negotiate with potential defendants through prefiling conferences, premerger clearances, and consent decrees. Cooperation with corporate interests led the National Federation of Independent Business to demand the removal of Federal Trade Commission (FTC) chair Edward F. Lowrey, whom it accused of being the attorney of record for several antitrust cases pending with the agency.[41]

Critical of the administration's cooperation with large corporations, William Langer, the North Dakota Republican, organized a Senate investigation of economic concentration in the electric power industry in 1953. Langer had been calling for a congressional inquiry into corporate mergers since 1947. Using his newly attained chairmanship of the Senate Judiciary Committee, he established the Subcommittee on Antitrust and Monopoly, appointed himself chair, and pledged to supplement its meager appropriations with his own earnings. At issue, the North Dakotan explained to a critic, was "a fight between monopoly and private business." The resulting *Monopoly in the Power Industry,* released in 1955, castigated the Eisenhower administration for subverting federal power policy and colluding with private interests in the construction of the Dixon-Yates electrical plant in Arkansas. It also pointed to the continued use of Wall Street utility holding companies and other monopoly devices. "Competition as a way of life" was "under constant attack," concluded the report.[42]

The Eisenhower administration elicited further controversy when Attorney General Brownell appointed a national committee to study the antitrust laws. The panel's 1955 report recommended use of the "rule of reason" and evaluation of "intent" before trade conspiracy prosecutions and called for repeal of "fair trade" laws. It also proposed eliminating the Robinson-Patman Act's "quantity discount rule," a measure that required the FTC to limit pricing concessions for bulk distributors. The attorney general's report, predicted the Bureau of Education on Fair Trade, "would promote monopoly at the expense of small business." It was "an insult to the intelligence of those who believe in a truly competitive economy," concurred the National Farmers Union. Wright Patman charged that the antitrust committee constituted a "lobby" for large corporate interests. Its conclusions were "contaminated," he testified before the House Judiciary Subcommittee on Monopoly and Antitrust, because half its members were attorneys who represented clients in pending antitrust suits.[43]

Three congressional committees held hearings on the disputed attorney general's report in 1955. The House judiciary subcommittee announced that three thousand businesses had disappeared in the "swelling merger tide" of the previous four years. Meanwhile, the panel's parent committee proposed legislation compelling federal agencies to disallow bank mergers that endangered competition. Similar versions of the measure won passage by voice votes in both houses the following year but could not be reconciled before adjournment. Another bill sought to require large corporations to notify the government of proposed mergers and empowered federal agencies to issue injunctions against them. After passage by a voice vote in the House, however, the measure died before the 1956 Senate adjourned.[44]

Attempts to control bank holding companies fared little better. After support from the Independent Bankers Association in 1954, the Senate passed Homer Capehart and Burnet S. Maybank's bill limiting federal sanction of new federal savings and loan branches. The House replaced the measure with a proposal that curtailed the expansion of all interstate bank holding companies and required them to divest nonbanking assets. Under pressure from the American Banking Association, however, the Senate exempted single-bank institutions and long-term trusts before agreeing to the bill in 1956. Meanwhile, independent bankers sought to limit mergers by demanding the Justice Department's prior approval. Joseph O'Mahoney encountered defeat in 1957 and 1959, however, when he tried to win Senate approval for an amendment establishing antitrust requirements for bank consolidations. Small business advocates were forced to settle for the Bank Merger Act of 1960, which compelled regulators to estimate the effects of mergers on competition before delivering written approval.[45]

While independent bankers complained of collusion between federal bureaucrats and powerful financial interests, the populist Estes Kefauver sought to keep the monopoly issue alive in the Senate. As chair of the Senate Judiciary Subcommittee on Antitrust and Monopoly between 1957 and 1963, Kefauver singlehandedly led exposés of administered prices in the drug, bread, automobile, steel, and other industries. Frequently inducing dramatic testimony under persistent cross-examination, the senator succeeded in demonstrating that dominant producers deliberately maintained prices without regard for market forces or inflationary consequences. Despite harsh attack from administration allies and corporate targets who sought to reduce his subcommittee funding, Kefauver continually admonished that the antitrust laws were "the best friend a business man has." Predictably, the senator's only legislative triumph came with the Kefauver-Harris Drug Act of 1962, a measure that dealt with pharmaceutical safety, not the freedom of enterprise he sought.[46]

✦ ✦ ✦

While opponents of collectivism battled amoral government bureaucrats, tax-exempt foundations, and economic monopolies in the 1950s, their greatest challenge proved to be federal involvement in civil rights. During World War II northern New Dealers and labor reformers joined black activists in focusing on racial justice, an apparent shift from earlier concerns with economic populism. In 1946 President Truman established the Civil Rights Commission. The commission's report the following year proposed that the government's wartime Fair Employment Practices Commission be made permanent and that Washington act to ensure racial desegregation and equal voting rights. Truman failed to implement this program but did desegregate the armed forces and place civil rights on the Democratic party's 1948 political agenda. Two years later the Supreme Court began to mandate racial integration in certain university graduate programs. In 1954 the *Brown* decision signaled the end of racially separated public education. The next year the Court ordered the integration of relevant schools with "all deliberate speed."[47]

Federal action on race relations collided with traditional notions of local control and states' rights. The controversy had surrounded congressional antilynching bills in the 1920s and 1930s and the Supreme Court's outlawing of the white primary in 1944. As a wartime alliance between southern Democrats and anti–New Deal Republicans emerged, civil rights opponents managed to mandate state control of absentee ballots in a voting bill. Fearing that policies from Washington might undermine the region's racial segregation and exclusion of blacks from the franchise, southern politicians adamantly opposed efforts to create a permanent Fair Employment Practices Commission, going so far as to picture the proposal as a disguised form of communism. By the 1950s the South perceived its troubles as emanating from outside the region and appeared to be moving toward the use of force to defend its customary way of life.[48]

Although racial prejudice framed much of the response to the struggle for civil rights, the conflict touched raw nerves for those suspicious of institutional concentrations of power. As early as 1946 John Flynn warned Francis J. Spellman, the archbishop of New York, that the intentions of those opposing discrimination were overshadowed by the movement's origins "in the minds of revolutionary and irreligious elements." President Truman's endorsement of civil rights, Flynn advised Senator Walter George of Georgia in 1949, was part of an effort to use the vote of southern blacks to convert the Democratic party into a socialist-labor movement. Flynn counseled Styles Bridges, a New Hampshire Republican, that Senate filibusters might be the "last weapon" to resist the socialist revolution imposed by a minority in the media and government. Distraught at the capture of the two parties by "One-Worlders and the New Dealers," Flynn worried in 1954 that his forces had "most certainly taken a thorough licking." Those in the North and South who still believed in private enterprise and a limited state, he concluded in 1956, needed a new party.[49]

John Flynn's calls for party restructuring were shared by such Republicans as Senator Karl Mundt and Robert Wood. Fearing the passions aroused by civil rights and its political consequences, President Eisenhower moved cautiously. Yet when mobs sought to prevent implementation of a federal court's school integration order in Little Rock, Arkansas, in 1957, the president deployed troops to defend civil order. Gallup polls showed that nearly two-thirds of Americans approved of Eisenhower's action to counter the violence. Nevertheless, 53 percent of the southern sample opposed the president's deployment, and more than two-thirds objected in principle to forced school integration. Northern antistatists like Flynn and Mundt joined white southerners in portraying government-sponsored integration as a "judicial usurpation" of the people's will. Critics from both regions charged that a remote and arbitrary central government had assumed unwarranted power over local control of public education, thereby violating basic principles of states' rights and home rule.[50]

Integration opponents believed that a "packed" Supreme Court had substituted the rational code of legal fiat for organic and timeworn standards of human relations. Enforced race-mixing was but a first step toward compulsory equality of association, a violation of the traditional principles that social status should be earned and that personal interaction should be voluntary. Intervention by a centralized, administrative state, critics asserted, obligated the government to employ force and compulsion in areas of personal and social relations. Such an invasion of private rights, they contended, amounted to bureaucratic and judicial tyranny over free society and was similar to communist absolutism. Reasoning of this sort led a Waco, Texas, physician to label Chief Justice Earl Warren a "sociocommunist," while Senator James O. Eastland from Mississippi referred to the Court as a "Revolutionary Tribunal." Federal administrative powers, Representative John V. Dowdy from East Texas warned in 1959, were necessary before communism or dictatorship could take control of the people.[51]

Opponents tied the civil rights issue to communism because they believed that intellectuals were using government coercion to erase human distinctions. In racial terms such anxiety addressed potential miscegenation and the emergence of one race. Integration, an East Texas lumber official opined in 1957, "means to make one of more than one . . . to mix-up and blend into one thing two or more separate things." In a broader

sense such fears reflected the belief that ethnic, national, and racial differences preserved the distinctive features of human personality and culture.
"Isn't the *basic* drive in civil rights to make the individual the mass, to make
everyone the same, . . . to make everyone dependent on big government?"
a Californian asked Senator Homer Capehart. References to the Supreme
Court's dictatorial attempts to create a "One World System" also revealed
the aversion to uniformity and collectivism in anti–civil rights protest.
Obliteration of racial distinctions seemed to convey a vision of mass depersonalization to those Americans frightened by the government's power
to mold relations between the races.[52]

Tensions over racial justice escalated when the Eisenhower administration introduced federal legislation in 1956. The bill proposed creating a
civil rights division in the Justice Department. Empowered with full investigatory powers, the attorney general could initiate civil suits to integrate
schools and public accommodations and end voting discrimination. The
measure provided that resulting contempt charges be tried by a federal
judge instead of a potentially biased jury. It also sought creation of a civil
rights commission to develop further legislation. President Eisenhower told
Senate majority leader Lyndon B. Johnson that the package was "the mild-
est civil rights bill possible." Response from the South was severe, however. Eighty-three southern members of Congress quickly signed a manifesto expressing "unqualified opposition to this iniquitous legislation." The
"*real* civil rights of Americans would be invaded," warned the representatives, by these proposals to launch sweeping inquiries based on the allegations of paid investigators.[53]

The Eisenhower bill passed the House in 1956 but died in Senator
James O. Eastland's Judiciary Committee. When the package came before the Senate the next year, Johnson's Texas mail ran an estimated 10
to 1 against it. Many of Johnson's constituents charged the senator with
betrayal and double-talk. A letter to the *Dallas News* complained bitterly of a federal "Gestapo to pry into our everyday lives." Little Rock,
a San Antonio correspondent chastised, "was merely the beginning of a
well organized plot . . . to cram Integration down our throats." A small-
town theater owner and supporter of Franklin Roosevelt accused Johnson
of using clever language reminiscent of "a diplomat in an alien country."
With a sense of despair and powerlessness, one Waco constituent pleaded for the senator to serve "grass roots Americans" by placing "*all your*
zeal behind the America we once knew."[54]

Realizing the importance of racial reform in modernizing the South's
social structure and economy, Lyndon Johnson privately told southern
colleagues that any attempt to kill the rights bill would paralyze both the
region and the Senate. Southern economic growth would be impossible,

he warned, if issues of status and morality remained unresolved and objects of constant challenge. Under Johnson's pressure, the Senate agreed to eliminate legislation on school integration and public accommodations. Federal judges, moreover, could now decide whether to impanel juries for contempt proceedings, and defendants could request juries for second trials. In 1957 these efforts resulted in passage of the first federal civil rights bill in eighty-two years. Three years later Johnson overcame a six-day filibuster by southern senators and pushed through a second rights bill by a 71-18 vote. This measure broadened the earlier law and authorized federal district judges to appoint referees to register qualified blacks where local authorities denied them voting rights.[55]

✦ ✦ ✦

Racial tensions escalated in 1960 when black college students organized sit-ins at segregated southern lunch counters. Following the election of President John F. Kennedy activists engaged in a series of "freedom rides" to propel the integration of interstate buses under federal protection. In 1962 Kennedy federalized the Mississippi National Guard and sent troops and marshals to ensure the integration of the state's leading university. One year later the physical presence of federal authorities forced Governor George C. Wallace to accede to the integration of the University of Alabama. Meanwhile, the Reverend Martin Luther King Jr. led massive demonstrations in Birmingham to force repeal of municipal segregation ordinances and gain minority hiring. These peaceful protests brought the use of fire hoses and dogs by local police, the arrest of nearly a thousand demonstrators, and the killing of four Sunday school students in the bombing of a black church. Such confrontations helped attract 200,000 civil rights protesters to the August 1963 March on Washington.[56]

Seeking orderly progress on civil rights, the Kennedy White House exerted political and economic pressure on southern business interests. Economic diversification, increased ties to the national marketplace, and the growth of African American consumer clout already gave the region's modern business elites a vested interest in social harmony and a fear of violent racial conflict. Faced with Governor Wallace's intransigence, the Kennedy administration used the machinery of the federal government to induce Alabama's corporate community to reason with the state leader. Top administrators in the Pentagon, the regulatory agencies, and the cabinet all were instructed to contact executives from a list of 375 Alabama businesses. Leading Kennedy officials also lobbied state defense contractors and major corporations with Alabama ties, such as U.S. Steel and Royal Crown Cola. Meanwhile, Assistant Attorney General for Civil Rights Burke Marshall prevailed on the president and cabinet members personally to contact Birmingham's "big mules," the seventy powerful business leaders who made up the city's Senior Citizens Committee.[57]

The Kennedy administration pursued desegregation and fair employment by organizing meetings with executives from leading drug store, theater, hotel, and retail chains. Through meetings of his Business Council, the president pressed corporate leaders to sign racial "plans for progress" and to participate in the creation of biracial councils in their communities. By the summer of 1963 Kennedy had placed his prestige behind a civil rights bill to desegregate public accommodations. The issue of racial justice "had become critical," he warned sixty business leaders, "and must be dealt with directly if the situation is to be kept within bounds." Following the Sunday school bombing of September 1963 Kennedy sent two retired military emissaries with strong corporate ties to work with Birmingham civic leaders of both races.[58]

The federal government's mild sponsorship of the civil rights revolution produced major upheavals in American political life. Within weeks of the 1954 *Brown* decision chapters of the White Citizens Council spread throughout Mississippi and Alabama. Members saw the groups as legal and respectable extensions of the town meeting. Using boycotts and pressures against blacks and uncooperative politicians, the loosely connected councils sought to stop or postpone school integration, keep blacks from voting, and demoralize such civil rights groups as the National Association for the Advancement of Colored People (NAACP). Meanwhile, remnants of the Ku Klux Klan, popular among lower-middle-class residents of the Alabama piedmont and the Southeast, went beyond the legal parameters of the citizens councils to resort periodically to shootings, beatings, bombings, and arson to protest prospective school integration.[59]

By 1961 twenty-five major national organizations had amassed over 300,000 followers devoted to uncompromising denunciations of New Deal statism, civil rights reform, and the continuing Communist threat. Portraying collectivism as the nation's prime enemy, protest groups such as the Manion Forum and the Christian Anti-Communism Crusade objected to the United Nations, federal aid to education, compulsory fluoridation of municipal drinking water, and nuclear disarmament. Many of the movement's southern, midwestern, and western followers drew their passion from strains of middle-class fundamentalism deeply suspicious of secular pluralism and Protestant reformism. They often shared the populist belief that the American dream had been betrayed by hidden conspiracies and that only the aroused masses of the nation could redeem it.[60]

Claiming fifty thousand members by 1964, the John Birch Society (JBS) became the most significant of the radical organizations. The JBS was founded in 1958 as a network of study clubs centered on the writings of its founder, Robert Welch, a New England candy manufacturer. Welch's works included "The Politician," an essay that he had privately distributed after 1954. This polemic portrayed socialism as "tyrannical altruism," an economic system imposed from the top. It described politicians as deceivers, intellectuals as traitors, and internationalists as betrayers of American interests. Because Dwight Eisenhower had sustained the globalist traditions of Franklin Roosevelt and George Marshall, argued Welch, he had become an agent of the Communist conspiracy. Further proof lay in the Eisenhower White House's alleged destruction of Joe McCarthy.[61]

The JBS built on accusations by 1950s anticommunists and nationalists that the American establishment cooperated with Communists in a global conspiracy to collectivize human life. Welch called for the United States to sever ties with the United Nations and NATO and to eliminate foreign aid and reciprocal trade agreements. At home he preached that secret organizations, pressure campaigns, and front groups were needed to combat the influence of Communists in government, public schools, mainstream churches, the media, and other social institutions. Arguing that political compromise was impossible in such a situation, Welch urged followers to purge all forms of collectivism from American life. The list extended from the Federal Reserve to the graduated income tax, mental health programs, and social security. "The United States is an insane asylum run by its worst patients," declared Welch in one speech. The civil rights movement, he insisted, was part of a worldwide Communist-controlled revolution ultimately directed at the United States. "Fully expose the 'civil rights' fraud," proclaimed Welch, "and you will break the back of the Communist conspiracy."[62]

Although the Birch Society attracted mainly a suburban and upper-middle-class following, its antiestablishment views placed it in the populist tradition of insurgence. Like the post–New Deal nationalists and anticommunists, Welch's supporters broadened the antielitist focus from finance to diverse centers of remote institutional power. As adherents of conspiracy imagery, they assumed that the truth was normally hidden from view and that things were precisely the opposite of what they appeared to be. This premise was buttressed by Welch's belief that Communists employed a "principle of reversal" to deceive and confuse adversaries by pretending to oppose what they really favored and vice versa. Given such stretches of imagination, the Birch Society's message makes more sense when treated as metaphor. When Welch exposed the insidious "insider's conspiracy," he seemed to be suggesting that the government functioned "as if" the Communists had taken over.[63]

The John Birch Society spoke to the powerlessness of nationalists and anticollectivists in an era in which their message appeared marginalized.

As critics of Truman's management of the cold war and his internal security policy, antiestablishment dissidents had received considerable public validation in the early 1950s. Yet the failures of McCarthyism, the foundations inquiry, antimonopoly agitation, and anti–civil rights activity left them relatively isolated in American political life. It would take a new generation of public figures to tap the insurgent legacy and translate it into majority politics.

13

The Populist Challenge to the
Established Order, 1964–92

"Just because we don't march," a Pueblo, Colorado, woman wrote to
President Lyndon Johnson in 1965, "doesn't mean we have no cause and
are not thinking." Although an overwhelming majority of Americans rejected the full implications of the John Birch Society's message, its assaults
on a bipartisan, liberal, eastern, and secular establishment tapped long-
standing regional and ideological animosities. From the 1960s onward a
variety of national political figures led a succession of antielitist and populist movements that defied conventional political categorization.[1] By the
1990s frustration with government management had become the defining
issue of American politics.

❖ ❖ ❖

Like Estes Kefauver, Wright Patman remained one of the few practitioners
of economic populism by the early 1960s. Although a loyal Democrat,
Patman used his chairmanship of the House Select Committee on Small
Business to reopen the investigation of tax-exempt foundations in 1962.
The Texan asserted that the nonprofit corporations enabled wealthy families and groups to escape taxes and maintain large segments of American
business in their own hands. Through stock ownership, declared Patman,
the foundations had taken control of the nation's industrial and commercial enterprises and had overwhelmed small business. He noted that surveyed institutions contributed only half of their aggregate receipts to charitable purposes. Because corporate dividends were untaxed when received
by tax-exempt bodies, foundations had been permitted to withhold almost
$7 billion from the Treasury Department between 1951 and 1960. Invok-

ing principles of public trust and equal treatment under the law, Patman called for limitations on foundation size, financial activities, and tenure.[2]

Chairman Patman resigned the leadership of the small business panel in 1963 to head its Special Subcommittee to Study Tax-Exempt Organizations. He now used Internal Review Service field audits to demonstrate how foundations functioned as securities dealers, business brokers, bankers, and mortgage traders. Patman claimed that 55 percent of surveyed nonprofit foundations violated Treasury Department regulations. A 1964 report detailed the "cozy tax shelters" provided for such families as the du Ponts. Because of the "indefensible apathy" and "archaic procedures" of the Treasury Department, it concluded, wealthy financial interests had exploited their tax-exempt status for personal gain. Patman's disclosures contributed to reform legislation requiring the compilation of a national foundations' registry. When the subcommittee chair filed his last report in 1969, however, he continued to insist that ordinary Americans were paying tax bills that properly belonged to the nonprofit corporations. Patman proposed that foundations be taxed 20 percent on gross income and be required to disburse net proceeds annually.[3]

The assault on charitable trusts was central to Wright Patman's populist outlook. "I have never abandoned my belief," he explained to constituents in 1965, "that our country belongs to the people, not to large industrial complexes, not to great accumulations of material wealth, and certainly not to the huge financial houses and commercial banks." As chair of the House Banking and Currency Committee between 1963 and 1974, the East Texan translated this creed into crusades against bank mergers, high interest rates, and collusion between federal regulators and bankers. In 1966 Patman pushed through an amendment to the Banking Holding Company Act that repealed exemptions for long-term trusts and registered investment companies, but he failed to stop a reworking of the Bank Merger Act permitting consolidations if "public interest" outweighed effects on competition. Meanwhile, Patman continued to harass the Federal Reserve Board. "It is a matter of gravest concern to me," he declared to a White House aide in 1965, "that the vast monetary machinery of this nation is run by a special private 'government'" apart from elected officials.[4]

Described as "the last of the great populists," Patman insisted that credit was a public resource that should be allocated for the needs of people. When the Federal Reserve Board increased discount rates to 4.5 percent late in 1965, the East Texan accused it of caving into the power of the large Wall Street banks and the "money trust." Accordingly, he introduced legislation to place interest ceilings on all commercial certificates of deposit. In turn, White House advisers predicted chaos in the financial markets if monetary restraint did not counter "excessive and inflationary demands for credit." The result was a substitute amendment to Patman's 1966 bill that asked the Federal Reserve Board to lower interest rates only when economic and market conditions warranted it. Tied personally and politically to President Johnson, the House Banking and Currency chair found himself unable to oppose the administration's financial concerns. By 1968 Patman had agreed to introduce a joint resolution removing interest rate limits on federal housing loans.[5]

While Patman articulated traditional hostility to "the money power," Karl Mundt, the South Dakota Republican, continued to give vent to long-standing nationalist and antistatist sentiments. Describing "the curse of modern government," Mundt bemoaned the departure from private ownership, meritocracy, individual initiative, and states' rights. He also worried about the effects of freeways, airlines, consolidated corporate power, and expensive social services on the survival of the small towns, in which more than half the American people still lived in the 1960s. Mundt assured small business groups that he stood for balanced federal budgets and lower taxes as well as the preservation of "local choice, local decision, and local control." He even cited Burton Wheeler's admonition that liberals had reversed their historical mission by abandoning the people and seeking more power for the executive branch of the federal government.[6]

Traditional resentment of centralized government intensified in the South, Midwest, and West in the 1960s. Responding to increasing Republican strength, thirty-two regional business leaders, lawyers, small-town newspaper publishers, oil entrepreneurs, and bankers held a meeting in 1961 to adopt a common party strategy. The conference produced a movement to draft Senator Barry Goldwater from Arizona as the Republican candidate for president in 1964. An admirer of both Robert La Follette and Robert Taft, Goldwater had been elected to the Senate in 1952. By the end of the decade he had become an open critic of the Eisenhower administration. Publishing *The Conscience of a Conservative* in 1960, Goldwater called for a unilateral foreign policy to defeat global communism, a scaling back of centralized government and the welfare state, and a reassertion of traditional moral and social values. By going outside normal party channels to use direct mail methods of fund-raising and communication, the Goldwater presidential campaign mounted an insurgency against the eastern Republican establishment. It also sought to realign American politics by uniting antistatist constituencies in both the North and South.[7]

White House strategists correctly anticipated that the Goldwater campaign would paint the Democrats as the party of "Big Business, Big Labor, and Big Government" and its own supporters as the "little people" and the "forgotten majority." Like most 1950s nationalists, Senator Goldwater saw internal threats as far more dangerous to the United States than Soviet aggression was. In particular he warned about the "totalitarian philosophy" behind excessive government and a powerful executive. Government should be no more than "an umpire" enforcing rules and contracts at home and abroad, preached Goldwater. Fiscal responsibility, he insisted, needed to run "deeper than the wheeler-dealer mentality of a card sharp." Opposed to "regimented, state-owned or run business and industry," the Arizonan warned that New Deal liberalism had shifted responsibility "from the family to the bureaucracy, from the neighborhood to the distant agency." Federal aid to education, he contended, amounted to unconstitutional intervention in local affairs. Besides, education was a matter of quality and standards, not quantity.[8]

Except in the South, where Goldwater received strong support from lower-middle-class whites, he fared best among those in upper-middle income brackets. These Americans appeared to respond to the candidate's insistence that deteriorating public morality was a major issue in American life. Because government philosophy ignored individual and family responsibility and upheld "the doctrine of the fast buck and the fast answer," declared the candidate, the nation was experiencing rising crime rates, juvenile delinquency, and scandalous grabs for power. "There is a mood of easy morals and uneasy ethics that is an aching truth in our land," Goldwater told a rally at the Illinois State Fair. The "fundamental moral and intellectual bankruptcy of modern-day liberalism," he proclaimed, would energize young people to reject the status quo and join the movement for moral renewal. Such thinking led a Goldwater follower to boast that by defeating the eastern establishment, the campaign was in a position "to save this country's soul" and establish "a whole new moral attitude."[9]

✦ ✦ ✦

Most Americans wanted to maintain basic government programs, such as social security, and continue bipartisan foreign policy. The result was a resounding 61 percent plurality for Lyndon Johnson, who had assumed the presidency following John Kennedy's assassination in 1963. Nevertheless, Goldwater skillfully touched on widespread uneasiness with the expansion of New Deal statism. He also succeeded in opposing government-sponsored racial integration on ideological terms by picturing civil rights legislation as a blatant violation of state prerogatives and a brutal assault on constitutional freedoms and property rights. Such schemes, he claimed, required "the creation of a police state" to enforce social behavior that should be influenced by evolving public attitudes and moral suasion. When

government sought to control equality in areas beyond law and civic order, insisted Goldwater, it produced only conformity. By capturing five
states in the Deep South, Republicans demonstrated that civil rights could
divide the region's New Deal Democrats and populists.[10]

Less than a year after Kennedy's death President Johnson won passage
of the Civil Rights Act. The federal government could now sue to desegregate public accommodations and schools and prohibit denial of equal
job opportunities in most businesses and unions. Yet racial tension persisted
with the murder of civil rights workers in Mississippi and Alabama and
the brutalization of protest marchers by state police. Invoking the words
of "We Shall Overcome," the anthem of the civil rights movement, Johnson
convened both houses of Congress in March 1965 to demand federal legislation to ensure equal access to the ballot box. The Voting Rights Act,
which provided government registrars in districts that prevented black
balloting, became law that summer.[11]

Like the Kennedy administration, the Johnson White House deployed
community relations agents to convince southern business and civic leaders to work for compliance with civil rights legislation. Federal representatives warned of the possibility of violence if ordinary whites were pro-
voked and the loss of local elites' reputations if resistance spiraled out of
control. Government emissaries also pointed out that Title 6 of the Civil
Rights Act prohibited the exclusion of racial and ethnic minorities from
all programs receiving federal financial aid. In response, the Mississippi
Economic Council issued a statement of principles in 1965 that called for
obedience to civil rights laws. After President Johnson met privately with
the officers of the Associated Industries of Alabama, U.S. Steel's Roger
Blough coordinated the publication of a similar manifesto. Meanwhile,
Blough and other industrial leaders lunched with the secretary of commerce
and Martin Luther King.[12]

As Washington used the corporate community to encourage racial ac-
commodation, Governor George Wallace of Alabama continued to orches-
trate resistance, going so far as to create his own state Democratic party.
Most white southerners bitterly resented what a Montgomery journalist
described as "the forcible disruption of their traditions by an all-power-
ful government." These Americans saw civil rights activists as rude outsiders seeking to impose social revolution on their communities. Sensing
that the levers of change originated at remote centers of power, racial traditionalists blamed radical intellectuals and government bureaucrats for
their powerlessness. Although 83 percent of a 1963 poll of southerners
believed that racial integration was inevitable, many whites worried that
Washington was "giving over to mass mob threats." An official of an Alabama grocers' association warned that government encouragement of civil

rights advocates would "only bring a harvest of ill will and maladjust-
ment." "If we try to solve all our problems in the streets," cautioned a
North Carolina woman in 1965, "we shall become a nation in riot."[13]

Troubled whites believed that civil rights programs extended special
privileges to blacks at their expense. The Civil Rights Act was "harsh legislation involving the morals, customs, and habits of our people," twenty-four signatories from an Alabama town protested to President Johnson
in 1964. "No one," proclaimed a petition from the residents of a Gulf
bayou community, "should be given any privileges without first earning
them." "No industry is being forced in placing my sons in jobs they would
like to have," a Sinton, Texas, woman complained to the White House.
The writer contended that federal laws "protect Negroes and permit them
to do acts our sons would be jailed for." A petition signed by 5,600 Alabama members of a paperworkers union local named after Franklin
Roosevelt protested that the civil rights bill would "take away our Constitutional Rights." As presidential aide George Reedy counseled Johnson,
many southern whites saw the equal opportunity features of civil rights
legislation as a means for blacks to inflict themselves on unwilling parties
and to take jobs away from those without political clout or influence.[14]

Aware of such sentiment, a Florida Chamber of Commerce official
warned the White House that efforts to solve the racial problem needed
to begin at the grass-roots and "should under no circumstances be handed down by dictatorial directive." Yet Democratic presidents of the 1960s
failed to envision alternatives to centralized management and reliance on
elite institutions. Assuming a concert of interests among ordinary Americans as well as a deference to the judgment of experts and leaders, policymakers expected that orderly change would benefit all parties in an expanding economy. Federal officials neglected to ask whether deep-seated
traditions could be easily replaced by legislation, regulatory bureaucracy,
and elite pressure. As George Reedy noted, there was little consensus over
racial justice for those who sensed a loss of control over their own lives
and communities. For such people the civil rights revolution threatened a
disruption of competitive standards and remained a symbol of their own
powerlessness.[15]

Corporate sponsorship of civil rights was by no means confined to the
South. In such northern cities as New York and Cleveland, the Ford Foundation subsidized voter registration and antipoverty research and action
groups. Fifty corporations financed a black power conference in Newark,
New Jersey, in 1967. Meanwhile, the Rockefeller, Carnegie, and Ford foundations contributed to the creation of the Urban Coalition, a consortium
of civil rights leaders and big-city mayors led by John Gardner, the former
president of the Carnegie Endowment. In the public sector the Economic

Opportunity Act of 1964 sought to fight a "war on poverty" by creating the Job Corps, Volunteers In Service to America (VISTA), and its own massive bureaucracy, all part of an effort to provide jobs, work training, education, health, and legal services for the poor. Within the first four years of its existence, however, the antipoverty program faced 140 congressional amendments and motions seeking to reduce funding and ensure that local politicians and agencies would control community action projects.[16]

As Mona Harrington has suggested, many Americans saw the Great Society as the product of the centralized authority of professional experts whose training and knowledge surpassed the abilities of ordinary citizens. Mid-1960s corporate and government subsidies also coincided with the outbreak of massive black rioting in northern cities. As a result, populist critics, such as Georgia's Lester Maddox, sharply attacked civil rights and antipoverty programs. A former leader of the White Citizens Council, Maddox telegrammed President Johnson in 1966 to assert that "your program of playing one group of American people against other Americans has brought more discord, violence, death, and property destruction than ever known to our nation." Elected governor, the Georgia restaurateur lambasted the White House for spending millions of federal dollars "to encourage, train, and finance the bums, criminals, and misfits who have brought near chaos to our country as they burn, kill, and wreck much of America." Maddox also complained that the War on Poverty spent millions on administration instead of aid to the poor.[17]

✦ ✦ ✦

Alabama's George Wallace mounted the most serious assault on the Great Society's race and poverty programs. Born to struggling farmers in the state's impoverished southeast corner, Wallace won two Golden Gloves championships. He made his way through the University of Alabama law school in the late 1930s as a legislative page, magazine seller, rabies inspector, boardinghouse waiter, and job recipient under the National Youth Administration. After serving as a flight engineer in the Pacific, Wallace returned to Alabama to practice law. His political career began when he won election to the state legislature in 1946 under the sponsorship of the populist "Big Jim" Folsom. Wallace supported the States Rights party of the "Dixiecrat" Strom Thurmond in 1948. Four years later voters selected him as a circuit court judge. After failing in a gubernatorial attempt in 1958, Wallace refused to obey a federal court order to turn over voting records to the new Civil Rights Commission. His acquittal on contempt charges and a pledge to "stand up for Alabama" facilitated a successful run for governor four years later.[18]

Adamantly opposed to interference by the central government and judiciary, Wallace refused to comply with a federal court injunction against interfering with the enrollment of black students at the University of Alabama in 1963. He denounced the Civil Rights Act as a mask for "uncontrolled federal executive power" and warned that government agencies would establish ethnic quotas for labor unions and businesses. Such violation of states' rights and local control, he warned, could only produce a tyranny fit for "a slave people." As Wallace began to broaden his message, he entered the 1964 Democratic presidential primaries. In North Carolina he received 100,000 qualifying signatures in less than two weeks. More significantly, the Alabama governor engineered strong showings in primaries in Maryland, Wisconsin, and Indiana. Adding to his strength in rural areas and affluent suburbs, Wallace scored heavily among white ethnic and blue-collar Democrats in the big cities. These voters deeply resented black militancy and feared that racial integration would jeopardize their neighborhoods and job seniority.[19]

To Wallace supporters, race was more a matter of black-white relationships than an expression of individual prejudice. The Alabama governor spoke to rivalries between the races in terms of access to power and influence, not mere competition for status. Angry at a federal government that assumed responsibilities once delegated to states and local bodies, Wallace followers believed that Washington had abandoned their interests. "I'm getting sick of hearing people holler 'minority' and get all the breaks in jobs and everything," one admirer confessed to the governor. The protest candidate played on the fear that black Americans appeared to be gaining political power and personal recognition by circumventing the rules of hard work and fair play. Many believed that the federal government had caved into black demands under threats of force. Wallace voters, as the sociologist Jody Carlson has shown, directed their rage of powerlessness toward an intrusive and distant central government that seemed to benefit hostile racial groups at their expense.[20]

Instead of targeting racial minorities, George Wallace argued that liberal lawyers, judges, academicians, media intellectuals, and government bureaucrats had imposed civil rights policy. He warned that this Democratic establishment held an authoritarian and statist agenda that threatened the party's lower middle class. "Let the people in Washington know that we want them to leave our houses, schools, jobs, businesses, and families alone," declared Wallace in 1964. Because civil rights mandates came from the federal bureaucracy and judiciary instead of elected officials, the Alabama governor succeeded in equating liberalism with insulated elitism. He particularly objected to the Department of Health, Education, and Welfare's guidelines for racial integration of schools and hospitals. Wallace complained about "the trend of pseudo-intellectual government," where "a select, elite group have written guidelines in bureaus and court decisions, have spoken from some pulpits, some college campuses, some newspaper offices, looking down their noses at the average man on the street . . . and the little businessman, saying to him that you do not know how to get up in the morning or go to bed at night unless we write you a guideline."[21]

By 1968, when Wallace announced his presidential candidacy on the American Independent ticket with General Curtis E. LeMay as his running mate, the Alabaman had widened the scope of his crusade. The former army sergeant framed his foreign policy views around support for U.S. involvement in the Vietnam War. Responding to the nationalist priority of anticommunist containment in Asia, the Kennedy and Johnson administrations gradually had brought the United States into a major air and land campaign in Indochina. The bloody stalemate drew bitter criticism from the intellectual and professional elites Joseph McCarthy had targeted. The controversial antiwar movement also extended to New Left revolutionaries, radical blacks, college activists, and adherents of "alternative" cultural lifestyles among middle-class youth. Although polls indicated that 71 percent of his supporters saw involvement in the war as a mistake, Wallace denounced antiwar protesters as cowards and traitors and insisted on treating the conflict as a test of patriotic duty.[22]

The Wallace campaign skillfully tied antiwar dissent to rampant disrespect for authority, sexual immorality, the deterioration of the work ethic, and general moral decline. Calling for domestic law and order, the candidate extolled traditional virtues of sacrifice, patriotism, military courage, loyalty, religious worship, and family cohesion, all of which he viewed as protections against the "slave-state philosophy" of "international collectivists." Wallace also addressed middle-class anxieties over rising taxes and inflation, condemning "nonproducers and welfare loafers" as well as the tax shelters and foundations of "the super-rich." He rounded off his appeal to the disenchanted by promising to protect "the little people" against "phony intellectuals and social engineers" in big government.[23]

While George Wallace attracted support from racial extremists and virulent anticommunists, two-thirds of his 1968 following came from northern union workers and southern Goldwater Democrats. Although many urban ethnics stayed with the Democratic party on election day, Wallace garnered nearly ten million votes (13.5 percent of the popular tally) and carried the Deep South. In the North upper-middle-class voters were more attracted to the candidate than were those in the lower middle class. But in the South, where he scored heavily with male residents of small towns and rural districts, Wallace won support from half of the skilled workers, a third of the less skilled, and a third of those in the lower middle strata.

Attracting younger voters across the nation, the Alabaman built a strong protest vote against the bastions of cultural and intellectual cosmopolitanism. His supporters appeared to be executing electoral vengeance against political elites and government itself.[24]

With the highest third-party vote since the La Follette insurgency of 1924, George Wallace fashioned a powerful new populism. Wallace's campaigns of the 1960s touched a widespread mood of defiance that transcended regional and class boundaries. He skillfully portrayed federal involvement in civil rights and welfare as a threat to the work ethic and other traditional values. By focusing on the reformers and "new class" intellectuals who supported these programs, the Alabama governor gave new urgency to long-standing fears of entrenched privilege, remote bureaucracy, and unseen and unaccountable centers of power. Like Huey Long and Joe McCarthy, Wallace offered followers a sympathetic airing of their grievances instead of tangible resolution. Nevertheless, the former boxer changed American politics by legitimizing and empowering former New Deal supporters and other ordinary Americans who felt increasingly alienated from the national power structure.[25]

❖ ❖ ❖

Richard Nixon successfully tapped the Wallace message in his triumphant 1968 presidential run. One of the leaders of the anticommunist purge in the early years of the cold war, Nixon faithfully served as vice president in the Eisenhower administration. Once John Kennedy defeated him for the presidency in 1960, the nation experienced eight years of Democratic rule marred by the Vietnam stalemate, urban race riots, student unrest, and the rise of the counterculture. Nixon pictured the Democratic party as paralyzed by its liberal, activist, culturally permissive, and rights-oriented elements. Expropriating the concerns Goldwater and Wallace initially raised, he set out to woo those unwilling to bear the financial and social costs of the new order. In what Jonathan Rieder has described as a crusade against the liberalism of the "well-born and well-placed," Nixon declared that "working Americans have become forgotten Americans . . . , they have become silent Americans."[26]

By downplaying social responsibility and extolling legitimate self-interest, the Republican candidate spoke to struggling Americans who feared that government spending, inflation, and taxation would eradicate the fruits of their efforts. As Thomas Edsall has noted, Richard Nixon tied these concerns to a new Republican strategy on race by supporting the principle of equality but opposing housing and public school integration imposed by federal courts and bureaucracies. Once in office, Nixon condemned such "liberal" institutions as the Supreme Court, Congress, the tax-exempt foundations, and the media as bastions of elitism that thwarted majority will. Vice President Spiro T. Agnew expanded the assault, referring to the liberal elite as a "haughty clique" that had "brought on a permissiveness that in turn has resulted in a shockingly warped sense of values."[27]

While Richard Nixon and Spiro Agnew sought out white southerners and blue-collar and ethnic Catholics of the Northeast and Midwest, George Wallace entered the 1972 Democratic presidential primaries as a law and order candidate. Wallace charged that a "suffocating bureaucracy in Washington" and the major political parties ignored the "average citizen who works each day for a living and pays the taxes that hold the country together." Sweeping to victories in Florida, Michigan, Tennessee, and Maryland, Wallace nevertheless dropped out of the race when he was paralyzed below the waist by an assassin's bullet. Meanwhile, Nixon and Agnew faced off against Senator George S. McGovern, a South Dakota Democrat who promised a negotiated peace in Vietnam and amnesty for draft evaders, supported abortion rights, and endorsed court-ordered mandates for racial integration. In an overwhelming victory, the Republicans swept to a 61 percent plurality, capturing nearly 80 percent of the Wallace vote and a majority of blue-collar, low-income, and Catholic ballots.[28]

Just as the Vietnam standoff dramatized the weakening of the United States, working-class Americans began to feel the economic effects of international competition, automation, and plant closings. As most new jobs fell within the menial service occupations, differences between low-income and managerial salaries and power levels dramatically widened. Meanwhile, white, middle-class employees desperately sought to hold onto hard-won status in the labor market, civil service, trade unions, and city government. As the working class and lower middle class appeared to converge in an era of downward mobility, rising energy costs and government spending fueled inflation until it reached a dizzying 13.5 percent in 1980. Inflation also pushed middle-class taxpayers into higher rate brackets. By 1973 individuals paid nearly 74 percent of all federal taxes, up from less than half during World War II. Middle-income people now turned over between one-fourth and one-fifth of their earnings in taxes, almost double the rate of the 1950s.[29]

Resentment about taxes corresponded to increasing impatience with the size and direction of government spending. Federal outlays reached $400 billion a year, one-third the gross national product, by the mid-1970s. Between 1965 and 1975 the number of households on welfare tripled, to nearly 3.5 million families; food stamp recipients multiplied four times between 1970 and 1975, to over 17.0 million. The distribution of scarce resources into social welfare and minority assistance meant that working-class and middle-class Americans were subsidizing the underclass and the professionals and bureaucrats serving it. As such critics as Peter Clecak and Thomas Edsall have suggested, taxes were extracted from those who worked and given to those who did not. Not surprisingly, the late 1970s witnessed a taxpayer revolt laced with strong hostility to government bureaucracy. California's Proposition 13, passed in 1978, fixed regressive property taxes at 1 percent of the actual value of the property and rolled back real estate assessments. Meanwhile, the Kemp-Roth proposal asked Congress to legislate a 30 percent federal income tax cut.[30]

Growing concern over government related to the nature of civil rights enforcement. The 1964 civil rights law enabled federal agencies to supervise half the American work force through antidiscrimination provisions and affirmative action plans. Through the 1970s the Justice Department compelled racial hiring and promotion preferences in the building trades and city police and fire departments. Race counting also influenced public school desegregation, integrated housing, college admissions, and the shape of electoral districts. Affirmative action appeared to penalize current white workers for past bias by employers and others. Critics consequently pictured group entitlements as "reverse discrimination" or "anti-egalitarian special preference." Because civil rights advocates believed that racism was too systemic to be addressed by law and open debate, they frequently resorted to administrative directives and court orders. Such methods only enhanced the image of government as elitist, undemocratic, and insensitive to ordinary Americans.[31]

Federal "giveaways" and racial enforcement quotas sometimes appeared to be rewards for socially destructive behavior. Critics asserted that civil rights legislation and welfare spending had failed to prevent the urban race riots of the mid-1960s, rising black crime and drug use, and the deterioration of African American family life. As Jonathan Rieder has reported, many white working-class people of the 1970s came to believe that welfare dependency and illegitimacy stemmed from the economic incentives of government programs as well as a ghetto culture that elevated pleasure over moral restraint. Rieder described a "volatile mix of race, morality, ethnicity, and class" among blacks and whites sharing the inner city. As national crime rates nearly tripled between 1960 and 1980, black street offenses soared. A 1974 government study revealed that 62 percent of robbery victims identified their attackers as black. Anxiety about threats to parental control as well as the safety of neighborhoods and children fed the grass-roots resistance to court-mandated public school busing that spread to such cities as Boston in the 1970s.[32]

Busing became the most divisive issue between working-class and reformist elements of the old New Deal political coalition. In Boston white ethnics saw themselves caught between the administrative expertise of the liberal elite and the perceived threat of the black underclass. Echoing the rhetoric of George Wallace, the antibusing activist Louise Day Hicks portrayed the struggle as a contest between "rich people in the suburbs" and "the workingman and woman, the rent payer, the home owner, the law-abiding, tax-paying, decent-living, hard-working, forgotten American." Neighborhood organizers expressed a deep alienation from an impersonal government they felt powerless to influence. Borrowing the civil rights movement's radical tactics of participatory democracy, they mounted school boycotts, street demonstrations, boisterous marches, and antiestablishment acts of civil disobedience.[33]

Busing, affirmative action, and government welfare all contributed to the impression that an antidemocratic elite customarily defended minority rights against the interests of average working people. As Washington relied on distributive mechanisms to secure advantages for poor blacks and other legally defined minorities, "fairness" appeared to signify favoritism toward special groups. New Deal liberalism once had offered a transcendent sense of justice and support for needy working people. As Thomas Edsall has argued, however, reformers had failed to appreciate that the imposition of true equality required a distribution of resources that placed substantial costs on the working- and lower-middle-class Americans who had constituted an essential part of the New Deal political coalition. Beholden to special interest groups representing feminists, labor unions, and civil rights organizations, Congress found itself allocating old resources instead of generating new ones. Opponents could now portray government activists as a new elite intent on imposing its own racial and social agenda on the nation.[34]

✤ ✤ ✤

By the late 1970s issues of cultural morality began to demand the attention already extended to race, rights, and taxes. For over a decade religious and philosophic traditionalists had opposed a self-indulgent youth culture, whose indiscriminate rebellion and alternative values appeared to defy moral restraints. Critics equated the counterculture with mindless euphoria, indiscriminate sex, drug use, and a rhetoric of violence and radicalism. They charged that an elite of culturally permissive liberals had taken control of education, the media, advertising, and the courts. By legitimating such practices as divorce, single parenting, feminism, homosexuality, pornography, and abortion, cultural leaders supposedly had blurred distinctions between right and wrong. Traditionalists insisted on individual initiative and self-discipline as well as such social virtues as duty, loyalty, deference, family feeling, religiosity, and patriotism. They insisted that humane local and national institutions could be sustained only by the propagation of such values.[35]

Television ministers, such as Pat Robertson and Jerry Falwell, carried the message of spiritual reawakening to large audiences of white evangelical and fundamentalist Christians, particularly in the South and West. Founded in 1979, Falwell's Moral Majority denounced American society as dominated by hedonism, permissiveness, and "secular humanism." The Virginia evangelist maintained that man had replaced God with a "super-state" in which all moral absolutes had disappeared. As evidence, Falwell pointed to America's perceived weakness in the face of global communism and threats to free enterprise at home. He also dramatized the nation's epidemics of drug and alcohol abuse, street crime, and violence. Falwell delivered his most impassioned plea on the secular government's control over life itself. He accomplished this by joining Roman Catholic clergy in denouncing *Roe v. Wade,* the Supreme Court decision of 1973 that prohibited states from banning abortions during the first three months of pregnancy. By 1980 physicians performed over 1.5 million legal abortions a year in the United States.[36]

Although many professional women had moved toward redefining gender roles by 1980, traditionalists looked upon feminism as a form of narcissism that placed individual needs above those of the family and society. Social conservatives, such as Phyllis Schlafly, insisted that family-tied privileges and protections provided the only safeguards for women in a male world. Threats to the venerated family were therefore dangerous to the welfare of both women and civilization. Believing in basic differences between the genders, Schlafly and others described women's role in terms of the nourishment of life. They warned that female control over fertility would upset social relationships between men and women. Antifeminists also held that sex was a procreative and sacred ritual that had to be protected from profanity and exploitation. Defenders of customary gender roles portrayed childbearing and nurture as natural processes inappropriate to planning. As such groups as the National Right to Life pointed to the sacredness of human existence and the rights of the unborn, social morality took on new importance in American politics.[37]

The rise of moral issues enabled opponents of the bureaucratic state to mount new coalitions against adversaries identified as the political and cultural establishment. Squeezed by economic stagnation, foreign competition, high labor costs, increased government social welfare, and expanded federal regulation, large American corporations responded in a hegemonic fashion. As Jerome Himmelstein has indicated, corporate conservatives of the 1970s organized lobbies, created ideological political action committees, commissioned advocacy advertising, and established their own think tanks and foundations. Significantly, attacks on taxation, organized labor, and government regulation appealed to working-class Democrats and Sun Belt evangelicals outraged at the "cultural permissiveness" of the "liberal establishment."[38]

Both urban ethnics and southern and western Protestants had historical animosities toward the established political elite. Seeking to exploit these roots, such conservative Republicans as Richard Viguerie, Howard Phillips, Jesse Helms, and Phyllis Schlafly organized to tap the George Wallace vote as early as 1973. Viguerie used the mails to raise money for Wallace during the next three years. By the end of the decade he had compiled computer data banks of fifteen million financial contributors. By melding a new political coalition of Wallace voters and mainstream Republicans outside the party's Wall Street wing, Viguerie succeeded in combining "insider" resources with the rhetoric of an outside challenger. The "New Right" transcended the elite conservatism of the Republican party by focusing on ideals of community, the producer ethic, and direct democracy.[39]

By incorporating widespread animosity toward high taxes, bureaucratic regulations, and judicial rulings, the New Right's organizers reached for a bipartisan majority frustrated with institutional liberalism's two decades of failure. "We are the radicals who want to change the existing power structure," a 1980 tract declared. "We are not conservative in the sense that conservative means accepting the status quo." As the political analyst William Schneider has observed, "antiestablishment populism" was "neither liberal nor conservative, but antielitist." Fed by the 1970s inflation and the social issues Barry Goldwater and George Wallace first popularized, Republican populists deflected resentment from the affluent to "new class" professionals and cultural leaders. Corporate funding helped to bolster the new movement. Yet as Christopher Lasch and Kevin Phillips have noted, it continued to sustain the distinctions between ordinary producers and privileged parasites first defined by the "radical conservatism" of Andrew Jackson.[40]

New Right coordinators such as Richard Viguerie saw themselves as enemies of wealth and privilege. Like the traditional progressives and nationalists of the 1930s and 1940s, however, they concentrated on the institutional ties between government and business. In *The Establishment vs. the People: Is a New Populist Revolt on the Way?* (1983), Viguerie attacked big business, large banks, the government, unions, and the media for participating in a system of public subsidies and bureaucratic regulation that threatened competition. He pointed out that foreign aid paid interest on international loans extended by private banks. Meanwhile, powerful lending institutions pressured government to bail out such large corporate debtors as Lockheed and Chrysler. "Big corporations are as bad as big government. They're in bed together," declared Paul Weyrich, the founder of the Committee for the Survival of a Free Congress.[41]

Viguerie and Weyrich portrayed collusion between government and business as symptomatic of a departure from American moral values. Viguerie charged that multinational banks and businesses that traded with the Soviet Union and supported the return of the Panama Canal were not concerned about patriotism or national security. He also blamed corporate leaders for the toleration of television sex and violence. Such concerns figured centrally in the New Right's portrait of itself as populist, which Viguerie defined as politics that placed the rights of the average citizen above elite concentrations of power. Viguerie approvingly quoted the observation of Jack Kemp, a Republican House member from New York, that populism expressed an "optimism about people and their willingness to respond to economic incentives as well as their ability to best control their own and their families' destinies. . . . Populism is basically the idea that you can trust people to make right decisions about their lives and about the country."[42]

A Wisconsinite of German Catholic and blue-collar background, Paul Weyrich pictured himself as a populist in the tradition of William Jennings Bryan. Unlike Bryan, Weyrich found liberal compassion condescending and patronizing. Instead, he extolled the virtues of a free enterprise that embodied "the Christian idea of stewardship" and permitted "the development of talents." Weyrich viewed the New Right as an expression of "conservative populism," which he described as "a hybrid amalgamation of generally accepted principles of limited government, free enterprise, strong national defense, and traditional fair values." Insisting that its principles transcended the atomistic philosophies of economic laissez-faire, Weyrich promised that the new politics would free Americans from elite liberalism, special corporate interests, and moral relativism.[43]

✦ ✦ ✦

Economic stagnation interacted with conservative, populist, nationalist, and insurgent values to frame presidential politics. Immobilized by an illegal cover-up of White House abuse of power in the Watergate scandals, Richard Nixon had resigned in 1974. The following year President Gerald Ford accepted the final U.S. withdrawal from Saigon and the reunification of Vietnam under Communist leadership. Addressing the mood of disillusionment, Jimmy Carter, the Democratic governor from Georgia, sought the presidency in 1976 by playing up his outsider role, attacking the federal bureaucracy, and promising to restore trust and openness in government. A member of the prestigious Trilateral Commission of international planners, Carter nevertheless exploited themes of populist anger when he insisted that "the people" ran the government, "not the other way around." On election day he won the popular vote by 2 percent and squeezed through the electoral college by a narrow vote of 291 to 241.[44]

Despite Jimmy Carter's standing as a southern populist and evangelical Christian, external factors mixed with poor political management to weaken his administration. During the late 1970s overseas challenges to the domestic auto and steel industries produced an overall 7.6 percent unemployment rate, which threatened social mobility and home ownership. When the international oil cartel raised energy prices by half in 1979, inflation soared to an annual 14 percent, and the Federal Reserve Board hiked interest rates to 15 percent. Since powerful corporate elements in the Democratic party supported tight money policies, regressive tax relief, and military spending, Carter's response to the impasse was limited. Having failed to protect working-class constituents, the Democratic party appeared to have abandoned its populist base. Meanwhile, the Soviet invasion of Afghanistan and the taking of fifty-three American hostages by the revolutionary Islamic government of Iran certified the president's image as the powerless leader of a declining nation.[45]

Former California governor Ronald Reagan skillfully exploited these vulnerabilities in the 1980 presidential race. Reared in a small Illinois town in the early century, Reagan worked as an Iowa sports announcer and then as a minor star in Hollywood dramas and comedies of the 1940s. As president of the Screen Actors Guild during the early years of the cold war, he began to see communism as a serious threat to personal liberty and government as a danger to the autonomy of individuals and local communities. When his movie career declined after 1950, Reagan hosted a weekly television western and then took on a public relations role for the military contractor General Electric. The former actor used this podium to call for lifting governmental restraints on people and the market. Taking his message into politics, Reagan supported Barry Goldwater with a 1964 television address called "A Time for Choosing." Two years later he won the California governorship by chiding "a few men in Washington" who think they "know better than we do what is good for us" and demanding a return of authority to local government and the common people.[46]

Governor Reagan declared that the nation needed a "spiritual rebirth" to overcome "the wave of hedonism" and "humanist philosophy" associated with 1960s youth and social ferment. As he entered the 1980 presidential contest, the Republican candidate emphasized the small-town values of his childhood. "Work and family are the center of our lives, the foundation of our dignity as a free people," he proclaimed in his nomination acceptance speech. Reagan promised that Republicans would "build a new consensus with all those across the land who share a community of values embodied in these words: family, work, neighborhood, peace, and freedom." As his campaign hit its final stride, the former governor assured a national television audience that "an era of national renewal" would revitalize such traditional precepts as individual autonomy, self-help, hard work, morality, religious observance, and patriotism.[47]

Despite Ronald Reagan's nostalgia for traditional verities, Christopher Lasch and others have pointed to the candidate's profound commitment to economic boosterism and technological progress. Rejecting the sense of limits implicit in the Carter presidency, Reagan personified consumer values of leisurely play and used the self-actualizing philosophies of contemporary psychology to privatize the meaning of freedom. By taking on the liberal establishment and government bureaucracy, the Republican nominee mounted the nation's first successful challenge of New Deal liberalism. Reagan's lyrical campaign advertisements announced that it was "morning in America" and time to "take the government off the backs of the people." Declaring that Great Society entitlements were an "abuse of power," he promised to free Americans from intrusive bureaucracy and slash federal taxes by 30 percent over three years. For Reagan, tax cuts were the most direct possible technique for transferring power from the government to the people.[48]

By portraying government bureaucracy as the establishment, Ronald Reagan united voters of all economic levels who opposed high taxes and federal regulation. The candidate skillfully equated liberal programs with special preferences, subsidies, and protections. Calling for an end to "reverse discrimination," he offered to cushion working people against the racial favoritism associated with cultural and social liberalism. Reagan also supported a constitutional amendment to ban abortions. His campaign supplemented these appeals with the use of computerized direct mail, tracking polls, focus groups, sophisticated marketing techniques, and television exposure. Reagan ultimately took 51 percent of the popular vote to 41 percent for Carter and swept to a stunning 489-89 victory in the electoral college. Significantly, a realignment of white fundamentalists helped bring seven southern states to the Republican column. In contrast more than one-fourth of the Democratic vote came from blacks. Republicans also took control of the Senate for the first time since 1952.[49]

President Reagan used his inaugural to announce that "government by an elite group" was not the solution to America's ills but "the problem" itself. The new president subscribed to a "supply-side economics" that held that government regulations and high taxes constrained production and inflated prices. Reagan argued that tax relief, reduced domestic spending, and deregulation would generate economic recovery. He promised that added revenues resulting from lower unemployment would decrease the federal budget deficit and help pay for an enhanced national defense. As the political journalist Sidney Blumenthal has suggested, the Reagan tax cut resembled free silver as a populist panacea for economic growth. It symbolized a faith in people's ability to generate vital expansion without inflation. Most centrally, Reaganomics promised a "national renewal" in which ordinary citizens would be liberated from bureaucratic tyranny and responsibility for the poor, who now appeared to be an unfortunate representation of government's inability to effect change.[50]

Through the Economic Recovery Act of 1981 Congress enacted a 25 percent cumulative personal income tax reduction, thereby releasing $749 billion into the market over three years. Most of the $35 billion cut from spending came from domestic programs. As a result, Aid to Families with Dependent Children (AFDC) lost 17 percent of its funding and eliminated 400,000 households from benefits. A 14 percent reduction in the food stamp program ended the eligibility of nearly a million families. Between 1980 and 1988 discretionary spending as a share of gross national product declined by more than one-third. Government civil rights agencies also narrowed enforcement to victims of personal discrimination. Although the cutbacks and policies of the "Reagan Revolution" disadvantaged the poor and racial minorities, they addressed the interests and aspirations of former Democrats and others alienated from big government. As unemployment declined from a high of 10.8 percent in 1982 and the longest peacetime economic expansion in U.S. history began to take hold, President Reagan insisted that his vision of America had prevailed.[51]

The Democrats turned to Carter's vice president, Walter F. Mondale, in the 1984 presidential election. Mondale, however, committed a fatal error when he offered to raise taxes without a revenue reform scheme that would redistribute the burden of the sacrifice. In contrast Ronald Reagan proposed to extend his first term's trimming of big government into a "second American Revolution." Accordingly, the Republicans won 59 percent of the popular vote and carried all but Minnesota and the District of Columbia. Exit polls revealed that Reagan had prevailed among four-fifths of the white evangelicals, equivalent to one-fourth of the national electorate. More telling, the Republicans succeeded in convincing young Americans that theirs was the party of economic opportunity and the future. Reagan and Vice President George Bush won a 55 percent plurality among voters between the ages of eighteen and twenty-nine.[52]

❖ ❖ ❖

After restating the call for a "second American Revolution" in the 1985 State of the Union address, President Reagan chose the 220th anniversary of Patrick Henry's "give me liberty" speech to outline a tax reform proposal at historic Williamsburg, Virginia. The chief executive expressed sympathy for the "cult of cheating" among American taxpayers and urged "rebellion" against Washington. "When we who are now there start talking about government as 'we' instead of 'they,'" he told his audience, "we've been there too long." Reagan's plan lowered rates for the most affluent, but it eliminated many deductions, reduced the number of income brackets, and shifted $120 billion of tax responsibility over five years from individuals to corporations. The president insisted that the scheme had been born of "popular resentment against a tax system that is unwise, unwanted, and unfair" and referred to targeted deductions as "special provisions that favor some at the expense of others." Campaigning against "Washington sophisticates" and "special interest lobbyists," Reagan extolled the "revolutionary" aspects of a plan ordinary citizens supported.[53]

Republican strategists sought to attract middle-class support by pitting the Reagan tax scheme against "wealthy and special interests." By doing so, they hoped to erase the party's "country-club image." "This Populism is anti-big government, pro-market, and pro-fairness," explained Secretary of the Treasury James A. Baker III. Many Americans held Reaganomics responsible for the creation of nearly twenty million jobs and low inflation. It was therefore not unreasonable for such supporters as the political analyst Jeffrey Bell to suggest that the former actor and governor was "the most completely populist president since Andrew Jackson."[54] Such judgments reflected far more than Reagan's anecdotal communications style and self-deprecatory humor. The president appeared to be an ordinary American because he embodied the concrete values and desires of the nation's majorities.

Ronald Reagan's identification with the American people often surfaced in foreign affairs, where he frequently moralized about impersonal forces in a manner reminiscent of the old progressives. Ever protective of U.S. interests, he had joined such nationalist Republicans as Jesse Helms in opposing the $1 billion "giveaway" of the 1978 Panama Canal Treaty. As president, Reagan articulated the lingering popular hostility to Communist dictatorships. Speaking to a 1983 convention of evangelical Christians in Orlando, Florida, he described the Soviet Union as "the focus of evil in the modern world" and an "evil empire." As Mona Harrington has suggested, Reagan's controversial Strategic Defense Initiative (SDI) sought to provide "a security shield" that would allow the nation to be free of outside pressures and threats from hostile regimes.[55]

Representing hope, faith, and belief in the fragmented American dream, Reagan won the affection of a generation hungry for a sense of national identity. The president made people feel good about themselves because he reiterated the possibility that the only constraints on human choice were self-imposed. "There is no left or right, only an up or down" between individual freedom and totalitarianism, he had declared in the aptly titled "A Time for Choosing" in 1964. Eighteen years later as president, Reagan offered a veterans' organization another challenge: "Americans must choose between two drastically different points of view. One puts faith in the pipe dreams and margin scribblers in Washington; the other believes in the collective wisdom of the people and their commitment to the American dream. One says tax and tax, spend and spend, and the other says have faith in the common sense of the people." Governments, the president told the 1984 Republican convention, either rule from pessimism, fear, and limits or from hope, confidence, and growth.[56]

Ronald Reagan's empowerment of the American people stemmed from his identification with their aspirations. As Daniel Rodgers has suggested, the president blended himself into both his audience and narrative by deferring to the collective dreams of his listeners. Americans were a nation of "unsung heroes . . . who reinvest those dreams in their children," he remarked in 1982. His administration was "motivated by a political philosophy that sees the greatness of America in you, her people," Reagan explained the next year. He complimented the Conservative Political Action Conference in 1985 for having spoken "for the permanent against the merely prevalent." But Reagan saw himself as the embodiment of a non-ideological national spirit. "Would you laugh," he confided to reporters on election eve in 1980, "if I told you that I think, maybe, the people see themselves and that I'm one of them? I've never been able to detach myself or think that I, somehow, am apart from them." Over eight years later Reagan received the highest public opinion rating ever recorded by a president leaving office.[57]

Republicans prevailed in the 1980 and 1984 presidential elections by taking advantage of the public's willingness to see the party as the agent of prosperity and individual opportunity. White evangelicals and southerners played a major role in these victories. Political scientists, however, failed to see a systemic realignment of the electorate. Party strategists acknowledged that the rewards of the 1980s economic recovery had not been distributed evenly. In fact Reagan Democrats, white working-class and lower-middle-class voters who voted Republican in 1980 and 1984, experienced no significant income improvement in the decade. As Vice President Bush sought to succeed Reagan in 1988, Lee Atwater, his campaign manager and central strategist, perceived that economic issues would not help Republicans among the white populists who held the balance of power in key states in the South. Believing that members of this important constituency were "conservatives on most social issues," Atwater hoped to unite the southern upper class and populists on the basis of traditional values. Such a strategy then could be applied to the national electorate.[58]

Social and demographic factors reinforced Republican strategy. By 1986 white suburbanites constituted 45 percent of the nation's voters, compared with 32 percent from the cities. The division between suburban and urban Americans widened in response to white perceptions of the inner city. Middle-income blacks had expanded from 20 percent of African American households in 1940 to over 55 percent in 1980. Yet an impoverished underclass still accounted for over 30 percent of the black population. Confined to inner-city ghettos, the black poor reinforced the most damaging racial stereotypes. Labor force participation by African American high school dropouts fell one-fourth between 1976 and 1986. By 1988 over 63 percent of black children were born out of wedlock. More blacks than whites were prisoners and AFDC recipients. Over 30 percent of violent crimes and 60 percent of robberies were committed by African Americans. Fifty-four percent of black assault felonies and 60 percent of robberies victimized whites.[59]

Republicans exploited the association between social disorder, race, and "liberal" philosophy. As Thomas Edsall has suggested, a "values barrier" pitted emphasis on commitment and responsibility against the expansion of individual and minority rights. Such "traditional values" as law and order, family discipline, and personal autonomy appeared to be lacking among a black underclass immersed in drug abuse and crime. Many whites came to believe that black disadvantages were the product of individual failures of motivation, willpower, and effort. Adherents of the work ethic also blamed a protectionist public welfare system that rewarded failure and locked the poor into unemployment and dependency. The Great Society was "a continuing, if well-intentioned, failure," James Pinkerton, a Bush planner, declared in an address to the Reason Foundation, because it "falsely assumes that experts, wise bureaucrats in league with university professors and politicians, can somehow administer supply and demand, prosperity and equality from an office building far away."[60]

✦ ✦ ✦

Despite George Bush's background as an eastern Republican from an elite family, Lee Atwater succeeded in bringing the populist cultural values of the 1980s to the presidential race. The task was facilitated when Michael Dukakis, the Democratic candidate, repeated Walter Mondale's rejection of economic populism. Bush attacked Dukakis as a Harvard elitist and a member of the American Civil Liberties Union (ACLU). He pointed out that the Massachusetts governor opposed the death penalty and had vetoed a bill requiring public school students to recite the Pledge of Allegiance. Visiting American flag factories, Bush declared, "I am not a card-carrying member of the ACLU. I am for the people." The president also condemned Dukakis for vetoing a bill prohibiting prison furloughs for first-degree murderers. Campaign commercials dramatized the case of Willie Horton, a black convict from Massachusetts who had disappeared on furlough while serving a life sentence for a killing. Horton had then pistol-whipped a Maryland man and twice raped the victim's fiancee.[61]

Accusing Dukakis of "coddling" dangerous criminals, Bush described his rival as a "know nothing, believe nothing, feel nothing" candidate, an "ice man." By placing himself on the side of popular opinion and castigating elites for being remote from the people, the vice president expropriated an important element of the insurgent tradition. Many Americans viewed the furlough controversy as an example of a rights-oriented government defying traditional standards and common sense. Polling showed that attacks on liberalism, the pledge veto, and the Willie Horton release were most effective among financially pressured whites skeptical of big government and corporate business, aging New Dealers in blue-collar jobs, and older and poor Democrats with strong feelings of patriotism. Identifying with the Reagan legacy and responding to George Bush's promise of no new taxes, these voters helped the Republicans overcome a 17 percent disadvantage. On election day Bush won 54 percent of the popular vote and prevailed by 426 to 112 in the electoral college.[62]

By manipulating cultural symbols and economic promises, the Republicans managed to win the suburban and southern votes essential to success. As Thomas Edsall has shown, the party succeeded in the 1980s because it constructed a nationwide "top-down" coalition. While Ronald Reagan and George Bush rewarded the wealthy and business classes with tax cuts and reduced federal regulation, they appealed for less affluent support by offering tax reductions and lower government spending on social services. Nevertheless, the economic consequences of the Reagan Revolution were far from populist. Edsall has described the 1980s as a period in which tax, spending, and regulatory policies produced "the most accelerated upwards redistribution of income in the nation's history." After-tax earnings of the top 1 percent of American families (under 700,000 households) rose 87 percent in the decade and accounted for three-fifths of the growth of such income between 1977 and 1989. Less than one-eighth of the nation's families controlled 38 percent of personal wealth by 1988.[63]

Reaganomics tax cuts and reduced federal regulation encouraged capital managers to turn to financial speculation and corporate mergers instead of productive investment. While this resulted in inflated executive fees and salaries, it narrowed working-class job opportunities to the menial service sector. These results, especially when combined with increased social security taxes and higher income taxes, were disastrous for ordinary Americans. The bottom two-fifths of American families experienced an actual decline in earnings after 1977. The 1980s after-tax income of the lowest 10 percent of families fell by more than 10 percent. As the national poverty rate jumped from 11.1 to 13.6 percent between 1973 and 1986, one-fifth of American children were counted among the poor. Meanwhile, higher defense spending aggravated the federal budget deficit, which reached over $200 billion by 1985, the same year the United States became a debtor nation for the first time since the outbreak of World War I. By the late 1980s Washington had a $2 trillion national debt and annual trade deficits of over $150 billion.[64]

Changes in the political system impeded response to the structural weaknesses of the national economy. The two major parties of the 1980s found themselves dominated by networks of elites that included interest groups, lobbyists, law firms, fund-raisers, and election specialists. By 1988 Democratic incumbents in the House of Representatives received more money from corporate political action committees (PACs) than did Republicans. Public trust of government suffered as national policy appeared to be dictated by negotiations between Washington's diverse "beltway" interests. Meanwhile, neither party tied the economic interests of the poor to the working and lower middle classes.[65]

As Americans entered the 1990s, the insurgent spirit appeared to be lost amid an array of populist cultural symbols and a negative politics that struck out blindly at remote and unseen enemies. The presidential campaign of 1992 generated an effort by George Bush to paint the Democratic nominee, Bill Clinton, as another liberal elitist. Bush reminded audiences that the Arkansas governor was a former Rhodes scholar who had opposed the Vietnam War and evaded the draft. Clinton fought back by emphasizing his roots as a southern Baptist in a struggling lower-middle-class family and identified with the legacy of John Kennedy. Meanwhile, the Texas billionaire H. Ross Perot mounted a third-party insurgency devoted to term limits and the return of government to the American people.[66]

The son of a cotton broker from Wright Patman's Texarkana, Ross Perot survived the 1930s depression and went on to graduate from Annapolis Naval Academy. After sales work for IBM, Perot founded Electronic Data Services (EDS) in 1962 and captured lucrative information processing contracts from Texas Blue Cross and Medicare. Investing his profits in a Wall Street brokerage, the feisty entrepreneur attracted public attention in 1969 by spending nearly $1 million in advertisements supporting President Nixon's Vietnam policy. Perot organized the delivery of gifts to American war prisoners three years later. He won further national acclaim in 1979 by financing a mission to rescue imprisoned EDS employees in revolutionary Iran. Eight years later he visited Vietnam to search for information on missing service members.[67]

Launching his 1992 candidacy on a cable television talk show, the home-spun Perot promised to get "under the hood" of gridlocked government and to "clean out the barn." By using action-oriented management and eliminating wasteful spending, the Texas billionaire pledged to lower the national debt and erase federal budget budgets. Cultivating the image of a nonpolitician, Perot insisted that his campaign had been organized by grass-roots volunteers, whom he addressed at "electronic town halls" and televised conference calls. With strongest backing from men and western-ers and those concerned with budget imbalances, he embodied the yearn-ing for nonpolitical alternatives to the governing stalemate of the 1990s and for a restoration of traditional producer values.[68]

In contrast to Perot, Bill Clinton pictured himself as a veteran political broker, whose slogan was "Putting People First." Advocating a mandate for "change" to reverse the sluggish economy, the Arkansas governor con-demned both Republican "trickle-down economics" and the "tax and spend" habits of the Democrats. Clinton promised to "reinvent govern-ment" and honor values of opportunity, responsibility, and community. On election day the Democrat took enough of the white, southern, and sub-urban vote to prevail with 43 percent of the popular tally to Bush's 37 percent and Perot's 19 percent. Significantly, the Perot ticket garnered the greatest percentage of votes for a third party since Theodore Roosevelt's effort in 1912.[69] A minority president without a strong mandate, Clinton found himself attempting to govern a nation whose people had lost faith in government's ability to represent democratic values.

Conclusion

The insurgent impulse has long had significant impact on the political culture of the United States. Creating a republic to meet the contradictory needs of order and liberty, Americans embraced an egalitarian individualism that nevertheless encouraged the creation of great wealth. As large corporations and banks consolidated access to the market in the late nineteenth century, populist reformers helped rally independent farmers and other producers against abusive monopoly, concentrated power, and special privilege. By the 1890s their demands had politicized the currency question and had broadened perceptions of the legitimate role of the federal government.

Populist agitators were succeeded by a group of progressives who addressed broad middle-class needs. Denouncing the dependence associated with the new economic order, anticorporate activists advanced traditional notions of economic individualism, democracy, and nationalism. Such producer values framed Progressive Era campaigns against the trusts, organized capital, and political bosses. They also explained the prominent role of senatorial reformers in crusades against involvement in World War I, the League of Nations, and postwar entanglements in Europe. Disturbed over easterners' economic domination, western insurgents played a particularly important role in opposing diplomatic and financial alliances with European colonialists.

By the 1920s a coalition of independent farmers and small enterprisers sought to tilt the federal government toward the needs of autonomous competitors. Deeply suspicious of monopolies and remote financial power, reformers bitterly denounced close ties between New Era presidencies and the corporate community. Many, however, individualized the evils they targeted and expressed ambivalence about the use of government coercion to neutralize excessive market power. Others objected to the hedonistic values of the era's consumer economy and to the cultural elites who appeared to legitimate them.

After the stock market crash of 1929 agitation for the protection of small farmers and independent merchants took on enhanced proportions. The Great Depression brought grass-roots campaigns to fight the "money power," combat chain stores, and contain monopolies. Nevertheless, fears of collectivism and disillusion with potential allies in government and organized labor turned many old progressives against the permanent features of the New Deal welfare state. By 1939 an emerging group of Republican insurgents sought to restrain liberal statism and reorient government to the preservation of middle-class opportunity.

As a second European military conflict emerged in the late 1930s, nationalists and noninterventionists once again moved to mobilize public opinion against the political, social, and economic consequences of U.S. involvement. Predictably, wartime concerns over collectivism, bureaucracy, and internationalism reinforced anti–New Deal sentiments. For both traditional progressives and a new generation of politicians, the federal government had become the leading threat to democracy and opportunity. Government critics now associated Washington's wartime intrusion into everyday life with the military alliance with the Soviet Union. The domestic regimentation, intellectual elites, and dictatorial regimes of the World War II period merged in the perceptions of insurgents to induce the purges of American public life during the cold war.

By the mid-1940s nationalist and noninterventionist fervor had evolved into bitter anticommunism. For the next forty-five years adversaries of the established order used communism as a metaphor for modern civilization's tendency toward abstract standards of justice, depersonalization, and collectivist values. Replacing opposition to concentrated economic power with demands for the protection of free enterprise and traditional morality, insurgents of the cold war era opposed coercive social and human rights programs as threats to independence and individual autonomy. Meanwhile, neopopulists provided new urgency to the denunciation of cultural elites by targeting "new class" professionals as the agents and legitimators of modern institutions and values.

✦ ✦ ✦

An overview of the history of twentieth-century insurgence suggests that the most radical critiques of corporate capitalism have originated with small competitors and independent enterprisers. Accepting the market economy as the key to individual opportunity and national prosperity, these Americans resented high finance, organized wealth, and international elites. The insurgent impulse conveyed their desire to use individual energies and resources to improve well-being in the face of the growing power of organizations and collectivities. Indeed, retailers, bankers, business leaders, and industrialists all have participated in the struggles outlined in this book. Their activism speaks to the Republican strategist Lawrence Dennis's observation that the two great issues of twentieth-century politics were individualism versus collectivism and isolationism versus internationalism.

Beyond economic grievances, small competitors and traditionalists maintained the producer values of work, discipline, and social propriety. These notions were tied to a social ethic that emphasized personal responsibility, merit achievement, local autonomy, and national identity. Many Americans sensed that their beliefs were threatened by the hedonistic and amoral dimensions of consumer capitalism and government policy. Perceiving their orthodox moral and economic codes as protectors against tyranny and depersonalization, they repeatedly fell back on them in times of crisis. Significantly, the third-party movements of Robert La Follette (1924), William Lemke and Father Charles Coughlin (1936), Philip La Follette (1938), George Wallace (1968), and Ross Perot (1992) all combined denunciations of a sterile and corrupt political order with the austere cultural traditions of producerism.

Although insurgent hostility to concentrated forms of power has been fairly consistent throughout the century, the political legacy of the struggle has been contradictory and confusing. Seeking to universalize their interests, Populists and progressives turned to the state to ensure competitive equality of opportunity between the 1890s and the 1930s. Yet they had difficulty applying the individualist values of producer republicanism to a corporate and urban society. Discomfort with concentrated privilege and collective organization turned many insurgents against the federal government itself. Once bureaucracy became linked with blueprints for social reorganization and experimentation, democratic dissidents rejected Washington's centralized rule as a danger to the autonomy and well-being of ordinary citizens.

The Great Depression also brought realignments that dramatically affected antiestablishment activism. Once the progressive coalition between farmers and labor evaporated with the interest politics of the 1930s, conflicts between working-class and middle-class elements appeared to be irrevocable. As the decade closed, electoral campaigns began to tie middle-class activists far closer to affluent elites than to working people and the poor. Not surprisingly, democratic populists increasingly shifted their focus from corporate and banking targets to the state and the professional elite.

* * *

The study of the insurgent legacy offered in these pages offers rewarding avenues of exploration for scholars. It would be useful, for example, to detail the manner in which the political establishment responded to democratic dissidence. Did insurgent influence limit the rationalization and corporatization of American society? How were insurgent concerns and protests translated into U.S. foreign policy? Did the deep cultural roots of anti-institutional politics encourage overtly conservative leaders to expropriate its rhetoric to defend established privileges? Did the insurgent legacy play a role in the tendency of some "insiders" to campaign as "outsiders?" How often did insurgent activists find themselves striking strategic alliances with elite groups and the establishment itself? What, in turn, were the difficulties dissidents experienced in maintaining control of the government instruments they occasionally created?

More central, however, are questions concerning the utility of the insurgent legacy to the nation's evolving needs. The renewed focus on domestic concerns in the post–cold war era initially appeared to offer an opportunity to reconceptualize the American political map. Yet the vast economic changes of the past two decades proved overwhelming. In addition to the problems of an unskilled underclass, semiskilled and part-time workers barely survive at the margins of the "postindustrial" information and service economy. In turn, the middle class finds itself squeezed by corporate belt-tightening and the reduced social mobility induced by global competition. Meanwhile, only the most affluent benefit from participation in international financial markets that seem to have no relation to the nation's production of goods and services.

Unable to offer solutions and palsied by the financial clout of powerful interest groups and lobbies, politicians of the 1990s often resorted to futile posturing and symbolic gestures. Millions of Americans responded to government taxation and debt, perceived favoritism, and bureaucratic intrusion with angry rejections of politics and a profound cynicism toward the state itself. In an era of declining voter participation and the growth of "people's militias" on the ideological fringes, the very legitimacy of democratic government appeared to be at stake.

Contemporary political journalists, such as E. J. Dionne Jr., Thomas Edsall, and Kevin Phillips, have sought remedies for the political gridlock and stalemate. Finding a mixture of "liberal instincts and conservative values" among voters distrustful of business and government alike, Dionne has argued that ordinary citizens support both equal opportunity and equal rights, self-reliance and social concerns, personal responsibility and individual rights. He has drawn on a presocialist language of democracy, community, and republicanism to outline a revitalized political centrism to express the needs and interests of the nation's "restive majority." In a similar approach Thomas Edsall has called for a refashioned "insurgency," built on "recognizably legitimate claims for an equal opportunity to participate and to compete." Meanwhile, Kevin Phillips has proposed regulation of financial markets, taxation of exorbitant executive salaries, and containment of lobbyists and campaign contributions as steps toward a refurbished populism of the center.[1]

By focusing on equality of opportunity as the central premise of American democracy, these writers provide a reminder that hostility to privilege lies at the core of the nation's republican heritage. Arguing that "liberals" no longer unite ordinary people around such economic concerns as progressive taxation and nonpreferential employment, all three seek the re-creation of "populist" coalitions to fulfill the common interests of the poor, working class, and middle class.

The reassertion of populist politics offers an intriguing way of addressing the despair and cynicism prevalent in American life. Yet it raises questions concerning the ability of the insurgent legacy to address the systemic problems plaguing the nation in the late twentieth century. Does the nation's heritage of democratic dissidence contain sufficient perspective, rationality, and vision to serve as a reference point and organizing strategy for those seeking to enhance the common welfare? To answer that question, additional queries need to be posed.

What are the roles of small enterprise and large corporations in American society? How are the consequences of market risk and failure to be absorbed? What is the legitimate place of centralized government in a complex and multilayered social and economic environment? Can the state act to promote democratic opportunities for ordinary Americans while protecting market and constitutional rights for competitors? What role do professional experts play in the articulation of societal challenges? Can ordinary people be empowered to participate in the consideration of major national issues?

In terms of equity, can a democratic politics respond to the impact of technological specialization and computer literacy on equal opportunity? Can the American dream of equitably distributed wealth coexist with market freedoms and the requirements of investment? What specific reforms can meet the desire of ordinary citizens for justice, equality, and opportunity without producing systemic favoritism or problems more vexing than the original challenges? How are the potential economic losses associated with global competition or environmental protection to be allocated democratically? Regarding social issues, can Americans learn to accept cultural and ethnic pluralism as a counterpart of equal economic opportunity? Can participation in a diverse global market be reconciled to spiritual identification with locality and a national culture? Will national loyalty prevent Americans from embracing worthy transnational endeavors? Can Americans ever reconcile corporate modes of organization with the traditional spiritual and political values of the nation's heritage?

The questions raised here address an insurgent tradition that is infused with a democratic spirit but is frequently defined by narrow economic interests, local and nationalist perspectives, anxieties over change, and the limits of ethnicity, race, and gender. Neopopulists will need to abandon exclusionary tactics to unify a fragmented society behind common goals. Although difficult, the task may be facilitated by the acknowledgment that the central American political debates of the twentieth century have not pitted ideological "liberalism" against "conservatism." Instead, the nation's democratic tradition has been framed by a healthy animosity to concentrated power and elitism, wherever it may be found. If the next century is to produce a vital national politics that defends ordinary citizens against arbitrary power and pursues reachable goals of justice, fair play, and equity, it likely will be one that replicates the most universal features of the insurgent legacy. For political democracy to survive in the United States, Americans must continue to move beyond left and right.

Notes

Preface

1. Thompson, *New York Herald Tribune*, 24 January 1938, quoted in Hawley, *New Deal and the Problem of Monopoly*, 472; ibid., 472–73; Hawley, "Discovery and Study of a 'Corporate Liberalism,'" 311; Himmelstein, *To the Right*, 1, 26. Other political definitions may be found in Doenecke, "Conservatism," 602, 607; Dionne, *Why Americans Hate Politics*, 268; Kazin, "Grass-Roots Right," 138; and Parenti, *Democracy for the Few*, 39–42.

2. Brinkley, "Writing the History of Contemporary America," 135–37; Brinkley, "Richard Hofstadter's *Age of Reform*," 462–80; Thelen, *Paths of Resistance*, 4; Lasch, *True and Only Heaven*, 468, 36–37; Lears, *No Place of Grace*, 307; Ribuffo, *Old Christian Right*, xii, xvii–xviii (quote on xvii).

3. Brinkley, "Writing the History of Contemporary America," 131–32; Bender, "Wholes and Parts," 125–29; Stock, *Main Street in Crisis*, 4–7; Thelen, *Paths of Resistance*, xiii; Lears, *No Place of Grace*, xx; Lasch, *True and Only Heaven*, 22. See also Lasch, "Beyond Left and Right," 21.

4. For populism, see J. Bell, *Populism and Elitism*; Phillips, *Post-Conservative America*, 31–52, 196–99; Shils, *Torment of Secrecy*, 98–102; Bunzel, *Anti-Politics in America*; Lasch, *True and Only Heaven*, 476–83; Kazin, "Grass-Roots Right," 141, 146, 154; and Kazin, *Populist Persuasion*. For conflict between upper and lower rungs of the middle class, see Hamilton, *Class and Politics in the U.S.*, 218. For "old" versus the "new" middle class, see Stock, *Main Street in Crisis*, 207. For previous books with the same title as this work, see Kostelanetz, ed., *Beyond Left and Right*; and Chickering, *Beyond Left and Right*.

Chapter 1: Producer Values, Corporate Culture, and Progressive Politics

1. *La Follette's Magazine,* July 1916, 1–2, quoted in Griffith, "Old Progressives and the Cold War," 336.

2. Diggins, *Lost Soul,* 5, 12, 14; Lustig, *Corporate Liberalism,* 2; J. Bell, *Populism and Elitism,* 15–16; Kloppenberg, "Virtues of Liberalism," 15–26; Nungent, "Tocqueville, Marx, and American Class Structure," 331.

3. Diggins, *Lost Soul,* 10; Kelley, *Cultural Pattern,* 42–44, 268; Lasch, *True and Only Heaven,* 14–15, 170–74; Pocock, *Politics, Language, and Time,* 92–98; Piott, *Anti-Monopoly Persuasion,* 5; Cayton and Onuf, *Midwest and the Nation,* 112.

4. Kelley, *Cultural Pattern,* 274–76, 56; Brinkley, *Voices of Protest,* 161; J. Bell, *Populism and Elitism,* 18; Piott, *Anti-Monopoly Persuasion,* 6.

5. Kelley, *Cultural Pattern,* 279; Kohl, *Politics of Individualism;* Zeigler, *Politics of Small Business,* l; Thelen, *Paths of Resistance,* 3, 173; D. Bell, *Cultural Contradictions of Capitalism,* xvi, 17, 55; Coben, *Rebellion against Victorianism,* 3–4, 25, 31; Cayton and Onuf, *Midwest and the Nation,* 118; M. Sklar, *Corporate Reconstruction,* 34.

6. Trachtenberg, *Incorporation of America,* 3–4; Piott, *Anti-Monopoly Persuasion,* 3, 55; Wiebe, *Search for Order,* 23; Keller, *Regulating a New Economy,* 2–3; Bruchey, *Wealth of the Nation,* 87.

7. Adams quoted in Trachtenberg, *Incorporation of America,* 3; M. Sklar, *Corporate Reconstruction,* 26, 23; Piott, *Anti-Monopoly Persuasion,* 10; Zunz, *Making America Corporate,* 12–14, 4–9, 39, 42; Keller, *Regulating a New Economy,* 5; Wiebe, *Search for Order,* xiii–xiv; Galambos, *Public Image of Big Business,* 3, 5. For corporate consolidation of administration, see Galambos and Pratt, *Rise of the Corporate Commonwealth,* 71–99.

8. Piott, *Anti-Monopoly Persuasion,* 3; Nungent, "Tocqueville, Marx, and American Class Structure," 327–28; Cassity, "Defending a Way of Life," iii, 26, 28, 70–72, 76, 67–71; Bender, *Community and Social Change,* 136; Zunz, *Making America Corporate,* 9; Wiebe, *Search for Order,* 112–13, 165–66, 297.

9. Green, *Shaping Political Consciousness,* 25–28, 41; M. Sklar, *Corporate Reconstruction,* 49.

10. M. Sklar, *Corporate Reconstruction,* 46, 96, 106–7, 110–12, 117–18, 123, 125–27, 181; Keller, *Regulating a New Economy,* 87.

11. M. Sklar, *Corporate Reconstruction,* 46, 127–28, 146–47, 150–51, 153.

12. Gibbs, *Great Silent Majority,* 7; Kunz, *Making America Corporate,* l; Cayton and Onuf, *Midwest and the Nation,* 104, 118; Wiebe, *Search for Order,* 44–47; Thelen, *Paths of Resistance,* xix; Bruchey, *Wealth of the Nation,* 91, 133; Kelley, *Cultural Pattern,* 282; Piott, *Anti-Monopoly Persuasion,* 152–53.

13. Wiebe, *Search for Order,* 52–53; Piott, *Anti-Monopoly Persuasion,* 9, 153; Bruchey, *Wealth of the Nation,* 131, 133 (quote); B. Palmer, "*Man over Money,*" 113–14, 122–23; Green, *Shaping of Political Consciousness,* 22–24.

14. Cleveland, Note, Post-war Foreign Policy, 1944–45, Special Case File, Box C-430, R. La Follette Jr. Papers; George, *Progress and Poverty.* For the single tax

movement, see Johnston, "Middle-Class Political Ideology in a Corporate Society," 355–99.

15. Bruchey, *Wealth of the Nation*, 90–94; Wiebe, *Search for Order*, 48; Ashby, *Bryan*, 29; Lustig, *Corporate Liberalism*, 43–44.

16. Lustig, *Corporate Liberalism*, 43–45; Lasch, *True and Only Heaven*, 217–18, 223; Thelen, *Paths of Resistance*, 205–7; B. Palmer, *"Man over Money,"* 9–14, 21–23, 31, 69–73, 77; Piott, *Anti-Monopoly Persuasion*, 11–21.

17. McMath, *Populist Vanguard*, 64–75; Turner, "Understanding the Populists," 358–59, 367–68; Goodwyn, *Populist Moment*, 294; M. Sklar, *Corporate Reconstruction*, 44 (first quote); Lustig, *Corporate Liberalism*, 45 (second quote).

18. Ashby, *Bryan*, 33–34; B. Palmer, *"Man over Money,"* 82, 85–86, 100–102, 105–7; Harvey, *Coin's Financial School*; Donnelly, *American People's Money*.

19. B. Palmer, *"Man over Money,"* xvi–xvii, 84.

20. Hicks, *Populist Revolt*, 442–44.

21. Ibid., 238–73, esp. 263 and 267; B. Palmer, *"Man over Money,"* 24, 212, 42; Lustig, *Corporate Liberalism*, 98; Lasch, *True and Only Heaven*, 219.

22. Ashby, *Bryan*, 49–55 (first quote on 53; second quote on 63). For the complete speech, see Ginger, ed., *Bryan*, 38–46.

23. Ashby, *Bryan*, xv, 1–3, 8, 26, 31, 32, 36–38. For Bryan as a "localist," see Harrington, *Dream of Deliverance*, 34–36.

24. Bryan, *Congressional Record* (hereafter *CR*), 53d Cong., 1st sess., 25 (16 August 1893), 409 (first quote), 410 (second quote), 401 (third quote).

25. Ashby, *Bryan*, 46, 49–55; Ginger, ed., *Bryan*, 42. For the fusion of the Populist and Democratic campaigns, see Ashby, *Bryan*, 55–57; and Hicks, *Populist Revolt*, 340–79.

26. Ashby, *Bryan*, 67; Cayton and Onuf, *Midwest and the Nation*, 114–15.

27. Bryan quoted in Ginger, ed., *Bryan*, 101–2, 112; Watson, *CR*, 52d Cong., 2d sess., 24 (16 April 1892), 3361; Bryan, *CR*, 53d Cong., 1st sess., 25 (16 August 1893), 405.

28. Bryan, *CR*, 53d Cong., 1st sess., 25 (16 August 1893), 405; Bryan, "Foreign Influence in American Politics," *Arena*, April 1898, in Ginger, ed., *Bryan*, 53–57.

29. Quoted in Cooper, "Progressivism and American Foreign Policy," 264; Bryan acceptance speech quoted in Ashby, *Bryan*, 85.

30. Ashby, *Bryan*, xv, 121–23; L. Gould, *Reform and Regulation*, 113–17.

31. Woodward, *Origins of the New South*, 373–83; Woodward, *Tom Watson*, 371, 401–50; Holmes, *White Chief*, 269–70, 279–80 (Vardaman quote on 270).

32. Noble, *Progressive Mind*, 103; Lustig, *Corporate Liberalism*, 74; Hicks, "Legacy of Populism," 225; Cooper "Progressivism and American Foreign Policy," 269; Cayton and Onuf, *Midwest and the Nation*, 116.

33. Fite, *Peter Norbeck*, 28–31; Marguiles, *Decline of the Progressive Movement*, 20–22, 42, 49, 52, 71; Maxwell, *La Follette and the Rise of Progressivism*, 18, 21, 50–51, 76, 81, 139.

34. Cayton and Onuf, *Midwest and the Nation*, 116; Thelen, *La Follette*, 22–23; Thelen, *Paths of Resistance*, xix, 239, 243–28; Fite, *Peter Norbeck*, 28–29.

35. Fite, *Peter Norbeck*, 31, 50–57, 62–63, 71–73, 80 (first quote on 62; second quote on 68). South Dakotans passed constitutional amendments authorizing state-owned flour mills, packing plants, and terminal elevators in 1918, but Norbeck and the legislature balked at implementing these measures.

36. Wilkins, "Middle Western Isolationism," 69–70; Wilkins, "Non-Partisan League and Upper Midwest Isolationism," 102; G. H. Smith, *Langer of North Dakota*, 213–14, 222 (quote on 214).

37. Wilkins, "Middle Western Isolationism," 70; Blackorby, *Prairie Rebel*, 24–25, 29–31 (quote on 31); Bennett, *Demagogues in the Depression*, 89; Fite, *Peter Norbeck*, 59.

38. Bennett, *Demagogues in the Depression*, 89; Blackorby, *Prairie Rebel*, 32–33; Remele, "Tragedy of Idealism," 80.

39. Townley quoted in R. Nye, *Midwestern Progressive Politics*, 314; Remele, "Tragedy of Idealism," 80–82; Blackorby, *Prairie Rebel*, 80.

40. Braeman, "Seven Progressives," 583; Wiebe, *Search for Order*, 166–81, 185–95, 210–11, 222–23, 296–97; Olin, *California's Prodigal Sons*, 43; Lustig, *Corporate Liberalism*; Gibbs, *Great Silent Majority*, 1–3; Thelen, *Paths of Resistance*, 253–58.

41. Croly, *Promise of American Life*.

42. Marguiles, *Decline of the Progressive Movement*, vi, 131–36, 139; Thelen, *La Follette*, 109–10, 117. Forty-three percent of the 1911 Wisconsin legislature had some college training. The "Wisconsin Idea" also spawned a "social center" movement that established five hundred public schools as forums for professionally led citizenship discussions. Thelen, *La Follette*, 108–9; and C. McCarthy, *Wisconsin Idea*.

43. L. Gould, *Reform and Regulation*, 76–95, 121–73; L. Gould, *Presidency of Theodore Roosevelt*; Roosevelt quoted in Olin, *California's Prodigal Sons*, 67; Lustig, *Corporate Liberalism*, 208–23.

44. L. Gould, *Reform and Regulation*, 173; Lustig, *Corporate Liberalism*, 203–8; J. Weinstein, *Corporate Ideal in the Liberal State*, xi–xii, 251–53; Thelen, *La Follette*, 103; M. Sklar, *Corporate Reconstruction*, 34, 81, 90, 167, 172, 203, 282, 325–31, 381–430, 441.

45. Maxwell, *La Follette and the Rise of Progressivism*, 179–80; Allen, "Republican Reformers and Geography and Politics," 223–24.

46. Lowitt, *Norris: 1861–1912*, 1, 8–9, 15, 20–21, 27–29, 36, 49, 78, 104–5, 107, 111, 121, 140–94; Zucker, *Norris*, 3.

47. Zucker, *Norris*, 153–59; Lowitt, *Norris: 1861–1912*, 166–88, 242; Lowitt, *Norris: 1913–1933*, 12–15.

48. Olin, *California's Prodigal Sons*, viii, 8–10, 22–23, 34–35; Feinman, *Twilight of Progressivism*, 6.

49. Olin, *California's Prodigal Sons*, 173–75; May, *Screening Out the Past*, 181; Duncan Aikman, "California: Progressivism without a Progressive Movement," *Today*, 13 January 1934, Political Campaign Material, 1934, Senatorial, Newspaper Articles, Carton 10, H. Johnson Papers.

50. Leuchtenburg, "Borah," *Dictionary of American Biography*, Supplement Two, 49–50; Borah quoted in Cooper, *Vanity of Power*, 140. For a critical view of Borah, see Cooper, "William E. Borah, Political Thespian," 148–49.

51. Leuchtenburg, "Borah," *Dictionary of American Biography,* Supplement Two, 50–51; C. Johnson, *Borah of Idaho,* 117–25; McKenna, *Borah,* 131–33.

52. P. La Follette, *Adventure in Politics,* 69; B. La Follette and F. La Follette, *La Follette,* vol. 1: vii, 46–48, 58–60, 68–89, 106–9, 116–28, 131–35; Marguiles, *Decline of the Progressive Movement,* 18–22, 42, 49, 93, 135–50; Maxwell, *La Follette and the Rise of Progressivism,* 58–59, 129, 132, 134, 138; Thelen, *La Follette,* 45, 96–98, 118–19; L. Gould, *Reform and Regulation,* 86, 143, 146–47, 157.

53. Thelen, *La Follette,* 102–4, 114, 116; R. La Follette Statement, Business Regulation, 1916, Box B-218, R. La Follette Papers.

Chapter 2: The Campaign against Internationalism, 1914–29

1. Norris Speech, 26 March 1917, quoted in Lowitt, *Norris: 1913–1933,* 68–71; Norris, *CR,* 65th Cong., 1st sess., 55 (4 April 1917), 213–15.

2. Cooper, "Progressivism and American Foreign Policy," 277; Grinder, "Progressives," 36; Clements, *Bryan,* 147–49; Borah to M. G. Reibeling, 26 April 1916, Preparedness, 1916–17, General Office File, Box 44, Borah Papers. See also Braeman, "Seven Progressives," 582, 588–91.

3. Wilkins, "Middle Western Isolationism," 69, 74; Wilkins, "Non-Partisan League and Upper Midwest Isolationism," 102; Remele, "Tragedy of Idealism," 82–83; James C. Knott to Borah, 26 February 1917, War Matters, 1916–17, General Office File, Box 45, Borah Papers.

4. Borah to Mansfield Storey, 6 December 1916, Foreign Affairs, 1916–17, General Office File, Box 40, Borah Papers; Grinder, "Progressives," 33, 36–37.

5. Cooper, *Vanity of Power,* 2–4; Borah to Paul U. Kellogg, 19 February 1917, and Borah to Charles Busey, 16 April 1917, Foreign Affairs, 1916–17, General Office File, Box 40, Borah Papers.

6. Cooper, *Vanity of Power,* 24–26, 30–32, 90 (Bryan quote).

7. Isaac Sherman, *CR,* 64th Cong., 2d sess., 53 (4 January 1916), 458–63, and Vardaman, *CR,* 64th Cong., 2d sess., 53 (2 March 1917), 4777–78, quoted in Cooper, *Vanity of Power,* 93, 181; Stone to Bennett Champ Clark, 1917, quoted by Clark, *CR,* 76th Cong., 1st sess., 84 (3 March 1939), 2212–13.

8. Clements, *Bryan,* 96, 98, 109–10, 114–15.

9. Ibid., 12, 15, 115–17; Ashby, *Bryan,* 159–65 (first and second quotes on 162; third quote on 162–63).

10. Wilkins, "Middle Western Isolationism," 71; Kent, "Portrait in Isolationism," 30–31 (quote on 31).

11. R. La Follette, *CR,* 64th Cong., 1st sess., 53 (20 July 1916), 11331; Cooper, *Vanity of Power,* 31 (first quote), 183 (second and third quotes); R. La Follette Speech Draft (fourth quote), Armed Ship Bill, 1917 (1), Box B-219, R. La Follette Papers.

12. R. La Follette quoted in Torelle, comp., *Political Philosophy of La Follette,* 407–8 (both quotes); R. La Follette, *CR,* 64th Cong., 1st sess., 53 (29 April 1916), 7018; Kent, "Portrait in Isolationism," 32–33; R. La Follette, *CR,* 64th Cong., lst sess., 53 (10 March 1916), 3886. Another war referendum proposal

introduced by Bryan's friend Walter Hensley, a Democrat from Missouri, received House hearings after February 1917. Gibbs, *Great Silent Majority,* 36n.

13. R. La Follette to Family, 2, 3, 4 February 1917, Box A-21, La Follette Family Papers.

14. Clements, *Bryan,* 121; R. La Follette to Family, 3, 6, 15, 17 February 1917, Box A-21, La Follette Family Papers.

15. Cooper, *Vanity of Power,* 179–82; Gibbs, *Great Silent Majority,* 26, 31; R. La Follette to Family, 6 March 1917, Box A-21, La Follette Family Papers; B. La Follette and F. La Follette, *La Follette,* vol. 1: 619 (quote).

16. B. La Follette and F. La Follette, *La Follette,* vol. 1: 641–42; R. La Follette Speech Draft, 3 (first quote), 1 (second quote), Armed Ship Bill, 1917 (1), Box B-219, R. La Follette Papers; Wilson quote in Sutton, "Bryan, La Follette, Norris," 620.

17. B. La Follette and F. La Follette, *La Follette,* vol. 1: 652–67; R. La Follette, *CR,* 65th Cong., 1st sess., 55 (4 April 1917), 223–34. La Follette's Wisconsin political constituency was not primarily German-American but was composed of urban laborers, middle-class progressives, and rural Scandinavians. Kent, "Portrait in Isolationism," 25, 112; Meyer, "Politics of Loyalty," 14, 20.

18. B. La Follette and F. La Follette, *La Follette,* vol. 1: 652 (first La Follette quote); La Follette to Family, 7 June 1917 (second La Follette quote), Box A-21, La Follette Family Papers; entry of 6 April 1917, in Levine, ed., "'Diary' of Hiram Johnson," 65; H. Johnson to Chester H. Rowell, 10 April, 17 September 1917, Johnson, 1917, Box 17, Rowell Papers.

19. Entry of 16 February 1918, in Levine, ed., "'Diary,' of Hiram Johnson," 67; H. Johnson to Johnson Jr., 27 July 1917, quoted in Lower, "Hiram Johnson," 506–7; Lower, "Hiram Johnson," 510, 514.

20. *CR,* 65th Cong., lst sess., 55 (27, 28 April 1917), 1354–63, 1442–46, 1481; Lowitt, *Norris: 1913–1933,* 78; H. Johnson to Johnson Jr., 23 July 1917, in Lower, "Hiram Johnson," 507–8 (first quote), 508 (second quote); Fitzpatrick, "Senator Hiram W. Johnson," 58; H. Johnson, *CR,* 65th Cong., 1st sess., 55 (19 April 1917), 840–41 (third quote). Between 60 and 70 percent of nationwide draft registrants applied for exemptions, and antidraft protests occurred in at least ten states. Gibbs, *Great Silent Majority,* 101–2.

21. Lower, "Hiram Johnson," 508; Lowitt, *Norris: 1913–1933,* 88; Borah to T. A. Davis, 14 April 1917, War Matters, 1916–17, General Office File, Box 46, Borah Papers; Edward C. Stokes to Borah, 31 July 1917, War Matters, 1916–17, General Office File, Box 46, Borah Papers. A banker himself, Stokes characterized the belief that Wilson had intervened to protect overseas loans as "unjust."

22. Borah to Prof. O. J. Penrose, 10 April 1917 (first and second quotes), War Matters—Peace Terms, 1916–17, General Office File, Box 45; Borah to J. H. Gipson, 7 May 1917, 1–3 (third and fourth quotes), Preparedness, 1916–17, General Office File, Box 44; and Borah to A. W. Ricker, 8 April 1918, Espionage, 1917–18, General Office File, Box 53, all in Borah Papers; H. Johnson, *CR,* 65th Cong., 2d sess., 56 (4, 24 April 1918), 4566–67, 5544. A former prosecutor, Johnson won approval for an amendment to the Sedition Act that placed

violations in civil courts instead of military tribunals. Fitzpatrick, "Senator Hiram W. Johnson," 60.

23. R. La Follette, *CR,* 65th Cong., 1st sess., 55 (21 August 1917), 6201 (first quote); R. La Follette, "People of Large Fortunes," War Revenue, 1917, Box B-163, R. La Follette Papers; R. La Follette, *CR,* 65th Cong., 1st sess., 55 (1, 3 September 1917), 6503–19, 6523–34; Lowitt, *Norris: 1913–1933,* 85–88; Borah to Early W. Bowmen, 30 August 1917, Revenue Bill, 1917–18, General Office File, Box 44, Borah Papers; H. Johnson, "Conscription of Wealth," 20 August 1917 (second quote), Speeches, Statements, and Press Releases, August 1917–March 1918, Carton 25, H. Johnson Papers; B. La Follette and F. La Follette, *La Follette,* vol. 2: 744–45; Fitzpatrick, "Senator Hiram W. Johnson," 62–63. For social profiles of war bond consumers, see Gibbs, *Great Silent Majority,* 81, 90.

24. Karl, *Uneasy State,* 41; R. La Follette to John Linten, 26 December 1917, and R. La Follette to Gilbert E. Roe, 21 December 1917, Box B-111, R. La Follette Papers; R. La Follette to Family, 16 November 1918, 1, 10, 24 (quote) December 1918, Box A-24, La Follette Family Papers.

25. Ray McKaig to Borah, 10 December 1917, Revenue Law, 1917–18, General Office File, Box 61; McKaig to Borah, 19 March 1918 (quote), Non-Partisan League, 1917–18, General Office File, Box 58; and Borah to W. J. Tapper, 8 May 1918, Profiteering, 1917–18, General Office File, Box 60, all in Borah Papers; Marguiles, *Decline of the Progressive Movement,* 214–16; Meyer, "Politics of Loyalty," 45–46, 49–50, 52, 57–58, 61 (Thompson quote on 49).

26. Cooper, *Vanity of Power,* 200, 202; Extract of Letter from John H. Rich, 1–2, attached to Henry Minor to Thomas J. Walsh, 13 July 1917 (first, second, and third quotes), Liberty Loans, Subject File B, Box 192, Walsh Papers; Arthur C. Townley Speech, Jamestown, N.D., 9 June 1917, Roll 14, Vol. 1, National Nonpartisan League Papers (hereafter National NPL Papers); National Nonpartisan League, *How to Finance the Great War* (1918), Reel 1, Vol. 1, National NPL Papers.

27. Larson, *Lindbergh of Minnesota,* 3–4, 17–19, 59–61, 69, 99, 117, 123; Pujo Committee Conclusion, quoted in Galambos and Pratt, *Rise of the Corporate Commonwealth,* 66–67.

28. Larson, *Lindbergh of Minnesota,* 189, 211–12, 282–85 (first quote on 61; second quote on 189); Lindbergh, *Why Is Your Country at War.*

29. Lindbergh to Eva Christie Lindbergh, n.d., Correspondence, January–March 1918, Box 2, Lindbergh Papers; Report of Agent Campbell, 6 June 1918, Report of Agent Murray, 10 June 1918, and Memo from Alfred Bettman, 13 October 1918, attached to Memo from Bettman, 25 July 1918, Item OG 1969371, Reel 82-B, Bureau of Investigation Files, National Archives, Washington, D.C.; George Perrine, "A Story of Charles A. Lindbergh, Sr.," postmarked 25 June 1942, in Miscellaneous, Folder 14, Box 5, Lindbergh Papers; Paul Seabury, "Charles Lindbergh: The Politics of Nostalgia," in *History,* 141.

30. Blackorby, *Prairie Rebel,* 77–78; R. La Follette to Judge James C. Kerwin, 5 January 1918, Box B-111, R. La Follette Papers; B. La Follette and F. La Follette, *La Follette,* vol. 2: 764, 767–78; R. La Follette Speech, Producers and Consumers' Convention, St. Paul, Minn., 20 September 1917, 5, 9, 13–18, 20–

30 (first quote on 16; second quote on 30), Roll 14, Vol. 1, National NPL Papers; P. La Follette, *Adventure in Politics,* 49. La Follette acknowledged U.S. grievances against Germany but characterized them as technical.

31. P. La Follette, *Adventure in Politics,* 49–50, 52–53, 156, 231–32, 84–85, 242 (first quote on 49); 65th Cong., 1st sess., U.S. Senate, Subcommittee of the Committee on Privileges and Elections, *Letter from the Secretary,* 2 (second quote); Meyer, "Politics of Loyalty," 36, 38–42; Marguiles, *Decline of the Progressive Movement,* 212–14, 204–6, 213 (third quote on 205–6); Maney, *"Young Bob" La Follette,* 24; B. La Follette and F. La Follette, *La Follette,* vol. 2: 842–46, 851–52, vol. 1: 651.

32. R. La Follette to Family, 27, 29 September 1917, Box A-21, La Follette Family Papers; Lincoln Steffens to R. La Follette, 7 October 1917, Special Correspondence, Box B-82, R. La Follette Papers; William Langer to R. La Follette, 24 October 1917, Special Correspondence, Box B-81, R. La Follette Papers; Eugene V. Debs to R. La Follette, 15 October, 26 November, 1917, and Warren G. Harding to Dr. William E. Arnold, 10 October 1917, Special Correspondence, Box B-80, R. La Follette Papers; R. La Follette to Family, 21 November 1918, and R. La Follette to Philip La Follette, 25 November 1918, Box A-24, La Follette Family Papers; U.S. Senate, Committee on Privileges and Elections, *Senator from Wisconsin;* P. La Follette, *Adventure in Politics,* 56.

33. Gibbs, *Great Silent Majority,* vii, 38–39, 41, 43–44.

34. R. La Follette to Family, 10 December, 10 November 1918, Box A-24; and R. La Follette to Family, 22 April 1919, Box A-27, all in La Follette Family Papers.

35. R. La Follette to Family, 27 November 1918, Box A-24; and R. La Follette to Family 7 April 1919 (first quote), 23 April 1919 (second quote), 17 April 1919 (third quote), Box A-27, all in La Follette Family Papers.

36. R. La Follette to Family, 23 April 1919 (first quote), 17 April 1919 (second quote), 1 May 1919 (third quote), Box A-27; and R. La Follette to R. La Follette, Jr., 3 June 1919, all in La Follette Family Papers.

37. R. La Follette to Family, 9 November 1918 (first quote), 15 November 1918 (second and third quotes), Box A-24; and R. La Follette to Family, 18 January 1919 (fourth quote), Box A-26, all in La Follette Family Papers.

38. R. La Follette to Family, 28 December 1918, Box A-24; and R. La Follette to Family, 6, 10 January 1919, Box A-26, all in La Follette Family Papers; H. Johnson Speech, November 1917, Speeches, Statements, and Press Releases, August 1917–March 1918, Carton 25, H. Johnson Papers.

39. Quoted in Lower, "Hiram Johnson," 516–24.

40. H. Johnson, *CR,* 65th Cong., 3d sess., 57 (29 January 1919), 2261 (first quote), 2266 (second quote), 2270 (third quote); Fitzpatrick, "Senator Hiram W. Johnson," 77–79; Lower, "Hiram Johnson," 517, 520.

41. Quoted in Lower, "Hiram Johnson," 524.

42. R. La Follette to Family, 5 November 1918 (first quote), 10 November 1918, Box A-24; R. La Follette to Sons, 15 June 1919 (second quote), 21 June 1919 (third quote), Box A-27; and R. La Follette to Family, 6 January 1919, Box A-26, all in La Follette Family Papers.

43. R. La Follette to Philip La Follette, 25 November 1918 (first quote), Box A-24; and R. La Follette to Family, 26 November 1918 (second quote), 3 December 1918, 26 October 1918 (third quote), 3 January 1919 (fourth quote), 9 January 1919 (fifth quote), Box A-26, all in La Follette Family Papers.

44. R. La Follette to Family, 5 May 1919 (first quote), 22 April 1919 (second, third, and fourth quotes), 8 May 1919 (fifth quote), and R. La Follette to Son, 29 June 1919 (sixth and seventh quotes), Box A-27, La Follette Family Papers. For an expansion of La Follette's views, see *CR,* 66th Cong., 1st sess., 58 (6 November 1919), 8001–11.

45. Stone, *Irreconcilables,* 4–99.

46. Guinsburg, *Pursuit of Isolationism,* 33–34, 37, 42–43, 48; Stone, *Irreconcilables,* 178.

47. Griffith, "Old Progressives and the Cold War," 336; H. Johnson to Chester H. Rowell, 27 March 1919 (first quote), 9 April 1919 (second quote), Johnson, 1918–30, Box 17, Rowell Papers; H. Johnson, *CR,* 66th Cong., 1st sess., 58 (2 June 1919), 509 (third quote); "Over the Top with Hiram Johnson, 'the Doughboy' of the Senate," *Boston Evening Transcript,* 12 July 1919 (fourth quote).

48. Marguiles, *Decline of the Progressive Movement,* 254–55; Guinsburg, *Pursuit of Isolationism,* 20–27; Stone, *Irreconcilables,* 100–127; Norris, *CR,* 66th Cong., 1st sess., 58 (15 July 1919), 2595; Borah to W. C. Birdwell, 31 January 1917, Peace Resolution, 1916–17 (1), General Office File, Box 43, Borah Papers; Borah to J. F. Kasanke, 2 February 1917, Peace Resolution, 1916–17 (2), General Office File, Box 43, Borah Papers; Borah to Frank T. Disney, 7 April 1917 (first quote), War Matters, 1916–17, General Office File, Box 76, Borah Papers; Borah to Pearl Wight, James T. Williams, 20 December 1918 (second quote), League to Enforce Peace, 1918–19, General Office File, Box 76, Borah Papers.

49. Guinsburg, *Pursuit of Isolationism,* 33–34; Stone, *Irreconcilables,* 128–77. For background on the treaty controversy, see Ambrosius, *Woodrow Wilson and the American Diplomatic Tradition.*

50. Guinsburg, *Pursuit of Isolationism,* 51–64, 73, 76; R. La Follette Statement, 1–3, World Court, 1923, Box B-201, R. La Follette Papers.

51. R. La Follette to Sons, 10 June 1919, 11 June 1919 (second quote), Box A-27, La Follette Family Papers; R. La Follette Statement, 3 (first quote), World Court, 1923, Box B-201, R. La Follette Papers. For the relationship between financiers and U.S. diplomacy, see Thomas Ferguson, "Industrial Conflict and the Coming of the New Deal," in Fraser and Gerstle, eds., *Rise and Fall of the New Deal Order,* 7–11.

52. Borah to Albert Beveridge, 27 June 1921 (quote), Funding of Foreign Debts, 1920–21, General Office File, Box 94; and Borah to George H. West, 31 January 1922, Funding of Foreign Debt, 1921–22, General Office File, Box 112, both in Borah Papers; R. La Follette, *CR,* 67th Cong., 4th sess., 64 (16 February 1923), 3742. For detail on the war debt agreement, see Hicks, *Republican Ascendancy,* 137–38.

53. Shipstead, "War," Correspondence, 1913, 1922–25, Box 1, Shipstead Papers; Norris to Rev. M. B. Carman, 20 January 1916, War Debts (1926), Box 46, Norris Papers.

54. Hard, "Benito and I Save the St. Paul," 224–25; Mabelle J. Talbert to Huey Long, and attachment, 7 May 1926, War Debts (1926), Box 46, Norris Papers.

55. Guinsburg, *Pursuit of Isolationism*, 83, 87, 91–92, 103–8.

56. Ibid., 105–8; Borah Form Letter to Constituents, 23 December 1923, International Court, 1923–24, General Office File, Box 155; Borah to J. B. Murray et al., 19 January 1925, 3–5, Borah to Ashmun Brown, 27 January 1925, and Borah to Moorfield Story, 8 April 1925 (first quote), International Court, 1924–25, General Office File, Box 180; Borah to R. W. Washburn, 8 August 1925 (second quote), International Court, 1925, General Office File, Box 180, all in Borah Papers. Borah never left the United States.

57. Borah to Commander F. D. McMillen, 6 June 1925, International Court, 1925, General Office File, Box 180, Borah Papers; Guinsburg, *Pursuit of Isolationism*, 100; R. La Follette Press Release, 26 April 1923, World Court, 1923, Box B-201, R. La Follette Papers; H. Johnson, *CR,* 69th Cong., 1st sess., 67 (19 January 1926), 2350–51.

58. Shipstead quoted in "Ten Senators on the World Court," 735; Shipstead, *CR,* 69th Cong., 1st sess., 67 (13 January 1926), 1956–65; Cole, *Senator Gerald P. Nye,* 60–61 (Nye quote on 61); Guinsburg, *Pursuit of Isolationism,* 108.

59. Rowell to H. Johnson, 23 February 1919, 2–5, January–April 1919, Box 4, Rowell Papers.

60. H. Johnson to Rowell, 27 March 1919, Johnson, 1918–30, Box 17, Rowell Papers; H. Johnson "Why 'Irreconcilables' Keep Out of Europe," 1.

61. Weekly Letter of U.S. Sen. Hiram W. Johnson, 24 January 1925, 1–2, Speeches, Statements, and Press Releases, January 1925–December 1927, Carton 25, H. Johnson Papers.

62. Ruetten, "Burton K. Wheeler," 53–56; G. H. Smith, *Langer of North Dakota,* 222–25; Ashby, *Spearless Leader,* 99–101; G. Nye, "Friendly Advise to Reactionaries," n.d., Addresses, 1928, Box 31, G. Nye Papers. For more on western colonial metaphors, see D. A. Horowitz, "Perils of Western Farm Politics," 95. Noninterventionist Montana remained a Democratic stronghold during the 1920s and 1930s.

63. Borchard, "Clash between Economic Interests Cause of War," *Yale News,* 24 October 1921, 1–2, in Special Correspondence, Box B-88; and R. La Follette, "The Flag Must Not Follow the Dollar," speech draft, 1921, Mexico, Speech Material, Box B-223, both in R. La Follette Papers. La Follette calculated that when interest, debt retirement, and pensions were included, 86 percent of federal spending was war related. R. La Follette, "How the President and Congress Are Spending Your Money," 1923, Box B-227, R. La Follette Papers.

64. Borah to Will H. Hays, and attachment, 19 February 1926, Movie Legislation, 1925–26, General Office File, Box 211, Borah Papers.

65. Ashby, *Spearless Leader,* 208; Lowitt, *Norris: 1913–1933,* 145; Norris, Pamphlet, National Citizens' Committee on Relations with Latin America, n.d., Misc. Correspondence, 1927, Box 1, Wheeler Papers.

66. Norris to Mr. and Mrs. O. D. Shaner, 14 February 1928 (first quote), and Norris to J. Nevin Sayre, 4 February 1928 (second quote), Hearst (Mexico),

1926–28, Box 34, Norris Papers; Borah, *CR,* 69th Cong., 2d sess., 68 (13 January 1927), 1555–56, 1558–60 (third quote on 1560).

67. Wheeler, *CR,* 69th Cong., 2d sess., 68 (13 January 1927), 2285; "'Dollar Diplomacy' in Nicaragua Is Bared by Shipstead's Keen Probe," *Labor,* 2 February 1927, 1, in Foreign Policy Clippings, Box 16, Shipstead Papers; "Nicaragua Fighting Rouses Congress to Attack Policy," *New York Times,* 5 January 1928, 1, 3; G. Nye, *CR,* 70th Cong., 1st sess, 69 (4 January 1928), 933–34; Cole, *Senator Gerald P. Nye,* 63; Blaine, *CR,* 70th Cong., 1st sess., 69 (3 February 1928), 2421–23; "Senate Insurgents Hit Marine Funds," *New York Times,* 19 April 1928, 12; O'Brien, "Senator John J. Blaine," 39–40.

68. Norris quoted in attachment to Agnes C. Watson to Norris, 28 March 1929, Hearst (Mexico), 1926–28, Box 34, Norris Papers; G. Nye Address, n.d., Addresses, 1928, Box 31, G. Nye Papers; Blaine, *CR,* 70th Cong., 1st sess., 69 (3 February 1928), 2421; O'Brien, "Senator John J. Blaine," 39.

Chapter 3: Anticorporate Progressives and the New Era, 1920–29

1. Moses, 7 November 1929, quoted in "Western Senators Vent Rage," *New York Times,* 9 November 1929, 1. For a colorful portrait of the insurgents, see Tucker and Barkley, *Sons of the Wild Jackass,* v.

2. Baruch, *American Industry in the War,* 104–7; Hawley, *Great War,* 2–27, 36–37, 45–48, 52–55; Ellis Hawley, "Three Facets of Hooverian Associationalism," in McCraw, ed., *Regulation in Perspective,* 95–102, 121; Hawley, "Discovery and Study of 'Corporate Liberalism,'" 310–11; D. A. Horowitz, "Visions of Harmonious Abundance"; Galambos, *Public Image of Big Business,* 181, 183, 186, 221, 261–64, 159.

3. R. La Follette Speech Draft, 4, Making of America, 1917, Box B-219, R. La Follette Papers.

4. Ibid., 4–6.

5. Dorfman, *Economic Mind in American Civilization,* vol. 3: 338–40; Galambos and Pratt, *Rise of the Corporate Commonwealth,* 68.

6. Borah to Fred C. Holbrook, 24 December 1920, and Borah to S. L. Hodgin, 21 August 1921, Federal Reserve Act, 1920–21, General Office File, Box 93; and Edward C. Stokes to Borah, 17 November 1919, Federal Reserve Bank, 1918–19, General Office File, Box 74, all in Borah Papers.

7. Norbeck to John T. Adams, 8 August 1921, Correspondence, 1921, Box 1, Norbeck Letters; Burdick, *CR,* 77th Cong., 1st sess., 87 (24 March 1941), 2531–32; Burdick, *CR,* 78th Cong., 2d sess., 90 (13 September 1944), 7741.

8. Memo, n.d., Stock Market—Editorials (3), Box 5, Norbeck Papers; D. P. Murray to Borah, and attachment, 1 December 1920, Federal Reserve Act, 1920–21, General Office File, Box 93, Borah Papers; McKelvie quoted in attachment to John P. Robertson to Samuel A. McKelvie, 19 September 1921, 2, Federal Reserve Board (1921–24), Box 27, Norris Papers; Borah to H. N. Owen, and attachment, 11 January 1922, Federal Reserve Act, 1921–22, General Office File, Box 111, Borah Papers.

9. Norris to Frederick C. Howe, 11 December 1922, Federal Reserve Board

(1921–24), Box 27, Norris Papers; R. La Follette Jr. Campaign Speech, 1925, Coolidge Administration, 1928, Box C-554, R. La Follette Jr. Papers; John Skelton Williams quoted in Press Release, National Board of Farm Organizations, 23 July 1921, 3–4, Federal Reserve Board (1921–24), Box 27, Norris Papers; Williams to Norris, 12 November 1921, Federal Reserve Board (1921–24), Box 27, Norris Papers.

10. Shipstead, *CR*, 69th Cong., 2d sess., 68 (16 February 1927), 3948–50; Norbeck to John T. Adams, 8 August 1921, Correspondence, 1921, Box 1, Norbeck Letters. For an eloquent statement of the agrarian position, see Phil R. Swing, *CR*, 67th Cong., 2d sess., 62 (23 May 1922), 7517.

11. Borah to Lot L. Feltham, 21 November 1922, Federal Reserve Act, 1921–22, General Office File, Box 111, Borah Papers; Keller, *Regulating a New Economy*, 53–54; Dorfman, *Economic Mind in American Civilization*, vol. 4: 20–21.

12. Dorfman, *Economic Mind in American Civilization*, vol. 4: 20–21; Keller, *Regulating a New Economy*, 53–54; R. La Follette to Sen. James A. Reed, 1 July 1922, 3–4, and G. L. Lynch to Richard Barny, 6 May 1922, Box B-118, R. La Follette Papers; Norris to George A. Ernst, and attachments, 16 January 1924, Federal Reserve Board (1921–24), Box 27, Norris Papers. La Follette Jr. later described the credit contraction and freight rate inflation as the "twin crimes of 1920." R. La Follette Jr. Campaign Speech, 1925, Coolidge Administration, 1928, Box C-554, R. La Follette Jr. Papers.

13. Marguiles, *Decline of the Progressive Movement*, 276 (first La Follette quote), 275 (second La Follette quote); Ruetten, "Burton K. Wheeler," 33–35.

14. "Farmers Want Old Time," *New York Times*, 2 February 1919, sec. 3: 2; R. La Follette, *CR*, 66th Cong., 1st sess., 58 (18 June 1919), 1284; Simpson to Asle J. Gronna, 15 July 1919, *CR*, 66th Cong., 1st sess., 58 (18 July 1919), 2817; Nina H. Weaver to Editor, *Chicago Tribune*, *CR*, 66th Cong., 1st sess., 58 (1 August 1919), 3505; Wiley Britton, *CR*, 66th Cong., 1st sess., 58 (1 August 1919), 3508–9.

15. "Congress for Repeal of Daylight Savings," *New York Times*, 19 June 1919, 15; "Daylight Issue up Again," *New York Times*, 2 August 1919, 14; "President Vetoes Daylight Repeal," *New York Times*, 16 August 1919, 7; "House Kills Veto of Daylight Law," *New York Times*, 20 August 1919, 17; "Daylight Saving Act Now Stands Repealed," *New York Times*, 21 August 1919, 1; *CR*, 66th Cong., 1st sess., 58 (19, 20 August 1919), 3980, 4009; Socolofsky, *Arthur Capper*, 148, 63, 94–95. The veto override carried by a 223-101 margin in the House and 57-19 in the Senate.

16. Hicks and Saloutos, *Agricultural Discontent in the Middle West*, 326–28, 334; Galambos, *Public Image of Big Business*, 191, 201.

17. Bruchey, *Wealth of the Nation*, 148–49.

18. Norbeck to John T. Adams, 21 July 1921, 2–3, and 8 August 1921, 3, Correspondence, 1921; Norbeck to Chas. N. Herreid, 15 September 1922, Correspondence, 1922; and Norbeck to Sen. James E. Watson, 29 August 1921, Correspondence, 1921, all in Box 1, Norbeck Letters.

19. Norbeck to Kent E. Keller, 8 March 1922, Correspondence, 1924; and H. Johnson to Norbeck, 10 August 1925, Johnson Correspondence Folder, 1924–32, both in Box 1, Norbeck Letters.

20. Norbeck to Kent E. Keller, 16 October 1923, 2, Correspondence, 1923; Norbeck to John T. Adams, 21 June 1921, Correspondence, 1921; and Norbeck to Tom Ayres, 5 April 1922, Correspondence, 1922, all in Box 1, Norbeck Letters.

21. Norbeck to M. Plin Beebe, 23 November 1921, 1–2, Correspondence, 1921; and Norbeck to Chas. N. Herreid, 15 September 1922, Correspondence, 1922, both in Box 1, Norbeck Letters.

22. Ashby, *Spearless Leader,* 221–22; Borah to Frederick William Wile, "The Future of the Progressive Movement," n.d., 4, Speeches and Statements, January–November 1925 and updated, Box 780, Borah Papers.

23. Borah to Edward T. Hubbell, 31 January 1922, Funding of Foreign Debt, 1921–22, Box 112, Borah Papers; Norbeck to Henry W. Rose, 9 November 1922, Correspondence, 1922, Box 1, Norbeck Letters; Norbeck to Chas. A. Aseth, 21 February 1924, Correspondence, 1924, Box 1, Norbeck Letters.

24. H. Johnson to Norbeck, 21 July, 11 September 1925, Correspondence, 1924–32, Box 1, Norbeck Letters.

25. Wheeler, *Yankee from the West,* 213–45; R. La Follette to Josephus Daniels, 19 April 1922, and Daniels to La Follette, 18 April 1922, Box B-118; and W. H. Gray to R. La Follette, and Gray to Senate of United States, 5 May 1922, Special Correspondence, Box B-94, all in R. La Follette Papers.

26. Wheeler, *Yankee from the West,* 213–45; Borah to Judge Abner P. Hayes, 26 February 1924, Teapot Dome, February 1924, General Office File, Box 169, Borah Papers.

27. Norris to Donald R. Richberg, 3 August 1931, 1–2, attached to Amos Pinchot to Norris, 19 August 1931, Progressive Conference, Box 38, Norris Papers; Norris, "The Repeal of Law by Executive Appointment," 1–2, Federal Trade Commission (1918–28), Box 26, Norris Papers; R. La Follette to Sons, 27 June 1919, Box A-27, La Follette Family Papers.

28. Norris, "Boring from Within," 297; Norris, "The Repeal of Law by Executive Appointment," 2 (first quote), and Norris to Basil M. Manly, 9 July 1925, 3 (second quote), FTC (1918–28), Box 26, Norris Papers; Lowitt, *Norris: 1913–1933,* 282.

29. R. La Follette, "Coolidge Slaughters the Federal Trade Commission" (first and second quotes), 1924, Box B-229, R. La Follette Papers; Thelen, *La Follette,* 175 (third quote).

30. Geelan, *Dakota Maverick,* 41; Morlan, *Political Prairie Fire,* 229–38; Martin W. Odland, "Building a Machine; Destroying a Party," Background Information and Family Materials, Box 1, M. Johnson Papers; National Nonpartisan League, *Origin, Purpose, and Method of Operation* (1917 pamphlet), 11, Reel 1, National NPL Papers.

31. "Sketch of Early Life of Henrik Shipstead," Biographical Data, Box 1, Shipstead Papers; Odland, "Building a Machine," Background Information and Family Materials, Box 1, M. Johnson Papers; R. La Follette, Note, Invisible Government, 1922, Box B-226, R. La Follette Papers; R. La Follette, "To the Voters of Minnesota," *New York Times,* 2 July 1923, 19. Kellogg had played a major role in the attempt to expel La Follette from the Senate. P. La Follette,

Adventure in Politics, 73. For 1920s progressivism and the farmer-labor movement, see Ashby, *Spearless Leader,* 91–92 .

32. Henry G. Teigan to J. A. H. Hopkins, 7 December 1922, Hopkins to Teigan, 28 March 1923, Teigan to John M. Baer, 17 April 1923, and Teigan to Lewis G. Vander Velde, 13 November 1922, Reel 11, National NPL Papers; Preamble, *Farmer-Labor Advocate,* 25 March 1924, 1–4, and "Need of a National Farmer-Labor Party," *Farmer-Labor Advocate,* 16 November 1926, Correspondence and Misc. Papers, 1918–May 1926, Box 1, Farmer-Labor Association Papers.

33. Borah Press Release, 21 July 1923, Speeches and Statements, July–December 1923, Box 780, Borah Papers; Ashby, *Spearless Leader,* 55. In 1922 progressives or populists won gubernatorial elections in Pennsylvania, Wisconsin, Nebraska, Oregon, and Oklahoma.

34. H. Johnson to Chester H. Rowell, 5 January 1917 (first quote), 2; H. Johnson to Rowell, 26 January 1917; Johnson to Matthew Hale, 29 January 1917, 4 (second quote); and Johnson to Meyer Lissner, 7 May 1919, 4, all in Johnson, 1918–30, Box 17, Rowell Papers.

35. Fitzpatrick, "Senator Hiram W. Johnson," 112–15, 120, 324.

36. Ibid., 115; H. Johnson to Jack Johnson, 1 May 1921, 16 December 1922, in Levine, ed., "'Diary,' of Hiram Johnson," 69, 71.

37. H. Johnson Press Notice, 16 November 1923, Speeches, Statements, and Press Releases, January–December 1923, Carton 25, H. Johnson Papers; Seth R. Brown et al., "To All Members of Organized Labor Who Are Registered as Republican Voters," ca. 1 April 1924, Political Campaign Material, 1924, Presidential Lists, Part 2, Carton 10, H. Johnson Papers; H. Johnson Speech, Cleveland, 3 January 1924, 5–6, Speeches, Statements, and Press Releases, January–December 1924, Carton 25, H. Johnson Papers; Fite, *Peter Norbeck,* 114–15; Norbeck to George W. Norris, 29 March 1924, Correspondence, 1924, Box 1, Norbeck Letters; Norbeck to A. H. Boynton, 15 February 1924, Norbeck Folder, Box 62, H. Johnson Papers; Blackorby, *Prairie Rebel,* 162; Langer to H. Johnson, 23 September 1920, Langer Folder, Box 49, H. Johnson Senate Papers.

38. H. Johnson Statement, 10 April 1924, Speeches, Statements, and Press Releases, January–December 1924, Carton 25, H. Johnson Papers; H. Johnson to H. Johnson Jr., 9 June 1924, in Burke, ed., *Diary Letters of Hiram Johnson,* vol. 4: 2, 4; H. Johnson Statement, n.d., Speeches, Statements, and Press Releases, January–December 1924, Carton 25, H. Johnson Papers.

39. R. La Follette to R. La Follette Jr., 13, 23 May 1919, Box A-27, La Follette Family Papers; R. La Follette Statement, 18 November 1922, Box B-112, R. La Follette Papers; R. Nye, *Midwestern Progressive Politics,* 327; Olssen, "Progressive Group in Congress," 244–63; Bryan to R. La Follette, 4 December 1922, Special Correspondence, Box B-93, R. La Follette Papers; Levine, *Defender of the Faith,* 213–16.

40. R. La Follette to R. La Follette Jr., 3 June 1919, Box A-27, La Follette Family Papers; William Hard to R. La Follette, 30 June, 9 July 1920, Special Correspondence, Box B-85, R. La Follette Papers; Meyer, "Politics of Loyalty, 14, 20–21, 63–65; Ashby, *Spearless Leader,* 122–36; Hicks and Saloutos, *Agricultural Discontent in the Middle West,* 357–59.

41. Hicks and Saloutos, *Agricultural Discontent in the Middle West,* 361–65; Tobin, *Organize or Perish,* 131–66; R. La Follette Press Release, 28 May 1924, attached to R. La Follette to Herman L. Ekern, 26 May 1924, Box A-31, La Follette Family Papers (quote).

42. R. Nye, *Midwestern Progressive Politics,* 335 (quote); MacKay, *Progressive Movement of 1924,* 148; Cott, *Grounding of Modern Feminism,* 251–52; Coben, *Rebellion against Victorianism,* 112–15, 125–35.

43. Ruetten, "Wheeler and the Montana Connection," 4–5; Wheeler, *Yankee from the West,* 58–62; Ruetten, "Burton K. Wheeler," 18–21, 28, 43; Ashby, *Spearless Leader,* 151–53; Norris to Wheeler, 7 September 1924, attached to James H. Baldwin to Norris, 11 September 1924, Progressives (1922–29), Box 298, Norris Papers.

44. Wheeler, *CR,* 69th Cong., 1st sess., 67 (20 June 1926), 11649–50; Wheeler Opening Speech, La Follette–Wheeler Campaign, Boston, 1 September 1924, 4, 20, and Wheeler 1924 Campaign Speech, Box 13, Wheeler Papers. For background on Wheeler, see Ruetten, "Burton K. Wheeler," 29–32.

45. Wheeler Opening Speech, Boston, 1 September 1924, 5, Box 13, Wheeler Papers; R. La Follette "How Wealth Dominates Legislation," address before People's Legislative Service, Washington, D.C., 16 April 1921, 1–2 (first quote), 1921, Box B-222, R. La Follette Papers; R. La Follette Speech Draft, Invisible Government, 1922, Box B-226, R. La Follette Papers; B. La Follette and F. La Follette, *La Follette,* vol. 2: 1133, 1146 (second quote); Wheeler, *Yankee from the West,* 263; MacKay, *Progressive Movement of 1924,* 143–61.

46. MacKay, *Progressive Movement of 1924,* 195–96; Ashby, *Spearless Leader,* 169–77; Hicks and Saloutos, *Agricultural Discontent in the Middle West,* 368.

47. Borah Press Release, 24 November 1924, 1, Speeches and Statements, January–December 1924, Box 780, Borah Papers; Wheeler, "Where are the Pre-War Radicals?" 561.

48. H. Johnson to Norbeck, 11 September 1925, H. Johnson Correspondence, Box 1, Norbeck Letters; People's Legislative Service, Press Release on Warren Nomination (1925), Box 48, Norris Papers.

49. Walsh to Richard Whelden, 6 April 1925, Warren Confirmation, Legislative File, Box 328, Walsh Papers; Norris to Clarence Reckmeyer, 30 March 1925, 3 (quote), Warren Nomination (1925), Box 48, Norris Papers. Warren's connections to the sugar trust had been researched by the People's Legislative Service, a progressive group affiliated with the La Follettes. R. La Follette Jr., Form Letter, n.d., Personal Correspondence, Basil Manly, 1925, Box C-2, R. La Follette Jr. Papers.

50. Norris to H. J. Kennedy, 17 March 1925, 2, Warren Nomination (1925), Box 48, Norris Papers; Norris, "Boring from Within," 297; H. Johnson to F. I. Drexler, 19 March 1925, H. Johnson Correspondence, 1924–32, Box 1, Norbeck Letters.

51. Ashby, *Spearless Leader,* 183–96; B. La Follette and F. La Follette, *La Follette,* vol. 2: 1161–63.

52. Borah and Wheeler, *CR,* 69th Cong., 1st sess., 67 (20 June 1925), 11648–50; Norris to Frank A. Harrison, 26 June 1925, attached to Mabeller J. Talbert

to R. La Follette Jr., 28 August 1925, Personal Correspondence, George W. Norris, 1925, Box C-2, R. La Follette Jr. Papers.

53. Maney, *"Young Bob" La Follette,* 39–43; Cole, *Senator Gerald P. Nye* 37–46; Rylance, "A Controversial Career," 8.

54. Thomas H. Brewer to Borah, 5 February, 14 March 1918 (quote), National Banks, 1917–18, General Office File, Box 57; Borah to M. M. Belknap, and attachment, 21 November 1922, Federal Reserve Act, 1921–22, General Office File, Box 111; and Association of Missouri Banks and Trust Companies Opposed to Branch Banking, *Shall We Allow Branch Banking to Supplant Independent Banking in the United States* (1922), 3, 8, Bank Legislation, 1921–22, General Office File, Box 108, all in Borah Papers.

55. Association of Missouri Banks and Trust Companies Opposed to Branch Banking, *Shall We Allow Branch Banking to Supplant Independent Banking in the United States* (1922), 3–5, 12–13, Bank Legislation, 1921–22, General Office File, Box 108, Borah Papers.

56. Ibid., 16; Committee of One Hundred, *Branch Banking Legislation,* Bulletin No. 3 (1926), Bank Legislation, 1925–26, General Office File, Box 198, Borah Papers; Borah to Ramsay M. Walker, and attachment, 14 December 1926, Bank Legislation, 1926–27, General Office File, Box 224, Borah Papers; Walsh to G. E. Bowerman, 17 January 1927, 1, Legislation-Banking, Legislative File, Box 263, Walsh Papers.

57. "A New McFadden Obstacle," *Journal of Commerce,* 31 January 1927, 1; "The Passage of the McFadden Branch Banking Bill," *Commercial and Financial Chronicle,* 29 January 1927, 545–48; Shipstead, *CR,* 69th Cong., 2d sess., 68 (16 February 1927), 3948–49.

58. Shipstead, *CR,* 68th Cong., 1st sess., 65 (1 February 1924), 87–88; Shipstead, *CR,* 68th Cong., 2d sess., 66 (21 January 1925), 2204 (quote). Industrial declines centered on iron and steel, coal, lumber, hides, shoes, autos, and construction.

59. Luthin, "Smith Wildman Brookhart of Iowa," 187–95; Cowing, "Sons of the Wild Jackass," 142–45.

60. Cowing, "Sons of the Wild Jackass," 144–45.

61. Ibid., 144n, 145, 145n, 147 (McMaster quote), 152 (Heflin quote). Supporters of the McMaster amendment included Blaine, Brookhart, Bronson M. Cutting, Clarrence C. Dill, Robert Howell, H. Johnson, La Follette Jr., G. Nye, Norris, Shipstead, and Elmer Thomas. Norbeck was absent but strongly favored the proposal. Ibid., 147n.

62. "Calls Progressives in Senate to Unite," *New York Times,* 15 September 1927, 1; "Senator Nye Outlines Insurgent Program," *New York Times,* 20 September 1927, 10; "Nye Paints Lowden as Still Untested," *New York Times,* 19 October 1927, 3. Portions of this and the next two paragraphs are from D. A. Horowitz, "Perils of Western Farm Politics," 96–98.

63. "Fail to Fix Course on Vare and Smith," *New York Times,* 3 December 1927, 2; "Insurgents Demand Republican Pledge," *New York Times,* 4 December 1927, 3; "Nye Thinks Curtis the Likely Winner," *New York Times,* 28 December 1927, 15; "Both Parties Watch Dakota Situation," *New York Times,* 29

January 1928, 2; L. C. Speers, "Seven Men Hold the Key to the Senate," *New York Times,* 4 December 1927, sec. 11: 1; Ashby, *Spearless Leader,* 218–21, 223–31, 235–37. .

64. Ashby, *Spearless Leader,* 268–70; Press Release, "Townley's Non-Partisan League," June 1928, Campaign and Transition, 1928–29, Hoover Presidential Papers; "Corn Belt Committee, 1928," Agriculture, 1928, Misrepresentations File, Hoover Presidential Papers; Fite, "Agricultural Issues in the Presidential Campaign of 1928," 653–73; Fausold, "President Hoover's Farm Policies," 364; Fite, *Peter Norbeck,* 132–33.

65. R. La Follette Jr., Minority Report on Platform, 1928 Kansas City Speech, Speeches and Articles, Box C-554, R. La Follette Jr. Papers; Maney, *"Young Bob" La Follette,* 59–61; Ashby, *Spearless Leader,* 268, 270, 275–76; John P. Robertson to Donald G. Hughes, 3 June 1928, and Telegram, Norris to Borah, 14 June 1928, Norris-for-President, 1927–31, Norris Papers; Fite, *Peter Norbeck,* 135.

66. R. La Follette Jr. to W. T. Rawleigh, 3 September 1929, Personal Correspondence, Box C-8, R. La Follette Jr. Papers; Fite, *Peter Norbeck,* 136–37; "Progressives of the Senate," 385–87.

67. Norris to E. A. Morse, 17 May 1926, Norris Recall (War Vote, 1928), Box 46, Norris Papers; Norris to Judson King, 13 July 1929, National Progressive League, Box 2, Norris Papers; Lowitt, *Norris: 1913–1933,* 197–216, 244–59, 330–47, 445–51, 457–67.

68. R. La Follette Jr. Radio Broadcast Draft, 1928, 1, Coolidge Administration, 1928, Speeches and Articles, Box C-554, R. La Follette Jr. Papers; Borah quoted in Frederick William Wile, "The Future of the Progressive Movement," n.d., 1, 5, Speeches and Statements, January–November 1925 and undated, Box 780, Borah Papers; Norbeck to William Hirth, 16 December 1929, Hirth Correspondence Folder, 1929–30, Box 1, Norbeck Letters; Hard, "In Bad All Around," 599; Hard, "Where Are the Pre-War Radicals?" 559; Ashby, *Spearless Leader,* 64–65.

69. Norris to Edward Keating, 5 August 1929, 1, Progressives (1922–29), Box 298, Norris Papers. For farmer-labor split, see Olssen, "Progressive Group in Congress"; and Ashby, *Spearless Leader,* 7, 11, 63, 65.

70. Quoted in Cowing, "Sons of the Wild Jackass," 155.

Chapter 4: Two Nations

1. "Klan Doctrine," *Imperial Night-Hawk,* 9 January 1924, 2–3.

2. Warren I. Susman, "Personality and the Making of Twentieth Century Culture," in Higham and Conkin, eds., *New Directions in American Intellectual History,* 220–21; May, *Screening Out the Past,* xii–xiii, 98, 116–17, 146, 197–99, 201–2. See also D. Bell, *Cultural Contradictions of Capitalism,* 67–68; Erenberg, *Steppin' Out;* Ostrander, *American Civilization in the First Machine Age;* and Fass, *Damned and the Beautiful.*

3. Lippmann quoted by Levine, "Progress and Nostalgia," in Levine and Middlekauff, eds., *National Temper,* 293; Lears, *No Place of Grace,* 54, 223. For the ethnocultural conflicts of the 1920s, see Hawley, *Great War,* 71–73, 107–10, 126–29.

4. Kirschner, *City and Country,* 21, 5–8, 136, 151–53, 168, 170, 183–201, 215, 238–39.

5. Burner, *Politics of Provincialism,* 4, 11, 77–79; Kirschner, *City and Country,* xix, 23–26, 40–41, 47–50, 60–62, 234–41; Hofstadter, *Age of Reform,* 294.

6. Kirschner, *City and Country,* 49 (quote); Lowitt, *Norris: 1913–1933,* 9 (first Norris quote), 324 (second Norris quote); R. La Follette to Family, 24 April 1919 (first La Follette quote), R. La Follette to R. La Follette Jr., 12 May 1919 (second La Follette quote), and R. La Follette to Family, 20 April 1919 (third La Follette quote), Box A-27, La Follette Family Papers.

7. H. Johnson to Hiram W. Johnson Jr., 2 July 1921, in Burke, ed., *Diary Letters of Hiram Johnson,* vol. 3: 1–2; H. Johnson to Archibald M. Johnson, 23 November 1929, in ibid., vol. 5: 2.

8. Ashby, *Spearless Leader,* 233, 238, 240–43, 257–57, 278–79; Kirschner, *City and Country,* 18; Mulder, *Insurgent Progressives,* 19; Maney, *"Young Bob" La Follette,* 70; Ruetten, "Burton K. Wheeler," 40; Petry, "Morality Legislation in North Dakota," 48; Blackorby, *Prairie Rebel,* 85.

9. Thelen, *Paths of Resistance,* 154; Levine, *Defender of the Faith,* 103–9.

10. Petry, "Morality Legislation in North Dakota," 13–27, 35–36, 48; Blue Laws, 1920–21, General Office File, Box 89, Borah Papers; "A Bill vs. Race Track Touts and Pimps—Not vs. News," (1922), Anti-Gambling Bills, 1921–22, Box 105, Borah Papers; Levine, *Defender of the Faith,* 209–10.

11. Flink, *Car Culture,* 144–45, 154, 157–59; quoted in Aikman, *Home Town Mind,* 37. For auto culture, see Brownell, "A Symbol of Modernity," 23–24; 33, 37–39, 42–43.

12. Marsden, *Fundamentalism and American Culture,* 141–95; Levine, *Defender of the Faith,* 254–92; Gerald B. Winrod, *Defender,* January 1928, quoted in Ribuffo, *Old Christian Right,* 91, 82–87.

13. Leuchtenburg, *Perils of Prosperity,* 217–21.

14. Clements, *Bryan,* 6, 10–11, 141–42; Levine, *Defender of the Faith,* 261–69, 279; Ashby, *Bryan,* 180, 183–84. Bryan misread Darwin's metaphor of natural selection as a survival of the strongest and most ruthless instead of a survival of the most "fit." S. Gould, "William Jennings Bryan's Last Campaign," 16ff.

15. Bender, *Community and Social Change,* 138; Ashby, *Bryan,* xvi (first Bryan quote), 184, 187 (second Bryan quote), 188–90, 192, 196.

16. Levine, *Defender of the Faith,* 220–28, 278, 294, 325–54 (first Bryan quote on 331; second on 228, fourth on 221); Clements, *Bryan,* 141–42; Bryan Speech before Democratic National Convention of 1924, in Ginger, ed., *William Jennings Bryan,* 222 (third Bryan quote).

17. Leuchtenburg, *Perils of Prosperity,* 222–23; Ashby, *Bryan,* 183–88, 196–202.

18. May, *Screening Out the Past,* xii, xv, 54, 98, 103–9, 125, 143, 145, 169–78, 211, 217, 223, 237, 253; Jowett, *Film, the Democratic Art,* 188–90; Press Release, Motion Picture Producers and Distributors Association, "Motion Pictures and Emotion by Dr. William M. Marston," 15 April 1929, 1, Part 1, Reel 1, Frame 168, Hays Papers; Vaughn, "Morality and Entertainment," 41; Kett, *Rites of Passage,* 258.

19. Pivar, *Purity Crusade*, 154–64, 265–66; Cott, *Grounding of Modern Feminism*, 87–91; Kirschner, *Paradox of Professionalism*, 32–40; Jowett, *Film, the Democratic Art*, 76–81, 113–18, 126–30; May, *Screening Out the Past*, 44–46, 49–59; Vaughn, "Morality and Entertainment," 39–40; Justice Hinman, Third Department of the Appellate Division of the New York Supreme Court, 6 July 1922, quoted in Chase, *Catechism on Motion Pictures*, 9; Chase, *Catechism on Motion Pictures*, 5.

20. *CR*, 64th Cong., 1st sess., 53 (20 April, 17 May 1916), 6476, 8221; *CR*, 66th Cong., 2d sess., 59 (7, 28 January, 17 May, 2, 4 June 1920), 1157, 1204, 2178–79, 7162, 8280, 8563; *CR*, 67th Cong., 1st sess., 61 (11 October 1921), 6247.

21. R. Sklar, *Movie-Made America*, 78–79, 132; May, *Screening Out the Past*, 179, 204–5; Jowett, *Film, the Democratic Art*, 164–79; Ellis Hawley, "Three Facets of Hooverian Associationalism: Lumber, Aviation, and Movies, 1921–1930," in McCraw, ed., *Regulation in Perspective*, 115–18; Ivy Lee to Will Hays, 25 April 1925, Part 1, Reel 21, Frame 989, Hays Papers; Olasky, "Failure of Movie Industry Public Relations," 163–75.

22. Olasky, "Failure of Movie Industry Public Relations," 163–75; Jowett, *Film, the Democratic Art*, 233–40; Vaughn, "Morality and Entertainment," 45–46, 48, 52–56.

23. Olasky, "Failure of Movie Industry Public Relations," 166; Jowett, *Film, the Democratic Art*, 154, 178; *Public Relations of the Motion Picture Industry*, 71–72; Federal Motion Picture Council in America (hereafter FMPC), *Motion Picture Leaflet*, 11 February 1939, Historical Data, Box 80, Gilman Papers; Henry L. Myers, "The Motion-Picture Industry," *CR*, 67th Cong., 2d sess., 72 (29 June 1922), 9657.

24. Elizabeth Gilman, "Catheryne Cooke Gilman, Social Worker," in Stuhler and Kreuter, eds., *Women of Minnesota*, 191–98, 203–5; Chambers, *Seedtime of Reform*, 92–93, 122, 127, 147–48; *Public Relations of the Motion Picture Industry*, 107–8; C. Gilman Address before National Conference of Social Work, 16 June 1931, and Motion Picture Leaflet, 11 February 1939, General Motion Pictures File, Box 62, Gilman Papers; Proposed Rider, National Council of Women, 2, attached to C. Gilman to Laura Dreyfus-Barney, 23 September 1929, Motion Picture Files, National Council of Women Correspondence, July–December 1929, Box 69, Gilman Papers; Rev. G. I. Humphreys quoted in press clipping, "Commercialization up at Women's Meet," 6 May 1930, Part 2, Reel 4, Frames 317–18, Hays Papers.

25. Excerpts from report of Professor Ernest Burgess for Chicago Motion Picture Commission, September 1920, and L. A. Averill, *Education Film Magazine* (July 1920), quoted in Chase, *Catechism on Motion Pictures*, 23–24; Historical Sketch, 2, Motion Picture Files, National Committee for the Study of Social Values in Motion Pictures, Box 70, Gilman Papers; Jowett, *Film, the Democratic Art*, 220–25; R. Sklar, *Movie-Made America*, 134–35; William H. Short to Gilman, and attachments, 13 May 1929, and Mark A. May to Gilman, 6 June 1929, Motion Picture Files, Correspondence, June–December 1929, Box 71, Gilman Papers; Vaughn, "Morality and Entertainment," 63; Eastman, "Our

Children and the Movies," 110. For a popularized version of the research sponsored by the Payne Foundation, see Forman, *Our Movie Made Children.* For similar critiques, see Eastman, "The Menace of the Movies."

26. Hampton, *History of the American Film Industry,* 260–64; Gomery, *Hollywood Studio System,* 2, 5; Huettig, *Economic Control of the Motion Picture Industry,* 63–64; Donahue, *American Film Distribution,* 21; R. Sklar, *Movie-Made America,* 144–48; Jowett, *Film, the Democratic Art,* 198; May, *Screening Out the Past,* 175–79, 253.

27. Preliminary Report of Arthur Butler Graham on Trade Practices Existing in the Motion Picture Industry in the United States of America to the Committee on Research of the Motion Picture Council, 3–7, Motion Picture Research Council (hereafter MPRC), Correspondence, 1932–33, Box 72, Gilman Papers; Donahue, *American Film Distribution,* 8–24; Huettig, *Economic Control of the Motion Picture Industry,* 63, 74–78, 116–25; George S. Schaffer to U.S. Attorney General and Sen. Thomas Walsh, 17 August 1930, and R. Souitteo to Walsh, n.d., Investigation Motion Pictures, Subject File B, Box 189, Walsh Papers.

28. Cohen quoted in Chase, *Catechism on Motion Pictures,* 5; Press Release, Motion Picture Theater Owners of America, 29 January 1925, 1–3, Part 1, Reel 20, Frames 19–23, Hays Papers; newspaper clipping, *Providence Bulletin,* 3 February 1925, Frame 787, Hays Papers; "Plan Movie 'Trust' Fight," *New York Times,* 6 March 1925, 22. For background on Cohen, see "Governor Is Firm on Censoring Films," *New York Times,* 1 April 1921, 17.

29. Donahue, *American Film Distribution,* 23; ASAMPE quoted in *Public Relations of the Motion Picture Industry,* 26, 43.

30. C. Gilman to Laura Dreyfus-Barney, 30 December 1927, Motion Picture Files, National Council of Women, Correspondence, 1927–28, Box 69; C. Gilman to William H. Short, 4 February 1928, Motion Picture Files, National Committee for the Study of Social Values in Motion Pictures, Correspondence, 1928, Box 71; and Graham Report, 6, 8, MPRC Correspondence, 1932–33, Box 72, all in Gilman Papers; Chase, *Case for the Federal Supervision of Motion Pictures,* 24–25, 30–31, 170–71.

31. Appleby, *CR,* 67th Cong., 2d sess., 62 (22 February 1922), 2917; entry on William D. Upshaw, *Dictionary of American Biography: Supplement Five,* 701; Upshaw, "The Child and the Motion Picture," address delivered before the National Education Association, Philadelphia, 29 June 1926, *CR,* 69th Cong., 1st sess., 67 (2 July 1926), 12841–42; Upshaw, *CR,* 68th Cong., 1st sess., 65 (2 February 1924), 2221; Swoope, *CR,* 68th Cong., 2d sess., 66 (14 February 1925), 3741–42; Swoope, *CR,* 69th Cong., 1st sess., 67 (8, 19 December 1925), 530, 1190–92; C[harles]. C. P[ettijohn] to Will H. Hays, 10 February 1927, Part 1, Reel 31, Frames 708–9, Hays Papers.

32. C. Gilman to Morey V. Kerns, 27 December 1927, Motion Picture Files, National Council of Women, Correspondence, 1927–28, Box 69, Gilman Papers; Hampton, *History of the American Film Industry,* 276–77, 365, 368, 391, 393; Simon N. Whitney, "Antitrust Policies and the Motion Picture Industry," in Kindem, ed., *American Movie Industry,* 163–64. The action against Warner Bros.

resulted in a jury acquittal in 1935. The government withdrew from the case against Fox in 1940.

33. Walsh, *CR*, 70th Cong., 1st sess., 69 (22 May 1928), 9429; Dill, *CR*, 71st Cong., 3d sess., 74 (3 March 1931), 7101–2; Brookhart, *CR*, 70th Cong., 2d sess., 70 (15 February 1929), 3554; Brookhart, *CR*, 71st Cong., 1st sess., 71 (2 May, 19 June 1929), 927–28, 3095–96; entry on Grant M. Hudson, *Who's Who in America*, 1190; Hudson, *CR*, 70th Cong., 1st sess., 69 (11 May 1928), 8479; Hudson, *CR*, 71st Cong., 2d sess., 72 (17 February, 26 May 1930), 3829, 6104–5, 9605–6; *Public Relations of the Motion Picture Industry*, 108–10. A summary of proposed legislation can be found in Morrison, "Movies before Congress," 646–47.

34. Editorial, *Washington Herald*, 20 March 1929; press clipping, "'The Churchman' Attacks Will Hays," 29 June 1929, Part 2, Reel 2, Frame 190, Hays Papers; *Churchman*, 13 July 1929, quoted in Olasky, "Failure of Movie Industry Public Relations," 167; Anna Garlin Spencer to C. Gilman, 15 June 1927, and C. Gilman to Spencer, 15 July 1927, Motion Picture Files, National Council of Women, Correspondence, 1927–28, Box 69, Gilman Papers; Mrs. Ambrose N. Diehl to H. C. Cose, 13 July 1928, 1–2, Part 1, Reel 41, Frames 682–86, Hays Papers; Press Release, MPPDA, 12 November 1929, 1, Part 1, Reel 3, Frames 325–27, Hayes Papers; C. Gilman to Mrs. B. S. Gadd, 21 January 1929, Motion Picture Files, National Council of Women, Correspondence, 1927–28, Box 69, Gilman Papers; Black, "Motion Picture Censorship," speech before National Board of Review of Motion Pictures, n.d., *CR*, 70th Cong., 2d sess., 70 (15 February 1929), 3554.

35. "Screen Ridicule of Protestant Ministry," *Imperial Night-Hawk*, 4 April 1923, 3; Chase, *Catechism on Motion Pictures*, 57, 115–17; Ribuffo, *Old Christian Right*, 5, 10–11; Kirschner, *City and Country*, 32–36; Ford, *International Jew*, quoted in G. S. Smith, *To Save a Nation*, 75–76. For an example of genteel anti-Semitism, see Eastman, "Who Controls the Movies?" 173.

36. Ford quoted in G. S. Smith, *To Save a Nation*, 75–76; Ribuffo, *Old Christian Right*, 45.

37. Entry of 20 September 1921, in Levine, ed., "'Diary' of Hiram Johnson," 70.

38. Kirschner, *City and Country*, 246, 252, 12–16, 27–30, 47–48, 35 (quote).

39. Leuchtenburg, *Perils of Prosperity*, 206–8.

40. Borah speech, *CR*, 69th Cong., 1st sess., 65 (14 April 1924), 6304; Norbeck to W. C. Gemmill, 20 May 1924, 1924 Correspondence, Box 1, Norbeck Letters; Capper, *CR*, 68th Cong., 1st sess., 65 (8 April 1924), 5823–24.

41. Norris quoted in Lowitt, *Norris: 1913–1933*, 326; H. Johnson, *CR*, 68th Cong., 1st sess., 65 (9 April 1924), 5951–52; Statement of U.S. Sen. Hiram W. Johnson, 30 April 1924, Speeches, Statements, and Press Releases, January–December 1924, Carton 25, H. Johnson Papers.

42. Leuchtenburg, *Perils of Prosperity*, 208; *CR*, 68th Cong., 1st sess., 65 (18 April 1924), 6649. The law originally tied immigration quotas to the 1890 Census but stipulated that later ratios would be based on 1920 figures.

43. Goldberg, *Grassroots Resistance*, 66–67, 70; Shawn Lay, "Introduction:

The Second Invisible Empire," in Lay, ed., *Invisible Empire in the West*, 3–9; Jackson, *Klan in the City*, 3–23. See also Blee, *Women of the Klan*.

44. Goldberg, *Grassroots Resistance*, 70; Jackson, *Klan in the City*, 15, 156–57, 190, 236–37; Frost, *Challenge of the Klan*, 22–23.

45. *Papers Read at the Meeting of Grand Dragons*, 124, 62; "Klan Doctrine," *Imperial Night-Hawk*, 9 January 1924, 2; Evans, "Klan's Fight for Americanism," 36, 54, 61; "The True Spirit of American Klansmen," *Imperial Night-Hawk*, 16 May 1923, 7; "American Government and Covenant Dependent on Protestant Anglo-Saxons," *Imperial Night-Hawk*, 12 March 1924, 2; Hiram Wesley Evans, "The Klan of Tomorrow," *Imperial Night-Hawk*, 15 October 1924, 2.

46. Evans, "Klan's Fight for Americanism," 36 (first quote), 54 (second quote); Evans, "Our Crusading Army," 3; "How the Klan Can Be Made a True Civic Asset in Every Progressive Community," *Imperial Night-Hawk*, 5 September 1923, 7; "Editorial Comment," *Imperial Night-Hawk*, 24 September 1924, 5.

47. Paul S. Etheridge, "Brief Interpretations of the By Laws and Constitution of the Klan," *Imperial Night-Hawk*, 3 September 1924, 3; Curry, *Klan under the Searchlight*, 8, 27, 41, 112; Simmons, *Klan Unmasked*, 89–90; "The Definition of Klannishness," *Imperial Night-Hawk*, 5 March 1924, 1; *Papers Read at the Meeting of Grand Dragons*, 49; Evans, *Public School Problem in America*, 3, 5; W. C. Wright, "A Klansman's Criteria of Character," *Imperial Night-Hawk*, 6 February 1924, 2; Evans, "Ballots behind the Ku Klux Klan," 246; "Klan Funeral Witnessed by Seven Thousand in Portage, Pa.," *Imperial Night-Hawk*, 5 March 1924, 6; "Sacred Music at Convention," *Imperial Night-Hawk*, 25 June 1924, 7; "Entertainment for Klaveliers," *Imperial Night-Hawk*, 25 June 1924, 8; Greenway, "Country-Western," 35–36. For Klan purity activities, see Coben, *Rebellion against Victorianism*, 136–39. Klan rules stipulated that masks could be worn only in the lodge, at public initiations, or in public parades by special permission. *Imperial Night-Hawk*, 30 May 1923, 7.

48. *Papers Read at the Meeting of Grand Dragons*, 70–73, 11–12, 60, 119–22, 125, 12; Evans, "Klan's Fight for Americanism," 39–40, 44–47; "Imperial Wizard Outlines Objectives," *Imperial Night-Hawk*, 18 July 1923, 6; Evans, *Menace of Modern Immigration*, 5, 16–17 (quotes), 22–24; Reverend Sam H. Campbell, "The Jewish Problem in the United States Discussed by Prominent Georgia Minister," *Imperial Night-Hawk*, 27 June 1923, 6; Curry, *Klan under the Searchlight*, 161–62; Evans, "The Klan of Tomorrow," *Imperial Night-Hawk*, 15 October 1924, 2.

49. *Papers Read at the Meeting of Grand Dragons*, 59–60 (first quote); Simmons, *Klan Unmasked*, 31–32 (second quote), 34 (third quote); Bohn, "The KKK Interpreted," 389 (fourth quote). For Klan nativism, see Evans, *Menace of Modern Immigration*, 18. For an analysis of Klan populism, see "Political Fundamentalism and Popular Democracy in the 1920s," 225–26.

50. Evans, "Klan's Fight for Americanism," 61; *Papers Read at the Meeting of Grand Dragons*, 117, 70–71, 25, 63.

51. Toy, "Ku Klux Klan in Oregon," 17; Tindall, *Emergence of the New South*, 192; Jackson, *Klan in the City*, 83; "The Klan's Attitude toward the Negro,"

Imperial Night-Hawk, 23 July 1924, 2; Evans, "Klan's Fight for Americanism," 37; Burner, *Politics of Provincialism*, 81n.

52. Evans, *Public School Problem in America*, 3 (first quote), 5 (second quote), 4 (third quote); Evans, "Klan's Fight for Americanism," 38–39 (fourth, fifth, and sixth quotes).

53. Evans, "Klan's Fight for Americanism," 39, 42–43, 49, 51; Evans, *Public School Problem in America*, 33–34; *Is the Ku Klux Klan Constructive or Destructive*, 2; Evans, "The Klan of Tomorrow," *Imperial Night-Hawk*, 15 October 1924, 1–3.

54. Coben, *Rebellion against Victorianism*, 136 (first quote); Blee, *Women of the Klan*, 80, 85, 103–18, 122; Loucks, *Klan in Pennsylvania*, 40–44; Grand Dragon, Realm of Oregon, in *Papers Read at the Meeting of Grand Dragons*, 82 (second quote); D. A. Horowitz, "Social Morality and Personal Revitalization," 371 (third quote); LaLande, "Beneath the Hooded Robe," 47; Snell, "Fiery Crosses," 269–70.

55. Protestant, "The Ku Klux Klan and Mer Rouge" (first quote), Ku Klux Klan, 1922–23, General Office File, Borah Papers; Jackson, *Klan in the City*, 67–68 (second quote on 67); *Papers Read at the Meeting of Grand Dragons*, 19, 55, 57; Alexander, *Klan in the Southwest*, 21, 27, 31, 35; *Marshfield News*, 24 December 1923, quoted in Saalfeld, *Forces of Prejudice in Oregon*, 10 (third quote).

56. Jenkins, "Ku Klux Klan in Youngstown, Ohio," 76–78; Jenkins, *Klan in Ohio's Mahoning Valley*, ix, 41; Goldberg, *Hooded Empire*, 19, 22, 24, 26, 29, 67, 166–67; Toy, "Ku Klux Klan in Oregon," 32–33; "Klan Letter Is Answered," *Morning Astorian*, 18 June 1922, 1, 5; Shawn Lay, "Imperial Outpost on the Border: El Paso's Frontier Klan No. 100," in Lay, ed., *Invisible Empire in the West*, 70–73.

57. Moore, *Citizen Klansmen*, 11–12, 79, 188–89, 191 (quote on 188).

58. Evans, "Klan's Fight for Americanism," 33–35, 38–39, 49, 55.

59. Moore, *Citizen Klansmen*, 188–90; Christopher N. Cocoltochos, "The Invisible Empire and the Search for Orderly Community: The Ku Klux Klan in Anaheim, California," in Lay, ed., *Invisible Empire in the West*, 102–3; Larry R. Gerlach, "A Battle of Empires: The Klan in Salt Lake City," in Lay, ed., *Invisible Empire in the West*, 127; Shawn Lay, "Imperial Outpost on the Border: El Paso's Frontier Klan No. 100," in Lay, ed., *Invisible Empire in the West*, 76; Alexander, *Klan in the Southwest*, 26–27; Goldberg, *Hooded Empire*, 118, 121–24, 128; Robert A. Goldberg, "Denver: Queen City of the Colorado Realm," in Lay, ed., *Invisible Empire in the West*, 37–38; Jackson, *Klan in the City*, 38–39, 47; Wald, "Visible Empire," 221; Woodward, *Tom Watson*, 468; D. A. Horowitz, "Klansman as Outsider," 15–18. For an example of Klan cooperation with African American voters, see Adkins, "Beale Street Goes to the Polls," 38–40. Alien land laws in Oregon, California, and Washington prohibited immigrants ineligible for citizenship from owning property in their own names and were directed at Japanese farmers and orchardists.

60. D. A. Horowitz, "Klansman as Outsider," 19; and David A. Horowitz, "Order, Solidarity, and Vigilance: The Ku Klux Klan in La Grande, Oregon," in Lay, ed., *Invisible Empire in the West*, 194–96; K.K.K. Statement, 1924, Box B-

230, R. La Follette Papers; B. La Follette and F. La Follette, *La Follette,* vol. 2: 1119–20; MacKay, *Progressive Movement of 1924,* 147, 215–16; Emil E. Holmes to Henry G. Teigan, 21 August 1926, Correspondence and Misc. Papers, June–August 1926, Box 1, Farmer-Labor Association Papers; Chas. K. Hankschu to Henrik Shipstead, 3 February 1926, Correspondence, 1926–34, Box 1, Shipstead Papers; Frank Vogel to G. Nye, postscript, 5 May 1926, Correspondence, May–December 1926, Box 66, G. Nye Papers. The KKK opposed the World Court because its membership was predominantly Roman Catholic and the Klan rejected European entanglements. Evans, "Ballots behind the Ku Klux Klan," 246.

61. Goldberg, *Grassroots Resistance,* 87–89, 79–82; Lay, "Conclusion," in Lay, ed., *Invisible Empire in the West,* 218–21; Burner, *Politics of Provincialism,* 89–90; Patton, "A Ku Klux Klan Reign of Terror," 53–54; Moore, *Citizen Klansmen,* 11; Goldberg, "Denver: Queen City of the Colorado Realm," in Lay, ed., *Invisible Empire in the West,* 52–54, 63, 69; Eckard Vance Toy, Jr., "Robe and Gown: The Ku Klux Klan in Eugene, Oregon," in Lay, ed., *Invisible Empire in the West,* 166; David A. Horowitz, "Order, Solidarity, and Vigilance: The Ku Klux Klan in La Grande, Oregon," in Lay, ed., *Invisible Empire in the West,* 195, 209; D. A. Horowitz, "Social Morality and Social Revitalization," 378–80.

62. Burner, *Politics of Provincialism,* 120–25; Leuchtenburg, *Perils of Prosperity,* 230–32; Bryan quoted in Ashby, *Bryan,* 181; Levine, *Defender of the Faith,* 309–16.

63. White quoted in Ashby, *Spearless Leader,* 272; *Christian Century* quoted in Leuchtenburg, *Perils of Prosperity,* 235; Lippmann quoted in Leuchtenburg, *Perils of Prosperity,* 240; Mencken quoted in Kirschner, *City and Country,* 51. For background on the Smith candidacy, see Burner, *Politics of Provincialism,* 187–93, 202–16.

64. Burner, *Politics of Provincialism,* 187; Leuchtenburg, *Perils of Prosperity,* 233–37; Levine, *Defender of the Faith,* 180.

65. Leuchtenburg, *Perils of Prosperity,* 223; Burner, *Politics of Provincialism,* 96–102; Kirschner, *City and Country,* 83, 246–55.

66. Kirschner, *City and Country,* 247, 251; D. Bell, *Contradictions of Capitalism,* xxii–xxv, 21–22.

Chapter 5: Farmers, the Money Power, and Depression Radicals, 1929–36

1. Lemke to Vanderbilt Jr., 5 May 1934, Folder 17, Box 11, Lemke Papers; Lemke Statement, quoted in Lynn Frazier, *CR,* 72d Cong., 2d sess., 76 (25 January 1933), 2517–18.

2. Shover, *Cornbelt Rebellion;* Hicks and Saloutos, *Agricultural Discontent in the Middle West,* 433, 448–50; R. Nye, *Midwestern Progressive Politics,* 359; Leuchtenburg, *Franklin D. Roosevelt,* 23–26; Stock, *Main Street in Crisis,* 128–47.

3. Borah to Ray McKaig, 18 February 1933, Ray McKaig, 1932–33, General Office File, Box 365, Borah Papers; G. Nye, interviewed by Charles P. Stewart, June 1932, reprinted in Nye Press Release, June 1932, Campaign File, Cam-

paign of 1932, Box 17C, G. Nye Papers; G. Nye, *CR,* 72d Cong., 1st sess., 75 (13 June 1932), 12769–70; Frank N. Briggs to Norris, 25 February 1933, and attachment, Spider Web of Wall Street, Box 298, Norris Papers.

4. Norbeck to William Habel, 9 January 1933, attached to Norbeck to Robert C. Hardy, 21 April 1933, Bank Reform (4), Box 1, Norbeck Papers; McNary, "View and Review of Legislation Affecting Agriculture," Part 1, 28 September 1932, 1–2, 4, 8–9, General Correspondence, 1929–33, Box 5, McNary Papers.

5. D. A. Horowitz, "Perils of Western Farm Politics," 99–103.

6. McNary, *CR,* 72d Cong., 1st sess., 75 (13 June 1932), 12768–69.

7. G. Nye, "What Progressives Hope for in 1932," radio address, 7 January 1932, "Addresses, 1932," Addresses and Speeches, Box 31, G. Nye Papers; Brookhart, *CR,* 72d Cong., 1st sess., 75 (13, 15 June 1932), 12770–72, 12997, 13000.

8. Hicks and Saloutos, *Agricultural Discontent in the Middle West,* 461–70; Feinman, *Twilight of Progressivism,* 60–61.

9. Feinman, *Twilight of Progressivism,* 61; McNary to Ella Stolz, 3 April 1933, General Correspondence, Box 1, McNary Papers; Fite, *Peter Norbeck,* 193; Wheeler, *CR,* 73d Cong., 1st sess., 77 (12, 19 April 1933), 1569.

10. Simpson, quoted in Fite, "Farmer Opinion and the Agricultural Adjustment Act," 660; Simpson to FDR, 24 October 1933, 1–2, Folder 12, October–December 1933, Box 11, Lemke Papers. For background on Simpson, see *Dictionary of American Biography,* vol. 17: 180–81.

11. Weeks, "Usher L. Burdick in Congress," 39; Blackorby, *Prairie Rebel,* 183.

12. Blackorby, *Prairie Rebel,* 3–4, 11, 28, 190n; Bennett, *Demagogues in the Depression,* 93, 194. Lemke's monetary theories are explained in Lemke, *You and Your Money.*

13. Lemke to Val P. Wolf, 18 March 1933 (first quote), and Lemke to C. H. Hyde, 18 March 1933 (second quote), Folder 8, January–March 1933, Box 11, Lemke Papers; Lemke, *CR,* 73d Cong., 2d sess., 78 (16 January 1934), 724 (third quote); Blackorby, *Prairie Rebel,* 191–95; Bennett, *Demagogues in the Depression,* 95 (fourth and fifth quotes).

14. Blackorby, *Prairie Rebel,* 190–91, 196; Lemke to W. H. Harvey, and attachments, 26 May 1934, Folder 17, Box 11, Lemke Papers.

15. Blackorby, *Prairie Rebel,* 180–85; Frazier, *CR,* 73d Cong., 1st sess., 77 (21, 22 April 1933), 2098–99, 2161; Lemke Press Release of NBC Radio Address, 16 April 1934, 3, Folder 16, April 1934, Box 11, Lemke Papers; Telegram, Stephen Early to FDR, and attachments, 9 April 1934, Office File (hereafter OF), 1038, FDR Library.

16. Rainey quoted in Stephen Early to FDR, and attachments, 9 April 1934; Telegram, FDR to Marvin H. McIntyre, 10 April 1934; Memo, John Dickinson to McIntyre, and attachments, 26 June 1934; Smith W. Brookhart to McIntyre, n.d.; Louis Howe to Fred R. Wolfe, and attachment and collection of telegrams and correspondence, 2 July 1934, all in OF 1038, FDR Library. The Lemke crusade is detailed in Bennett, *Demagogues in the Depression,* 96–97; and Blackorby, *Prairie Rebel,* 198–201.

17. Blackorby, *Prairie Rebel,* 207–8.

18. Ibid., 207–10; Charles G. Binderup et al. to FDR, 18 July 1935, OF 1038, FDR Library; Binderup, *CR,* 74th Cong., 1st sess., 79 (9 July 1935), 10864–65.

19. Blackorby, *Prairie Rebel,* 180–81; Bennett, *Demagogues in the Depression,* 97–98.

20. Lemke to Repr. Isabella Greenway, January 1935, quoted in Bennett, *Demagogues in the Depression,* 98; Lemke Statement, in Remarks of Lynn Frazier, *CR,* 72d Cong., 2d sess., 76 (25 January 1933), 2517–18.

21. Bennett, *Demagogues in the Depression,* 99–100; John L. Shuff to McIntyre, 6 May 1936, OF 1038, FDR Library; Farm Credit Administration, "Summary of Attached Analysis of HR 2066," n.d., attached to W. I. Myers to FDR, 26 March 26, 1937, OF 1038, FDR Library.

22. Blackorby, *Prairie Rebel,* 211–15; Bennett, *Demagogues in the Depression,* 98, 100–101; Lemke to T. K. Bergland, and attachment, 23 November 1936, Folder 14, October–November 1936, Box 2, Lemke Papers.

23. Editorial, "The Senate at Its Worst," *New York Herald Tribune,* 14 February 1930, 18; "Some of Senator Hiram W. Johnson's Recent Services to California," Political Campaign Material, 1934, Senatorial, Miscellaneous Papers, Carton 10, H. Johnson Papers; Fite, *Peter Norbeck,* 172. The six Hughes Senate opponents were John J. Blaine, Robert La Follette Jr., Norris, Borah, Brookhart, and Nye.

24. Fite, *Peter Norbeck,* 170, 174–76 (first quote on 174; second on 176), 178; Leuchtenburg, *Franklin D. Roosevelt,* 59; R. La Follette Jr. Radio Address, 9 June 1933, 9, Speeches and Articles, Box C-557, R. La Follette Jr. Papers; Lowitt, *Norris: 1913–1933,* 451.

25. R. La Follette Jr. and Edward P. Costigan to FDR, 8 March 1933, attached to R. La Follette Jr. to Hiram W. Johnson, 8 March 1933, Personal Correspondence, Box C-11, R. La Follette Jr. Papers; Feinman, *Twilight of Progressivism,* 58; Lemke to J. A. Gray, 31 March 1933, Folder 8, January–March 1933, Box 11, Lemke Papers.

26. Leuchtenburg, *Franklin D. Roosevelt,* 60; Brinkley, *Voices of Protest,* 55–56; P. La Follette, Message to Special Session of Legislature, 24 November 1931, "Quotations from Some of the Addresses of Governor La Follette," Control of Credit (1938), Press Releases, November–December 1938, Box 129, P. La Follette Papers.

27. R. La Follette Jr. Radio Address, 9 June 1933, 6, Speeches and Articles, Box C-557, La Follette Jr. Papers; Leuchtenburg, *Franklin D. Roosevelt,* 59, 90–91, 158–61; Mulder, "Progressive Insurgents," 116–17.

28. Wood to R. La Follette Jr., 7 March, 10 April 1933, Correspondence File, Box 9, Wood Papers.

29. Wood to R. La Follette Jr., 17 March, 18 May 1933, Correspondence File, Box 9; Wood to FDR, 27 January 1933, Correspondence File, Box 15; Wood to William H. Woodin, 17 March 1933, attached to Wood to R. La Follette Jr., 7 April 1933, Correspondence File, Box 9; Wood to R. La Follette Jr., 10 April 1933, Correspondence File, Box 9, all in Wood Papers.

30. Wood to R. La Follette Jr., 13 April 1933 (first quote), 18 May 1933, Correspondence File, Box 9; Wood to FDR, 24 October 1934 (second quote), Correspondence File, Box 15, all in Wood Papers.

31. Bennett, *Demagogues in the Depression,* 151–69; Bennett, *Party of Fear,* 249–51.

32. Press Release, 4 January 1932, Box 12, Wheeler Papers; Hawley, *New Deal and the Problem of Monopoly,* 316; Leuchtenburg, *Franklin D. Roosevelt,* 82; Ruetten, "Wheeler and the Montana Connection," 11; Ruetten, "Burton K. Wheeler," 113, 115, 118–19.

33. Ruetten, "Burton K. Wheeler," 118–19, 123, 125–26; Wheeler "Dishonest Bankers," radio address, 25 February 1933, Box 14 (40), Wheeler Papers; Leuchtenburg, *Franklin D. Roosevelt,* 50, 82.

34. Leuchtenburg, *Franklin D. Roosevelt,* 78–81; Wheeler, *CR,* 73d Cong., 1st sess., 77 (22 April 1933), 2148–49; Ruetten, "Burton K. Wheeler," 125–26; Borah to B. F. Miller, 13 January 1934, Currency and Money Question, December 1933–March 1934, Subject File, Box 761, Borah Papers.

35. Borah to H. G. Pine, 23 April 1934, attached to Pine to Borah, 20 April 1934, Currency and Money Question, April–May 1934, Subject File, Box 761, Borah Papers; Leuchtenburg, *Franklin D. Roosevelt,* 83; Ruetten, "Burton K. Wheeler," 135–37, 140, 143; Burton K. Wheeler Press Release, 1935, Box 12, Wheeler Papers.

36. Wright Patman entry, *Current Biography, 1946,* 461; Schmelzer, "Early Life and Early Congressional Career of Wright Patman," 2, 8, 10, 14, 16–17, 23–24, 34, 40, 48, 51, 53–55.

37. Schmelzer, "Early Life and Early Congressional Carreer of Wright Patman," 57–67, 69–74, 115; Patman, *CR,* 71st Cong., 1st sess., 71 (21 October 1929), 4697–98; Patman, *CR,* 72d Cong. 1st sess., 75 (13 April 1932), 8098.

38. Schmelzer, "Early Life and Early Congressional Career of Wright Patman," 126, 80, 87, 90, 99, 141; "Again Congress Faces Veterans' Legislation," *Congressional Digest* 11 (November 1932), 257, 267–68; Mulder, *Insurgent Progressives,* 97–98, 126; Leuchtenburg, *Franklin D. Roosevelt,* 13–16, 147; entry on Usher L. Burdick, *Current Biography, 1946,* 461. Patman's radio address on the bonus bill can be found in *CR,* 74th Cong., 1st Sess., 79 (21 February 1935), 2435–36.

39. Patman, *Banketeering, Bonuseering, Melloneering,* introduction.

40. Ibid., 7, 12, 15–17, 19–21, 25–30.

41. Hemphill and Owen quoted in Burdick, Notes on Monetary Conference, 20 February 1935, 2–4, Folder 36, Economics: Monetary Policy 1935, Box 6; Burdick, "Interest and How It Works" (quote), Folder 29, Economics: Interest 1940, Box 6; and Burdick, "Who Wants to be President?" n.d., Folder 32, Legislation: Presidential Powers, Box 13, all in Burdick Papers. For Owen's complete statement, see *CR,* 74th Cong., 1st sess., 79 (May 4, 1935), 6973–74.

42. Judge Richard McCarten to Lemke, 28 March 1933, Folder 8, January–March 1933; Lemke to Carl D. Thompson, May 1934, 16, 28, Folder 17, May 1934; and Lemke Radio Address, 26 May 1934, Folder 17, May 1934, all in Box 11, Lemke Papers; Blackorby, *Prairie Rebel,* 180–81, 234, 237.

43. Woodin to Sen. Duncan U. Fletcher, 3 May 1933, 2, Folder 10, May–June 1933, Box 11, Lemke Papers; Brinkley, *Voices of Protest,* 138–39; Patman Statement, *CR,* 74th Cong., 1st sess., 79 (1 May 1935), 6713; G. Nye, *CR,* 74th Cong., 1st sess., 79 (25 July 1935), 11842–43. Nye's Senate efforts were duplicated in the House by Ohio Democrat Martin Sweeney.

44. G. Nye, *CR*, 74th Cong., 1st sess., 79 (26 July 1935), 11906; Mulder, *Insurgent Progressives*, 112; Bennett, *Demagogues in the Depression*, 76; *CR*, 75th Cong., 3d sess., 83 (10, 24 January 1938), 303, 1010–11; entry on Wright Patman, *Current Biography*, 1946, 462.

45. Brinkley, *Voices of Protest*, 90–92, 94–97, 110, 119–20; Bennett, *Demagogues in Depression*, 50–51 (quote on 51).

46. Brinkley, *Voices of Protest*, 110–13; Telegram, Coughlin to FDR, 6 August 1933, attached to Marvin H. McIntyre to Coughlin, 8 August 1933, OF 306, FDR Library; Coughlin Form Letter, September 1934, OF 306, FDR Library. For Coughlin's monetary notions, see Coughlin, *New Deal in Money*.

47. G. S. Smith, *To Save a Nation*, 5, 7, 23 (Coughlin quote); Brinkley, *Voices of Protest*, 150; Bennett, *Demagogues in the Depression*, 52, 60–63, 66. Some 40 percent of the delegates to the 1936 National Union for Social Justice convention were women. Bennett, *Demagogues in the Depression*, 16.

48. Brinkley, *Voices of Protest*, 150.

49. Quoted in ibid., 126; *Detroit Evening Times*, 4 March 1935; *Detroit News*, 4 March 1935.

50. Quoted in Brinkley, *Voices of Protest*, 133 (first quote), 137 (second and third quotes).

51. "The National Union for Social Justice, 1935–1936," Public Works and Relief Projects (1931–38), Carton 9, H. Johnson Papers. For the complete text, see "Father Coughlin's Preamble and Principles of the National Union for Social Justice," in Brinkley, *Voices of Protest*, 287–88.

52. Brinkley, *Voices of Protest*, 287–88.

53. Ibid., 112–13, 175–77, 179; G. S. Smith, *To Save a Nation*, 36 (Coughlin quote).

54. G. S. Smith, *To Save a Nation*, 36, 38–39 (Coughlin quote on 39); Bennett, *Demagogues in the Depression*, 72–76; Brinkley, *Voices of Protest*, 103, 121, 138–39.

55. Brinkley, *Voices of Protest*, 187; W. L. Slattery to Postmaster General, 19 March 1935, OF 306, FDR Library; Shenton, "Coughlin Movement," 367; Marx, "Depression Era Extremist," 62–64, 94–95.

56. Paul W. Rieker to FDR, 30 March 1933, and A. M. Brinker to FDR, 29 October 1933, OF 306, FDR Library.

57. William Montague O'Neill to FDR, 3 March 1935, OF 306, FDR Library.

58. Brinkley, *Voices of Protest*, 17–22. For Long's background, see also Jeansonne, *Messiah of the Masses*.

59. Brinkley, *Voices of Protest*, 24–31.

60. Bennett, *Demagogues in the Depression*, 119–20; Brinkley, *Voices of Protest*, 27–29, 44 (first quote); Long Form Letter, 7 March 1933 (second quote), OF 1403, FDR Library.

61. Brinkley, *Voices of Protest*, 70–71; poster advertisement for *American Progress*, attached to Long to FDR, 27 July 1933, President's Personal Files (hereafter PPF) 2337, FDR Library.

62. Brinkley, *Voices of Protest*, 71–73; Bennett, *Demagogues in the Depression*, 120–21.

63. Long, "Our Blundering Government," radio address, NBC, 7 March 1935, 2–3, OF 1403, FDR Library; Brinkley, *Voices of Protest*, 71, 169.

64. Brinkley, *Voices of Protest*, 73, 158; Bennett, *Demagogues in the Depression*, 121.

65. Bennett, *Demagogues in the Depression*, 122–26; Brinkley, *Voices of Protest*, 74, 148–50, 181–82, 206; Burdick to Earle J. Christenberry, 21 January 1936, attached to Christenberry to Burdick, 10 January 1936, Folder 5, Huey Long, Box 17, Burdick Papers.

66. Brinkley, *Voices of Protest*, 229–33.

67. Ibid., 45–46, 78, 128, 174, 235–37; Statement of H. Johnson, ca. 10 September 1935, Speeches, Statements, and Press Releases, June 1932–January 1937, Carton 26, H. Johnson Papers; Burdick to R. G. Jenkins, 14 January 1935, Folder 5, Huey Long, Box 17, Burdick Papers.

68. Brinkley, *Voices of Protest*, 174–75, 207–9, 249–50, ix, 139–40, 144–45, 150, 177, 198, 212–13; Bennett, *Demagogues in the Depression*, 189–92, 196. Boston's Thomas Charles O'Brien, a former lawyer for the Brotherhood of Railway Trainmen and district attorney, accepted the party's vice presidential spot.

69. Bennett, *Demagogues in the Depression*, 14, 108–9, 193–94, 205–6 (quote on 193); McCoy, *Angry Voices*, 116–17, 145.

70. Bennett, *Demagogues in the Depression*, 13, 230 (Coughlin quotes); Blackorby, *Prairie Rebel*, 218.

71. Blackorby, *Prairie Rebel*, 228–30; Brinkley, *Voices of Protest*, 246–48, 257. For Lemke's working-class support, see Marx, "Depression Era Extremist," 32; and Bennett, *Party of Fear*, 261–63.

72. Bennett, *Demagogues in the Depression* 271; Brinkley, *Voices of Protest*. ix, 144–45, 150–56, 161, 168, 196, 282–83.

Chapter 6: "Natural Man vs. Corporate Man"

1. F. Harper, "'New Battle on Evolution,'" 422n; Ribuffo, *Old Christian Right*, xii.

2. Melvin T. Copeland, "Marketing," in Committee on Recent Economic Changes of the President's Conference on Unemployment, *Recent Economic Changes*, vol. 1: 362–69; Boorstin, *Americans*, 110; "Chains Now Do Sixth of Total Retail Sales," *Spectator* 48 (7 February 1931), 3; Lebhar, *Chain Stores*, 163; F. Harper, "'New Battle on Evolution,'" 410.

3. Loe, "Chain Store Distribution," 7–8; R. W. Lyons, "The Economic Aspects of the Chain Store," address delivered before the Economic Club of Chicago, 11 April 1929, Subject File, Chain Stores 1929–30, Hoover Presidential Papers; Hoover Acceptance Address, Palo Alto, Calif., 11 August 1928, in Hoover, *New Day*, 34.

4. Ryant, "Kentucky and the Movement to Regulate Trade Stores," 273–74; F. Harper, "'New Battle on Evolution,'" 409; J. Palmer, "Economic and Social Aspects of Chain Stores," 276.

5. Lebhar, *Chain Stores*, 139–42; Martin, "Independent, et al., versus the Chains," 47–56.

6. Webb, *Divided We Stand,* 57 (first quote); Filene, *Next Steps Forward in Retailing,* 22; F. Harper, "'New Battle on Evolution,'" 409–10; Lebhar, *Chain Stores,* 170; Flynn, "Chain Stores," 270–71; "War on the Chain Store," 544 (second quote). For background on the antichain movement, see Ryant, "South and the Movement against Chain Stores," 207–22; and Ryant, "Merchandising in the New Era," 202–10.

7. Rhodes, "The Mushroom Growth Chain a Liability to a Community," *Oregon Merchant's Magazine,* April 1930, 17; Jennie E. Applegate to FDR, 15 April 1933, OF 288, FDR Library.

8. H. C. Featherstone to Ray P. Chase, 18 January 1929, 24, Chain Stores, Box 6, Chase Papers; Flowers, *America Chained,* 76 (first quote), 81 (second quote), 83 (third quote).

9. C. C. McCall, quoted in "Live and Let Live," *Duncan's Trade Register,* April 1930, 12; Telegram, Texas Anti-Chain Association to Hoover, 7 February 1930, Subject File, Chain Stores, 1929–30, Box 74, Hoover Presidential Papers; Mimeograph Release #2, Independent Merchants of Minnesota, n.d., 1–20 March 1933, Gehan Papers.

10. Sterrett, "Robert G. Duncan," 33; "Fightin' Bob Duncan Speaking," *Duncan's Trade Register,* March 1930, 1–2; "Official Platforms and Slogans," *Oregon Voter,* 22 April 1922, 6; Malcolm Clark Jr., "Self-appointed Anti-chain Lobbyist Attacked Task with Fervor of Wildcat," *Oregonian,* 30 December 1982, sec. B: 7; "This Infernal Oligarchy," *Duncan's Trade Register,* April 1930, 2 (quote); "Third and Last Call," *Duncan's Trade Register,* 3.

11. Duncan quoted in Malcolm Clark Jr., "Self-Appointed Anti-chain Lobbyist Attacked Task with Fervor of Wildcat," *Oregonian,* 30 December 1982, sec. B: 7; "Chain Store Fight," *Oregon Voter,* 22 March 1930, 416–19; "Robert Gordon Duncan," *Oregon Voter,* 10 May 1930, 19–20 (quote); "Robert G. Duncan to Serve Sentence," *Oregonian,* 2 June 1931, 1; "Duncan out of Jail," *Oregonian,* 16 November 1931, 9.

12. "Station KSVP Broadcasting," *Duncan's Trade Register,* April 1930, 6 (first quote); "Stinking Advice; It's Free," *Duncan's Trade Register,* 11–12 (second quote); "Natural Man and Corporate Man," *Duncan's Trade Register,* March 1930, 5 (remaining quotes).

13. Henderson quoted in F. Harper, "'New Battle on Evolution,'" 414; Henderson speech, *CR,* 71st Cong., 2d sess., 72 (23 May 1930), 9433–36 (second and third quotes). A portrait of Henderson appears in Flynn, "Chain Stores," 270–71.

14. F. Harper, "'New Battle on Evolution,'" 414, 424; Ryant, "Kentucky and the Movement to Regulate Chain Stores," 275; Lee, *Anti–Chain Store Tax Legislation.* For the ideological component of the antichain movement, see D. A. Horowitz, "Crusade against Chain Stores," 341–68.

15. Sen. Res. 224, *CR,* 70th Cong., 1st sess., 69 (5 May 1928), 7857; *CR,* 71st Cong., 2d sess., 72 (9 December 1929), 325–33; Kelly speech, "Will Kelly Price Fixing Bill Prevent Monopolies?" *Congressional Digest* 9 (August–September 1930), 205.

16. Capper, *CR,* 72d Cong., 1st sess., 75 (9 July 1932), 14976–78. For a contemporary summary of antichain politics, see Flynn, "Up against the Chains," 8–9ff.

17. Capper, *CR,* 72d Cong., 1st sess., 75 (9 July 1932), 14977 (first, second, and third quotes), 14978 (fourth quote); *CR,* 72d Cong., 2d sess., 76 (21 December 1932), 826; *CR,* 72d Cong., 1st sess., 75 (17 May 1932), 10455–56; Copeland, *CR,* 72d Cong., 1st sess., 75 (11 July 1932), 14989.

18. G. Nye, "Our Industries Must Be Saved," *CR,* 71st Cong., 3d sess., 74 (24 January 1931), 2059–64, 3059 (first and second quotes), 3063 (third quote); "Federal Trade Commission and Antitrust Laws," *CR,* 72d Cong., 1st sess., 75 (5 January 1932), 1287–89; "Two Witnesses Back Federal Trade Bills," *New York Times,* 19 March 1932, 2 (fourth quote).

19. Bellows, "Mystery of the Chains," 19–20, 41; Federal Trade Commission, *Final Report on Chain Store Investigation,* 91.

20. Federal Trade Commission, *Chain Stores,* 117–18; Federal Trade Commission, *Final Report on Chain Store Investigation,* 23–24, 28–29, 64–65, 85, 96–97 (quote on 64).

21. Hawley, *New Deal and the Problem of Monopoly,* 249–50, 295–60; Brand, *Corporatism and the Rule of Law,* 173; U.S. House of Representatives, Committee on Investigation of American Retail Federation, *Investigation of the Trade Practices,* 5, 23, 52; Patman quoted in "The Patman Investigation," *Southern Pharmaceutical Journal* 28 (September 1935), 15.

22. Schmelzer, "Early Life and Early Congressional Career of Wright Patman," 126–27; Hawley, *New Deal and the Problem of Monopoly,* 251; Patman, *CR,* 74th Cong., 2d sess., 80 (14 February 1936), 2064–66; Robinson, *CR,* 74th Cong., 2d sess., 80 (30 April 1936), 6430 (quote); Institute of Distribution, "Who Pays for Advertising," quoted by Patman, *CR,* 74th Cong., 2d sess., 80 (9 March 1936), 3446; Wood to M. H. McIntyre, 21 February 1936, attached to McIntyre to Robinson, 7 March 1936, OF 288, FDR Library; Filene to FDR, 1 April 1936, OF 288, FDR Library.

23. "Price-Discrimination Battle," *Business Week,* 25 January 1936, 11; "Odds on Price-Control Law," *Business Week,* 7 March 1936, 9; "Independents Ask Chain Store Curb," *New York Times,* 5 March 1936, 32; Patman Press Release, 7 March 1936, OF 288, FDR Library; Patman CBS Radio Address, 18 April 1936, *CR,* 74th Cong., 2d sess., 80 (20 April 1936), 5728–29; *CR,* 74th Cong., 2d sess., 80 (29, 30 April, 27, 28 May, 19 June 1936), 6346–49, 6436, 8111–40, 8223, 8242, 10,700. Colorful accounts of Patman's activities can be found in "Passing the Buck on Price Bill," *Business Week,* 9 May 1936, 32; and "Alarmed by Patman Bill Victory," *Business Week,* 13 June 1936, 13–14.

24. *CR,* 74th Cong., 2d sess., 80 (1, 3 June 1936), 8433, 8871; *CR,* 75th Cong., 1st sess., 81 (11 March, 3 August 1937), 2133, 8143; Miller, *CR,* 75th Cong., 1st sess., 81 (19 April 1937), A873 (first quote), A874 (second and third quotes).

25. Patman, *CR,* 75th Cong., 3d sess., 83 (14 February, 7 March 1938), A598–602, A866–87; "Retail Grocers O.K. Patman Chain Tax," *Oregon Merchant's Magazine,* August 1938, 7; "Absentee Ownership: Turn on the Light," *Vital Speeches of the Day* 5 (November 1938), 72.

26. Patman, *CR,* 76th Cong., 1st sess., 84 (24 January, 27 February 1939), 713 (first quote), A751 (second quote); Patman, *CR,* 76th Cong., 3d sess., 86 (7

March 1940), A1272. The first Roosevelt quote was from a 10 October 1937 speech at Grand Coulee Dam and the second from Jackson Day Dinner remarks on 8 January 1938.

27. Ryant, "Kentucky and the Movement to Regulate Chain Stores," 284; Max A. Miller to Norris, 12 December 1938, attached to Norris to Miller, 16 December 1938, Chain Stores Taxes, Box 147, Norris Papers; Paul H. Nystrom to Borah, 30 March 1936, Legislation/Borah–Van Nuys Bill, 1936, General Office File, Box 444, Borah Papers; Griffin, "Economic Significance of Recent Price Legislation," 371.

28. Fuller, "Case for the Independent Merchant," 11–12; Grether, "Consumer Attitudes as to Chain and Independent," 206, 212; Brief of Manning and Harvey, in Support of Appellant, Supreme Court of State of Oregon, March Term 1934, quoted in D. A. Horowitz, "The Crusade against Chain Stores," 363; Celler quoted by Lynne M. Lamm, "Patman Bill Still Argued," *Progressive Grocer* 18 (March 1939), 72. For the Celler-Patman radio debate, see *CR,* 76th Cong., 3d sess., 86 (9 April 1940), A1945–59.

29. Editorial, *Labor World,* 1 April 1936, *CR,* 74th Cong., 2d sess., 80 (30 April 1936), 6430; *CR,* 76th Cong., 1st sess., 84 (16, 27 February 1939), A583–85, A755; FDR to John A. Logan, and attachments, 30 September 1939, and FDR to T. Blair Willison, and attachments, 9 November 1939, OF 288, FDR Library.

30. Neuberger, "Restriction of Chain Stores," 9; Lynne M. Lamm, "Patman Bill Still Argued," *Progressive Grocer* 11 (March 1932), 76; Patman to FDR, 30 July 1940, OF 288, FDR Library.

31. Webb, *Divided We Stand,* 54; "Methodists Score Movies and Novels," *New York Times,* 8 May 1930, 18; *Public Relations of the Motion Picture Industry,* 149; Carl E. Milliken to Rev. Harold McA. Robinson, 27 July 1932, 1, Part 2, Reel 8, Frame 336, Hays Papers; Jowett, *Film, the Democratic Art,* 244–56; R. Sklar, *Movie-Made America,* 173.

32. C. Gilman to Margaret S. Gould, 7 June 1934, Federal Motion Picture Council (hereafter FMPC), Correspondence, January–May 1934, Box 85, Gilman Papers; "Reforms Sought by Presbyterians," *New York Times,* 29 May 1934, 12; Hays Press Release, 22 June 1934, Part 2, Reel 12, Frame 6, Hays Papers; John B. Lewis Press Release, 12 July 1934, Part 2, Reel 12, Frame 179, Hayes Papers; Vaughn, "Morality and Entertainment," 39–65.

33. Douglas Gomery, "Hollywood, the National Recovery Administration, and the Question of Monopoly Power," in Kindem, ed., *American Movie Industry,* 206, 209; Elizabeth Gilman, "Catheryne Cooke Gilman: Social Worker," in Stuhler and Kreuter, eds., *Women of Minnesota,* 205–6; C. Gilman to Mrs. Frederick P. Bagley, 31 December 1934, FMPC, Correspondence, June–December 1934, Box 85, Gilman Papers; C. Gilman to William H. Short, 23 November 1933, Motion Picture Research Council, Correspondence, 1932–33, Box 72, Gilman Papers; Patman, *CR,* 73d Cong., 2d sess., 78 (16 March 1934), 4718; Chase to Board of Directors and Advisory Committee, 16 February 1934, and Chase to C. Gilman, 16 February 1934, FMPC, Correspondence, January–May 1934, Box 85, Gilman Papers; C. Gilman to Margaret S. Gould, 7 June 1934, and Chase to Short, 10 October 1934, FMPC, Correspondence, June–December 1934, Box 85, Gilman Papers.

34. "Francis D. Culkin, Congressman, 68," *New York Times*, 5 August 1943, 15; Culkin, "The Crime-Breeding Movies," *CR*, 74th Cong., 1st sess., 78 (2 July 1935), 10668 (first quote), 10666 (second and third quotes); Jowett, *Film, the Democratic Art*, 276–77.

35. Entry on Matthew W. Neely, *Dictionary of American Biography, Supplement Six*, 472–73; quoted in U.S. Senate, Committee on Interstate Commerce, *Hearings on Anti "Block-Booking,"* 5.

36. William Green to Sen. Alben W. Barkley, 13 July 1939, *CR*, 76th Cong., 1st sess., 84 (14 July 1939), 9144; Conant, *Antitrust in the Motion Picture Industry*, 94–106, 152.

37. C. Gilman to Grace H. Bagley, 21 December 1934, FMPC, Correspondence, June–December 1934, Box 85, Gilman Papers.

38. Brand, *Corporatism and the Rule of Law*, 11–12, 22–23, 89, 92, 206; Hawley, *New Deal and the Problem of Monopoly*, 35, 47–50, 136. For background on Borah's assault on the NRA, see D. A. Horowitz, "Senator Borah's Crusade," 693–708.

39. Quoted in Cole, *Roosevelt and the Isolationists*, 46.

40. Borah to Byrd Trego, 1 June 1933, Legislation/Industrial Recovery, 1932–33, General Office File, Box 363, Borah Papers; Brand, *Corporatism and the Rule of Law*, 87–88; Borah, *CR*, 73d Cong., 1st sess., 77 (7 June 1933), 5162–66; Borah quoted in "Roosevelt Trims Program," *New York Times*, 8 June 1933, 1.

41. Borah, *CR*, 73d Cong., 1st sess., 77 (7 June 1933), 5162 (first quote), 5163 (second quote); Borah quoted in "Roosevelt Trims Program," *New York Times*, 8 June 1933, 4 (third quote); Borah amendment in Brand, *Corporatism and the Rule of Law*, 88.

42. "Borah, Nye Refuse NRA Board Posts," *New York Times*, 27 December 1933, 6; Hawley, *New Deal and the Problem of Monopoly*, 76–81; "Roosevelt Order Aids 'Little Man,'" *New York Times*, 21 January 1934, 1, 20; *CR*, 73d Cong., 2d sess., 78 (2 February 1934), 1824; Borah, *CR*, 73d Cong., 2d sess., 78 (8 February 1934), 2158; "Anti-Trust Drive Is Urged by Borah," *New York Times*, 8 February 1934, 13.

43. Hawley, *New Deal and the Problem of Monopoly*, 84, 96–97; FTC Report quoted in *CR*, 73d Cong., 2d sess., 78 (21 March 1934), 5001; "Steel Code Cruel, Borah Declares," *New York Times*, 22 March 1934, 4; Borah, *CR*, 73d Cong., 2d sess., 78 (21 March 1934), 5000; "Darrow Board Finds Monopoly," *New York Herald Tribune*, 21 May 1934, sec. 1: 8–9.

44. Borah to Abraham S. Weissman, 11 April 1934, N.R.A./Small Business, 1933–34, General Office File, Box 391, Borah Papers; Borah to Repr. Allen T. Treadway, 19 July 1934, N.R.A./Small Business, 1933–34 (3), General Office File, Box 392, Borah Papers; "Idaho Baker Defies NRA," *New York Times*, 4 August 1934, 1.

45. D. A. Horowitz, "Senator Borah's Crusade," 693–94; George J. Michaelson to Borah, 27 May 1934, attached to Borah to Michaelson, 1 June 1934 (first quote), and Frederick Neudorff to Borah, 16 July 1934 (second quote), N.R.A./Small Business, 1933–34 (3), General Office File, Box 392, Borah Papers; Alfred Germain to Borah, 3 August 1934 (third quote), N.R.A./Small Business, 1933–

34 (4), General Office File, Box 392, Borah Papers; John Borden to Borah, 23 January 1935 (fourth quote), National Recovery Administration—Small Business, 1935, General Office File, Box 424, Borah Papers.

46. Borah, *CR,* 73d Cong., 2d sess., 78 (8 February 1934), 2156–58; Borah to president of Malad Chamber of Commerce, 1 March 1934, N.R.A./Investigations, Monopolies, 1933–34 (2), General Office File, Box 393, Borah Papers; E. A. Talbot to Borah, 1 February 1934 (first quote), and F. L. Saffell to Borah, 11 April 1934 (second quote), N.R.A./Small Business, 1933–34, General Office File, Box 391, Borah Papers; Edward J. Ramsey to Borah, 18 February 1935, and W. F. Grossenbach to Borah, 16 February 1935, National Recovery Administration—Monopoly Investigation (1), General Office File, Box 424, Borah Papers

47. Ernest F. Du Brul to Borah, 26 April 1934, and H. L. Mills to Borah, 2 June 1934, N.R.A./Small Business, 1933–34, General Office File, Box 391; and George W. Schryver to Borah, 19 February 1935, National Recovery Administration—Monopoly Investigation (1), General Office File, Box 424, all in Borah Papers.

48. Brand, *Corporatism and the Rule of Law,* 183–81; R. G. Johnson to Borah, 19 April 1934, and J. L. McLaughlin to Borah, 16 June 1934, N.R.A./Small Business, 1933–34, General Office File, Box 391, Borah Papers; "Board Takes a Hand," *New York Times,* 17 February 1935, 17 (quote).

49. A. A. Parker to Borah, 11 May 1934, N.R.A./Small Business, 1933–34 (2), General Office File, Box 391; and R. W. Johnson to Borah, and attachment, 28 April 1934, N.R.A./Small Business, 1933–34, General Office File, Box 391, both in Borah Papers.

50. Borah to E. W. Hamman, 7 October 1934, N.R.A./Small Business, 1933–34 (5), General Office File, Box 392, Borah Papers; "NRA Profiteering Assailed by Borah," *New York Times,* 16 November 1933, 8; Borah, *CR,* 73d Cong., 2d sess., 78 (18 January, 8 February 1934), 866–71, 2156–58; "Borah and Glass Attack NRA Codes," *New York Times,* 19 January 1934, 22.

51. Mulder, *Insurgent Progressives,* 55–60; Telegram, Coughlin to FDR, 24 September 1933, OF 306, FDR Library; Sullivan, "Presenting the Case for 'Little Business,'" *Congressional Digest* 14 (January 1935), 22–23.

52. Feinman, *Twilight of Progressivism,* 72; Borah, *CR,* 74th Cong., 1st sess., 79 (10 January 1935), 250; "Borah Takes a Hand," *New York Times,* 17 February 1935, 17; Richberg quoted in "Borah Denounces Choosing Trusts," *New York Times,* 25 February 1935, 2; "More Trade Curbs Seen by Johnson," *New York Times,* 8 March 1935, 5.

53. Borah quoted in "Committee Starts to Draft New NIRA," *New York Times,* 9 March 1935, 8. For the entire speech, see Borah, *CR,* 74th Cong., 1st sess., 79 (8 March 1935), 3197–204.

54. Borah, *CR,* 74th Cong., 1st sess., 79 (21 March 1935), 4165–70, 4183; "Roosevelt Fails of NRA Solution," *New York Times,* 1 May 1935, 1–2; "2-Year NRA Plan Proposed in House," *New York Times,* 21 May 1935, 1, 8; "Anti-Trust Issue Threatens Battle on NRA Extension," *New York Times,* 9 June 1935, 1, 28; "One Man in House Again Blocks NRA," *New York Times,* 14 June 1935, 1–2; *CR,* 74th Cong., 1st sess., 79 (14, 15 June 1935), 9291, 9311–19, 9351,

9414; "Long Filibuster Lasts 15½ Hours," *New York Times,* 14 June 1935, 2; "Skeleton NRA Is Extended," *New York Times,* 15 June 1935, 1–2; Hawley, *New Deal and the Problem of Monopoly* 126–28. For the *Schechter* case, see Karl, *Uneasy State,* 143–45.

55. Tugwell, *Democratic Roosevelt,* 405.

56. "Borah Opens War on 'Bureaucracy' under New Deal," *New York Times,* 5 July 1934, sec. 1: 13; "Monopolies Retard Upturn, Says Borah," *New York Times,* 25 July 1934, 20; Turner Catledge, "Republicans Line Up for Sensational Battle," *New York Times,* 16 February 1936, sec. 4: 3; Borah speech, 9 April 1936, quoted in McKenna, *Borah,* 339.

57. "Borah Not Joining Block," *New York Times,* 9 June 1936, 14 (first quote); "Declares Landon 'Sound' on Money," *New York Times,* 14; R. L. Duffus, "Cleveland Platform Shows Shift since '32," *New York Times,* 14 June 1936, sec. 4: 4 (second quote); "Landon Demands Monopolies' End and Escape from Bureaucracy," *New York Times,* 9 June 1936, 1 (third quote).

58. *CR,* 74th Cong., 1st sess., 79 (10 January, 5, 6 August 1935), 250, 255–56, 12551–57; "Anti-Trust Fight Opened by Borah," *New York Times,* 11 January 1935, 8; Borah, *CR,* 75th Cong., 1st sess., 81 (19 March 1937), 2477 (first quote); O'Mahoney Radio Address, 25 August 1935, *CR,* 74th Cong., 1st sess., 79 (26 August 1935), 14701–2 (second quote).

59. O'Mahoney, *CR,* 75th Cong., 2d sess., 82 (30 November 1937), 494–98; O'Mahoney, *CR,* 75th Cong., 3d sess., 83 (25 February 1938), 2446–49; "Federal Licensing of Business Urged," *New York Times,* 1 December 1937, 1, 15; Jackson quoted in "Congress Smiles on Trust Attack," *New York Times,* 28 December 1937, 1; "President and Borah Discuss Monopolies," *New York Times,* 29 January 1938, 2; Felix Belair Jr., "Expect Roosevelt to Define 'Abuses,'" *New York Times,* 30 January 1938, 1, 4; "Roosevelt 'Agrees' with Borah on Plans for Anti-Monopoly Laws," *New York Times,* 23 April 1938, 1–2; FDR Address to Congress, 29 April 1938, quoted in Hawley, *New Deal and the Problem of Monopoly,* 412.

60. Charles W. Hurd, "Long Study of Monopolies to Precede New Legislation," *New York Times,* 1 May 1938, 7; Roosevelt quoted in Frederick R. Barkley, "Monopoly Inquiry Holds Vast Possibility," *New York Times,* 19 June 1938, 3; Hawley, *New Deal and the Problem of Monopoly,* 410–19, 460–65; Thorp quoted in "'Monopoly' Inquiry Is Told It Hunts a Business Rarity," *New York Times,* 3 December 1938, 1–2.

61. *CR,* 76th Cong., 1st sess., 84 (5 January 1939), 88. For the complete TNEC report, see U.S. Senate, Temporary National Economic Committee, *Final Report and Recommendations.*

62. Quoted in Ewin L. Davis to Stephen Early, and attachments, 21 February 1935, OF 101–A, FDR Library; "Trade Board Fights Use of President's Likeness," *New York Times,* 22 February 1935, 12.

63. Henry S. Dennison, "The Platform of the Small and Middle-Size Business Man," 3, attached to M. H. McIntyre to Dennison, 6 August 1936 (first quote), OF 172–A; V. W. Dennen to FDR, 18 August 1935, OF 172–A; Frank T. Renick to FDR, 11 May 1933 (second quote), attached to Louis Howe to Renick, 25

May 1933, OF 288; and E. J. Byman to FDR, 17 May 1934 (third quote), attached to Howe to Byman, 29 May 1934, OF 172–A, all in FDR Library.

64. Fred Roth to FDR, 4 February 1938, 1–3, OF 172–A, FDR Library. For government small business definitions, see K. Mayer, "Small Business as a Social Institution," 334.

65. "5 Groups in Field of Small Business," *New York Times,* 5 February 1939, sec. 3: 9; "Program Outlined by Small Business," *New York Times,* 11 December 1941, 37; entry on C. Wilson Harder, *Who's Who in America, 1950–1951,* 1133; Hamilton, *Restraining Myths,* 243–47; Zeigler, *Politics of Small Business,* 13–20.

66. Hawley, *New Deal and the Problem of Monopoly,* 266–68, 466–67, 140–41, 263.

67. Hirth, *Chain Stores,* 10, attached to Hirth to M. H. McIntyre, 22 December 1936, OF 288; and H. L. Brown to FDR, 22 February 1936, attached to M. H. McIntyre to Brown, 26 February 1936, OF 172–A, both in FDR Library. Similar themes are explored in Brinkley, *Voices of Protest,* 146–48, 156.

68. Two hundred nonbanking corporations owned nearly one-fourth of the nation's wealth in the period under discussion. Berle and Means, *Modern Corporation and Private Property,* 19.

Chapter 7: The Last Progressives

1. Ballinger, "The Efficiency of Big Business," attached to Ballinger to Alfred S. Dashiell, 11 July 1941, B Correspondence, Box 17, Flynn Papers.

2. Feinman, *Twilight of Progressivism,* 23–24, 27, 32, 40–41, 45, 49, 51, 61–62, 65, 80, 75; Norris to J. D. Ream, 24 March 1931, Progressive Conference, 1931, Box 38, Norris Papers; Mulder, "Progressive Insurgents," 107–9, 113–15; H. Johnson to Flynn, 22 November 1932, Senate, Flynn Papers.

3. Feinman, *Twilight of Progressivism,* 91–93, 95; Mulder, "Progressive Insurgents," 117–20.

4. "Borah Demands a Rebuilt Party," *New York Times,* 9 November 1934, 2 (first quote); "Borah Asks Republicans to Reorganize the Party," *New York Times,* 2 December 1934, 1; Benjamin W. Oppenheim, "Why Doesn't Borah Run for the Presidency?" 2, 6, 10–13 (second quote on 13), attached to Borah to J. M. Lampert, 27 July 1935, Personal/Presidency (2), General Office File, Box 428, Borah Papers; White quoted in Feinman, *Twilight of Progressivism,* 98; Arthur Krock, "Hostile Bloc Places Borah on Offensive," *New York Times,* 9 February 1936, sec. 4: 2; McKenna, *Borah,* 319–36; Feinman, *Twilight of Progressivism,* 99–113.

5. Norris to Conference of Progressives, 11 September 1936, Progressives (Third Party), Box 39, Norris Papers; R. La Follette Jr. Radio Address, 2 November 1936, Speeches and Articles, Box C-558, R. La Follette Jr. Papers; Wheeler Campaign Speech, North Dakota, n.d., Box 15, Wheeler Papers.

6. Mulder, *Insurgent Progressives,* 158–59, iii; Patterson, *Congressional Conservatism and the New Deal,* 80–71; Cole, *Roosevelt and the Isolationists,* 207–8; Feinman, *Twilight of Progressivism,* 117–35. Norris sat as a Senate Independent, La Follette as a Progressive, and Henrik Shipstead as a Farmer-Laborite.

7. R. La Follette Jr. Radio Address, 13 February 1937, 8, 10–11, Supreme Court—Radio, Speeches, and Articles, Box C-559, La Follette Jr. Papers; Maney, *"Young Bob" La Follette,* 189, 192–93; Pinchot, Open Letter to Members of Congress, 13 February 1937, 2–3, Supreme Court—Outside, February 1937, Special Correspondence, Box C-363, R. La Follette Jr. Papers; Borah Radio Address, 1 February 1937, *CR,* 75th Cong., 1st sess., 81 (3 February 1937), A131–33; Borah to Ray McKaig, 6 March 1937 (first quote), and Borah to Thomas Morgan, 6 March 1937 (second quote), Supreme Court, 1937 (4), General Office File, Borah Papers.

8. Feinman, *Twilight of Progressivism,* 123–28; Borah to Frank D. Ryan, 13 April 1937 (first and second quotes), Supreme Court, 1937 (5), General Office File, Box 483, Borah Papers; Mulder, *Insurgent Progressives,* 185–86.

9. Mulder, *Insurgent Progressives,* 184–86; Wheeler to Frank Finnegan, 2 December 1939, Montana A–M Misc. Correspondence, Box 3, Wheeler Papers; Wheeler, "The Supreme Court," radio address, 21 February 1937 (first quote), Box 16, Wheeler Papers; Press Release, 3 April 1937 (second quote), Box 12, Wheeler Papers.

10. Newspaper clipping, attached to T. M. Smith to R. La Follette Jr., 26 February 1937, Supreme Court, February 1937, Special Correspondence, Box C-361, R. La Follette Jr. Papers; MacColl, "Supreme Court and Public Opinion," 235, 347, 195, 404, 197, 406, 354.

11. G. R. Killen to FDR, 7 February 1937, Unfavorable, K, OF 41, FDR Library; O. Gunvaldsen to R. La Follette Jr., 14 July 1934, attached to Wheeler to Gunvaldsen, 18 August 1937, A–L Misc. Correspondence, Box 2, Wheeler Papers; Mrs. C. B. Nichols to G. Nye, 18 February 1937, Court Packing Correspondence (A), Box 10, G. Nye Papers.

12. R. A. Edgar to R. La Follette Jr., 10 February 1937, Supreme Court Letters Against, February 1937, Box C-362, R. La Follette Jr. Papers; Mabell Frank to G. Nye, 22 February 1937, Court Packing Correspondence (C), Box 10, G. Nye Papers; Anonymous to FDR, n.d., Unfavorable, A, OF 41, FDR Library; Fred Brenckman to Philip La Follette, 4 March 1937, attached to Brenckman to Borah, 4 March 1937, Supreme Court, 1937 (4), General Office File, Box 483, Borah Papers.

13. H. L. Prestholdt to G. Nye, 15 February 1937, Court Packing Correspondence (A), Box 10, G. Nye Papers; [illegible] to Nye, 23 February 1937, Court Packing Correspondence (D), Box 10, G. Nye Papers; Russel C. Burton to FDR, 15 March 1937, Unfavorable, B, OF 41, FDR Library; M. G. Whitney to Borah, 6 March 1937 (quote), attached to Borah to Whitney, 8 March 1937, Supreme Court, 1937 (3), General Office File, Box 483, Borah Papers.

14. Ned Baumarten to FDR, 18 March 1937, Unfavorable, B, OF 41, FDR Library; George L. Heays to Norris, 22 June 1937, attached to Norris to Heays, 24 June 1937, Supreme Court (1937), Box 117, Norris Papers; Macey F. Deming to FDR, 5 March 1937, Unfavorable, D, OF 41, FDR Library; G. G. Kendall to Borah, 6 June 1937, Supreme Court Reorganization, 2–14 June 1937, Public Opinion File, Box 744, Borah Papers; K. N. Dahle to FDR, 5 March 1937, Unfavorable, D, OF 41, FDR Library; Katharine and Edgar Rowe to G. Nye, 17 February 1937, Court Packing Correspondence (A), Box 10, G. Nye Papers.

15. Feinman, *Twilight of Progressivism*, 132–34; Patterson, *Congressional Conservatism and the New Deal*, 119–24; Wheeler quoted by Mulder, *Insurgent Progressives*, 209.

16. Wood to Marvin H. McIntyre, 17 July 1937, attached to McIntyre to Wood, 20 July 1937, PPF 1365, FDR Library; "Wheeler Asserts Party Is Not Split," *New York Times*, 23 August 1937, sec. 1: 5. For insight into Wheeler's politics, see Catledge, "Liberal Who Fights New Deal Liberalism," 3.

17. Ruetten, "Burton K. Wheeler," 232–33 (first quote), 244; Mulder, *Insurgent Progressives*, 220, 239–40, 293–95; Cole, *Senator Gerald P. Nye*, 142–43 (second quote); Norbeck to James S. Milloy, 11 June 1935, NRA (6), Box 57, Norbeck Papers.

18. Miller, *Governor Philip F. La Follette*, 113; Judge Vince A. Day to Wheeler, 21 January 1940, attached to Wheeler to Day, 17 January 1940, D Misc. Correspondence, Box 4, Wheeler Papers; Fritz Lehmberg Sr. to Shipstead, 18 June 1938, Correspondence, June–December 1938, Box 2, Shipstead Papers.

19. Maney, *"Young Bob" La Follette*, 170, 176; H. Johnson quoted in Fitzpatrick, "Senator Hiram W. Johnson," 264; Wheeler to Harold Putman, 4 January 1940, P Misc. Correspondence, Box 6, Wheeler Papers; Borah to W. B. Russell, 6 May 1937, and Borah to Richard L. Neuberger, 14 April 1937, Strikes/Automobile, 1937, General Office File, Box 483, Borah Papers; Borah press releases for Associated Press, 18 March and 6 April 1937 (second quote), Speeches and Statements, January–December 1937, Box 783, Borah Papers. For the unsuccessful Byrnes amendment to condemn sit-downs, see *CR,* 75th Cong., 1st sess., 81 (17 March 1937), 2337.

20. Mulder, *Insurgent Progressives*, 224–26; R. F. Lovejoy to Borah, 9 June 1938, Wages and Hours Bill, April–June 1938, General Office File, Box 506, Borah Papers; Resolution, Legislative Committee of Norristown Chamber of Commerce, 3 June 1938, attached to Edgar E. Schmidt to Borah, 7 June 1938, Wages and Hours Bill, April–June 1938, General Office File, Box 506, Borah Papers.

21. Borah quoted in Mulder, *Insurgent Progressives*, 226; H. Johnson to H. Johnson Jr., 1 August 1937, quoted in Levine, ed., "'Diary' of Hiram Johnson," 74; Mulder, *Insurgent Progressives*, 225.

22. Cole, *Roosevelt and the Isolationists*, 102–4, 109, 95–96; "Congress and the Reciprocal Trade Treaties," *Congressional Digest* 18 (December 1939), 291; Henry Carter, "Politics and the Trade Agreement," 8–9.

23. Feinman, *Twilight of Progressivism*, 75–77; H. Johnson quoted in Cole, *Roosevelt and the Isolationists*, 103; Borah, *CR,* 73d Cong., 2d sess., 78 (17 May, 4 June 1934), 9006–10 (first quote on 9007), 10376 (second quote).

24. Mulder, *Insurgent Progressives*, 245–46; Borah to E. S. Trask, 11 October 1937, Foreign Affairs/Reciprocal Trade Agreements, 1937, General Office File, Box 468, Borah Papers; Kent, "Portrait in Isolationism," 268–69; *CR,* 75th Cong., 1st sess., 81 (9, 25 February 1937), 1064–65, 1612.

25. Allen T. Treadway, "The Administration's Ruinous Trade Treaty Program," *CR,* 76th Cong., 1st sess., 84 (5 August 1939), 4061; Millard D. Brown, "Should Congress Extend the Act Empowering the President to Make Recipro-

cal Trade Treaties," *Congressional Digest* 18 (December 1939), 315; Cole, *Roosevelt and the Isolationists,* 103, 109–12.

26. Feinman, *Twilight of Progressivism,* 140–41; Borah quoted in Mulder, *Insurgent Progressives,* 254; "Wheeler for Curb on Reorganization," *New York Times,* 9 March 1938, sec. 1: 4. For background on the politics of executive reorganization, see *Congressional Digest* 16 (October 1937), 225–56.

27. FDR quoted in Farley, *Jim Farley's Story,* 257; Melvin D. Hildreth to Marvin H. McIntyre, 24 June 1938, OF 300, North Dakota, FDR Library; Repr. Harry Sauthoff to P. La Follette, 22 April 1938, Correspondence, 22–23 April 1938, Box 97, P. La Follette Papers; poll of 8 April 1938, Gallup, *Gallup Poll,* vol. 1: 96.

28. Feinman, *Twilight of Progressivism,* 139–42; Mulder, *Insurgent Progressives,* 254–61, 288–89.

29. Capper quoted in Mulder, *Insurgent Progressives,* 273–74; Wheeler, *Yankee from the West,* 352; Staff Memo, 18 March 1940, 1–3, Bureaucracy, 1938–40, Box 503, Taft Papers.

30. Research Division, Republican National Committee, "The Tyranny of New Deal Taxation," August 1938, 2, 4–6, Taxation, 1938, Box 119, Taft Papers; Mulder, *Insurgent Progressives,* 264–65; "Norris to Fight for Profits Tax," *New York Times,* 6 April 1938, 13.

31. Poll of 6 January 1939, Gallup, *Gallup Poll,* vol. 1: 134; Shipstead, "We Must Reduce Interest Rates," *CR,* 73d Cong., 2d sess., 78 (8 February 1934), 2182; H. Johnson quoted in Mulder, *Insurgent Progressives,* 250–51.

32. Patterson, *Congressional Conservatism and the New Deal,* 333–34; G. Nye, "Reminiscences of Senate Career," 1971, 13, Box 40, G. Nye Papers; Shipstead to E. M. Ferguson, 28 March 1939, quoted in Mulder, *Insurgent Progressives,* 299.

33. Lemke quoted in Mulder, *Insurgent Progressives,* 240–41; Elyden and Elizabeth Babcock to R. La Follette Jr., 17 August 1937, Black Nomination, 1937, General Office File, Box C-35, R. La Follette Jr. Papers; Charles Edgar Haupt to Shipstead, 24 April 1939, Correspondence, 21–30 April 1939, Box 3, Shipstead Papers.

34. Mr. and Mrs. C. O. Johnson to Shipstead, 8 February 1939, Correspondence, 1–13 February 1939, Box 2; and Midi Kogl to Shipstead, 11 June 1939, Correspondence, 1–18 June 1939, Box 3, both in Shipstead Papers.

35. Mulder, *Insurgent Progressives,* 261, 266–67, 271, 281; Patterson, *Congressional Conservatism and the New Deal,* 295–96, 315; Fitzpatrick, "Senator Hiram W. Johnson," 263.

36. Mulder, *Insurgent Progressives,* 245–49.

37. Miller, *Governor Philip F. La Follette,* 272–73, 277–78; H. Johnson to Harry Flood Byrd, 18 August 1938, 2, Box 18, H. Johnson Papers; poll of 9 September 1938, Gallup, *Gallup Poll,* vol. 1: 117.

38. Leuchtenburg, *Franklin D. Roosevelt,* 25, 36, 95; Olson quoted in Brinkley, *Voices of Protest,* 227.

39. Geelan, *Dakota Maverick,* 59, 61–, 63–66; Blackorby, *Prairie Rebel,* 192–93; Hjalmervik, "William Langer's First Administration," 14.

40. Hjalmervik, "William Langer's First Administration," 20, 39; Langer quoted in G. Mayer, *Political Career of Floyd B. Olson,* 154; Geelan, *Dakota Maverick,* 69–78; Blackorby, *Prairie Rebel,* 202–10. Langer's wife replaced him in the 1934 election and lost to the Democratic candidate, who was then disqualified because of state residency requirements.

41. Blackorby, *Prairie Rebel,* 261–63; G. H. Smith, *Langer of North Dakota,* 39. Langer was tried for a perjury charge stemming from the first trial but was acquitted.

42. Meyer, "Politics of Loyalty," 75–77, 104–10; P. La Follette quoted in *Washington Daily News,* 17 January 1931; "La Follette Takes Wisconsin's Breath," *New York Times,* 25 January 1931, sec. 3: 8.

43. Feinman, *Twilight of Progressivism,* 81–84; R. La Follette Jr. Address at Progressive Conference, 19 May 1934, Fund Du Lac, Wisconsin, Progressive Party, Speeches and Articles, Box C-558, R. La Follette Jr. Papers; P. La Follette quoted in Miller, "Philip La Follette," 68.

44. Press Release of Lynn Frazier, 4 October 1934, 1, Publications and Speeches, May–December 1934, Box 119, P. La Follette Papers; P. La Follette, *Adventure in Politics,* 215.

45. Brinkley, *Voices of Protest,* 229; "La Follette Plan Makes Scant Gains," *New York Times,* 2 May 1938, 11; McCoy, "National Progressives of America," 75, 79.

46. Miller, "Philip La Follette," 71, 73–76; Brinkley, *Voices of Protest,* 229–30; Lerner, "Phil La Follette," 552–53; "La Follette Plan Makes Scant Gains," *New York Times,* 2 May 1938, 11.

47. P. La Follette, *Adventure in Politics,* 252; "La Follette Plan Makes Scant Gains," *New York Times,* 2 May 1938, 11 (first quote); Lerner, "Phil La Follette," 552–53 (second and third quotes); Draft of Speech at Harvard School of Business Administration Alumni Banquet, 17 June 1937, 8, 10–11, 21, Articles and Speeches, January–July 1937, Box 119, P. La Follette Papers; Mimeograph of Economic Club Dinner Speech, New York, 28 February 1938 (fourth quote), Articles and Speeches, August 1937–March 1938, Box 99, P. La Follette Papers; Miller, "Philip La Follette," 75.

48. P. La Follette Form Letters, 28 March 1938, Correspondence, April 1938, Box 93; John Gamper to P. La Follette, 9 March 1938, Correspondence, 9–10 March 1938, Box 94; Repr. Henry G. Teigan to P. La Follette, 22 April 1938, Correspondence, 22–23 April 1938, Box 97; J. C. Hallett to P. La Follette, 17 March 1938, Correspondence, 16–17 March 1938, Box 94; W. J. Sawyer to FDR, 19 March 1938, attached to Sawyer to P. La Follette, 19 March 1938, Correspondence, 19–21 March 1938, Box 95; Albert Strey to P. La Follette, 25 April 1938 (quote), and other samples, Correspondence, April 1938, Box 93; William H. Hanchett to P. La Follette, 31 March 1938, Correspondence, April 1938, Box 93; and Harry A. Kovenock to P. La Follette, 5 April 1938, Correspondence, April 1938, Box 98, all in P. La Follette Papers. Correspondence relating to La Follette's meetings in May and April 1938 can be found in Box 94, P. La Follette Papers.

49. Adolph Maassen to P. La Follette, 4 April 1938 (first quote), Correspon-

dence, April 1938, Box 98, P. La Follette Papers; McCoy, "National Progressives of America," 81; "Blames Roosevelt for Present Slump," *New York Times,* 21 April 1938, 3 (second quote); Mimeographs, radio speeches of 21 April 1938, 1–2 (third quote), 3 (fourth quote), and 22 April 1938, 2, Articles and Speeches, April 1938, Box 119, P. La Follette Papers.

50. P. La Follette Form Letter, 22 April 1938, Correspondence, April 1938, Box 98, P. La Follettee Papers; Miller, "Philip La Follette," 80; Conference of the National Progressives of America, "A New Movement . . . the National Progressives of America . . . Is Under Way," pamphlet, 28 April 1938, 3–5, Articles and Speeches, April 1938, Box 119, P. La Follette Papers. For details of the speech and event, see "National Progressive Party," *New York Times,* 29 April 1938, 1, 12; "Text of La Follette's Speech," *New York Times,* 12; and "Get Rich First, Squabble Later, Says La Follette," *Life* 4 (9 May 1938), 9.

51. "Text of La Follette's Speech," *New York Times,* 29 April 1938, 12.

52. Ibid.

53. McCoy, "National Progressives of America," 85, 88; R. La Follette Jr. Press Release, 8 October 1938, Press Releases, October 1938, Box 129, P. La Follette Papers; Samuel Levin to P. La Follette, 19 April 1938, Correspondence, April 1938, Box 98, P. La Follette Papers; Lerner, "Phil La Follette," 554–55.

54. "La Follette Thunder," 492–93; "New Progressives," 519–20; McCoy, "National Progressives of America," 85–86, 89; Judge Arthur P. McNulty to P. La Follette, 26 April 1938, Correspondence, 24–26 April 1938, Box 97, P. La Follette Papers; "La Follette Plan Makes Scant Gains," *New York Times,* 2 May 1938, 6; "Progressives, What Now?" 3; State Sen. T. V. Smith to P. La Follette, 20 April 1938, Correspondence, 20–21 April 1938, Box 97, P. La Follette Papers. The response to the NPA was described in Aldric P. Revell, "La Follette Party," *New York Times,* 23 April 1939, sec. 4: 10; and Brown, "Phil La Follette Sounds Off," 16.

55. Everett Case to Robert M. Hutchins, 3 May 1938, attached to Hutchins to P. La Follette, 6 May 1938, Correspondence, 5–6 May 1938, Box 99; William Benton to P. La Follette, 25 April 1938, Correspondence, 24–26 April 1938, Box 97; and Bruno [?] to P. La Follette, 3 May 1938, Correspondence, 3–4 May 1938, Box 99, all in P. La Follette Papers; Lerner, "Phil La Follette," 552; Bruce Bliven to P. La Follette, and attachment, 10 May 1938, Correspondence, 10–11 May 1938, Box 100, P. La Follette Papers.

56. Lerner, "Phil La Follette," 552–54; "Progressives, What Now?" 4; Arthur H. Harlow to P. La Follette, 29 April 1938, Correspondence, 29–30 April 1938, Box 97, P. La Follette Papers.

57. Thompson, "The National Progressives," *New York Herald Tribune,* 2 May 1938, 17.

58. Maney, *"Young Bob" La Follette,* 206–7 (first quote); "Progressives, What Now?" 4; Bruno [?] to P. La Follette, 3 May 1938 (second quote), Correspondence, 3–4 May 1938, Box 99, P. La Follette Papers; FDR to Ambassador William Phillips, 18 May 1938, quoted in McCoy, "National Progressives of America," 87 (third quote); Thompson, "The National Progressives," *New York Herald Tribune,* 2 May 1938, 17 (fourth quote).

59. Gallup, "New Third Party Found to Be Weak," *New York Times*, 27 May 1938, 6; poll of 27 May 1938, Gallup, *Gallup* Poll, vol. 1: 104; Miller, *Governor Philip F. La Follette*, 146; J. Vernon Burke to P. La Follette, 5 May 1938, and Repr. Jerry Voorhis to La Follette, 6 May 1938, 2, Correspondence, 5–6 May 1938, Box 99, P. La Follette Papers; "Wisconsin to Name Slates Tomorrow," *New York Times*, 19 September 1938, 14.

60. Aldric P. Revell, "La Follette Party," *New York Times*, 23 April 1939, sec. 4: 10; Joe Van Nordstand to Harold Peterson, 29 February 1940 (first quote), Correspondence and Misc. Papers, 1940, Box 5, Farmer-Labor Association Papers; P. La Follette Address before Farmer-Labor Convention, Rochester, Minn., 8 March 1940 (second quote), Papers, Articles, and Letters, January–December 1940, Box 120, P. La Follette Papers; Miller, "Philip La Follette," 81; Miller, *Governor Philip F. La Follette*, 127.

61. Green, *Shaping Political Consciousness*, 119–34; Stock, *Main Street in Crisis*, 207, 217.

62. Brinkley, *Voices of Protest*, 156–57; G. S. Smith, *To Save a Nation*, 77–78, 99; Ribuffo, *Old Christian Right*, 17–18.

63. Lasch, *True and Only Heaven*, 68, 70; Galambos, *Public Image of Big Business*, 261, 267; Mulder, *Insurgent Progressives*, i, iv, 11, 182, 212, 300. For progressives and the old middle class, see Graham, *An Encore for Reform*, 24–25, 39–40, 48, 68–69, 182–83.

64. Mulder, *Insurgent Progressives*, 301, 274–76.

65. Ruetten, "Burton K. Wheeler," 232–33; Mulder, *Insurgent Progressives*, 276, 256n; Shipstead Statement (1940 campaign), Speeches, News Releases, Statements, Folder 3, Box 21, Shipstead Papers; Ickes, *Secret Diary: 1936–1939*, 643, 707; Ickes, *Secret Diary: 1939–1941*, 284; Feinman, *Twilight of Progressivism*, 191.

66. Feinman, *Twilight of Progressivism*, 143–44 (first quote); Wheeler, *Yankee from the West*, 197, 428 (second quote). Similar issues were explored in Wheeler, "Liberalism," radio address before Carolina Political Union, Chapel Hill, N.C., 23 April 1940, *CR*, 76th Cong., 3d sess., 86 (29 April 1940), A2467; and Wheeler, "Nazism vs. Americanism," address in Chicago, 11 June 1937, 5, 8, 13, Box 16, Wheeler Papers.

67. Mundt, "The America I Want," address before Women's National Republican Club, New York, 14 January 1939, *CR*, 76th Cong., 1st sess., 84 (18 January 1939), A188 (first quote); Mundt, "This Tyranny Called Liberalism," address before Knife and Forkers, Sioux Falls, S.D., 4 December 1939, 1, 5, Folder 3, Speeches—Liberalism, 1939, Box DB 1228, Mundt Papers; Mundt, "The Republican Formula—'A Fair Chance for a Free People,'" radio address, 22 April 1939, *CR*, 76th Cong., 1st sess., 84 (26 April 1939), 6749 (second quote).

68. Feinman, *Twilight of Progressivism*, 143–44; "Platform Drafted By 'Grass Rooters,'" *New York Times*, 9 October 1935, 1–2; polls of 9 July and 2 April 1939, Gallup, *Gallup Poll*, vol. 1: 164, 148.

Chapter 8: The Noninterventionist Insurgency, 1935–41

1. Wheeler, *CR*, 77th Cong., 1st sess., 87 (28 July 1941), 6335.

2. Cole, *Roosevelt and the Isolationists,* 81, 86–87; Vinson, "War Debts and Peace Legislation," 206–9.

3. Vinson, "War Debts and Peace Legislation," 206, 208; Cole, *Roosevelt and the Isolationists,* 87–88.

4. Cole, *Roosevelt and the Isolationists,* 88–94; Vinson, "War Debts and Peace Legislation," 214, 217–18; poll of 18 March 1938, Gallup, *Gallup Poll,* vol. 1: 94.

5. Cole, *Roosevelt and the Isolationists,* 119–21; Guinsburg, *Pursuit of Isolationism,* 155–59.

6. John F. O'Ryan to H. Johnson, 17 December 1931, National World Court Folder, Box 61, H. Johnson Papers; Mulder, "Progressive Insurgents," 110; Wheeler, "World Court," radio address, 29 January 1935, 2, Box 15, Wheeler Papers.

7. Cole, *Roosevelt and the Isolationists,* 121–24; Brinkley, *Voices of Protest,* 134–37.

8. Cole, *Roosevelt and the Isolationists,* 141–47; Cole, *Senator Gerald P. Nye,* 66–72.

9. G. Nye, "The Profits of War and Preparation—A Challenge to Peace," radio address, 1 September 1934, 1, and G. Nye Radio Address, National Radio Forum, 2 October 1934, 1, 3, Addresses, Box 53, G. Nye Papers; G. Nye, "Should Governments Exercise Direct Control of Munitions Industries?" *Congressional Digest* 13 (November 1934), 266; G. Nye Radio Address, 15 April 1935, 3, Addresses, Box 53, G. Nye Papers.

10. Cole, *Senator Gerald P. Nye,* 73, 75, 79, 93; Wiltz, "Nye Committee Revisited," 218–20, 214; 159; Munitions Committee Summary, n.d., 2, History of Munitions Hearings Folder, Box 23, G. Nye Papers.

11. Munitions Committee Summary, n.d., 10 (first quote), 4, 152, History of Munitions Hearings Folder, Box 23, G. Nye Papers; Cole, *Senator Gerald P. Nye,* 94 (second quote); "Nye Denies Inquiry 'Cleared' Morgan," *New York Times,* 10 February 1936, 4 (third quote).

12. Cole, *Senator Gerald P. Nye,* 88–90, 94–95; Munitions Committee Summary, n.d., 3, 12–13, 10, History of Munitions Hearings Folder, Box 23, G. Nye Papers.

13. Cole, *Roosevelt and the Isolationists,* 141, 167; G. Nye quoted in Hutchinson, "Arms Inquiry," 662.

14. Memorandum, Sen. Clark and Sen. Nye to Sen. Pittman, 10 July 1935, Munitions Committee Memoranda, 1934–41, and undated folder, Box 23, G. Nye Papers; Cole, *Roosevelt and the Isolationists,* 170–79 (Johnson quote on 177).

15. G. Nye Press Release, 26 January 1936, 1–2, Addresses, Box 54, G. Nye Papers; Cole, *Roosevelt and the Isolationists,* 184–86.

16. Cole, *Roosevelt and the Isolationists,* 228–34.

17. Ibid., 267–68, 240–43, 251–52.

18. Borah to Robert Reed, 9 November 1937, quoted in Cole, *Roosevelt and the Isolationists,* 170; Shipstead Radio Address, 16 November 1937, *CR,* 75th Cong., 2d sess., 82 (1 December 1937), A257–58; Cole, *Roosevelt and the Isolationists,* 253–54; Ludlow to FDR, 21 December 1936, attached to FDR to Ludlow, 29 December 1936, 2, OF 274, FDR Library.

19. Cole, *Roosevelt and the Isolationists,* 256–61; Comments of Major General William C. Rivers, Ludlow Press Release, 22 December 1937, and FDR to William B. Bankhead, 6 January 1938, OF 3084, FDR Library.

20. Polls of 2, 14 October 1938, 13 March, 14 April 1939, Gallup, *Gallup Poll,* vol. 1: 120, 121, 145, 149; Cole, *Roosevelt and the Isolationists,* 275, 319, 312–14.

21. Cole, *Roosevelt and the Isolationists,* 315–16, 319; G. Nye to Walter Lippmann, 1 May 1939, Neutrality, Correspondence, 1938–39, Box 24, G. Nye Papers; R. La Follette Jr. Radio Address, 13 July 1939, 2, Speeches and Articles, Box C-561, R. La Follette Jr. Papers.

22. Poll of 4 October 1939, Gallup, *Gallup Poll,* vol. 1: 149; G. Nye quoted in Guinsburg, *Pursuit of Isolationism,* 213; H. Johnson, *CR,* 76th Cong., 2d sess., 84 (20 October 1939), 1074; Borah to Charles Brown, 13 October 1939, and Borah to George Wharton Pepper, 20 September 1939, Foreign Affairs–Neutrality, September–November 1939, General Office File, Box 513, Borah Papers.

23. Feinman, *Twilight of Progressivism,* 183–87 (Borah quote on 184; Johnson quote on 181).

24. Poll of 4 December 1939, Gallup, *Gallup Poll,* vol. 1: 193; Cole, *Roosevelt and the Isolationists,* 363–64, 304–5, 367–68, 370, 372–73, 375.

25. Press Release, 23 June 1940, American Institute of Public Opinion, OF 1413, FDR Library; Wheeler to Lockwood Thompson, and attachment, 5 July 1940, T Misc. Correspondence, Box 7, Wheeler Papers; poll results, Public Opinion Research Project, attached to memoranda, FDR to Lowell Mellett, 12 August and 30 September 1940, PPF 4721, FDR Library; Thomas to FDR, 24 July 1940 (first quote), PPF 4840, FDR Library; Louis N. Cavanaugh to Stephen T. Early, 4 September 1940 (second quote), OF 1413 Misc., FDR Library; Louise Rice-Carter to Charles L. McNary, 24 July 1940 (third quote), Levi T. Pennington to McNary, 8 July 1940 (fourth quote), attached to Telegram, McNary to Pennington, 13 July 1940, and Hugh Sheehan to McNary, 24 July 1940 (fifth quote), General Correspondence, Box 10, McNary Papers. Pennington was the president of Pacific College in Oregon.

26. G. Nye, "Universal Compulsory Military Training Now?" draft of article for *Washington Daily News,* 29 June 1940, 2, Addresses, Box 56, G. Nye Papers; Wheeler Speech before a Mass Meeting Opposing Military Conscription in Peace Time, Washington, D.C., 1 August 1940, 1, Box 17, Wheeler Papers; Wheeler Radio Address, 15 August 1940, *CR,* 76th Cong., 3d sess., 86 (21 August 1940), A5148–50; Cole, *Roosevelt and the Isolationists,* 377–79.

27. Poll of 4 December 1938, Gallup, *Gallup Poll,* vol. 1: 129; Wheeler to Joseph H. Griffin, 30 December 1939, F–L Misc. Correspondence, Box 3, Wheeler Papers; Wheeler to Peter Rorvik, 9 April 1940, Montana R Misc. Correspondence, Box 6, Wheeler Papers.

28. Ruetten, "Burton K. Wheeler," 286, 311 (first quote), 295 (third quote); Wheeler, radio address, 7 June 1940, quoted in Wheeler, *Yankee from the West,* 20–21 (second quote); Wheeler, "Keep Out of War," radio address, 30 June 1940, 3 (fourth quote), 6, Box 17, Wheeler Papers.

29. Telegram, P. La Follette to Wheeler, 6 July 1940, attached to Wheeler to

La Follette, 6 July 1940, L Misc. Correspondence, Box 5; Wheeler to Barry Bingham, 6 January 1940, B Misc. Correspondence, Box 4; Governor John Moses to Wheeler, 25 November 1939, Box 2; Linn A. E. Gale to Wheeler, 30 June 1940, attached to Wheeler to Gale, 3 July 1940, G Misc. Correspondence, Box 5; and Wheeler to Mrs. O. W. Anderson, 21 August 1940, A Misc. Correspondence, Box 4, all in Wheeler Papers. Ernest Lundeen, Minnesota's Farmer-Labor senator, chaired the Make Europe Pay War Debts Committee.

30. Cole, *Roosevelt and the Isolationists,* 390–93; G. Nye Address in Support of Candidacy of Arthur H. Vandenberg for Presidency, Nebraska Primary, 6 April 1940, 5, 7, 9–10, Addresses, Box 56, G. Nye Papers; Shipstead Statement, "How Willkie the 'New Deal' Democrat Won Republican Leadership," Speeches, News Releases, Statements, Folder 5, Box 21, Shipstead Papers; Burdick, "Mr. Willkie and the Draft," 1949, Folder 10, Foreign Policy: Foreign Affairs 1951–56, Box 7, Burdick Papers.

31. Cole, *Roosevelt and the Isolationists,* 391–93, 400.

32. Feinman, *Twilight of Progressivism,* 190–93; G. Nye Radio Address, 6 April 1940, 1, 6, Addresses, Box 56, G. Nye Papers; H. Johnson, "Senator Johnson Says Third Term Greater Crisis Than War," radio address and campaign pamphlet, 18 October 1940, 6, Political Campaign Material 1940, Senatorial Misc. Papers, H. Johnson Papers; H. Johnson Statement, 16 August 1940, Speeches, Statements, and Press Releases, July 1940–January 1941, Carton 26, H. Johnson Papers; G. Nye Press Release, 19 August 1940, Correspondence, July–October 10, 1940, Box 6, Shipstead Papers.

33. R. Bailey Stortz to Donald D. Dahl, 15 January 1940, D Misc. Correspondence, Box 4, Wheeler Papers; Wheeler to William Green, and attachments, 30 November 1939, Box 2, Wheeler Papers; Ruetten, "Burton K. Wheeler," 291–92; Ruetten, "Wheeler and the Montana Connection," 17; Leuchtenburg, *Franklin D. Roosevelt,* 321; H. Johnson, diary entry of 19 January 1941, in Levine, ed., "'Diary' of Hiram Johnson," 76.

34. Justus D. Doenecke, "Power, Markets, and Ideology: The Isolationist Response to Roosevelt Foreign Policy, 1940–41," in Liggio and Martin, eds., *Watershed of Empire,* 132–35, 150–52, 161n; Chadwin, *Hawks of World War II,* 68.

35. Memorandum, Stephen T. Early to FDR, 27 September 1939, Neutrality, January–September 1939, OF 1561, FDR Library; Chadwin, *Hawks of World War II,* 43–48, 54–70, 78; Press Release of Telegram to FDR, 26 December 1940, attached to Early to Ulric Bell, 26 December 1940, Box 4, OF 4193, Misc., FDR Library; Memorandum, Early to Marguerite LeHand, and attachments, 3 January 1941, Box 4, OF 4193, Misc., FDR Library.

36. Thompson to Borah, 26 September 1939, 1–3, Foreign Affairs–Neutrality, September–November 1939, Box 513, Borah Papers; Richberg to R. La Follette Jr., 25 September 1939, 2, General, 1939, General Office File, Box C-35, R. La Follette Jr. Papers.

37. Lamont to FDR, 15 June 1940, PPF 70, FDR Library; Cole, *Roosevelt and the Isolationists,* 366–37; FDR to Thomas, 17 October 1939, PPF 4840, FDR Library; FDR to White, December 1939, 2, PPF 1196, FDR Library; FDR to Thomas, 31 July 1940, 1, PPF 4840, FDR Library.

38. Marie Luhrs to Stephen T. Early, 27 December 1940, 1–2 (first quote), OF 4193 Misc., FDR Library; Marshall to D. M. Linnard, 21 January 1941 (third quote), NFWC–History, Box 7, Marshall Papers; Telegram, Marshall to FDR, 28 December 1940, 2 (second quote), and Telegram, Marshall to FDR, 29 December 1940, OF 4193 Misc., FDR Library; G. S. Smith, *To Save a Nation,* 164 (fourth quote).

39. Mark M. Jones to Bronson Batchelor, and attachments, 26 February 1941, NFWC—Organization and Operations, Box 7, Marshall Papers; Cole, *Roosevelt and the Isolationists,* 379–80; Wood to FDR, 7 February 1941, PPF 1365, FDR Library; Cole, *America First,* 84–85.

40. Cole, *America First,* 17–34; Memorandum from J. Edgar Hoover re America First Committee, 1 March 1941, 1–2, 4–5, attached to Memorandum, Stephen T. Early to Hoover, 21 February 1941, OF 4330, FDR Library.

41. Cole, *America First,* 37–38, 57.

42. Ibid., 69–71; Justus D. Doenecke, "Power, Markets, and Ideology," in Liggio and Martin, eds., *Watershed of Empire,* 143, 150; P. La Follette Speech before Phi Beta Kappa of New York, 18 December 1940, 1, Press Releases, 1940–42, Box 130, P. La Follette Papers; G. Nye, "Reminiscences of Senate Career," 1971, 7, Box 40, G. Nye Papers; G. Nye, "Should We Turn to 'Isolation'?" 1–2.

43. Robert E. Smith to Wheeler, 8 July 1940, S Misc. Correspondence, Box 7, Wheeler Papers; Cole, *Roosevelt and the Isolationists,* 8.

44. Justus D. Doenecke, "Power, Markets, and Ideology," in Liggio and Martin, eds., *Watershed of Empire,* 139–40, 143, 150–52; Doenecke, "Anti-Interventionist Tradition," 8.

45. National Association of Manufacturers Statements, "Governmental Aid to Countries at War" and "National Defense," 24 January 1940, Correspondence, January 1940, Box 5, Shipstead Papers; Wood to Stephen T. Early, and attachment, 6 November 1939, OF 1561, FDR Library.

46. Borah to John T. Flynn, 10 January 1938, Senate, Flynn Papers; Emil Trunk to G. Nye, 2 August 1941, Propaganda and Censorship, Box 43, G. Nye Papers.

47. Boyle, "Roots of Isolationism," 43; Carl P. Dick To Borah, 1 October 1939, 5, attached to Dick to Borah, 2 October 1939, Foreign Affairs–Neutrality, September–November 1939, General Office File, Box 513, Borah Papers; Burt Owens to Shipstead, 16 October 1939, Correspondence, 10–31 October 1939, Box 5, Shipstead Papers; Judge C. F. Schweigert to Burdick, 23 July 1941, attached to Burdick to Schweigert, 28 July 1941, Folder 12, Foreign Policy: Foreign Affairs Misc., 1941, Box 7, Burdick Papers.

48. R. La Follette Jr. Form Letter, 24/25 October 1940, War, 1940, General Office File, Box C-35A, R. La Follette Jr. Papers; Rehge L. Rolle to McNary, 15 June 1940, and McNary Form Letter, June 1940, General Correspondence, Box 9, McNary Papers; G. Nye draft of newspaper article, 15 October 1939, Addresses, Box 56, G. Nye Papers; Shipstead to Rosalind B. Judd, 8 January 1939, Correspondence, January 1939, Box 2, Shipstead Papers; Shipstead Speech Draft, 4 July 1941, 5, Speeches, News Releases, Statements, Folder 1, Box 21, Shipstead Papers; P. La Follette Speech before Phi Beta Kappa of New York, 18 December 1940, 2, Press Releases, 1940–42, Box 130, P. La Follette Papers.

49. Gipson, *State of the Nation,* 2–3; "Lindbergh, Willkie, and the Jews," *Chicago Daily Tribune,* 13 September 1941; Shipstead to Rev. T. F. Gullixson, 1 February 1940, Correspondence, February 1940, Box 5, Shipstead Papers; Wheeler, "Let's Go to War Now—An Answer," radio address, 20 August 1940, *CR,* 76th Cong., 3d sess. 86 (21 August 1940), A5153.

50. Poll of 8 November 1939, Gallup, *Gallup Poll,* vol. 1: 189; R. La Follette Jr. Statement, 15 August 1941, 1, attached to La Follette Jr. to Richard Neuberger, 15 August 1941, Personal Correspondence, Box C-18, R. La Follette Jr. Papers; H. Johnson, *CR,* 76th Cong., 2d sess., 84 (29 October 1939), 1072–73.

51. P. La Follette, speech before America First Meeting, Kenosha, Wis., Press Release, 26 May 1941 (first quote), Press Releases, 1940–42, Box 130, P. La Follette Papers; McNary Form Letter, May 1939, General Correspondence, Box 5, McNary Papers; Burdick, "United States Neutrality," speech, 25 September 1939, 1, Folder 21, Foreign Policy: Foreign Affairs 1939–54, Box 7, Burdick Papers; A. E. Bomgren to Shipstead, 22 October 1941 (second quote), Correspondence, 18–23 October 1941, Box 8, Shipstead Papers; Wheeler radio commentary, 12 January 1941, quoted in Cole, *Roosevelt and the Isolationists,* 415 (third quote).

52. Cole, *Roosevelt and the Isolationists,* 411–13 (quotes), 421–22.

53. Ibid., 414–15, 458; Wheeler, *CR.,* 77th Cong., 1st sess., 87 (21 January 1941), A178–79; Shipstead quoted in Feinman, *Twilight of Progressivism,* 194; R. La Follette Jr. Radio Address, 3 March 1941, 3–4, 6, Speeches and Articles, Box C-561, R. La Follette Jr. Papers; G. Nye Radio Address, 19 January 1941, and G. Nye Address before Mass Meeting of America First, New York, 20 February 1941, Addresses, Box 57, G. Nye Papers.

54. Guinsburg, *Pursuit of Isolationism,* 266; Cole, *Roosevelt and the Isolationists,* 414, 416–17, 419 (quotes).

55. Extracts from Minority Report of House Foreign Affairs Committee on Lend-Lease Bill, 1–2, File Material on Criticism of Lend-Lease Bill, OF 4193, FDR Library; Cole, *Roosevelt and the Isolationists,* 419–21.

56. Lindbergh quoted in Paul Seabury, "Charles Lindbergh: The Politics of Nostalgia," in *History,* 130; Lindbergh, "Letter to Americans," 14–15 (quote on 15), 77. For background on Lindbergh, see Cole, *Charles A. Lindbergh,* 2–94.

57. Cole, *Roosevelt and the Isolationists,* 461, 434–35; "Lindbergh Assails Tie with Russia," *New York Times,* 2 July 1941, 2 (first quote); Cole, *Charles A. Lindbergh,* 80 (second quote).

58. Larson, *Lindbergh of Minnesota,* 214; Lindbergh Address at Fort Wayne, Ind., 3 October 1941, clipping from *Chicago Daily Tribune,* 4 February 1941, Lindbergh Clippings, Box 19, Shipstead Papers; Roger Butterfield, "Lindbergh," *Life* 7 (11 August 1941), 65.

59. Lindbergh's *Reader's Digest* article quoted in Cole, *Charles A. Lindbergh,* 165; Program, America First Committee, Minneapolis Auditorium, 10 May 1945, Correspondence, May–August 16, 1941, Box 8, Shipstead Papers; Lindbergh quoted in Paul Seabury, "Charles Lindbergh: The Politics of Nostalgia," in *History,* 138.

60. Lindbergh quoted in Cole, *Charles A. Lindbergh,* 186 (first quote), 191 (third quote), 166 (fifth quote); Cole, *Roosevelt and the Isolationists,* 289; Lindbergh Address at Fort Wayne, Ind., 3 October 1941 (second quote), Lindbergh Clippings, Box 19, Shipstead Papers; "Lindbergh Cheered on Pledge to Talk as Long as Allowed," *Minneapolis Sunday Star,* 11 May 1941, 1 (fourth quote).

61. Lindbergh quoted in Cole, *Charles A. Lindbergh,* 56, 80–81, 171–73. The Des Moines speech referred to the "British and Jewish races."

62. Wheeler to Will Hays, 13 January 1941, attached to Hays to FDR, 17 January 1941, PPF 1945, FDR Library; Cole, *Roosevelt and the Isolationists,* 474–75; Cole, *Senator Gerald P. Nye,* 185–86 (Nye quoted on 186).

63. B. Clark testimony, 10 September 1941, in U.S. Senate, Subcommittee of the Committee on Interstate Commerce, *Propaganda in Motion Pictures,* 70–71 (quote on 71); G. Nye testimony, 9 September 1941, ibid., 47 (first Nye quote), 37, 35–36, 6 (second Nye quote).

64. G. Nye testimony, 9 September 1941, ibid., 37 (first quote), 42, 44 (second quote), 38; Willkie to D. Worth Clark, 8 September 1941, ibid., 19–21; Richard E. Gutstadt to Philmore J. Haber, 19 September 1941, 1, attached to Gustadt Form Letter, 17 September 1941, Charles A. Lindbergh, Correspondence, etc., 1941 (2), Box 34, Jewish Community Relations Council of Minnesota (hereafter JCRCM) Papers.

65. G. Nye to William Stern, 29 August 1941, 2, Anti-Semitism, 1941, Box 1, G. Nye Papers; Harry Weinberger to D. Worth Clark, 12 September 1941, America First: Motion Picture and Radio Investigation, Flynn Papers; Hyman Jaffe to G. Nye, 18 September 1941, Anti-Semitism, September 1941, Box 1, G. Nye Papers; Arthur Brin to Robert E. Wood, 14 September 1941, Charles A. Lindbergh, Correspondence, etc., 1939 (l), Box 34, JCRCM Papers; Thompson, "Contradictions of Lindbergh's Claim," *Washington Evening Star,* 17 September 1941; Ribuffo, *Old Christian Right,* 185.

66. Cole, *America First,* 132–38; Flynn to Robert E. Wood, 5 June 1941, 1, Wood Correspondence, America First Committee Files, Flynn Papers; Neuberger to Bailey Stortz, 15 September 1941, War or Peace, Box 38, Neuberger Papers.

67. Flynn to Wood, 5 June 1941, 1, Wood Correspondence, America First Committee Files, Flynn Papers; Bennett, *Party of Fear,* 265, 269–70; Robert Edward Edmondson, "The Jewish System Indicted," 15 September 1937, Anti-Semitism, 1937–39, Box 1, G. Nye Papers; H. Johnson to H. Johnson Jr., 11 February 1939, quoted in Cole, *Roosevelt and the Isolationists,* 308.

68. G. S. Smith, *To Save a Nation,* 4; Dr. F. E. Kosanke to Gerald P. Nye, 2 August 1941 (first quote), Propaganda and Censorship, Box 43, G. Nye Papers; Josephine Remer to Borah, 24 November 1938 (second quote), Jewish Refugees and Immigration Laws, November 1938, Subject File, Box 766, Borah Papers; Ribuffo, *Old Christian Right,* 9, 11; Langer ms., "The Jews" (third quote), attached to "TO WHOM IT MAY CONCERN," 3 September 1941, Folder 3, Speeches 1949–50, Box 274, Langer Papers.

69. Rankin quoted in G. S. Smith, *To Save a Nation,* 170; Holman quoted in "Bankers Behind War Drive," *New York Daily News,* 5 March 1941, 2; Report on Usher L. Burdick, n.d., 6, 7, 23, Burdick Folder, 1944–54, Box 9, JCRCM

Papers; Wheeler Speech, 3 March 1941, cited in FBI Report 1158, 13 February 1942, OF 10–B, FDR Library; Guinsburg, *Pursuit of Isolationism*, 265.

70. Flynn to Lindbergh, 15 September 1941, 1–3, America First: Lindbergh Speech, Flynn Papers; Cole, *Charles A. Lindbergh,* 171–72, 180, 185; Paul Seabury, "Charles Lindbergh: The Politics of Nostalgia," in *History,* 141.

71. Cole, *Roosevelt and the Isolationists,* 397 (first quote), 424–26, 432, 461 (second and third quotes), 462, 470–71 (fourth quote); Steele, "Franklin D. Roosevelt and His Foreign Policy Critics," 18–19, 32; Cole, *America First,* 135.

72. Cole, *Roosevelt and the Isolationists,* 436–41, 490, 443–44, 450–53; Wheeler to Flynn, 14 November 1941, Flynn Papers; MacNider quoted in Cole, *America First,* 197–98.

73. Lindbergh to Wood, 24 September 1941, Correspondence File, Box 10, Wood Papers; P. La Follette quoted in Cole, *America First,* 181–82; Lindbergh, draft of speech to be delivered 12 December 1941, 2, attached to Lindbergh to Wood, 6 December 1941, Correspondence File, Box 10, Wood Papers.

74. Lindbergh, draft of speech to be delivered 12 December 1941, 3, attached to Lindbergh to Wood, 6 December 1941, Correspondence File, Box 10, Wood Papers; Cole, *Roosevelt and the Isolationists,* 504–6; Spritzer, "B. K. Wheeler and Jim Murray," 27; Cole, *America First,* 193–96.

75. Wood to Lindbergh, 12 December 1941, Correspondence File, Box 10, Wood Papers; Doenecke, "Anti-Interventionist Tradition," 8.

Chapter 9: Democratic Nationalism and the Assault on Collectivism, 1941–46

1. Lindbergh, *Wartime Journals of Charles A. Lindbergh,* xv; Wheeler, "America, You Will Love War!" radio address, 22 February 1941, *CR,* 77th Cong., 1st sess., 87 (25 February 1941), A831.

2. Lemke, "Government by Bureaucracy," *CR,* 78th Cong., 1st sess., 89 (29 March 1943), A1541; G. Nye to R. Douglas Stuart Jr., 19 January 1942, America First Committee Correspondence, 1942 and undated, Box 1, G. Nye Papers.

3. Taft quoted in Polenberg, *War and Society* 269; Taft, "Is This a Conservative War?" 2; Peek to Repr. Roy O. Woodruff, 10 December 1941, Folder 1330, Peek Papers; Fish, "Campaign of Abuses Has Started," *CR,* 78th Cong., 2d sess., 90 (29 February 1944), A1020; Dennis to Robert Wood, 23 January 1943, Correspondence File, Box 3, Wood Papers.

4. Bureau of Intelligence, Office of Facts and Figures (OFF), *Survey of Intelligence Materials,* 27 (10 June 1942), 1, 2, 5, 14, PSF OWI; Gallup, "An Analysis of American Public Opinion regarding the War" (American Institute of Public Opinion), 10 September 1942, 8, PPF 4721; and Bureau of Intelligence, OFF, *Survey of Intelligence Materials,* 12 (2 March 1942), 3–4, and 28 (17 June 1942), 8a, PSF OWI, all in FDR Library.

5. Bureau of Intelligence, OFF, *Survey of Intelligence Materials,* 27 (10 June 1942), 13, 17–19, and 12 (2 March 1942), 5, PSF OWI; Gallup, "An Analysis of American Public Opinion regarding the War" (American Institute of Public Opinion), 10 September 1942, 8, PPF 4721; and Bureau of Intelligence, OFF,

Survey of Intelligence Materials, 28 (17 June 1942), 8a, PSF OWI, all in FDR Library.

6. Shipstead, "The 'Four Freedoms' Alliance (Ltd.)," statement, n.d., 2, Speeches, News Releases, Statements, Folder 4, Box 21, Shipstead Papers; Brooks, "Political Aims of Russia and England," *CR,* 78th Cong., 2d sess., 90 (13 December 1944), 9309; O'Donnell, "Capitol Stuff," *Washington Times-Herald,* 14 December 1944, *CR,* 78th Cong., 2d sess., 90 (14 December 1944), 4750–51.

7. Memorandum, FDR to R. La Follette Jr., and attachment, 20 February 1942, Personal Correspondence, Box C-20, R. La Follette Jr. Papers; Darilek, *A Loyal Opposition,* 51 (Churchill quote), 125–26; Young, *Congressional Politics,* 161–62.

8. Ickes to FDR, 23 June 1941, War, Secretary of Interior File, Box 373, Ickes Papers; "The Two Russias," *Chicago Tribune, CR,* 77th Cong., 2d sess., 88 (11 June 1942), A2222; Wood to R. Douglas Stuart, 20 December 1944, Correspondence File, Box 17, Wood Papers.

9. Darilek, *A Loyal Opposition,* 127–28, 97–98, 143.

10. "Sacrifices to Communism," *Chicago American,* 22 November 1943, *CR,* 78th Cong., 1st sess., 89 (22 November 1943), A5009–10.

11. Darilek, *A Loyal Opposition,* 32–34, 129 (Fish quote); Albert B. Chandler, 17 May 1943, quoted in Young, *Congressional Politics,* 152.

12. Charles I. Faddis, *CR,* 77th Cong., 2d sess., 88 (28 September 1942), 7550–51; "Communist League Has Abandoned Old Label," *Tablet,* 23 October 1943, *CR,* 78th Cong., 1st sess., 89 (28 October 1943), A4612; "Fourth Term Urged by District of Columbia and Maryland Communists," *Washington Daily News,* 3 February 1944, *CR,* 78th Cong., 2d sess., 90 (4 February 1944), A587; Davis, quoted by Karl E. Mundt, "Head of War Information Warns against Communist Propaganda," *CR,* 77th Cong., 2d sess., 88 (24 July 1942), A2954.

13. Martin Dies to FDR, 1 October 1941, 1 (first and second quotes), 5 (third quote), 2 (fourth quote), OF 263, FDR Library; Dies, *CR,* 77th Cong., 2d sess., 88 (15 January 1942), 410.

14. Fish, "Communist Camouflage—New Labels for Old," *CR,* 78th Cong., 1st sess., 89 (28 October 1943), A4612; "Communist League Has Abandoned Old Label," *Tablet,* 23 October 1943, *CR,* 78th Cong., 1st sess., 89 (28 October 1943), A4612; Eastman, "To Collaborate Successfully We Must Face the Facts about Russia," *Reader's Digest,* July 1943, *CR,* 78th Cong., 1st sess., 89 (1 July 1943), A3440.

15. Dies, *CR,* 77th Cong., 2d sess., 88 (28 January 1942), 800; Memorandum, Maude D. Poulton to Stephen T. Early, and attachments, 5 February 1942, OF 133, FDR Library; *CR,* 77th Cong., 2d sess., 88 (28 January, 9 February, 30 April 1942), 791, 1139, 3806.

16. Busbey, "Red Art Propaganda," *CR,* 78th Cong., 1st sess., 89 (30 June 1943), 6892; Dennis to Robert Wood, 23 January 1943, Correspondence File, Box 3, Wood Papers; Wheeler, "American Communists's Attitude toward Certain American Citizens," *CR,* 77th Cong., 2d sess., 88 (11 May 1942), A1682; "The Two Russias," *Chicago Tribune, CR,* 77th Cong., 2d sess., 88 (11 June 1942), A2222; Bureau of Intelligence, OFF, *Survey of Intelligence Materials,* 19

(19 April 1942), 8, 11–12, and 28 (17 June 1942), 5–6, PSF OWI, FDR Library; Ribuffo, *Old Christian Right,* 184–87.

17. Ribuffo, *Old Christian Right,* 187; Memorandum, Stephen T. Early to J. Edgar Hoover, 21 May 1940, OF 10–B, FDR Library; Cole, *Roosevelt and the Isolationists,* 460, 486–87, 531; Memorandum, FDR to Francis Biddle, 17 November 1941, Justice Department, 1938–44, PSF, FDR Library; "America First Committee," 13 February 1942, 14–19, attached to J. Edgar Hoover to Edwin M. Watson, 13 February 1942, FBI Report 1158, OF 10–B, FDR Library.

18. G. S. Smith, *To Save a Nation,* 126–28, 136; Charles E. Coughlin, "Persecution—Jewish and Christian," 20 November 1938, OF 4330, FDR Library; Brinkley, *Voices of Protest,* 267.

19. Bureau of Intelligence, OFF, *Survey of Intelligence Materials,* 19 (19 April 1942), 8, PSF OWI, FDR Library; Ribuffo, *Old Christian Right,* 174, 188–89, 193–98, 125–27.

20. Dennis to Wood, 30 July 1944, Correspondence File, Box 3, Wood Papers; G. Nye, *CR,* 78th Cong., 1st sess., 89 (14 January 1943), 149; Langer quoted in Elizabeth Donahue, "Langer Champions Sedition Suspects," *PM,* 10 September 1945 (first Langer quote), Langer, 1944–47, JCRCM Papers; Langer, *CR,* 78th Cong., 2d sess., 90 (8 September 1944), 7624 (second Langer quote).

21. Memorandum, James Rowe Jr. to Attorney General Biddle, 25 February 1943 (quote), Justice Department Folder, Francis Biddle Papers, 1941–43, PSF, FDR Library; Memorandum, Herbert Wechsler to Biddle, 16 June 1945, Domestic Propaganda Folder, Francis Biddle Papers, 1941–43, PSF, FDR Library; Ribuffo, *Old Christian Right,* 193–95, 215, 256.

22. H. A. Wallace, "The Price of Free World Victory," address before the Free World Association, 8 May 1942, 1, New York City, attached to Wallace to FDR, 4 May 1942, OF 12, FDR Library; Blum, *V Was for Victory,* 21–34; Winkler, *Politics of Propaganda.*

23. Starnes, *CR,* 78th Cong., 1st sess., 89 (18 June 1943), 6133–34; Bridges, "Tribute to the Press—Criticism of Office of War Information," *CR,* 78th Cong., 1st sess., 89 (15 June 1943), 5863.

24. Winkler, *Politics of Propaganda,* 66–68 (quote on 66); Fish, "AFL and CIO List OWI as Communist," *CR,* 78th Cong., 1st sess., 89 (12 October 1943), A4249; Bradley, *CR,* 78th Cong., 1st sess., 89 (1 April 1943), 2821.

25. Winkler, *Politics of Propaganda,* 68–71, 149; *CR,* 78th Cong., 1st sess., 89 (18, 30 June 1943), 6133, 6137, 6143, 6814, 6828; C. P. Trussell, "Roosevelt Signs Six Big Fund Bills," *New York Times,* 13 July 1943, 1, 26; *CR,* 78th Cong., 1st sess., 89 (17 September, 4 November 1943), 7637, 9171.

26. Chapman, *Contours of Public Policy,* 168–74; Bradley, "Office of Civilian Defense Used as Propaganda Agency," *CR,* 78th Cong., 1st sess., 89 (11 October 1943), 8194–95.

27. Abrahamson, *American Home Front,* 132–33, 139; Karl, *Uneasy State,* 209–12, 214–15.

28. Herbert J. Rushton to Fred Chase, 14 January 1943, 1, 9, Time Controversy—1943, C–G, Box 76; Thomas J. Jerbert to Marvin A. Kelly, Opinion No. 4788, 2 February 1942, Daylight, H–M, Box 77; Samuel F. Brown to Ohio Leg-

islature, 6 February 1943 (first quote), attached to Bricker to Brown, 8 February 1943, Time Controversy—1943, A–B, Box 76; Dr. B. F. Lamb to Bricker, 2 March 1943, attached to Bricker to Lamb, 8 March 1943, Time Controversy—1943, H–L; Ethyl Allard to Bricker, 24 February 1943 (second quote), Time Controversy—1943, A–B; and Judge Frank L. Johnson to Attorney General Thomas Herbert, 23 February 1943, attached to Bricker to Johnson, 1 March 1943, Time Controversy, H–L, all in Bricker Papers.

29. Vatter, *U.S. Economy in World War II,* 89, 92, 98–99; Chapman, *Contours of Public Policy,* 145–46, 179–85, 224–25; Bureau of Intelligence, OFF, *Survey of Intelligence Materials,* 20 (22 April 1942), 9, PSF OWI, FDR Library. Rationing of gasoline, coffee, and canned foods stemmed from shortages of tires, ships, and tin.

30. C. P. Trussell, "Congress Recesses until September 14," *New York Times,* 9 July 1943, 1; Chapman, *Contours of Public Policy,* 226–28.

31. Chapman, *Contours of Public Policy,* 218–23; Leff, "Politics of Sacrifice," 1299–1301, 1306; G. Nye Form Letter, 14 May 1943, Addresses, Box 59, G. Nye Papers; *CR,* 78th Cong., 1st sess., 89 (23 March 1943), 2347.

32. Chapman, *Contours of Public Policy,* 214–15; U.S. House of Representatives, Select Committee to Investigate Acts of Executive Agencies beyond the Scope of Their Authority, *Second Intermediate Report,* 11.

33. Bureau of Intelligence, OFF, *Survey of Intelligence Materials,* 35 (7 August 1942), 15, PSF OWI, FDR Library; Walter H. Judd to Frank V. LaVelle, and attachments, 17 February 1943, OPA, February 1943; Ferris B. Martin to Judd, 11 January 1943, and Paul A. Best to Judd, 23 January 1943, OPA, January 1943; Judd to Lewis Shawhan, and attachments, 2 March 1943, OPA, March 1943; Judd to W. S. Moscrip, 13 February 1943, OPA, February 1943; and Judd to Leif Edon, 19 January 1943, and Judd to Robert L. Wilson, and attachments, 10 January 1943, OPA, January 1943, all in Box 37, Judd Papers.

34. Dirksen, "Powers of the Courts Must Be Restored to Review Regulations and Orders of OPA," *CR,* 78th Cong., 1st sess., 89 (22 September 1943), A3949–50; Jennings, 78th Cong., 2d sess., 90 (10 June 1944), 5714–15; Lemke quoted in Blackorby, *Prairie Rebel,* 195; Martin Dies, *CR,* 77th Cong., 2d sess., 88 (15 January 1942), 408–9.

35. Sikes, "Failure of the OPA," 78th Cong., 1st sess., 89 (6 May 1943), A3410 (first and second quotes), A3411 (third quote); Judd to Beatrice Lindgren, 17 March 1943, Republican Party, March–June 1943, Box 49, Judd Papers; Judd to Bernard G. Rice, 2 March 1943, OPA, March 1943, Box 37, Judd Papers; Vursell, "OPA and Small Business," *CR,* 78th Cong., 1st sess., 89 (27 May 1943), A2634–35; "Senator Langer Cites Record," *New York Times,* 1 July 1943, *CR,* 78th Cong., 1st sess., 89 (1 July 1943), A3362.

36. Dirksen, 78th Cong., 1st sess., 89 (18 June 1943), 6111–12, 6122–26, 6140–41; Chapman, *Contours of Public Policy,* 215–16.

37. Dennis, "Grand Strategy for the Republican Party until 1944," 1 December 1942, 6, Political File, Box 70, Bricker Papers; Charles Le Bleu to FDR, 4 June 1942, 1–4, L Misc. Folder (LEB–LOM), Box 48, H. Johnson Papers.

38. Bureau of Intelligence, OFF, *Survey of Intelligence Materials,* 28 (17 June 1942),

8–8a, and 64 (26 February 1943), 4–5, PSF OWI, FDR Library; Schwabe, "Stop Bureaucracy, or What?" *CR,* 79th Cong., 1st sess., 91 (27 September 1945), A4065.

39. Robsion, "Cut Down Waste and Inefficiency," *CR,* 78th Cong., 1st sess., 89 (22 September 1943), 7760 (first quote); Tydings, "Activities of Government Press Agencies," *CR,* 77th Cong., 2d sess., 88 (28 May 1942), 4684 (second quote); Philip A. Bennett, *CR,* 77th Cong., 2d sess., 88 (24 February 1942), A679 (third quote); Woodruff, "Paying for Past Follies," *CR,* 78th Cong., 1st sess., 89 (19 November 1943), A4988 (fourth and fifth quotes), 4989 (sixth quote).

40. Jones, "Agencies under White House Control," *CR,* 77th Cong., 2d sess., 88 (27 April 1942), A1541; Shipstead quoted in Guinsburg, *Pursuit of Isolationism,* 243; Judd to L. D. Sargent, 9 July 1943, Bureaucracy, 1943–44, Box 8, Judd Papers; Wherry, *CR,* 79th Cong, 1st sess., 91 (18 June 1945), 6236.

41. Ludlow, *CR,* 78th Cong., 2d sess., 90 (10, 15 May 1944), 4293, 4525; Lemke, "Government by Bureaucracy," *CR,* 78th Cong., 1st sess., 89 (29 March 1943), A1541.

42. Maney, *"Young Bob" La Follette,* 253; R. La Follette Jr., "A Senator Looks at Congress," 91.

43. Chapman, *Contours of Public Policy,* 92–97, 102–3 (Walters quote on 96).

44. Ibid., 211–14; Polenberg, *War and Society,* 194–95 (Dies quote on 194); C. P. Trussell, "Congress Recesses until September 14," *New York Times,* 9 July 1943, 13.

45. Young, *Congressional Politics,* 19, 33, 41, 38, 36; Chapman, *Contours of Public Policy,* 261, 135–37, 147–68; 233–41, 241–45, 248–50, 252, 256–59; Polenberg, *War and Society,* 79–85.

46. Patman, "Surplus Property and Small Business," *CR,* 78th Cong., 2d sess., 90 (16 August 1944), 7025; Polenberg, *War and Society,* 8, 12–13, 77–78; Abrahamson, *American Home Front,* 135–36, 150.

47. Bruchey, *Wealth of the Nation,* 180–81; Vatter, *U.S. Economy in World War II,* 55–60; Zeigler, *Politics of Small Business,* 2–3.

48. Murray, *CR,* 76th Cong., 3d sess., 86 (22 August 1940), 10708; FDR to Murray, and attachments, 7 October 1940, OF 172, FDR Library; *CR,* 76th Cong., 3d sess., 86 (9 September, 8 October 1940), 11793–94, 13367, 13370, 13372; *CR,* 77th Cong., 1st sess., 87 (4 December 1941), 9428; Zeigler, *Politics of Small Business,* 81–82.

49. Heath, "American War Mobilization," 298, 308–10, 316; Special Committee to Study Problems of American Small Business, Rept. 479, Part 2 and 3, in Murray, *CR,* 77th Cong., 2d sess., 88 (5 February 1942), 1044–47, 1595–96; U.S. Senate, Special Committee to Study Problems of American Small Business, *American Small Business,* 1–2, 5–6, 12–16, 18 (first quote on 6); Murray to FDR, 24 August 1942, Diary of Henry Morgenthau Jr., Book 564, 140, and Murray to Morgenthau Jr., 2 October 1942 (second quote), Diary of Henry Morgenthau Jr., Book 582, 436, FDR Library.

50. Blum, *V Was for Victory,* 126–30; Memorandum, Smaller War Plants Corporation, 7 December 1943, attached to R. La Follette Jr. to S. Abbot Smith, 21 December 1943, Smaller War Plants Corp., Government Department File, Box C-252, R. La Follette Jr. Papers.

51. Vatter, *U.S. Economy in World War II,* 61–66; Dahlstrom, "'Remote Bigness' as a Theme," 24–26; Stromer, *Making of a Political Leader,* 103.

52. *CR,* 78th Cong., 2d sess., 90 (12 May, 22 June, 1, 11 December 1944), 4370–74, 6478, 8708, 9097; Blum, *V Was for Victory,* 124–31.

53. U.S. Senate, Temporary National Economic Committee, *Final Report and Recommendations,* 24–29.

54. Patman, "The Republican Party . . . Bad for Small Business," *CR,* 78th Cong., 2d sess., 90 (8 June 1944), A2868–69; Patman, "Surplus Property and Small Business," *CR,* 78th Cong., 2d sess., 90 (16 August 1944), 7025–30; "Fate of the Small Business Committee," *St. Louis Globe-Democrat,* 27 November 1945, *CR,* 79th Cong., 1st sess., 91 (10 December 1945), A5401.

55. Zeigler, *Politics of Small Business,* 81–82; Taft, "We Must Remove Restrictions on Business," *Philadelphia Inquirer,* 7 May 1944, cited by Harold Ickes, "On Free Enterprise," 8, draft for *Everybody's Digest,* 23 June 1944, Articles, Secretary of Interior File, Box 116, Ickes Papers; Virkus quoted in Report on Frederick A. Virkus, 220, 224–25, 228, Conference of Small Business Organizations, 1944, Box 13, JCRCM Papers; *CR,* 79th Cong., 1st sess., 91 (12 December 1945), 11891–99.

56. "The Bretton Woods Proposals," OF 5549, FDR Library; Blum, *V Was for Victory,* 307–9.

57. Morgenthau Radio Address, 23 July 1944, 1–4 (first and second quotes on 3; third quote on 2), attached to Morgenthau to FDR, 29 July 1944, OF 5549, FDR Library.

58. Wagner, *CR,* 79th Cong., 1st sess., 91 (15 February 1945), 1114–15; H. J. Kahout and family to Shipstead, 18 July 1945, Correspondence, 18–26 July 1945, Box 12, Shipstead Papers; Undelivered Shipstead Speech, 1946, 4–7, Speeches, News Releases, Statements, Folder 5, Box 21, Shipstead Papers; Geelan, *Dakota Maverick,* 116; Elmer Thomas et al. to FDR, 21 June 1944, attached to FDR to Thomas, 13 July 1944, OF 5549, FDR Library.

59. Dennis, "Grand Strategy for the Republican Party until 1944," 1 December 1942, 7–11 (first quote on 7; second quote on 11), Political File, Box 70, Bricker Papers. Although there is no author listed in the Bricker files, Dennis's name appears on a copy attached to Dennis to Robert E. Wood, 19 November 1942, Correspondence, Box 3, Wood Papers.

60. Flynn, "You Better Know about Bretton Woods," 5, 7, 10, National Economic Council, June 1945, Economic Council Papers, Vol. 3, No. 12, A5335, Box 27, Shipstead Papers.

61. Taft quoted in Blum, *V Was for Victory,* 308, and Taft Press Release, 3–4, Bretton Woods Agreement, 1944–45, Box 496, Taft Papers; *CR,* 79th Cong., 1st sess., 91 (7 June, 19 July 1945), 5723, 7780.

62. Willis quoted in Darilek, *A Loyal Opposition,* 67; Wherry, *CR,* 79th Cong., 1st sess., 91 (18 June 1945), 6237; Dahlstrom, "'Remote Bigness' as a Theme," 30; Peek to Roy O. Woodruff, 25 March 1942, *CR,* 77th Cong., 2d sess., 88 (7 May 1942), A1672; Peek to G. Nye, 19 January 1943, Folder 1407, Peek Papers.

63. Wiley, *CR,* 79th Cong., 1st sess., 91 (20 June 1945), 6352; Langer, *CR,* 78th Cong., 1st sess., 89 (28 May 1943), 5025.

64. Darilek, *A Loyal Opposition,* 67; *CR,* 78th Cong., 1st sess., 89 (13 May, 2 June 1943), 4378, 5203; Frederick R. Barkley, "Gives Truman Right to Reduce Tariffs," *New York Times,* 20 June 1945, 1, 15; *CR,* 79th Cong., 1st sess., 91 (26 May, 12, 20 June 1945), 5166, 5968, 6358–59, 6361–64; Barkley, "Senate Extends Trade Law," *New York Times,* 21 June 1945, 1, 15.

65. Vandenberg Jr. quoted in Darilek, *A Loyal Opposition,* 59; Darilek, *A Loyal Opposition,* 65–68; Flynn to Vandenberg, 18 August 1943, Senate, Flynn Papers; O'Donnell, "Capitol Stuff," *Washington Times-Herald,* 29 February 1944, *CR,* 78th Cong., 2d sess., 90 (29 February 1944), A1005.

66. Bureau of Intelligence, Office of Facts and Figures, *Survey of Intelligence Materials,* 17 (1 April 1942) 1–3, and 27 (10 June 1942), 14–15, PSF OWI, FDR Library; Gallup poll, cited in Divine, *Second Chance,* 68–69; McCoy, "Republican Opposition during Wartime," 184; Darilek, *A Loyal Opposition,* 69, 139–40.

67. Darilek, *A Loyal Opposition,* 82 (Fulbright quote), 70–74, 120–23.

68. Burdick Speech Draft, n.d., 3, Folder 12, Foreign Policy, Foreign Affairs Misc. 1941, Box 7, Burdick Papers; Hoffman, *CR,* 77th Cong., 2d sess., 88 (13 January 1942), 310; Wheeler, "Americanism versus Internationalism in the Post-War Picture," *CR,* 78th Cong., 1st sess., 89 (8 April 1943), A1716; Wheeler to Wood, 21 April 1944, Correspondence File, Box 21, Wood Papers.

69. Flynn, *As We Go Marching,* 252 (first quote); Flynn, "What Is the President's Foreign Policy and What Is Wrong with It?" 12 June 1944, 2 (second quote), 5 (third quote), Foreign Policy, Box 26, Flynn Papers; G. Nye, *CR,* 78th Cong., 1st sess., 89 (4 November 1943), 9084, 9089–90; G. Nye, *CR,* 78th Cong., 2d sess., 90 (19 December 1944), 9688 (fourth quote).

70. G. Nye, *CR,* 78th Cong., 2d sess., 90 (19 December 1944), 9688; Darilek, *A Loyal Opposition,* 126–27; Thad F. Wasielewski, "The Yalta Agreement," *CR,* 79th Cong., 1st sess., 91 (23 March 1945), 2697.

71. Young, *Congressional Politics,* 195–96; Wheeler, *CR,* 79th Cong., 1st sess., 91 (24 July 1945), 7973; Shipstead Speech, 14 July 1945, 3, Speeches, News Releases, Statements, Folder 3, Box 21, Shipstead Papers; *CR,* 79th Cong., 1st sess., 91 (28 July 1945), 8190; Langer to M. Jane Mann, 4 October 1945, Folder 4, United Nations Charter 1945, Box 146, Langer Papers.

72. Polenberg, *War and Society,* 187–89; Stromer, *Making of a Political Leader,* 3–4, 12; Dahlstrom, "'Remote Bigness' as a Theme," 25, 31–32.

73. Dennis, "Grand Strategy for the Republican Party until 1944," 1 December 1942, 14–15 (first quote), 7 (second quote), Political File, Box 70, Bricker Papers.

74. Wood to Dennis, 19 January 1943, Political File, Box 70, Bricker Papers; Darilek, *A Loyal Opposition,* 43–45, 144–49; Flynn to B. Carroll Reece, 21 April 1942, House, Flynn Papers; Wood to Karl E. Mundt, 12 November 1943, Correspondence File, Box 12, Wood Papers; Wood to Isabel B. La Follette, 18 December 1944, Correspondence File, Box 9, Wood Papers.

75. Chapman, *Contours of Public Policy,* 263; Feinman, *Twilight of Progressivism,* 206–8; Rylance, "A Controversial Career," 14–18; Winkler, *Home Front,* 81–84; Meyer, "Politics of Loyalty," 129, 132, 136–40, 143–45; P. Jones, "Wash-

ington Can't Cure Everything," 112; Wheeler, *Yankee From the West,* 389; P. La Follette quoted in Miller, *Governor Philip F. La Follette,* 177–78. For the importance of the 1946 elections, see Griffith, "Old Progressives and the Cold War," 337; and Cole, *Roosevelt and the Isolationists,* 553–55.

Chapter 10: Crisis of the Old Order

1. House Military Affairs Committee Report, 29 June 1945, cited in "Communists Still Active," *Washington Post,* 30 June 1945, *CR,* 79th Cong., 1st sess., 91 (30 June 1945), A3176–77.

2. Miller, "Advice to OPA," *CR,* 79th Cong., 1st sess., 91 (26 June 1945), A3021; Jenkins, "Greatest Menace is Propaganda," *CR,* 79th Cong., 1st sess., 91 (19 December 1945), A5675; O'Daniel, *CR,* 79th Cong., 1st sess., 91 (10 December 1945), 11706; poll of 4 March 1946, Gallup, *Gallup Poll,* vol. 1: 561.

3. Dahlstrom, "'Remote Bigness' as a Theme," 27–28; Stromer, *Making of a Political Leader,* 79; Press Release, Senate Small Business Committee, 29 November 1945, Small Business Committee, Legislative File, Box C-342, R. La Follette Jr. Papers; Resolution, Minnesota Small Business Commission, 4 February 1946, Small Business Committee, 1946–47, Box 51, Judd Papers; Press Release, Tiffin, Ohio, 9 October 1946, 2–3 (quote on 3), Press Releases and Speeches, September–November 1946, Campaign for U.S. Senate, Box 86A, Bricker Papers.

4. John D. Morris, "OPA Compromise Sent to President," *New York Times,* 29 June 1946, 1; Bertram D. Hulen, "OPA Price Controls End," *New York Times,* 30 June 1946, 1, 9; Morris, "House Votes Bill to Control Prices," *New York Times,* 24 July 1946, 1–2; Hamby, *Beyond the New Deal,* 79–80.

5. Bricker to C. W. Freer, 6 March 1947, and Fred L. Crawford to Bricker, and attachments, 10 March 1947, Correspondence, Box 86B, Bricker Papers; *CR,* 80th Cong., 1st sess., 93 (28 February, 24 March 1947), 1526, 2437, 2448; *CR,* 80th Cong., 2d sess., 94 (20 February, 23, 31 March 1948), 1445, 3271–72, 3770–72; Dahlstrom, "'Remote Bigness' as a Theme," 30–31.

6. Bricker entries, *Current Biography, 1943,* 73, and *Current Biography, 1956,* 77; Bricker Speech before Republican State Convention, Columbus, Ohio, 11 September 1946, 2–3 (first quote on 2), Bricker Press Release, Elyria, Ohio, 16 October 1946 (second quote), and Bricker Press Release, Ashland, Ohio, 24 October 1946, Press Releases and Speeches, September–November 1946, Campaign for U.S. Senate, Box 86A, Bricker Papers.

7. Bricker Speech before Republican State Convention, Columbus, Ohio, 11 September 1946, 2 (first quote), 4–5 (second quote on 5), Bricker Press Release, Cleveland, 22 October 1946, 4, and Bricker Press Release, Toledo, 18 October 1946 (third and fourth quotes), Press Releases and Speeches, September–November 1946, Campaign for U.S. Senate, Box 86A, Bricker Papers.

8. Shipstead, "Economic Trends," 199 (first quote), 201 (second quote); Judd to Frank P. Leslie, 22 July 1946, Republican Party, June–July 1946, Box 56, Judd Papers; McCarran, *CR,* 80th Cong., 1st sess., 93 (24 April 1947), 3898.

9. Wheeler to Joe Bauer, 4 June 1946, Misc. Correspondence, Box 8, Wheeler Papers; Wheeler, *CR,* 79th Cong., 1st sess., 91 (27 November 1945), 11034

(quote); Shipstead Speech Draft, 1946, Speeches, News Releases, Statements, Folder 2, Box 22, Shipstead Papers; P. La Follette, "A Sound American Policy," radio address, 18 October 1946, Papers, Publications, and Speeches, 1942–61, Box 120, P. La Follette Papers.

10. Wheeler to Flynn, 31 December 1943, cited in Ribuffo, *Old Christian Right*, 193; "La Follette Leads Isolationist Bolt," *New York Times*, 9 May 1944, 1; R. La Follette Jr., *CR*, 79th Cong., 1st sess., 91 (31 May 1945), 5315–32; R. La Follette Jr. quoted in Maney, *"Young Bob" La Follette*, 268.

11. Dondero, *CR*, 79th Cong., 1st sess., 91 (8 March 1945), A1093; Joseph P. McLaughlin to Matthew J. Connelly, 1 May 1950, 1950 Folder, OF 263–Misc., Truman Library; Burdick to George Wall, 10 May 1951 (quote), Folder 2, Communism as a Political Dictatorship in Russia, Box 23, Burdick Papers; Burdick, "Communism," Folder 31, Socialist-Communist Ideology Dupes Americans, Box 23, Burdick Papers; Bricker, "Mobilizing for World Leadership," speech before National Industrial Conference Board, 28 May 1947, 6, Press Releases, Speeches, 1947–48, Box 86B, Bricker Papers.

12. Flynn to Taft, 9 October 1946, Senate, Flynn Papers; Taft, "Return to Liberty," speech to Missouri Republican Club, Kansas City, Mo., 12 February 1946, *CR*, 79th Cong., 2d sess., 92 (1 March 1946), A1047–49; Martin quoted in Theoharis, *Yalta Myths*, 45.

13. Reece quoted in Theoharis, *Yalta Myths*, 51; Martin quoted in Griffith, *Politics of Fear*, 11, 38; Taft quoted in Theoharis, *Yalta Myths*, 11; Vursell quoted in Theoharis, *Yalta Myths*, 52.

14. Wherry quoted in Oshinsky, *A Conspiracy So Immense*, 50, 52; Athan Theoharis, Introduction, in Theoharis, ed., *Truman Presidency*, ii (second quote); Dallek, *American Style of Foreign Policy*, 157; Theoharis, *Seeds of Repression*, 18–20; Meyer, "Politics of Loyalty," 129–48.

15. R. La Follette Jr., "Turn the Light on Communism," 73–74; Maney, *"Young Bob" La Follette*, 307 (quote), 309; A. Harper, *Politics of Loyalty*, 20–23.

16. Polls of 6 July, 26 August 1946, Gallup, *Gallup Poll*, vol. 1: 587, 593–94; George H. Earle to Truman, 26 February 1947, attached to Truman to Earle, 28 February 1947, 1945–47 Folder, OF 263, Truman Library.

17. Reeves, *Life and Times of Joe McCarthy*, 206; Thomas to Truman, 23 April 1947, quoted in A. Harper, *Politics of Loyalty*, 46; Spellman and J. Hoover quoted in Dallek, *American Style of Foreign Policy*, 168.

18. A. Harper, *Politics of Loyalty*, 24–44; G. S. Smith, "Isolationism, the Devil and Second World War," 85.

19. A. Harper, *Politics of Loyalty*, 62–63; Bourke B. Hickenlooper, *CR*, 80th Cong., 1st sess., 93 (24 March 1947), 2451; Anthony Leviero, "Lilienthal's Fate Uncertain," *New York Times*, 12 February 1947, 6; "Owen Young Aids Lilienthal," *New York Times*, 24 February 1947, 3; "M'Kellar Resumes Lilienthal Battle," *New York Times*, 18 February 1947, 17; Cabell Phillips, "Lilienthal Case Becomes a Political Issue," *New York Times*, 16 February 1947, sec. 4: 3; "Lilienthal Scored at Senate Meeting," *New York Times*, 11 February 1947, 10.

20. Anthony Leviero, "Lilienthal Rejects Red Aims," *New York Times*, 5 February 1947, 1, 3; Leviero, "Lilienthal's Fate Uncertain," *New York Times*,

12 February 1947, 1, 6; Leviero, "Lilienthal 'Veto' Asked by McKellar," *New York Times,* 6 February 1947, 1 (quote).

21. McCraw, *Morgan vs. Lilienthal,* 72–73, 79, 82, 107; Telegram, Morgan to Robert A. Taft, n.d., Series 4, B4, Morgan Papers; Morgan to Taft, 4 March 1947, attached to Morgan *Vita,* Atomic Energy, 1945–48, Box 491, Taft Papers. Taft explained his opposition to Morgan in *CR,* 80th Cong., 1st sess., 93 (2 April 1947), 3024.

22. Telegram, Morgan to Taft, n.d. (first quote), and Morgan, *Antioch Notes,* 24 (15 March 1947), n.p. (second quote), Series 4, B4, Morgan Papers; Morgan to Taft, 4 March 1947, attached to Morgan *Vita,* Atomic Energy, 1945–48, Box 491, Taft Papers; "A. E. Morgan Explains Opposition to Lilienthal," *Yellow Springs News,* 27 March 1947, 1–2.

23. A. Harper, *Politics of Loyalty,* 63; "Lilienthal Scored at Senate Meeting," *New York Times,* 11 February 1947, 10; "Truman to Back Lilienthal," *New York Times,* 13 February 1947, 1, 12; Cabell Phillips, "Lilienthal Case Becomes a Political Issue," *New York Times,* 16 February 1947, sec. 4: 3 (first quote); Taft, Statement of 22 February 1947, in "Text of Taft and Compton Messages," *New York Times,* 22 February 1947, 4 (Taft quotes).

24. "Text of Taft and Compton Messages," *New York Times,* 22 February 1947, 4 (Taft quotes).

25. Kenneth McKellar, *CR,* 80th Cong., 1st sess., 93 (3 April 1947), A1463.

26. Ferguson entry, *Current Biography, 1943,* 202; Ferguson, *CR,* 80th Cong., 1st sess., 93 (26 March 1947), 2594–95.

27. Ferguson, *CR,* 80th Cong., 1st sess., 93 (26 March 1947), 2594.

28. Anthony Leviero, "Lilienthal Wins Senate Vote," *New York Times,* 10 April 1947, 1; A. Harper, *Politics of Loyalty,* 65–66. For the Senate vote to confirm, see *CR,* 80th Cong., 1st sess., 93 (9 April 1947), 3241.

29. Griffith, *Politics of Fear,* 40–41.

30. Carr, *House Committee on Un-American Activities,* 21–36.

31. Ibid., 37–50; Theoharis, *Seeds of Repression,* 120–21; HUAC report of 1948 quoted in Latham, *Communist Controversy in Washington,* 381; Stripling, *Red Plot against America,* 175, 194, 203; Budenz quoted in Carr, *House Committee on Un-American Activities,* 36n.

32. Carr, *House Committee on Un-American Activities,* 56 (Rankin and Thomas quotes), 55–56, 60–69.

33. Ibid., 70–77; Navasky, *Naming Names, ,* 80–83, 113; poll of 30 November 1947, Gallup, *Gallup Poll,* vol. 1: 689–90. Six of the Hollywood Ten were Jewish.

34. Rogin, *Intellectuals and McCarthy,* 216; Edward Cox, 2 May 1946, quoted in Athan Theoharis, "Unanswered Questions," in Theoharis, ed., *Beyond the Hiss Case,* 271; Carr, *House Committee on Un-American Activities,* 68–92.

35. Carr, *House Committee on Un-American Activities,* 93–97; Chambers HUAC testimony quoted in Stripling, *Red Plot against America,* 98; Carr, *House Committee on Un-American Activities,* 93–97. White died of a heart attack days after his HUAC testimony.

36. Carr, *House Committee on Un-American Activities,* 97–126.

37. Fried, *Nightmare in Red,* 19–21.

38. Mundt Press Release, n.d., 1, Folder 1, Remarks by K.E.M. in the House and Senate, 1949, Box DB 12110, Mundt Papers; Mundt, "What the Hiss Trial Actually Means," *CR,* 81st Cong., 2d sess., 96 (15 January 1950), 890–91 (quote on 891); "Bridges and Hiss and an Awakening People," *Detroit Free Press,* 6 April 1950, 6.

39. Navasky, *Naming Names,* 21, 4 (quote), 7–8; Latham, *Communist Controversy in Washington,* 8, 320.

40. Mundt, "What the Hiss Trial Actually Means," *CR,* 81st Cong., 2d sess., 96 (25 January 1950), 893; HUAC quoted in Fried, *Nightmare in Red,* 80; Theoharis, *Seeds of Repression,* 133–35.

41. Special Folder Con, OF 263A; Nancut B. Naguen to Truman, 20 November 1947 (first quote), Special Folder Pro, OF 263A; Jim Ducas to Truman, 19 December 1947 (second quote), attached to Matthew J. Connelly to Department of Justice, 29 December 1947, 1945–47 Folder, OF 263; and Mike McDonald to Truman, 13 January 1948 (third quote), 1945–49 Folder, OF 263, all in Truman Library.

42. Quoted in Dallek, *American Style of Foreign Policy,* 176; polls of 6 August 1947, 28 February, 5 July 1948, Gallup, *Gallup Poll,* vol. 1: 664, 714, 742; Mundt to Flynn, 12 September 1948, U.S. Congress, House, Flynn Papers.

43. Jeanette O'Neal to Truman, 6 August 1948 (first quote), attached to Matthew J. Connelly to O'Neal, 22 October 1948; Harriet F. Backus to Truman, 19 August 1948 (second quote), attached to Connelly to Backus, 22 October 1948; Charles E. Bennett to Truman, 16 September 1948 (third quote), attached to Connelly to Bennett, 22 October 1948; A. B. Hale to Truman, 7 August 1948 (fourth quote), attached to Connelly to Hale, 22 October 1948; James E. Larned to Truman, 9 September 1948 (fifth quote), attached to Connelly to Larned, 22 October 1948; and Jim Mackin to Connelly, 30 August 1948 (sixth quote), attached to Connelly to Mackin, 31 August 1948, all in "Red Herring" Remarks Folder, OF 263–Misc., Truman Library.

44. Navasky, *Naming Names,* 26; Rogin, *Ronald Reagan,* 67; Mundt quoted in Carr, *House Committee on Un-American Activities,* 82–83.

45. Mundt, "World Affairs—A Look Ahead," address before the 36th Annual Meeting, Chamber of Commerce of the United States, 28 April 1948, 6, Mundt Speeches, vol. 2, Mundt Papers; polls of 19 April 1947 and 18 August 1948, Gallup, *Gallup Poll,* vol. 1: 640, 751; William R. Tanner and Robert Griffith, "Legislative Politics and 'McCarthyism': The Internal Security Act of 1950," in Griffith and Theoharis, eds., *Specter,* 177–78; Taft to Charles E. Mason, 26 May 1948, Communists, 1948, Box 894, Taft Papers.

46. FTC Statement to House Small Business Committee, 1 July 1946 (first quote), in Federal Trade Commission, *Present Trend of Corporate Mergers and Acquisitions,* 39, 1; Federal Trade Commission, *Merger Movement,* 17; U.S. Senate, Special Committee to Study Problems of American Small Business, *Independent Business,* 5, 9–11; 1948 Report of the Joint Committee to Congress quoted in Report of the Joint Committee on the Economic Report on the January 1949 Economic Report of the President, 1 March 1949, 50–51 (second and third quotes), Economic Controls Bill—HR 2756, Box 88, Bricker Papers.

47. Ed Wimmer to William Langer, 18 May 1948 (first quote), attached to Langer to Wimmer, 4 June 1948, Folder 8, Sheyenne Dam/Small Business, 1947–48, Box 223, Langer Papers; Fred A. Virkus to Members of 83d Congress, January 1953, Folder 2, Small Business, Social Security 1953–54, Box 517, Langer Papers; Stromer, *Making of a Political Leader,* 104, 107; Zeigler, *Politics of Small Business,* 60, 66, 68–69, 84, 139; U.S. Senate, Special Committee to Study Problems of American Small Business, *Independent Business,* 5 (second and third quotes), 9–11.

48. Stromer, *Making of a Political Leader,* 108–10; Taft, *CR,* 81st Cong., 1st sess., 95 (9 September 1949), 12759–61, 12764; Patterson, *Mr. Republican,* 191, 330; Green, *Shaping Political Consciousness,* 175, 183–85, 189; "Senator Taft as a Liberal," Policy Chairman, 1948–49, Box 750, Taft Papers; Taft, "Return to Liberty," speech to Missouri Republican Club, Kansas City, 12 February 1946, *CR,* 79th Cong., 2d sess., 92 (1 March 1946), A1049; Taft, "My Political Credo," 1–4, 1948 Campaign Miscellany—Publicity and Speech Material, Credo, Box 238, Taft Papers.

49. Morton to Samuel N. Rinaker, 14 October 1947, attached to Rinaker to Taft, 18 October 1947, Marshall Plan, 1947, Box 714, Taft Papers; McCormick to Robert E. Wood, 19 February 1947, Correspondence File, Box 11, Wood Papers; McCormick to Taft, 30 June 1948 (McCormick quote), attached to Taft to C. Wayland Brooks, 12 January 1948, Senators Correspondence, 1948, Box 899, Taft Papers; Wheeler to Wood, 12 April 1948, Correspondence File, Box 21, Wood Papers.

50. Statement by Clarence J. Brown, 3 May 1948, 1948 Campaign Miscellany—Publicity and Speech Material, Box 238, Taft Papers; Press Release, Excerpts from Speech from Senator John W. Bricker Nominating Senator Robert A. Taft for the Presidency of the United States, n.d., 1 (first and second quotes), 4 (third quote), Press Releases, Speeches, 1947–48, Box 86B, Bricker Papers; Patterson, *Mr. Republican,* 387–88, 395–411.

51. Patterson, *Mr. Republican,* 405–7, 412–16; poll of 14 April 1948, Gallup, *Gallup Poll,* vol., 1: 725; Taft, "Case against President Truman," 18–19, 141 (quote on 18); Hamby, *Beyond the New Deal,* 209–12.

52. Green, *Shaping Political Consciousness,* 178; Doenecke, *Not to the Swift,* 11, 164–65; Doenecke, "Strange Career of American Isolationism," 79–81; Wood to Douglas MacArthur, 4 September 1945, Correspondence File, Box 10, Wood Papers; Wood to Robert A. Taft, 30 November 1946, Correspondence File, Box 18, Wood Papers; Griffith, "Old Progressives and the Cold War," 338–39, 344–45.

53. Doenecke, *Not to the Swift,* 58–62; "Ballyhoo for Britain," *Wall Street Journal,* 13 November 1945, *CR,* 79th Cong., 1st sess., 91 (12 December 1945), A5460; Bennett, "Santa Claus Rides Again," *CR,* 79th Cong., 1st sess., 91 (12 December 1945), A5476; Gavin, "Proposed Loan to Great Britain," *CR,* 79th Cong., 1st sess., 91 (12 December 1945), A5512; Landis, "Back to Solvency," *CR,* 79th Cong., 1st sess., 91 (19 December 1945), A5673; Mundt, *CR,* 79th Cong., 1st sess., 91 (20 December 1945), A5684; Emanuel Celler, "The British Loan—Opposition Mounting," *CR,* 79th Cong., 1st sess., 91 (12 December

1945), 11927–28; Brooks, "Analysis of Terms of Proposed Loan to Great Britain," *CR,* 79th Cong., 1st sess., 91 (17 December 1945), 12151–57; Knutson, *CR,* 79th Cong., 1st sess., 91 (11 September 1945), 8511–12; Capehart, "Speech of Professor Laski and the Proposed Loan to Great Britain," *CR,* 79th Cong., 1st sess., 91 (7 December 1945), 11611–12.

54. Langer quoted in Brekke, "Usher L. Burdick," 1–2; G. H. Smith, *Langer of North Dakota,* 118–19, 123–25, 128, 154–55; Wilkins, "Langer and National Priorities," 44; Langer, "The Loan to England," speech ms., n.d. [1945], 1, 3–5, Folder 3, Speeches 1949–50, Box 274, Langer Papers. For background on Langer's foreign policy views, see D. A. Horowitz, "North Dakota Noninterventionists," 34–36.

55. G. H. Smith, *Langer of North Dakota,* 129–30; Wilkins, "Middle Western Isolationism," 71; Paul Schilla to Langer, 5 March 1946 (quote), Folder 6, British Loan, March–April 1946, Box 144, Langer Papers; poll of 6 March 1946, Gallup, *Gallup Poll,* vol. 1: 561; John H. Crider, "Closure Is Barred on Loan to Britain," *New York Times,* 8 March 1946, 1, 9; John H. Crider, "British Loan Foes Fail," *New York Times,* 9 May 1946, 1, 16; "British Loan Vote Is Set," *New York Times,* 10 May 1946, 1, 10; "Loan Vote 46 to 34," *New York Times,* 11 May 1946, 1–2; C. P. Trussell, "Danger to British Loan Seen," *New York Times,* 4 July 1946, 1, 22; Crider, "House, 219 to 155," *New York Times,* 14 July 1946, 1, 3. Two-thirds of the remaining World War II Senate noninterventionists voted against the British loan. Doenecke, *Not to the Swift,* 75.

56. Doenecke, *Not to the Swift,* 73–75, 86 (quote on 74); Langer to A. F. Lehr, 18 August 1947, and Langer to T. E. Savagean, 15 April 1947, Folder 17, Greece 1946–47, Box 178, Langer Papers; Wilkins, "Langer and National Priorities," 43–45; Bricker, "Mobilizing for World Leadership," speech before National Industrial Conference Board, 28 May 1947, 3–4, 7–8, and Bricker Statement on the Greek and Turkish "Loan" Vote, 22 April 1947, Press Releases, Speeches, 1947–48, Box 86B, Bricker Papers.

57. Doenecke, *Not to the Swift,* 75; Taft quoted in Radosh, *Prophets on the Right,* 152, 157; Taft, "Return to Liberty," speech to Missouri Republican Club, 12 February 1946, *CR,* 79th Cong., 2d sess., 92 (1 March 1946), A1048.

58. Villard to Taft, and attachments, 22 December 1947, Compulsory Military Training, 1947, Box 885, Taft Papers; "Address of the President of the United States," *CR,* 80th Cong., 2d sess., 94 (17 March 1948), 2996–97; polls of 16 February, 13 June, 25 July 1947, 9 April 1948, Gallup, *Gallup Poll,* vol. 1: 626, 653–54, 661, 723; Taft, "Universal Military Training and National Defense," address at Fremont, Nebr., 7 April 1948, *CR,* 80th Cong., 2d sess., 94 (20 April 1948), A2359–60; Taft, "Case against President Truman," 144.

59. *CR,* 80th Cong., 2d sess., 94 (7, 10, 18 June 1948), 7260–61, 7678–81, 8828–29; C. P. Trussell, "Senate Filibuster Bars Draft Action," *New York Times,* 19 June 1948, 1–2; *CR,* 80th Cong., 2d sess., 94 (19 June 1948), 9253, 9276–77; C. P. Trussell, "21–Month Draft in 90 Days Voted by Congress," *New York Times,* 20 June 1948, 1, 34. For Langer's views on the draft, see G. H. Smith, *Langer of North Dakota,* 70–85; and G. H. Smith, "Senator William Langer and Military Conscription," 16, 18, 23.

60. Report of the Joint Committee on the Economic Report on the January 1949 Economic Report of the President, 1 March 1949, 10, Economic Controls Bill—HR 2756, Box 88, Bricker Papers; Langer, "American Foreign Policy," *CR,* 81st Cong., 1st sess., 95 (17 February 1949), 1343–44; Langer to Malone, n.d., and Malone to Senate Colleagues, August 1949, Folder 18, Trade/Truman Doctrine 1949–50, Box 275, Langer Papers.

61. Doenecke, *Not to the Swift,* 114–21; poll of 2 November 1947, Gallup, *Gallup Poll,* vol. 1: 683; Bryniarski, "Against the Tide," 7–8, 176, 178–79; Taft to John R. Murray, 20 October 1947, attached to Taft to Murray, 20 November 1947, Foreign Policy, 1947, Box 887, Taft Papers; Radosh, *Prophets on the Right,* 160–62.

62. Lenn J. Oare to Capehart, 14 February 1948, and Capehart to Mr. and Mrs. Arthur G. Bobbitt, 10 March 1948, Capehart's European Recovery Program, 1948, Box 104, Capehart Papers; Capehart, "American Principle Applied to a Joint European Recovery Program," address before Peoria and Illinois Bar Associations, Peoria, Ill., 7 February 1948, 4–5, Europe Post–World War II, Box 104, Capehart Papers; Langer, "European Recovery Program," speech draft, 8 March 1948, 5, 17, Folder 3, Speeches, 1949–50, Box 274, Langer Papers; Langer to James J. Hill, 22 January 1948, Folder 6, Marshall Plan, 1947–48, Box 218, Langer Papers.

63. Bryniarski, "Against the Tide," 11–14, 176, 178–79; Homer E. Capehart to DeWitt Emery, and attachment, 27 January 1948, General Correspondence, 1948, C–J, Box 17a, Capehart Papers; "The Marshall Plan," resolution adopted by Executive Board of National Association of Retail Grocers, n.d., attached to William Langer to R. M. Kiefer, 6 February 1948, Folder 1, Marshall Plan/ Maternity Bill, 1949–50, Box 262, Langer Papers; Editorial, "Wall Street Effrontery," *Chicago Tribune* (2 January 1948), 12.

64. Bryniarski, "Against the Tide," 8–9; Langer, *CR,* 80th Cong., 1st sess., 93 (4, 16 December 1947), 11029, 11437; Langer, *CR,* 80th Cong., 2d sess., 94 (11 February 1948), 1263; Taft, press release of address before Live Stock Exchange, South Omaha, Nebr., 13 February 1948, 7, Agriculture–Brannon, 1948, Box 484, Taft Papers.

65. Capehart entry, *Current Biography, 1947,* 90–91; Bryniarski, "Against the Tide," 180–84; *CR,* 80th Cong., 2d sess., 94 (9, 11 March 1948), 2364, 2516–22, 2523–24, 2773–75.

66. *CR,* 80th Cong., 2d sess., 94 (4, 11, 13 March 1948), 2126, 2521–23, 2775, 2793; Bryniarski, "Against the Tide," 184–88; Doenecke, *Not to the Swift,* 115.

67. Burger to Robert A. Taft, and attachment, 9 January 1948, European Recovery Program, 1948, Box 603, Taft Papers; Homer E. Capehart to H. D. LaMont, and attachments, 24 February 1949, Economic Cooperation Administration (hereafter ECA), 1949, Box 7, Capehart Papers; Jenner, *CR,* 81st Cong., 1st sess., 95 (28 March 1949), 3265.

68. James W. Phillips to J. T. Hogsett, 18 October 1949, ECA, 1949, Box 88, Bricker Papers; Capehart to Lawrence Johnson, and attachments, 9 February 1949, and Capehart to H. D. LaMont, and attachments, 24 February 1949,

Economic Cooperation Administration, 1949, Box 7, Capehart Papers; Taft to B. K. Leach, 14 June 1949, attached to Leach to Taft, 16 June 1949, Reciprocal Trade Agreements, 1949, Box 911, Taft Papers; McGregor to Patman, 10 October 1949, ECA, 1949, Box 88, Bricker Papers. For background on the aluminum controversy, see "The ECA-Aluminum Blunder Still a Mystery," *Modern Metals,* January 1949, 13–15.

69. Doenecke, *Not to the Swift,* 156; poll of 28 March 1949, Gallup, *Gallup Poll,* vol. 2: 800.

70. L. H. Smith, *CR,* 81st Cong., 1st sess., 95 (17 August 1949), 11670; G. H. Smith, *Langer of North Dakota,* 185–91; Langer Draft for Radio Address on Atlantic Pact, n.d., Folder 4, Speeches 1949–50, Box 274, Langer Papers; Langer Form Letter, 25 July 1949 (quote), Folder 3, North Atlantic Pact 1949–50, Box 265, Langer Papers.

71. Quoted in Doenecke, *Not to the Swift,* 155; Bryniarski, "Against the Tide," 274, 281; Taft quoted in Radosh, *Prophets on the Right,* 168. The entire Taft speech is in *CR,* 81st Cong., 1st sess., 95 (11 July 1949), 9204–10.

72. Taft quoted in Radosh, *Prophets on the Right,* 169; Bryniarski, "Against the Tide," 277–80; Doenecke, *Not to the Swift,* 155–56. Homer Capehart and Karl Mundt supported NATO.

73. Doenecke, *Not to the Swift,* 171–72 (quote), 156; Griffith, *Politics of Fear,* 46–47.

74. Green, *Shaping of Political Consciousness,* 168–69, 178.

Chapter 11: The Nationalist Critique of Bipartisan Foreign Policy, 1949–55

1. J. McCarthy, speech of 9 December 1949, quoted in Oshinsky, *A Conspiracy So Immense,* 84.

2. Griffith, *Politics of Fear,* 46–47; poll of 11 January 1950, Gallup, *Gallup Poll,* vol. 1: 881.

3. Vandenberg Jr. to A. V. Vandenberg, 7 August 1949, quoted in Doenecke, *Not to the Swift,* 177; Judd, "America's New Role in World Affairs," Ohio Chamber of Commerce, Columbus, Ohio, 3 November 1949, 4–5, Folder 66, Box 209, Judd Papers; Wherry quoted in Oshinsky, *A Conspiracy So Immense,* 104; Doenecke, *Not to the Swift,* 171, 179.

4. Malone Press Release, 4 March 1948, Folder 5, Marshall Plan 1947–48, Box 218, Langer Papers; Langer, "American Foreign Policy," *CR,* 81st Cong., 1st sess., 95 (17 February 1949), 1339; Taft radio speech, 8 January 1950, quoted in A. Harper, *Politics of Loyalty,* 118. Only 26 percent of a national sample knew what *bipartisan* meant. Poll of 2 June 1950, Gallup, *Gallup Poll,* vol. 2: 915.

5. Doenecke, *Not to the Swift,* 165, 183, 197–201; Doenecke, "Strange Career of Isolationism," 80–81; Bryniarski, "Against the Tide," 14; Lawrence A. Smith, *CR,* 81st Cong., 1st sess., 95 (17 August 1949), 11671.

6. Taft quoted in Himmelstein, *To the Right,* 35. The entire Taft speech is in *CR,* 82d Cong., 1st sess., 97 (5 January 1951), 55–69. See also Taft, *A Foreign Policy for Americans.*

7. Wherry speech of 30 March 1951 quoted in Stromer, *Making of a Political Leader,* 134; poll of 4 April 1951, Gallup, *Gallup Poll,* vol. 2: 974.

8. J. McCarthy, *CR,* 81st Cong., 2d sess., 96 (20 February 1950), 1954. The speech in the *Record* probably was made days after Wheeling. Allen J. Matusow, "McCarthy and the State Department," in Matusow, ed., *Joseph R. McCarthy,* 20.

9. J. McCarthy, *CR,* 81st Cong., 2d sess., 96 (20 February 1950), 1954 (first and third quotes), 1957 (second quote).

10. Ibid.; Oshinsky, *A Conspiracy So Immense,* 112–14, 161 (quote); Truman quoted in Theoharis, *Seeds of Repression,* 164.

11. Griffith, *Politics of Fear,* 58–60, 65–74.

12. Ibid., 76–78 (quotes on 77).

13. Ibid., 78–81 (McCarthy quote on 79; Budenz quote on 81).

14. Ibid., 82–84, 87–90; Agnes M. Lewis to Truman, 25 March 1950, Subcommittee on Loyalty (Pro) Folder, OF 419–K Misc., Truman Library; O'Donnell, "Capitol Stuff," *New York Daily News,* 25 April 1950; McCarthy quoted in Oshinsky, *A Conspiracy So Immense,* 157. For typical McCarthy rhetoric, see Address to Midwest Council of Young Republicans, *CR,* 81st Cong., 2d sess., 96 (9 May 1950), A3426–28.

15. Griffith, *Politics of Fear,* 90–93; L. V. Lathrop to Truman, 24 March 1950, Harry Wolfe Jr. to Truman, 31 March 1950, and Nancy Luciano to Truman, 23 February 1950, Subcommittee on Loyalty (Pro) Folder, OF 419–K Misc., Truman Library.

16. Poll of 21 May 1950, Gallup, *Gallup Poll,* vol. 2: 911–12; Jesse W. Barrett to Kem, 22 June 1950, Folder 6713, Kem Papers; poll of 7 July 1950, Gallup, *Gallup Poll,* vol. 2: 924.

17. Oshinsky, *A Conspiracy So Immense,* 169–71 (first and second quotes on 169; third on 170); Jenner, *CR,* 81st Cong., 2d sess., 96 (21 July 1950), 10792. See also Jenner, *CR,* 81st Cong., 2d sess., 96 (20 July 1950), 10686–717.

18. LaFeber, *America, Russia, and the Cold War,* 91–92, 99–101, 113–16.

19. Reichard, *Politics as Usual,* 71; Burdick, "Red Tape and Foreign Wars," Folder 50, Economics: Small Business, 1951–52, Box 6, Burdick Papers; Paul Van Middlesworth to Capehart, 23 November 1952, Price Controls, 1952, Box 7, Capehart Papers; Malone Press Release, 23 July 1951, 2, Folder 10, Speeches 1951–52, Box 491, Langer Papers; Kem to C. E. Conrad, 21 July 1950, Folder 6715, Kem Papers.

20. Tanner, "Passage of the Internal Security Act," 318–19; Theoharis, *Seeds of Repression,* 137 (first quote), 141–42 (second quote); Fried, *Nightmare in Red,* 115–16.

21. Mundt, "America's Major Problem," *Daughters of the American Revolution Magazine,* January 1949, 1–4; Mundt, "What Lies Ahead of the American Enterprise System?" address before International Acetylene Association, Pittsburgh, 25 April 1949, 8, 14 (first Mundt quote), Folder 1, Box DB 1220, Mundt Papers; Theoharis, *Seeds of Represssion,* 141–42 (second Mundt quote); Tanner, "Passage of the Internal Security Act," 4–12, 284.

22. Georgia Amsler to Truman, 14 August 1930, attached to William D.

Hassett to Amsler, 24 August 1950, Folder A, OF 263B; Elliott Earl to Sen. Henry C. Lodge Jr., 21 July 1950, attached to Donald S. Dawson to Earl, 15 June 1950, Folder 1945–50, OF 2750; Katherine Moore to Truman, 11 August 1950, attached to Hassett to Moore, 25 August 1950, Folder B, OF 263B; Mr. and Mrs. F. G. Francis to Truman, 9 August 1950, attached to Hassett to Francis, 26 August 1950, Folder F, OF 263B; Ruth Yunker to Truman, 16 August 1950, Folder 1950, OF 263–Misc.; and "Housewife Launches Movement," newspaper clipping attached to Hassett to Mrs. J. L. Bagaugh, 25 August 1950, Folder B, OF 263B, all in Truman Library.

23. Judd to Rev. G. Eugene Durham, 15 May 1950, Unamerican Activities, 1950–52, Box 171, Judd Papers; Theoharis, *Seeds of Repression,* 119; Wilkins, "Langer and National Priorities," 55–56; Langer to Truman, 18 September 1950, attached to Truman to Langer, 23 September 1950, PPF 5491, Truman Library.

24. Robert A. Patterson to Truman, 25 September 1950, and B. E. Myers to Truman, 26 September 1950, Internal Security Act Veto Folder, Con, OF 2750–C, Truman Library.

25. Fried, *Nightmare in Red,* 153–54, 145–46; "Interview with Senator McCarran," *U.S. News and World Report* 31 (16 November 1951), 24, 28; Theoharis, *Seeds of Repression,* 107–8, 170; A. Harper, *Politics of Loyalty,* 181–82; Fried, *Nightmare in Red,* 146–48 (quote on 146).

26. J. McCarthy, *CR,* 81st Cong., 2d sess., 96 (6 July 1950), 9715–16; Reeves, *Life and Times of Joe McCarthy,* 223, 335; McCarthy quoted in Griffith, *Politics of Fear,* 123. For the campaign against Tydings, see Griffith, *Politics of Fear,* 124.

27. Polls of 6 December 1950, 22 January, 2 February, 2 March, 5 November 1951, Gallup, *Gallup Poll,* vol. 2: 951, 960, 963, 968, 1019.

28. D. A. Horowitz, "North Dakota Noninterventionists," 34; Sponberg, "North Dakota and the Korean War," vii–viii, 98–99, 151–55; Mrs. Otto Gajewski to M. Young, 1 September 1950, and W. R. Buchholz to Langer, 1 April 1951, quoted in Sponberg, "North Dakota and the Korean War," 36, 191–92; Wilkins, "Langer and National Priorities," 72.

29. Dick English to Matthew J. Connelly, 12 December 1950, attached to Connelly to English, 14 December 1950, Acheson Comments Folder, OF 20–Misc., Truman Library; Olivia Marie O'Grady to Truman, 28 April 1952, and Joseph Short to O'Grady, 21 May 1952, 1951–53 Folder, OF 263, Truman Library.

30. Mrs. Carl Medford to Truman, 23 April 1951, MacArthur Dismissal (Con) Folder M, OF 584; Mrs. William H. Bell to Truman, 25 July 1950, Acheson (Con) Folder B, OF 20–Misc.; Edwin C. Anderson to Truman, 5 January 1951, Acheson (Con) Folder A, OF 20–Misc.; and Mrs. Ambie C. Mitchell to Truman, n.d. [1951], MacArthur Dismissal (Con) Folder M, OF 584, all in Truman Library.

31. Doenecke, *Not to the Swift,* 124; James S. Elmore to P. La Follette, 16 November 1947, and P. La Follette to George T. Davis, 11 November 1947, Correspondence, MacArthur for President Club, May 1947–January 1948, Box 144, P. La Follette Papers; P. La Follette to Harold E. Stassen, 25 March 1948, and La Follette Form Letter, 27 March 1948, Correspondence, MacArthur for President Club, March 25–31, Box 145, P. La Follette Papers; Miller, *Governor Philip F. La Follette,* 176, 171.

32. Robert E. Wood to Douglas MacArthur, 16 June 1947, MacArthur to Wood, 16 November 1947, Wood to MacArthur, 15 April 1948, and Wood to MacArthur, 6 May 1948, Correspondence File, Box 10, Wood Papers; Doenecke, *Not to the Swift*, 124; Kaufman, *Korean War*, 33–40.

33. MacArthur, *Reminiscences*, 379 (first quote), 380–82, 386 (second and third quotes), 390.

34. Ibid. 414.

35. Poll of 3 May 1951, Gallup, *Gallup Poll*, vol. 2: 981; Walker, "Bricker and McCarthy," 77; Taft to J. B. Walter, 30 April 1951, MacArthur, 1951, Box 995, Taft Papers; "Total Letters and Telegrams Re MacArthur Dismissal," 8 May 1951, MacArthur Dismissal Folder #1, May 1951, OF 584, Truman Library.

36. Mrs. John A. Unger to Truman, 11 April 1951, Charles F. Unger to Truman, 11 April 1951, and Franklin R. Uhlig to Truman, 12 April 1951, Folder U, OF 2750–C, Truman Library.

37. Granville Rice to Wherry, 26 April 1951, quoted in Stromer, *Making of a Political Leader*, 77; Lawrence J. Moyse to Truman, 27 April 1951, MacArthur Dismissal (Con) Folder M; C. I. Price to Repr. Arthur G. Klein, 15 May 1951, attached to Truman to Klein, 21 May 1951, MacArthur Dismissal (Con) Folder K; W. R. Umbreit to Truman, 11 April 1951, MacArthur Dismissal (Con) Folder U; and Orrin L. Browning, "Football Rules a la Truman," *Cleveland American*, 19 April 1951, attached to Memo for Mr. Short, 28 May 1951, MacArthur Dismissal Folder #2, May 1951, all in OF 584, Truman Library.

38. J. McCarthy, 12 April and 21 June 1951, quoted in Oshinsky, *A Conspiracy So Immense*, 194; McCarthy Statement, 11 June 1951, MacArthur Dismissal Folder #2, May 1951, OF 584, Truman Library.

39. Jenner, *CR*, 82d Cong., 1st sess., 97 (11 April 1951), 3619; Mundt to Mrs. Andrew Nelson, 19 January 1951, Folder 7, Foreign Relations—General Correspondence 1951, Box DB 479, Mundt Papers; Mundt to Andrew Kuehn II, 24 April 1951, Folder 1, Legislation—Foreign Relations Committee, Box DB 480, Mundt Papers; Langer Telegram to Glenn Flint, 19 April 1951, Folder 2, MacArthur 1951–52, Box 483, Langer Papers; Judd, "MacArthur Dismissal Threatens United States Peace and Security," *CR*, 82d Cong., 1st sess., 97 (11 April 1951), 3684–85; Taft to George Gunderson, 3 May 1951, attached to Taft to George C. Rhoderick Jr., 3 May 1951, MacArthur, 1951, Box 995, Taft Papers.

40. A. Harper, *Politics of Loyalty*, 113; Goldman, *Crucial Decade*, 124; Stromer, *Making of a Political Leader*, 112, 121–24. For Wherry's views on Acheson, see *CR*, 81st Cong., 1st sess., 95 (18 January 1949), 463–65.

41. Capehart, *CR*, 81st Cong., 1st sess., 95 (18 January 1949), 462; V. E. Artman to Truman, 13 January 1949, Acheson (Con) Folder A, OF 20–Misc., Truman Library; Langer Speech Draft, n.d., Folder 5, Speeches 1949–50, Box 274, Langer Papers; G. H. Smith, *Langer of North Dakota*, 51.

42. Hoffman, *CR*, 81st Cong., 1st sess., 95 (20 September 1949), 13060; Judd to Warren F. Chapman, 12 February 1951, Communism, 1951–52, Box 103, Judd Papers; Judd to Axel O. Rapp, 3 April 1950, Foreign Affairs Committee, January–July 1950, Box 114, Judd Papers; Butler quoted in Goldman, *Crucial Decade*, 125.

43. "Hiss Is Sentenced to Five-Year Term," *New York Times,* 26 January 1950, 1; Judd Press Release, 26 January 1950, Communism, 1951–52, Box 103, Judd Papers; Herman F. Healy to Truman, Acheson (Con) Folder H, OF 20–Misc., Truman Library; Frank Audino to Truman, 26 January 1950, Acheson-Hiss (Con) Folder A, OF 20–Misc., Truman Library.

44. Catherine Buehler to Truman, 25 July 1950, H. J. Bobbitt to Truman, 30 July 1950, and Mrs. A. W. Bradfield to Truman, 14 September 1950, Acheson (Con) Folder B, OF 20–Misc., Truman Library; poll of 22 December 1950, Gallup, *Gallup Poll,* vol. 2: 953–54; J. J. Carrol to Truman, 27 November 1950, Acheson (Con) Folder C, OF 20–Misc., Truman Library; Helem Amen to Truman, 1 December 1950, and Arthur J. Arenholz to Truman, 10 December 1950, Acheson (Con) Folder A, OF 20–Misc., Truman Library.

45. Mrs. Elner Bouchard to Truman and William Brown to Truman, 4 May 1951, Acheson (Con) Folder B, OF 20–Misc.; Chas. V. Magnus to Truman, 24 April 1951, MacArthur Dismissal (Con) Folder M, OF 584; and John H. Beekler to Truman, 20 April 1951, James C. Bell to Truman, 14 April 1951, and George S. Brown to Truman, 31 May 1951, Acheson (Con) Folder B, OF 20–Misc., all in Truman Library.

46. Report on Committee for Constitutional Government, n.d., Committee for Constitutional Government, undated (1), Box 11, JCRCM Papers; Judd to Repr. Richard B. Wigglesworth, 16 July 1951, Foreign Affairs Committee, May–December 1951, Box 115, Judd Papers; Capehart Statement, n.d., 6, Ideologies—Releases, 1950, Box 151, Capehart Papers; Burdick to Mrs. Frances Beier, 31 March 1952, Folder 4, Korean War, Box 23, Burdick Papers; Mundt, *CR,* 82d Cong., 1st sess., 97 (5 May 1951), 5080.

47. Stromer, *Making of a Political Leader,* 50–60, 63–64, 69–73.

48. Dallek, *American Style of Foreign Policy,* 184; Taft quoted in Radosh, *Prophets on the Right,* 174; Langer, *CR,* 81st Cong., 2d sess., 96 (23 September 1950), 15656–57; Wherry quoted in Stromer, *Making of a Political Leader,* 43.

49. Green, *Shaping Political Consciousness,* 203; Taft quoted in Reichard, *Politics as Usual,* 79; Doenecke, *Not to the Swift,* 222; polls of 16 April 1951 and 13 February 1952, Gallup, *Gallup Poll,* vol. 2: 977, 1041.

50. Doenecke, *Not to the Swift,* 211, 217, 222; Wood to McCormick, 2 May 1952, and McCormick to Wood, 3 May 1952, Correspondence File, Box 11, Wood Papers; Wood to Douglas MacArthur, 6 July 1952, MacArthur Presidential Candidacy, 1952–53, Box 43, Wood Papers; Taft Memo on 1952 Campaign, quoted in Griffith, "Eisenhower and the Corporate Commonwealth," 99–100.

51. Oshinsky, *A Conspiracy So Immense,* 230, 236–38, 242–43; "Text of Address by McCarthy Accusing Governor Stevenson of Aid to Communist Cause," *New York Times,* 28 October 1952, 26 (McCarthy quote); Dallek, *American Style of Foreign Policy,* 187 (Eisenhower quote); Reichard, *Politics as Usual,* 82 (Dulles quote).

52. Griffith, "Eisenhower and the Corporate Commonwealth," 97; Green, *Shaping of Political Consciousness,* 209–13, 221; Oshinsky, *A Conspiracy So Immense,* 346.

53. Lindbergh to Robert E. Wood, 16 August 1952, Correspondence File, Box

10, Wood Papers; Flynn to Robert R. McCormick, 21 January 1953, McCormick, Flynn Papers; Ralph C. Tobin to Bricker, 17 April 1953, attached to Bricker to Tobin, 19 May 1953, Constitutional Amendment, 16–31 May 1953, Box 92, Bricker Papers; Kohlberg to Board of Directors, American Telephone and Telegraph Company, 29 May 1954, Consitutional Amendment, 13–30 June 1954, Box 102, Bricker Papers.

54. Oshinsky, *A Conspiracy So Immense,* 261; John F. Ryan to Homer E. Capehart, 15 January 1953, John Foster Dulles, 1946–1959, Box 137, Capehart Papers; Rushmore, "Senator from Moscow (Idaho)," 141–42; Welker, "American Policy toward the Government of Communist China," *CR,* 83d Cong., 2d sess., 100 (14 January 1954), 250–52; "Does New Look at China Mean Recognition?" *U.S. News and World Report* 34 (29 January 1954), 66–69.

55. Kaufman, *Trade and Aid,* 17–26, 116–19, 127–28, 208.

56. G. H. Smith, *Langer of North Dakota,* 49 (first quote), 50, 109–10, 45 (second and third quotes).

57. Langer Press Release, 31 December 1951, quoted in G. H. Smith, *Langer of North Dakota,* 112; Langer, Minority Views on H.R. 9678, in 83d Cong., 2d sess., Report 1799, Part 2, "The Mutual Security Act of 1954" (13 July 1954), 7–8, 16, 49 (first quote), Folder 10, Mutual Security 1953–54, Box 510, Langer Papers; Langer speech, 25 January 1955, quoted in G. H. Smith, *Langer of North Dakota,* 52, 159–60, 179–81; Langer Statement on the Mutual Security Act of 1956, n.d., 1–2 (second quote), Folder 11, William Langer Speeches: 26 January 1950–55, Box 610, Langer Papers.

58. Kaufman, *Trade and Aid,* 54, 55 (quote), 111, 69–70, 104–10, 133–35, 197, 206. For Jenner's complete speech, see "Bankers' Profits from Foreign Aid," 33–38.

59. Poll of 18 August 1954, Gallup, *Gallup Poll,* vol. 2: 1262; Reichard, *Politics as Usual,* 91; Kaufman, *Trade and Aid,* 208; Doenecke, *Not to the Swift,* 234 (quote).

60. Doenecke, *Not to the Swift,* 235; Zahniser, "Bricker Reflects upon Bricker Amendment," 322–23, 328–29; Bricker, "Should the Constitution Be Amended to Curb Use of the Treaty Power?" *Congressional Digest* 31 (November 1952), 270; Thatcher, "Bricker Amendment," 107–8; Holman quoted in Sumner Gerard Form Letter, December 1955, Folder 6218, Misc. Correspondence, Donnelly Papers; Bricker to Eberhard P. Deutsch, 5 November 1951, Constitutional Amendment, Correspondence, 1951–52, Box 160, Bricker Papers. For more on Bricker's views, see Bricker, "Four Current Misrepresentations," *CR,* 83d Cong., 2d sess., 100 (22 January, 28 April 1954), 633–39, 5698–700.

61. Zahniser, "Bricker Reflects upon Bricker Amendment," 330–31; Thatcher, "Bricker Amendment," 108, 111–16; poll of 7 October 1953, Gallup, *Gallup Poll,* vol. 2: 1176; Reichard, *Reaffirmation of Republicanism,* 60, 67.

Chapter 12: On the Edge

1. Schlamm, "Across McCarthy's Grave," 470.

2. Oshinsky, *A Conspiracy So Immense,* 263, 355–56; Fried, *Nightmare in Red,* 148, 179–80 (quote on 180).

3. Fried, *Nightmare in Red,* 179, 171–72 (quotes), 115.

4. Oshinsky, *A Conspiracy So Immense,* 233–34, 245; Meyer, "Politics of Loyalty," 177–79, 204–5; Griffith, *Politics of Fear,* 213, 201–2; J. McCarthy, *CR,* 83rd Cong., 1st sess., 99 (25 March 1953), 2291–92.

5. Griffith, *Politics of Fear,* 201–4.

6. Ibid., 216; Reeves, *Life and Times of Joe McCarthy,* 502–3; J. McCarthy, *CR,* 83rd Cong., 1st sess., 99 (9 July 1953), 8277.

7. Oshinsky, *A Conspiracy So Immense,* 334 (first quote), 338–39, 344 (second quote).

8. Ibid., 348–50, 354, 356 (quote on 349).

9. Ibid., 365–77 (first quote on 376; second on 377).

10. Ibid., 378–79 (first quote), 392 (second and third quotes), 394–95 (fourth quote).

11. Ibid., 400, 403–7, 413–16, 442–45.

12. Rovere, *Senator Joe McCarthy,* 28 (first, second, and third quotes); Oshinsky, *A Conspiracy So Immense,* 429–32 (fourth quote on 431).

13. Quoted in Rovere, *Senator Joe McCarthy,* 26.

14. Eisenhower quoted in Oshinsky, *A Conspiracy So Immense,* 433 (first quote), 434 (second quote); Reeves, *Life and Times of Joe McCarthy,* 639–40; poll of 9 June 1954, Gallup, *Gallup Poll,* vol. 2: 1241; Griffith, *Politics of Fear,* 270–72.

15. Eisenhower quoted in Griffith, *Politics of Fear,* 103; Griffith, "Eisenhower and the Corporate Commonwealth," 97, 113–14; Oshinsky, *A Conspiracy So Immense,* 197–200 (second quote on 197), 264, 358.

16. Oshinsky, *A Conspiracy So Immense,* 473–74 (McClellan quote on 474), 475 (Capehart quote), 481 (third quote); Griffith, *Politics of Fear,* 270–72.

17. Quoted in Oshinksy, *A Conspiracy So Immense,* 483. The entire speech is in *CR,* 83rd Cong., 2d sess., 100 (10 November 1954), 15952–54.

18. J. McCarthy, *CR,* 83rd Cong., 2d sess., 100 (10 November 1954), 15964; Griffith, *Politics of Fear,* 102–3, 312–13; Bricker to Robert S. Lame, 10 June 1953, Communism, Box 91, Bricker Papers; Bricker to O. A. Hafely, 10 December 1953, Communism, Box 95, Bricker Papers; Bricker, *CR,* 83rd Cong., 2d sess., 100 (12 November 1954), 16000 (first quote); Mrs. H. C. Baker to Bricker, 10 August 1954 (second quote), For McCarthy Letters, Box 111, Bricker Papers; Flynn to Karl E. Mundt, 9 December 1954 (third quote), Senate, Flynn Papers; Doenecke, *Not to the Swift,* 233. Bricker and Homer Capehart opposed censure but paired themselves with Senate supporters of the measure. Ironically, McCarthy had supported Truman's European containment programs and backed Eisenhower against Taft in 1952. Griffith, *Politics of Fear,* 13.

19. Wheeler quoted in Doenecke, *Not to the Swift,* 233; Oshinsky, *A Conspiracy So Immense,* 302–3; Rovere, *Senator Joe McCarthy,* 19 (quote), 21–22.

20. Oshinsky, *A Conspiracy So Immense,* 308, 222, 507, 304; Viereck, "New American Radicals," 42.

21. T. Parsons, "McCarthyism and American Social Tension," 242 (first quote); Meyer, "Politics of Loyalty," 184, 187 (second quote), 227–28. For McCarthy as a populist, see Shils, *Torment of Secrecy,* 13, 30–32, 98–101; and Bunzel, *Anti-Politics in America,* 60–62.

22. Oshinsky, *A Conspiracy So Immense,* 55–57; Rovere, *Senator Joe McCarthy,* 19; Daniel Bell, "The Dispossessed," in D. Bell, ed., *Radical Right,* 7, 12, 15–16, 21–22. Since the cold war was a "postmodern" conflict in which the management of imagery and propaganda often took precedence over direct military conflict, the loyalty of intellectuals was particularly essential. The Wilsonian progressive George Creel noted that post-1945 liberals sneered at patriotism as old-fashioned while talking of "'revolution' as calmly as though they were ordering a sundae." Quoted in Graham, *Encore for Reform,* 90.

23. Meyer, "Politics of Loyalty," 186 (first quote); Shils, *Torment of Secrecy,* 37, 43, 100 (second quote), 15, 120–22, 181–84, 78, 46, 205–7.

24. Himmselstein, *To the Right,* 73–74, 77 (first quote), 78 (second quote); George E. Deatherage to Bricker, 20 December 1952, attached to Bricker to Deatherage, 9 January 1953, Constitutional Amendment, 1–15 January 1953, Box 91, Bricker Papers.

25. Rogin, *Intellectuals and McCarthy,* 5, 30–31, 65, 72, 171; Francis, "Evil That Men Don't Do," 16–21.

26. Repr. Wint Smith quoted in Rogin, *Intellectuals and McCarthy,* 228; Schlamm, "Across McCarthy's Grave," 470.

27. Steve Fraser, "The Labor Question," in Fraser and Gerstle, eds., *Rise and Fall of the New Deal Order,* 73; J. Bell, *Populism and Elitism,* 62–63; Himmelstein, *To the Right,* 100, 146. For resentment toward "new class" professionals, see Lasch, *True and Only Heaven,* 509–29.

28. Fried, *Nightmare in Red,* 159; Introduction, in Reeves, ed., *Foundations under Fire,* 26–27; Griffith, *Politics of Fear,* 87n, 143; U.S. House of Representatives, Select Committee to Investigate and Study Educational and Philanthropic Foundations and Other Comparable Organizations Which Are Exempt from Federal Income Tax, *Final Report,* 6–7; B. Carroll Reece, *CR,* 83rd Cong., 1st sess., 99 (27 July 1953), 10016. For background on the foundations controversy, see Lankford, *Congress and the Foundations,* 35–52.

29. Kohlberg Memorandum, "Sound Public Thinking Precedes Sound Eisenhower Foreign Policy," n.d., 2, and Kohlberg to Archibald Roosevelt, 13 January 1953, attached to Kohlberg to Flynn, 26 December 1952, K Correspondence; Flynn to Reece, 20 April 1953, House; and Flynn to Robert H. Harriss, 24 March 1954, Harriss, Box 18, all in Flynn Papers.

30. Hawley, *New Deal and the Problem of Monopoly,* 415; Lankford, *Congress and the Foundations,* 54, 58, 86–87; Reece, *CR,* 83rd Cong., 1st sess., 99 (23 April, 27 July 1953), 3726–28, 10015 (first quote), 10030; U.S. House of Representatives, Special Committee to Investigate Tax-Exempt Foundations and Comparable Organizations, *Relations between Foundations and Education and between Foundations and Government,* 469 (second quote), 467 (third quote). The Ohio Democrat Wayne L. Hays led critics in attacking committee staff for permitting little oral testimony by foundations. Written statements were solicited once the hearings ended.

31. U.S. House of Representatives, Special Committee to Investigate Tax-Exempt Foundations and Comparable Organizations, *Tax-Exempt Foundations: Final Report,* 39 (quote), 40–45, 85–91, 147–51; Leo Egan, "Number and Size

of Foundations Up," *New York Times,* 3 March 1954, 20; "Foundations Investigation," *Congressional Quarterly Almanac (CQA)* 10 (1954), 239; Wormser, *Foundations,* 196–99. For background on the economic and social origins of American foundations, see Quigley, *Tragedy and Hope,* 935–38, 947–50.

32. "Foundations Investigation," *CQA* 10 (1954), 239 (first quote); René A. Wormser, "Foundations: Their Power and Influence," in Reeves, ed., *Foundations under Fire,* 104 (second quote); U.S. House of Representatives, Special Committee to Investigate Tax-Exempt Foundations and Comparable Organizations, *Tax-Exempt Foundations: Final Report,* 75, 85–91.

33. U.S. House of Representatives, Special Committee to Investigate Tax-Exempt Foundations and Comparable Organizations, *Relations between Foundations and Education and between Foundations and Government,* 475 (first and second quotes), 477 (third and fourth quotes), 480 (fifth quote), 483 (sixth and seventh quotes).

34. U.S. House of Representatives, Special Committee to Investigate Tax-Exempt Foundations and Comparable Organizations, *Tax-Exempt Foundations: Final Report,* 31–32, 60 (first Hobbs quote), 61–66, 68–71, 87–88; Reece, *CR,* 83rd Cong., 1st sess., 99 (27 July 1953), 10016; Wormser, *Foundations,* 196; U.S. House of Representatives, Special Committee to Investigate Tax-Exempt Foundations and Comparable Organizations, *Tax-Exempt Foundations: Hearings,* 113, 117, 123, 126 (second Hobbs quote), 130 (third Hobbs quote).

35. U.S. House of Representatives, Special Committee to Investigate Tax-Exempt Foundations and Comparable Organizations, *Tax-Exempt Foundations: Hearings,* 132, 139 (first quote); René Wormser, "Foundations: Their Power and Influence," in Reeves, ed., *Foundations under Fire,* 100 (second quote), 101 (third quote).

36. "Foundations," *CQA* 10 (1954), 239; U.S. House of Representatives, Special Committee to Investigate Tax-Exempt Foundations and Comparable Organizations, *Tax-Exempt Foundations: Final Report,* 20–22; Introduction, in Reeves, ed., *Foundations under Fire,* 26; Lankford, *Congress and the Foundations,* 88.

37. Dallek, *American Style of Foreign Policy,* 188; "The Story of Federal Action," *Congressional Digest* 35 (December 1956), 292; "The Small Business Administration," *Congressional Digest* 35 (December 1956), 293; "Small Business Administration," *CQA* 9 (1953), 428ff.; "Small Business Agency," *CQA* 11 (1955), 468–70; "Small Business," *CQA* 14 (1958), 623; "Small Business Agency," *CQA* 14 (1958), 257–58; Zeigler, *Politics of Small Business,* 80, 104–12, 134, 122.

38. U.S. House of Representatives, Select Committee on Small Business, *Fair Trade,* 1; *Fair Trade Newsletter,* 18 April 1952, attached to Usher L. Burdick to John A. McGuire, 25 April 1952, Economics: Fair Trade (McGuire Bill), Box 6, Burdick Papers; "Washington Report" Brochure, "Economic Considerations in 'Fair Trade' Price Fixing," 8 July 1952, Economics: Fair Trade (McGuire Bill), Box 6, Burdick Papers; Herschel D. Newsom to Burdick, 19 March 1952, attached to Burdick to Newsom, 21 March 1952, Economics: Fair Trade (McGuire Bill), Box 6, Burdick Papers; Summary of Statement by John W. Anderson, Pres-

ident of the American Fair Trade Council, before the House Judiciary Committee, 22 February 1952, 1–3, Economics: Fair Trade (McGuire Bill), Box 6, Burdick Papers; Statement by Ed Wimmer before Special Subcommittee on the Study of Monopoly Power, House Committee on the Judiciary, n.d., 4–5, Economics: Fair Trade (McGuire Bill), Box 6, Burdick Papers.

39. Armin F. Rohde to Burdick, 19 March 1952, Folder 9, Economics: Fair Trade (McGuire Bill), Box 6; T. M. McLaughlin to Burdick, 30 April 1953 (first quote), attached to Burdick to McLaughlin, 4 May 1953, Folder 47, Economics: Robinson-Patman Act, Box 6; Nicholas J. Janson to Burdick, 23 March 1956 (second quote), Folder 52, Economics: Anti-Trust, 1955, Box 5; and Patman Address before the Golden Anniversary Convention of the National Food Brokers Association, Atlantic City, N.J., 21 January 1954, 1–5, 9 (third quote), attached to R. H. McVay to Burdick, 23 February 1954, Folder 46, Economics: Robinson-Patman Act, Box 6, all in Burdick Papers.

40. Luther A. Huston, "Price Cuts Held Little Man's Foe," *New York Times,* 30 April 1955, 7; "Price Discrimination," *CQA* 12 (1956), 522–23; Patman, *CR,* 84th Cong., 2d sess., 102 (13 March, 12 April 1956), 4634–48, 6269–70; "Proposals to Set Aside Court Decisions," *CQA* 14 (1958), 288, 623; "Price Discrimination," *CQA* 14 (1958), 559–60.

41. Jowett, *Film, the Democratic Art,* 333–53; Simon N. Whitney, "Antitrust Policies and the Motion Picture Industry," in Kindem, ed., *American Movie Industry,* 186; Griffith, "Eisenhower and the Corporate Commonwealth," 104–5; George J. Burger to President, 6 April 1955, reprinted in NFIB Press Release, 8 April 1955, 2–3, attached to John Sparkman to Karl E. Mundt, 25 April 1955, Folder 3, Committee on Small Business 1955, Box 675, Mundt Papers.

42. Langer, *CR,* 80th Cong., 1st sess., 93 (19 June 1947), 7286; Langer to Judge Homer Bone, 6 December 1955, Langer Press Release, 14 December 1955, and Langer to John H. Faunce, 22 February 1955 (first quote), Folder 7, Judiciary Subcommittee—Anti-Trust and Monopoly, 1955–56, Box 538, Langer Papers; U.S. Senate, Subcommittee of the Committee on the Judiciary, *Monopoly in the Power Industry,* 4–9, 10 (second quote), 22–24.

43. "Antitrust Investigations," *CQA* 11 (1955), 545–59, 552–54; "Ending 'Fair Trade' Laws," *New York Times,* 1 April 1955, 1, 15; "Opinions Divided on 'Fair Trading,'" *New York Times,* 1 April 1955 (first quotes), 14; National Farmers Union Press Release, 1 April 1955 (second quote), attached to Angus McDonald to Usher L. Burdick, 5 April 1955, Folder 52, Economics: Anti-Trust, 1955, Box 5, Burdick Papers; Patman Address before the Golden Anniversary Convention of the National Food Brokers Association, Atlantic City, N.J., 21 January 1954, 9, attached to R. H. McVay to Usher L. Burdick, 23 February 1954, Folder 46: Economics: Robinson-Patman Act, Box 6, Burdick Papers; Luther A. Huston, "Patman Attacks Antitrust Study," *New York Times,* 11 May 1955, 20 (third quote); Lawrence O'Kane, "Patman Attacks Trade Law Study," *New York Times,* 21 October 1955, 22.

44. "Antitrust Investigations," *CQA* 11 (1955), 546; "Antitrust Law," *CQA* 12 (1956), 524 (quote); "Antitrust Measures," *CQA* 11 (1955), 468; "Antitrust Law," *CQA* 12 (1956), 523–27; "Pro-Merger Notice," *CQA* 12 (1956), 525–27.

45. "Bank Holding Companies," *CQA* 9 (1953), 436; "Savings, Loan Branches," *CQA* 10 (1954), 520; "Bank Companies," *CQA* 11 (1955), 477–79; "Bank Holding Companies," *CQA* 12 (1956), 557–59; "Bank Mergers," *CQA* 16 (1960), 301; "Antitrust Measures," *CQA* 11 (1955), 468; "Antitrust Law," *CQA* 12 (1956), 523–27.

46. Statement of Ben DuBois before the House Judiciary Committee, 8 March 1957, 1–5, attached to Karl E. Mundt to Herbert E. Cheever, 22 April 1957, Folder 2, Banking and Currency Committee, 1957, Box 407, Mundt Papers; Gorman, *Kefauver,* 300–308 (Kefauver quote on 300); "Antitrust Matters," *CQA* 14 (1958), 76.

47. Lawson, *Running for Freedom,* 1–40.

48. Chapman, *Contours of Public Policy,* 264–66; Lerche, "Southern Congressmen and the 'New Isolationism,'" 335–36.

49. Flynn to Spellman, 29 January 1946, S Correspondence; Flynn to George, 24 March 1949, and Styles Bridges, March 1949, Senate; Flynn to Robert H. Harriss, 24 March 1954, Harriss, Box 18; and Flynn to James F. Byrnes, 17 May 1956, B Correspondence, Box 17, all in Flynn Papers.

50. Griffith, "Eisenhower and the Corporate Commonwealth," 115–16; polls of 4 October and 13 January 1957, Gallup, *Gallup Poll,* vol. 2: 1517, 1465; Flynn to James F. Byrnes, 17 May 1956, B Correspondence, Box 17, Flynn Papers; T. G. Tilford, "Common Sense and Integration," *Daily Sentinel* (Nacogdoches, Tex.), 14 August 1957, in Civil Rights—Correspondence relating to LBJ's Senate Bill, Box 3, LBJ Senate Papers relating to Civil Rights.

51. T. G. Tilford, "Integration," *Daily Sentinel,* 14 August 1957, in Civil Rights—Correspondence relating to LBJ's Senate Bill, Box 3, LBJ Senate Papers relating to Civil Rights; Carleton Putnam, "My Dear Mr. President," 13 October 1958, advertisement reprint, 1959 Subject Files, Civil Rights—A, Box 652, LBJ Senate Papers; Dr. John R. Brown to President, 29 September 1957, Faubus File Opposing Eisenhower, A–D, Box 394, LBJ Senate Papers; Dr. Paul H. Power to LBJ, 21 September 1957, Civil Rights—Correspondence relating to LBJ's Senate Bill, Box 3, LBJ Senate Papers relating to Civil Rights; "Southern Congressmen Present Segregation Manifesto," *CQA* 12 (1956), 416–17; "Dowdy Says Forecast by Red May Be True," *Dallas Morning News,* 27 July 1959, 1959 Subject Files, Civil Rights—W, Box 654, LBJ Senate Papers. Portions of this and the following sections are from D. A. Horowitz, "White Southerners' Alienation and Civil Rights," 173–79.

52. T. G. Tilford, "Integration," *Daily Sentinel,* 14 August 1957 (first quote), Civil Rights—Correspondence relating to LBJ's Senate Bill, Box 3, LBJ Senate Papers relating to Civil Rights; Paul C. Rudolph to Homer E. Capehart, 26 July 1957 (second quote), Civil Rights, 1957, Box 136, Capehart Papers; Mrs. J. H. Bondeson to LBJ, 27 January 1960, File B, Box 13, LBJ Senate Papers relating to Civil Rights; E. K. Snider to LBJ, 11 January 1957 (third quote), "Segregation," Box 15, LBJ Senate Papers relating to Civil Rights.

53. Griffith, "Eisenhower and the Corporate Commonwealth," 115 (first quote); "83 Southern Representatives Issue Civil Rights Manifesto," *CQA* 12 (1956), 462 (second and third quotes).

54. Lawson, *Black Ballots,* 56; Note, Civil Rights Correspondence relating to LBJ's Senate Bill, 2 of 2, Box 3, LBJ Senate Papers relating to Civil Rights; A. V. Grant, "Gestapo Set Up on Civil Rights," *Dallas News,* 8 September 1957 (first quote); C. B. Howze to LBJ, 15 October 1957 (second quote), and Velva Otts to LBJ, 26 September 1957 (third quote), Civil Rights Correspondence relating to LBJ's Senate Bill, 2 of 2, Box 3, LBJ Senate Paper relating to Civil Rights; Maisie Turner Waters to LBJ, 11 May 1959 (fourth quote), 1959 Subject Files, Civil Rights—W, Box 654, LBJ Senate Papers.

55. Kearns, *Lyndon Johnson and the American Dream,* 146–48, 151; Lawson, *Black Ballots,* 165–202, 222–46.

56. Lewis, *King,* 172–96, 226–27.

57. Cramer, "School Desegregation and New Industry," 384–89; Wirt, *Politics of Southern Equality,* 137, 217–18, 254, 305; Memorandum of Conversations, Department of Defense, 29 May 1963, Alabama Notebook, May–June 1963, Alabama File, Burke Marshall Papers; Description of Procedure regarding University of Alabama, 28 May 1963, Alabama File, Burke Marshall Papers; Memorandum, Lee C. White to JFK, 11 July 1963, 2, Civil Rights File, L. White Papers; L. White to JFK, 14 May 1963, Alabama, Subject File, President's Office Files (hereafter POF), JFK Library; Anthony Lewis, transcript of interview with Burke Marshall, 20 June 1964, 99–101, Oral History Program, JFK Library. This and following sections are from D. A. Horowitz, "White Southerners' Alienation and Civil Rights," 180–200.

58. Memorandum, Lee C. White to JFK, 11 July 1963, Business Council Meetings, 3–19 July 1963, Civil Rights Files, L. White Papers; J. Kennedy quote in Memorandum, Frederick R. Kappel, n.d., 3, attached to Louis F. Oberdorfer to White, 19 July 1963, Civil Rights Files, L. White Papers; John Krider to JFK, 5 June 1963, Meetings with President, 5–19 June 1963, Civil Rights Files, L. White Papers; Memorandum, Berl I. Bernhard to Theodore Sorenson and Lee White, 15 May 1963, Civil Rights, May 1963, Attorney General's Correspondence, R. Kennedy Papers; Memorandum to Attorney General, 23 May 1963, Civil Rights: Meetings with Business Leaders, May 1963, R. Kennedy Papers; Proposed Press Release, 4 June 1963, EX HU 2, 26 December 1962–20 June 1963, White House Central Files (hereafter WHCF), JFK Library; Form Letter, Attorney General to Participants in 4 June 1963 Conference, 5 June 1963, Civil Rights: Meetings with Business Leaders, June 1963, Attorney General's Correspondence, R. Kennedy Papers; Kenneth C. Royall and Earl H. Blaik, Report to JFK, 10 October 1963, Civil Rights, Alabama, 17 May–10 October 1963, POF, JFK Library.

59. Halberstam, "White Citizens Councils," 293–94, 299–301; Cater, "Civil War in Alabama's Citizens' Councils," 19–21; Chalmers, *Hooded Americanism,* 354–55, 349–50.

60. Danzig, "Radical Right and the Rise of the Fundamentalist Minority," 291–97; Westin, "Deadly Parallels," 25–27.

61. Himmelstein, *To the Right,* 66; Welch quoted in Powers, "Robert Welch on Dwight Eisenhower."

62. Himmelstein, *To the Right,* 67–68; Allan F. Westin, "John Birch Society,"

in D. Bell, ed., *Radical Right*, 203, 205, 207–8; Forster and Epstein, *Danger on the Right*, 93, 108 (first quote), 96 (second quote), 156, 158, 163.

63. Forster and Epstein, *Danger on the Right*, 197, 126; Powers, "Robert Welch on Dwight Eisenhower" (quote).

Chapter 13: The Populist Challenge to the Established Order, 1964–92

1. H. B. McConnell to President, 29 March 1965, Box 179, Civil Rights, Public Opinion Mail, LBJ Library; Maurice Isserman and Michael Kazin, "The Failure and Success of the New Radicalism," in Fraser and Gerstle, eds., *Rise and Fall of the New Deal Order*, 236.

2. U.S. House, Select Commitee on Small Business, *Tax-Exempt Foundations and Charitable Trusts* (1962), vi–vi, 1, 9–13, 17–19, 51, 133–35; Lankford, *Congress and the Foundations*, 93–101; Introduction, in Reeves, ed., *Foundations under Fire*, 19–20, 25.

3. U.S. House, Select Committee on Small Business, *Tax-Exempt Foundations and Charitable Trusts* (1963), iii, 5–15; U.S. House, Select Committee on Small Business, *Tax-Exempt Foundations and Charitable Trusts* (1964), iii (first quote), 4 (second quote); Introduction, in Reeves, ed., *Foundations under Fire*, 28–29; Patman Statement before House Ways and Means Committee, 18 February 1969, *CR*, 91st Cong., 1st sess., 115 (18 February 1969), 3780–81; Patman, "Should Investment Earnings of Charitable Foundations Be Subject to Federal Taxation," *Congressional Digest* 48 (May 1969), 148, 150, 152, 154.

4. Patman's 1490th Weekly Letter, 4 November 1965 (first quote), Patman Name File, 1 July 1965–31 December 1965, WHCF, LBJ Library; Sherrill, "Last of the Great Populists," 24; "Banking Holding Company Exemptions Changed" and "Bank Merger Law Revised," *CQA* 22 (1966), 762–66, 767–72; Patman to Lee C. White, 11 March 1965 (second quote), attached to White to Patman, 23 March 1965, EX FI 9–1, Federal Reserve System, Box 55, WHCF, LBJ Library.

5. Sherrill, "Last of the Great Populists," 23 (first quote); Patman, "ABCs of American Money System," *CR*, 88th Cong., 2d sess., 110 (3 August 1964), 17253–61; Kay, "Warrior from Patman's Switch," 155–56, 178; Patman to LBJ, 15 January 1965, attached to Lawrence F. O'Brien to Patman, 16 January 1964, EX LE/FI 9, Box 51, WHCF, LBJ Library; Patman Speech Draft, 10 June 1965, 18 (second quote), attached to W. Marvin Watson to LBJ, 9 June 1965, EX FG 233, Box 282, WHCF, LBJ Library; Memorandum, Arthur M. Okun to LBJ, 26 May 1966, EX LE/FI 2, 22 February 1966–, Box 48, WHCF, LBJ Library; Memorandum, Garden Ackley to LBJ, and attachments, 29 July 1966 (third quote), CF FG 233, Federal Reserve System, Box 32, WHCF, LBJ Library; Memorandum, Patman to Citizens Interested in Returning Our Monetary System to the People of the United States, 15 September 1966, Patman Name File, 1 July–31 December 1966, WHCF, LBJ Library; Barefoot Sanders to President, 1 February 1968, Patman Name File, 1 January 1968–, WHCF, LBJ Library.

6. Mundt, "The Key to the Future of American Politics," address before South Carolina State Bankers Association, Greenville, S.C., 5 May 1956, *CR*, 84th Cong., 2d sess., 102 (4 June 1956), 9443 (first quote); Mundt, *CR*, 86th Cong.,

1st sess., 105 (8 September 1959), 18572–74; Mundt, Draft of Letter to National Small Business Men's Association, April 1960 (second quote), Folder 8, National Business Men's Association, 1960, Total Centralization, Senate Small Business Committee, Box 675, Mundt Papers; Mundt, "Question for the 1962 'Liberal': Whatever Happened to Freedom From . . . ?" speech draft, n.d., Folder 4, Speeches—General, Liberalism 1962–?, Box DB 1228, Mundt Papers; Mundt, "The New 'Liberals': Are They Really '20th-Century Tories'?" *U.S. News and World Report* 54 (25 March 1963), 108.

7. Edsall, *Chain Reaction,* 7, 39–42.

8. Leonard Coe Scruggs to Harry C. McPherson, 22 July 1964 (first quote), attached to Memorandum, Horace Busby to Jack Valenti, 11 August 1964, EX PL 2, 6 August–14 August 1964, Box 83, WHCF, LBJ Library; Goldwater Address to Thirty-second Women's Patriotic Conference on National Defense, Inc., cited in *Washington Evening Star,* 1 February 1958, in "What Goldwater Said," 260, Box 28, Reedy Office Files, LBJ Library; Goldwater, speech of 21 September 1964, Charlotte, N.C., in "What Goldwater Has Said," 14 (second quote), 17 (sixth quote), Supplement D, 15 September–30 September 1964, Box 26, Reedy Office Files, LBJ Library; Goldwater Speech before Retail Merchants Association of Baltimore, 19 May 1954, *CR,* 83rd Cong., 2d sess., 100 (25 May 1954), A3807 (third quote); Goldwater, remarks to Texas Republican Convention, 15 June 1964 (fourth and fifth quotes), in "What Goldwater Said," 296, Box 28, Reedy Office Files, LBJ Library; Goldwater, *Conscience of a Conservative,* 34, 78–79.

9. Hamilton, *Restraining Myths,* 66–67, 123, 158–59; Goldwater, speech of 10 September 1964 (first quote), Minneapolis, Minn., in "What Goldwater Has Said," 6, Supplement E—Additional September Quotes, Box 26; Goldwater, speech of 19 August 1964 (second quote), Illinois State Fair, quoted in *Chicago Tribune,* 20 August 1964, in Goldwater Quotes, 5, 1–15 September 1964, Supplement C, Box 28; and Goldwater, *San Francisco Examiner,* 6 July 1963 (third quote), in "What Goldwater Said," 445, Box 28, all in Reedy Office Files, LBJ Library; Bunzel, *Anti-Politics in America,* 88 (fourth quote).

10. Louis Harris, The Harris Survey, 5 October 1964, PL 2, 3 October–6 October 1964, Box 98, WHCF, LBJ Library; Edsall, *Chain Reaction,* 40–42; Goldwater Position Papers, Goldwater for President Committee, 1964, "What Goldwater Said," 202, 206, Box 28, Reedy Office Files, LBJ Library; Goldwater, *CR,* 88th Cong., 2d sess., 110 (18 June 1964), 13825 (quote); Goldwater, speech of 16 October 1964, Conrad Hilton Hotel, Chicago, quoted in *Washington Post,* 18 October 1964, in "What Goldwater Has Said," 6, Supplement D—1–16 October 1964, Box 26, Reedy Office Files, LBJ Library.

11. Lewis, *King,* 264–93.

12. Wirt, *Politics of Southern Equality,* 137, 187, 242, 254, 305; "What We Believe and Where We Stand . . . ," 15 April 1965, attached to Memorandum, LeRoy Collins to LBJ, 14 April 1965, EX HU 2/ST 1, Box 24, LBJ Library; John W. Nixon to LBJ, 23 May 1966, attached to Harry C. McPherson Jr. to Nixon, 8 June 1966, HU 2/ST 1, 2 December 1965–, Box 29, WHCF, LBJ Library. For publication of manifesto, see *Wall Street Journal,* 15 April 1965.

13. Don F. Wasson, "Selma Inscribes Notes of Reason in History Text," *Montgomery Advertiser,* 31 January 1965 (first quote); poll of 19 July 1963, Gallup, *Gallup Poll,* vol. 3: 1820; Lois W. Dew to LBJ, 11 June 1963 (second quote), Civil Rights—1–17 June 1963, Box 5, LBJ Vice Presidential Papers relating to Civil Rights; Milton R. Durrett to Repr. Carl Elliott, 20 May 1963 (third quote), attached to Lee C. White to Elliott, 3 June 1963, EX HU 2/ST 1, WHCF, JFK Library; Elizabeth F. Lassiter to LBJ, 25 March 1965 (fourth quote), Box 145, Civil Rights Public Opinion Mail, LBJ Library.

14. Walter H. Roberts and twenty-three others to LBJ, 15 February 1964 (first quote), and petition to LBJ, 25 February 1964 (second quote), Exhibit Letters, LE/HU 2, 30 January–19 February 1964, Box 67, WHCF; Mrs. Richard Kunitz Jr. to LBJ, 1 May 1964 (third quote), Box 180, Civil Rights Public Opinion Mail; Albert B. Crane to LBJ, 6 March 1964 (fourth quote), LE/HV2, 20 February–12 March 1964, Box 67, WHCF; and Confidential Memorandum, Reedy to LBJ, Confidential Memoranda—Reedy, Box 6, LBJ Vice Presidential Papers Open for Civil Rights, all in LBJ Library.

15. John Krider to JFK, 5 June 1963, Meetings with President, 5 June–19 June 1963, Civil Rights Files, L. White Papers; Confidential Memorandum, Reedy to LBJ, Confidential Memoranda—Reedy, Box 6, LBJ Vice Presidential Papers Open for Civil Rights.

16. D. Horowitz and Kolodney, "Foundations," 44; Memorandum, Richard S. Franzen to Bertrand M. Harding, and attachments, 3 October 1968, GOP Obstructionism on OEO Legislation, Box 31, Gaither Office Files; Sundquist, *Politics and Policy,* 145–46.

17. Harrington, *Dream of Deliverance,* 237; Telegram, Maddox to LBJ, 23 June 1966, Maddox Name File, WHCF, LBJ Library; Maddox to LBJ, 10 July 1968, Exhibit Letters, WHCF, LBJ Library.

18. Wallace, *Stand Up for America,* 10–11, 19, 21–22, 24, 26, 43, 51, 53, 55, 57, 63, 65–69.

19. Ibid., 69, 72, 75, 78–79, 81, 83, 86 (first quote), 88, 90, 96; Carlson, *George C. Wallace,* 30 (second quote), 33–33, 64–66.

20. Carlson, *George C. Wallace,* 6, 15–17, 277–28 (quote on 16).

21. Wallace quoted in ibid., 31; Wallace quoted in Novak, *Rise of the Unmeltable Ethnics,* 16; Edsall, *Chain Reaction,* 9–10, 74, 77–78, 85.

22. Dionne, *Why Americans Hate Politics,* 44, 79; Gallup poll of 14 July 1968, cited in Memorandum, Fred Panzer to LBJ, 21 July 1968, EX PL / Wallace, George, Box 27, WHCF, LBJ Library.

23. Wallace, *Stand Up for America,* 82 (first quote), 86–87 (fourth quote), 92, 122 (third quote), 124; Wallace quoted in "Governor George Wallace / The War on Poverty," *Birmingham Independent,* 3 March 1965, 3 (second quote); Jonathan Rieder, "The Rise of the Silent Majority," in Fraser and Gerstle, eds., *Rise and Fall of the New Deal Order,* 249–51.

24. Jack Nelson and Nicholas C. Chriss, "Radical Rightists Play Key Roles in Wallace Drive," *L.A. Times,* 17 September 1968, in EX PL / Wallace, George, Box 27, WHCF, LBJ Library; Memorandum, Fred Panzer to LBJ, 22 October 1968, and Panser Memorandum to LBJ, 12 July 1968, EX PL / Wallace, George,

Box 27, WHCF, LBJ Library; Edsall, *Chain Reaction,* 77; Hamilton, *Restraining Myths,* 160–62.

25. Carlson, *George C. Wallace,* 7.

26. Rieder, "The Rise of the Silent Majority," in Fraser and Gerstle, eds., *Rise and Fall of the New Deal Order,* 260–61, 244, 248.

27. Ibid., 260–63 (quote on 262); Edsall, *Chain Reaction,* 97–98, 75.

28. Rieder, "The Rise of the Silent Majority," in Fraser and Gerstle, eds., *Rise and Fall of the New Deal Order,* 244 (first quote), 260 (second quote), 262–63; Wallace, *Stand Up For America,* 153–55, 165–66 (third quote on 166); Himmelstein, *To the Right,* 72.

29. Himmelstein, *To the Right,* 6; Rieder, "The Rise of the Silent Majority," in Fraser and Gerstle, eds., *Rise and Fall of the New Deal Order,* 254–55; Lasch, *True and Only Heaven,* 482, 485; Clecak, *Crooked Paths,* 90, 80–81. By 1970, 36 percent of the work force consisted of manual laborers. Anderson, "Language of Class in Twentieth-Century America," 367.

30. Clecak, *Crooked Paths,* 73, 80–81, 90–91, 94, 131–32; Edsall, *Chain Reaction,* 11, 17–18, 106, 214.

31. Edsall, *Chain Reaction,* 127, 122–24, 14 (first quote), 187 (second quote); Fuchs, *American Kaleidoscope,* 406–42.

32. Edsall, *Chain Reaction,* 15, 121, 236, 11–13; Rieder, "The Rise of the Silent Majority," in Fraser and Gerstle, eds., *Rise and Fall of the New Deal Order,* 255–57 (quote on 256).

33. Formisano, *Boston against Busing;* Lasch, *True and Only Heaven,* 496–505, 478 (Hicks quote).

34. Edsall, *Chain Reaction,* 3–9, 122, 206, 263–64. 281–82; Dionne, *Why Americans Hate Politics,* 178–79, 107, 142, 321. For the importance of McGovern reform rules in consolidating upper-middle-class influence on Democratic politics, see Dionne, *Why Americans Hate Politics,* 49, 51, 144.

35. Dionne, *Why Americans Hate Politics,* 110–11; Edsall, *Chain Reaction,* 5, 20, 108–9, 122, 258–59; Nash, *Conservative Intellectual Movement in America,* 250–51, 300; Himmelstein, *To the Right,* 6, 71; Klatch, *Women of the New Right,* 127–29; Phillips, *Post-Conservative America,* 193–95; Lasch, *True and Only Heaven,* 24, 33–34, 171.

36. Entry on Jerry Falwell, *Current Biography Yearbook, 1981,* 139–43; Falwell quoted in Himmelstein, *To the Right,* 98; U.S. Department of Commerce, *Statistical Abstract of the United States, 1987,* table 102, 67.

37. Himmelstein, *To the Right,* 6, 97–126; Phillips, *Post-Conservative America,* xvii–xviii; Luker, *Abortion and the Politics of Motherhood;* Klatch, *Women of the New Right,* 127–29; Lasch, *True and Only Heaven,* 488–92.

38. Himmelstein, *To the Right,* 97, 132–64, 63–64, 71; Phillips, *Post-Conservative America,* xvii, xx, 14, 31–32.

39. Himmelstein, *To the Right,* 8, 80–92, 63–64; Judis, "Pop-Con Politics," 19–20; J. Bell, *Populism and Elitism,* 165; Phillips, *Post-Conservative America,* xx, 31–32, 46–50.

40. Weyrich quoted in Viguerie, *New Right,* 59 (first quote); William Schneider, "The Political Legacy of the Reagan Years," in Blumenthal and Ed-

sall, ed., *The Reagan Legacy,* 64 (second quote); Himmelstein, *To the Right,* 92; Lasch, *True and Only Heaven,* 505, 509; Phillips, *Post-Conservative America,* 14.

41. Viguerie, *Establishment vs. the People,* 8–9, 41, 61, 64–65, 70; Weyrich quoted in Neuhaus, "Right to Fight," 555, 559 (quote).

42. Viguerie, *Establishment vs. the People,* 41, 61, 64–65, 70, 14, 182 (Kemp quote).

43. Quoted in Neuhaus, "Right to Fight," 555–59 (first quote on 559); Viguerie, *Establishment vs. the People,* 186 (second quote).

44. "1976 Elections," *CQA* 32 (1976), 819–22 (quotes on 819).

45. Edsall, *Chain Reaction,* 27, 135; Ferguson and Rogers, *Right Turn,* 195–96.

46. Harrington, *Dream of Deliverance,* 260; Lasch, *True and Only Heaven,* 38–39; Dallek, *Ronald Reagan,* 28.

47. Reagan quoted in J. White, *New Politics of Old Values,* 50 (first quote); Dallek, *Ronald Reagan,* 7, 27; Reagan Acceptance Speech, Republican National Convention, 17 July 1980, in Reagan, *Ronald Reagan Talks,* 70 (second and third quotes); Reagan, "A Vision for America," television speech of 3 November 1980, quoted in J. White, *New Politics of Old Values,* 50 (fourth quote).

48. Lasch, *True and Only Heaven,* 38–39; Rodgers, "Ronald Reagan's Rhetoric"; Edsall, *Chain Reaction,* 24; Reagan quoted in Harrington, *Dream of Deliverance,* 261.

49. Edsall, *Chain Reaction,* 10–14, 21, 24, 144–46, 162; "Reagan Buries Carter," *CQA* 36 (1980), 3–6B; J. Bell, *Populism and Elitism,* 156–57.

50. Reagan Inaugural Address, 20 January 1981, in Reagan, *Speaking My Mind,* 61 (first quote), 63 (second quote); Dallek, *Ronald Reagan,* 63–64; J. Bell, *Populism and Elitism,* 100–101; Green, *Shaping Political Consciousness,* 254–55.

51. Edsall, *Chain Reaction,* 22, 159, 192, 23, 187; J. Bell, *Populism and Elitism,* 174; "Congress Enacts President Reagan's Tax Plan," *CQA* 37 (1981), 91–104; "Fiscal 1982 Reconciliation Cuts," *CQA* 37 (1981), 256–66; "Reagan's Seven-Year Record," *CQA* 44 (1988), 187; "Economic Policy," *CQA* 38 (1982), 27.

52. "Landslide Victory by Reagan," *CQA* 40 (1984), 3–6B; J. Bell, *Populism and Elitism,* 159; Dionne, *Why Americans Hate Politics,* 248.

53. George Skelton, "Reagan on Tax System: 'It's Time We Rebelled,'" *Los Angeles Times,* 31 May 1985, 1 (first and second quotes), 11 (third quote); Robert S. McIntyre, "President Plays Populist," *Los Angeles Times,* 2 June 1985, sec. 4: 1 (fourth quote); Skelton, "Tide of Mail Backs Tax Plan," *Los Angeles Times,* 1 June 1985, 4 (fifth quote); "Congress Enacts Sweeping Overhaul of Tax Law," *CQA* 42 (1986), 491–98. Top tax rates on individuals were reduced from 50 to 28 percent, while the highest corporate rates fell from 46 to 34 percent.

54. Tom Redburn, "Reagan Plans Big Tax Reform Push," *Los Angeles Times,* 26 May 1985, 10 (first and second quotes); J. Bell, *Populism and Elitism,* 174, 190 (third quote).

55. J. Bell, *Populism and Elitism,* 111–12; Reagan remarks at the Annual Convention of the National Association of Evangelicals, Orlando, Fla., 8 March

1983, in "Excerpts from President's Speech," *New York Times,* 9 March 1983, 18; Harrington, *Dream of Deliverance,* 271–72.

56. Reagan, "A Time for Choosing," in Reagan, *Ronald Reagan Talks,* 4; "Remarks on Accepting the GOP Nomination," 23 August 1984, in Reagan, *Speaking My Mind,* 200.

57. Rodgers, "Reagan's Rhetoric"; Reagan, speech of 26 January 1982, quoted in J. White, *New Politics of Old Values,* 60; Reagan remarks at Evangelicals Convention, 8 March 1983, in Reagan, *Speaking My Mind,* 171; Reagan remarks at the Conservative Political Action Conference, Washington, D.C., 1 March 1985, in Reagan, *Speaking My Mind,* 274; Reagan remarks to reporters, in Reagan, *Ronald Reagan Talks,* 169.

58. Himmelstein, *To the Right,* 166, 197; Atwater quoted in Edsall, *Chain Reaction,* 221.

59. Edsall, *Chain Reaction,* 227, 16, 118, 235, 241, 242, 113, 236.

60. Ibid., 16, 258, 259 (quote), 273, 244, 283, 276; James Pinkerton, "The New Paradigm," an address before the Reason Foundation, Los Angeles, 23 April 1990, quoted in ibid., 274.

61. J. Bell, *Populism and Elitism,* 161–63; Edsall, *Chain Reaction,* 224–25; Blumenthal, *Pledging Allegiance,* 262–64 (quote on 264).

62. Blumenthal, *Pledging Allegiance,* 264–66 (quote on 264), 284–86, 291, 295–96, 307–8; J. Bell, *Populism and Elitism,* 163; Edsall, *Chain Reaction,* 224–26; Himmelstein, *To the Right,* 207–9; "Bush Victory," *CQA* 44 (1988), 3–7A.

63. Edsall, *Chain Reaction,* 21–23, 225, 6 (quote), 11, 23, 220; Sylvia Nasar, "The 1980s: A Very Good Time for the Very Rich," *New York Times,* 5 March 1992, 1.

64. Sylvia Nasar, "The 1980s: A Very Good Time for the Very Rich," *New York Times,* 5 March 1992, 1; Harrington, *Dream of Deliverance,* 270; Edsall, *Chain Reaction,* 275; Hodding Carter, *Reagan Years,* 59–60, 45, 49, 85, 55; McIntyre, "President Plays Populist," *Los Angeles Times,* 2 June 1985, sec. 4: l; "Deficit Limited Reagan's Options in 1988 Budget," *CQA* 44 (1988), 181; "Congress Cleans Plan for $1.1 Trillion Budget," *CQA* 44 (1988), 193; U.S. Department of Commerce, *Statistical Abstract of the United States, 1989,* table 489, 303.

65. Thomas Byrne Edsall, "The Changing Shape of Power: A Realignment in Public Policy," in Fraser and Gerstle, eds., *Rise and Fall of the New Deal Order,* 269–71; Edsall, *Chain Reaction,* 25–27, 267–68, 30.

66. "Democrats Reclaim Electoral College," *CQA* 48 (1992), 3–5A.

67. "The Man and the Myth," *Newsweek,* 15 June 1992, 21–22; "How He Might Govern," *Newsweek,* 15 June 1992, 26; "Issues: Filling in the Blanks," *Newsweek,* 15 June 1992, 24.

68. "The Man and the Myth," *Newsweek,* 15 June 1992, 20 (quotes), 24; "The Other Side of Perot," *Time,* 29 June 1992, 39; "Wiring Up the Age of Technopolitics," *Newsweek,* 15 June 1992, 25; Laurence I. Barrett, "Making Sense of the Polls," *Time,* 29 June 1992, 48; Brinkley, "Roots," 44–45.

69. Clinton quoted in Howard Fineman, "The Torch Passes," *Newsweek,*

special election issue, November/December 1992, 8–9; "Democrats," *CQA* 48 (1992), 3–5A.

Conclusion

1. Dionne, *Why Americans Hate Politics,* 14 (first quote), 97, 246, 326, 329 (second quote), 353–54; Edsall, *Chain Reaction,* 286 (third quote); Phillips, *Arrogant Capital.*

Bibliography

Manuscripts

Biddle, Francis. Papers. Franklin D. Roosevelt Presidential Library, Hyde Park, N.Y.

Borah, William E. Papers. Library of Congress, Washington, D.C.

Bricker, John W. Papers. Ohio Historical Society, Columbus.

Burdick, Usher L. Papers. Orin G. Libby Manuscript Collection, Department of Special Collections, Chester Fritz Library, University of North Dakota.

Capehart, Homer E. Papers. Indiana State Library, Indianapolis.

Chase, Ray P. Papers. Minnesota Historical Society, St. Paul.

Donnelly, Phil M. Papers. Western Historical Manuscripts, University of Missouri at Columbia.

Farmer-Labor Association. Papers. Minnesota Historical Society, St. Paul.

Flynn, John T. Papers. University of Oregon Special Collections, Eugene.

Gaither, James. Office Files. Lyndon Baines Johnson Presidential Library, Austin, Tex.

Gehan, George H. Papers. Minnesota Historical Society, St. Paul.

Gilman, Robbins, and Catheryne Cooke Gilman. Papers. Minnesota Historical Society, St. Paul.

Hays, Will. Papers (microform). Edited by Douglas Gomery. Frederick, Md.: University Publications of America, 1988.

Hoover, Herbert C. Presidential Papers. Herbert Hoover Presidential Library, West Branch, Iowa.

Ickes, Harold L. Papers. Library of Congress, Washington, D.C.

Jewish Community Relations Council of Minnesota. Papers. Minnesota Historical Society, St. Paul.

Johnson, Hiram W. Papers. Bancroft Library, University of California at Berkeley.

Johnson, Lyndon B. Senate Papers relating to Civil Rights, Senate Papers, Vice-Presidential Papers, Vice Presidential Papers Open for Civil Rights, and Presidential Papers. Lyndon Baines Johnson Presidential Library, Austin, Tex.

Johnson, Magnus. Papers. Minnesota Historical Society, St. Paul.

Judd, Walter H. Papers. Minnesota Historical Society, St. Paul.

Kem, James P. Papers. Western Historical Manuscripts, University of Missouri at Columbia.

Kennedy, John F. Presidential Papers. John F. Kennedy Presidential Library, Boston, Mass.

Kennedy, Robert F. Papers. John F. Kennedy Presidential Library, Boston, Mass.

La Follette, Philip F. Papers. State Historical Society of Wisconsin, Madison.

La Follette, Robert M. Papers. Library of Congress, Washington, D.C.

La Follette, Robert M., Jr. Papers. Library of Congress, Washington, D.C.

La Follette Family Papers. Library of Congress, Washington, D.C.

Langer, William. Papers. Department of Special Collections, Orin G. Libby Manuscript Collection, Chester Fritz Library, University of North Dakota.

Lemke, William. Papers. Department of Special Collections, Orin G. Libby Manuscript Collection, Chester Fritz Library, University of North Dakota.

Lindbergh, Charles A., Sr. Papers. Minnesota Historical Society, St. Paul.

Marshall, Burke. Papers. John F. Kennedy Presidential Library, Boston, Mass.

Marshall, Verne. Papers. Herbert Hoover Presidential Library, West Branch, Iowa.

McNary, Charles L. Papers. Library of Congress, Washington, D.C.

Morgan, Arthur E. Papers. Special Collections, Antioch College Library, Yellow Springs, Ohio.

Mundt, Karl E. Papers. Dakota State College, Madison, S.D.

National Nonpartisan League. Papers. Minnesota Historical Society, St. Paul.

Neuberger, Richard. Papers. University of Oregon Special Collections, Eugene.

Norbeck, Peter. Letters, 1921–36. Western Historical Manuscripts, University of Missouri at Columbia.

————. Papers. University of South Dakota Archives, Vermillion.

Norris, George W. Papers. Library of Congress, Washington, D.C.

Nye, Gerald P. Papers. Herbert Hoover Presidential Library, West Branch, Iowa.

Oral History Program. John F. Kennedy Presidential Library, Boston, Mass.

Peek, George N. Papers. Western Historical Manuscripts, University of Missouri at Columbia.

Reedy, George E. Office Files. Lyndon Baines Johnson Presidential Library, Austin, Tex.

Roosevelt, Franklin D. Presidential Papers. Franklin D. Roosevelt Presidential Library, Hyde Park, N.Y.

Rowell, Chester H. Papers. Bancroft Library, University of California at Berkeley.

Shipstead, Henrik. Papers. Minnesota Historical Society, St. Paul.

Taft, Robert A. Papers. Library of Congress, Washington, D.C.

Truman, Harry S. Presidential Papers. Harry S. Truman Presidential Library, Independence, Mo.

Walsh, Thomas J. Papers. Library of Congress, Washington, D.C.

Wheeler, Burton K. Papers. Montana Historical Society, Helena.

White, Lee C. Papers. John F. Kennedy Presidential Library, Boston, Mass.

Wood, Robert E. Papers. Herbert Hoover Presidential Library, West Branch, Iowa.

Newspapers and News Magazines

Birmingham Independent, 1965
Boston Evening Transcript, 1919
Business Week, 1936
Chicago Tribune, 1941–48
Commercial and Financial Chronicle, 1927
Congressional Digest, 1930–69
Congressional Quarterly Almanac, 1953–92
Detroit Evening Times, 1935
Detroit Free Press, 1950
Detroit News, 1935
Duncan's Trade Register, 1930
Imperial Night-Hawk, 1923–24
Journal of Commerce, 1927
Life, 1938–41
Los Angeles Times, 1985
Minneapolis Star, 1941
Modern Metals, 1949
Montgomery Advertiser, 1965
Morning Astorian (Astoria, Oreg.), 1922
Newsweek, 1992
New York Daily News, 1950
New York Herald Tribune, 1934–38
New York Times, 1915–92
Oregonian, 1931–82
Oregon Merchants Magazine, 1930–38
Oregon Voter, 1922–30
Progressive Grocer, 1932–39
Southern Pharmaceutical Journal, 1935
Spectator, 1931
Time, 1992
U.S. News and World Report, 1951–63
Vital Speeches of the Day, 1938
Wall Street Journal, 1965
Washington Daily News, 1931
Washington Evening Star, 1941
Yellow Springs (Ohio) *News,* 1947

Public Documents

Congressional Record. Washington, D.C.: Government Printing Office, 1893–1956.
Department of Commerce, Bureau of the Census. *Statistical Abstract of the United States, 1987.* Washington, D.C.: Government Printing Office, 1987.

————. *Statistical Abstract of the United States, 1989.* Washington, D.C.: Government Printing Office, 1989.

Federal Trade Commission. *Chain Stores, Chain Store Price Policies.* Washington, D.C.: Government Printing Office, 1934.

————. *Final Report on the Chain Store Investigation.* Washington, D.C. Government Printing Office, 1935.

————. *The Merger Movement: A Summary Report.* Washington, D.C.: Government Printing Office, 1948.

————. *The Present Trend of Corporate Mergers and Acquisitions.* Washington, D.C.: Government Printing Office, 1947.

U.S. House of Representatives. Committee on Investigation of American Retail Federation. *Investigation of the Trade Practices of Big Scale Retail and Wholesale Buying and Selling Organizations.* Washington, D.C.: Government Printing Office, 1935.

U.S. House of Representatives. Committee on Small Business. *Small Business Organizations.* Washington, D.C.: Government Printing Office, 1950.

U.S. House of Representatives. Select Committee on Fair Trade. *Fair Trade: The Problem and the Issues.* Washington, D.C.: Government Printing Office, 1952.

U.S. House of Representatives. Select Committee on Small Business. *Tax-Exempt Foundations and Charitable Trusts: Their Impact on Our Economy.* Chairman's Report. Washington, D.C.: Government Printing Office, 1962.

————. *Tax-Exempt Foundations and Charitable Trusts: Their Impact on Our Economy.* Subcommittee Chairman's Report to Subcommittee No. 1. Washington, D.C.: Government Printing Office, 1963.

————. *Tax-Exempt Foundations and Charitable Trusts: Their Impact on Our Economy.* Chairman's Report to Subcommittee No. 1. Washington, D.C.: Government Printing Office, 1964.

U.S. House of Representatives. Select Committee to Investigate Acts of Executive Agencies beyond the Scope of Their Authority. *Second Intermediate Report.* Washington, D.C.: Government Printing Office, 1943.

U.S. House of Representatives. Select Committee to Investigate and Study Educational and Philanthropic Foundations and Other Comparable Organizations Which Are Exempt from Federal Income Tax. *Final Report.* Washington, D.C.: Government Printing Office, 1953.

U.S. House of Representatives. Special Committee to Investigate Tax-Exempt Foundations and Comparable Organizations. *Relations between Foundations and Education and between Foundations and Government.* Staff Report No. 3. Washington, D.C.: Government Printing Office, 1954.

————. *Tax-Exempt Foundations: Final Report.* Washington, D.C.: Government Printing Office, 1954.

————. *Tax-Exempt Foundations: Hearings before the Special Committee to Investigate Tax-Exempt Foundations and Comparable Organizations.* Washington, D.C.: Government Printing Office, 1954.

U.S. Senate. Committee on Interstate Commerce. *Hearings on Anti "Block-Booking" and "Blind Selling" in the Leasing of Motion-Picture Films.* Washington, D.C.: Government Printing Office, 1939.

U.S. Senate. Committee on Privileges and Elections. *Senator from Wisconsin.* Report No. 614. Washington, D.C.: Government Printing Office, 1918.

U.S. Senate. Special Committee to Study Problems of American Small Business. *American Small Business.* Additional Report Pursuant to Senate Resolution 298, 5 February 1942. Washington, D.C.: Government Printing Office, 1942.

———. *Independent Business—Its Struggle for Survival.* Washington, D.C.: Government Printing Office, 1949.

U.S. Senate. Subcommittee of the Committee on Interstate Commerce. *Propaganda in Motion Pictures: Hearings before a Subcommittee of the Committee on Interstate Commerce.* Washington, D.C.: Government Printing Office, 1942.

U.S. Senate. Subcommittee of the Committee on the Judiciary on Antitrust and Monopoly. *Monopoly in the Power Industry.* Interim Report. Washington, D.C.: Government Printing Office, 1955.

U.S. Senate. Subcommittee of the Committee on Privileges and Elections. *Letter from the Secretary of the Minnesota Commission of Public Safety to Senator Frank B. Kellogg.* Washington, D.C.: Government Printing Office, 1917.

U.S. Senate. Temporary National Economic Committee. *Final Report and Recommendations.* Washington, D.C.: Government Printing Office, 1942.

Articles, Pamphlets, and Books

Abrahamson, James L. *The American Home Front.* Washington, D.C.: National Defense University Press, 1983.

Aikman, Duncan. *The Home Town Mind.* New York: Minton and Balch, 1926.

Alexander, Charles C. *The Ku Klux Klan in the Southwest.* Lexington: University of Kentucky Press, 1965.

Allen, Howard. "Republican Reformers and Geography and Politics: Voting on Reform Issues in the United States Senate, 1911–1916." *Journal of Southern History* 27 (October 1961): 216–28.

Ambrosius, Lloyd E. *Woodrow Wilson and the American Diplomatic Tradition: The Treaty Fight in Perspective.* New York: Cambridge University Press, 1987.

Anderson, Margo. "The Language of Class in Twentieth-Century America." *Social Science History* 12 (Winter 1988): 349–75.

Ashby, LeRoy. *The Spearless Leader: Senator Borah and the Progressive Movement in the 1920s.* Urbana: University of Illinois Press, 1972.

———. *William Jennings Bryan: Champion of Democracy.* Boston: Twayne, 1987.

Association of Missouri Banks and Trust Companies Opposed to Branch Banking. *Shall We Allow Branch Banking to Supplant Independent Banking in the United States.* St. Louis: Research Advertising Bureau, 1922.

Baruch, Bernard. *American Industry in the War: A Report of the War Industries Board.* New York: Prentice-Hall, 1941.

Bell, Daniel. *The Cultural Contradictions of Capitalism.* New York: Basic Books, 1978.

———, ed. *The Radical Right: The New American Right.* Garden City, N.Y.: Doubleday, 1963.

Bell, Jeffrey. *Populism and Elitism: Politics in the Age of Equality.* Washington, D.C.: Regnery Gateway, 1992.

Bellows, F. M. "The Mystery of the Chains." *System and Business Management* 63 (January 1934): 19–21ff.

Bender, Thomas. *Community and Social Change in America.* New Brunswick, N.J.: Rutgers University Press, 1968.

———. "Wholes and Parts: The Need for Synthesis in American History." *Journal of American History* 73 (June 1986): 120–36.

Bennett, David H. *Demagogues in the Depression: American Radicals and the Union Party, 1932–1936.* New Brunswick, N.J.: Rutgers University Press, 1969.

———. *The Party of Fear: From Nativist Movements to the New Right in American History.* Chapel Hill: University of North Carolina Press, 1988.

Berle, Adolf A., Jr., and Gardiner C. Means. *The Modern Corporation and Private Property.* 1932. Reprint, New York: Macmillan, 1948.

Blackorby, Edward C. *Prairie Rebel: The Public Life of William Lemke.* Lincoln: University of Nebraska Press, 1963.

Blee, Kathleen M. *Women of the Klan: Racism and Gender in the 1920s.* Berkeley: University of California Press, 1991.

Blum, John Morton. *V Was for Victory: Politics and American Culture during World War II.* New York: Harcourt Brace Jovanovich, 1976.

Blumenthal, Sidney. *Pledging Allegiance: The Last Campaign of the Cold War.* New York: Harper Collins, 1990.

Blumenthal, Sidney, and Thomas Byrne Edsall, eds. *The Reagan Legacy.* New York: Pantheon Books, 1988.

Blumer, Herbert. "Moulding of Mass Behavior through the Motion Pictures." *American Sociological Society Publication 29* 3 (August 1935): 115–27.

Boas, Ralph Phillip. "Jew Baiting in America." *Atlantic Monthly* 127 (May 1921): 658–65.

Bohn, Frank. "The KKK Interpreted." *American Journal of Sociology* 30 (January 1925): 385–407.

Boorstin, Daniel J. *The Americans: The Democratic Experience.* New York: Random House, 1973.

Boyle, Peter G. "The Roots of Isolationism: A Case Study." *Journal of American Studies* 6 (April 1972): 41–50.

Braeman, John. "Seven Progressives." *Business History Review* 35 (Winter 1961): 581–92.

Brand, Donald R. *Corporatism and the Rule of Law: A Study of the National Recovery Administration.* Ithaca, N.Y.: Cornell University Press, 1988.

Brinkley, Alan. "Richard Hofstadter's *The Age of Reform*: A Reconsideration." *Reviews in American History* 13 (September 1985): 462–80.

———. "Roots." *New Republic* 207 (27 July 1992): 44–45.

———. *Voices of Protest: Huey Long, Father Coughlin, and the Great Depression.* New York: Alfred A. Knopf, 1982.

———. "Writing the History of Contemporary America: Dilemmas and Challenges." *Daedalus* 113 (Summer 1984): 121–41.

Brown, Heywood. "Phil La Follette Sounds Off." *New Republic* 95 (11 May 1938): 16ff.

Brownell, Blaine A. "A Symbol of Modernity: Attitudes toward the Automobile in Southern Cities in the 1920s." *American Quarterly* 24 (March 1972): 20–44.

Bruchey, Stuart. *The Wealth of the Nation: An Economic History of the United States.* New York: Harper and Row, 1988.

Bunzel, John H. *Anti-Politics in America: Reflections on the Anti-Political Temper and Its Distortions of the Democratic Process.* New York: Alfred A. Knopf, 1967.

Burke, Robert E. "A Friendship in Adversity: Burton K. Wheeler and Hiram W. Johnson." *Montana: The Magazine of Western History* 36 (Winter 1986): 12–25.

———, ed. *The Diary Letters of Hiram Johnson, 1917–1945.* 7 vols. New York: Garland, 1983.

Burner, David. *The Politics of Provincialism: The Democratic Party in Transition, 1918–1932.* New York: Alfred A. Knopf, 1968.

Cahnman, Werner J. "Socio-Economic Causes of Antisemitism." *Social Problems* 5 (July 1957): 21–29.

Carlson, Jody. *George C. Wallace and the Politics of Powerlessness: The Wallace Campaigns for the Presidency, 1964–76.* New Brunswick, N.J.: Transaction Books, 1981.

Carr, Robert K. *The House Committee on Un-American Activities, 1945–1950.* Ithaca, N.Y.: Cornell University Press, 1952.

Carter, Henry. "Politics and the Trade Agreement." *Wharton Review* 11 (February 1938): 8–9.

Carter, Hodding. *The Reagan Years.* New York: George Braziller, 1988.

Cater, Douglass. "Civil War in Alabama's Citizens' Councils." *Reporter* 14 (17 May 1956): 19–21.

Catledge, Turner. "The Liberal Who Fights New Deal Liberalism." *New York Times Magazine* (8 August 1937): 3ff.

Cayton, Andrew R. L., and Peter S. Onuf. *The Midwest and the Nation: Rethinking the History of a Region.* Bloomington: Indiana University Press, 1990.

Chadwin, Mark Lincoln. *The Hawks of World War II.* Chapel Hill: University of North Carolina Press, 1968.

Chalmers, David M. *Hooded Americanism: The First Century of the Ku Klux Klan, 1865–1965.* Garden City, N.Y.: Doubleday, 1965.

Chambers, Clarke A. *Seedtime of Reform: Social Service and Social Action.* Minneapolis: University of Minnesota Press, 1963.

Chapman, Richard N. *Contours of Public Policy, 1939–1945.* New York: Garland, 1981.

Chase, William Sheafe. *The Case for the Federal Supervision of Motion Pictures.* Brooklyn, N.Y.: n.p., 1927.

———. *Catechism on Motion Pictures in Interstate Commerce.* 3d ed. New York: New York Civic League, 1922.

Chickering, A. Lawrence. *Beyond Left and Right: Breaking the Political Stalemate.* San Francisco: ICS Press, 1993.

Clark, Malcolm, Jr. "The Bigot Disclosed: Ninety Years of Nativism." *Oregon Historical Quarterly* 75 (June 1974): 109–90.

Clecak, Peter. *Crooked Paths: Reflections on Socialism, Conservatism, and the Welfare State.* New York: Harper and Row, 1977.

Clements, Kendrick A. *William Jennings Bryan: Missionary Isolationist.* Knoxville: University of Tennessee Press, 1982.

Coben, Stanley. "The Assault on Victorianism in the Twentieth Century." *American Quarterly* 27 (December 1975): 604–25.

———. *Rebellion against Victorianism: The Impetus for Cultural Change in 1920s America.* New York: Oxford University Press, 1991.

———. "A Study in Nativism: The American Red Scare of 1919–20." *Political Science Quarterly* 79 (March 1964): 52–75.

Cole, Wayne S. *America First: The Battle against Intervention, 1940–1941.* Madison: University of Wisconsin Press, 1953.

———. *Charles A. Lindbergh and the Battle against American Intervention in World War II.* New York: Harcourt Brace Jovanovich, 1974.

———. *Roosevelt and the Isolationists, 1932–45.* Lincoln: University of Nebraska Press, 1983.

———. *Senator Gerald P. Nye and American Foreign Relations.* Minneapolis: University of Minnesota Press, 1962.

Coletta, Paolo. *William Jennings Bryan: Political Evangelist, 1860–1908.* Lincoln: University of Nebraska Press, 1964.

Committee on Recent Economic Changes of the President's Conference on Unemployment. *Recent Economic Changes.* Report. 2 vols. New York: McGraw-Hill, 1929.

Conant, Michael. *Antitrust in the Motion Picture Industry.* Berkeley: University of California Press, 1960.

Cooper, John Milton, Jr. "Progressivism and American Foreign Policy: A Reconsideration." *Mid-America* 51 (October 1969): 260–76.

———. *The Vanity of Power: American Isolationism and the First World War, 1914–1917.* Westport, Conn.: Greenwood, 1969.

———. "William E. Borah, Political Thespian." *Pacific Northwest Quarterly* 56 (October 1965): 145–53.

Cott, Nancy F. *The Grounding of Modern Feminism.* New Haven, Conn.: Yale University Press, 1987.

Coughlin, Charles E. *The New Deal in Money.* Royal Oak, Mich.: League of the Little Flower, 1933.

Cowing, Cedric B. "Sons of the Wild Jackass and the Stock Market." *Business History Review* 33 (Summer 1959): 138–55.

Cramer, Richard M. "School Desegregation and New Industry: The Southern Community Leaders' Viewpoints." *Social Forces* 41 (May 1963): 384–89.

Croly, Herbert. *The Promise of American Life.* 1909. Reprint, New York: Dutton, 1963.

Current Biography. New York: H. W. Wilson, 1940–.

Current Biography Yearbook. New York: H. W. Wilson, 1940–.

Curry, Leroy A. *The Ku Klux Klan under the Searchlight: An Authorative,*

Dignified and Enlightened Discussion of the American Klan. Kansas City, Mo.: Western Baptist Publishing, 1924.

Dahlstrom, Harl A. "'Remote Bigness' as a Theme in Nebraska Politics: The Case of Kenneth S. Wherry." *North Dakota Quarterly* 38 (Summer 1970): 23–32.

Dallek, Robert. *The American Style of Foreign Policy: Culture, Politics, and Foreign Policy.* New York: Alfred A. Knopf, 1983.

———. *Ronald Reagan: The Politics of Symbolism.* Cambridge, Mass.: Harvard University Press, 1984.

Danbom, David B. *World of Hope: Progressives and the Struggle for an Ethical Public Life.* Philadelphia: Temple University Press, 1987.

Danzig, David. "The Radical Right and the Rise of the Fundamentalist Minority." *Commentary* 33 (April 1962): 291–98.

Darilek, Richard E. *A Loyal Opposition in Time of War: The Republican Party and the Politics of Foreign Policy from Pearl Harbor to Yalta.* Westport, Conn.: Greenwood, 1976.

Dictionary of American Biography. 22 vols. New York: Charles Scribner's Sons, 1946, and supplements.

Diggins, John P. *The Lost Soul of American Politics: Virtue, Self-Interest, and the Foundation of Liberalism.* New York: Basic Books, 1984.

Dionne, E. J., Jr. *Why Americans Hate Politics.* New York: Simon and Schuster, 1991.

Divine, Robert A. *Second Chance: The Triumph of Internationalism in America during World War II.* New York: Atheneum, 1967.

Doenecke, Justus D. "The Anti-Interventionist Tradition: Leadership and Perceptions." *Literature of Liberty* 4 (Summer 1981): 7–67.

———. "Conservatism: The Impassioned Sentiment—A Review Essay." *American Quarterly* 28 (Winter 1976): 601–9.

———. "The Isolationists and a Usable Past: A Review Essay." *Peace and Change* 5 (Spring 1978): 67–73.

———. *Not to the Swift: The Old Isolationists in the Cold War.* Lewisburg, Penn.: Bucknell University Press, 1979.

———. "The Strange Career of American Isolationism, 1944–1954." *Peace and Change* 3 (Summer–Fall 1975): 79–83.

———, ed. *Danger Undaunted: The Anti-Interventionist Movement of 1940–1941 as Revealed in the Papers of the America First Committee.* Stanford, Calif.: Hoover Institution Press, 1990.

Donahue, Suzanne Mary. *American Film Distribution: The Changing Marketplace.* Ann Arbor, Mich.: UMI Research Press, 1987.

Donnelly, Ignatius. *The American People's Money.* Chicago: Laird and Leer, 1895.

Dorfman, Joseph. *The Economic Mind in American Civilization.* 5 vols. New York: Viking, 1949–59.

Eastman, Fred. "The Menace of the Movies." *Christian Century* 47 (15 January 1930): 75–78.

———. "Our Children and the Movies." *Christian Century* 47 (22 January 1930): 110–12.

———. "What's to Be Done with the Movies?" *Christian Century* 47 (12 February 1930): 202–4.

———. "Who Controls the Movies?" *Christian Century* 47 (5 February 1930): 173–75.

Edsall, Thomas Byrne, with Mary D. Edsall. *Chain Reaction: The Impact of Race, Rights, and Taxes on American Politics.* New York: W. W. Norton, 1991.

Erenberg, Lewis A. *Steppin' Out: New York Nightlife and the Transformation of American Culture, 1890–1930.* Chicago: University of Chicago Press, 1981.

Evans, Hiram Wesley. "The Ballots behind the Ku Klux Klan." *World's Work* 55 (January 1928): 243–52.

———. "The Catholic Question as Viewed by the Ku Klux Klan." *Current History* 26 (July 1927): 563–68.

———. "The Klan's Fight for Americanism." *North American Review* 223 (March 1926): 33–63.

———. *The Menace of Modern Immigration.* Dallas: n.p., 1923.

———. "Our Crusading Army." *Kourier Magazine* 2 (October 1926): 2–5.

———. *The Public School Problem in America: Outlining Fully the Policies and the Program of the Knights of the Ku Klux Klan toward the Public School System.* Atlanta: Knights of the Ku Klux Klan, 1924.

Farley, James A. *Jim Farley's Story: The Roosevelt Years.* New York: Whittlesey House, 1948.

Fass, Paul S. *The Damned and the Beautiful: American Youth in the 1920s.* New York: Oxford University Press, 1979.

Fausold, Martin L. "President Hoover's Farm Policies." *Agricultural History* 51 (April 1978): 362–77.

Feinman, Ronald L. *Twilight of Progressivism: The Western Republican Senators and the New Deal.* Baltimore: Johns Hopkins University Press, 1981.

Ferguson, Thomas, and Joel Rogers. *Right Turn: The Decline of the Democrats and the Future of American Politics.* New York: Hill and Wang, 1986.

Filene, Edward A. *Next Steps Forward in Retailing.* New York: Harper and Row, 1937.

Filler, Louis. *Dictionary of American Conservatism.* New York: Philosophic Library, 1987.

Fite, Gilbert C. "The Agricultural Issues in the Presidential Campaign of 1928." *Mississippi Valley Historical Review* 37 (March 1951): 653–72.

———. "Farmer Opinion and the Agricultural Adjustment Act of 1933." *Mississippi Valley Historical Review* 48 (March 1962): 656–73.

———. *Peter Norbeck: Prairie Statesman.* Columbia: University of Missouri Press, 1948.

Flink, James J. *The Car Culture.* Cambridge, Mass.: MIT Press, 1976.

Flowers, Montaville. *America Chained: A Discussion of "What's Wrong with the Chain Store."* Pasadena, Calif.: Montaville Flowers Publicists, 1931.

Flynn, John T. *As We Go Marching.* Garden City, N.Y.: Doubleday, Doran, 1944.

———. "Chain Stores: Menace or Promise." *New Republic* 66 (15 April–13 May 1931): 223–26, 270–73, 298–301, 324–26, 350–53.

———. "The Marines Land in Wall Street." *Harper's* 169 (July 1934): 149–50.

———. "Up against the Chains." *Collier's* 83 (27 April 1929): 8–9ff.

Forman, Henry James. *Our Movie Made Children.* New York: Macmillan, 1933.

Formisano, Ronald P. *Boston against Busing: Race, Class, and Ethnicity in the 1960s and 1970s.* Chapel Hill: University of North Carolina Press, 1991.

Forster, Arnold, and Benjamin R. Epstein. *Danger on the Right.* New York: Random House, 1964.

Francis, Samuel. "The Evil That Men Don't Do: Joe McCarthy and the American Right." *Chronicles* 10 (September 1986): 16–21.

Fraser, Steve, and Gary Gerstle, eds. *The Rise and Fall of the New Deal Order, 1930–1980.* Princeton, N.J.: Princeton University Press, 1989.

Fried, Richard M. *Nightmare in Red: The McCarthy Era in Perspective.* New York: Oxford University Press, 1990.

Frost, Stanley. *The Challenge of the Klan.* Indianapolis: Bobbs-Merrill, 1924.

———. "The Masked Politics of the Klan." *World's Week* 55 (February 1928): 399–407.

———. "When the Klan Rides." *Outlook* 135 (23 December 1923): 716–18.

Fuchs, Lawrence H. *The American Kaleidoscope: Race, Ethnicity, and the Civic Culture.* Hanover, N.H.: University Press of New England, 1990.

Fuller, James H. "The Case for the Independent Merchant." *California Journal of Development* 21 (June 1931): 11–12ff.

Galambos, Louis. *The Public Image of Big Business America, 1880–1940: A Quantitative Study in Social Change.* Baltimore: Johns Hopkins University Press, 1975.

Galambos, Louis, and Joseph Pratt. *The Rise of the Corporate Commonwealth: United States Business and Public Policy in the Twentieth Century.* New York: Basic Books, 1988.

Gallup, George H. *The Gallup Poll: Public Opinion, 1935–1971.* 3 vols. New York: Random House, 1972.

Garson, Robert A. "Political Fundamentalism and Popular Democracy in the 1920s." *South Atlantic Quarterly* 76 (Spring 1977): 219–33.

Gatewood, Willard B., Jr. "Politics and Piety in North Carolina: The Fundamentalist Crusade at High Tide, 1925–1927." *North Carolina Historical Review* 42 (July 1965): 275–90.

Geelan, Agnes. *Dakota Maverick: The Political Life of William Langer.* Fargo, N.D.: Geelan, 1975.

George, Henry. *Progress and Poverty.* 1897. Reprint. New York: Schalkenbach, 1992.

Gibbs, Christopher C. *The Great Silent Majority: Missouri's Resistance to World War I.* Columbia: University of Missouri Press, 1988.

Ginger, Ray, ed. *William Jennings Bryan: Selections.* Indianapolis: Bobbs-Merrill, 1967.

Gipson, J. H. *The State of the Nation.* Caldwell, Idaho: Caxton, 1940.

Goldberg, Robert A. *Grassroots Resistance: Social Movements in Twentieth Century America.* Belmont, Calif.: Wadsworth, 1991.

———. *Hooded Empire: The Ku Klux Klan in Colorado.* Urbana: University of Illinois Press, 1981.

Goldman, Eric F. *The Crucial Decade and After: America, 1945–1960.* New York: Alfred A. Knopf, 1960.

Goldwater, Barry. *Conscience of a Conservative.* Sheperdsville, Ky.: Victor, 1960.

Gomery, Douglas. *The Hollywood Studio System.* New York: St. Martin's, 1986.

Goodwyn, Lawrence F. *The Populist Moment: A Short History of the Agrarian Revolt in America.* New York: Oxford University Press, 1978.

Gorman, Joseph Bruce. *Kefauver: A Political Biography.* New York: Oxford University Press, 1971.

Gould, Lewis L. *The Presidency of Theodore Roosevelt.* Lawrence: University of Kansas Press, 1991.

———. *Reform and Regulation: American Politics from Roosevelt to Wilson.* New York: Alfred A. Knopf, 1986.

Gould, Stephen Jay. "William Jennings Bryan's Last Campaign." *Natural History* 96 (November 1987): 16ff.

Graham, Otis L., Jr. *An Encore for Reform: The Old Progressives and the New Deal.* New York: Oxford University Press, 1967.

Green, David. *Shaping Political Consciousness: The Language of Politics in America from McKinley to Reagan.* Ithaca, N.Y.: Cornell University Press, 1987.

Greenway, John. "Country-Western: The Music of America." *American West* 5 (November 1968): 32–41.

Grethers, E. T. "Consumer Attitudes as to Chain and Independent." *Commonwealth—Part Two* 7 (14 July 1931): 185–214.

Griffin, C. E. "The Economic Significance of Recent Price Legislation." *Journal of Marketing* 3 (April 1939): 371ff.

Griffith, Robert. "Dwight D. Eisenhower and the Corporate Commonwealth." *American Historical Review* 87 (February 1982): 87–122.

———. "Old Progressives and the Cold War." *Journal of American History* 66 (September 1979): 334–47.

———. *The Politics of Fear: Joseph R. McCarthy and the Senate.* Rev. ed. Amherst: University of Massachusetts Press, 1987.

Griffith, Robert, and Athan Theoharis, eds. *The Specter: Original Essays on the Cold War and the Origins of McCarthyism.* New York: Franklin Watts, 1974.

Grinder, Robert D. "Progressives, Conservatives, and Imperialism: Another Look at the Senate Republicans, 1913–1917." *North Dakota Quarterly* 41 (Autumn 1973): 28–39.

Guinsburg, Thomas N. *The Pursuit of Isolationism in the United States Senate from Versailles to Pearl Harbor.* New York: Garland, 1982.

Hahn, Steven. *The Roots of Southern Populism: Yeomen Farmers and the Transformation of the Georgia Upcountry, 1850–1890.* New York: Oxford University Press, 1983.

Halberstam, David. "The White Citizens Councils: Respectable Means for Unrespectable Ends." *Commentary* 22 (October 1956): 293–302.

Hamby, Alonzo L. *Beyond the New Deal: Harry S. Truman and American Liberalism.* New York: Columbia University Press, 1973.

Hamilton, Richard F. *Class and Politics in the U.S.* New York: John Wiley and Sons, 1972.

———. *Restraining Myths: Critical Studies of U.S. Social Structure and Politics.* New York: John Wiley and Sons, 1975.

Hampton, Benjamin B. *History of the American Film Industry: From Its Beginnings to 1931*. 1931. Reprint, New York: Dover, 1970.

Hard, William. "Benito and I Save the St. Paul." *Nation* 122 (3 March 1926): 224–25.

———. "In Bad All Around." *Nation* 119 (3 December 1924): 599.

———. "Where Are the Pre-War Radicals?" *Survey* 55 (1 February 1926): 559.

Harper, Alan D. *The Politics of Loyalty: The White House and the Communist Issue, 1946–1952*. Westport, Conn.: Greenwood, 1969.

Harper, F. J. "'A New Battle on Evolution': The Anti-Chain Store Trade-at-Home Agitation of 1929–1930." *Journal of American Studies* 16 (December 1982): 407–26.

Harrington, Mona. *The Dream of Deliverance in American Politics*. New York: Random House, 1986.

Harvey, William. *Coin's Financial School*. 1894. Reprint. Cambridge, Mass.: Harvard University Press, 1963.

Harwood, William L. "The Ku Klux Klan in Grand Forks, North Dakota." *South Dakota History* 1 (Fall 1971): 301–35.

Hawley, Ellis W. "The Discovery and Study of a 'Corporate Liberalism.'" *Business History Review* 52 (Autumn 1978): 309–20.

———. *The Great War and the Search for a Modern Order: A History of the American People and Their Institutions, 1917–1933*. New York: St. Martin's, 1979.

———. *The New Deal and the Problem of Monopoly: A Study in Economic Ambivalence*. Princeton, N.J.: Princeton University Press, 1966.

Hays, Will. *Will Hays Papers*. Edited by Douglas Gomery. Frederick, Md.: University Publications of America, 1988.

Heath, Jim F. "American War Mobilization and the Use of Small Manufacturers, 1939–1943." *Business History Review* 46 (Autumn 1972): 295–319.

Hesseltine, William B. "Robert M. La Follette and the Principles of Americanism." *Wisconsin Magazine of History* 31 (March 1948): 261–67.

Hicks, John D. "The Legacy of Populism in the Western Middle West." *Agricultural History* 23 (October 1949): 225–36.

———. *The Populist Revolt: A History of the Farmers' Alliance and the People's Party*. Minneapolis: University of Minnesota Press, 1931.

———. *Republican Ascendancy, 1921–1933*. New York: Harper and Brothers, 1960.

Hicks, John D., and Theodore Saloutos. *Agricultural Discontent in the Middle West, 1900–1939*. Madison: University of Wisconsin Press, 1951.

Higham, John, and Paul K. Conkin, eds. *New Directions in American Intellectual History*. Baltimore: Johns Hopkins University Press, 1979.

Himmelstein, Jerome L. *To the Right: The Transformation of American Conservatism*. Berkeley: University of California Press, 1990.

History. New York: Meridian Books, 1960.

Hofstadter, Richard. *The Age of Reform: From Bryan to F.D.R.* New York: Alfred A. Knopf, 1955.

———. *The American Political Tradition*. New York: Random House, 1948.

Holmes, William F. *The White Chief: James Kimble Vardaman*. Baton Rouge: Louisiana State University Press, 1970.

Holsinger, M. Paul. "The Oregon School Controversy, 1922–25." *Pacific Historical Review* 27 (August 1968): 327–41.

Hoover, Herbert. *The New Day: Campaign Speeches of Herbert Hoover*. Stanford, Calif.: Stanford University Press, 1928.

Horowitz, David. "Sinews of Empire." *Ramparts* 8 (October 1969): 32–43.

Horowitz, David, and David Kolodney. "The Foundations." *Ramparts* 7 (April 1969): 38–48ff.

Horowitz, David A. "The Crusade against Chain Stores: Portland's Independent Merchants, 1928–1935." *Oregon Historical Quarterly* 89 (Winter 1988): 341–68.

———. "The Klansman as Outsider: Ethnocultural Solidarity and Antielitism in the Oregon Ku Klux Klan of the 1920s." *Pacific Northwest Quarterly* 80 (January 1989): 12–20.

———. "North Dakota Noninterventionists and Corporate Culture." *Heritage of the Great Plains* 17 (Summer 1984): 30–42.

———. "The Perils of Western Farm Politics: Herbert Hoover, Gerald P. Nye, and Agricultural Reform, 1926–1932." *North Dakota Quarterly* 53 (Fall 1985): 92–110. Also in *Herbert Hoover and the Republican Era: A Reconsideration*, edited by Carl Krog and William R. Tanner. Lanham, Md.: University Press of America, 1984.

———. "Senator Borah's Crusade to Save Small Business from the New Deal." *Historian* 55 (Summer 1993): 693–708.

———. "Social Morality and Personal Revitalization: Oregon's Ku Klux Klan in the 1920s." *Oregon Historical Quarterly* 90 (Winter 1989): 365–84.

———. "White Southerners' Alienation and Civil Rights: The Response to Corporate Liberalism, 1956–1965." *Journal of Southern History* 54 (May 1988): 173–200.

Howe, Daniel Walker. "American Victorianism as a Culture." *American Quarterly* 27 (December 1975): 507–32.

Huettig, Mae D. *Economic Control of the Motion Picture Industry: A Study on Industrial Organization*. Philadelphia: University of Pennsylvania, 1944.

Hummings, Neville March. *Film Censors and the Law*. London: George Allen and Unwin, 1967.

Hutchinson, Paul. "The Arms Inquiry." *Christian Century* 52 (15 May 1935): 643–64.

Ickes, Harold L. *The Secret Diary of Harold L. Ickes: The Inside Struggle, 1936–1939*. New York: Simon and Schuster, 1954.

———. *The Secret Diary of Harold L. Ickes: The Lowering Clouds, 1939–1941*. New York: Simon and Schuster, 1954.

Is the Ku Klux Klan Constructive or Destructive: A Debate between Imperial Wizard Evans, Israel Zangwill and Others. Girard, Kans.: Haldeman-Julius, 1924.

Jackson, Kenneth T. *The Ku Klux Klan in the City, 1915–1930*. New York: Oxford University Press, 1967.

Jeansonne, Glen. *Messiah of the Masses: Huey P. Long and the Great Depression*. New York: Harper Collins, 1992.

Jenkins, William D. *The Ku Klux Klan in Ohio's Mahoning Valley*. Kent, Ohio: Kent State Press, 1990.

———. "The Ku Klux Klan in Youngstown, Ohio: Moral Reform in the Twenties." *Historian* 41 (November 1978): 76–93.

Jenner, William E. "The Bankers' Profits from Foreign Aid." *American Mercury* 86 (April 1958): 33–38.

Johnson, Claudius O. *Borah of Idaho*. 1936. Reprint, Seattle: University of Washington Press, 1967.

Johnson, Guy B. "A Sociological Interpretation of the New KKK Movement." *Social Forces* 1 (May 1923): 440–45.

Johnson, Hiram W. "Why 'Irreconcilables' Keep Out of Europe, Told by Hiram Johnson." *New York Times Magazine* (14 January 1923): 1ff.

Jones, Paul. "Washington Can't Cure Everything." *Saturday Evening Post* 217 (18 November 1944): 112.

Jowett, Garth. *Film, the Democratic Art*. Boston: Little, Brown, 1976.

Judis, John B. "Pop-Con Politics." *New Republic* 191 (3 September 1984): 18–20.

Karl, Barry D. *The Uneasy State: The United States from 1915 to 1945*. Chicago: University of Chicago Press, 1983.

Kaufman, Burton I. *The Korean War: Challenges in Crisis, Credibility, and Command*. Philadelphia: Temple University Press, 1986.

———. *Trade and Aid: Eisenhower's Foreign Economic Policy, 1953–61*. Baltimore: Johns Hopkins University Press, 1982.

Kay, Hubert. "The Warrior from Patman's Switch." *Fortune* 71 (April 1965): 155–56ff.

Kazin, Michael. "The Grass-Roots Right: New Histories of U.S. Conservatism in the Twentieth Century." *American Historical Review* 97 (February 1992): 136–55.

———. *The Populist Persuasion: An American History*. New York: Basic Books, 1995.

Kearns, Doris. *Lyndon Johnson and the American Dream*. New York: Harper and Row, 1976.

Keller, Morton. *Regulating a New Economy: Public Policy and Economic Change in America, 1900–1933*. Cambridge, Mass.: Harvard University Press, 1990.

Kelley, Robert. *The Cultural Pattern in American Politics: The First Century*. New York: Alfred A. Knopf, 1979.

Kett, Joseph F. *Rites of Passage: Adolescence in America, 1790 to the Present*. New York: Basic Books, 1977.

Kindem, Gorham, ed. *The American Movie Industry: The Business of Motion Pictures*. Carbondale: Southern Illinois University Press, 1982.

Kirschner, Don S. *City and Country: Rural Responses to Urbanization in the 1920s*. Westport, Conn.: Greenwood, 1970.

———. *The Paradox of Professionalism: Reform and Public Service in Urban America, 1900–1940*. Westport, Conn.: Greenwood, 1986.

Klatch, Rebecca E. *Women of the New Right.* Philadelphia: Temple University Press, 1987.

Kloppenberg, James T. "The Virtues of Liberalism: Christianity, Republicanism, and Ethics in Early American Political Discourse." *Journal of American History* 74 (June 1987): 9–33.

Kohl, Lawrence Frederick. *The Politics of Individualism: Parties and the American Character in the Jacksonian Era.* New York: Oxford University Press, 1989.

Kostelanetz, Richard, ed. *Beyond Left and Right: Radical Thought for Our Times.* New York: William Morrow, 1968.

Krog, Carl, and William R. Tanner, eds. *Herbert Hoover and the Republican Era: A Reconsideration.* Lanham, Md.: University Press of America, 1984.

LaFeber, Walter. *America, Russia, and the Cold War, 1945–1990.* New York: McGraw-Hill, 1991.

La Follette, Belle Case, and Fola La Follette. *Robert M. La Follette.* 2 vols. New York: Macmillan, 1953.

La Follette, Philip. *Adventure in Politics: The Memoirs of Philip La Follette.* Edited by Donald Young. New York: Holt, Rinehart, and Winston, 1970.

La Follette, Robert M., Jr. "A Senator Looks at Congress." *Atlantic Monthly* 172 (July 1943): 91ff.

———. "Turn the Light on Communism." *Collier's* 119 (8 February 1947): 73–74.

"La Follette Thunder." *Nation* 146 (30 April 1938): 492–93.

Lagemann, Ellen Condliff. *The Politics of Knowledge: The Carnegie Corporation, Philanthropy, and Public Policy.* Middletown, Conn.: Wesleyan University Press, 1989.

LaLande, Jeff. "Beneath the Hooded Robe: Newspapermen, Local Politics, and the Ku Klux Klan in Jackson County, Oregon, 1921–1923." *Pacific Northwest Quarterly* 83 (April 1992): 42–52.

Lankford, John. *Congress and the Foundations in the Twentieth Century.* River Falls: Wisconsin State University, 1964.

Larson, Bruce L. *Lindbergh of Minnesota: A Political Biography.* New York: Harcourt Brace Jovanovich, 1973.

Lasch, Christopher. "Beyond Left and Right: Political Change in America." *Old Oregon* 69 (Winter 1989): 18–26.

———. *The True and Only Heaven: Progress and Its Critics.* New York: W. W. Norton, 1991.

Latham, Earl. *The Communist Controversy in Washington: From the New Deal to McCarthy.* Cambridge, Mass.: Harvard University Press, 1966.

Lawson, Steve F. *Black Ballots: Voting Rights in the South, 1944–1969.* New York: Columbia University Press, 1976.

———. *Running for Freedom: Civil Rights and Black Politics in America since 1941.* New York: McGraw-Hill, 1991.

Lay, Shawn, ed. *The Invisible Empire in the West: Toward a New Historical Appraisal of the Ku Klux Klan of the 1920s.* Urbana: University of Illinois Press, 1992.

Lears, Jackson. *No Place of Grace: Antimodernism and the Transformation of American Culture, 1880–1930.* New York: Pantheon Books, 1981.

Lebhar, Godfrey M. *Chain Stores in America, 1859–1962.* 3d ed. New York: Chain Store Publication, 1963.

Lee, Maurice W. *Anti-Chain Store Tax Legislation.* Chicago: University of Chicago Press, 1939.

Leff, Mark H. "The Politics of Sacrifice on the American Home Front in World War II." *Journal of American History* 77 (March 1991): 1296–1318.

Lemke, William. *You and Your Money.* Philadelphia: W. H. Dorrance, 1938.

Lerche, Charles O., Jr. "Southern Congressmen and the 'New Isolationism.'" *Political Science Quarterly* 75 (September 1980): 321–37.

Lerner, Max. "Phil La Follette—An Interview." *Nation* 146 (14 May 1938): 552–55.

Leuchtenburg, William E. *Franklin D. Roosevelt and the New Deal, 1932–1940.* New York: Harper and Row, 1963.

———. *The Perils of Prosperity, 1914–1932.* Chicago: University of Chicago Press, 1958.

Levine, Lawrence W. *Defender of the Faith, William Jennings Bryan: The Last Decade, 1915–1925.* New York: Oxford University Press, 1965.

———, ed. "The 'Diary' of Hiram Johnson." *American Heritage* 20 (August 1969): 64–76.

Levine, Lawrence W., and Robert Middlekauff, eds. *The National Temper: Readings in American Culture and Society.* 2d ed. New York: Harcourt Brace Jovanovich, 1972.

Lewis, David L. *King: A Biography.* 2d ed. Urbana: University of Illinois Press, 1978.

Liggio, Leonard P., and James P. Martin, eds. *Watershed of Empire: Essays on the New Deal.* Colorado Springs, Colo.: Ralph Myles, 1976.

Lindbergh, Charles A. "Aviation, Geography, and Race." *Reader's Digest* 35 (November 1939): 64–67.

———. "Letter to Americans." *Collier's* 107 (29 March 1941): 14–15ff.

———. *The Wartime Journals of Charles A. Lindbergh.* New York: Harcourt Brace Jovanovich, 1970.

Lindbergh, Charles A., Sr. *Why Is Your Country at War and What Happens to You after the War and Related Subjects.* Washington, D.C.: National Capital Press, 1917.

Loe, Kelley. "Chain Store Distribution Is Sound Economy." *Everybody's Business* 1 (15 October 1935): 7–8.

Loucks, Emerson H. *The Ku Klux Klan in Pennsylvania: A Study in Nativism.* New York: Telegraph Press, 1936.

Lower, Richard Coke. "Hiram Johnson: The Making of an Irreconcilable." *Pacific Historical Review* 41 (November 1972): 505–26.

Lowitt, Richard. *George W. Norris: The Making of a Progressive, 1861–1912.* Syracuse, N.Y.: Syracuse University Press, 1963.

———. *George W. Norris: The Persistence of a Progressive, 1913–1933.* Urbana: University of Illinois Press, 1971.

Luker, Kristin. *Abortion and the Politics of Motherhood.* Berkeley: University of California Press, 1984.

Lustig, R. Jeffrey. *Corporate Liberalism: The Origins of Modern American Political Theory, 1890–1920.* Berkeley: University of California Press, 1982.

Luthin, Reinhard H. "Smith Wildman Brookhart of Iowa: Insurgent Agrarian Politician." *Agricultural History* 25 (October 1951): 187–97.

MacArthur, Douglas. *Reminiscences.* New York: McGraw-Hill, 1964.

MacKay, Kenneth Campbell. *The Progressive Movement of 1924.* New York: Columbia University Press, 1947.

Maney, Patrick J. *"Young Bob" La Follette: A Biography of Robert M. La Follette, Jr., 1895–1953.* Columbia: University of Missouri Press, 1978.

Marguiles, Herbert F. *The Decline of the Progressive Movement in Wisconsin, 1890–1928.* Madison: State Historical Society of Wisconsin, 1968.

Marsden, George M. *Fundamentalism and American Culture: The Shaping of Twentieth-Century Evangelism, 1870–1925.* New York: Oxford University Press, 1980.

Martin, Boyce F. "The Independent, et al., versus the Chains." *Harvard Business Review* 9 (October 1930): 47–56.

Matusow, Allen J., ed. *Joseph R. McCarthy.* Englewood Cliffs, N.J.: Prentice-Hall, 1970.

Maxwell, Robert S. *La Follette and the Rise of Progressivism in Wisconsin.* Madison: State Historical Society of Wisconsin, 1956.

May, Lary. *Screening Out the Past: The Birth of Mass Culture and the Motion Picture Industry.* New York: Oxford University Press, 1980.

————, ed. *Recasting America: Culture and Politics in the Age of the Cold War.* Chicago: University of Chicago Press, 1989.

Mayer, George H. *The Political Career of Floyd B. Olson.* Minneapolis: University of Minnesota Press, 1951.

Mayer, Kurt. "Small Business as a Social Institution." *Social Research* 14 (September 1947): 332–49.

McCarthy, Charles. *The Wisconsin Idea.* New York: Macmillan, 1912.

McCarthy, Joseph R. *McCarthyism: The Fight for America.* New York: Devin-Adair, 1952.

McCoy, Donald R. *Angry Voices: Left-of-Center Politics in the New Deal Era.* Lawrence: University of Kansas Press, 1958.

————. "The National Progressives of America, 1938." *Mississippi Valley Historical Review* 44 (June 1957): 75–93.

————. "Republican Opposition during Wartime, 1941–1945." *Mid-America* 49 (July 1967): 174–89.

McCraw, Thomas K. *Morgan vs. Lilienthal: The Feud within the TVA.* Chicago: Loyola University Press, 1970.

————, ed. *Regulation in Perspective: Historical Essays.* Cambridge, Mass.: Harvard University Press, 1981.

McKenna, Marian C. *Borah.* Ann Arbor: University of Michigan Press, 1961.

McMath, Robert C., Jr. *Populist Vanguard: A History of the Southern Farm Alliance.* Chapel Hill: University of North Carolina Press, 1975.

Mecklin, John Moffatt. *The Ku Klux Klan: A Study of the American Mind.* 1924. Reprint, New York: Russell and Russell, 1963.

Miller, John E. *Governor Philip F. La Follette, the Wisconsin Progressives, and the New Deal, 1930–1939.* Columbia: University of Missouri Press, 1982.

———. "Philip La Follette: Rhetoric and Reality." *Historian* 45 (November 1982): 65–83.

Moore, Leonard J. *Citizen Klansmen: The Ku Klux Klan in Indiana, 1921–1928.* Chapel Hill: University of North Carolina Press, 1991.

———. "Historical Interpretation of the 1920s Klan: The Traditional View and the Populist Revision." *Journal of Social History* 24 (Winter 1990): 341–57.

Morrison, Charles Clayton. "The Movies before Congress." *Christian Century* 47 (21 May 1930): 646–47.

Moum, Kathleen. "The Social Origins of the Nonpartisan League." *North Dakota History* 53 (Spring 1986): 18–22.

Mowry, George E. *The Urban Nation, 1920–1960.* New York: Hill and Wang, 1965.

Mulder, Ronald A. *The Insurgent Progressives in the United States Senate and the New Deal, 1933–1939.* New York: Garland, 1979.

———. "The Progressive Insurgents in the United States Senate, 1935–36: Was There a Second New Deal?" *Mid-America* 57 (April 1975): 106–25.

Murphy, Paul L. "Sources and Nature of Intolerance in the 1920s." *Journal of American History* 51 (June 1964): 60–76.

Nash, George. *The Conservative Intellectual Movement in America since 1945.* New York: Basic Books, 1979.

Navasky, Victor S. *Naming Names.* New York: Penguin Books, 1980.

Neuberger, Richard. "Restriction of Chain Stores." *Everybody's Business* 1 (25 October 1935): 9.

Neuhaus, Richard John. "The Right to Fight." *Commonweal* 108 (9 October 1981): 555–59.

"The New Progressives." *Nation* 146 (7 May 1938): 519–20.

Neymeyer, Robert. "The Ku Klux Klan of the 1920s in the Midwest and West: A Review Essay." *Annals of Iowa* 51 (Fall 1992): 625–33.

Noble, David W. *The Progressive Mind, 1890–1917.* Boston: Rand McNally, 1970.

Norris, George W. "Boring from Within." *Nation* 121 (16 September 1925): 297–99.

Novak, Michael. *The Rise of the Unmeltable Ethnics: Politics and Culture in the Seventies.* New York: Macmillan, 1971.

Nungent, Walter. "Tocqueville, Marx, and American Class Structure." *Social Science History* 12 (Winter 1988): 327–46.

Nye, Gerald P. "Should We Turn to 'Isolation'?" *New York Times Magazine* (14 January 1940): 1–2ff.

Nye, Russel B. *Midwestern Progressive Politics: A Historical Study of Its Origins and Development, 1870–1958.* New York: Harper and Row, 1959.

O'Brien, Patrick G. "Senator John J. Blaine: An Independent Progressive during 'Normalcy.'" *Wisconsin Magazine of History* 60 (Autumn 1976): 25–41.

Olasky, M. N. "The Failure of Movie Industry Public Relations, 1921–1934." *Journal of Popular Film and Television* 12 (Winter 1984–85): 163–75.

Olin, Spencer C., Jr. *California's Prodigal Sons: Hiram Johnson and the Progressives, 1911–1917.* Berkeley: University of California Press, 1968.

Olssen, Erik. "The Progressive Group in Congress, 1922–29." *Historian* 42 (February 1980): 244–63.

Oshinsky, David A. *A Conspiracy So Immense: The World of Joe McCarthy.* New York: Free Press, 1983.

Ostrander, Gilman M. *American Civilization in the First Machine Age, 1890–1940.* New York: Harper, 1972.

Palmer, Bruce. *"Man over Money": The Southern Populist Critique of American Capitalism.* Chapel Hill: University of North Carolina Press, 1980.

Palmer, James L. "Economic and Social Aspects of Chain Stores." *Journal of Business* 2 (July 1929): 272–90.

Papers Read at the Meeting of Grand Dragons, Knights of the Ku Klux Klan, at Their First Annual Meeting Held at Asheville, North Carolina, July 1923. New York: Arno, 1977.

Parenti, Michael. *Democracy for the Few.* New York: St. Martin's, 1995.

Parsons, Stanley B. *The Populist Context: Rural versus Urban Poor on a Great Plains Frontier.* Westport, Conn.: Greenwood, 1973

———. "Who Were the Populists?" *Nebraska History* 44 (June 1963): 83–99.

Parsons, Talcott. "McCarthyism and American Social Tension: A Sociologist's View." *Yale Review* 44 (Winter 1955): 226–45.

Patman, Wright. *Banketeering, Bonuseering, Melloneering.* Paris, Tex.: Peerless, 1934.

Patterson, James T. *Congressional Conservatism and the New Deal: The Growth of the Conservative Coalition in Congress, 1933–1939.* Lexington: University of Kentucky Press, 1967.

———. *Mr. Republican: A Biography of Robert A. Taft.* Boston: Houghton Mifflin, 1972.

Patton, R. A. "A Ku Klux Klan Reign of Terror." *Current History* 28 (April 1928): 51–55.

Phillips, Kevin P. *Arrogant Capital: Washington, Wall Street, and the Frustration of American Politics.* Boston: Little, Brown, 1994.

———. *The Politics of Rich and Poor: Wealth and the Electorate in the Reagan Aftermath.* New York: Random House, 1990.

———. *Post-Conservative America: People, Politics, and Ideology in a Time of Crisis.* New York: Random House, 1982.

Piott, Steven L. *The Anti-Monopoly Persuasion: Popular Resistance to the Rise of Big Business in the Midwest.* Westport, Conn.: Greenwood, 1985.

Pivar, David J. *Purity Crusade: Sexual Morality and Social Control, 1868–1900.* Westport, Conn.: Greenwood, 1973.

Pocock, J. G. A. *Politics, Language, and Time: Essays on Political Thought and History.* New York: Atheneum, 1971.

Polenberg, Richard. *War and Society: The United States, 1941–1945.* Philadelphia: J. B. Lippincott, 1972.

Pollock, Norman. *The Populist Response to Industrial America: Midwestern Populist Thought.* Cambridge, Mass.: Harvard University Press, 1962.

Pratt, William C. "Radicals, Farmers, and Historians: Some Recent Scholarship about Agrarian Radicalism in the Upper Midwest." *North Dakota History* 52 (Fall 1985): 12–25.

"The Progressives of the Senate." *American Mercury* 16 (April 1929): 385–93.

"Progressives, What Now?" *Common Sense* 7 (June 1938): 3.

The Public Relations of the Motion Picture Industry. New York: Department of Research and Education, Federal Council of the Churches of Christ in America, 1931.

Quigley, Carroll. *Tragedy and Hope: A History of the World in Our Time.* New York: Macmillan, 1966.

Radosh, Ronald. *Prophets on the Right: Profiles of Conservative Critics of American Globalism.* New York: Simon and Schuster, 1975.

Reagan, Ronald. *Ronald Reagan Talks to America.* Old Greenwich, Conn.: Devin-Adair, 1983.

———. *Speaking My Mind: Selected Speeches.* New York: Simon and Schuster, 1989.

Reeves, Thomas C. *The Life and Times of Joe McCarthy.* New York: Stein and Day, 1982.

———. ed. *Foundations under Fire.* Ithaca, N.Y.: Cornell University Press, 1970.

Reichard, Gary W. *Politics as Usual: The Age of Truman and Eisenhower.* Arlington Heights, Ill.: Harlan Davidson, 1988.

———. *The Reaffirmation of Republicanism: Eisenhower and the Eighty-third Congress.* Knoxville: University of Tennessee Press, 1975.

Remele, Larry. "The Tragedy of Idealism: The National Nonpartisan League and American Foreign Policy, 1917–1919." *North Dakota Quarterly* 42 (Autumn 1974): 78–95.

Ribuffo, Leo P. *The Old Christian Right: The Protestant Far Right from the Great Depression to the Cold War.* Philadelphia: Temple University Press, 1983.

Rogin, Michael P. *The Intellectuals and McCarthy: The Radical Specter.* Cambridge, Mass.: MIT Press, 1967.

———. *Ronald Reagan, the Movie and Other Episodes.* Berkeley: University of California Press, 1987.

Rovere, Richard H. *Senator Joe McCarthy.* New York: Harcourt Brace Jovanovich, 1959.

Ruetten, Richard T. "Burton K. Wheeler and the Montana Connection." *Montana: The Magazine of Western History* 27 (Summer 1977): 2–19.

Rushmore, Howard. "The Senator from Moscow (Idaho)." *American Mercury* 81 (July 1955): 141–42.

Ryant, Carl. "Kentucky and the Movement to Regulate Chain Stores, 1925–1945." *Filson Club History Quarterly* 57 (July 1983): 270–85.

———. "Merchandising in the New Era: Change in the Kentucky Retail Trade during the 1920s." *Journal of Kentucky Studies* 1 (July 1984): 202–10.

———. "The South and the Movement against Chain Stores." *Journal of Southern History* 39 (May 1973): 207–22.

Rylance, Daniel. "A Controversial Career: Gerald P. Nye, 1925–1946." *North Dakota Quarterly* 36 (Winter 1968): 5–19.

Saalfeld, Lawrence J. *Forces of Prejudice in Oregon, 1920–1925.* Portland, Oreg.: Archdiocesan Historical Commission, 1984.

Safianow, Allen. "Konklave in Kokomo Revisited." *Historian* 50 (May 1988): 329–47.

Schlamm, William S. "Across McCarthy's Grave." *National Review* 3 (18 May 1957): 469–70.

Seabury, William Marston. *The Public and the Motion Picture Industry.* New York: Macmillan, 1926.

Shenton, James P. "The Coughlin Movement and the New Deal." *Political Science Quarterly* 73 (September 1958): 352–73.

Sherrill, Robert. "The Last of the Great Populists." *New York Times Magazine* (16 March 1969): 24–25ff.

Shils, Edward A. *The Torment of Secrecy: The Background and Consequences of American Security Policies.* Glencoe, Ill.: Free Press, 1956.

Shipstead, Henrik. "Economic Trends. " *Medical Annals of the District of Columbia* 15 (May 1946): 199–203.

Shover, John L. *Cornbelt Rebellion: The Farmers' Holiday Association.* Urbana: University of Illinois Press, 1965.

Simmons, William Joseph. *The Klan Unmasked.* Atlanta: William E. Thompson, 1924.

Sklar, Martin J. *The Corporate Reconstruction of American Capitalism, 1890–1916: The Market, the Law, and Politics.* New York: Cambridge University Press, 1988.

Sklar, Robert. *Movie-Made America: A Cultural History of American Movies.* New York: Random House, 1975.

Slichter, Sumner H. "Undermining the Foundations." *Atlantic Monthly* 194 (September 1954): 50–54.

Smith, Geoffrey S. "Isolationism, the Devil and the Advent of the Second World War: Variations on a Theme." *International History Review* 4 (February 1982): 55–89.

———. *To Save a Nation: American Countersubversives, the New Deal, and the Coming of World War II.* New York: Basic Books, 1973.

Smith, Glenn H. *Langer of North Dakota: A Study in Isolationism, 1940–1959.* New York: Garland, 1979.

———. "Senator William Langer and Military Conscription, 1945–1959." *North Dakota Quarterly* 37 (Autumn 1969): 14–24.

Snell, William R. "Fiery Crosses in the Roaring Twenties: Activities of the Revised Klan in Alabama, 1915–1930." *Alabama Review* 23 (October 1970): 256–76.

Socolofsky, Homer E. *Arthur Capper: Publisher, Politician, and Philanthropist.* Lawrence: University of Kansas Press, 1962.

Spritzer, Donald E. "B. K. Wheeler and Jim Murray: Senators in Conflict." *Montana: The Magazine of Western History* 23 (April 1973): 16–33.

Steele, Richard W. "Franklin D. Roosevelt and His Foreign Policy Critics." *Political Science Quarterly* 94 (Spring 1979): 15–32.

Sterrett, Frank. "Robert G. Duncan: 'The Oregon Wild Cat.'" *Oregonian Northwest Magazine* (17 April 1966): 33ff.

Stock, Catherine McNicol. *Main Street in Crisis: The Great Depression and the Old Middle Class on the Northern Plains.* Chapel Hill: University of North Carolina Press, 1992.

Stone, Ralph A. *The Irreconcilables: The Fight against the League of Nations.* Lexington: University of Kentucky Press, 1970.

Stripling, Robert E. *The Red Plot against America.* 1949. Reprint. New York: Arno, 1977.

Stromer, Marvin E. *The Making of a Political Leader: Kenneth S. Wherry and the United States Senate.* Lincoln: University of Nebraska Press, 1969.

Stuhler, Barbara, and Gretchen Kreuter, eds. *Women of Minnesota: Selected Biographical Essays.* St. Paul: Minnesota Historical Society, 1977.

Sundquist, James L. *Politics and Policy: The Eisenhower, Kennedy, and Johnson Years.* Washington, D.C.: Brookings Institution, 1968.

Sutton, Walter A. "Bryan, La Follette, Norris—Three Midwestern Politicians." *Journal of the West* 8 (October 1969): 613–30.

Taft, Robert A. "The Case against President Truman." *Saturday Evening Post* 221 (25 September 1948): 18–19ff.

———. *A Foreign Policy for Americans.* Garden City, N.Y.: Doubleday, 1951.

———. "Is This a Conservative War?" *University of Chicago Roundtable* 260 (14 March 1943): 2ff.

"Ten Senators on the World Court." *Nation* 121 (30 December 1925): 751ff.

Thatcher, Terrence L. "The Bricker Amendment: 1952–54." *Northwest Ohio Quarterly* 49 (Summer 1977): 107–17.

Thelen, David. *Paths of Resistance: Tradition and Democracy in Industrializing Missouri.* 2d ed. Columbia: University of Missouri Press, 1991.

———. *Robert M. La Follette and the Insurgent Spirit.* Boston: Little, Brown, 1976.

Theoharis, Athan. *Seeds of Repression: Harry S. Truman and the Origins of McCarthyism.* Chicago: Quadrangle Books, 1971.

———. *The Yalta Myths: An Issue in U.S. Politics, 1943–1955.* Columbia: University of Missouri Press, 1970.

———, ed. *Beyond the Hiss Case: The FBI, Congress, and the Cold War.* Philadelphia: Temple University Press, 1982.

———, ed. *The Truman Presidency: The Origins of the Imperial Presidency and the National Security State.* Stanfordville, N.Y.: M. Coleman Enterprises, 1979.

Tindall, George Brown. *The Emergence of the New South, 1913–1945.* Baton Rouge: Louisiana State University Press, 1967.

Tobin, Eugene M. *Organize or Perish: America's Independent Progressives, 1913–1933.* Westport, Conn.: Greenwood, 1986.

Torelle, Ellen, comp. *The Political Philosophy of Robert M. La Follette as Revealed in His Speeches and Writings.* Madison, Wis.: Robert M. La Follette Company, 1920.

Trachtenberg, Alan. *The Incorporation of American Culture and Society in the Gilded Age.* New York: Hill and Wang, 1982.

Tucker, Ray, and Frederick R. Barkley. *Sons of the Wild Jackass*. 1932. Reprint, Seattle: University of Washington Press, 1970.

Tugwell, Rexford G. *The Democratic Roosevelt*. Garden City, N.Y.: Doubleday, 1957.

Turner, James. "Understanding the Populists." *Journal of American History* 67 (September 1980): 354–73.

Tyack, David B. "The Perils of Pluralism: The Background of the Pierce Case." *American Historical Review* 74 (October 1968): 74–98.

Vatter, Harold G. *The U.S. Economy in World War II*. New York: Columbia University Press, 1985.

Vaughn, Stephen. "Morality and Entertainment: The Origin of the Motion Picture Production Code." *Journal of American History* 77 (June 1990): 39–65.

Viereck, Peter. "The New American Radicals." *Reporter* 11 (December 1954): 41–42.

Viguerie, Richard A. *The Establishment vs. the People: Is a New Populist Revolt on the Way?* Chicago: Regnery Gateway, 1983.

———. *The New Right: We're Ready to Lead*. Falls Church, Va.: Viguerie Company, 1980.

Vinson, John C. "War Debts and Peace Legislation: The Johnson Act of 1934." *Mid-America* 50 (July 1968): 206–22.

Wald, Kenneth D. "The Visible Empire: The Ku Klux Klan as an Electoral Movement." *Journal of Interdisciplinary History* 11 (Autumn 1980): 217–34.

Wallace, Anthony F. C. "Revitalization Movements: Some Theoretical Considerations for Their Comparative Study." *American Anthropologist* 58 (April 1956): 264–81.

Wallace, George C. *Stand Up for America*. Garden City, N.Y.: Doubleday, 1976.

"War on the Chain Store." *Nation* 130 (7 May 1930): 544–45.

Webb, Walter Prescott. *Divided We Stand: The Crisis of a Frontierless Democracy*. New York: Farrar and Rinehart, 1937.

Weinstein, Allen. *Perjury: The Hiss-Chambers Case*. New York: Alfred A. Knopf, 1978.

Weinstein, James. *The Corporate Ideal in the Liberal State, 1900–1918*. Boston: Beacon, 1968.

Westin, Allan F. "Deadly Parallels: Radical Right and Radical Left." *Harper's Magazine* 224 (April 1962): 25–32.

Wheeler, Burton K. "Where Are the Pre-War Radicals?" *Survey* 55 (1 February 1926): 561.

———, with Paul F. Healy. *Yankee from the West*. Garden City, N.Y.: Doubleday, 1962.

White, John Kenneth. *The New Politics of Old Values*. Hanover, N.H.: University Press of New England, 1988.

Who's Who in America. Chicago: A. N. Marquis, 1932, 1950.

Wiebe, Robert. *The Search for Order, 1877–1920*. New York: Hill and Wang, 1967.

Wilkins, Robert P. "Middle Western Isolationism: A Re-examination." *North Dakota Quarterly* 24 (Summer 1957): 69–76.

———. "The Non-Partisan League and Upper Midwest Isolationism." *Agricultural History* 39 (April 1965): 102–9.

———. "Senator William Langer and National Priorities: An Agrarian Rebel's View of American Foreign Policy, 1945–1952." *North Dakota Quarterly* 42 (Autumn 1974): 42–59.

Wiltz, John E. "The Nye Committee Revisited." *Historian* 23 (February 1961): 211–33.

Winkler, Allan M. *Home Front U.S.A.: America during World War II*. Arlington Heights, Ill.: Harlan Davidson, 1986.

———. *The Politics of Propaganda: The Office of War Information, 1942–1945*. New Haven, Conn.: Yale University Press, 1978.

Wirt, Frederick M. *The Politics of Southern Equality: Law and Social Change in a Mississippi County*. Chicago: Aldine, 1970.

Woodward, C. Vann. *Origins of the New South, 1877–1913*. Baton Rouge: Louisiana State University Press, 1951.

———. *Tom Watson, Agrarian Rebel*. 1938. Reprint, New York: Rinehart, 1955.

Wormser, René A. *Foundations: Their Power and Influence*. New York: Devin-Adair, 1958.

Young, Roland. *Congressional Politics in the Second World War*. New York: Columbia University Press, 1956.

Zahniser, Marvin R. "John W. Bricker Reflects upon the Fight for the Bricker Amendment." *Ohio History* 87 (Summer 1978): 322–33.

Zeigler, Harmon. *The Politics of Small Business*. Washington, D.C.: Public Affairs Press, 1961.

Zucker, Norman L. *George W. Norris: Gentle Knight of American Democracy*. Urbana: University of Illinois Press, 1966.

Zunz, Olivier. *Making America Corporate, 1870–1920*. Chicago: University of Chicago Press, 1990.

Unpublished Works

Adkins, Walter P. "Beale Street Goes to the Polls." M.A. thesis, Ohio State University, 1935.

Brekke, Earl J. "Usher L. Burdick and Mid-West Isolationism: A Study in Foreign Policy." M.A. thesis, University of North Dakota, 1964.

Bryniarski, Joan Lee. "Against the Tide: Senate Opposition to the Internationalist Foreign Policy of Presidents Franklin D. Roosevelt and Harry S. Truman, 1943–1949." Ph.D. diss., University of Maryland, 1972.

Cassity, Michael J. "Defending a Way of Life: The Development of Industrial Market Society and the Transformation of Social Relationships in Sedalia, Missouri, 1850–1900." Ph.D. diss., University of Missouri, 1973.

Fitzpatrick, John James, III. "Senator Hiram W. Johnson: A Life History, 1866–1945." Ph.D. diss., University of California at Berkeley, 1975.

Hjalmervik, Gary L. "William Langer's First Administration, 1932–1934." M.A. thesis, University of North Dakota, 1966.

Horowitz, David A[lan]. "Visions of Harmonious Abundance: Corporate Ideology in the 1920s." Ph.D. diss., University of Minnesota, 1971.

Howson, Embrey B. "The Ku Klux Klan in Ohio after World War One." M.A. thesis, Ohio State University, 1951.

Johnston, Robert Douglas. "Middle-Class Political Ideology in a Corporate Society: The Persistence of Small-Propertied Radicalism in Portland, Oregon 1883–1926." Ph.D. diss., Rutgers University, 1993.

Kent, Alan Edmund. "Portrait in Isolationism: The La Follettes and Foreign Policy." Ph.D. diss., University of Wisconsin, 1957.

MacColl, E. Kimbark. "The Supreme Court and Public Opinion: A Study of the Court Fight of 1937." Ph.D. diss., University of California at Los Angeles, 1953.

Marx, Gary T. "The Social Basis of the Support of a Depression Era Extremist: Father Charles E. Coughlin." M.A. thesis, University of California at Berkeley, 1962.

Meyer, Karl Ernest. "The Politics of Loyalty: From La Follette to McCarthy in Wisconsin, 1918–1952." Ph.D. diss., Princeton University, 1956.

Petry, Jerome M. "Morality Legislation in North Dakota, 1920–1954." M.A. thesis, University of North Dakota, 1967.

Powers, Richard G. "Robert Welch on Dwight Eisenhower, 'A Dedicated, Conscious Agent of the Communist Conspiracy.'" Paper presented before the Twenty-first Annual Meeting of the Popular Culture Association, San Antonio, Tex., 28 March 1991.

Recken, Stephen L. "A Reinterpretation of the Oregon School Bill of 1922: The Concept of the Common School in Progressive America." M.A. thesis, Portland State University, 1973.

Rodgers, Daniel. "Ronald Reagan's Rhetoric." Paper presented at 104th Annual Meeting of the American Historical Association, San Francisco, Calif., 30 December 1989.

Ruetten, Richard T. "Burton K. Wheeler: A Progressive between the Wars." Ph.D. diss., University of Oregon, 1961.

Schmelzer, Janet Louise. "The Early Life and Early Congressional Career of Wright Patman: 1894–1941." Ph.D. diss., Texas Christian University, 1978.

Sponberg, Michael R. "North Dakota and the Korean War, 1950–1951: A Study in Public Opinion." M.A. thesis, University of North Dakota, 1969.

Tanner, William R. "The Passage of the Internal Security Act of 1950." Ph.D. diss., University of Kansas, 1971.

Toy, Eckard Vance, Jr. "The Ku Klux Klan in Oregon: Its Character and Program." M.A. thesis, University of Oregon, 1959.

Walker, William O. "John W. Bricker and Joseph R. McCarthy: The Cold War at Home and Abroad, 1950–54." M.A. thesis, Ohio State University, 1970.

Weeks, Irwin John. "Usher L. Burdick in Congress, 1934–1944: A Liberal on Domestic Issues." M.A. thesis, University of North Dakota, 1971.

Index